Mazar Adventure

Sylhet and Beyond

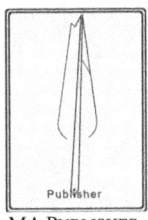

MAYAR AKASH

MA PUBLISHER

Published by MA Publishing (Penzance) 2021
Published January 2021
ISBN-13: 978-1-910499-68-9

Cover designed by Mayar Akash
Typeset in Times New Roman
All photos belong to Mayar Akash

Paper printed on is FSC Certified, lead free, acid free, buffered paper made from wood-based pulp. Our paper meets the ISO 9706 standard for permanent paper. As such, paper will last several hundred years when stored.

Dedication

My father
Late Hajji Mohammad Mashuk Miah

&

My Mother
Hajjah Asiah Khatun

Who unreservedly supported,
financed and facilitated me in this journey.

Rabbir ham huma
Kama rabbayani sageera

"My Lord, have mercy upon them
As they brought me up [when I was] small"
Surah Al-Israh (17:24)

Thank you to all who have helped me in this journey,
gratitude to you all,
wherever you may be.

Content

Introduction

It's been sometime since I thought about moving on from the books I published on Hazrat Shah Jalal and his Mazar, and I also published a website too [it's no longer available]. It's been playing on my mind to compile a book and list all the Mazars that I went to and those that were not featured in any of the previous attempts. They did not do justice to what really happened, what I did, the personal reason for doing it.

Neither of the previous two attempts justifies the sheer number of places and shrines I visited around the district of Sylhet and its four sub-districts, Sylhet, Hobigonj, Moulvibazar, Gulapgoinj, and it did not end there, I also went to Dhaka, the capital city of Bangladesh.

The countless discoveries that I made for myself, were educational and invigorating for me. I was having my own adventure, searching, researching it was an unfolding joy. This inadvertent adventure turned out to be my Spiritual journey, and one that helped and prepared me to meet my maker.

In late 2009 I was diagnosed with a rare disease and that there was no cure for it; and that, at the time; the information was that I had 4 years of life span left; and during this time my immune system was going slowly kill me off.

The disease was known as Wegener's Granulomatosis, a disease discovered by a German scientist during the 2nd world war 75 years ago then. Yet, after 75 year [2009], there was no cure, and no proper facility other than 3 research labs. This was not positive, optimistic or hopeful news.

I was prescribed steroids to manage the pain and symptoms, this particular auto immune disease attacked the small veins in the upper part of the body, hip up; so it starts from the left eye and then works itself down. It attacked me in my left eye and managed to get to my left ear, thank fully I got intervention quick and the further deterioration was halted. The medicine did more than that, it took a toll on me; I was weak, tired, lethargic, gaining weight, dishevelled.

So with all of that going on within a short period of time, my older brother intimated to me to go to Bangladesh where our mum and dad were at the time, going to them meant at least there, I will receive the parental love, attention and care that he could not provide me.

I weighed up my options, it didn't take long, an instant decision, he booked a ticket for me and by February I was on a flight heading to my parents in Bangladesh.

So the disease was diagnosed in December 2009 and by 2010, February I was heading home, by that time there were few visit made to the Moorfields Eye hospital; who were looking into my illness and also prescribed the medicine and how to administer it.

During this time, while all that was taking place I was searching on-line for as much information as possible. The information did not do justice and left me "raw," this information needed to be explained by either a professional who knows or other sufferers.

I found a group on-line and they were very helpful and with the burden of the knowledge that I acquired, it was a downhill disease and I was going to die. Facing with that new reality of my life, it took a nosedive into reality checks, and in that process so much was happening at all level.

I was shedding so much, dreams, hopes, aspirations, all long term plans just broke off and disappeared; so many other baggages that I was carrying, such as my children, that I won't be able to be there for them, fathering them, the negative feelings I had from the experiences of divorce and many others. There were a lot of detachments from myriads of things that once mattered and at that moment lost the cause. It lightened me and the load that I had in my mind and on my shoulders.

Inadvertently and as well as learning that I was going to die, this knowledge drained the blood out of me, in every apart and aspects, physically and in all hopes, feelings and dream, reflecting back, I was like a corpse.

So this journey to Bangladesh was a journey "one way," and I knew at that time that I was not returning back. I was going there to live out the remaining days to die, and all that concerned me was how I was going manage the pain and the knowledge of my deterioration, my demise.

> *"So with this knowledge, my resolve was that I was going back home to die and off load all burdens, responsibilities and expectations."*

Once I got over there, it was an emotion tsunami for me, and my parents were affected too, they were on their own emotional roller coaster ride. My parents have already lost a child, my sister who was two and half year older than me. And now for them to lose another child before them will have been devastating. Unbeknown to us my father had lung cancer and no one could detect it, in Bangladesh.

One of the other facts of life for a child from the Muslim background is the pilgrimage to Makkah; and as it were I wasn't up to it, nor was there any money of mine to finance one. So there and then I consciously made a decision to visit all the 360 missionaries, as my pilgrimage. And this is the entire collection from those visits.

Notes

The title/recognition, "Hazrat," has been omitted from the page title, for the purpose of indexing more accurately. This is no way in disrespect nor to dilute the reverences given to the many prominents in this list, no one is on equal footing and nor does this purport to doing so.

Also reverence and respect is subjective and that remains with the people. The names are marked with asterisk:
***= the Main Man,
**= verified by 8 sided plaque,
*= reference made to the companions,
pages that have no asterisks are as they are, unverified.

By adding all these names in the list does not equal them to the revered saints, it is just my list of places I visited – organised and listed in the book as a timeline-noting the date and the time.

There are many that ended up in the list inadvertently – simply because they came to sight as a result of my targeted journeys to the verified sites of the companions of Hazrat Shah Jalal Yemini.

This list is an authoritative one of my personal trip and is for information purpose only; I express my views and opinions from the observation and experience. Interpretation is subjective to the reader, to that end, this book or I, are not promoting "shirk," if anyone with mental disposition to think that, then stop.

I hope, those of you viewing this book find what you are looking for.

Sharing the knowledge

After I returned back to UK 11 months after in 2011, I wrote about Hazrat Shah Jalal and about his Mazar and in 2020 about my illness.

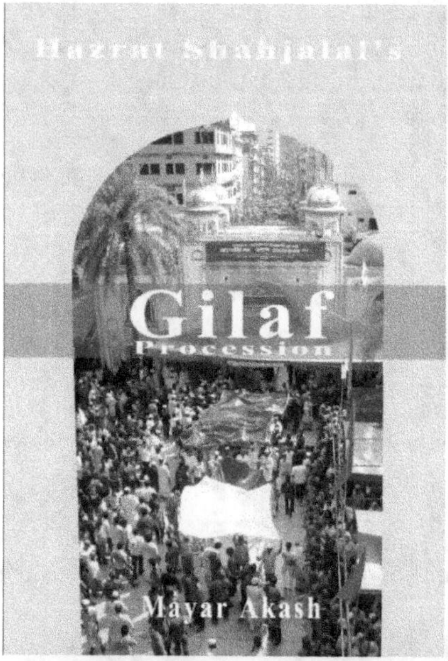
Hazrat Shahjalal's
Gilaf
Procession
Mayar Akash

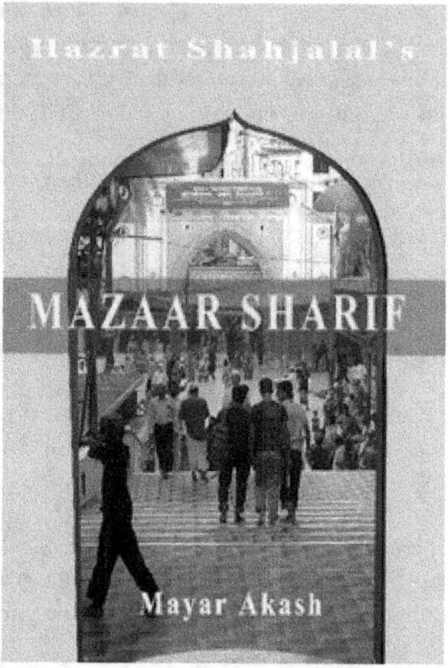
Hazrat Shahjalal's
MAZAAR SHARIF
Mayar Akash

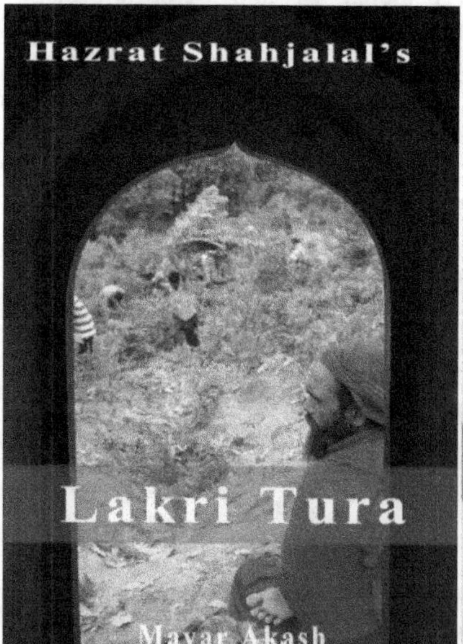
Hazrat Shahjalal's
Lakri Tura
Mayar Akash

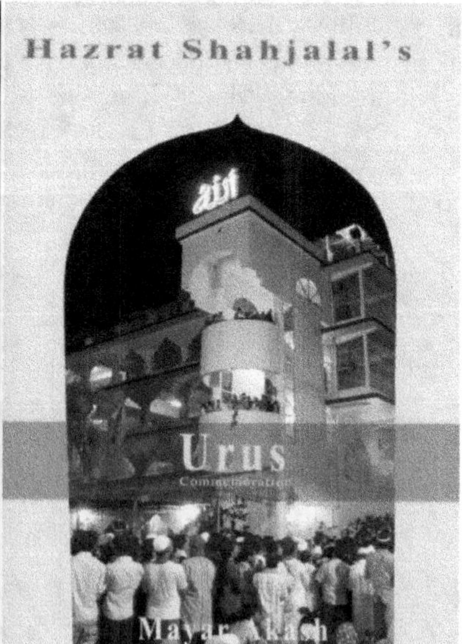
Hazrat Shahjalal's
Urus
Mayar Akash

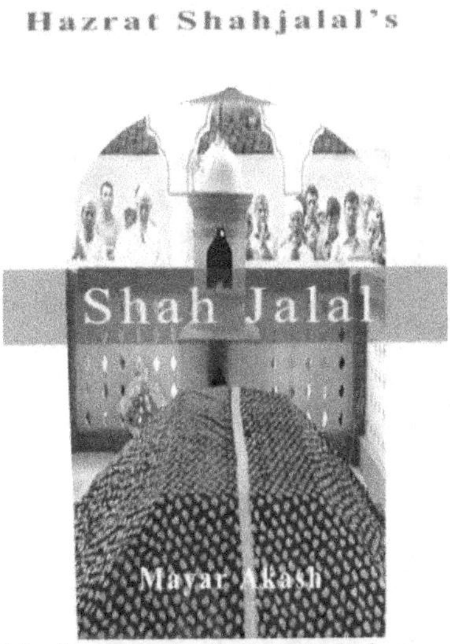
Hazrat Shahjalal's
Shah Jalal
Mayar Akash

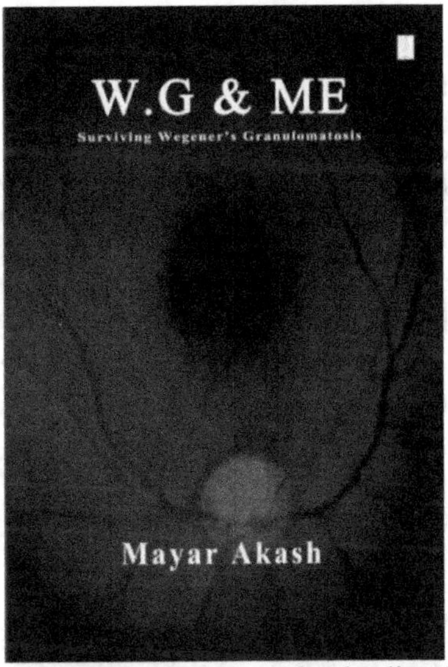
W.G & ME
Surviving Wegener's Granulomatosis
Mayar Akash

My journey in Bangladesh begun with the list from theses two books listed below. There were many inaccuracies in

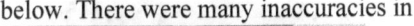

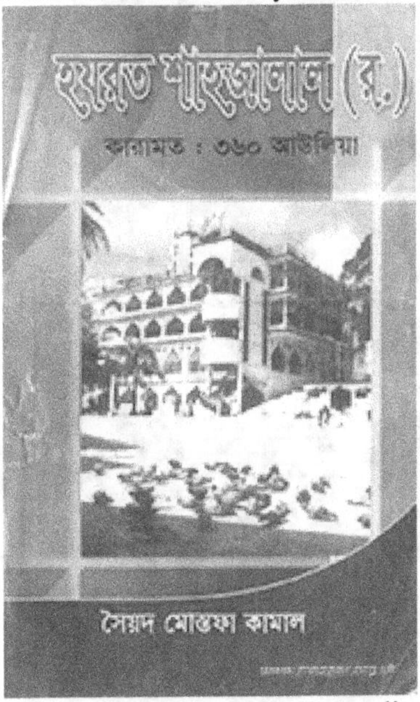
হযরত শাহজালাল (র.)
কারামত : ৩৬০ আউলিয়া
সৈয়দ মোস্তফা কামাল

1. Title: Shah Jalal and 360 Auwliyas
By Syed Mustafa Kamal

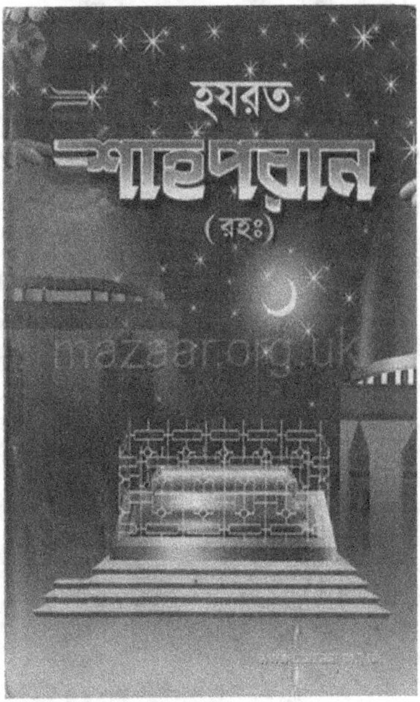
হযরত
শাহপরান
(রহঃ)
mazaar.org.uk

2. Title: Hazrat Shah Poran
by S. M. Shoriot Ullah

List of names extracted from these books. The list differs with according to the authors.

Website

I also created a website and put a lot of work in, it was up for few years and came off-line 2020. Following are screenshots of the pages. S. M. Shoriot Ullah SMSU List.

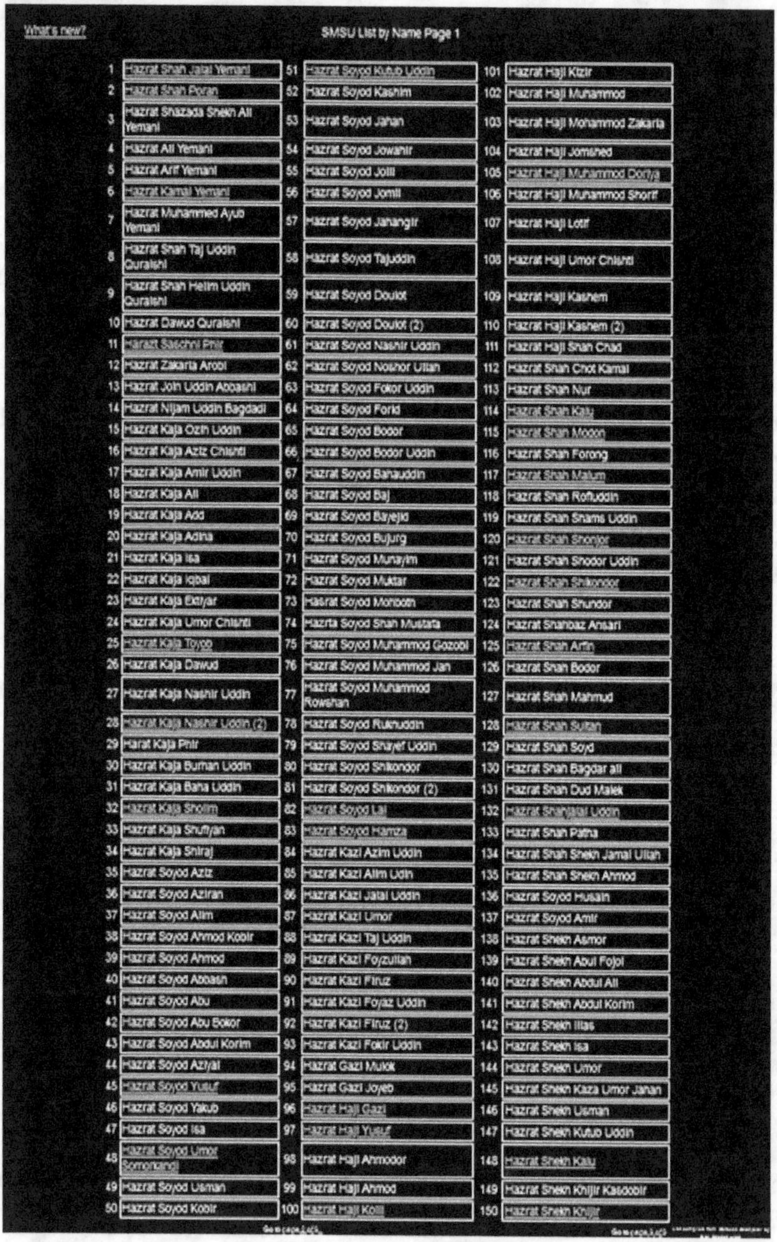

What's new?

SMSU List by Name Page 1

1	Hazrat Shah Jalal Yemani	51	Hazrat Soyod Kutub Uddin	101	Hazrat Haji Kizir
2	Hazrat Shah Poran	52	Hazrat Soyod Kashim	102	Hazrat Haji Muhammod
3	Hazrat Shazada Shekh Ali Yemani	53	Hazrat Soyod Jahan	103	Hazrat Haji Mohammod Zakaria
4	Hazrat Ali Yemani	54	Hazrat Soyod Jowahir	104	Hazrat Haji Jomshed
5	Hazrat Arif Yemani	55	Hazrat Soyod Jolil	105	Hazrat Haji Muhammod Dorya
6	Hazrat Kamal Yemani	56	Hazrat Soyod Jomil	106	Hazrat Haji Muhammod Shorif
7	Hazrat Muhammed Ayub Yemani	57	Hazrat Soyod Jahangir	107	Hazrat Haji Lotif
8	Hazrat Shah Taj Uddin Quraishi	58	Hazrat Soyod Tajuddin	108	Hazrat Haji Umor Chishti
9	Hazrat Shah Helim Uddin Quraishi	59	Hazrat Soyod Doulot	109	Hazrat Haji Kashem
10	Hazrat Dawud Quraishi	60	Hazrat Soyod Doulot (2)	110	Hazrat Haji Kashem (2)
11	Harazt Sachnli Phir	61	Hazrat Soyod Nashir Uddin	111	Hazrat Haji Shah Chad
12	Hazrat Zakaria Arobi	62	Hazrat Soyod Noshor Ullah	112	Hazrat Shah Chot Kamal
13	Hazrat Join Uddin Abbashi	63	Hazrat Soyod Fokor Uddin	113	Hazrat Shah Nur
14	Hazrat Nijam Uddin Bagdadi	64	Hazrat Soyod Forid	114	Hazrat Shah Kalu
15	Hazrat Kaja Ozih Uddin	65	Hazrat Soyod Bodor	115	Hazrat Shah Modon
16	Hazrat Kaja Aziz Chishti	66	Hazrat Soyod Bodor Uddin	116	Hazrat Shah Forong
17	Hazrat Kaja Amir Uddin	67	Hazrat Soyod Bahauddin	117	Hazrat Shah Malum
18	Hazrat Kaja Ali	68	Hazrat Soyod Baj	118	Hazrat Shah Rofiuddin
19	Hazrat Kaja Add	69	Hazrat Soyod Bayejid	119	Hazrat Shah Shams Uddin
20	Hazrat Kaja Adina	70	Hazrat Soyod Bujurg	120	Hazrat Shah Shonjor
21	Hazrat Kaja Isa	71	Hazrat Soyod Munayim	121	Hazrat Shah Shodor Uddin
22	Hazrat Kaja Iqbal	72	Hazrat Soyod Muktar	122	Hazrat Shah Shikondor
23	Hazrat Kaja Ektiyar	73	Hasrat Soyod Mohobbth	123	Hazrat Shah Shundor
24	Hazrat Kaja Umor Chishti	74	Hazrta Soyod Shah Mustafa	124	Hazrat Shahbaz Ansari
25	Hazrat Kaja Toyob	75	Hazrat Soyod Muhammod Gozobi	125	Hazrat Shah Arifin
26	Hazrat Kaja Dawud	76	Hazrat Soyod Muhammod Jan	126	Hazrat Shah Bodor
27	Hazrat Kaja Nashir Uddin	77	Hazrat Soyod Muhammod Rowshan	127	Hazrat Shah Mahmud
28	Hazrat Kaja Nashir Uddin (2)	78	Hazrat Soyod Ruknuddin	128	Hazrat Shah Sultan
29	Harat Kaja Phir	79	Hazrat Soyod Shayef Uddin	129	Hazrat Shah Soyd
30	Hazrat Kaja Burhan Uddin	80	Hazrat Soyod Shikondor	130	Hazrat Shah Bagdar ali
31	Hazrat Kaja Baha Uddin	81	Hazrat Soyod Shikondor (2)	131	Hazrat Shah Dud Malek
32	Hazrat Kaja Sholim	82	Hazrat Soyod Lal	132	Hazrat Shahjalal Uddin
33	Hazrat Kaja Shufiyan	83	Hazrat Soyod Hamza	133	Hazrat Shah Patha
34	Hazrat Kaja Shiraj	84	Hazrat Kazi Azim Uddin	134	Hazrat Shah Shekh Jamal Ullah
35	Hazrat Soyod Aziz	85	Hazrat Kazi Alim Udin	135	Hazrat Shah Shekh Ahmod
36	Hazrat Soyod Aziran	86	Hazrat Kazi Jalal Uddin	136	Hazrat Soyod Husain
37	Hazrat Soyod Alim	87	Hazrat Kazi Umor	137	Hazrat Soyod Amir
38	Hazrat Soyod Ahmod Kobir	88	Hazrat Kazi Taj Uddin	138	Hazrat Shekh Asmor
39	Hazrat Soyod Ahmod	89	Hazrat Kazi Foyzullah	139	Hazrat Shekh Abul Fojol
40	Hazrat Soyod Abbash	90	Hazrat Kazi Firuz	140	Hazrat Shekh Abdul Ali
41	Hazrat Soyod Abu	91	Hazrat Kazi Foyaz Uddin	141	Hazrat Shekh Abdul Korim
42	Hazrat Soyod Abu Bokor	92	Hazrat Kazi Firuz (2)	142	Hazrat Shekh Ilias
43	Hazrat Soyod Abdul Korim	93	Hazrat Kazi Fokir Uddin	143	Hazrat Shekh Isa
44	Hazrat Soyod Aziyat	94	Hazrat Gazi Mulok	144	Hazrat Shekh Umor
45	Hazrat Soyod Yusuf	95	Hazrat Gazi Joyeb	145	Hazrat Shekh Kaza Umor Jahan
46	Hazrat Soyod Yakub	96	Hazrat Haji Gazi	146	Hazrat Shekh Usman
47	Hazrat Soyod Isa	97	Hazrat Haji Yusuf	147	Hazrat Shekh Kutub Uddin
48	Hazrat Soyod Umor Somorkandi	98	Hazrat Haji Ahmodor	148	Hazrat Shekh Kalu
49	Hazrat Soyod Usman	99	Hazrat Haji Ahmod	149	Hazrat Shekh Khijir Kasdobir
50	Hazrat Soyod Kobir	100	Hazrat Haji Kolil	150	Hazrat Shekh Khijir

SMSU List by Name Page 2

151	Hazrat Shekh Gorib	201	Hazrat Muhammod Malik	251	Hazrat Korim Dad Rumi
152	Hazrat Shekh Jokai	202	Hazrat Muhammod Yasin	252	Hazrat Kamal Uddin
153	Hazrat Shekh Jamal	203	Hazrat Muhammod Shohotyal	253	Hazrat Kala Mian
154	Hazrat Shekh Jamil	204	Hazrat Muhammod Saleh	254	Hazrat Kutub Alom
155	Hazrat Shekh Ziauddin	205	Hazrat Muhammod Seladar	255	Hazrat Kasim Boddegi
156	Hazrat Shekh Tahir	206	Hazrat Muhammod Janedi	256	Hazrat Gorib Khaki
157	Hazrat Shekh Nosrot	207	Hazrat Muhammod Toki	257	Hazrat Goni Muhammod
158	Hazrat Shekh Niyamot Ali	208	Hazrat Muhammod Nur	258	Hazrat Goypi Phir
159	Hazrat Shekh Musa	209	Hazrat Muhammod Lotif	259	Hazrat Gulam
160	Hazrat Shekh Mohammod Kibabi	210	Hazrat Muhammod Sahabani	260	Hazrat Dilwar Khotib
161	Hazrat Shekh Mohammod Dana	211	Hazrat Muhammod Hazi	261	Hazrat Dawr Boksh Khotib
162	Hazrat Shekh Shomos	212	Hazrat Muhammod Shikondor	262	Hazrat Dada Phir
163	Hazrat Shekh Shorof Uddin	213	Hazrat Muhammod Shahbal	263	Hazrat Doulot Goni
164	Hazrat Shekh Shahoda	214	Hazrat Muhammod Shuja	264	Hazrat Doulot Gazi
165	Hazrat Shekh Sabu	215	Hazrat Muhammod Noki	265	Hazrat Doulot Mahiri
166	Hazrat Shekh Solim	216	Hazrat Muhammod Kaberi	266	Hazrat Nur Mulok
167	Hazrat Shekh Saleh	217	Hazrat Muhammod Dorrya	267	Hazrat Nur Ullah
168	Hazrat Shekh Shiraj Uddin	218	Hazrat Muhammod Min	268	Hazrat Nurul Huda
169	Hazrat Shekh Shodor	219	Hazrat Muhammod Soyod	269	Hazrat Nur Ali
170	Hazrat Shekh Helim Uddin	220	Hazrat Mauwlana Keyam Uddin	270	Hazrat Nijam Uddin Kermani
171	Hazrat Shekh Hussain	221	Hazrat Mokdum Habib	271	Hazrat Nijam Uddin Bagdadi
172	Hazrat Shekh Hussain (2)	222	Hazrat Mokdum Rohim Uddin	272	Hazrat Phir Amin
173	Hazrat Aziz Chishti	223	Hazrat Mokdum Nijamuddin Semani	273	Hazrat Phir Mulok
174	Hazrat Shukur Ullah	224	Hazrat Mokdum Jafor Gojonoi	274	Hazrat Ziauddin
175	Hazrat Mujaffor Bihari	225	Hazrat Modsuddin	275	Hazrat Porbot Gan Phir
176	Hazrat Mujaffor	226	Hazrat Moshud Mulok	276	Hazrat Forid Ansari
177	Hazrat Helim Uddin Bihari	227	Hazrat Mohiuddin	277	Hazrat Rowshan Serag
178	Hazrat Hasan Uddin Bihari	228	Hazrat Mohin Ali	278	Hazrat Suleman Foteh Gazi
179	Hazrat Adom Khaki	229	Hazrat Mowdud	279	Hazrat Firuj Atabi
180	Hazrat Azim Ashraki	230	Hazrat Maruf Seidar	280	Hazrat Foru Jayed
181	Hazrat Arif Multani	231	Hazrat Burhan Uddin Burhan	281	Hazrat Dewan Foteh Muhammod
182	Hazrat Alauddin	232	Hazrat Burhan Uddin Ahmod	282	Hazrat Ahmod
183	Hazrat Ahmod Abbasi	233	Hazrat Burhan Uddin Kattal	283	Hazrat Kanda Jokmok
184	Hazrat Ahmod Nishan Bordar	234	Hazrat Bodor Mulok	284	Hazrat Tin Salami
185	Hazrat Abu Turab	235	Hazrat Dawud Mulok	285	Hazrat Babu doulot
186	Hazrat Abul Hassan	236	Hazrat Taj Mulok	286	Hazrat Bahar Ashkari
187	Hazrat Abul Khayer	237	Hazrat Joyn Uddin	287	Hazrat Rukon Uddin Ansari
188	Hazrat Abul Adir	238	Hazrat Joyn Uddin Ansari	288	Hazrat Sultan Shah Shikondor
189	Hazrat Abu Bokkor	239	Hazrat Joyn Uddin Muhammod	289	Hazrat Shikondor Tobilyaz
190	Hazrat Abdul Aziz	240	Hazrat Zia Ullah	290	Hazrat Shuna Gazi
191	Hazrat Abdul Jolil	241	Hazrat Zinda Phir	291	Hazrat Shahab Uddin
192	Hazrat Abdul Malik	242	Hazrat Junaid Gujrati	292	Hazrat Maleh Malek
193	Hazrat Abdul Shukur	243	Hazrat Ismail Umori	293	Hazrat Shikondor Solim
194	Hazrat Abdul Hekim	244	Hazrat Isa Chisti	294	Hazrat Lal Shaheb
195	Hazrat Abdul Rohim	245	Hazrat Imam Uddin	295	Hazrat Ullah
196	Hazrat Abdul Mali	246	Hazrat Elim Shah	296	Hazrat Hobib Gazi
197	Hazrat Abdul Ali	247	Hazrat Kari Emiah	297	Hazrat Hafiz Muhammod
198	Hazrat Muhammod Ansari	248	Hazrat Usman Uddin	298	Hazrat Helim Uddin Nurnali
199	Hazrat Muhammod Amin	249	Hazrat Usman Uddin (2)	299	Hazrat Hamid Faruki
200	Hazrat Muhammod Ashik	250	Hazrat Umor Dorrya	300	Hazrat Haydor Gazi

What's New?

SMSU List by Name Page 3

301	Hazrat Hashem Chisti	351		
302	Hazrat Hojjot Malek	352		
303	Hazrat Husamuddin??	353		
304	Hazrat Hisan Uddin	354		
305	Hazrat Hasan Shohid	355		
306	Hazrat Hafez Foshi	356		
307	Hazrat Gulam (2)	357		
308	Hazrat Sufi Husen	358		
309	Hazrat Dewan Kolli	359		
310	Hazrat Hazi Jomshed Khotib	360		
311	Hazrat Shekh Nosor			
312	Hazrat Mokdum Shaheb			
313	Hazrat Kazi Shah Dewan			
314	Hazrat Shorif Ajmiri			
315	Hazrat Lal Shaheb (2)			
316	Hazrat Sufi Husen (2)			
317	Hazrat Mad Soyod			
318	Hazrat Gorum Dewan			
319	Hazrat Muktar Shohid			
320	Hazrat Shams Uddin Bihari			
321	Hazrat Doriyah Phir			
322	Hazrat Soyod Buruj			
323	Hazrat Soyod Ujran			
324	Hazrat Hasan Uddin			
325	Hazrat Habullah Khotit			
326	Hazrat Maruf Siladar			
327	Hazrat Forid Uddin Rushon Siraj			
328	Hazrat Mauwlana Keyamuddin			
329	Hazrat Taj Mali			
330	Hazrat Kaja Fayar			
331	Hazrat Shekh Bej			
332	Hazrat Adom Khaki (2)			
333	Hazrat Imam Uddin (2)			
334	Hazrat Muhammod Ayub Imam			
335	Hazrat Jamil			
336	Hazrat Hamid Uddin Narayon			
337	Hazrat Zia Uddin Ahmod			
338	Hazrat Soyod Abdul korim			
339	Hazrat Goni Ahmod			
340	Hazrat Toyob Selami			
341	Hazrat Amin			
342	Hazrat Shekh Shorif			
343	Hazrat Shah Giyash Ali			
344	Hazrat Muhammod Noki Babul Doulot			
345	Hazrat Hafiz Muhammod			
346	Hazrat Shah Baba Mian			
347	Hazrat Bondu Shah Dawd ?			
348	Hazrat Baba Aiynuddin			
349	Hazrat Shah Mojlish Amin			
350				

ENGLAND

Produced, Researched and Created by Mayar Akash, 2010. Managed by Little England Ventures 2002-2010. Photography by Mayar Akash

Soyod Mustafa Kamal (SMK) List

SMK List by Name Page 1

1	Hazrat Shah Jalal Yemani	51	Hazrat Kaza Jamil	101	Hazrat Kaza Selim
2	Hazrat Shayek Haji Ahmod	52	Hazrat Kaza Jownor	102	Hazrat Shayek Shadu
3	Hazrat Soyod Ahmed Kobir	53	Hazrat Kaza Jahangir	103	Hazrat Shayek Shunagazi
4	Hazrat Shayek Haji Ahmod	54	Hazrat Shayek Jamal	104	Hazrat Shayek Shorof Uddin
5	Hazrat Kaza Ahmod	55	Hazrat Shayek Jogal	105	Hazrat Shayek Kaji Shah Dewan
6	Hazrat Kaza Aziyal	56	Hazrat Shayek Makdum Jaffor Gajonor	106	Hazrat Shayek Imam Shukurullah
7	Hazrat Kaza Abul Fozol	57	Hazrat Shayek Kaji Jahan	107	Hazrat Shayek Haji Shorif
8	Hazrat Shayek Aman Ullah	58	Hazrat Shayek Haji Jomened	108	Hazrat Shayek Shah Shamsuddin Mohammod Bihari
9	Hazrat Shayek Ahmod	59	Hazrat Shayek Jalal Uddin	109	Hazrat Shayek Shihab Uddin
10	Hazrat Shayek Kaji Amin Uddin	60	Hazrat Shayek Junaid Quraishi	110	Hazrat Shayek Shorif Ajmiri
11	Harazt Shayek Muhammod Ayub Imam	61	Hazrat Shayek Chashni Phir	111	Hazrat Shayek Shahbaz Ansari
12	Hazrat Kaza Iqbal	62	Hazrat Kaza Hamza	112	Hazrat Shayek Shamsuddin
13	Hazrat Kaza Adina	63	Hazrat Kaza Helim Uddin Namuli	113	Hazrat Shayek Saleh Muluk
14	Hazrat Kaza Amir Uddin	64	Hazrat Shayek Husen	114	Hazrat Kaza Sufiyan
15	Hazrat Kaza Ektyar	65	Hazrat Shayek Makdum Habib	115	Hazrat Shayek Shodru
16	Hazrat Shayek Imam Uddin	66	Hazrat Shayek Hujjaten Muluk	116	Hazrat Kaza Ziauddin Muhammod
17	Hazrat Shayek Ismail Umor	67	Hazrat Shayek Husen Shohid	117	Hazrat Shayek Shah Ziauddin
18	Hazrat Shayek Ahmod Abbas	68	Hazrat Shayek Habib Gazi	118	Hazrat Shayek Ziaullah
19	Hazrat Shayek Abul Hasan	69	Hazrat Shayek Husam Uddin Bihari	119	Hazrat Shayek Tahir
20	Hazrat Shayek Abul Khayer	70	Hazrat Shayek Hasan Sufi	120	Hazrat Shayek Tayab Gilani
21	Hazrat Shayek Abu Soyd	71	Hazrat Kaza Kholilullah	121	Hazrat Kaza Abdul Jolil
22	Hazrat Shayek Abu Ariz	72	Hasrat Kaza Kholil	122	Hazrat Kaza Umor Somorkondi
23	Hazrat Shayek Adom Khaki	73	Hazrat Shayek Haji Kholil	123	Hazrat Kaza Abdul Muyall
24	Hazrat Shayek Elias	74	Hazrat Shayek Kholil Dewana	124	Hazrat Shayek Ali Yemani
25	Hazrat Kaza Amir	75	Hazrat Shayek Haji Khijir	125	Hazrat Shayek Shahzada Ali Yemani Sani
26	Hazrat Kaza Ahmod Sani	76	Hazrat Shayek Khijir	126	Hazrat Kaza Abdul Korim
27	Hazrat Kaza Abu Bokor	77	Hazrat Shayek Khasdobir	127	Hazrat Kaza Isa
28	Hazrat Kaza Abu Abbas	78	Hazrat Kaza Doulot	128	Hazrat Shayek Abdul Aziz
29	Harat Kaza Abu Bokor Sani	79	Hazrat Shayek Dauwd Quraishi	129	Hazrat Shayek Usman
30	Hazrat Shayek Ahmod Nishan Bordar	80	Hazrat Shayek Delawar Khotib	130	Hazrat Kaza Isa (2)
31	Hazrat Kaza Bodor Uddin	81	Hazrat Shayek Daur Bokth Khotib	131	Hazrat Shayek Abdul Malik
32	Hazrat Kaza Bujurg	82	Hazrat Shayek Dud Muluk	132	Hazrat Shayek Isa
33	Hazrat Kaza Bayezid	83	Hazrat Kaza Daud	133	Hazrat Shayek Alauddin
34	Hazrat Kaza Babu	84	Hazrat Douloten Muniri	134	Hazrat Shayek Abdullah
35	Hazrat Kaza Bodor	85	Hazrat Shayek Diyar Phir	135	Hazrat Shayek Abdul Korim
36	Hazrat Shayek Baj	86	Hazrat Shayek Babu Doulot	136	Hazrat Shayek Abdul Shakur
37	Hazrat Shayek Bahauddin	87	Hazrat Shayek Zakaria Hafiz	137	Hazrat Kaza Aziz Chisti
38	Hazrat Shayek Bodor Muluk	88	Hazrat Shayek Zakaria Arbi	138	Hazrat Shayek Arif Multani
39	Hazrat Kaza Bahauddin	89	Hazrat Kaza Ruknuddin	139	Hazrat Kaza Alom
40	Hazrat Kaza Burhan Uddin Kattal	90	Hazrat Shayek Makdum Rokonuddin	140	Hazrat Aziz
41	Hazrat Shayek Burhan Uddin Burhana	91	Hazrat Shayek Rukon Uddin Ansari	141	Hazrat Shayek Abdul Rohim
42	Hazrat Shayek Bahar Askori	92	Hazrat Shayek Joinuddin Abbasi	142	Hazrat Shayek Abdul Halim
43	Hazrat Phiren Yemani	93	Hazrat Shayek Joinuddin Zakaria	143	Hazrat Shayek Ariz Askori
44	Hazrat Phiren Prithi Jahan	94	Hazrat Shayek Sultan Shikondor Gazi	144	Hazrat Kaza Ali
45	Hazrat Phiren Muluk	95	Hazrat Shayek Shikondor Muhammod	145	Hazrat Shayek Umor
46	Hazrat Kaza Piyar	96	Hazrat Kaza Saifuddin	146	Hazrat Shayek Usman Uddin
47	Hazrat Kaza Soyod Shah Tajuddin	97	Hazrat Shayek Selim	147	Hazrat Shayek Umor Dowri
48	Hazrat Shayek Kaji Tajuddin	98	Hazrat Shayek Siraj Uddin	148	Hazrat Shayek Haji Umor Chisti
49	Hazrat Shayek Taj A Muluk	99	Hazrat Shayek Shikondor	149	Hazrat Shayek Haji Usman Dowri
50	Hazrat Kaza Jolal Uddin	100	Hazrat Kaza Siraj	150	Hazrat Kaza Umor Jahan

This list was compiled from book 1 (listed on page 21) purchased in Sylhet at the Dorga gate avenue.

This is the list of books that were written about Sylhet and the Mazars.

Title	Author	Isbn / ref. No. / Date
Hazrat Shah Jalal & Shah Poran	M.M Mizanur Rohman Jahery	2009
Rowjaye Shah Jalal	Kadim Moin Uddin Jaifor Khan	1722
Riyajursh Salatin	Gulam Hussain Solim	1786
Suhel E Yemen	Nasir Uddin Hyder	1860
Tarikeh Jalali	Mubashir Ali Dobir	1868
Torfeh Itihash	Soyod Abdul Agfor	1885
Shrihot dorfon	Moulovi Muhammad Ahmod	1886
Rajmala	Kewlashchondro shingho	1895
Shrihoter Itihash	Sri Muhini Muhon Dash Gupta	1903
Shrihoter Shah Jalal	Abdul Wahab Choudhury	1905
Shrihoter Itibrikto	Osutto Soron Choudhury totunidi	1910
Kasareh Itihash	Upendro Sondro Guhon	1910
Shrihot Bijoy Kabeh	Abu Jekaria Ibrahim Ali	1911
Sokreh Pani Dukko	Boshonto Kumar Sen Gupta	1919
Hazrat Shah Jalaler kescha	Ashraf Hussain Shahitant	1929
Shrihoteh Islam Jowti	Mufti Ajhar Uddin Ahmod	1938
Shrihoter Prasin Itihash	Komlakont Gupta Choudhury	1940
Purbo Pakistaner Islam	Dr. Muhammad Enamul Hoque	1948
Bangali Musolmander Shamagik Itihash	Dr. Abdul Korim	1959
Shrihot Jowti	Muhammad Riasot Ali	1962
Hazrat Shahjalal & Sylheter Itihash	Soyod Murtoza Ali	1965
Purbopakistaneh Islamer Alo	Choudhury Shamsur Rohman	1965
Banglar Musolman	Kondokar Fojole Rabbi	1968
Bongobaroter Itihash	Oddehpok Md. Ish hak	1972
Muslim Banglai Bideshi Porjotok	Dr. Wakib Ahmod	1977
Bangladesher Itihash	Abdul Monnan Talib	1980
Dorgai Dorbesh	Monuwar Hussain	1980

Islami Shahshon Bebosta	Shakaoatul Ambia	1980
Jalalbader Kota	Dewan Nurul Anuwar Hussain Choudhury	1983
Nobigoinj Itikota	Motiyar Rohman	1985
Shonkito Islami Bishokush	Islamic Foundation	1985
Sylheter Itihash	Muhammad Ashraf Hussain	1990
Boreno Sylhet	Fozlur Rahman	1990
Sylheter Mati Sylheter Manush	Fozlur Rahman	1991
Hazrat Shah Jalal - Koramoth 360 Auwlia	Soyod Mustafa Kamal	1992
Brihoktor Sylheter oidotrinik Shadkogon	Dewan Muhammad Ajrof	1992
Habigoinj Porikroma	Dr Muhammad Afjol	1994
Sylheter Islam	Dewan Muhammad Afjal	1995
Shunamgoinj Jelar Itihash & Tottito	Abu Ali Sajjad Hussain	1995
Gulapgoinj Itihash & Tottito	Anuwar Shah Jahan	1996
Brihonktor Sylheter Itihash	Muhammad Abdul Aziz Shompadith	1997
Jogonathpur Kotha	Ragib Hussain Choudhury	1997
JalalbaderShonkritik Totito	Choudhury Gulam Akbar	1998
Sylhet Bibager Proshahon & Bumi Bebsha	Md. Hafizur Rahman Buiya	1998
Jokigoinj Itihash	Abarok Hussain	2000
Shofor Nama ibn Botuta	Muhammad Nasir Ali	2000
Hazrat Shah Poran r.	S. M. Shoriot Ullah	2000
Sylhet Bibager itibritto	Muhammad Muminur Hoque	2001
Shunamgoinj Porisiti	Muhammad Ali Khan (Shompadit)	2002
Sylhet Bidi info dot com	Himadri Sikor Rai	2002

Home Page

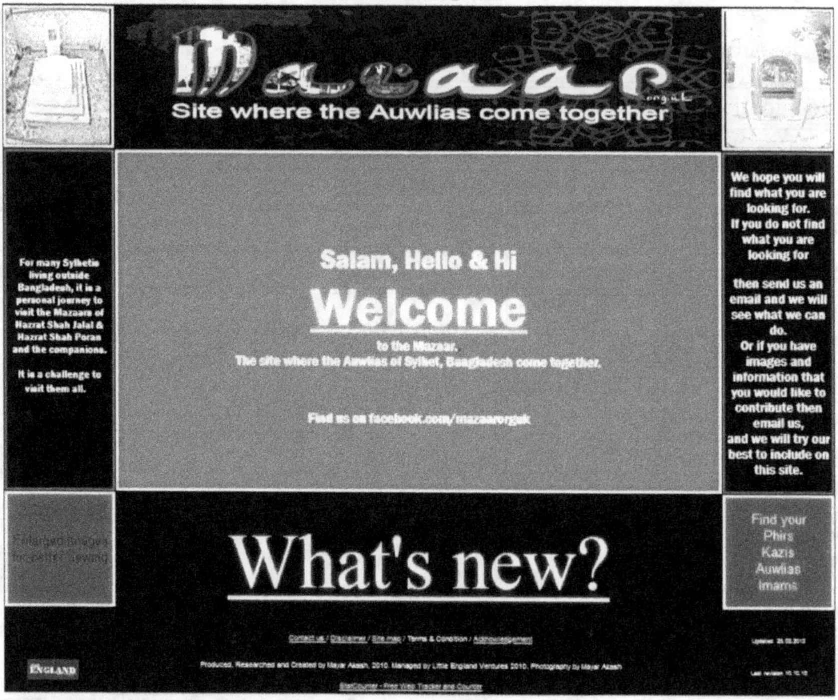
Mazaar
Site where the Auwlias come together
For many Sylhetis living outside Bangladesh, it is a personal journey to visit the Mazaars of Hazrat Shah Jalal & Hazrat Shah Poran and the companions.
It is a challenge to visit them all.
Salam, Hello & Hi
Welcome
to the Mazaar.
The site where the Auwlias of Sylhet, Bangladesh come together.
Find us on facebook.com/mazaarorguk
We hope you will find what you are looking for.
If you do not find what you are looking for
then send us an email and we will see what we can do.
Or if you have images and information that you would like to contribute then email us, and we will try our best to include on this site.
What's new?
Find your Phirs Kazis Auwlias Imams
ENGLAND

I created this site while I was in Bangladesh and had time on my hand to do it. It didn't get completed as I didn't get to visit all 360 Mazars because I returned back to UK after 11 months of stay. As you will see a lot of work went in to create a comprehensive site.

What's new page.

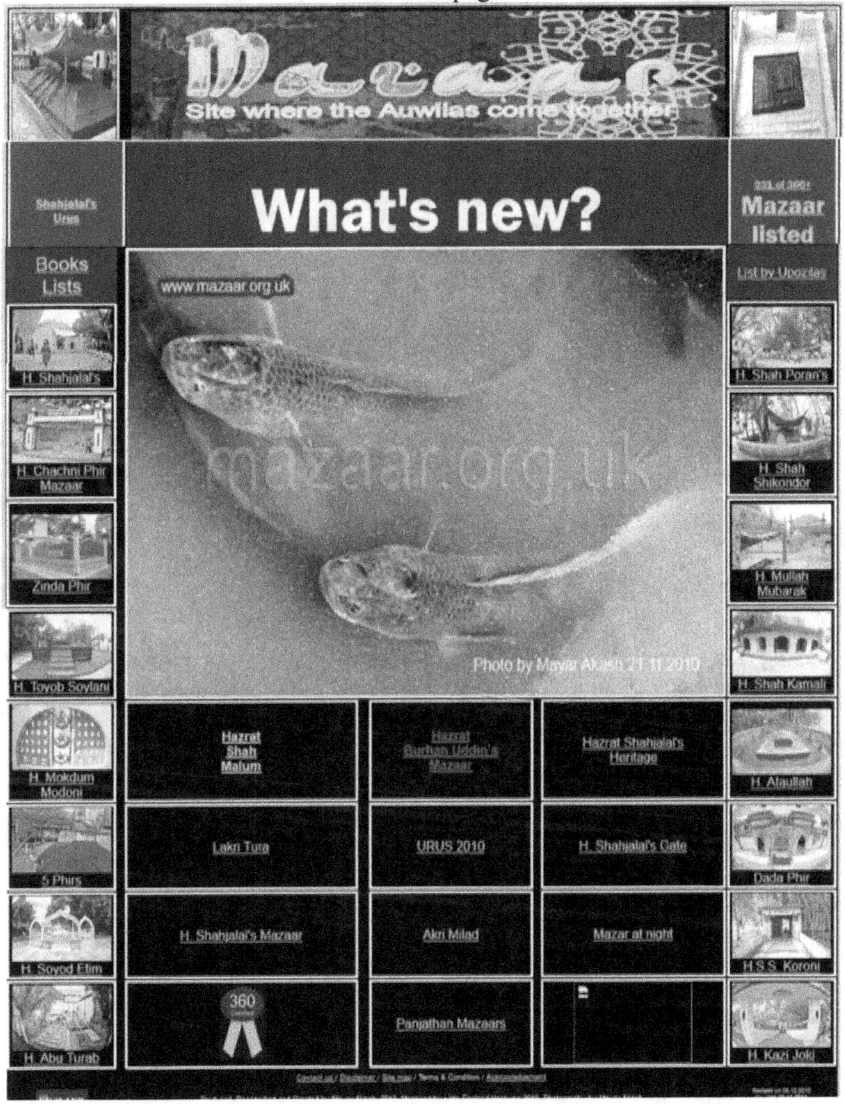
Site where the Auwlias come together
What's new?
Mazaar
listed
Books
Lists
List by Upozilas
www.mazaar.org.uk
mazaar.org.uk
H. Shahjalal's
H. Chachni Phir
Mazaar
Zinda Phir
H. Toyob Soylani
H. Mokdum
Modoni
5 Phirs
H. Soyod Elim
H. Abu Turab
H. Shah Poran's
H. Shah
Shikondor
H. Mullah
Mubarak
H. Shah Kamali
H. Ataullah
Dada Phir
H.S.S. Koroni
H. Kazi Joki
Hazrat
Shah
Malum
Hazrat Shahjalal's
Heritage
Lakri Tura
URUS 2010
H. Shahjalal's Gate
H. Shahjalal's Mazaar
Akri Milad
Mazar at night
360
Panjathan Mazaars

This was the "What's New?" page with images of places visited so far and dissecting the information about my findings.

Index Page

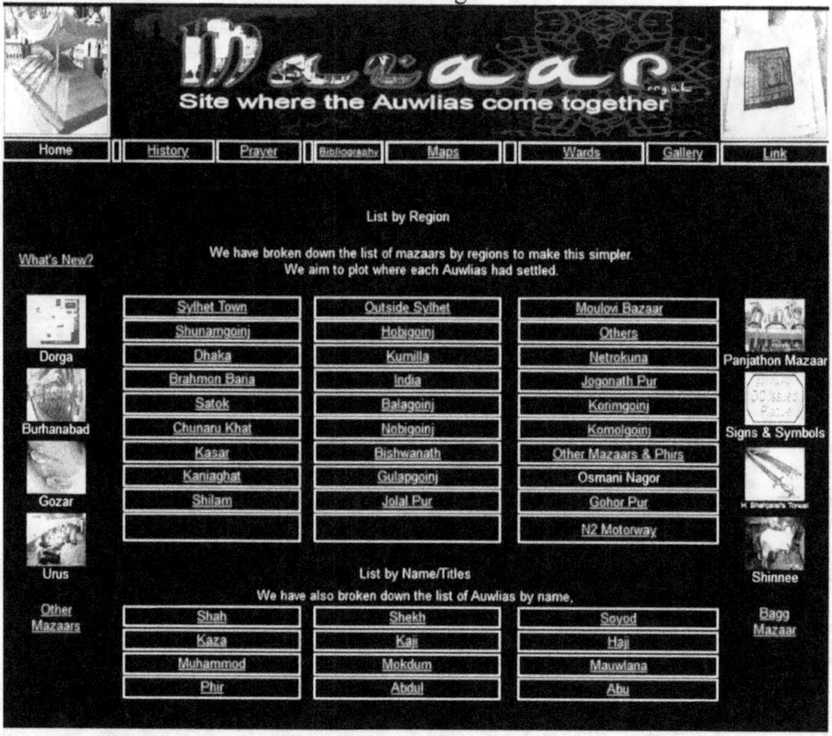
Site where the Auwlias come together
Home
History
Prayer
Bibliography
Maps
Wards
Gallery
Link
List by Region
What's New?
We have broken down the list of mazaars by regions to make this simpler.
We aim to plot where each Auwlias had settled.
Sylhet Town
Outside Sylhet
Moulovi Bazaar
Shunamgoinj
Hobigoinj
Others
Dhaka
Kumilla
Netrokuna
Brahmon Baria
India
Jogonath Pur
Satok
Balagoinj
Korimgoinj
Chunaru Khat
Nobigoinj
Komolgoinj
Kasar
Bishwanath
Other Mazaars & Phirs
Kaniaghat
Gulapgoinj
Osmani Nagor
Shilam
Jolal Pur
Gohor Pur
N2 Motorway
Dorga
Burhanabad
Gozar
Urus
Other Mazaars
Panjathon Mazaar
Signs & Symbols
Shinnee
Bagg Mazaar
List by Name/Titles
We have also broken down the list of Auwlias by name.
Shah
Shekh
Soyod
Kaza
Kaji
Haji
Muhammod
Mokdum
Mauwlana
Phir
Abdul
Abu

A lot of extensive research and dissecting of information has gone into this page to make it easy for users to navigate.

Sylhet Town Page

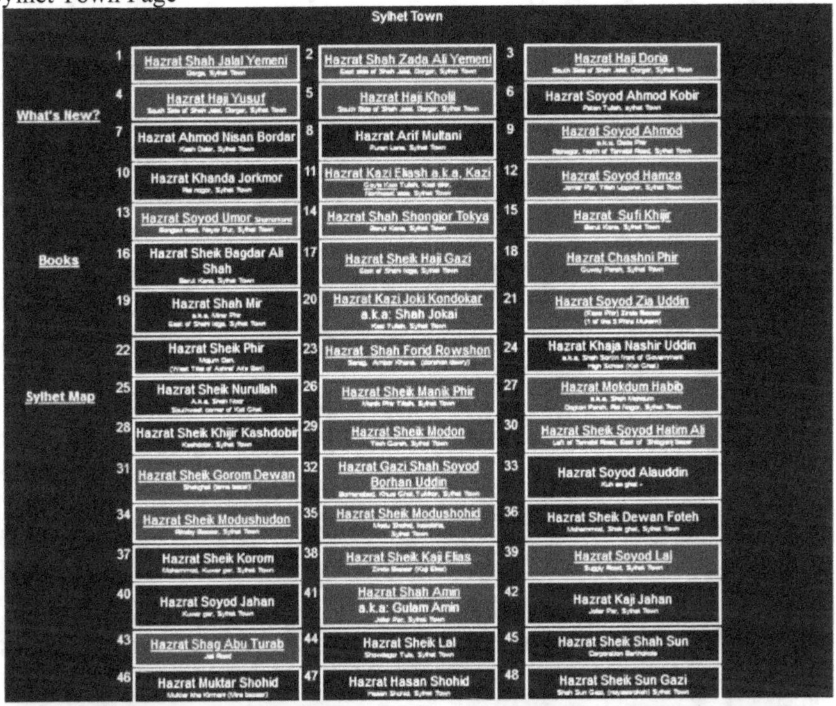
Sylhet Town
What's New?
Books
Sylhet Map
1 Hazrat Shah Jalal Yemeni
2 Hazrat Shah Zada Ali Yemeni
3 Hazrat Haji Doria
4 Hazrat Haji Yusuf
5 Hazrat Haji Kholil
6 Hazrat Soyod Ahmod Kobir
7 Hazrat Ahmod Nisan Bordar
8 Hazrat Arif Multani
9 Hazrat Soyod Ahmod
10 Hazrat Khanda Jorkmor
11 Hazrat Kazi Eliash a.k.a. Kazi
12 Hazrat Soyod Hamza
13 Hazrat Soyod Umor
14 Hazrat Shah Shongjor Tokya
15 Hazrat Sufi Khijir
16 Hazrat Sheik Bagdar Ali Shah
17 Hazrat Sheik Haji Gazi
18 Hazrat Chashni Phir
19 Hazrat Shah Mir
20 Hazrat Kazi Joki Kondokar a.k.a: Shah Jokai
21 Hazrat Soyod Zia Uddin
22 Hazrat Sheik Phir
23 Hazrat Shah Forid Rowshon
24 Hazrat Khaja Nashir Uddin
25 Hazrat Sheik Nurullah
26 Hazrat Sheik Manik Phir
27 Hazrat Mokdum Habib
28 Hazrat Sheik Khijir Kashdobir
29 Hazrat Sheik Modon
30 Hazrat Sheik Soyod Hatim Ali
31 Hazrat Sheik Gorom Dewan
32 Hazrat Gazi Shah Soyod Borhan Uddin
33 Hazrat Soyod Alauddin
34 Hazrat Sheik Modushudon
35 Hazrat Sheik Modushohid
36 Hazrat Sheik Dewan Foteh
37 Hazrat Sheik Korom
38 Hazrat Sheik Kaji Elias
39 Hazrat Soyod Lal
40 Hazrat Soyod Jahan
41 Hazrat Shah Amin a.k.a: Gulam Amin
42 Hazrat Kaji Jahan
43 Hazrat Shag Abu Turab
44 Hazrat Sheik Lal
45 Hazrat Sheik Shah Sun
46 Hazrat Muktar Shohid
47 Hazrat Hasan Shohid
48 Hazrat Sheik Sun Gazi

Outside Sylhet town

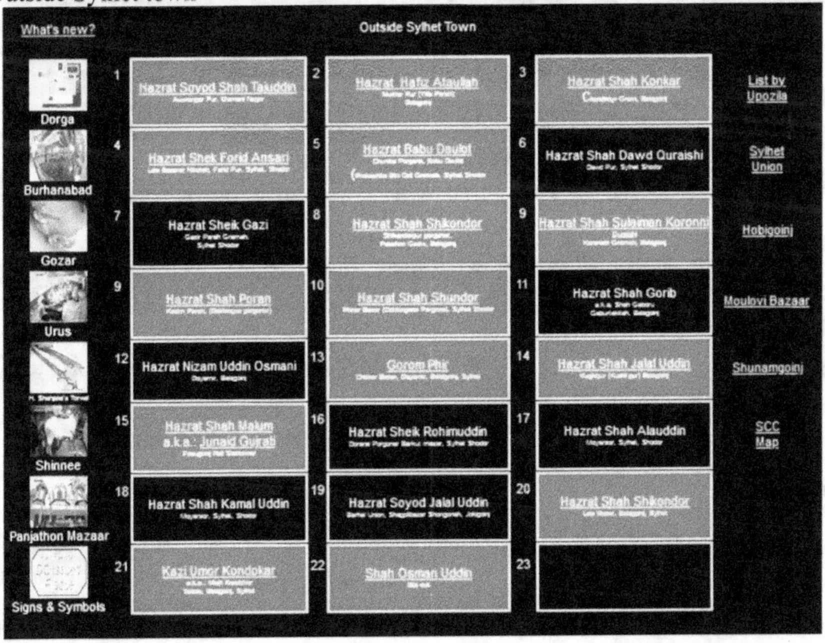
What's new?
Outside Sylhet Town
Dorga
Burhanabad
Gozar
Urus
Shinnee
Panjathon Mazaar
Signs & Symbols
1 Hazrat Soyod Shah Tajuddin
2 Hazrat Hafiz Ataullah
3 Hazrat Shah Konkar
4 Hazrat Shek Forid Ansari
5 Hazrat Babu Daulot
6 Hazrat Shah Dawd Quraishi
7 Hazrat Sheik Gazi
8 Hazrat Shah Shikondor
9 Hazrat Shah Sulaiman Koronni
9 Hazrat Shah Poran
10 Hazrat Shah Shundor
11 Hazrat Shah Gorib
12 Hazrat Nizam Uddin Osmani
13 Gorom Phir
14 Hazrat Shah Jalal Uddin
15 Hazrat Shah Malum a.k.a.: Junaid Gujrati
16 Hazrat Sheik Rohimuddin
17 Hazrat Shah Alauddin
18 Hazrat Shah Kamal Uddin
19 Hazrat Soyod Jalal Uddin
20 Hazrat Shah Shikondor
21 Kazi Umor Kondokar
22 Shah Osman Uddin
23
List by Upozila
Sylhet Union
Hobigoinj
Moulovi Bazaar
Shunamgoinj
SCC Map

Moulovi Bazaar

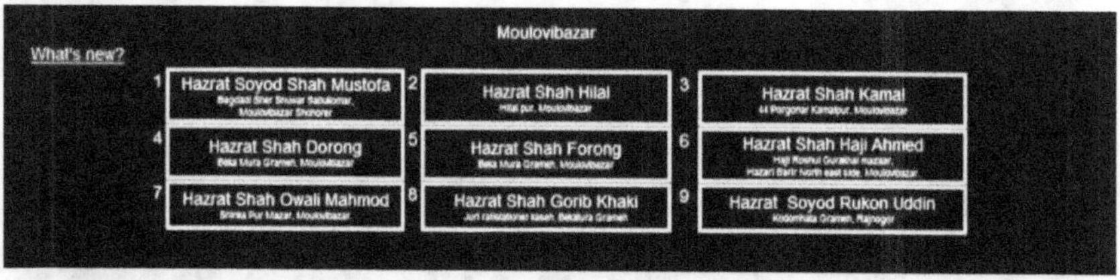
Moulovibazar
What's new?
1 Hazrat Soyod Shah Mustofa
2 Hazrat Shah Hilal
3 Hazrat Shah Kamal
4 Hazrat Shah Dorong
5 Hazrat Shah Forong
6 Hazrat Shah Haji Ahmed
7 Hazrat Shah Owali Mahmod
8 Hazrat Shah Gorib Khaki
9 Hazrat Soyod Rukon Uddin

Shunamgoinj

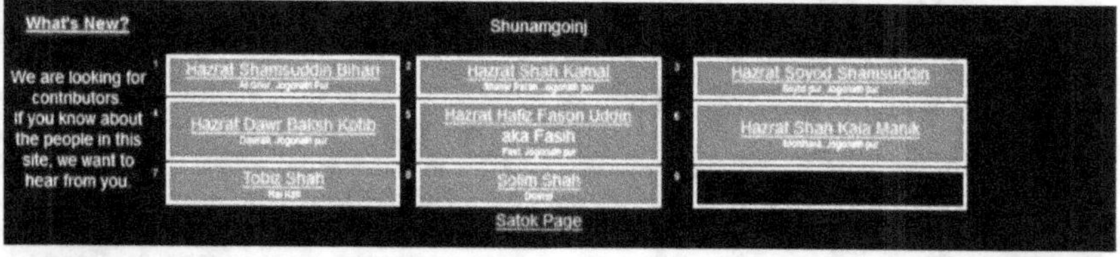
What's New?
Shunamgoinj
We are looking for contributors. If you know about the people in this site, we want to hear from you.
Hazrat Shamsuddin Bihari
Hazrat Shah Kamal
Hazrat Soyod Shamsuddin
Hazrat Dawr Baksh Kotib
Hazrat Hafiz Fason Uddin aka Fasih
Hazrat Shah Kala Manik
Tobiz Shah
Solim Shah
Satok Page

Hobigonj

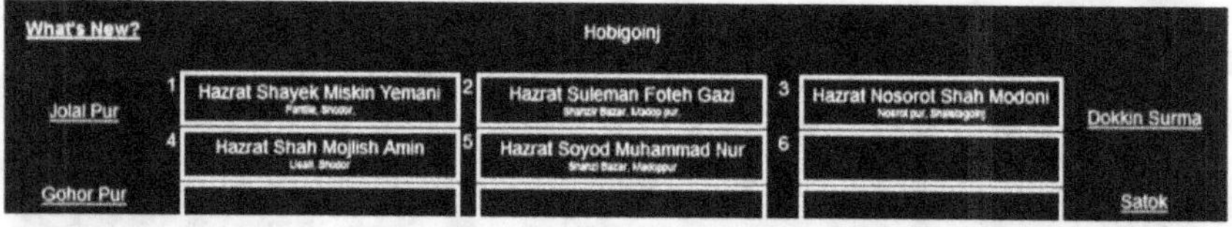
What's New?
Hobigoinj
Jolal Pur
Gohor Pur
1 Hazrat Shayek Miskin Yemani
2 Hazrat Suleman Foteh Gazi
3 Hazrat Nosorot Shah Modoni
4 Hazrat Shah Mojlish Amin
5 Hazrat Soyod Muhammad Nur
6
Dokkin Surma
Satok

Others

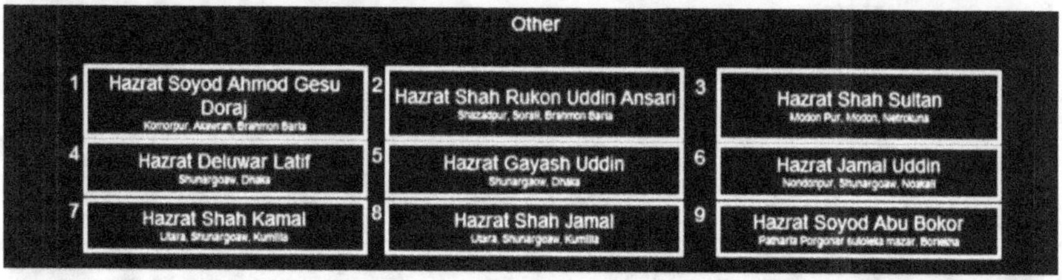
Other
1 Hazrat Soyod Ahmod Gesu Doraj
2 Hazrat Shah Rukon Uddin Ansari
3 Hazrat Shah Sultan
4 Hazrat Deluwar Latif
5 Hazrat Gayash Uddin
6 Hazrat Jamal Uddin
7 Hazrat Shah Kamal
8 Hazrat Shah Jamal
9 Hazrat Soyod Abu Bokor

Bishwanath

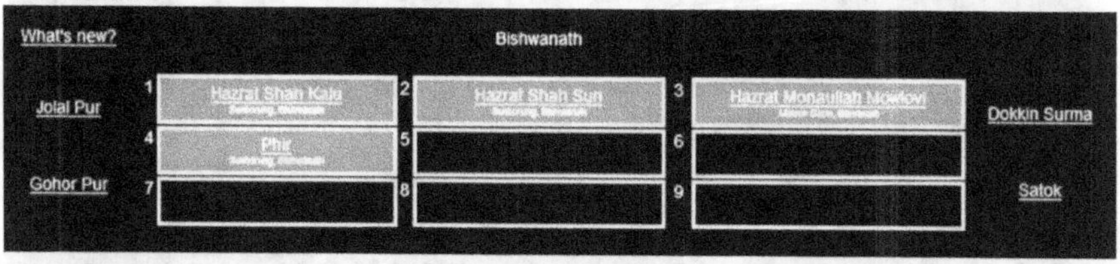
What's new?
Bishwanath
Jolal Pur
Gohor Pur
1 Hazrat Shah Kala
2 Hazrat Shah Sun
3 Hazrat Monaullah Mowlovi
4 Phir
5
6
7
8
9
Dokkin Surma
Satok

Gohor Pur

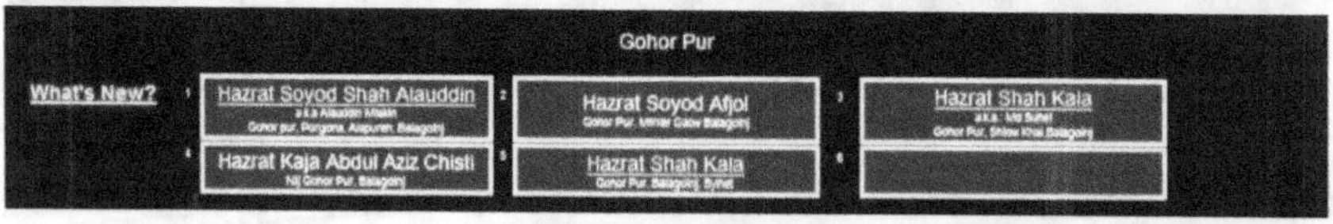
Gohor Pur
What's New?
Hazrat Soyod Shah Alauddin
Hazrat Soyod Afjol
Hazrat Shah Kala
Hazrat Kaja Abdul Aziz Chisti
Hazrat Shah Kala

Chunaru Ghat

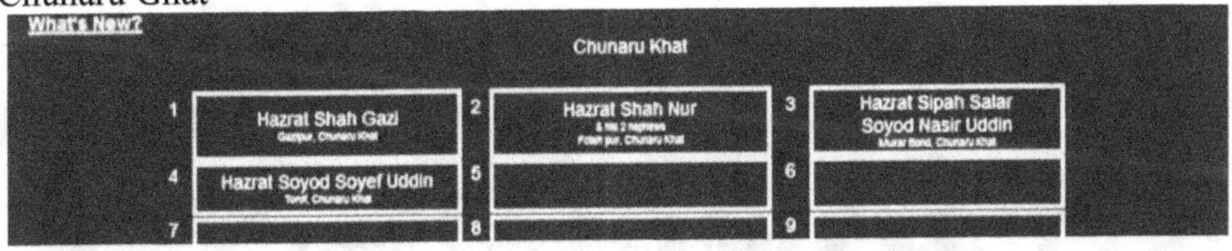
What's New?
Chunaru Khat
1
Hazrat Shah Gazi
2
Hazrat Shah Nur
3
Hazrat Sipah Salar Soyod Nasir Uddin
4
Hazrat Soyod Soyef Uddin
5
6
7
8
9

Gulapgoinj

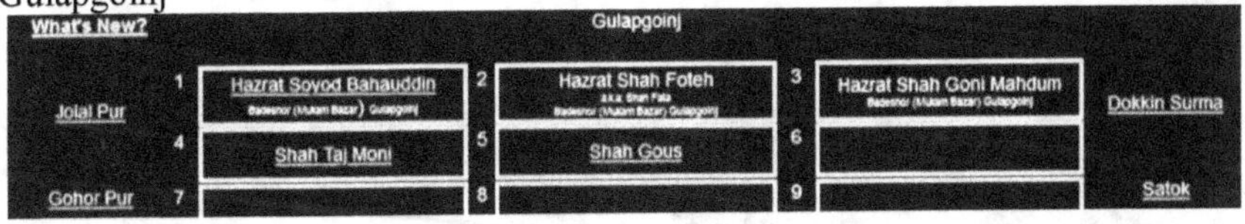
What's New?
Gulapgoinj
Jolal Pur
Gohor Pur
1
Hazrat Soyod Bahauddin
2
Hazrat Shah Foteh
3
Hazrat Shah Goni Mahdum
4
Shah Taj Moni
5
Shah Gous
6
7
8
9
Dokkin Surma
Satok

Kanaighat

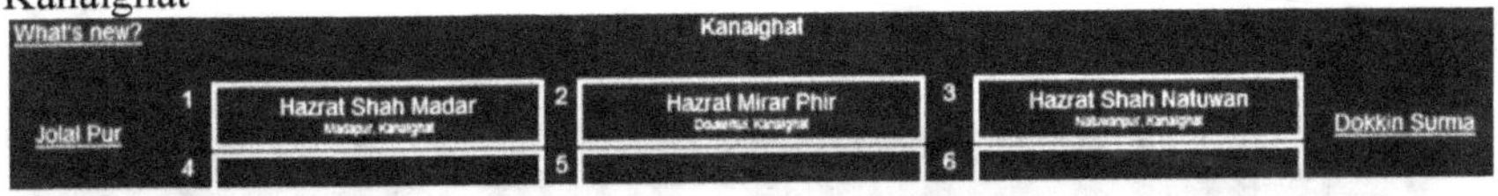
What's new?
Kanaighat
Jolal Pur
1
Hazrat Shah Madar
2
Hazrat Mirar Phir
3
Hazrat Shah Natuwan
4
5
6
Dokkin Surma

Kasar

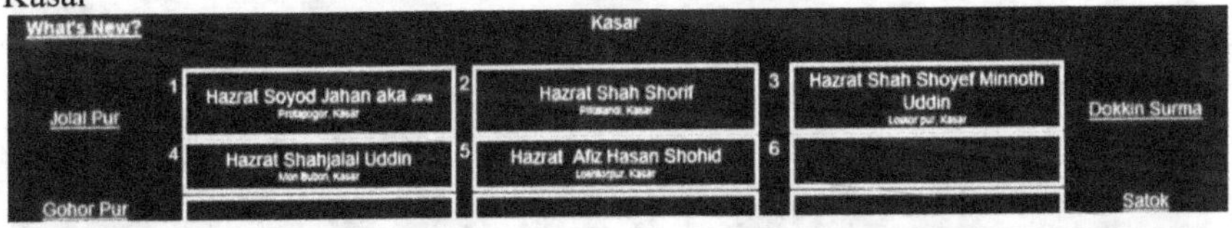
What's New?
Kasar
Jolal Pur
Gohor Pur
1
Hazrat Soyod Jahan aka
2
Hazrat Shah Shorif
3
Hazrat Shah Shoyef Minnoth Uddin
4
Hazrat Shahjalal Uddin
5
Hazrat Afiz Hasan Shohid
6
Dokkin Surma
Satok

Komolgoinj

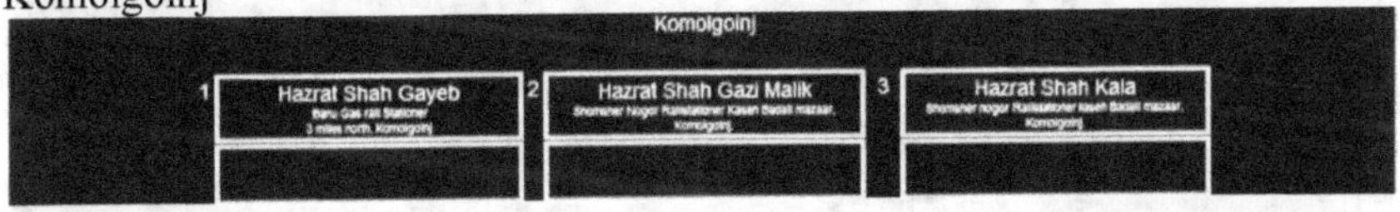
Komolgoinj
1
Hazrat Shah Gayeb
2
Hazrat Shah Gazi Malik
3
Hazrat Shah Kala

Korimgoinj

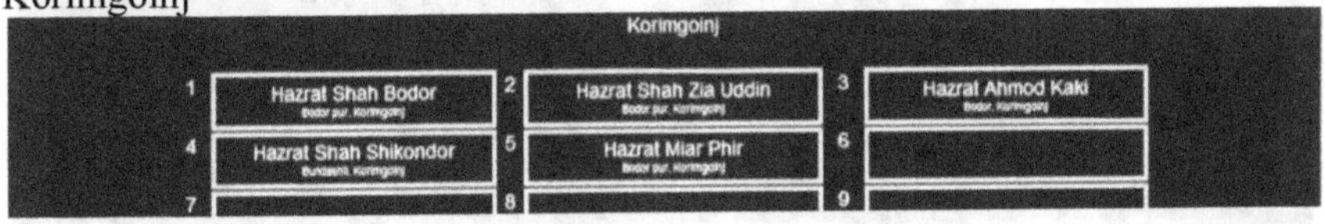
Korimgoinj
1
Hazrat Shah Bodor
2
Hazrat Shah Zia Uddin
3
Hazrat Ahmod Kaki
4
Hazrat Shah Shikondor
5
Hazrat Miar Phir
6
7
8
9

N2 Motorway

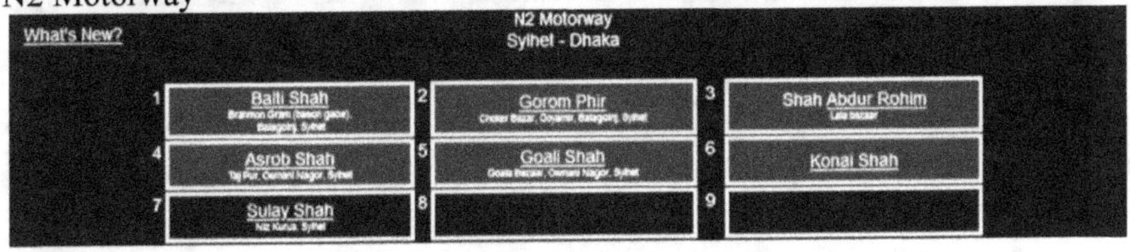
What's New?
N2 Motorway
Sylhet - Dhaka
1
Balti Shah
2
Gorom Phir
3
Shah Abdur Rohim
4
Asrob Shah
5
Goali Shah
6
Konai Shah
7
Sulay Shah
8
9

Nobigoinj

What's new?

Nobigoinj

1	Hazrat Shah Taj Uddin Qureshi Chowti, Nobigoinj		Hazrat Shekh Shodor a.k.a Shodor Uddin Qureshi Shotorsoni, Nobigoinj		Hazrat Hafiz Zakaria Pitua, Nobigoinj
4	Hazrat Shah Mahmud Urdu Bazar, Nobigoinj	5	Hazrat Shah Shohid Loskor Pur, Nobigoinj	6	
7		8		9	

Shilam

What's New?

Shilam

Jolal Pur	1	Hazrat Toyob Sulaiman a.k.a. Toyob Soylani & Toyob salim Bornor Bari, Shilam, Sylhet Shodor	2	Kaza Bu Ali Gaud Gaon, Shilam, Dokkin Surma	3	Hazrat Shah Shikondor Teli Para, Shilam, Sylhet	Dokkin Surma
	4	Hazrat Shah Jafor Gojonby Gudrali Porgona, Mohamod pur Gram, Sylhet Shodor	5	Dilbor Shah Muttar Pur, Gorom Tolla, Shilam, Sylhet	6	A Ali Kadip Pur, Shilam, Sylhet	
Gohor Pur	7	Bibir Mukam Kadipur, Shilam, Sylhet	8	Shah Kidur Rajanagar Pur, Shilam, Sylhet	9		Satok

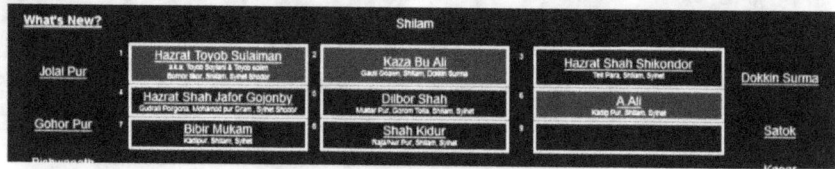

These are the other Mazars that are not confirmed as part of the 360 missionary groups.

Other Mazaars & Phirs

1	Shah Mullah Mubarak Shab Mullah Parah, Osmani Nagor	2	Hazrat Shah Kolomdor Poschim Gaow, Shikondor Pur	3	Hazrat Shah Konai Phir Pub Gaow, Shikondor Pur, Osmani Nagor
4	Hazrat Shah Koronshi Koronshi, Goala Bazar, Osmani Nagor	5	Hazrat Kolim Shah Nayopr pur, Sylhet	6	Hazrat Kura Kuri Ratnager
7	H. Goali Shah Kadimpur & Koronshi point, Goala Bazaar.	8	Dudraj Kalisadar Bari, Raja Pur, Buaijur Bazaar	9	Doi Kura Buaijur Bazaar, Balagonj
10	Lari Bibir Mazaar Muttar Pur, Burunga, Osmani Nagor	11	Uzir Shah Pochim Tilla Para, Burunga, Osmani Nagor	12	Shah Siddique Fasi Para, Balagonj
13	Shah Aziz Doeh Hull, Balagonj	14	Hazrat Shah Miah Sandai Sandair Parah, Balagonj	15	Hazrat Shah Miah Roshai Sandair Parah, Balagonj
16	Fokir Moib Ullah Off Robi Dash Rd, Tajpur, Osmani Nagor	17	Unknown Mazaar Doeh Hull, Balagonj	18	Shodai Shuhag Maz para, Shilam, Sylhet
19	Obuj Shah Isa Moith, Sylhet	20	Shah Shikondor Olir Teli Parah, Shilam, Sylhet	21	Balti Shah Brammon Gram (bawon gaow), Balagonj, Sylhet
22	Bangi Jolal	23	Iship Pur Uttor Pur, Osmani Nagor, Balagonj, Sylhet	24	Abdul Gofur Khan Chondito.
25	Monnan Shah Raja Pur, Sylhet	26	Bangi Kutub	27	Phir Md Abdul Malik
28	Mulog & Tulshi Soyod Bari Rasta, Lesu Bagan, Purbo Phir Moholla, Sylhet Town	29	Jiboi Kha Fokir Fokirtansor, Lala Bazar, Sylhet	30	Khatuna Jahanath Borhanabad, Khueni Ghat, Sylhet Town
31	Mir Mohi Uddin Abdit Pur, Fokir Parah, Lala Bazar, Balagonj, Sylhet	32	Kotali Shah Aurongor Pur, Osmani Nagor, Sylhet	33	Etim Shah Nobigoinj
34	Shah Soyod Fenugonj	35			

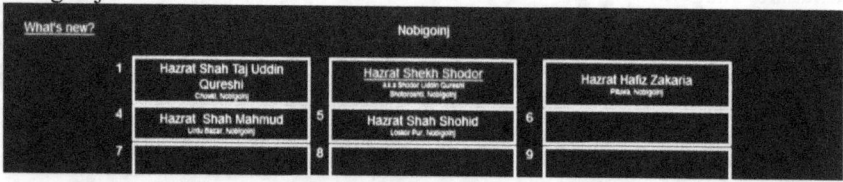

List by Sylhet District Upozilas

We have broken down the list of mazaars by regions to make this simpler.
We aim to plot where each Auwlias had settled.

Sylhet Districts/Zilas		
Sylhet	Shunamgoinj	Moulovibazaar
	Hobigoinj	
	Sylhet Upozilas	
Sylhet Shodor	Fensugoinj	Guyain Ghat
Kanai Ghat	Joynta Pur	Bishwanath
Balagoinj	Biani Bazaar	Gulapgoinj
Companygoinj	Jokigoinj	N2 Motorway
Within Sylhet Upozila there are 98 unions		
	Shunamgoinj Upozilas	
Shunamgoinj Shodor	Satok	Jogonath Pur
Dirai	Shallah	Dormo Pasha
Bishombor Pur	Tahir Pur	Jamal Goinj
	Duwara Bazaar	
Within Shunamgoinj Upozilas there are 81 unions		
	Mowlovibazar Upozilas	
Mowlovibazar Shodor	Kulaura	Borlekha
Komolgoinj	Srimongol	Rajnogor
Within Mowlovibazar Upozilas there are 67 unions		
	Hobigoinj Upozilas	
Hobigoinj Shodor	Nobigoinj	Chunarughat
Banyasong	Bahubol	Madop Pur
Ajmirigoinj	Lakai	
Within Hobigoinj Upozilas there are 77 unions		

Mazars organised by wards.

Sylhet Wards

Ward 1	Ward 2	Ward 3
* Ambarkhana * Dargah Mahalla * Darshan Deury * Dargah Gate * Jharnarpar * Mirer Maidan * Miah Fazil Chist * Purba Subidbazar * Rajargali	* Dairapar * Jallapara * Tripara * Kazi Eliaspara * Lama Bazar (Sarasfur) * Mirza Jangal * Zindabazar	* Kajal Shah * Keyapara * Munshipara * Subid Bazar
Ward 4	**Ward 5**	**Ward 6**
* Ambarkhana * Dattapara * Housing Estate * Lichi Bagan, Majudari	* Barabazar * Electric Supply * Goypara (Chachnipara) * Khush Dabir	* Badam Bagicha * Choukidighi * Eliaskandi * Syedmognj
Ward 7	**Ward 8**	**Ward 9**
* Bam Kalapara * Fazal Chisti * Jalalabad * Kalapara * Pir Mahalla * Sayaif Khan Road * Subid Bazar	* Brahman Shashan * Hauldar Para * Kucharpara * Korarpar * Noapara * Panitala * Pathantala * Uttar Pir Mahalla	* Akhalia * Baghibari * Danukhter * Kuliapar * Kanisail * Modina Market * Nehari Para * Pathan Tola * Sagardigir Par
Ward 10	**Ward 11**	**Ward 12**
* Dhar * Gasitala * Kalapara * Majumder Para * Molla Para * Nabab Road * Wapda	* Bhatalia * Bil Par * Kajalshah * Lala Dighirpar * Madhu Shahid * Noapara * Rekabi Bazar	* Bhangatikar * Itakhola * Kuarpar * Saudagartala * Sekhghat

Though I started this on the website, I've not yet gone round doing that.

Ward 13

* Chandighat
* Dakshin Taltala
* Kazi Bazar
* Khulia Para
* Lama Bazar
* Mirza Jangal
* Mogal Tala Masu Dighirpar
* Raner Dighirpar
* Sheikhghat
* Surma Market
* Topkhana
* Tali-Hour

Ward 14

* Bandar Bazar
* Brahmandi Bazar
* Chali Bandar, Chorarpar
* Hasan Market
* Dak Bangla Road
* Dhupra Dighirpar
* Jallar Par
* Jamtala
* Houkers Market
* Kastagarh
* Kamal Garh
* Kalighat
* Lal Dighirpar
* Paura Biponi
* Paura Mirzajangal
* Shah Chatt Road
* Uttar Talitala
* Zinda Bazar

Ward 15

* Bandar Bazar
* Baruth Khana
* Chali Bandar
* Churi Patti
* Hasan Market
* Jail Road
* Joynagar
* Jaiarpur
* Nayarpool
* Noapara
* Suphani Ghat
* Puran Lane
* Uttar Dhopa Dighirpar
* Zinda Bazar

Ward 16

* Charadigirpar
* Dhoper Digirpar
* Hauapara
* Kahan Daura
* Kumarpara
* Purba Zinda Bazar
* Naya Sarak
* Saudagar Tola
* Tantipara

Ward 17

* Ambarkhana
* Abdulla
* Chandan Tala
* Chauhatta
* Kazi Jalaluddin Mahalla
* Kazi Tala
* Mir Boxtala

Ward 18

* Brajahat Tila
* Evergreen
* Jharharpar
* Jherjheri Para
* Kumar Para
* Mira Bazar
* Mousumi
* Sabuj Bagh
* Serak
* Shahi Eidgah
* Shakhari Para

Ward 19

* Chandani Tila
* Daptari Para
* Darjee Band
* Darjee Para
* Goner Para
* Kahar Para
* Raynagar
* Sonapara

Ward 20

* Balichhara South
* Kharadi Para
* Lama Para
* Majumder Para
* Roynagar
* Senpara
* Sonarpara
* Shibganj

Ward 21

* Bhatatikr
* Brahman Para
* Gopal Tila
* Hatimbagh
* Lakri Para
* Sadipur
* Shaplabagh
* Tilaghar

Ward 22

* Block-A
* Block-B
* Block-C
* Block-D
* Block-E
* Block-F
* Block-G
* Block-H
* Block-I
* Block-J
* Bangladesh Bank Colony

Ward 23

* Machimpur
* Mehendibagh

Ward 24

* Hatimbagh
* Kurshi Ghat
* Lamapara
* Mirapara
* Sadatikar
* Sarderpara
* Shapla Bagh
* Sadipur-2
* Tero Ratan
* Tuliikar

Ward 25

* Boroikandi
* Barthokhola
* Godnail
* Khojarkhola
* Mominkhola

Ward 26

* Jalopara
* Kadamtala

Ward 27

* Alampur
* Gotatikar

Maps

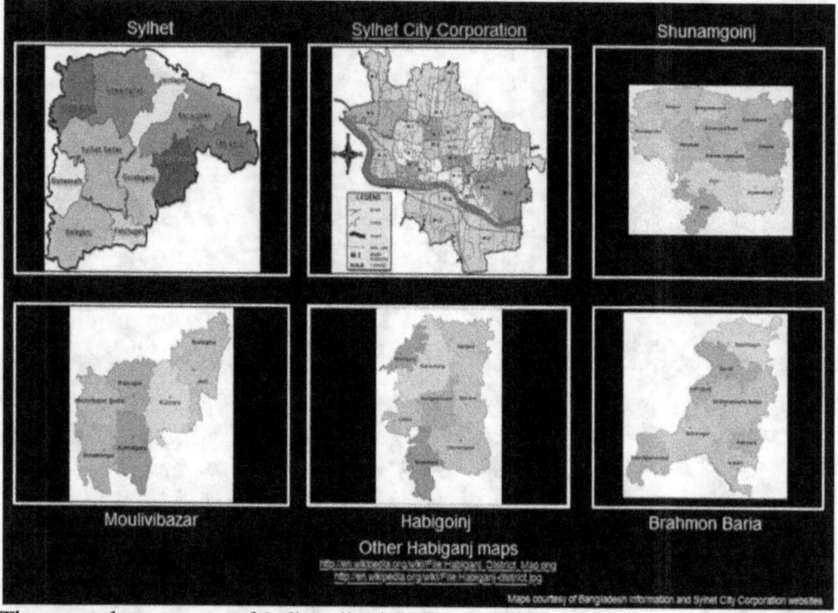
Sylhet
Sylhet City Corporation
Shunamgoinj
Moulivibazar
Habigoinj
Brahmon Baria
Other Habiganj maps
Maps courtesy of Bangladesh information and Sylhet City Corporation websites

These are the segment of Sylhet district with its boroughs.

Let the Journey Begin!

The journey was not in any particular order, and I started off with my own ancestral one in Mullah Para from my paternal side and Shikondor pur from my maternal side.

What you should know to understand the content of the book. After independence from the British, and Sylhet fell into the East Pakistan side, the government then audited the Mazars and issued the genuine Mazar of the companions of Hazrat Shah Jalal with an eight sided plaque.

The eight sided plaque was issued by the Pakistani Government to authenticate the mazar to have been a companion of Hazrat Shah Jalal and a members of the 360 missionary.

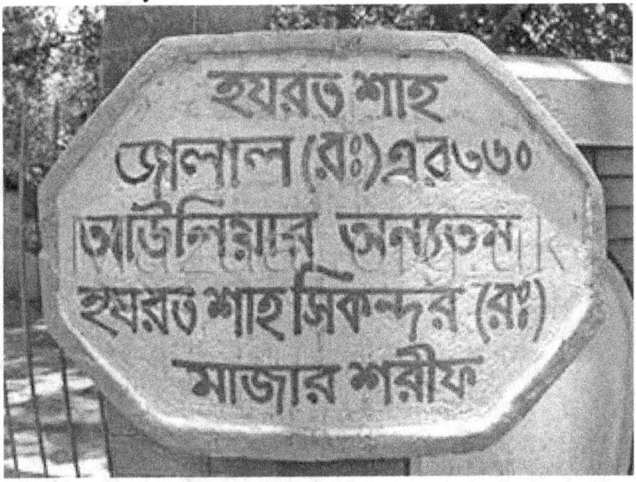
হযরত শাহ
জালাল (রঃ) এর ৩৬০
আউলিয়ার অন্যতম
হযরত শাহ জিকন্দর (রঃ)
মাজার শরীফ

Where I have found an 8 sided plaque, I have captured it and thus being the authentication of the mazar site and the name. There is also two asterisks **, after the authenticated names, the header and in the content list, for a quick ID.

There are also sites that are claimed to be part of the 360 missionaries, and those I have marked with one *, asterisks. I have learnt and also have proof, that people cannot make a false claim for number of reason, it will go against the religious beliefs. Also false claims have been challenged; we have photographed couple in the books.

All other sites are listed as they are. If there isn't any mention that they are validated or there are no asterisks after their names or there couldn't be any verification, then they are not part of the companions.

This book is subjective to everyone, so this books content is not formal or legal, but as a self learning reference only. Please do your own due diligence to seek whatever are the facts for you.

Shah Mullah Mubarak Shahab*

- Mullah Para, Osmani Nagor, Sylhet.

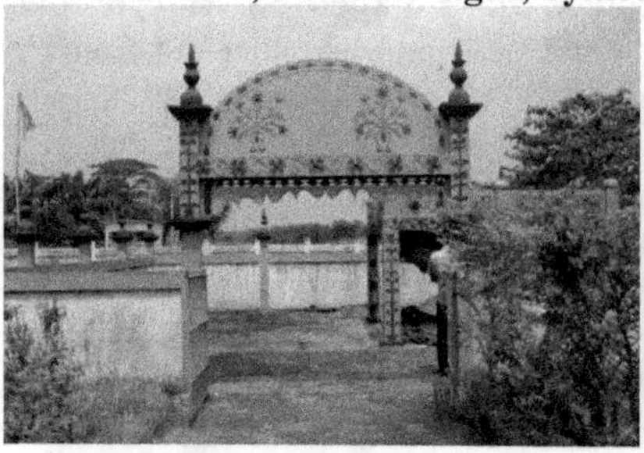

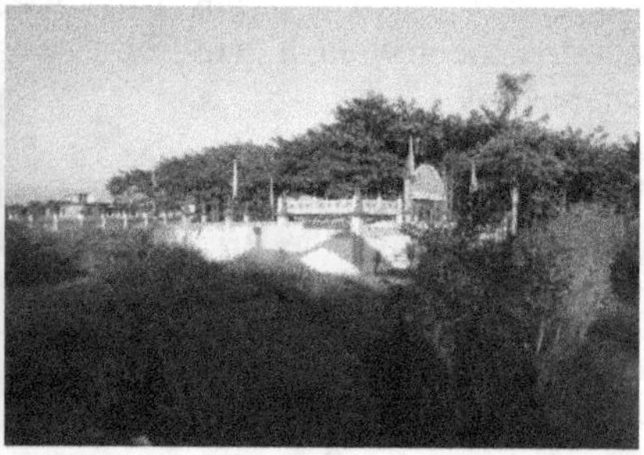

11.1.2004 14:37

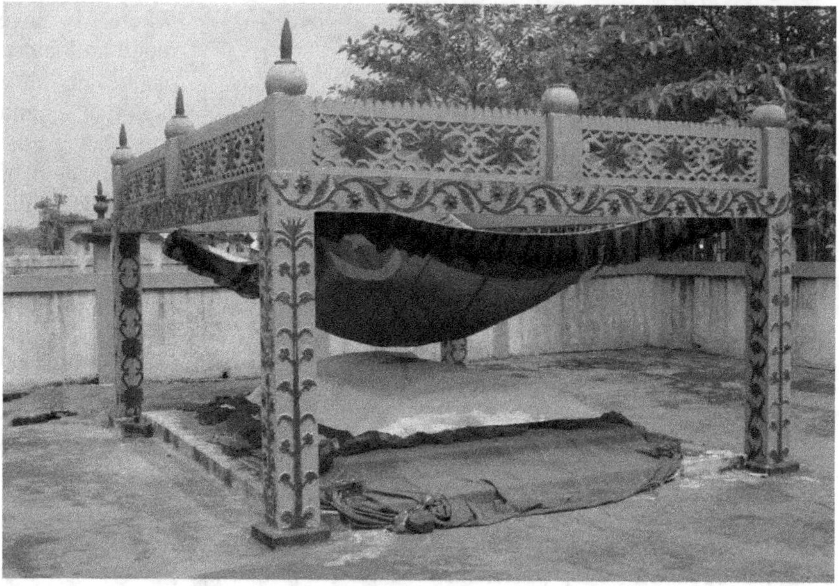

This mazar is my paternal ancestral linage. This was the first place I went and did my salaam.

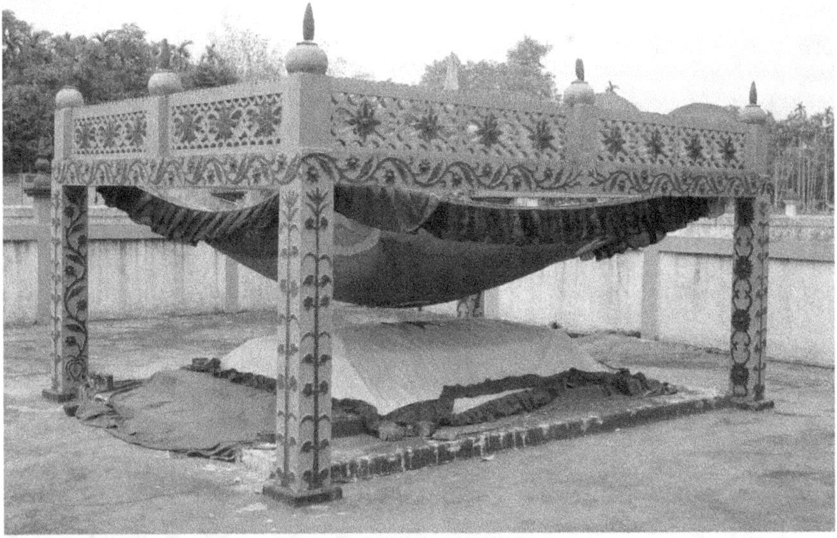

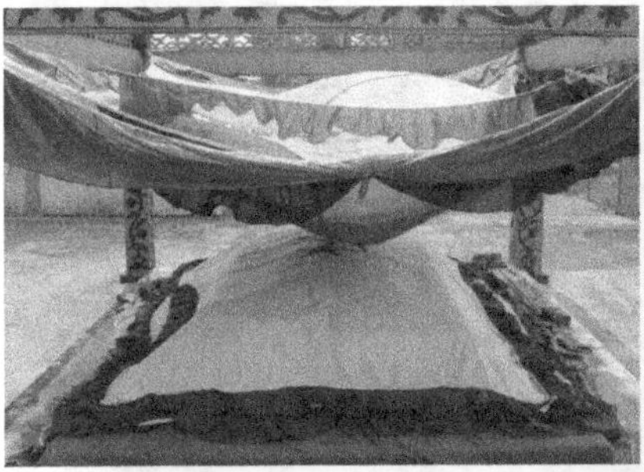

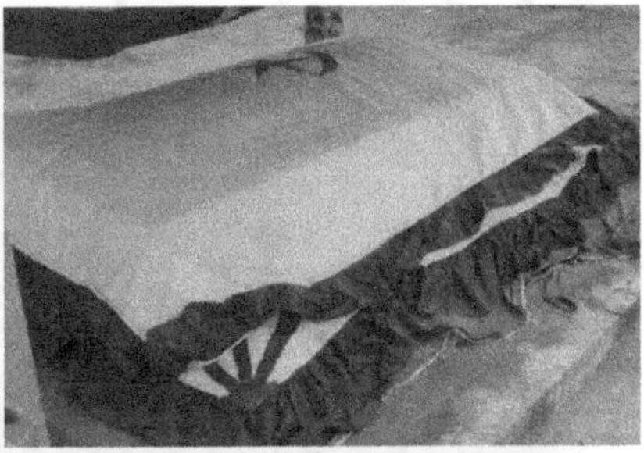

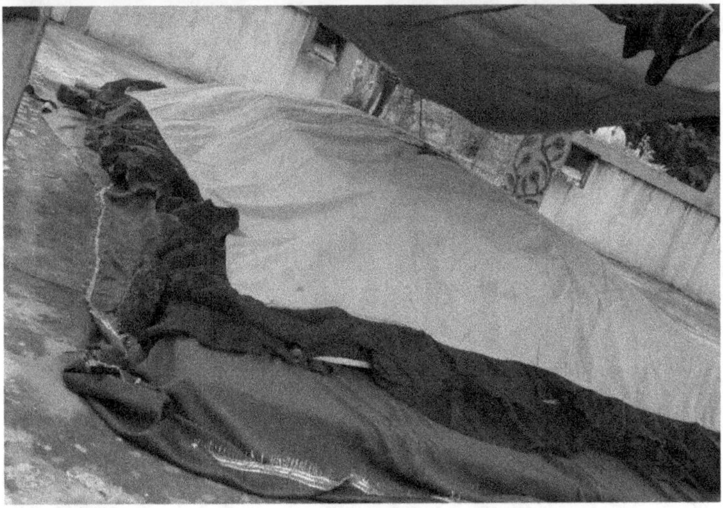

April 2010

Akanji

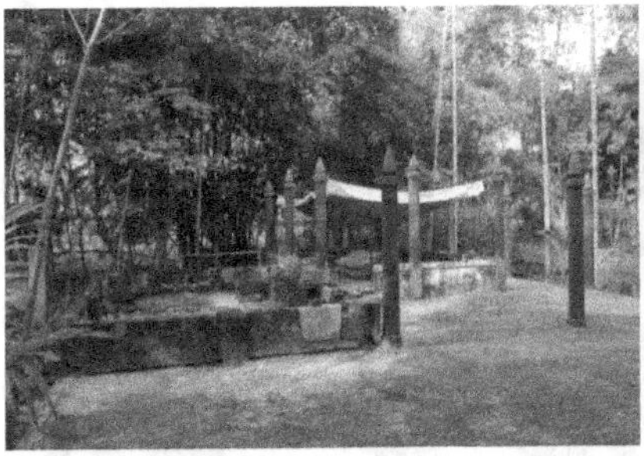

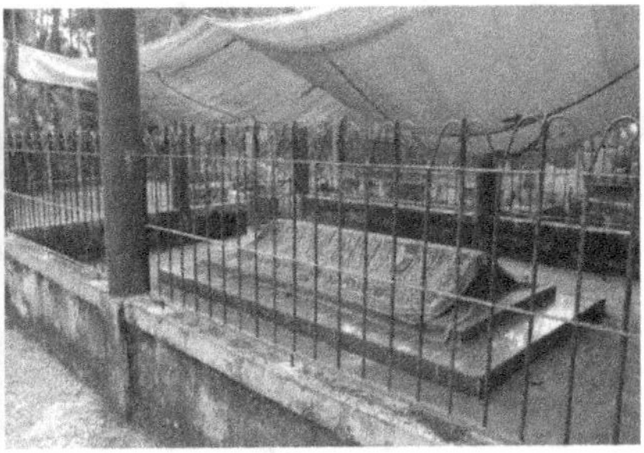

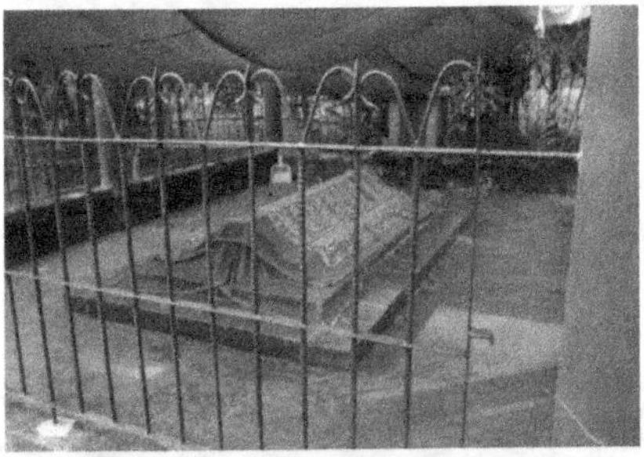

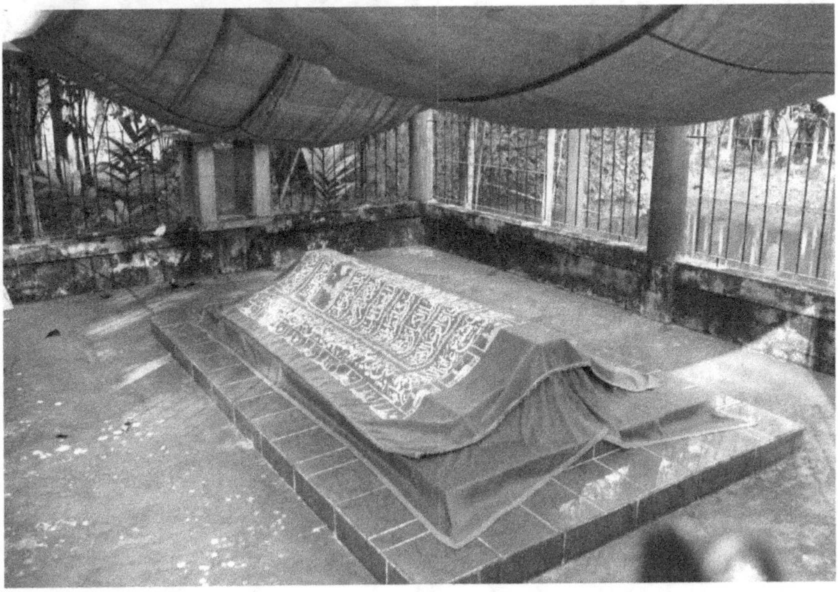

3.4.2011, 13:17:06

Shah Dilal Uddin*

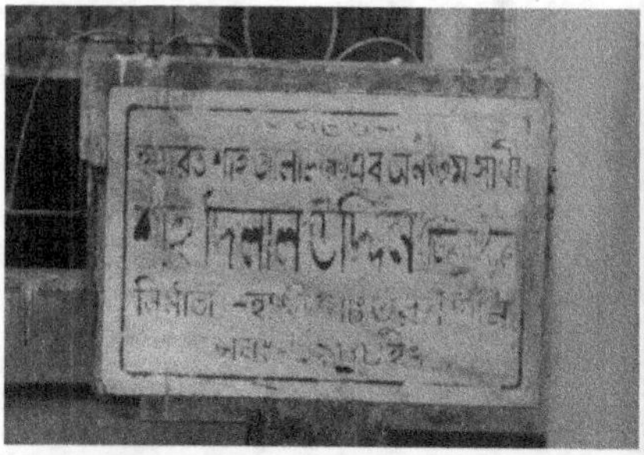

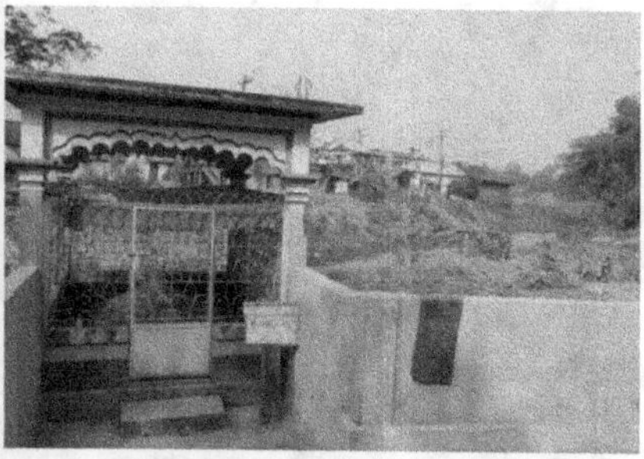

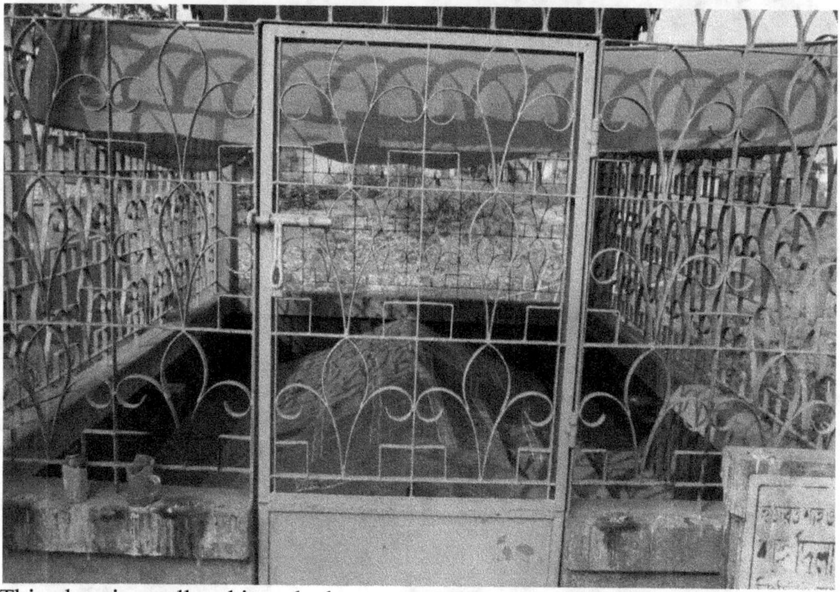

This place is small and is tucked away, very easy to miss.

3.4.2010, 17:44

Jolal Ahmod **

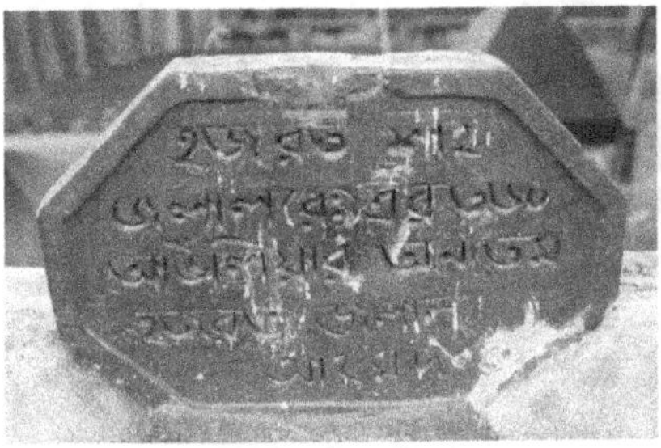

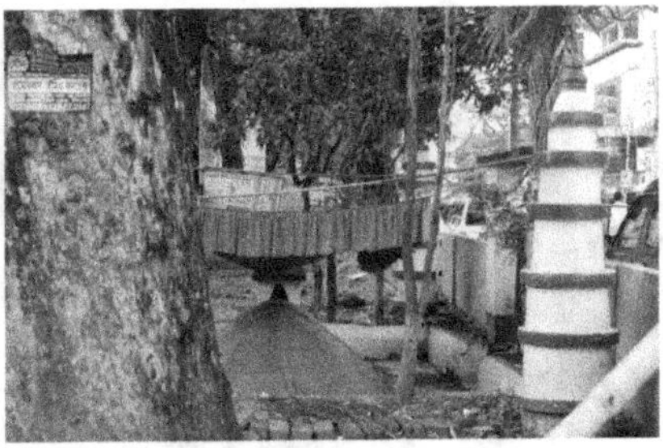

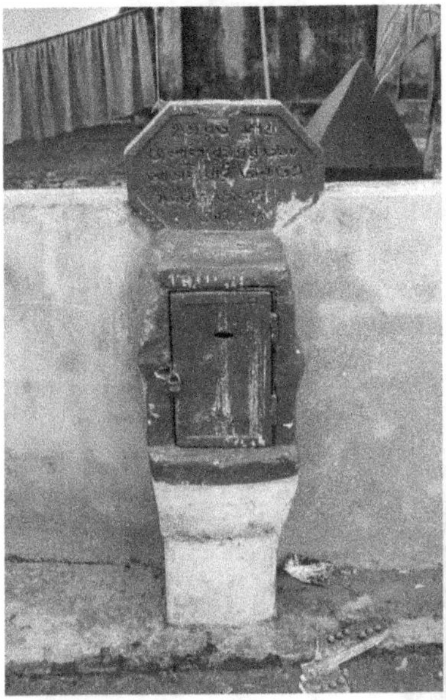

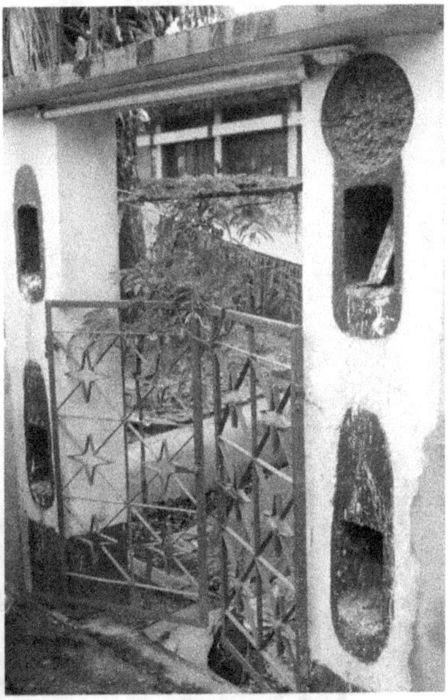

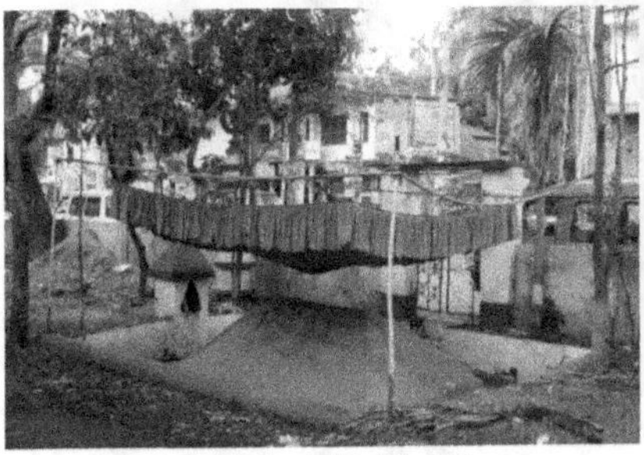

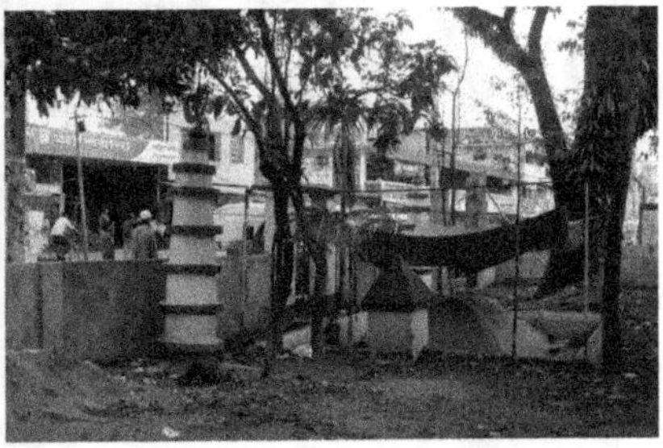

30.4.2010, 12:41:00

Modu Shudon**

Sylhet Town Stadium Mazar

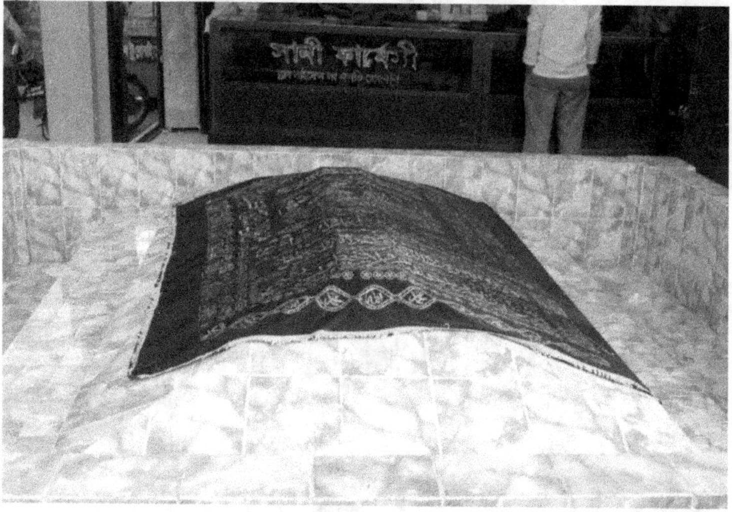

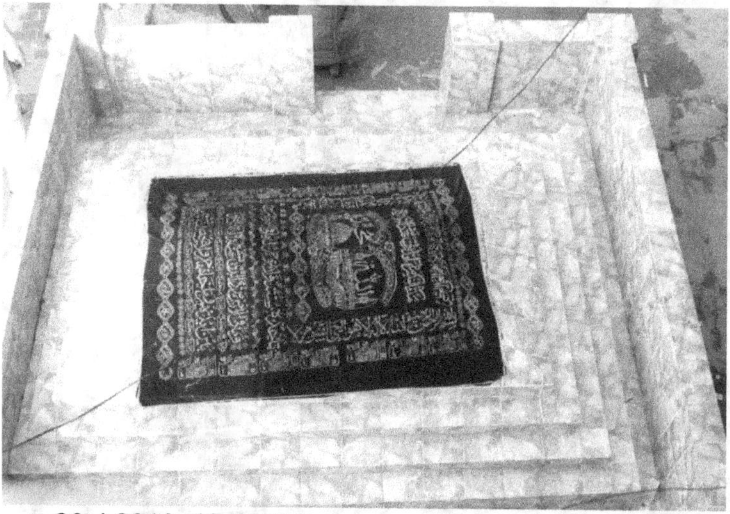

30.4.2010, 12:19:56

This was a strange place; it is situated on the side of the stadium in the Sylhet.

Modu Shohid**

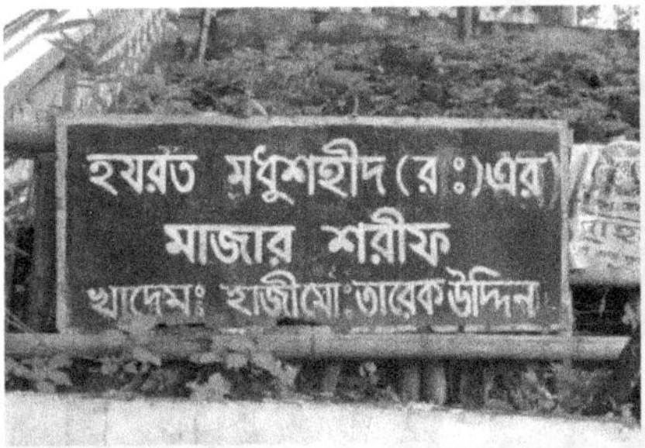
হযরত মধুশহীদ(রঃ)এর
মাজার শরীফ
খাদেমঃ হাজীমোঃ তারেক উদ্দিন

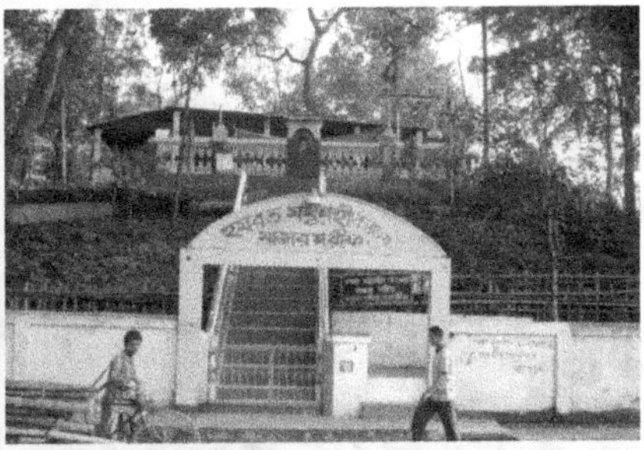

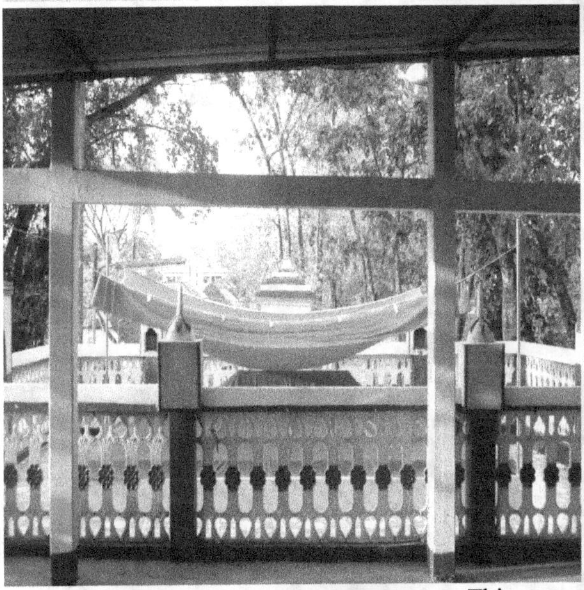

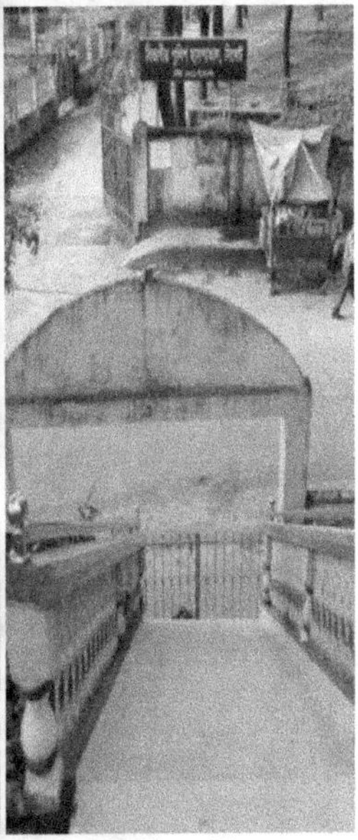

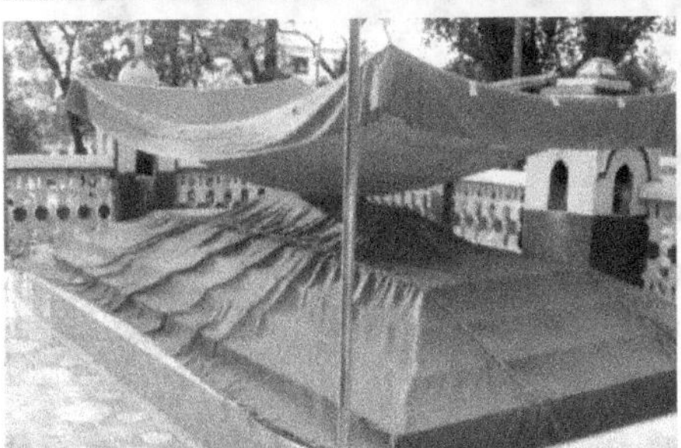

This mazar is in Sylhet Town, and is situated on top of a hill. With the hustle and bustle of the commuter, the place still gave that serenity.

30.4.2010, 12:30:00

Manik Phir**

Manik Phir Tilla, Sylhet Town

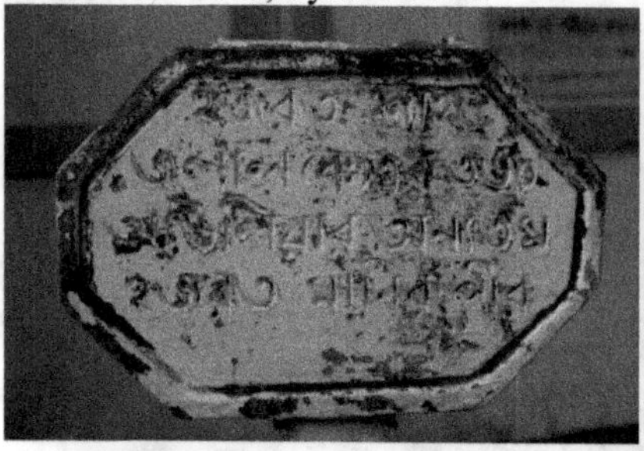

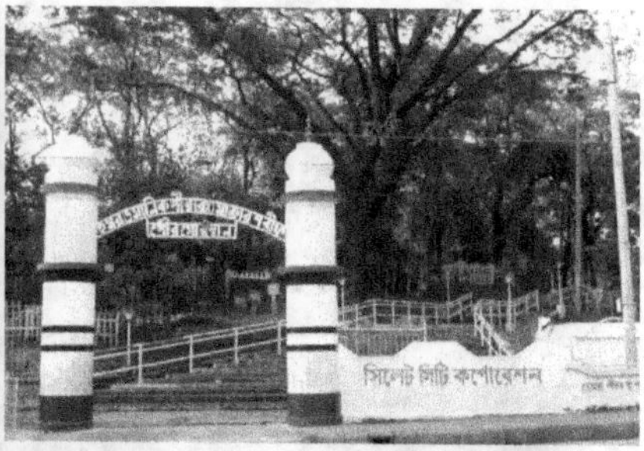
সিলেট সিটি কর্পোরেশন

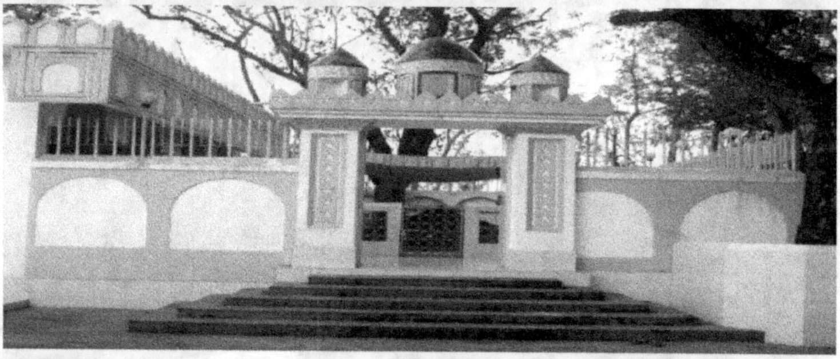

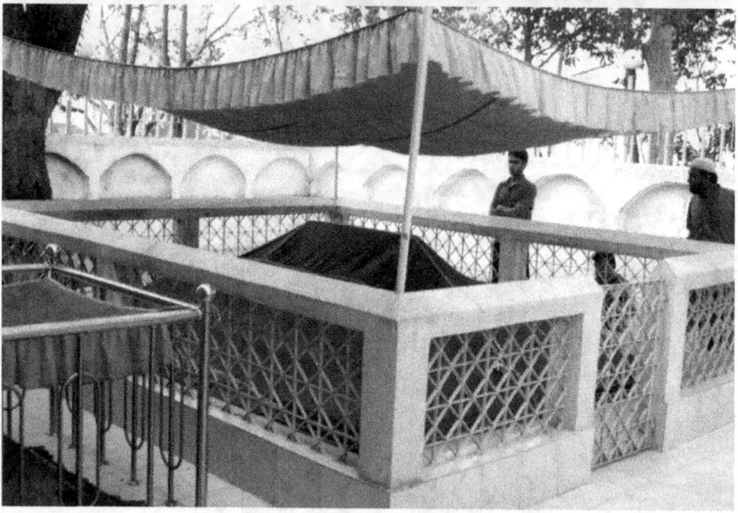

30.4.2010, 13:03:40

This place is well known and is home to many burials. To reach this mazar, there is a walk up to the hill top and then through the gates. Where you are received by the white tiled sanctum, where the zapped feeling transcends.

Shah Kolim

Nayorful, Sylhet

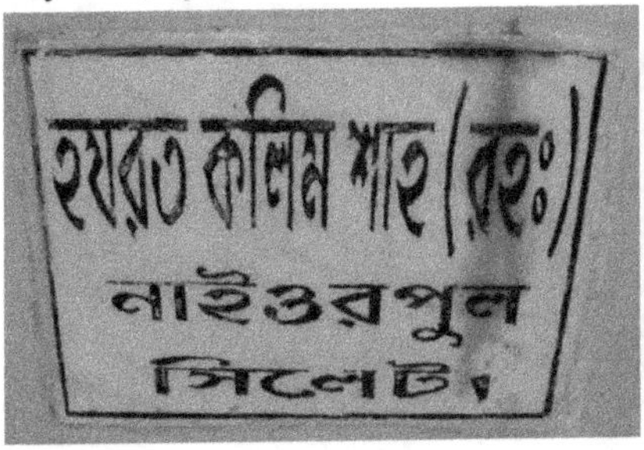
হযরত কলিম শাহ (রহঃ)
নাইওরপুল
সিলেট।

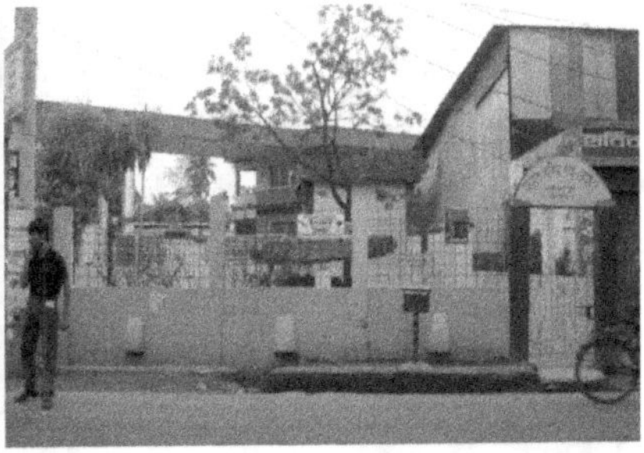

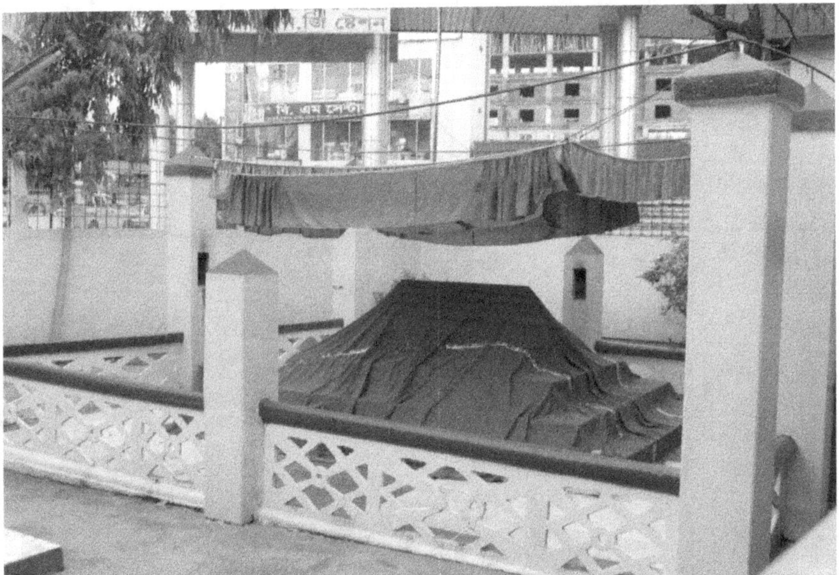

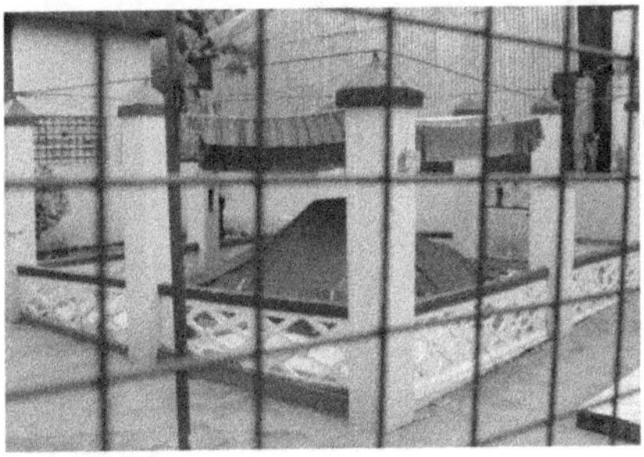

30.4.2010, 13:18:42

June 2010

Shah Jalal Yemeni mazar

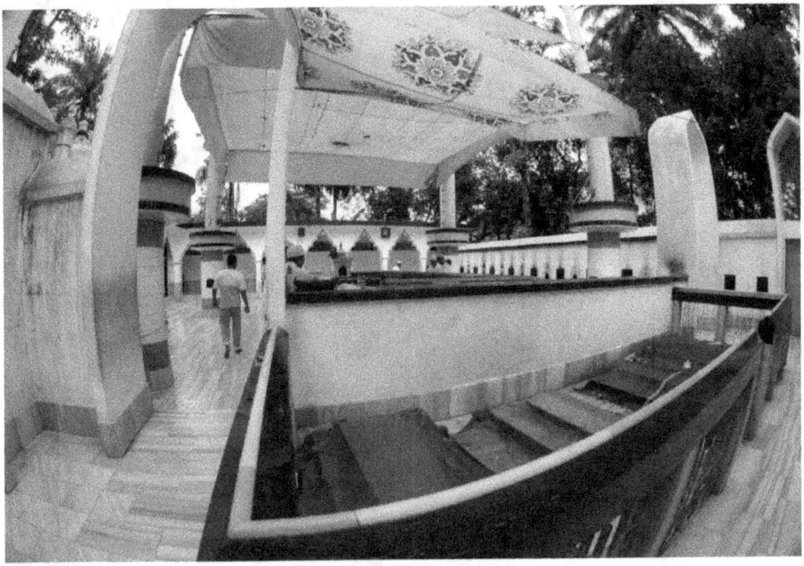

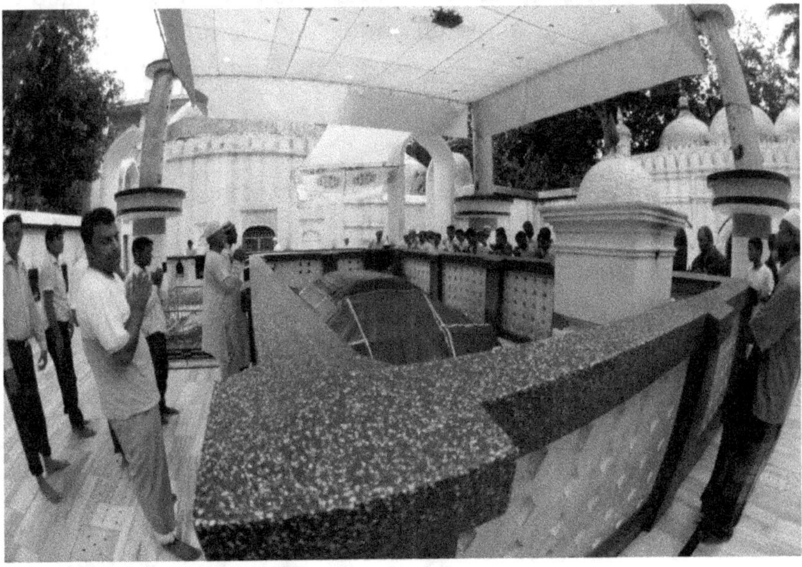

22.6.2010, 12:27:10

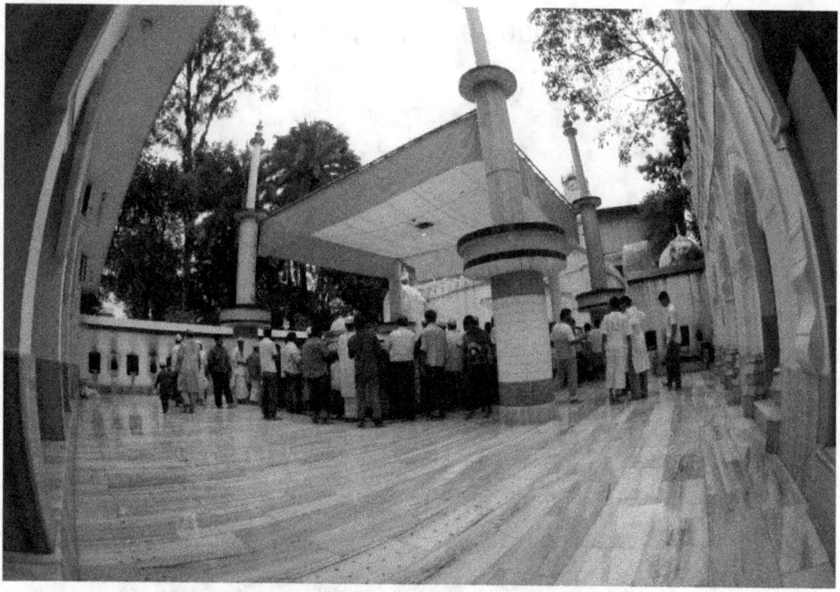

This was the first visit I made to the Dorga in 2010. I just wanted to capture the setting. I sat in the far corner and took the picture, yet I could have sat their hours. It was so grounding; warm, tranquil, energy was bouncing off these walls, for sure.

July 2010

Kazi Joki Kondokar**

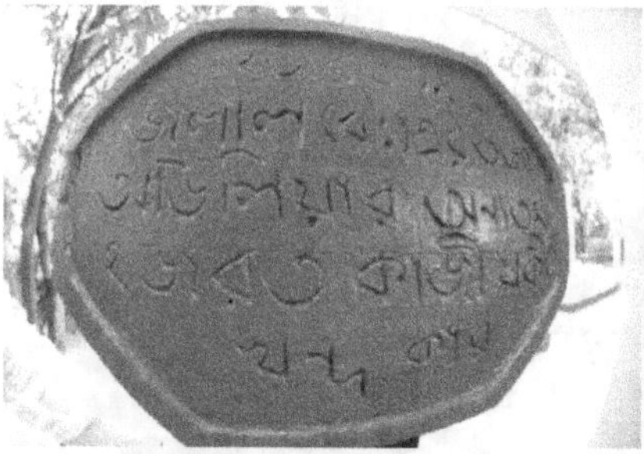

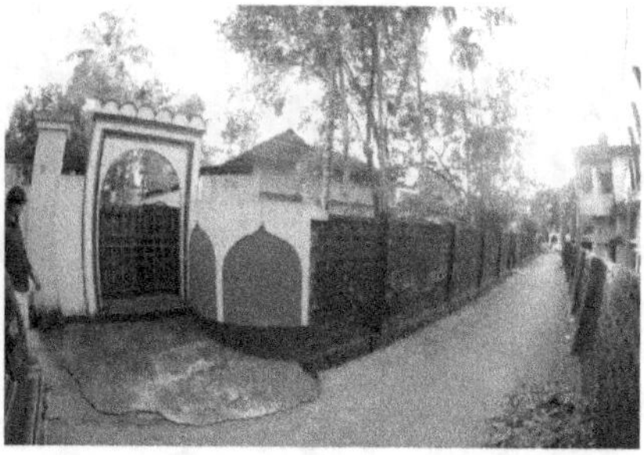

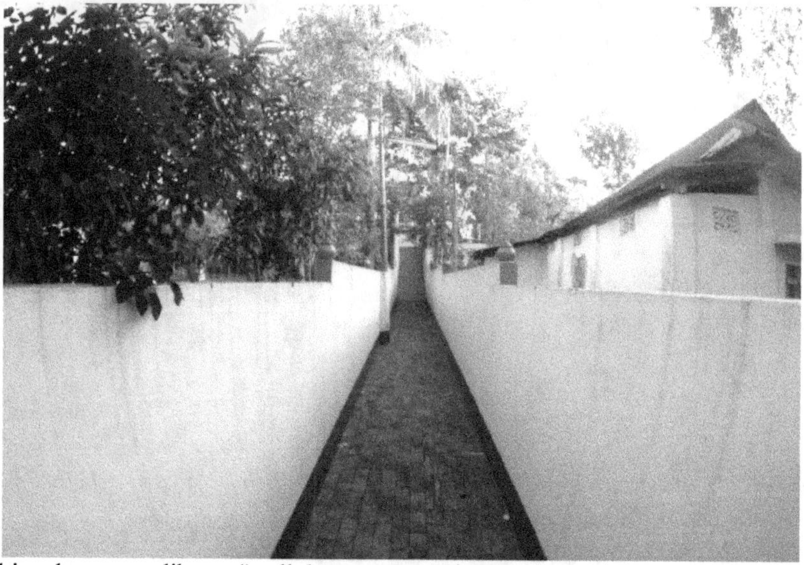

This place was like a "well kept secret," it was located in an estate, long pathways as you can see. Once you enter the gate, you have a well maintained path that leads you to some steps to the mazar. When you enter the inner sanctum, you are greeted with and opulent garden, set in marble.

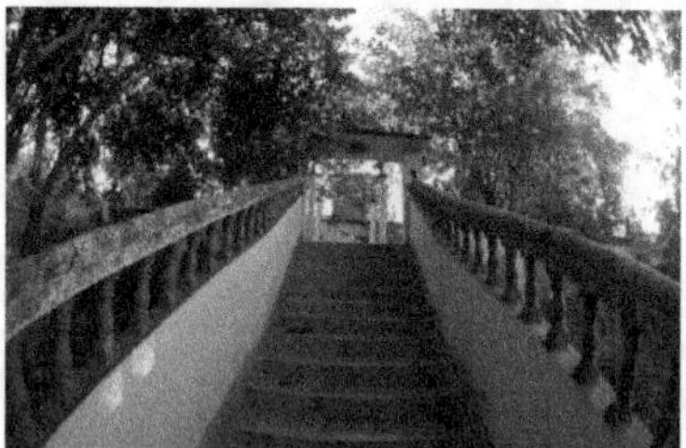

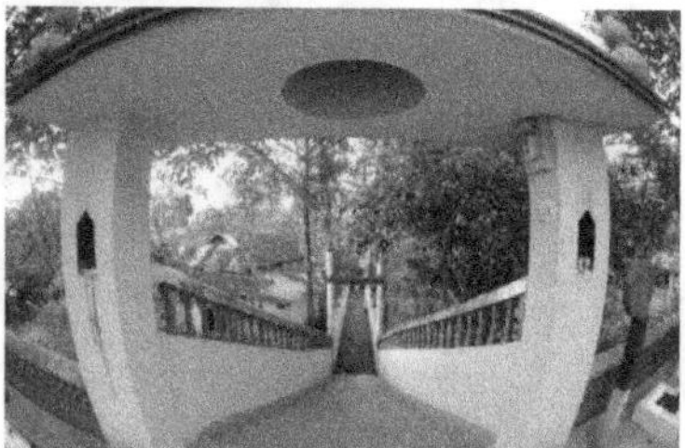

These are bottom of the steps up and top down view, very ornate and neat.

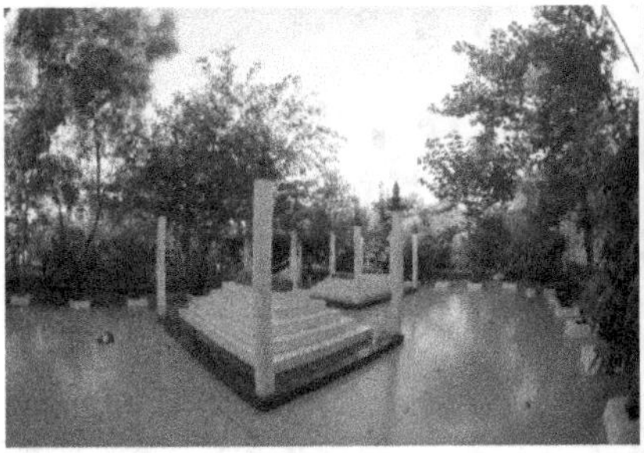

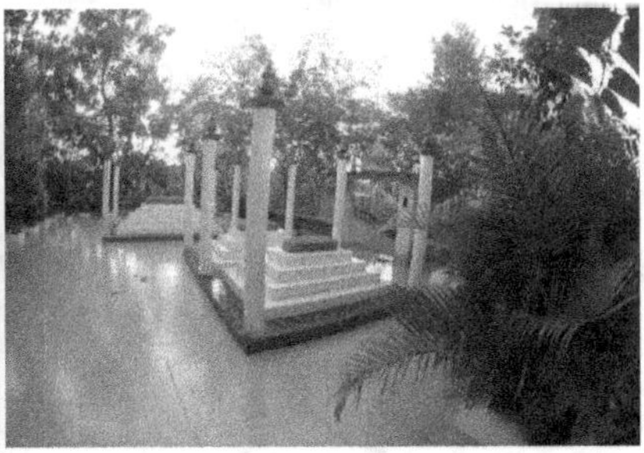

I was impressed with this place, it was well maintained, all tiled up and the plants are boxed in too.

On seeing this space, it was a pleasant surprise; it was if it was a personal garden, courtyard inside your house.

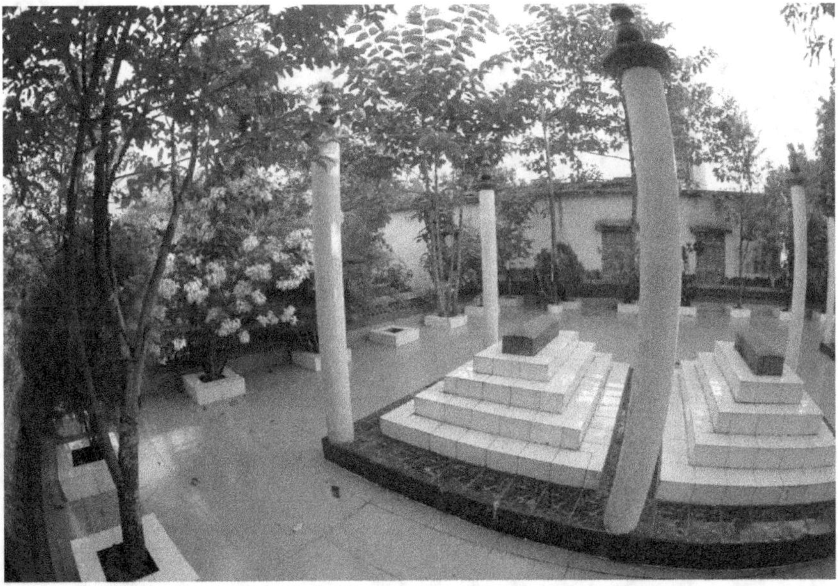

I took pictures from all angles to capture the work, effort and the devotion from the descendants.

The only shame was, I didn't take a lot of time there, to soak up the peace.

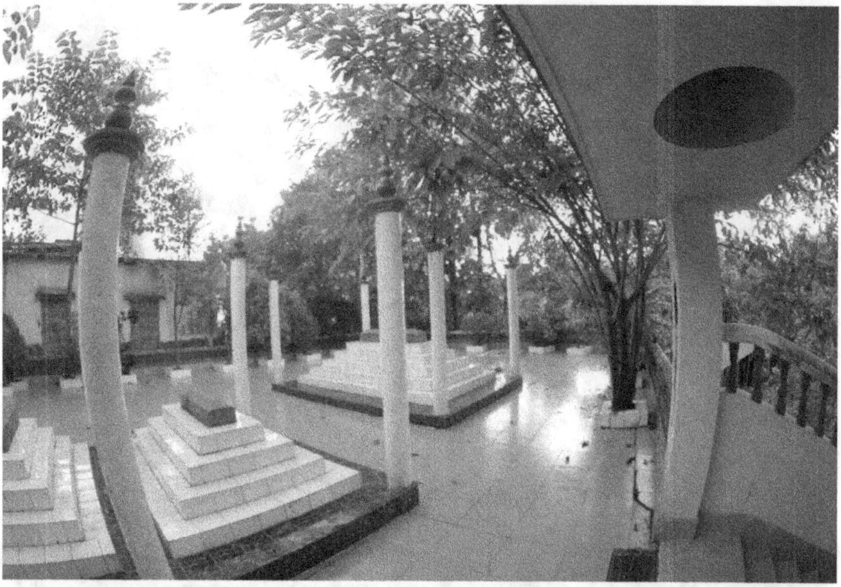

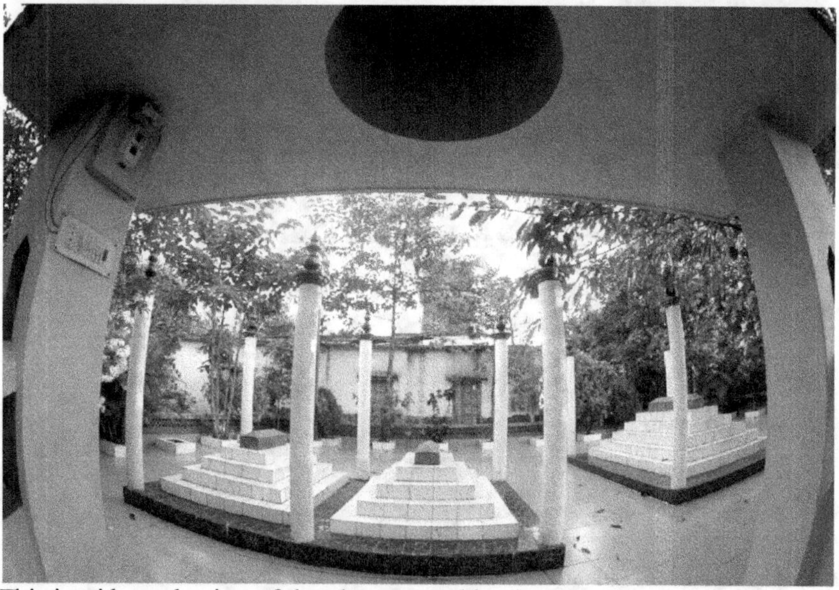

This is wide angle view of the place, everything is covered up with marble and concrete - there is no mud or earth exposed other than edges were trees and plants are, and the overhanging trees from adjacent garden, land.

12.7.2010, 08:08:42

Sufi Khijir**

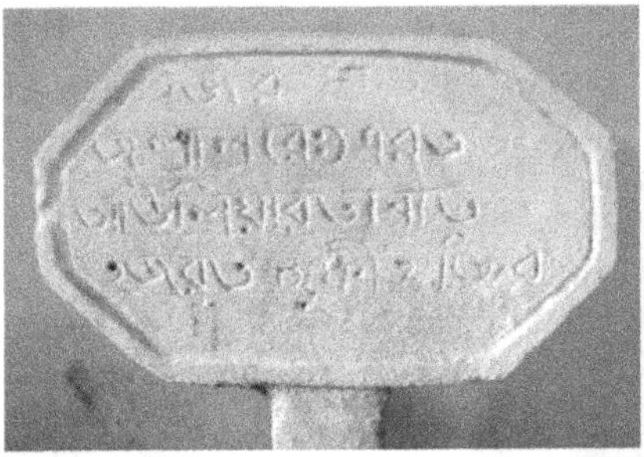

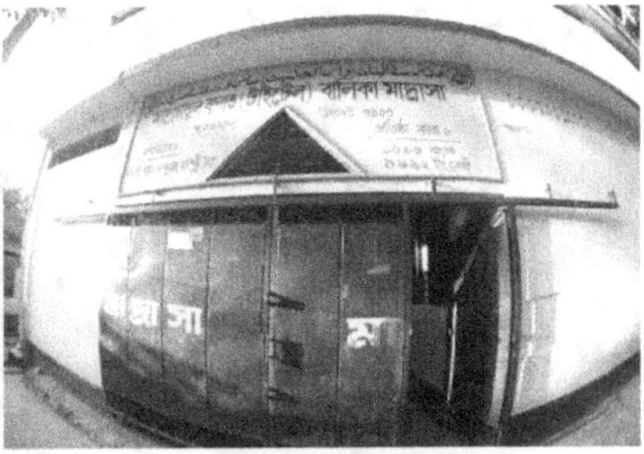

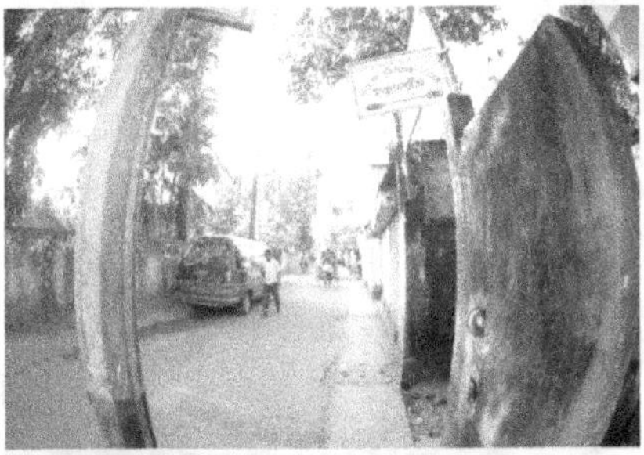

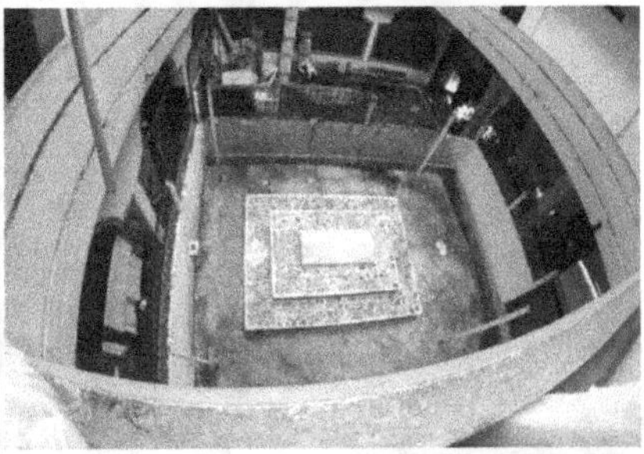

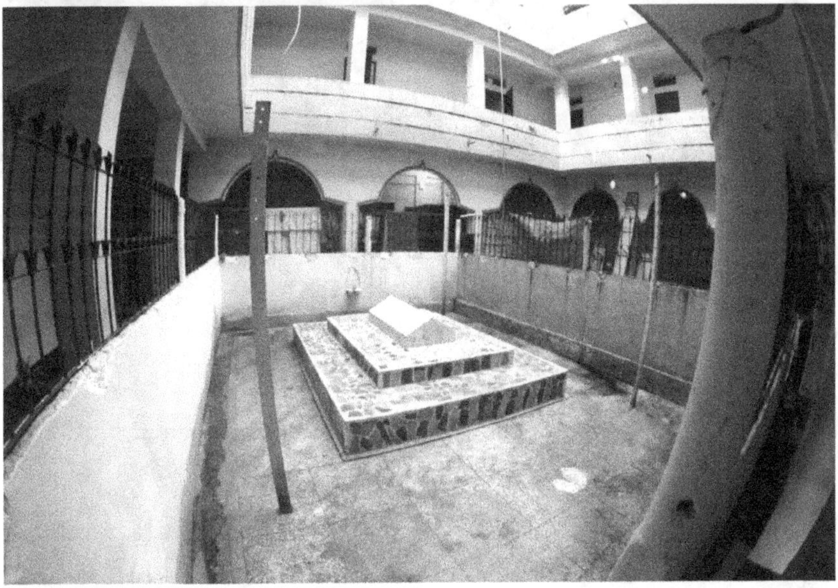

12.7.2010

This place is inside a building complex.

Soyod Imam**

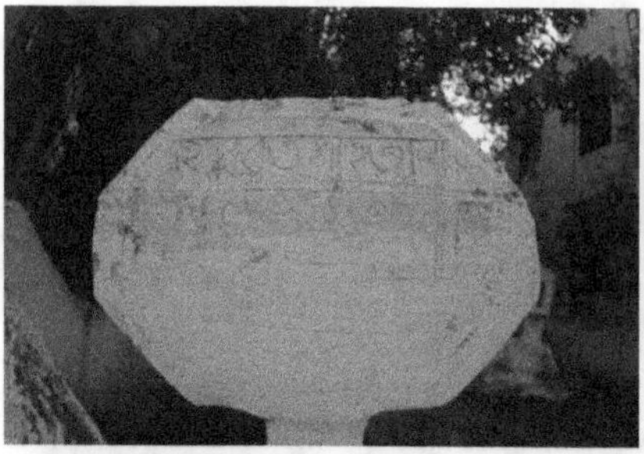

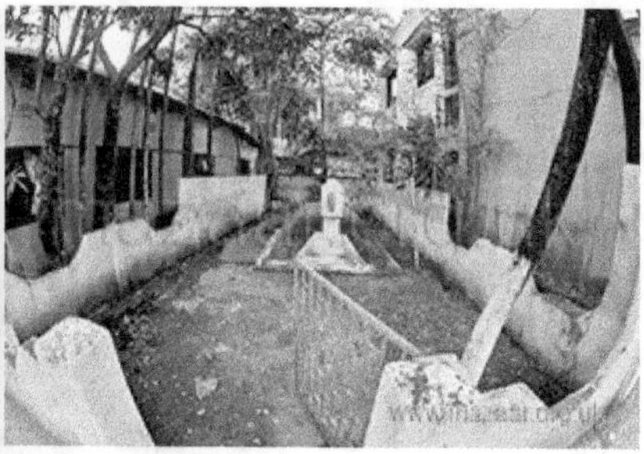

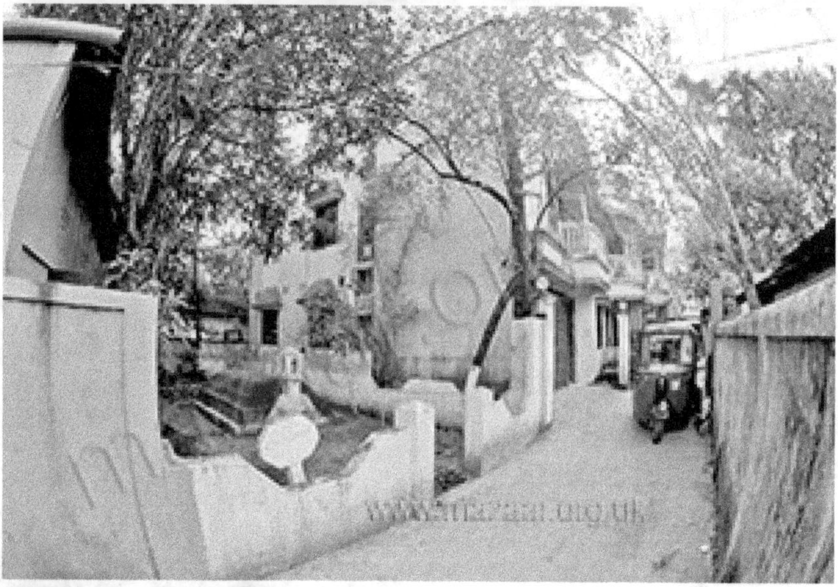

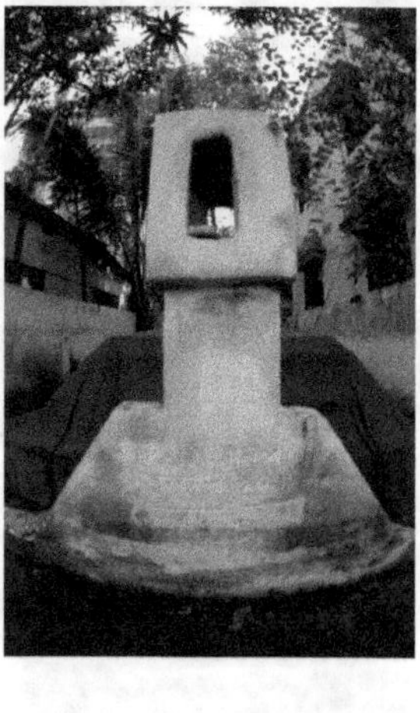

This site was off the beaten tracks, it was in an estate; within the building complex in its own plot.

12.7.2010, 19:28:12

Shah Sonjor Tokiya**

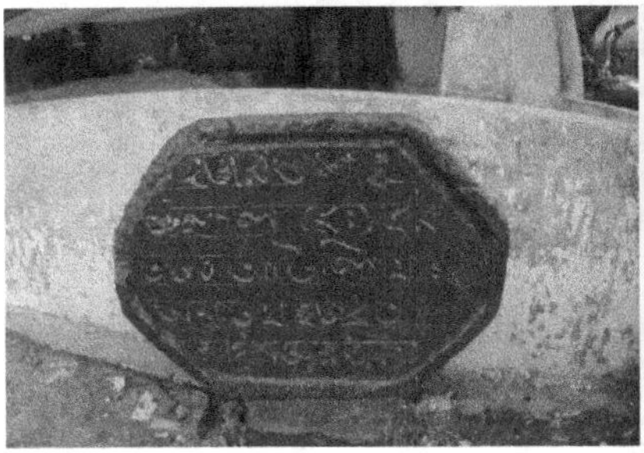

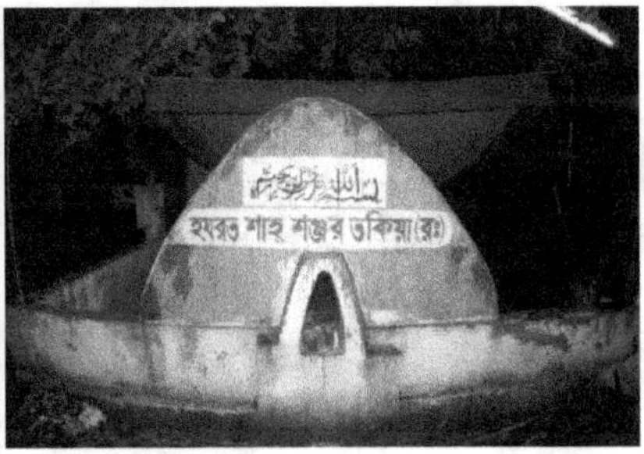
হযরত শাহ শঞ্জর তকিয়া(রঃ)

20.9.2010,

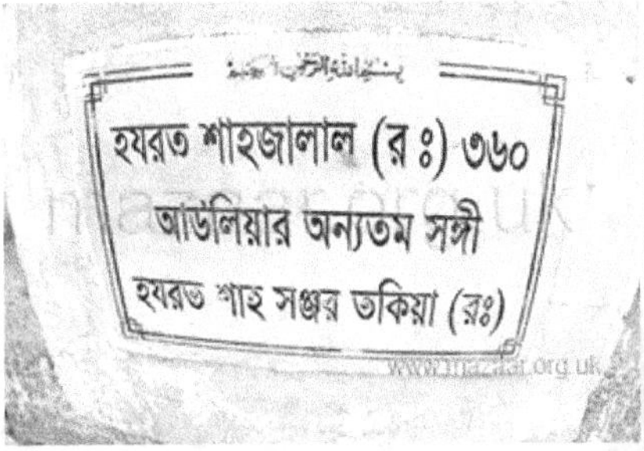
হযরত শাহজালাল (র ঃ) ৩৬০
আউলিয়ার অন্যতম সঙ্গী
হযরত শাহ সঞ্জর তকিয়া (রঃ)
www.mazar.org.uk

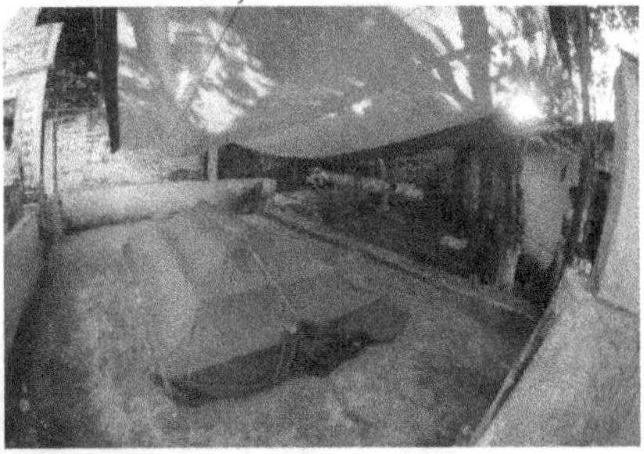

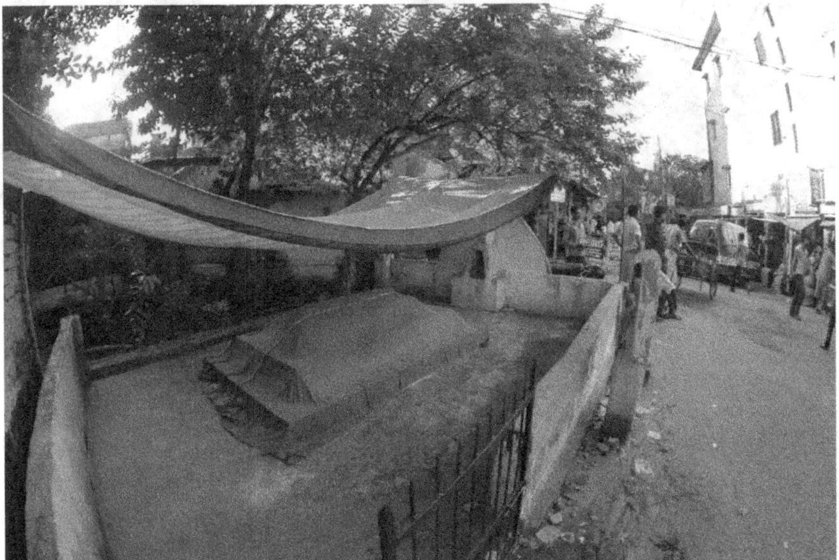

12.7.2010 19:33:10

Mahbub Shah

Jail Road, Sylhet Town

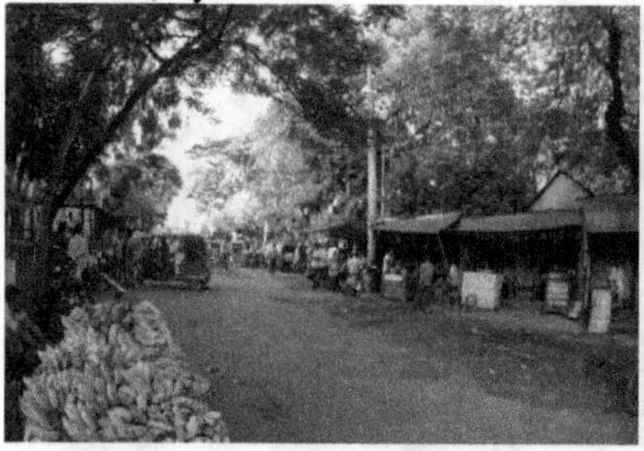

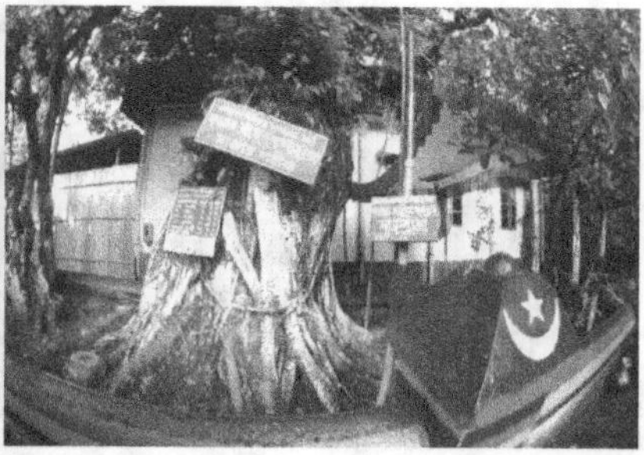

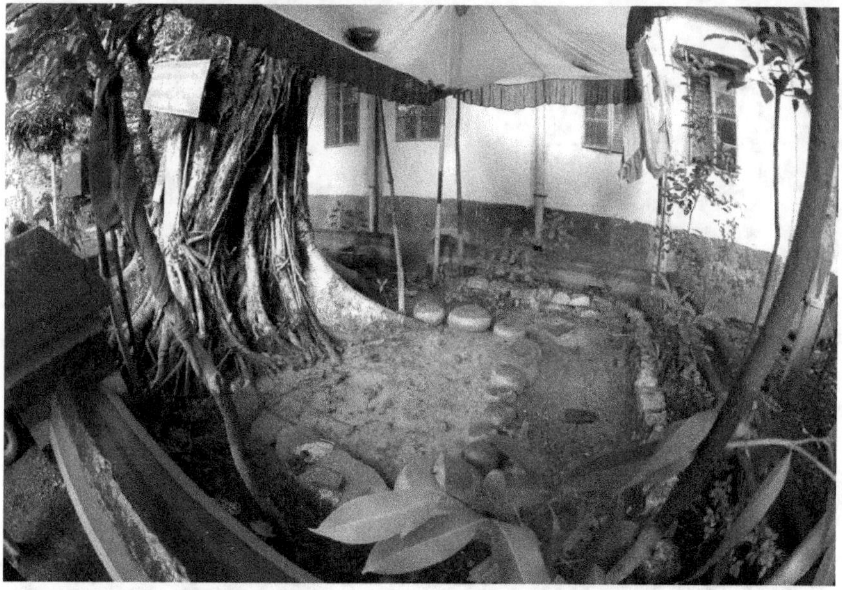

12.7.2010, 19:41:30

Thugai Phir*

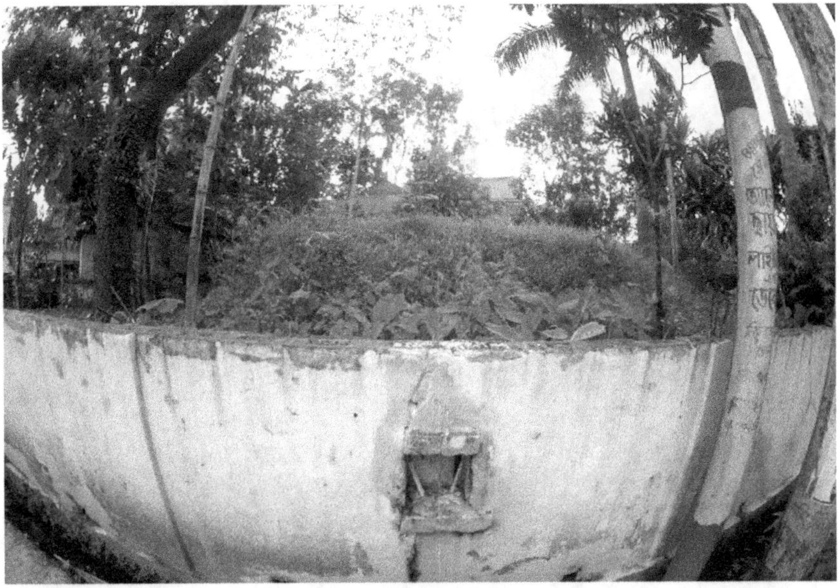

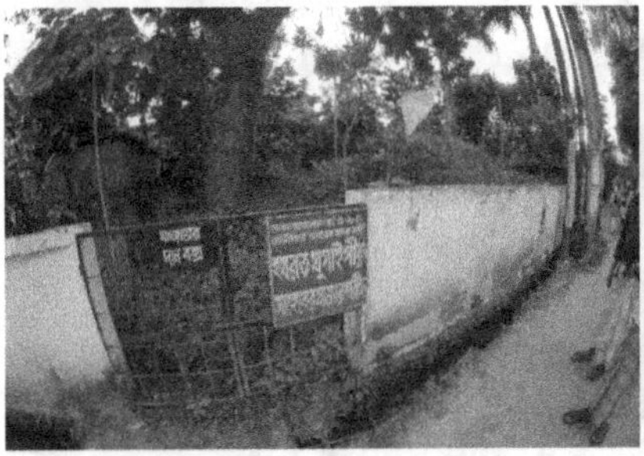

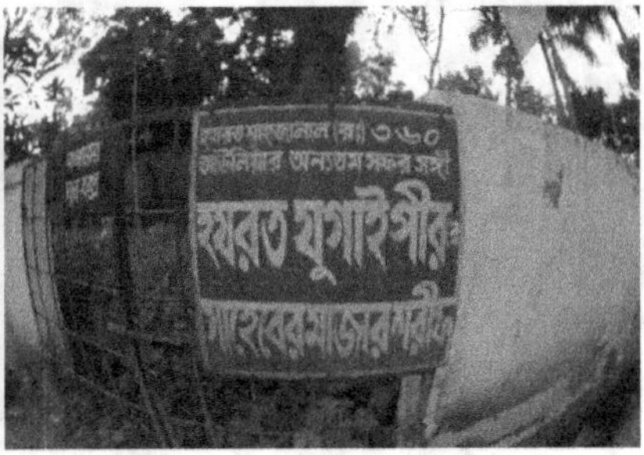

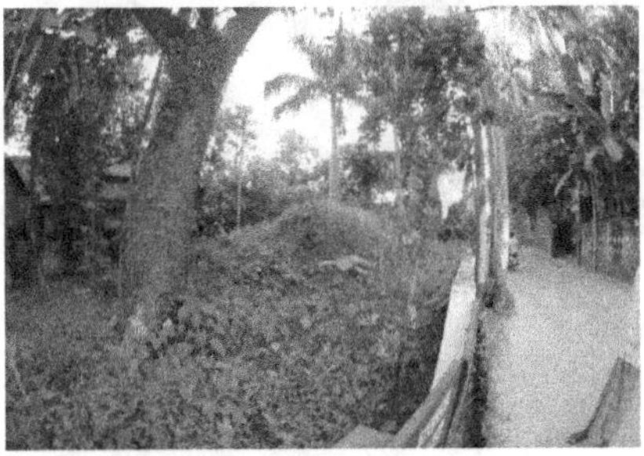

12.7.2010, 20:28:24

Soyod Kala Shah

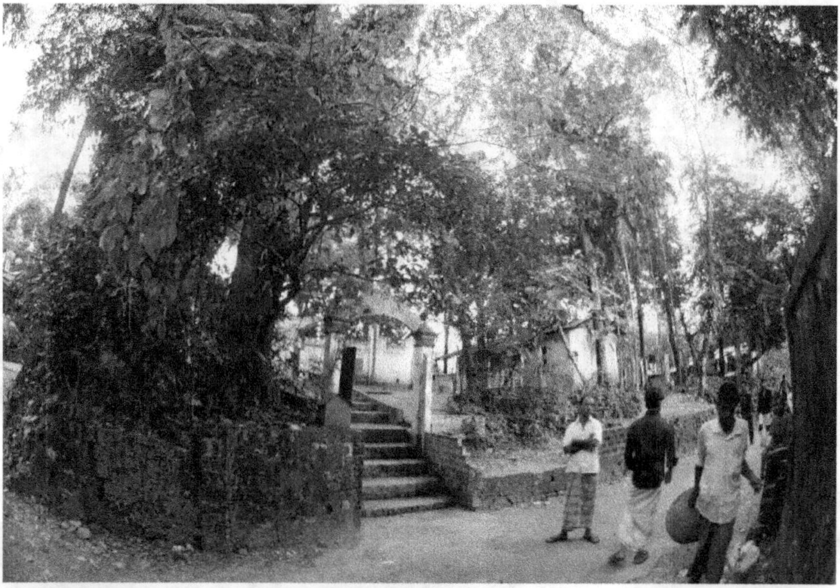
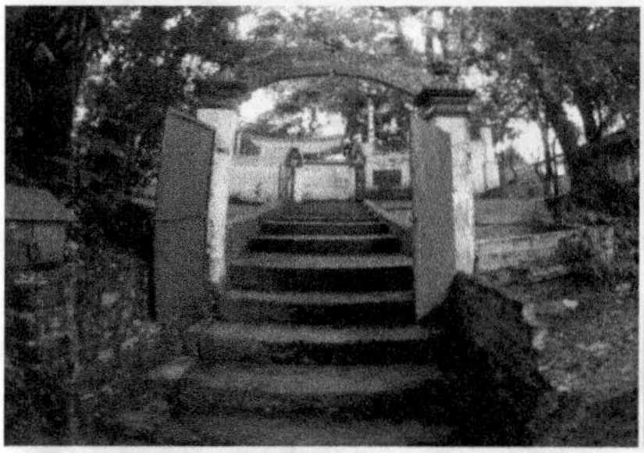
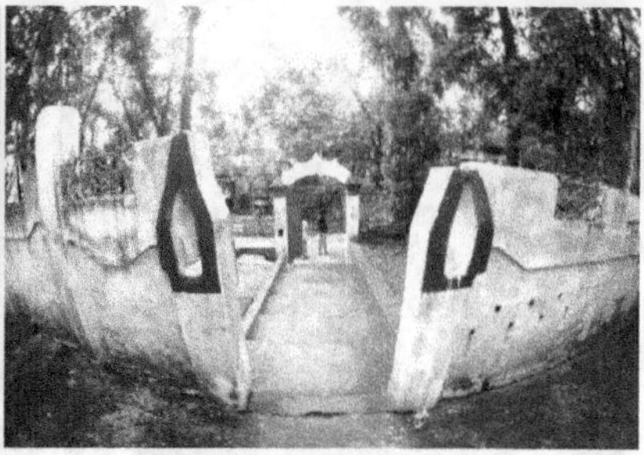
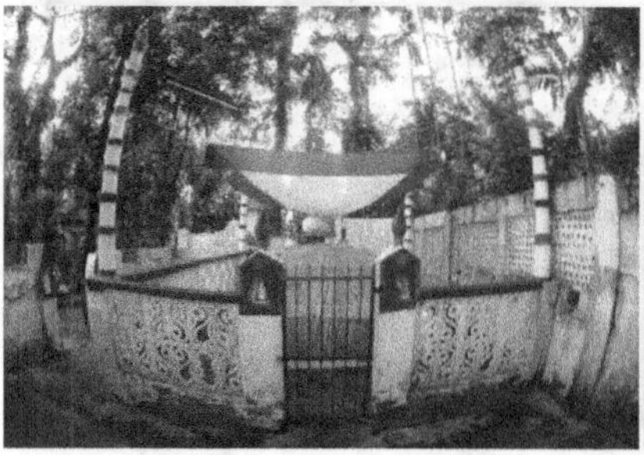
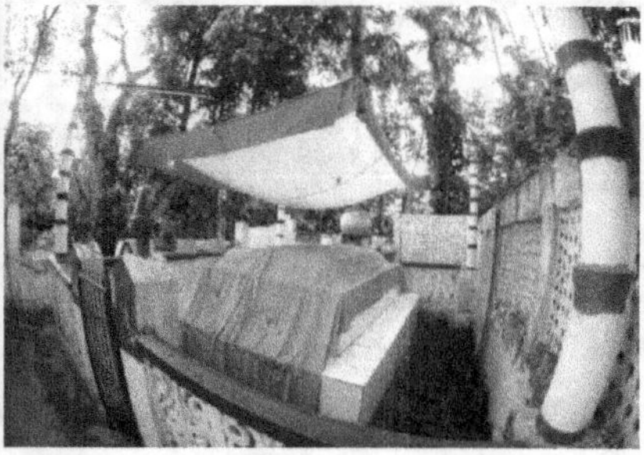

12.7.2010, 20:33:18

Soyod Najim Shah Qureshi*

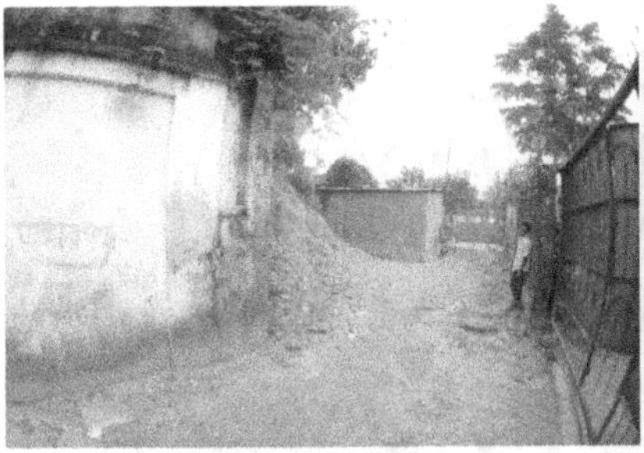

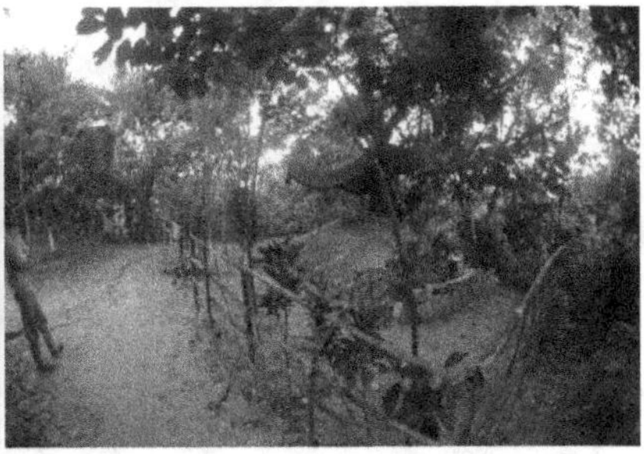

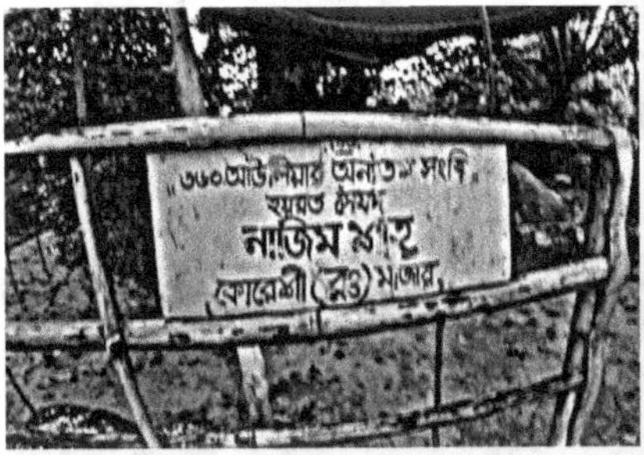
হযরত সৈয়দ
নাজিম শাহ্
কোরেশী (রঃ) মাজার

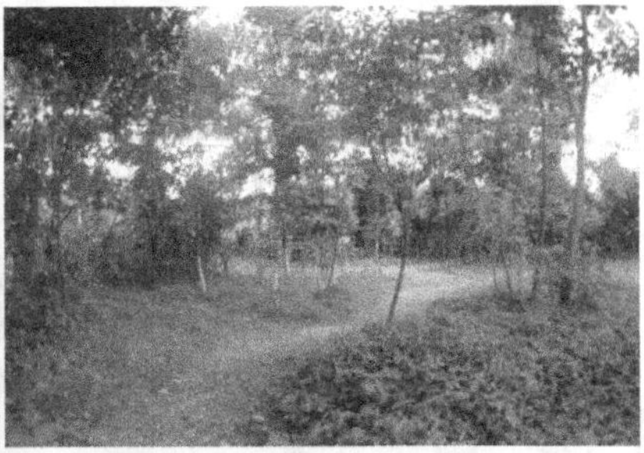

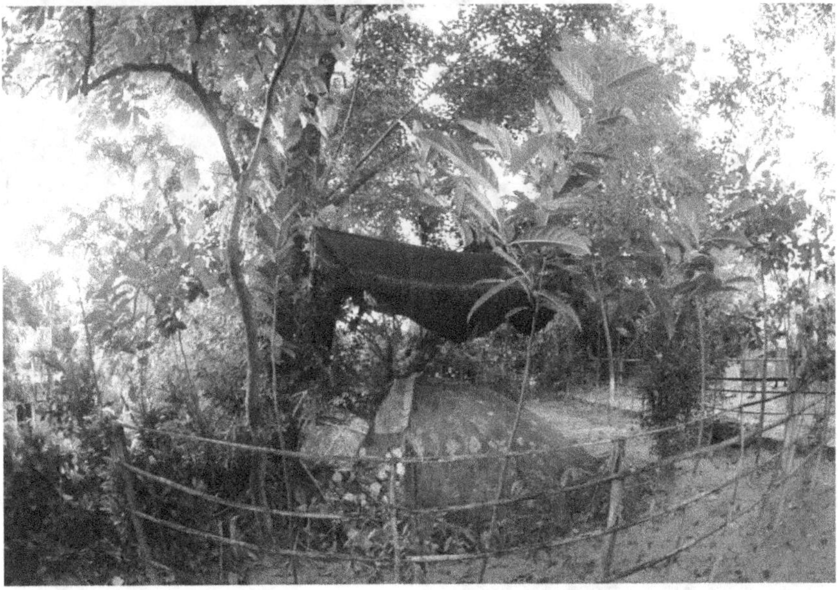

12.7.2010, 20:40:16

Moshkil Ashsan

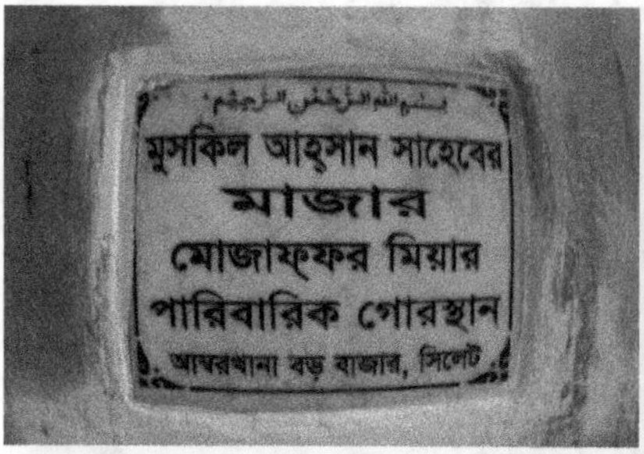
بسم الله الرحمن الرحيم
মুসকিল আহ্সান সাহেবের
মাজার
মোজাফ্ফর মিয়ার
পারিবারিক গোরস্থান
আম্বরখানা বড় বাজার, সিলেট

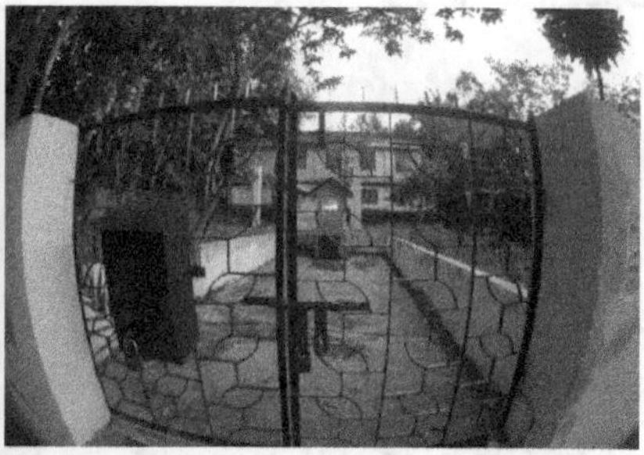

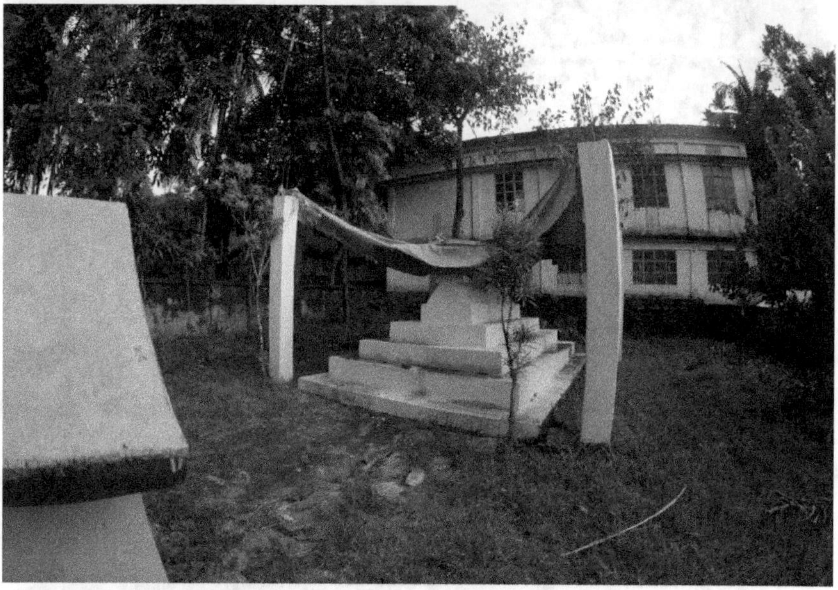

12.7.2010, 20:48:14

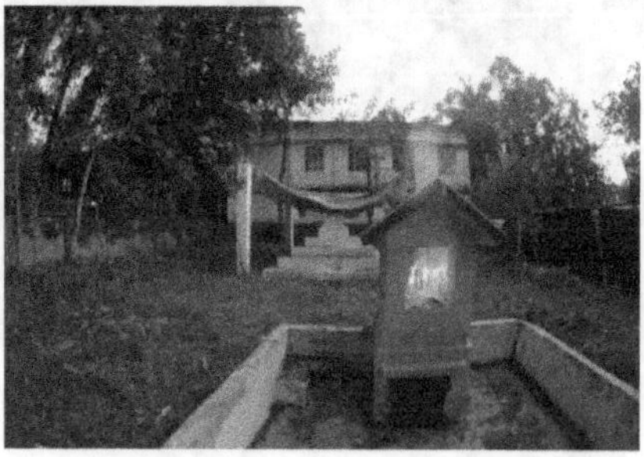

Shamalal Shah

Kodom Toli, Doriyar Mazar 25.9.2010.

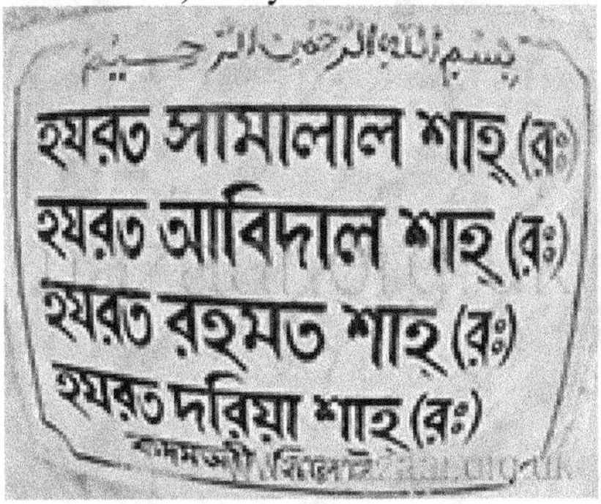
بسم الله الرحمن الرحيم
হযরত সামালাল শাহ্ (রঃ)
হযরত আবিদাল শাহ্ (রঃ)
হযরত রহমত শাহ্ (রঃ)
হযরত দরিয়া শাহ (রঃ)

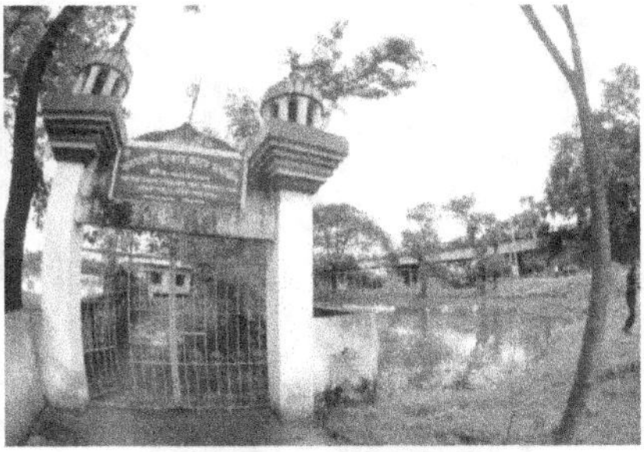

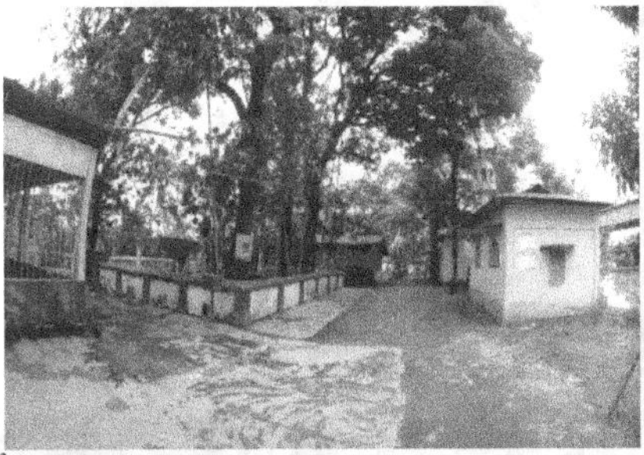

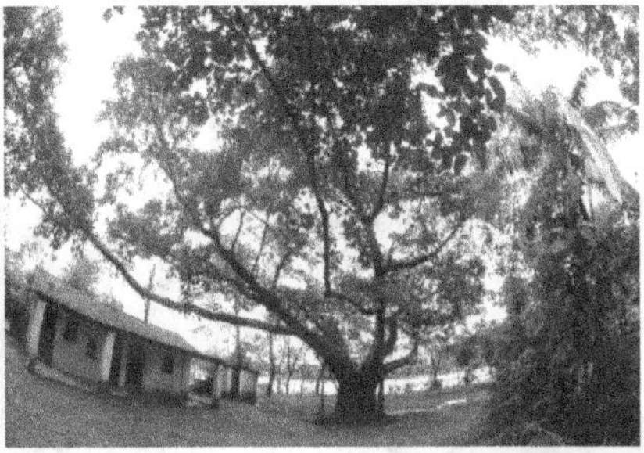

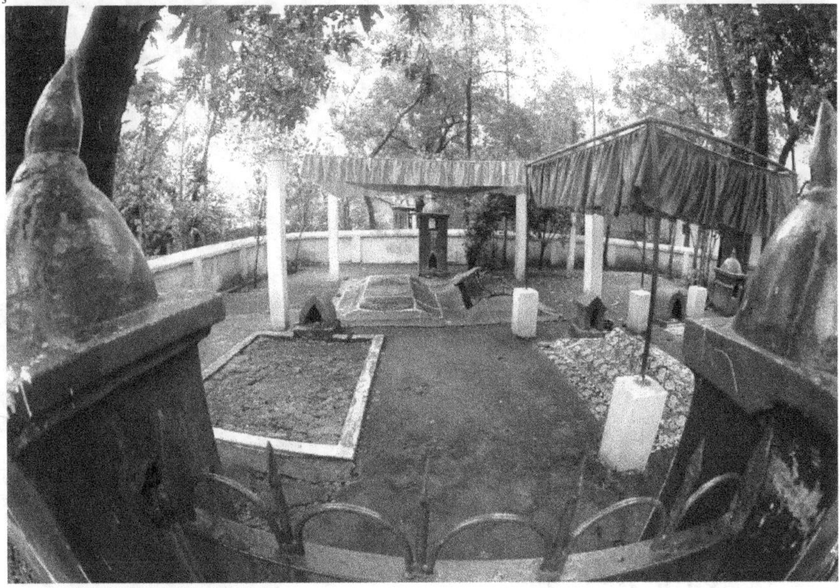

14.7.2010, 16:41:24

Abidal Shah

same plot as Shamalal, Kodom Toli, Doriyar Mazar

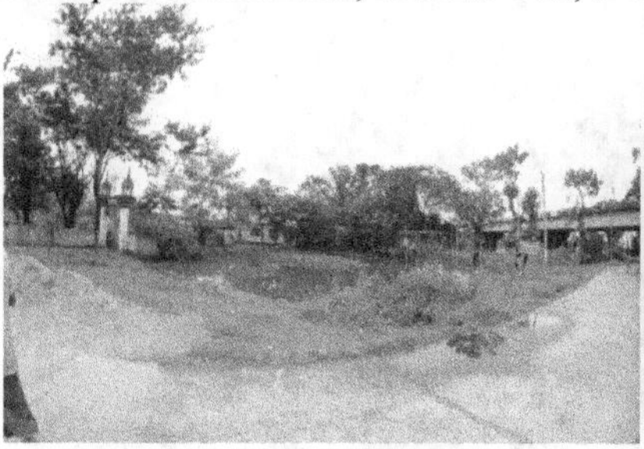

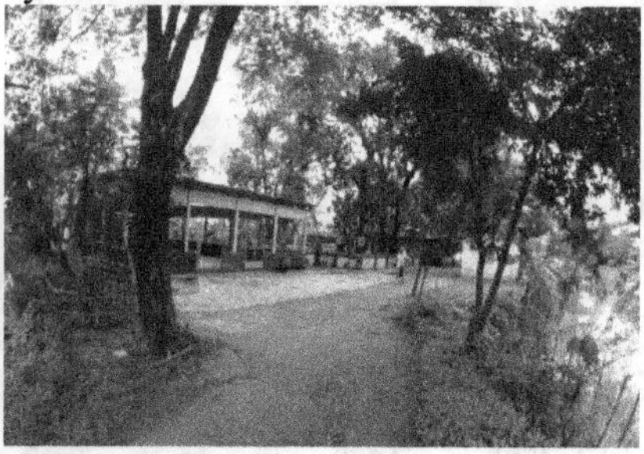

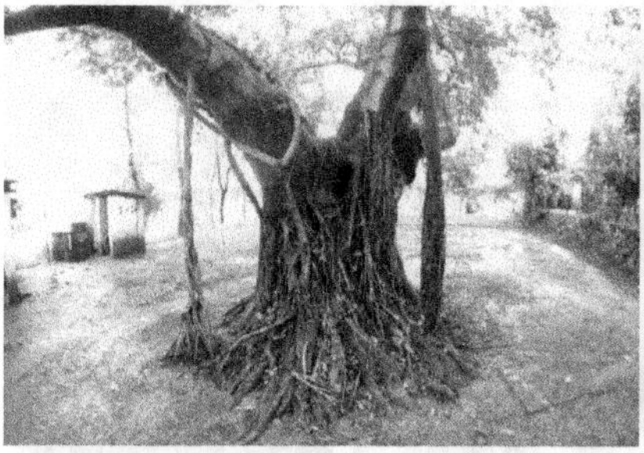

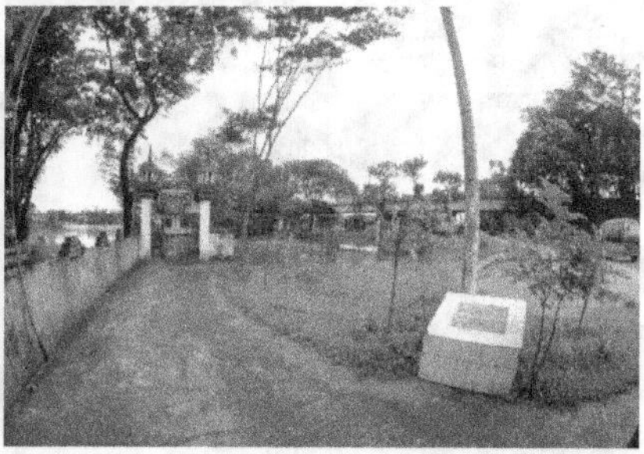

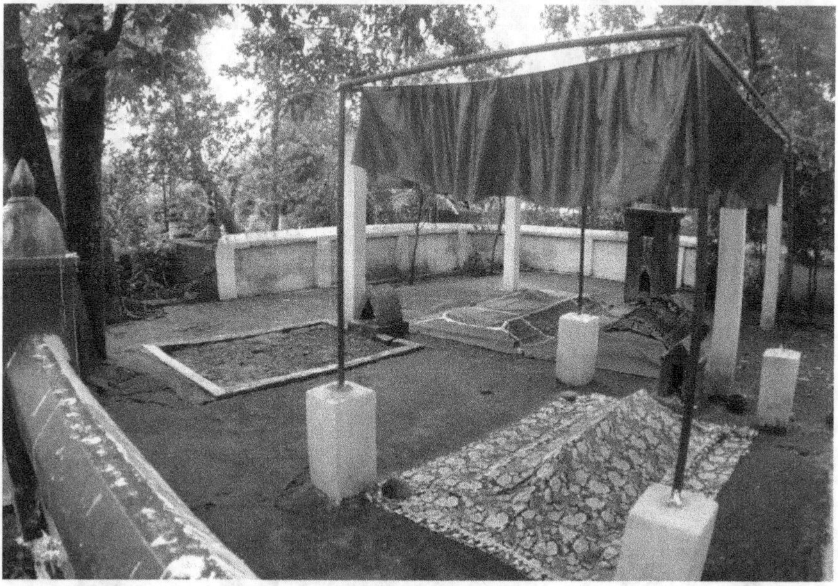

14.7.2010, 16:41:24

Suliye Panja**

Guta Tikor, Suley Panjer Road,

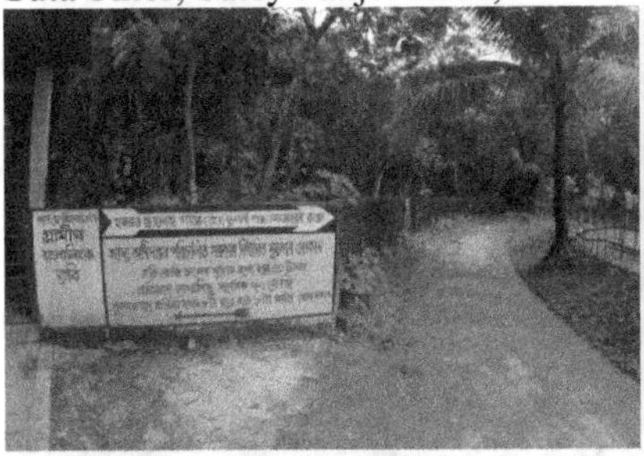

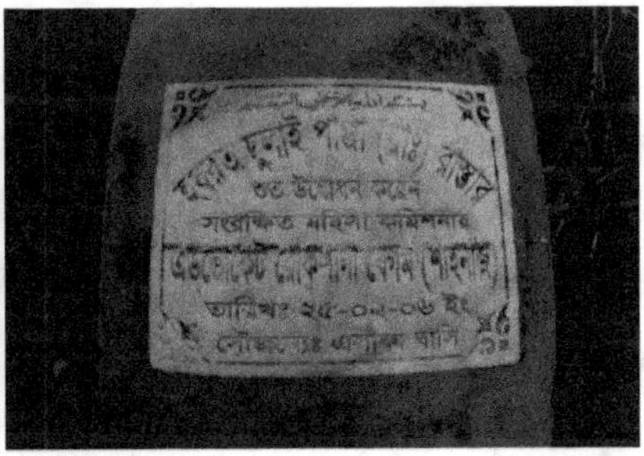

Suleh Panjer was the cook for the 360 Auwliyas.

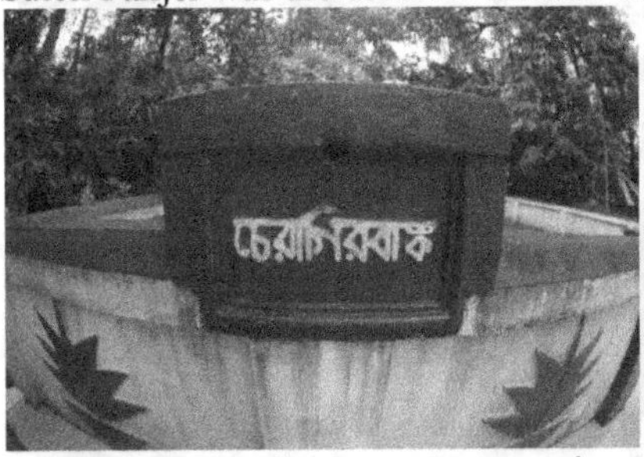

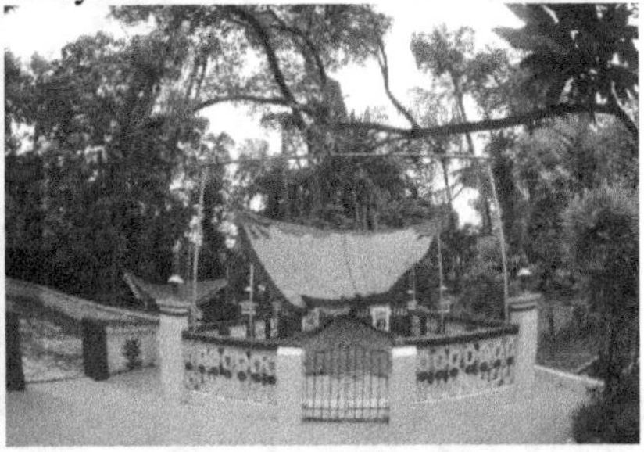

He's Mazar boasts a massive 500 year + Bott Gass (tree)

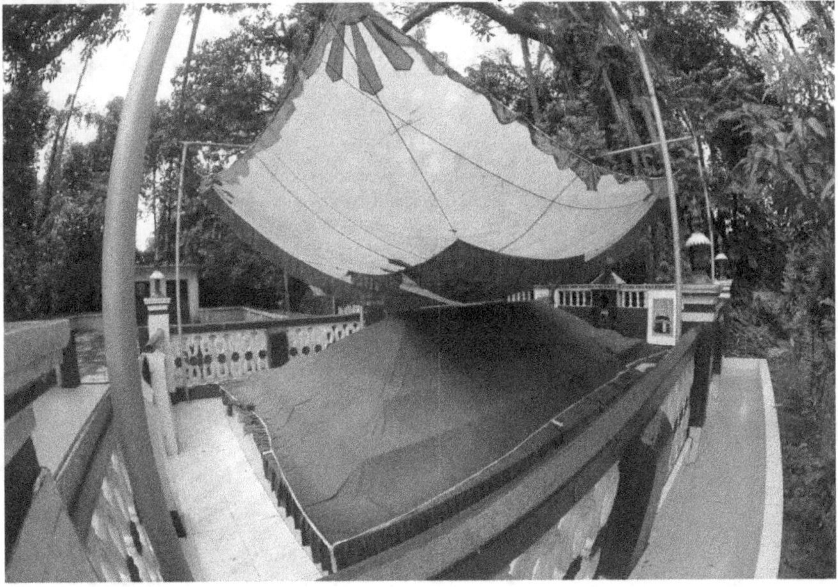

14.7.2010, 16:59:20

Shah Amin*

Sylhet Town

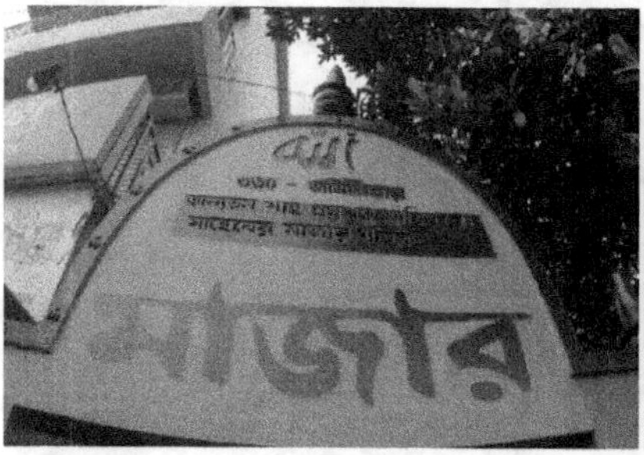
মাজার

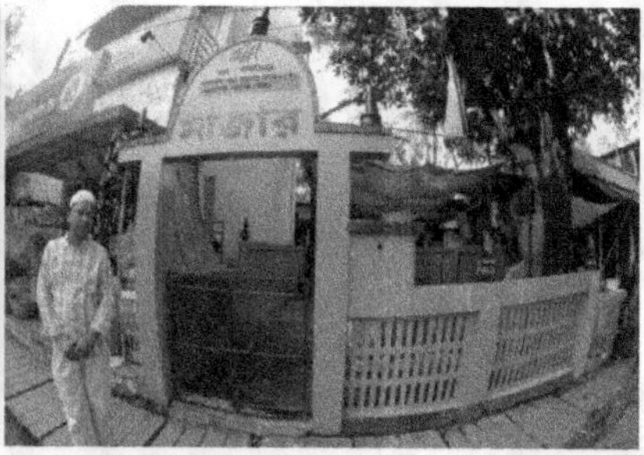

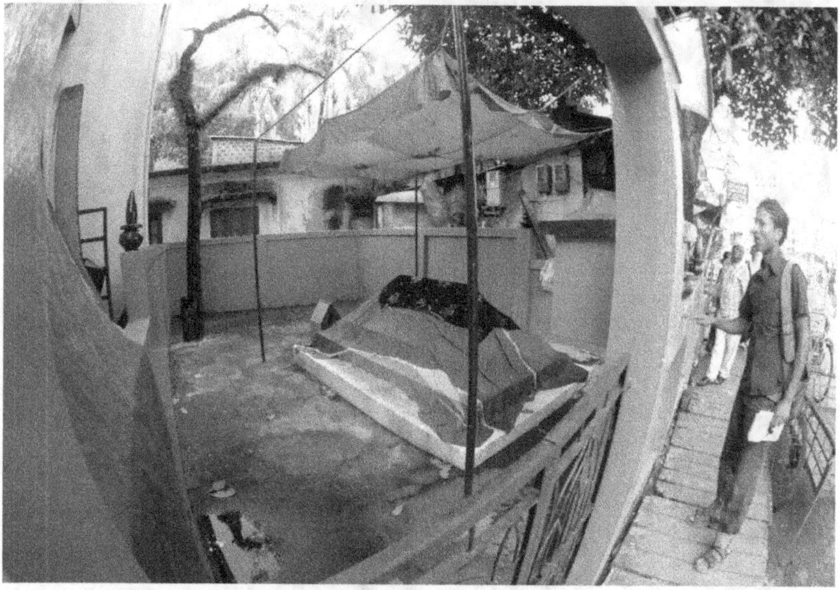

This site in Sylhet City, on the main street, this was not a calm site, and while I knew I was at a mazar, I was conscious of everything else around me.

14.7.2010, 17:04:12

Muhib Uddin

a.k.a,

Anfor Shah

Nuar Gaow, Shadipur

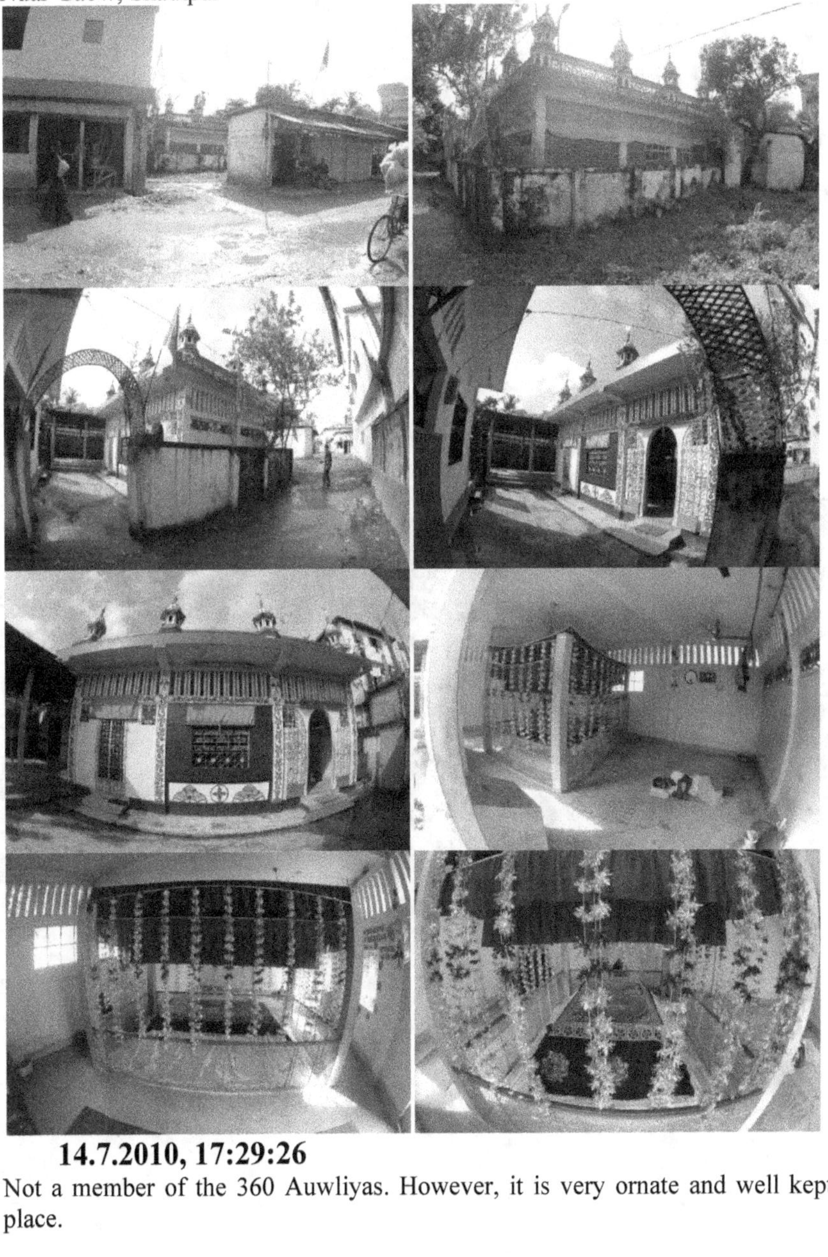

14.7.2010, 17:29:26

Not a member of the 360 Auwliyas. However, it is very ornate and well kept place.

Jolfu Shah

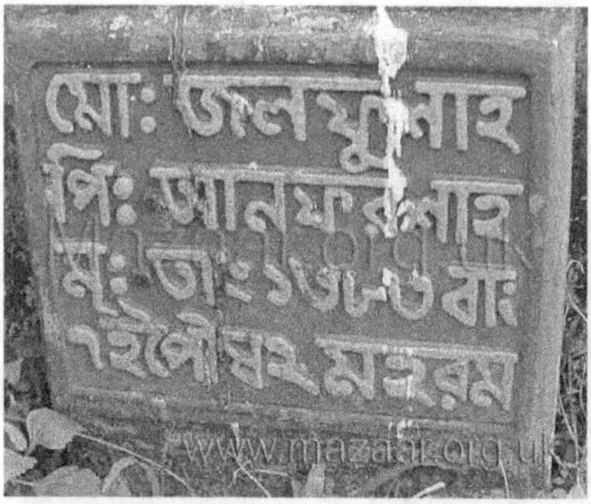

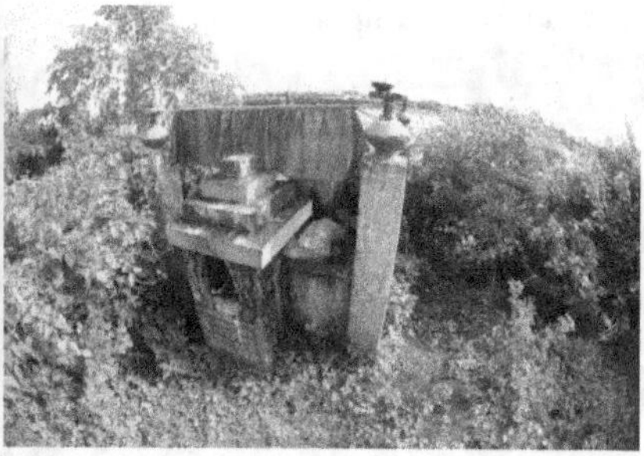

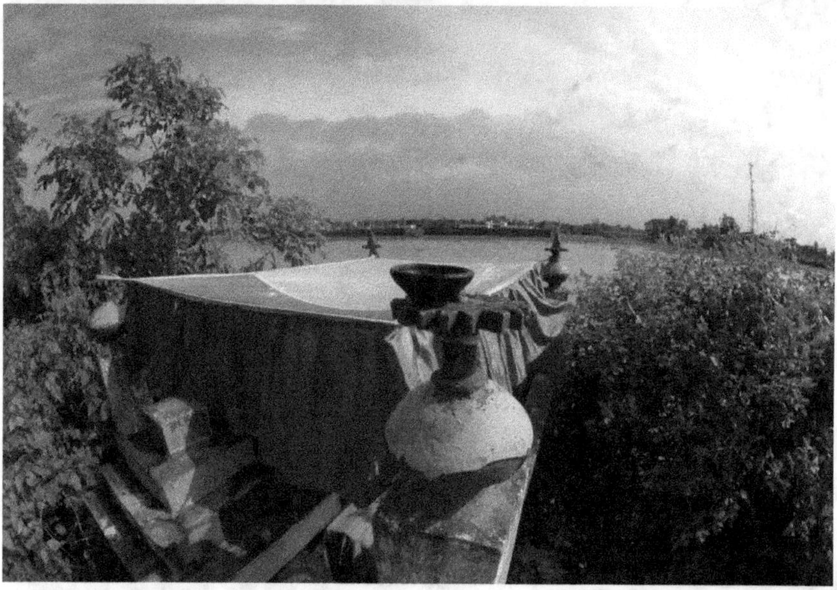

14.7.2010, 17:40:12

On the riverbank of Surma River

Shah Gazi Soyod Burhan Uddin#

Burhanabad, Kishi Ghat, Tul Tiker, Sylhet.

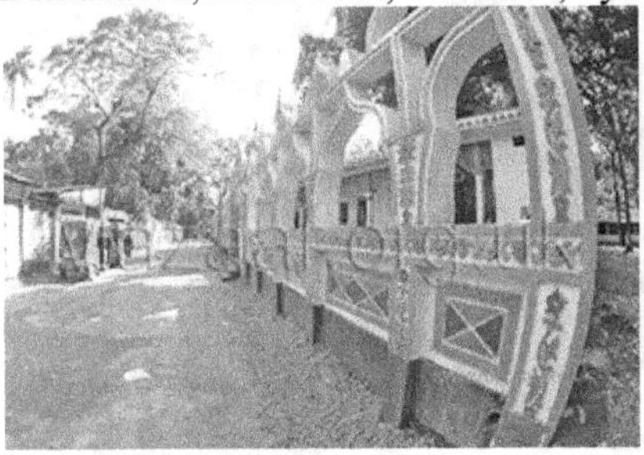
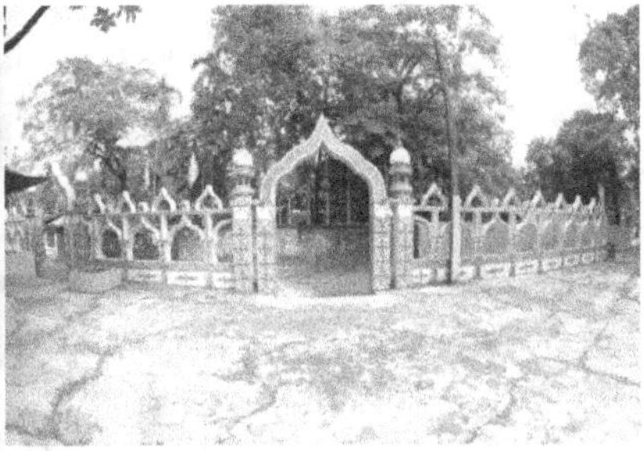
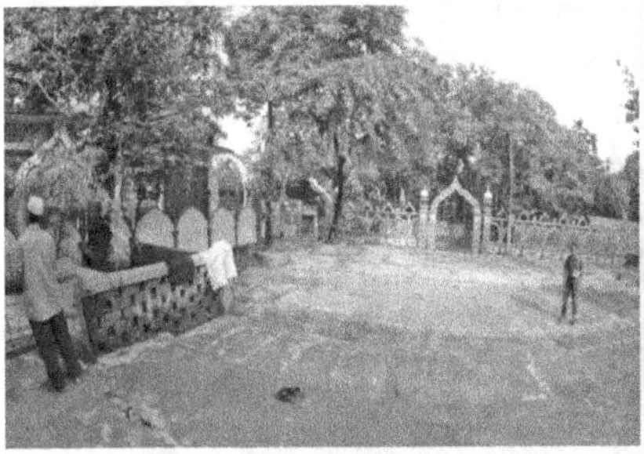
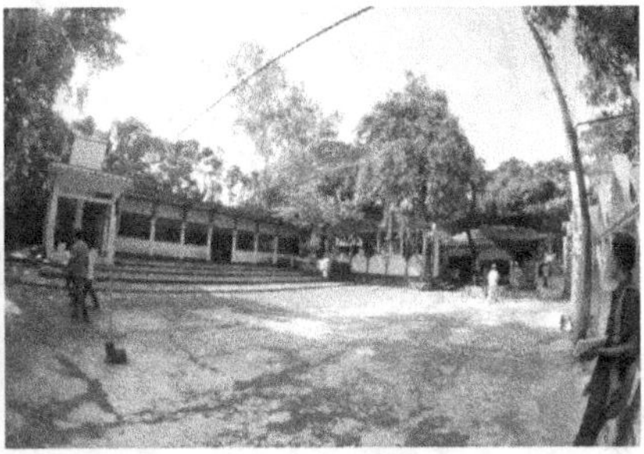
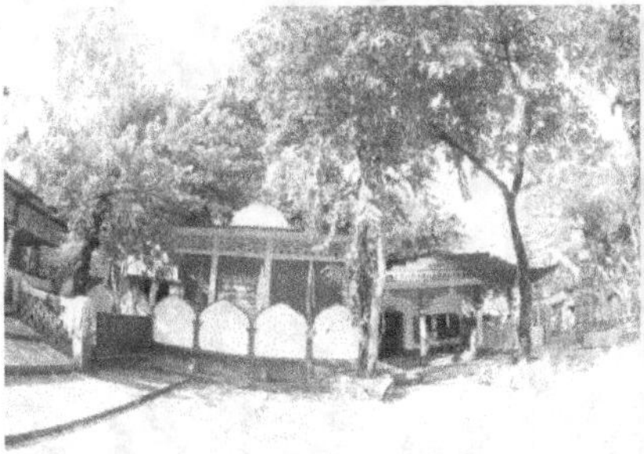
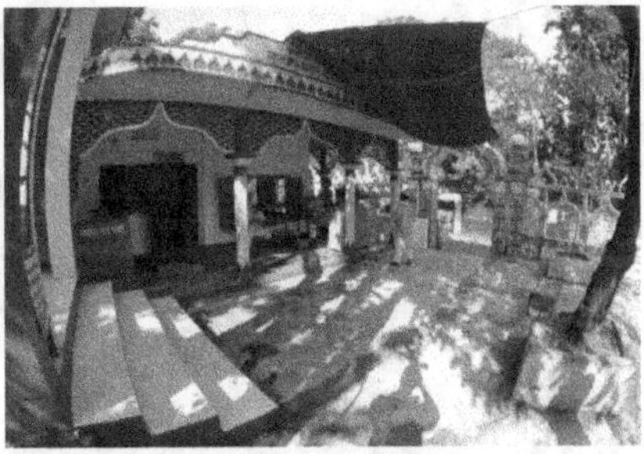
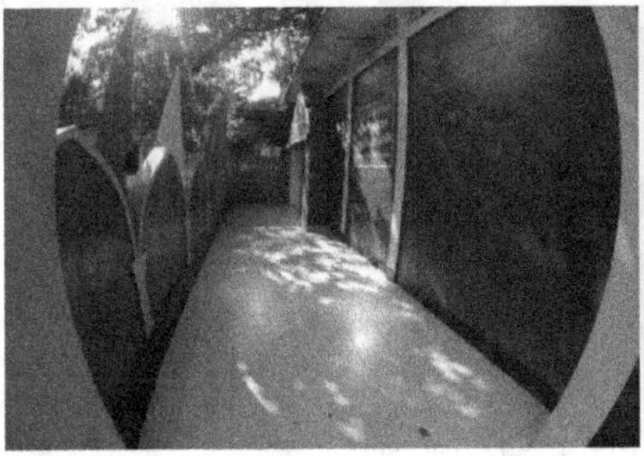
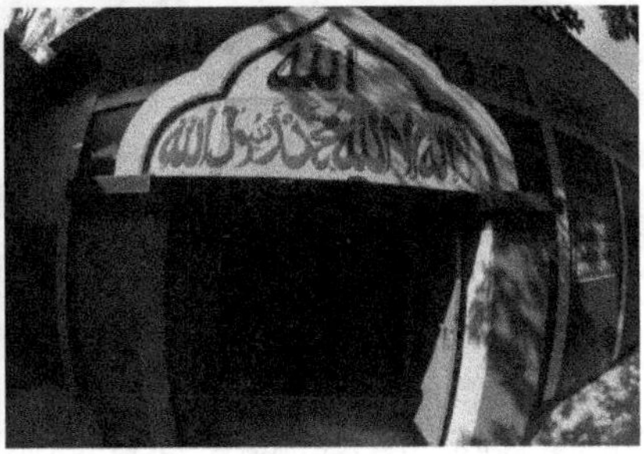

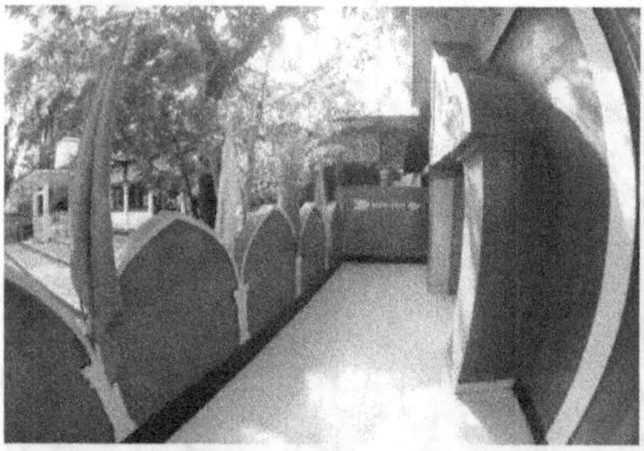

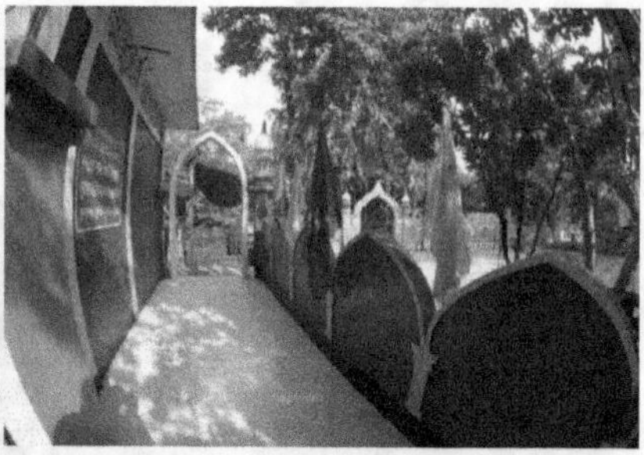

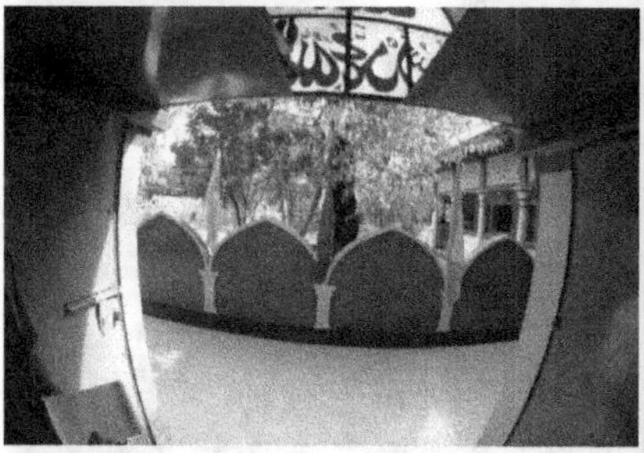

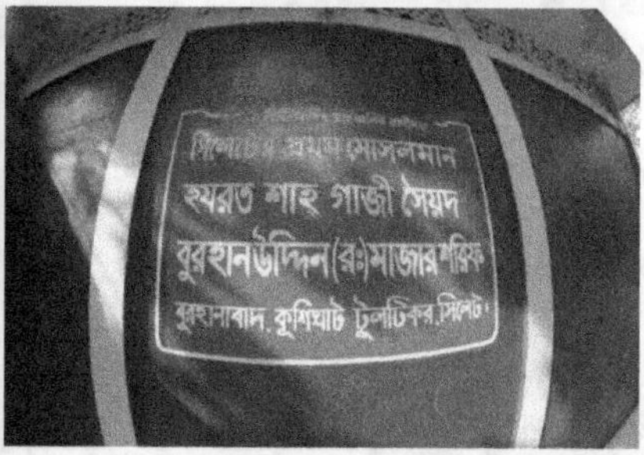
হযরত শাহ গাজী সৈয়দ
বুরহানউদ্দিন (রঃ) মাজার শরিফ
বুরহানাবাদ, কুশিঘাট টুলটিকর, সিলেট।

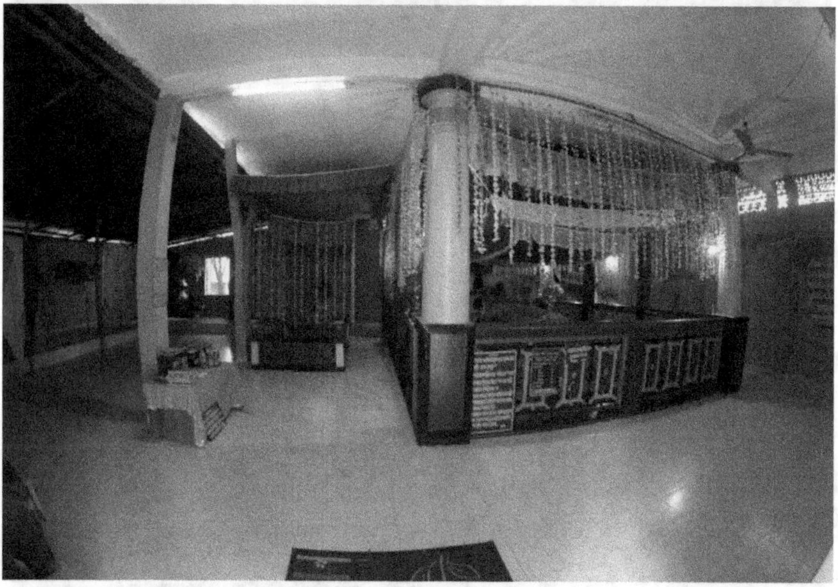

14.7.2010, 18:03:32

Burhan Uddin lived in the Sylhet region, before Hazrat Shah Jalal's.

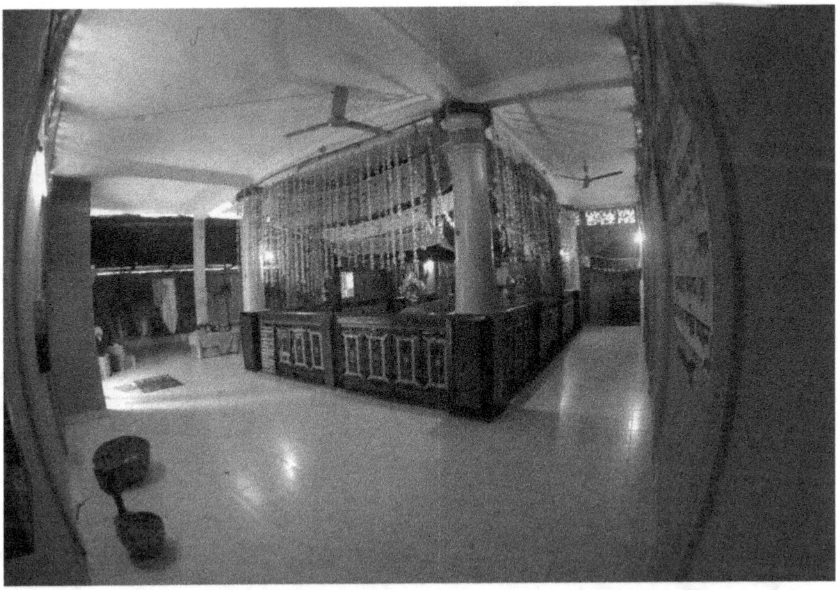

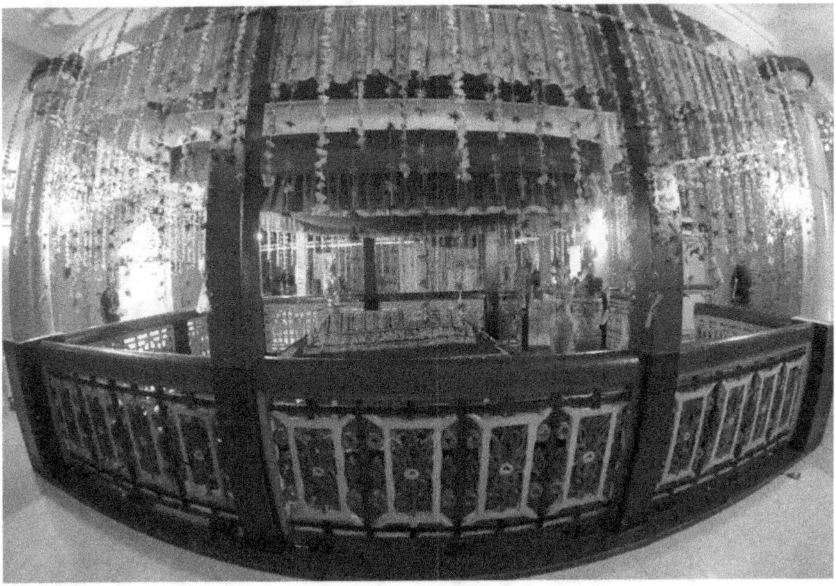

Burhan Uddin is one of the reasons why Shah Jalal and the 306 missionaries went to Sylhet. Hazrat Shah Jalal was a Sufi contingent with the army of Firuz Shah, Nephew of Nizam Uddin auwliya of Delhi at the time.

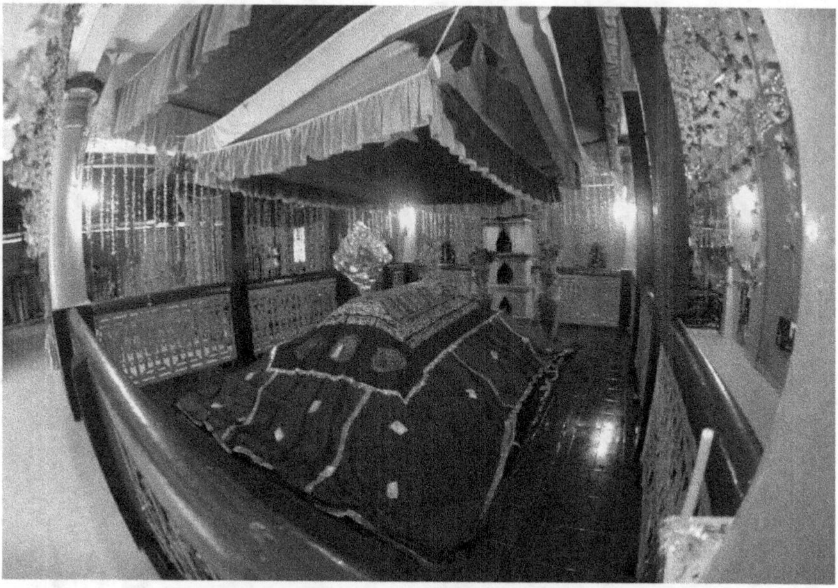

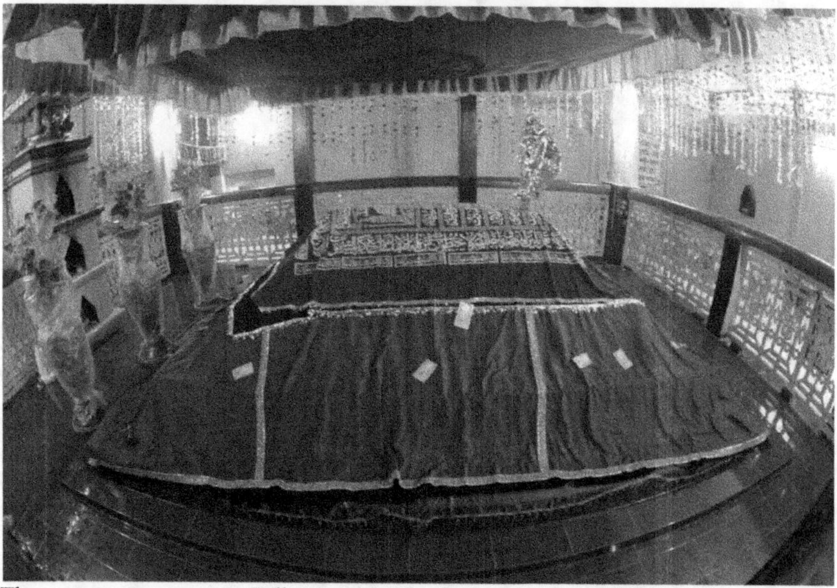

The army was sent to Sylhet region to get Justice for Killing of his son and cutting of his hand by the regional Hindu King, Guar Govind.

He and his family are the bedrock of Shah Jalal's journey in propagating Sufism in Sylhet and the surrounding areas.

Shohid Guljar Alom

Burhanabad, Kishi Ghat, Tul Tiker

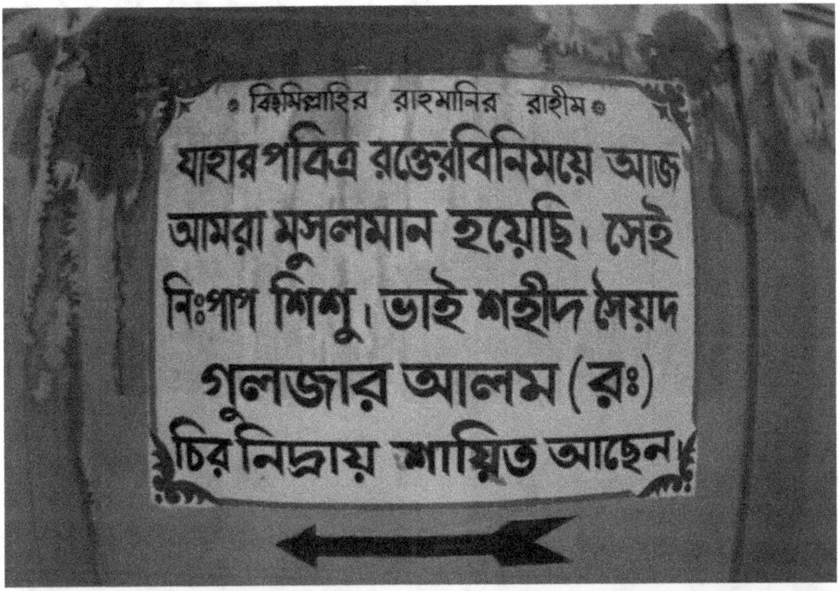
বিসমিল্লাহির রাহমানির রাহীম
যাহার পবিত্র রক্তের বিনিময়ে আজ
আমরা মুসলমান হয়েছি। সেই
নিঃপাপ শিশু। ভাই শহীদ সৈয়দ
গুলজার আলম (রঃ)
চির নিদ্রায় শায়িত আছেন।

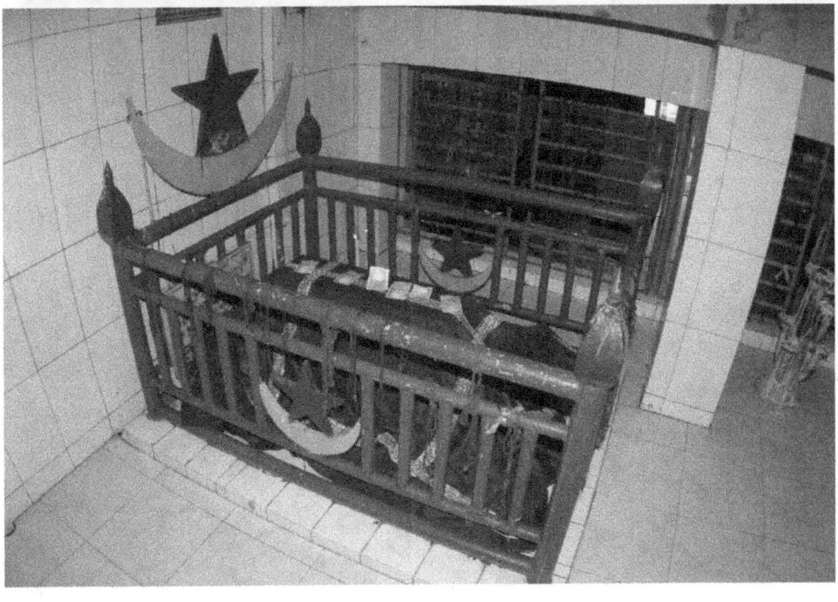

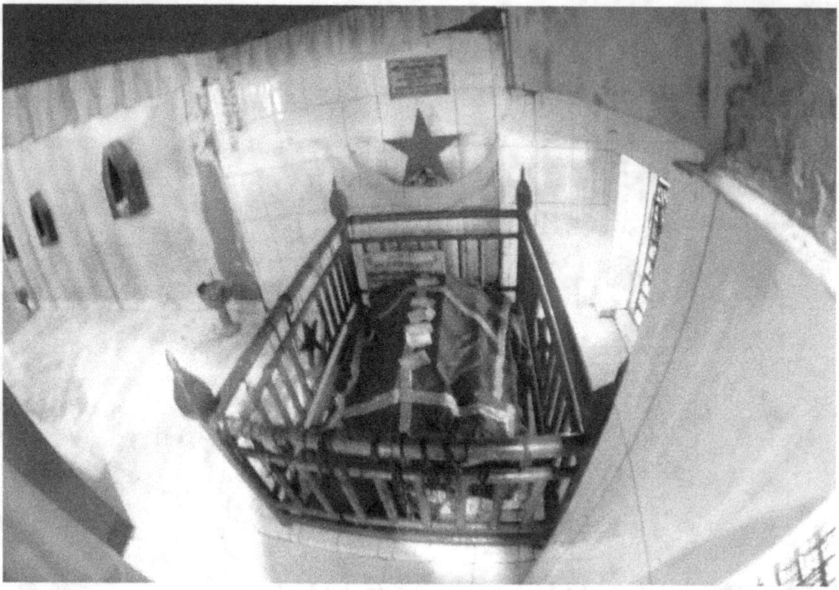

14.7.2010, 17:57:56

He is the first Muslim to be killed in Sylhet. He was killed by Gaur Govinda Raja.

His death was the beginning of the downfall of the Hindu King.

And the beginning of the military campaign from Delhi, to seek justice for the execution of Guljar and the cutting of his dad's hand, Burhan Uddin.

Several attempts were made to get to Sylhet and were met with opposition and they failed and returned without getting justice.

Justice and the downfall of the Hindu King came when Hazrat Shah Jalal accompanied the army sent my Delhi and entered Sylhet in 1303.

It be interesting to identify when the ""360 missionary's" was coined, that has now become synonymous with Hazrat Shah Jalal.

Khatuna Jahanath#

Burhan Uddin's wife

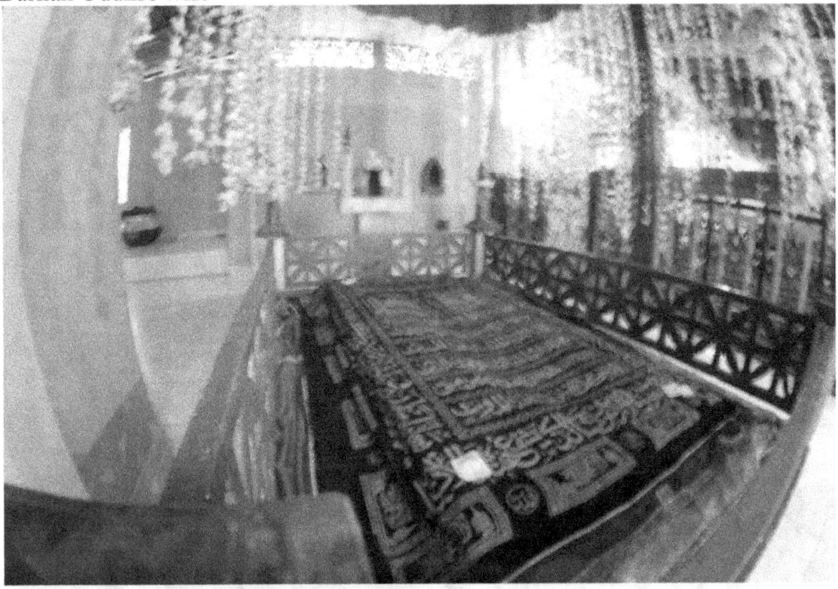

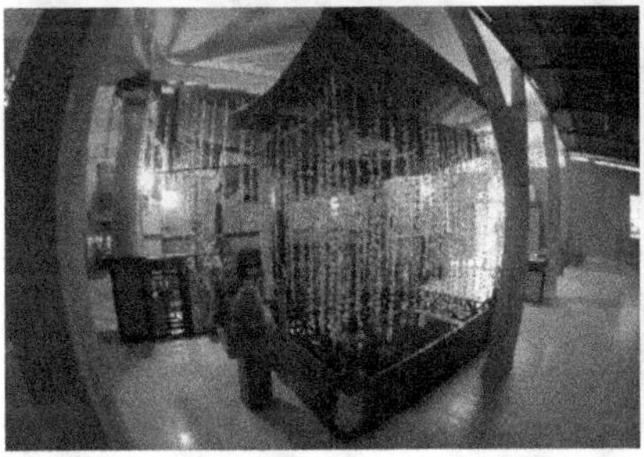

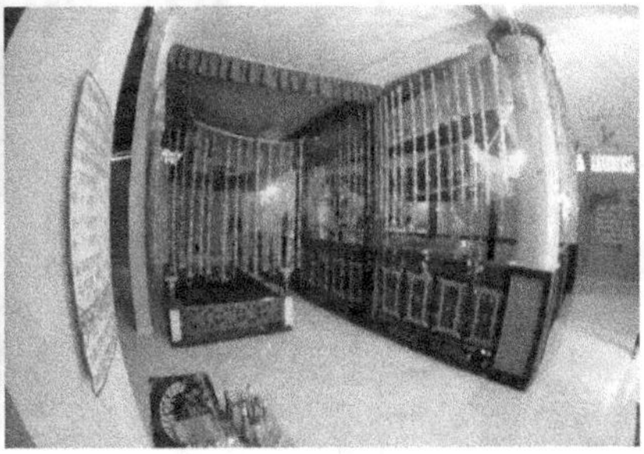

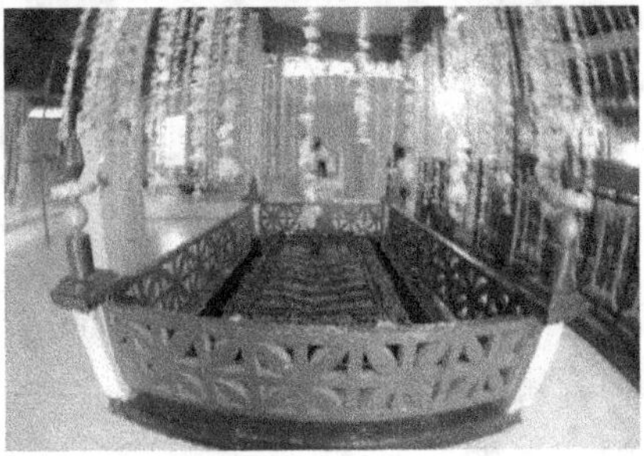

14.7.2010, 18:00:24

Shekh Nasir Uddin

Kuar Parah Point, Shekh Parah, Sylhet Town, off main road, behind shops.

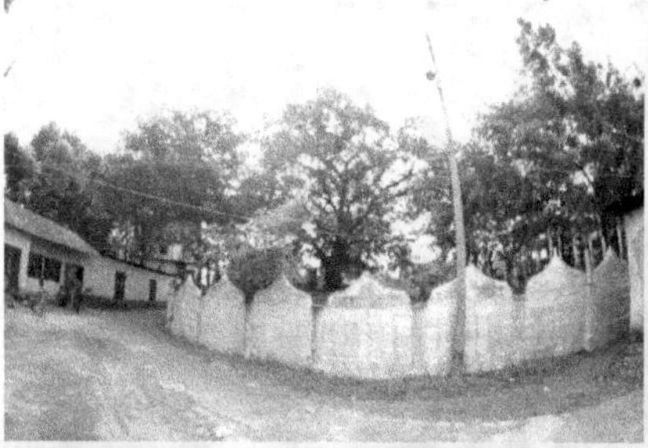

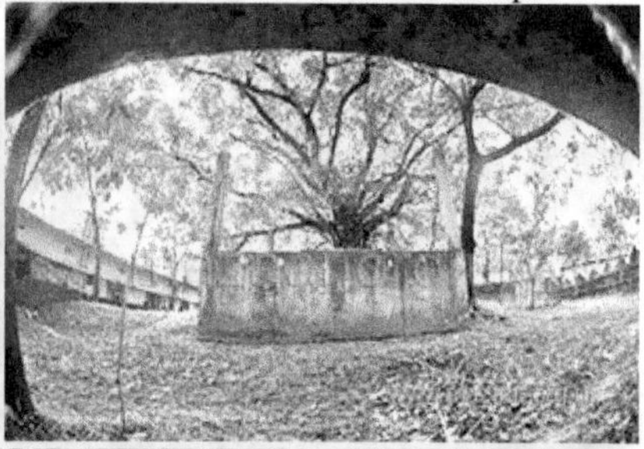

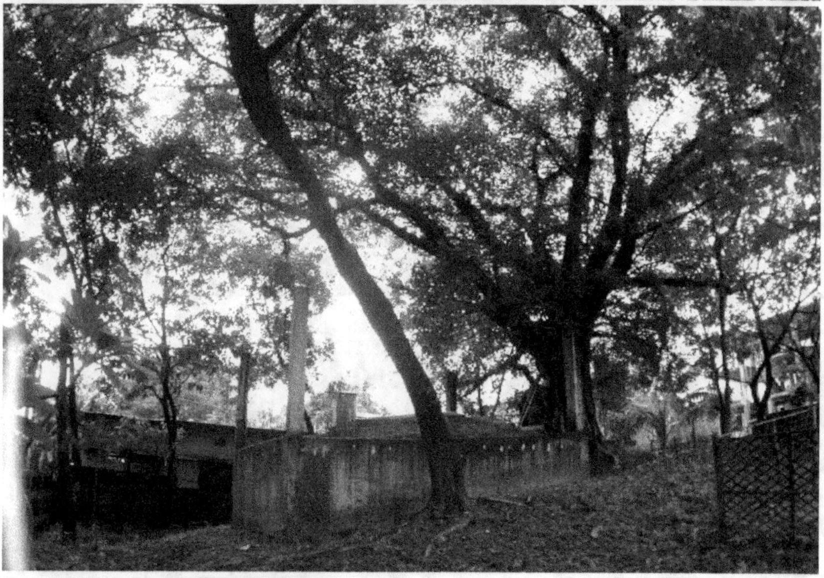

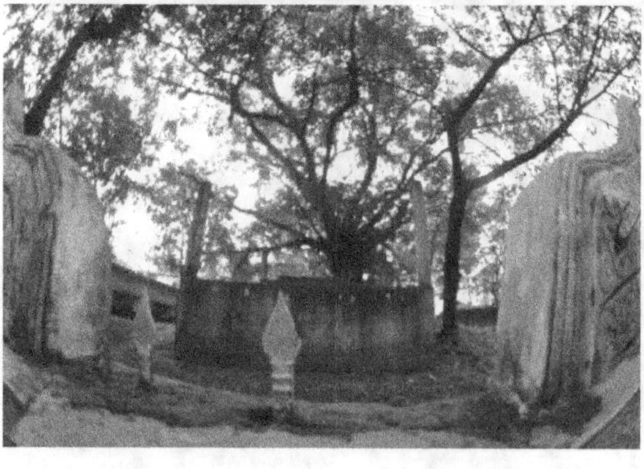

This site is in Sylhet town and located off road site, you enter into a secluded space. While there has been some work done in the past, it is not maintained as other examples. This site is not bright and welcoming, as are many.

14.7.2010, 18:30:10

Gulam*

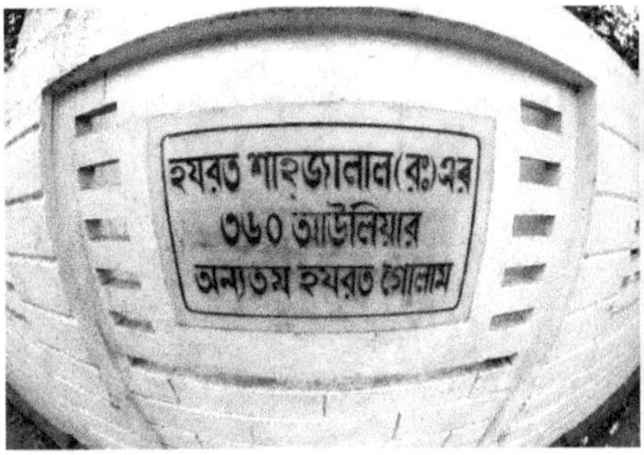
হযরত শাহ্‌জালাল(রঃ)এর
৩৬০ আউলিয়ার
অন্যতম হযরত গোলাম

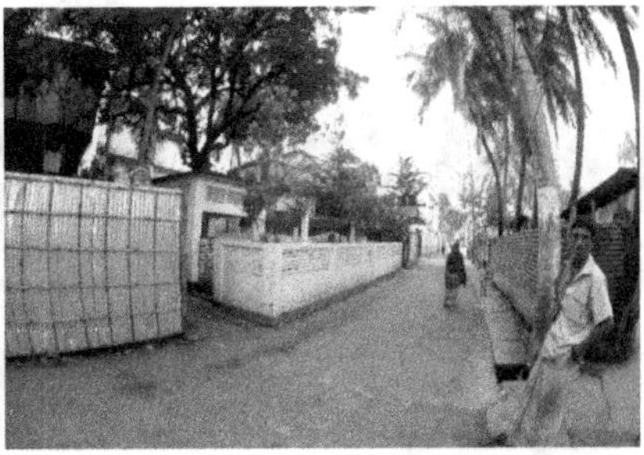

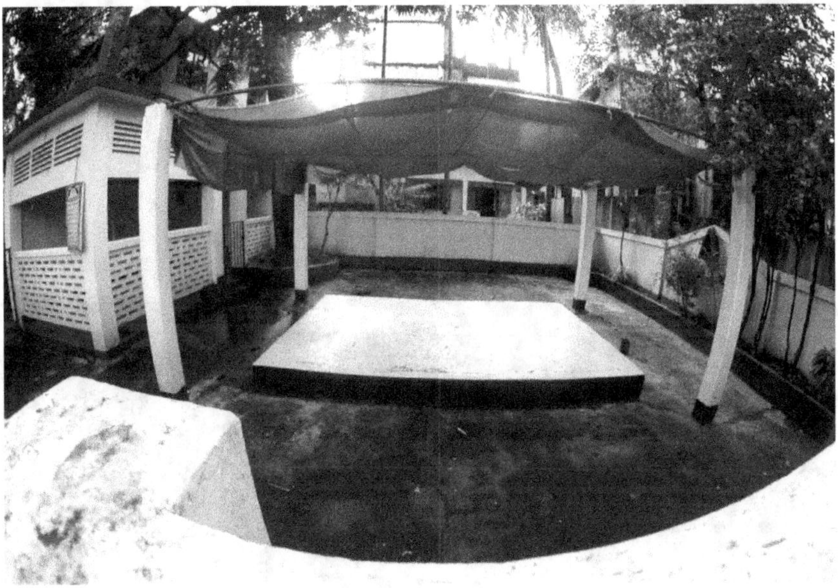

14.7.2010 19:16

Here is anther of the beaten tracks and in an estate street. This backs on to a property and looks like a garden.

There is a claim on the plaque that this person was part of the 360 missionaries, but there are no 8 sided plaques that the Pakistani Government authenticated the site with during their reign of Bangladesh, in the East Pakistan era.

Soyod Jamal Phir*

Monipuri Rajbari

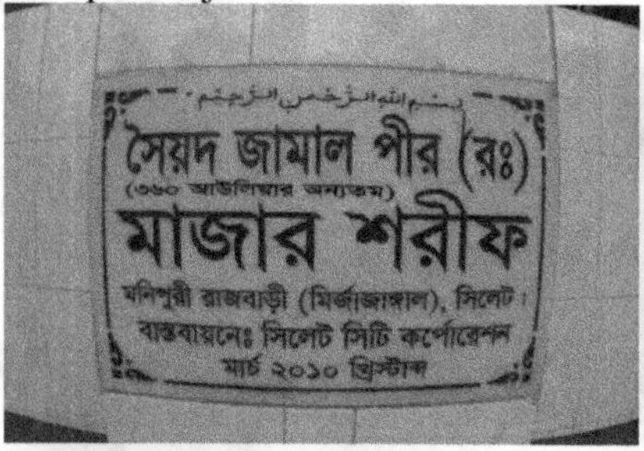
সৈয়দ জামাল পীর (রঃ)
(৩৬০ আউলিয়ার অন্যতম)
মাজার শরীফ
মনিপুরী রাজবাড়ী (মির্জাজাঙ্গাল), সিলেট।
বাস্তবায়নেঃ সিলেট সিটি কর্পোরেশন
মার্চ ২০১০ খ্রিস্টাব্দ

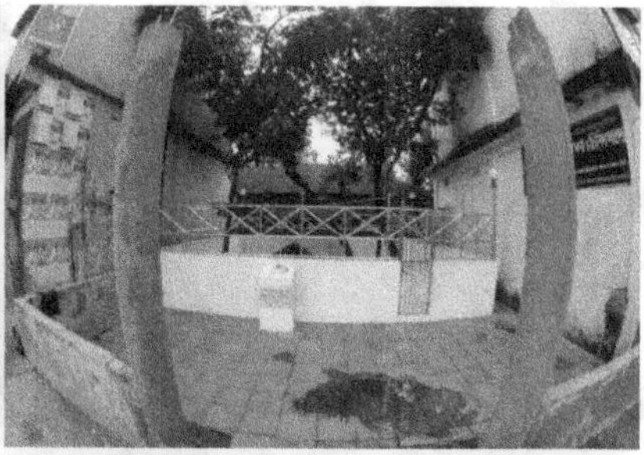

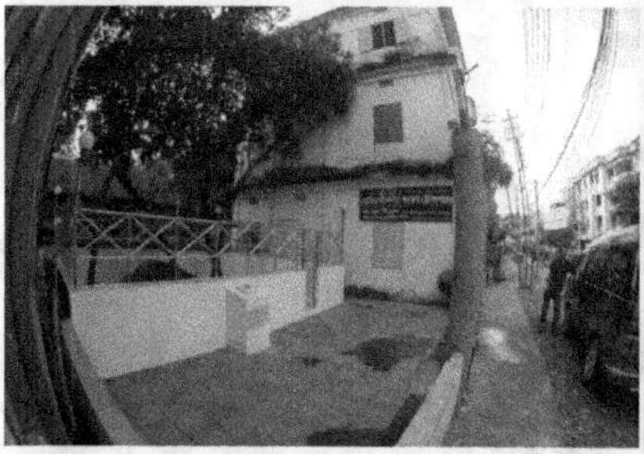

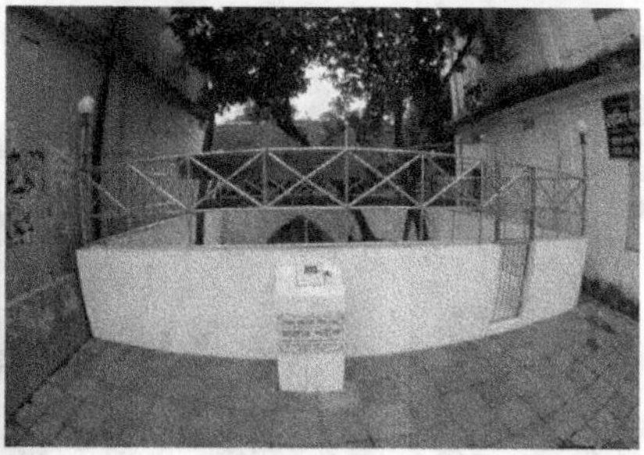

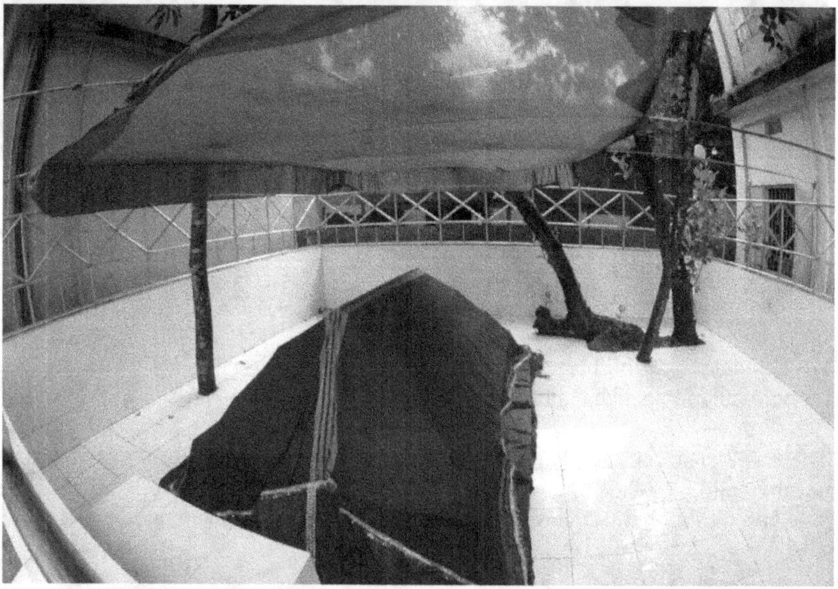

14.7.2010, 19:29:22

Goybi Phir

Lama Bazar, Sylhet

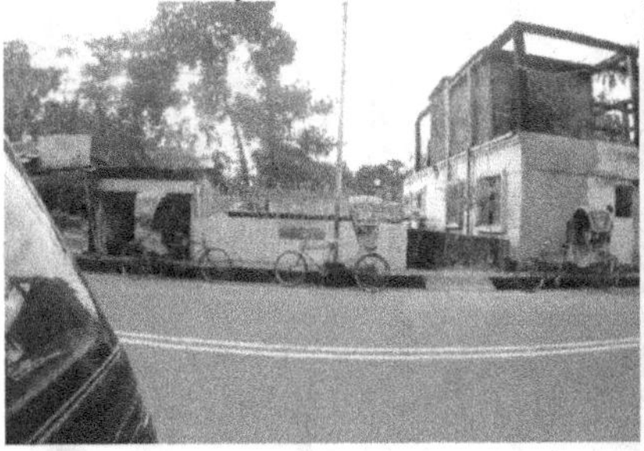

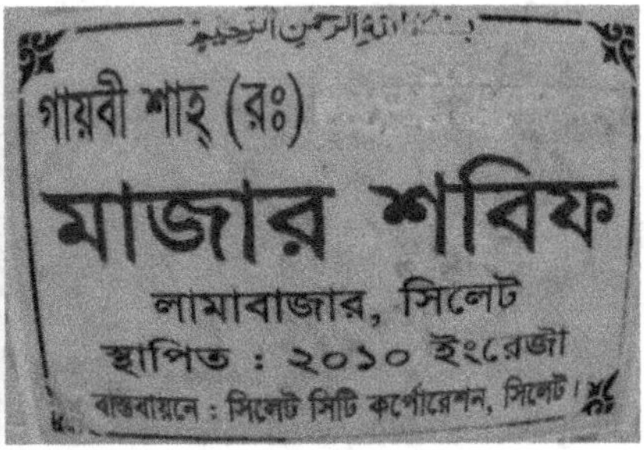
গায়বী শাহ্ (রঃ)
মাজার শরিফ
লামাবাজার, সিলেট
স্থাপিত : ২০১০ ইংরেজী
বাস্তবায়নে : সিলেট সিটি কর্পোরেশন, সিলেট।

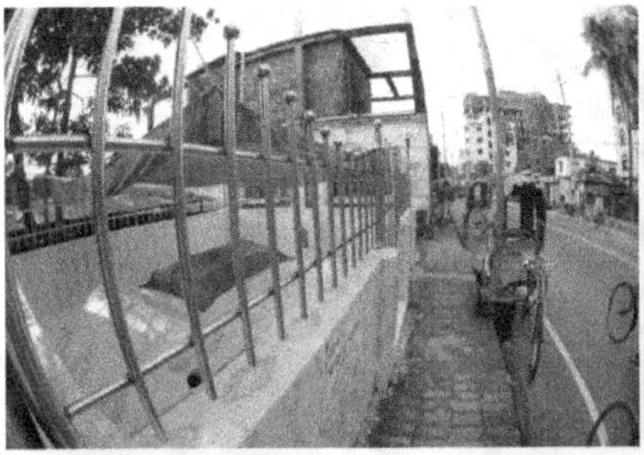

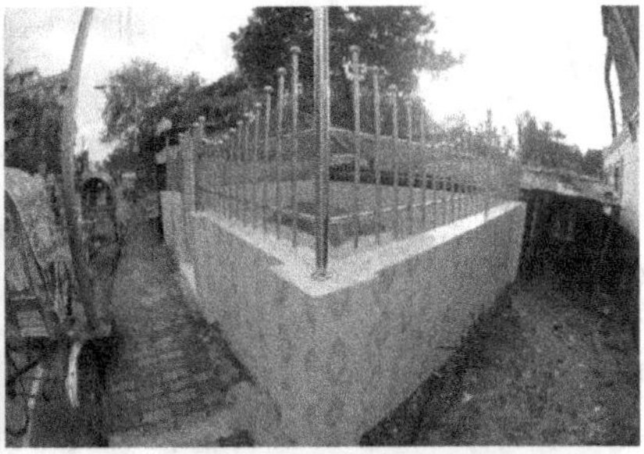

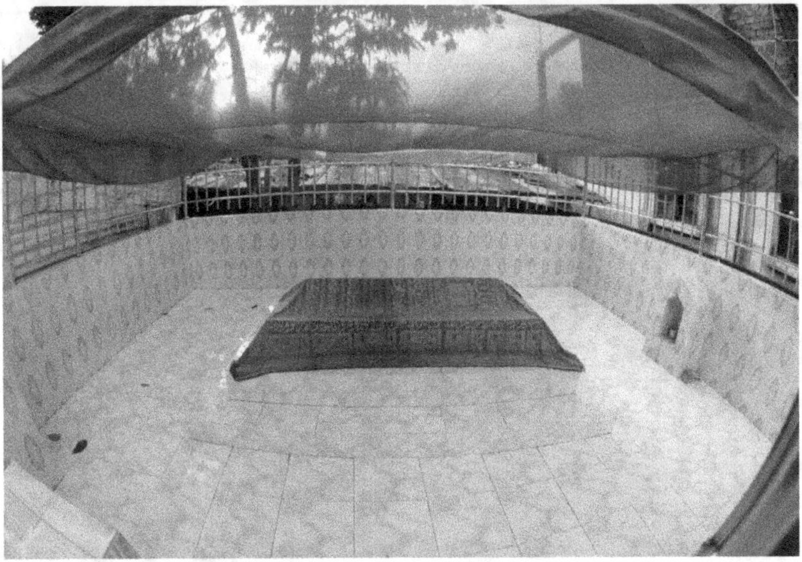

14.7.2010, 19:34:08

Here is evidence, that they claimed this person to be of the 360 missionaries, but it has been deleted off the plaque.

Shah Soyod Lal

a.k.a,

Soyod Jahan

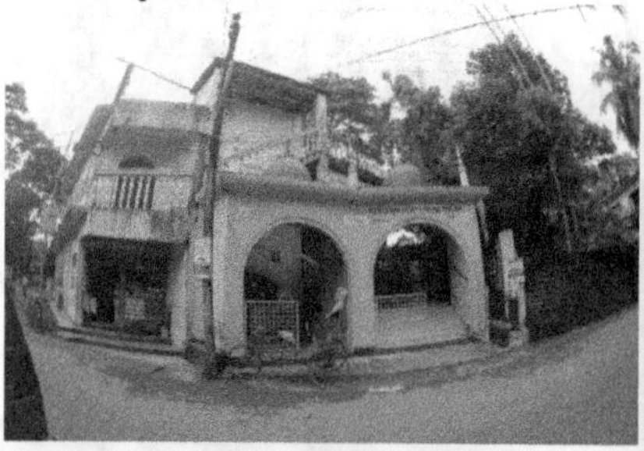

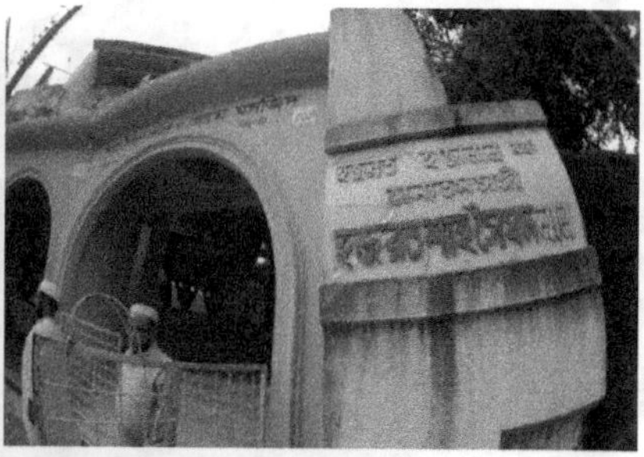

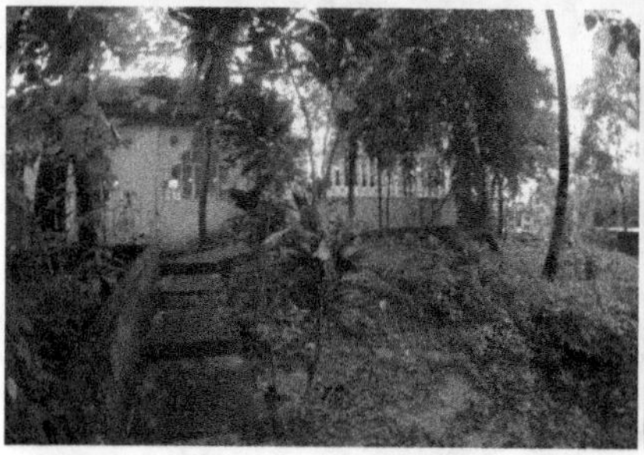

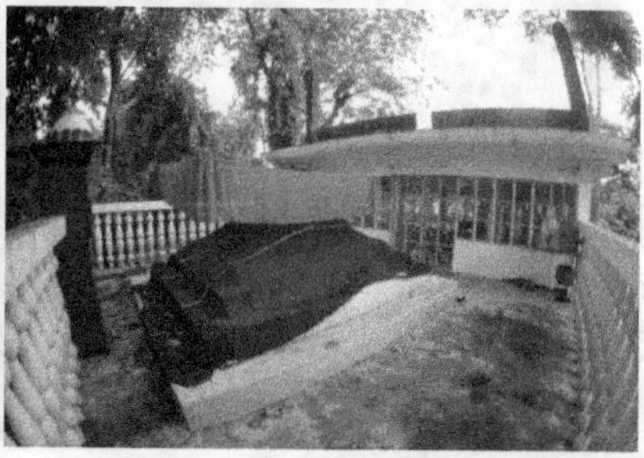

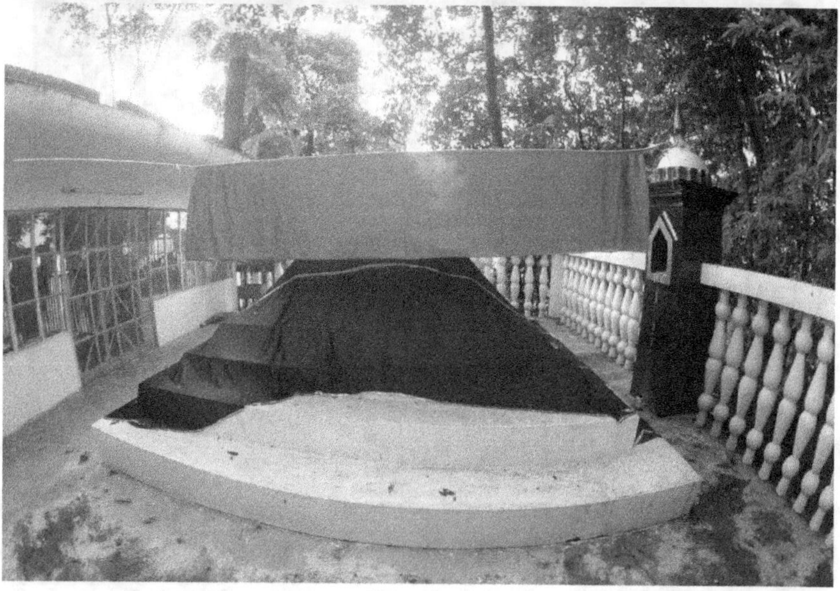

14.7.2010, 19:44:12

Soyod Ingu Lal

Ingulal Road.

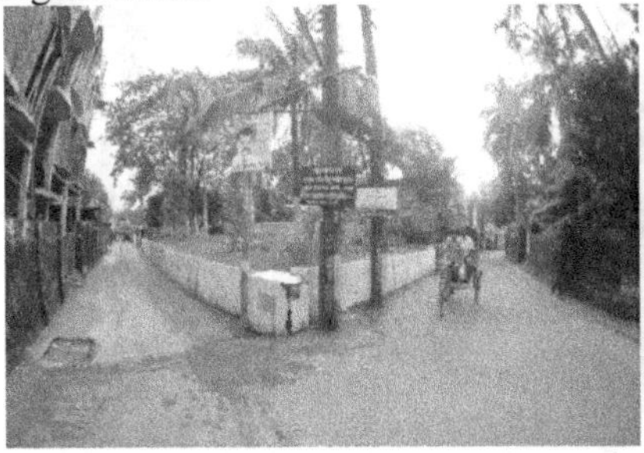

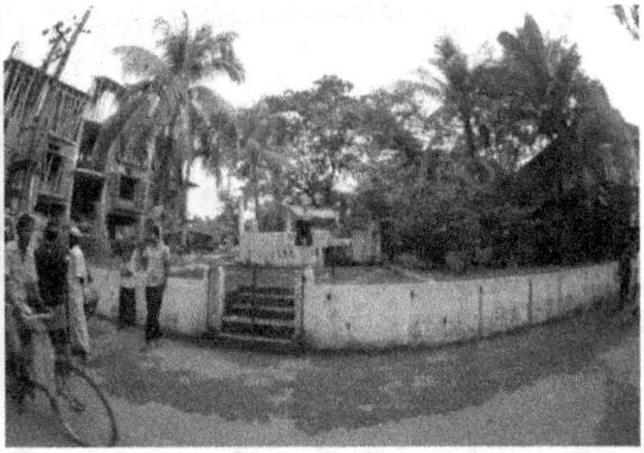

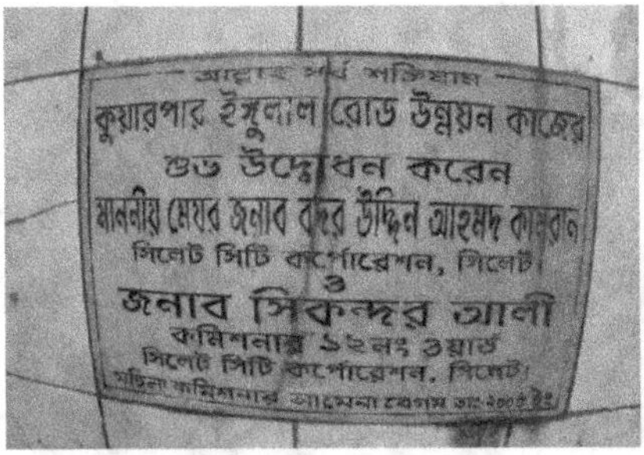
কুয়ারপার ইঙ্গুলাল রোড উন্নয়ন কাজের
শুভ উদ্বোধন করেন
সিলেট সিটি কর্পোরেশন, সিলেট।
ও
জনাব সিকন্দর আলী
কমিশনার ১২নং ওয়ার্ড
সিলেট সিটি কর্পোরেশন, সিলেট।

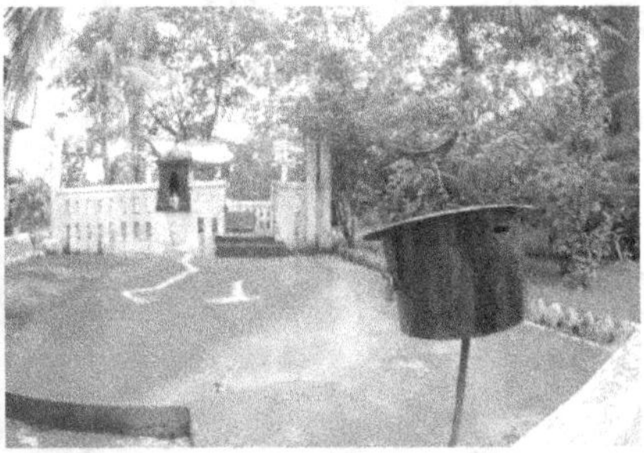

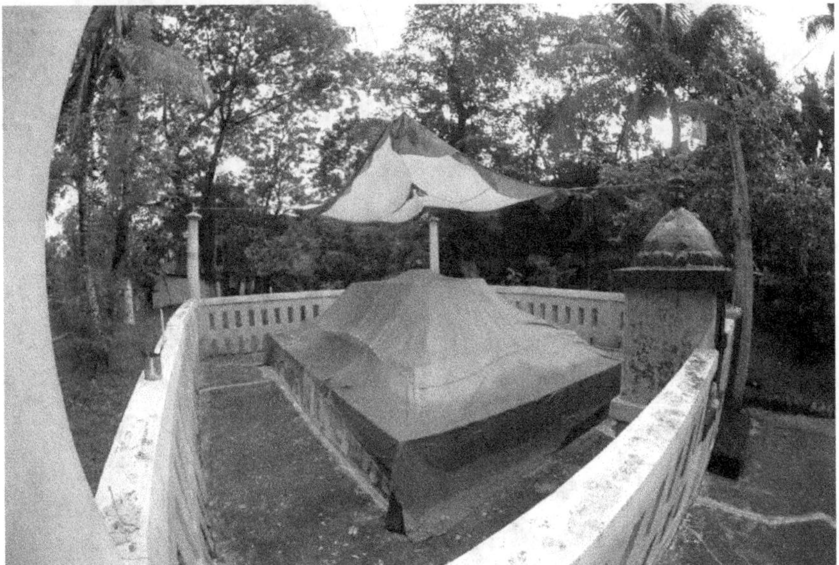

14.7.2010, 19:53:14

Shah Bondeh Ali

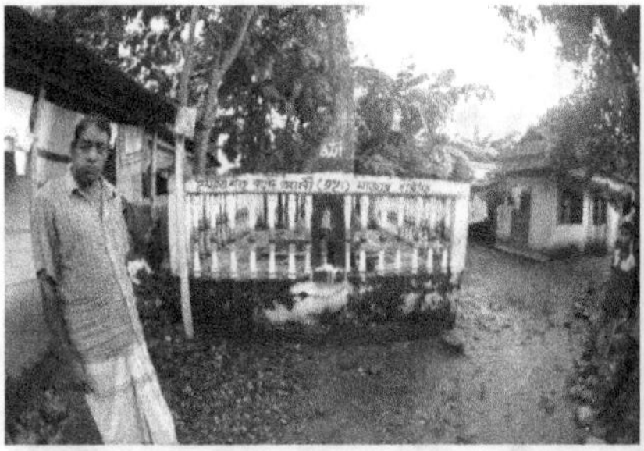

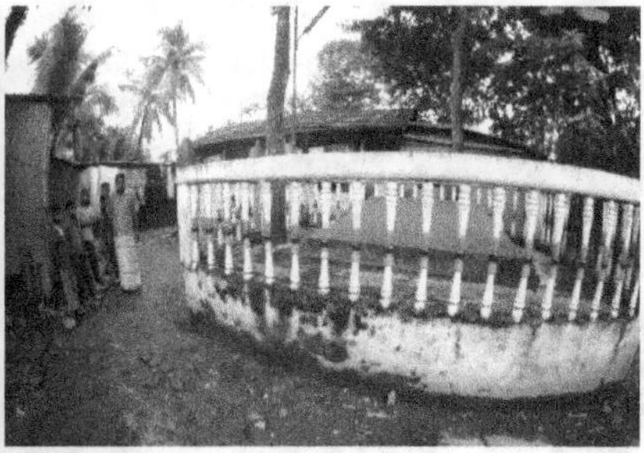

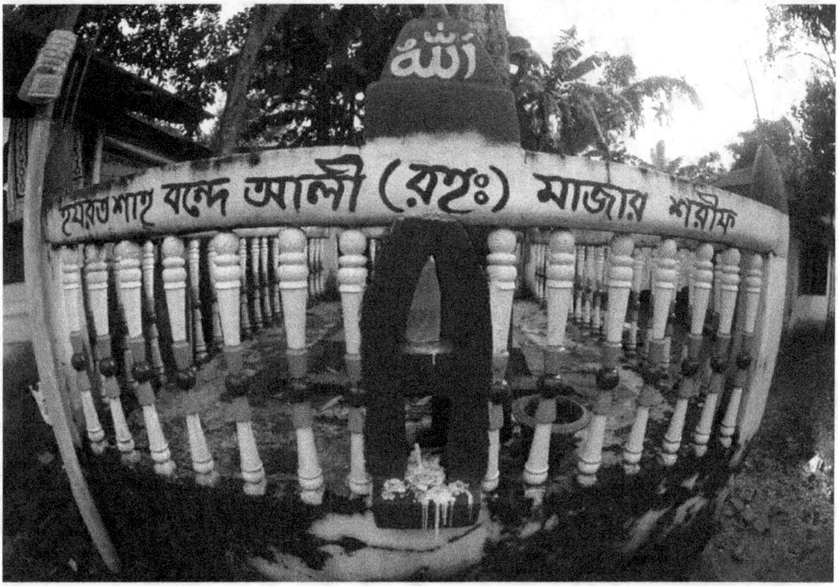
الله
হযরত শাহ্ বন্দে আলী (রহঃ) মাজার শরীফ

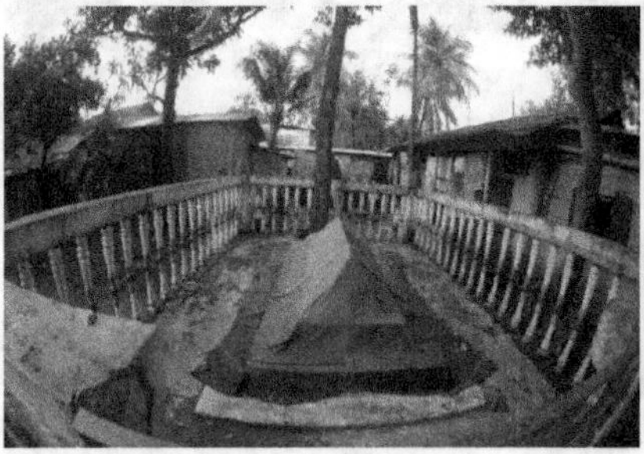

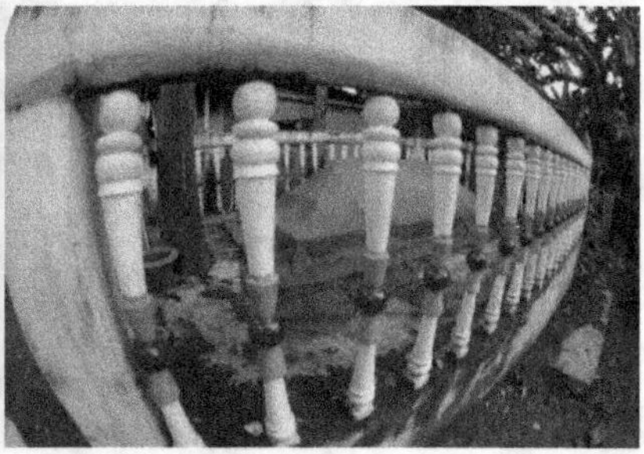

14.7.2010, 19:59:48

Not a member of the 360 group.

Obuj Shah

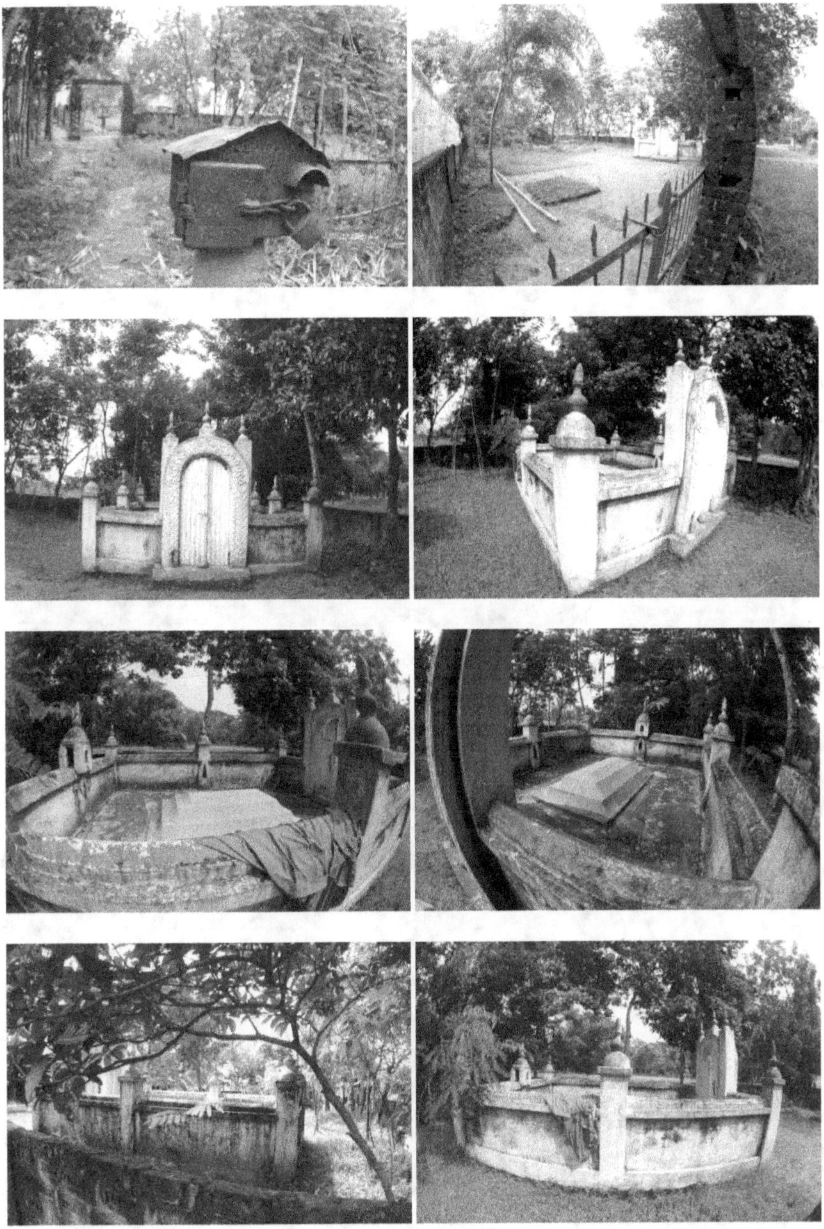

16.7.2010, 16:26:12

Mohammad Suhel**

a.k.a.

Kalashah

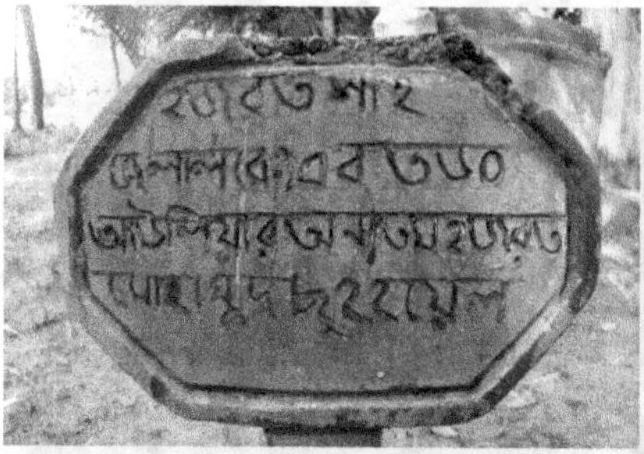
হযরত শাহ
জেলাল(রঃ)এর ৩৬০
আউলিয়ার অন্যতম হযরত
মোহাম্মদ ছুহয়েল

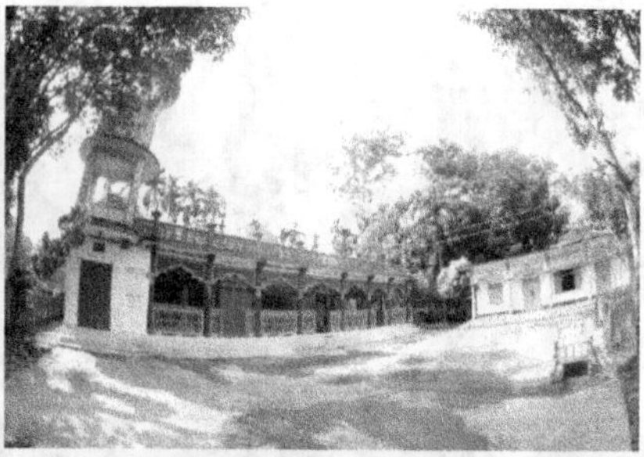

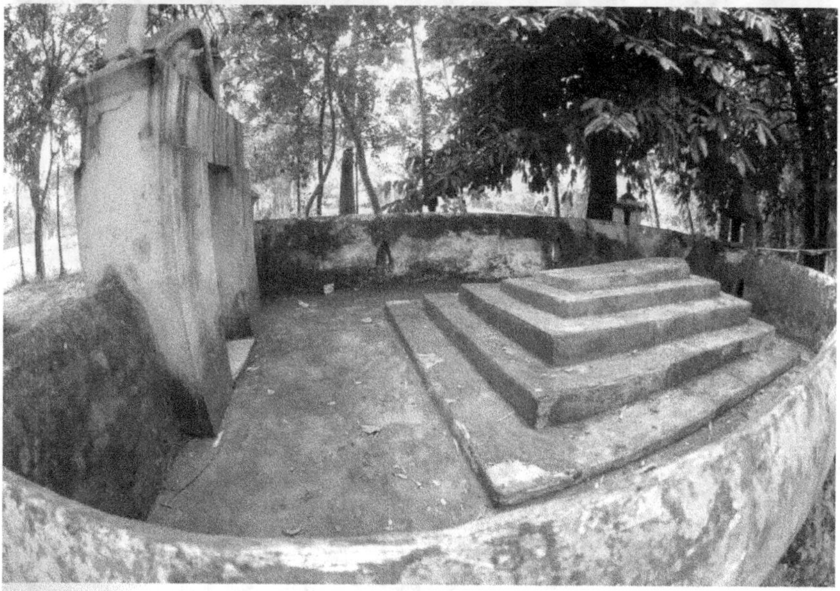

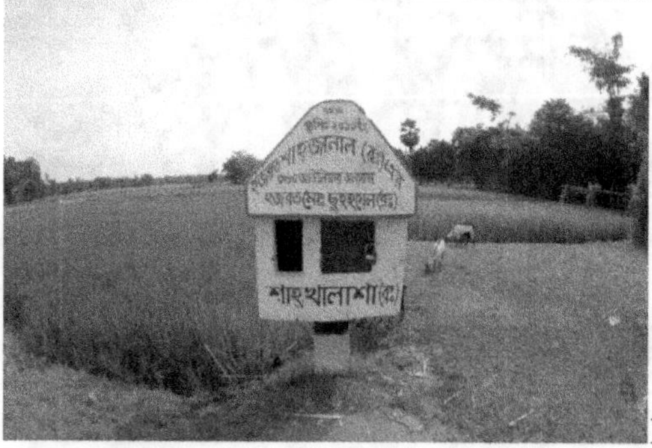
শাহখালাশা(রঃ)

16.7.2010, 16:48:48

Shah Soyod Basir

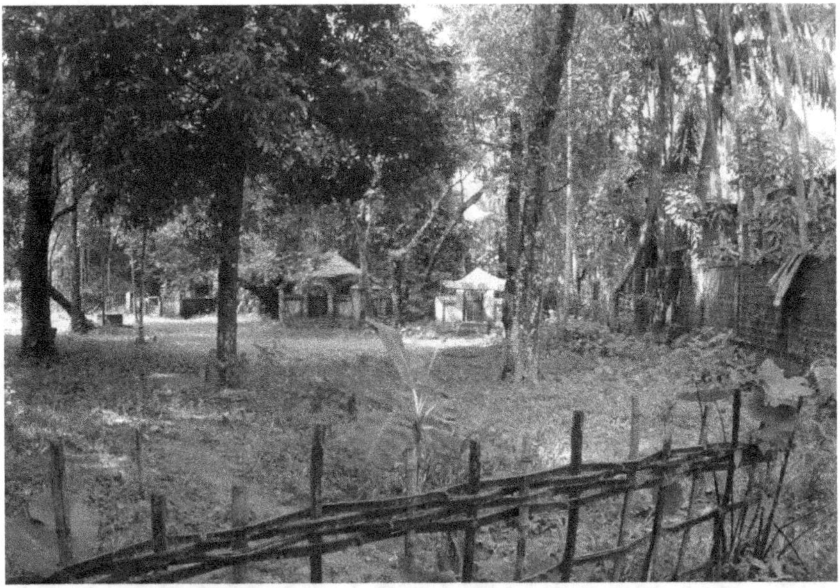

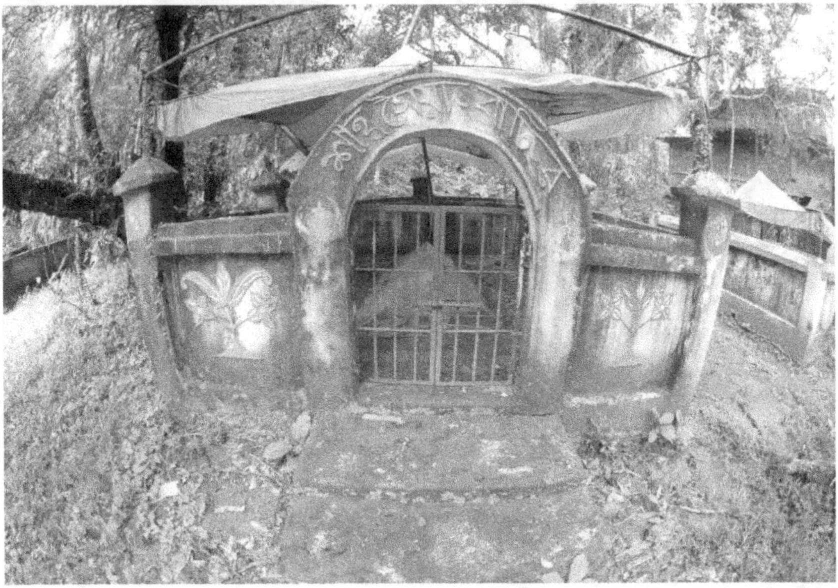

16.7.2010, 17:27:18

Mohamod Nosir Shah

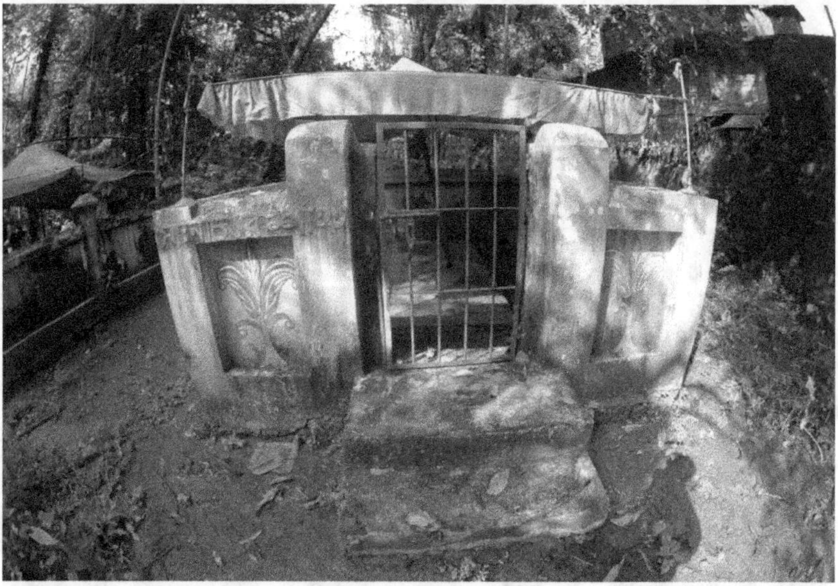

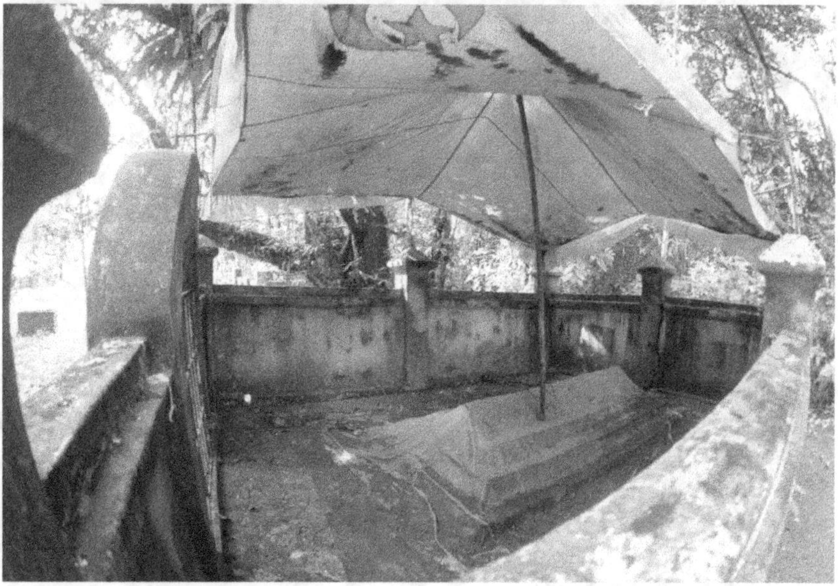

16.7.2010, 17:28:12

Dada Phir**

Tamabil Road, Sylhet Town

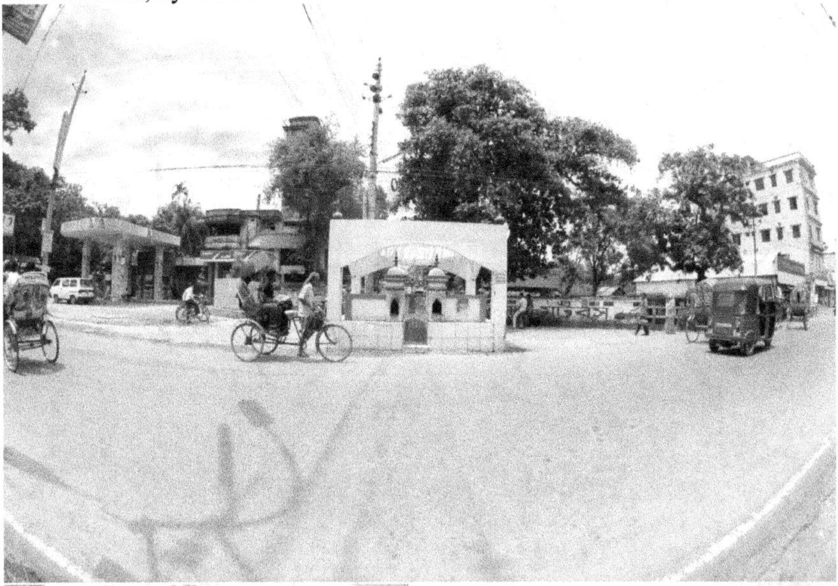

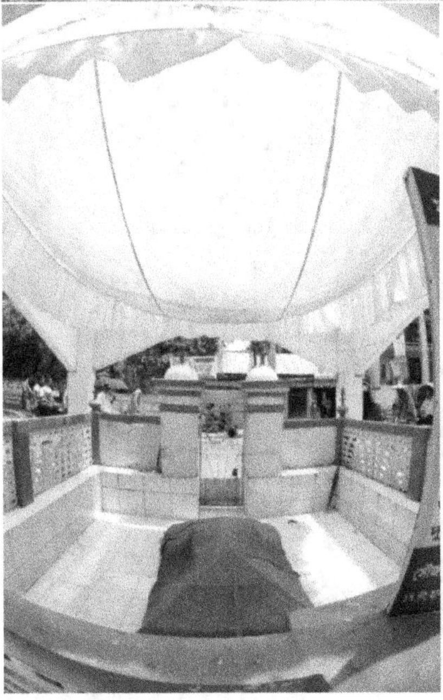

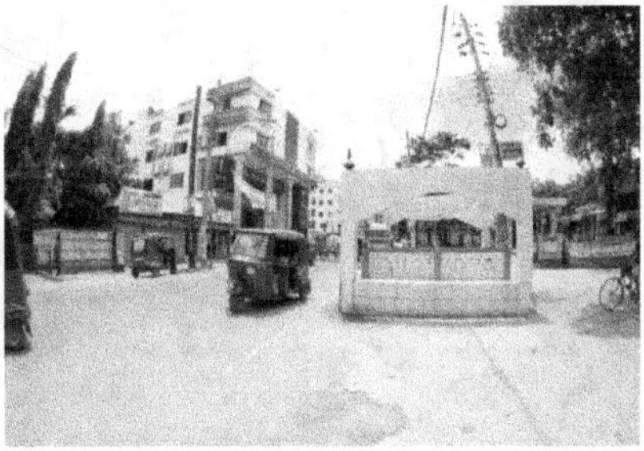

This was a weird situation, the mazar was in the middle of the road, main road, and as the road would have it, you are at your own peril, but you are OK if you have your vehicle stationed next to it.
This site is kept and maintained.

16.7.2010 17:52

Shah Kala**

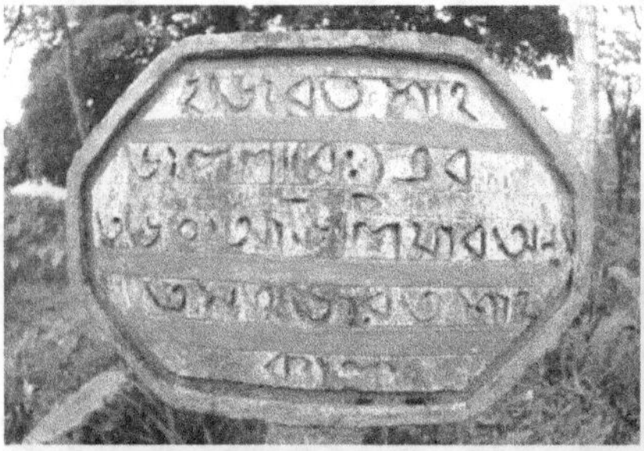
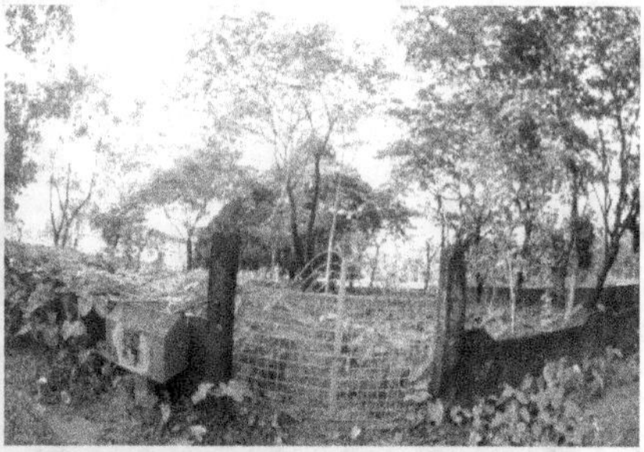
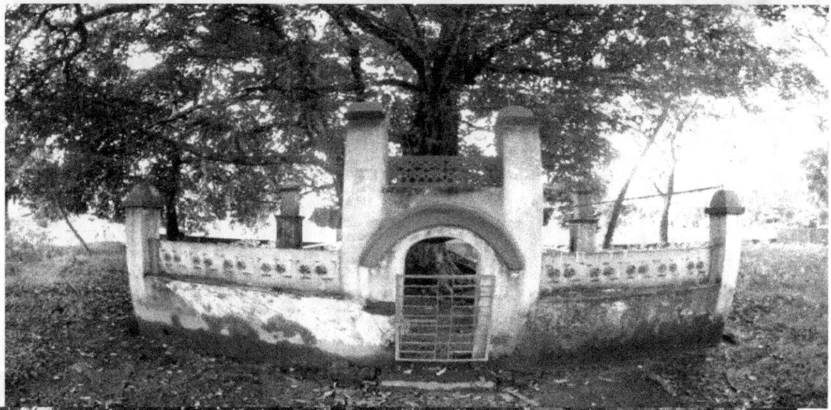
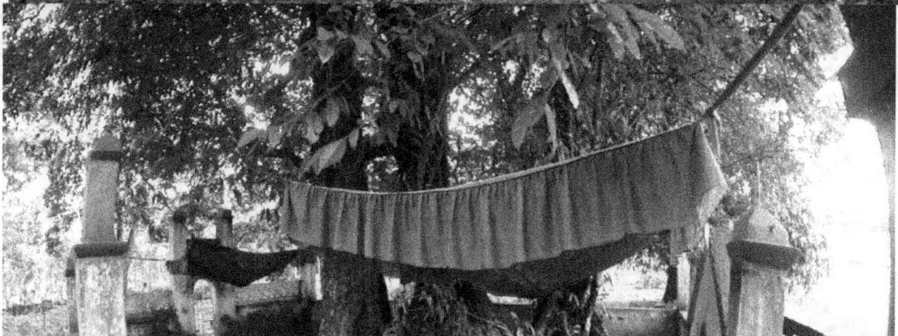

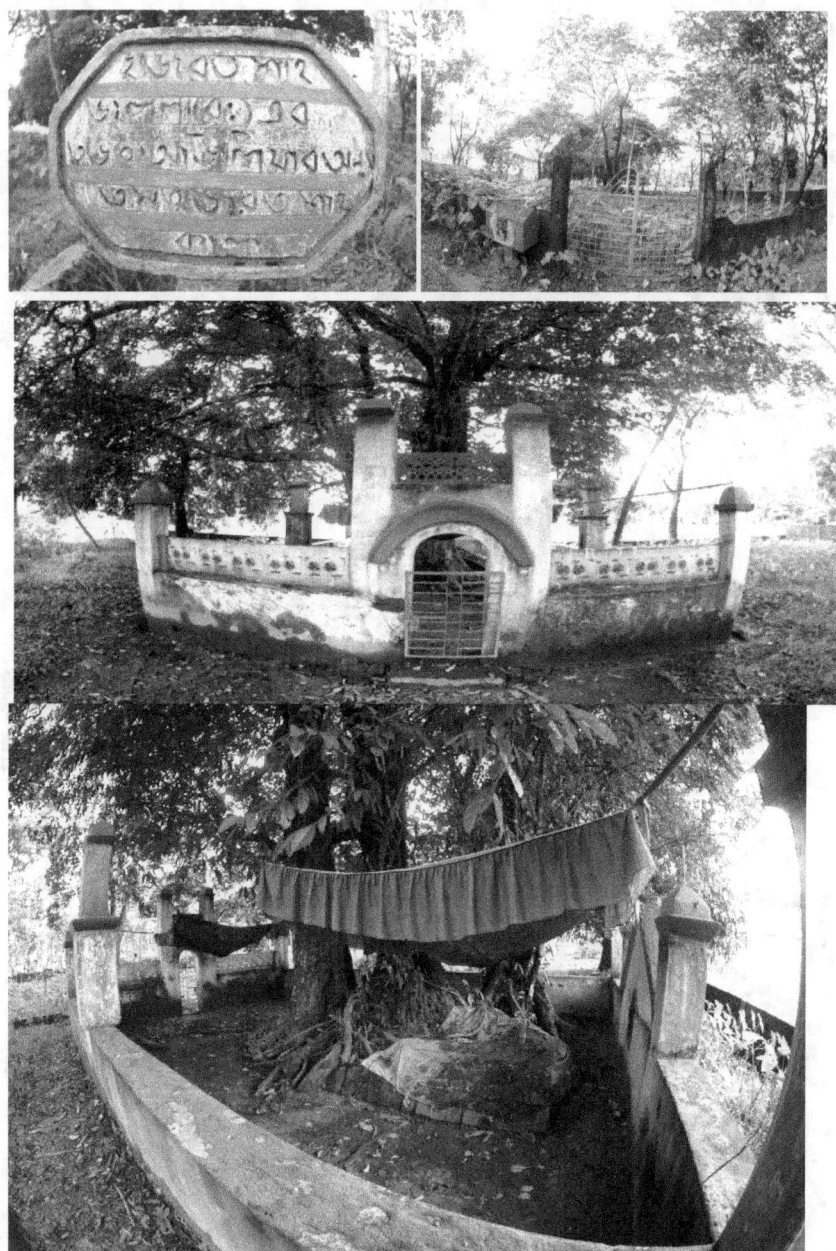

16.7.2010, 18:01:30

It looks wild, and there is low maintenance, but it has the peace.

Shah Sultan**

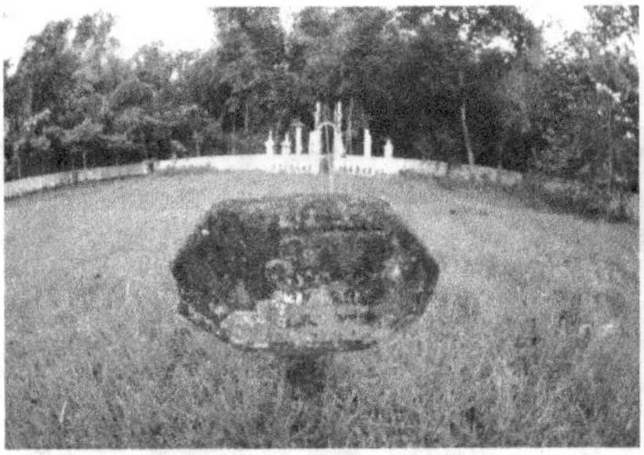
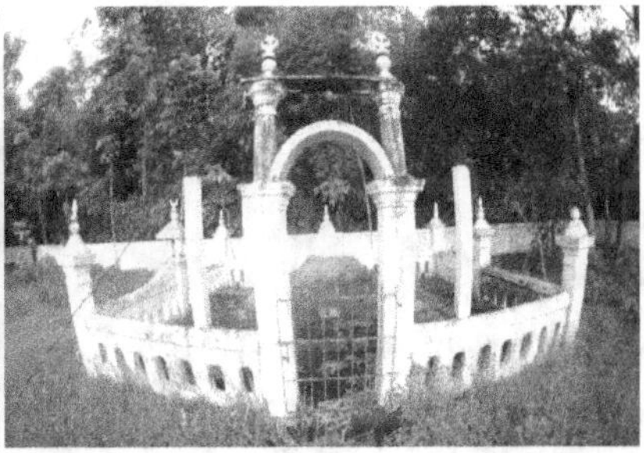
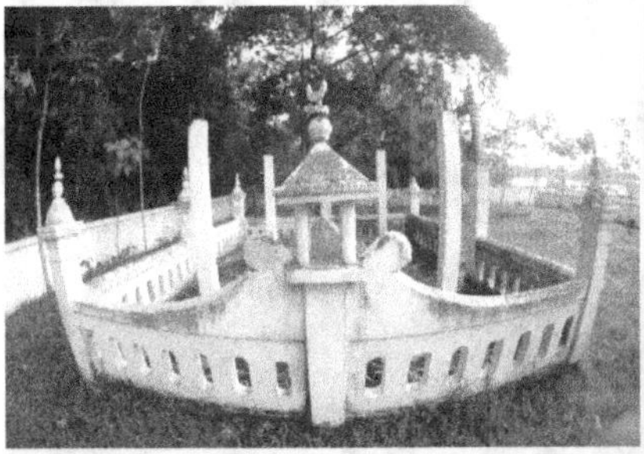
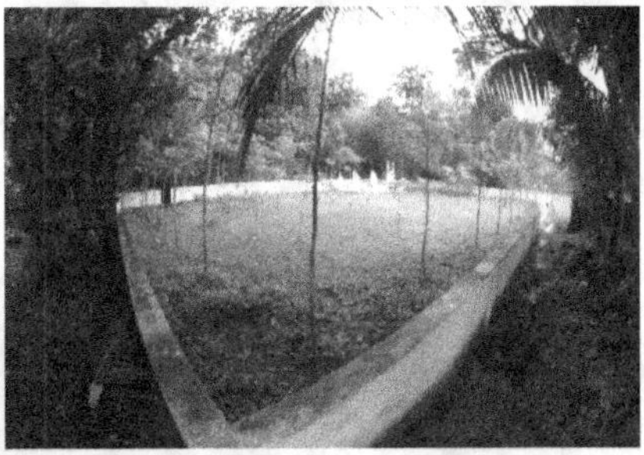
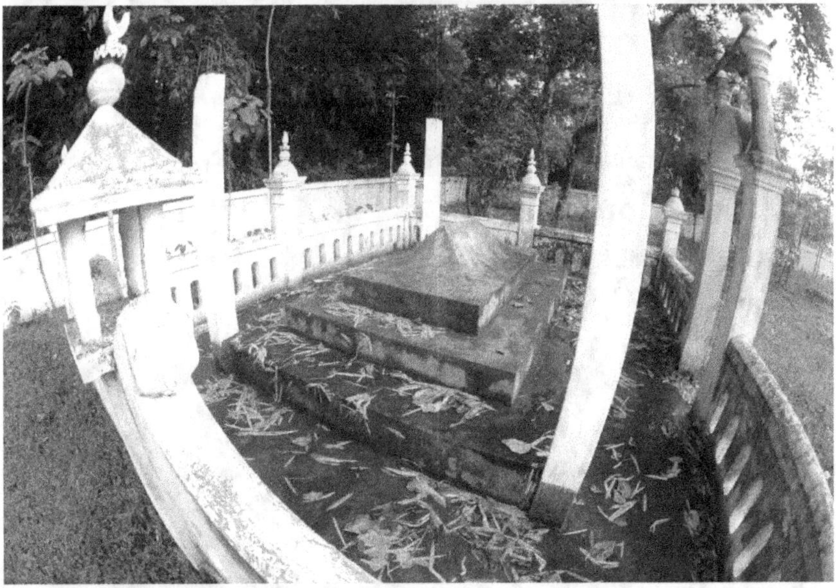

16.7.2010, 19:02:42

Alauddin Miskin

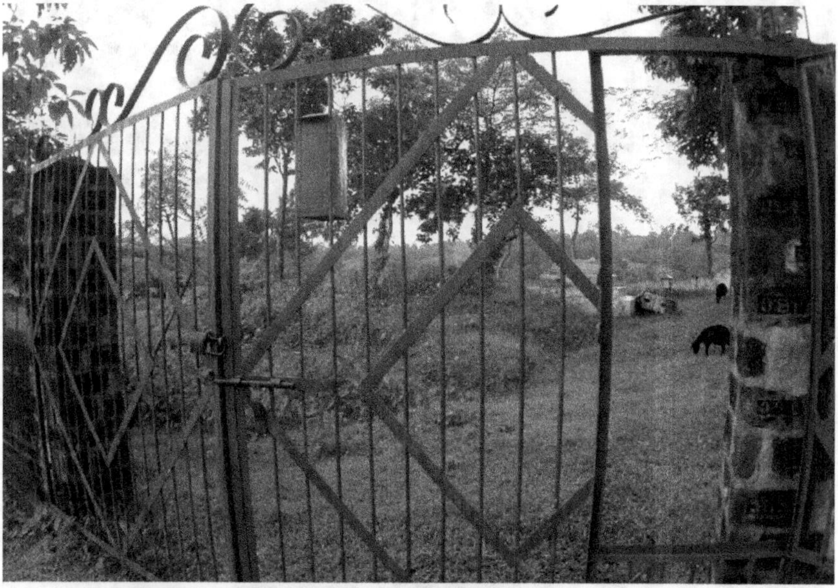

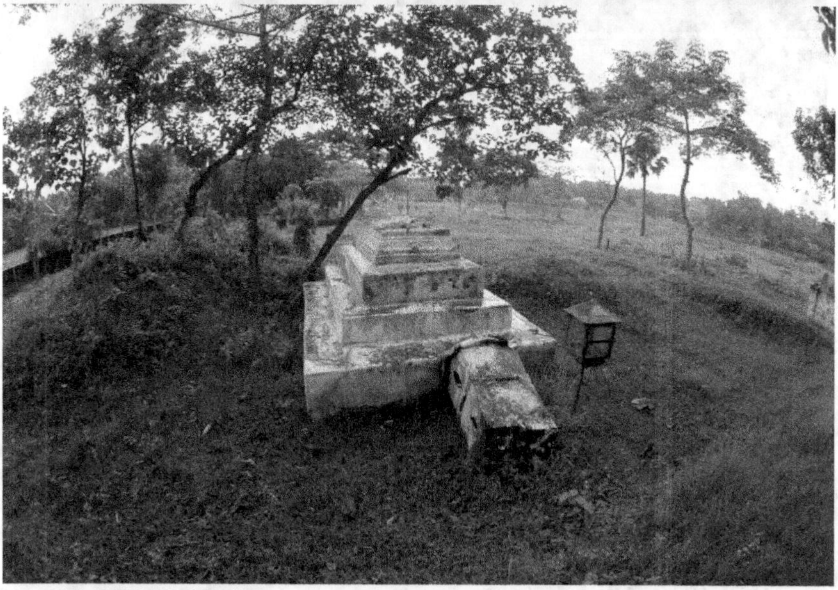

16.7.2010 18:46

This place was a bit of a wild goose chase - it was in the middle of a field - there is natural calmness. As you can see, the site is not maintained and area left for the animals to graze. It is not an inviting place.

Shah Jalal Dorga

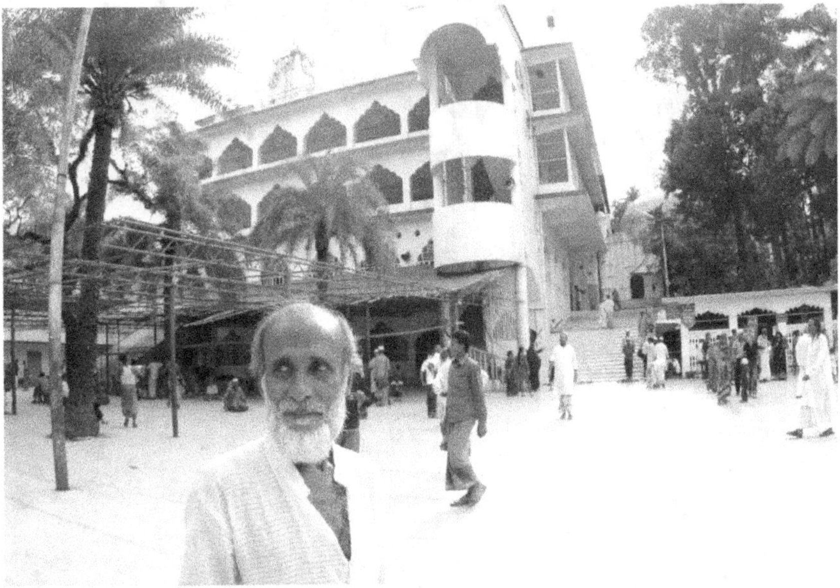

26.7.2020, 11:00:46

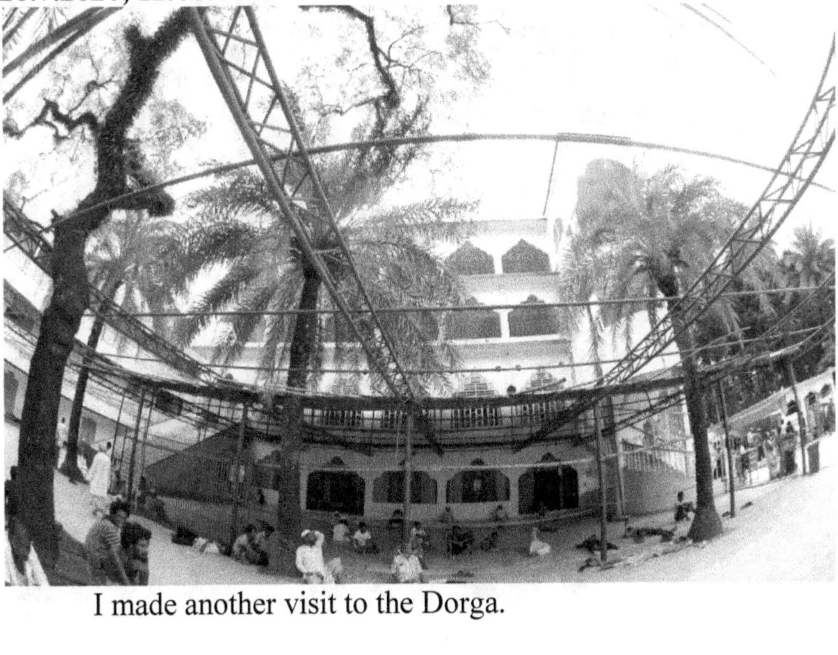

I made another visit to the Dorga.

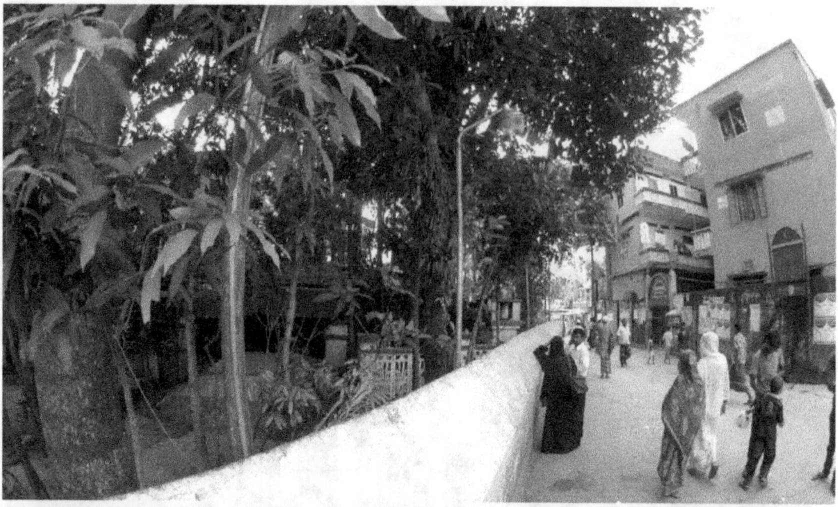

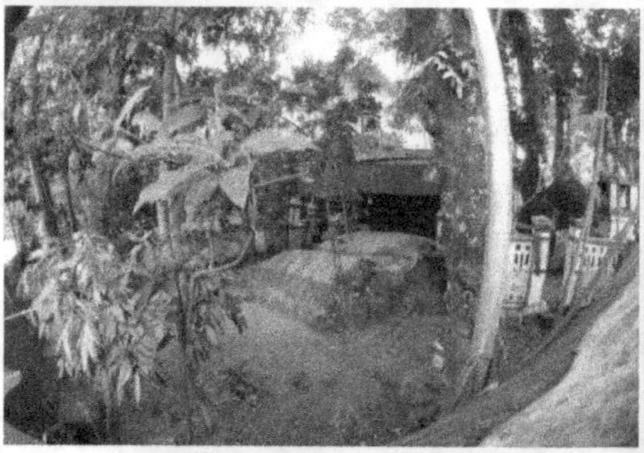

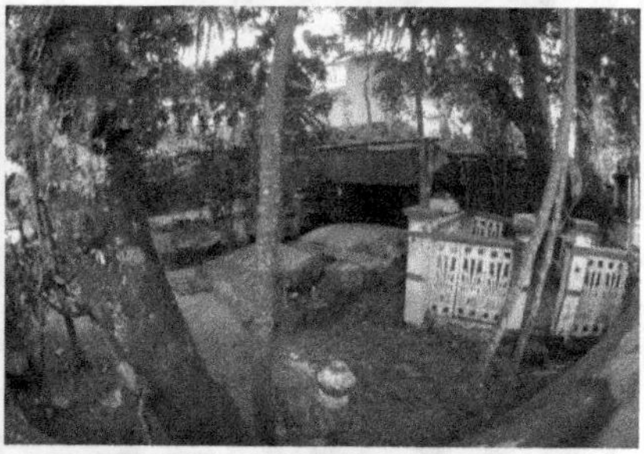

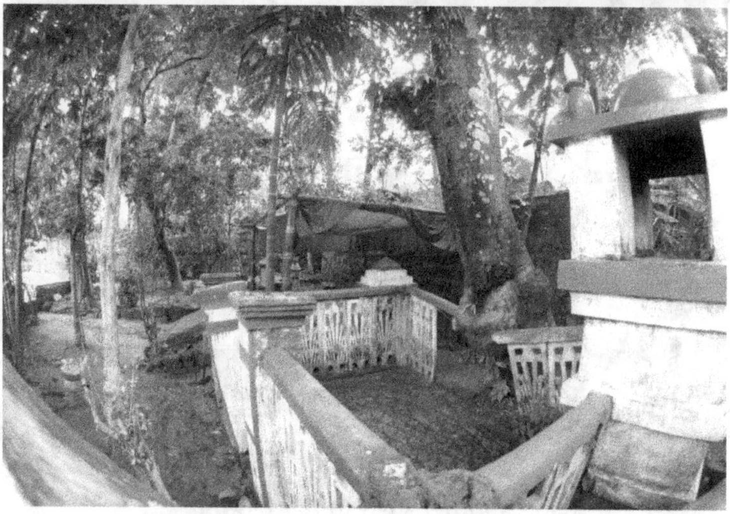

Haji Gazi Shah Miraji

Shahi Idga side, Sylhet Town

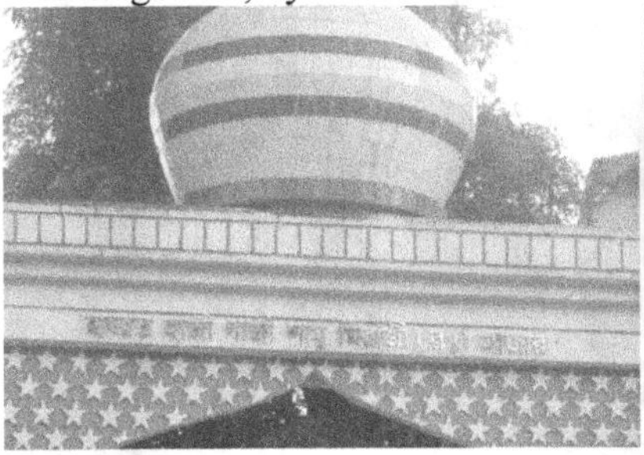

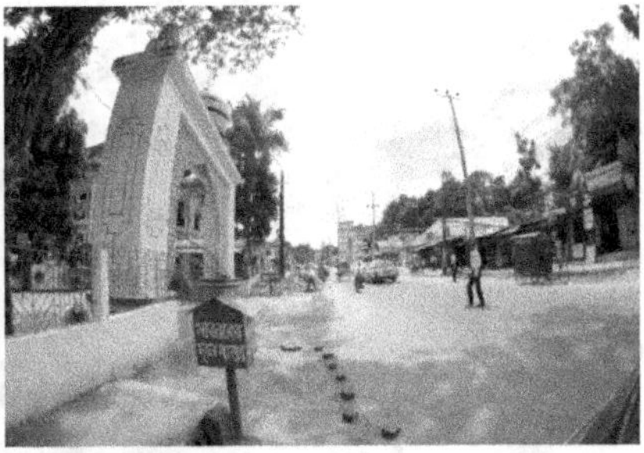

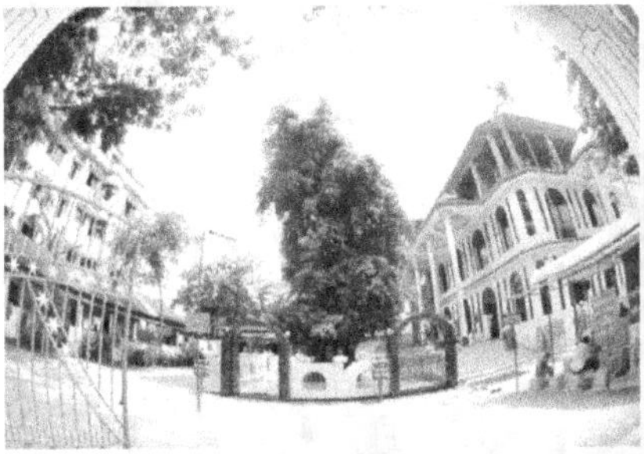

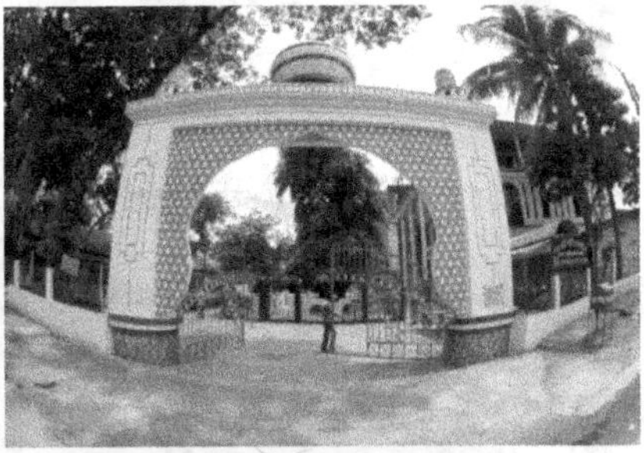

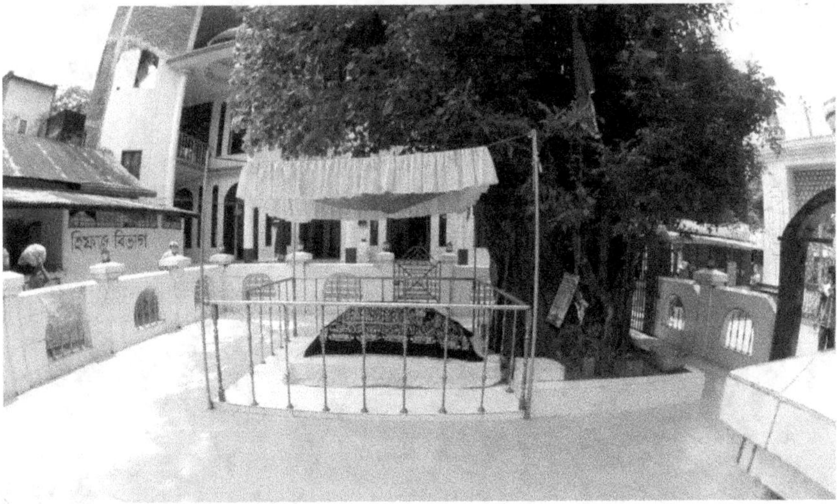

26.7.2010, 18:10:32

This is the city, Eid Gha - very well managed, very pristine. This site oozes peace, serenity and tranquillity.

Shah Poran [Forhan]**

Kadim Nagar, Sylhet town (**26.7.2010 7pm**)

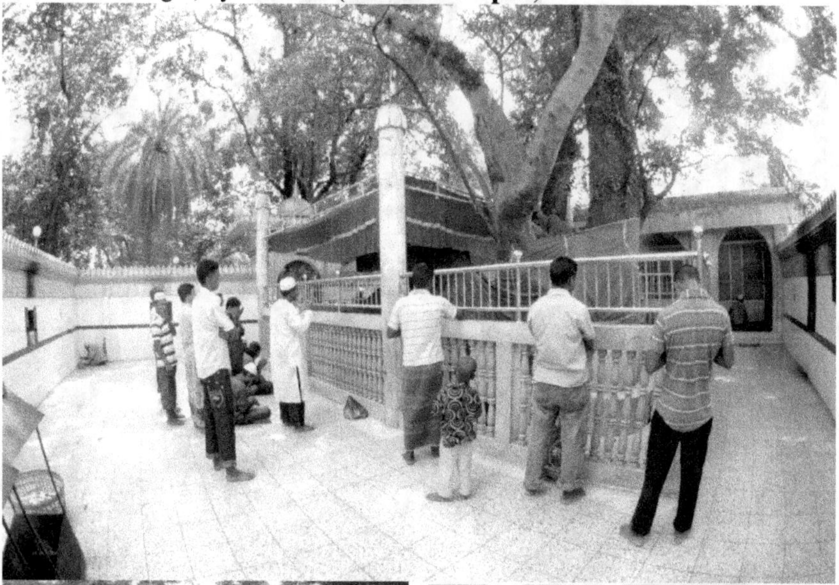

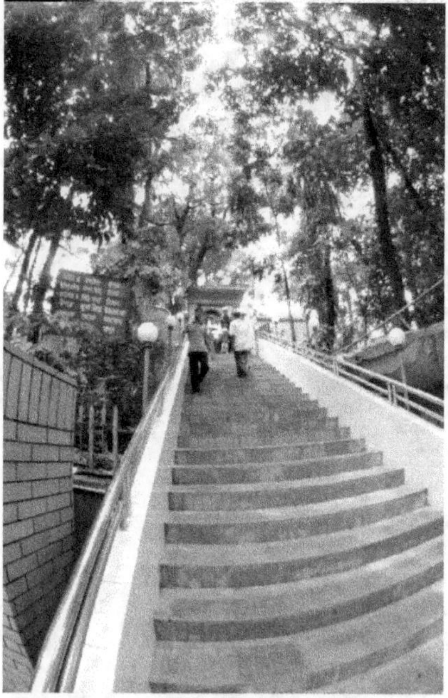

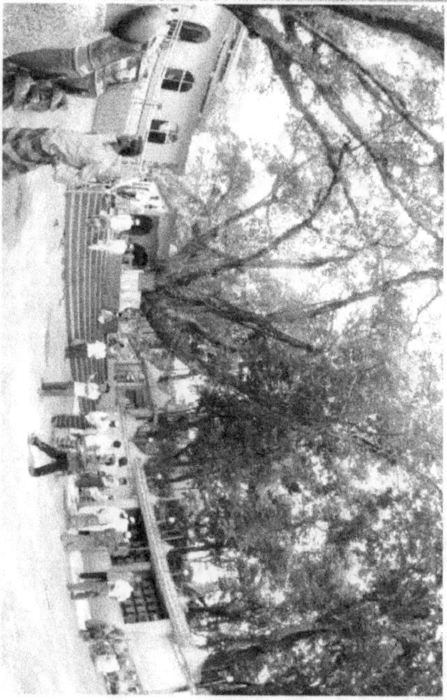

The famous steps going up to the Mazar.

Kura Kuri

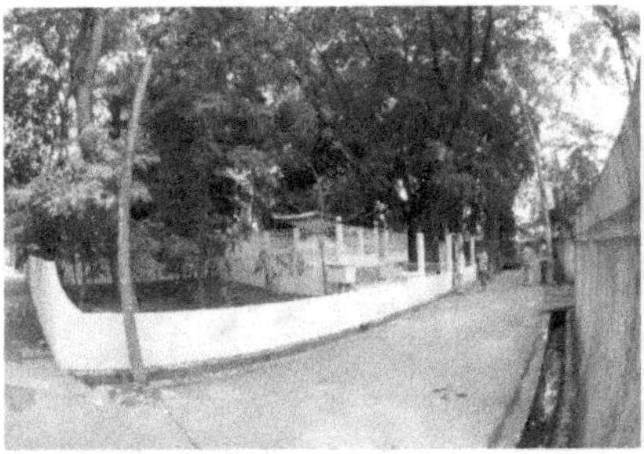
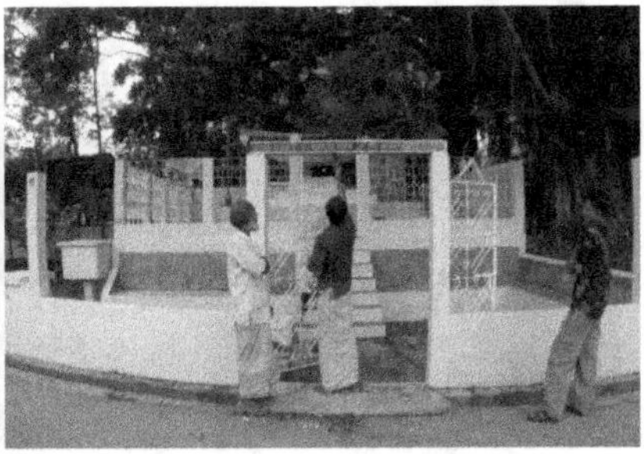

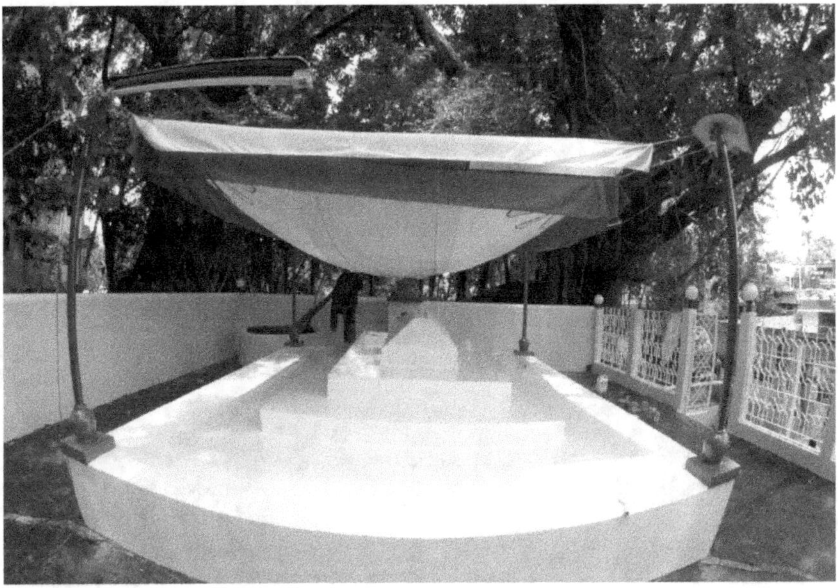

26.7.2010, 19:31:58

Lal Soyod

Electric Road, Sylhet

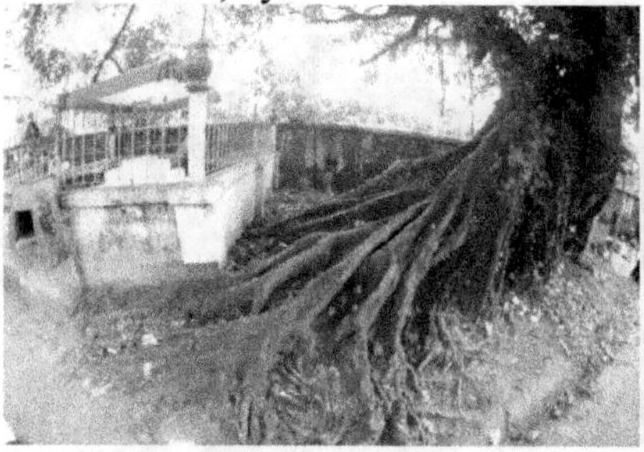

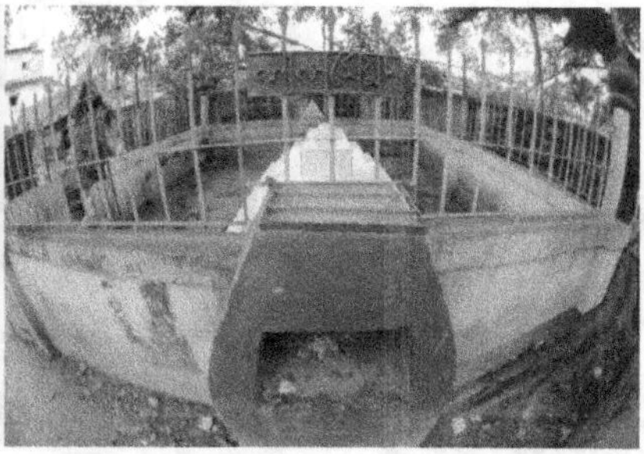

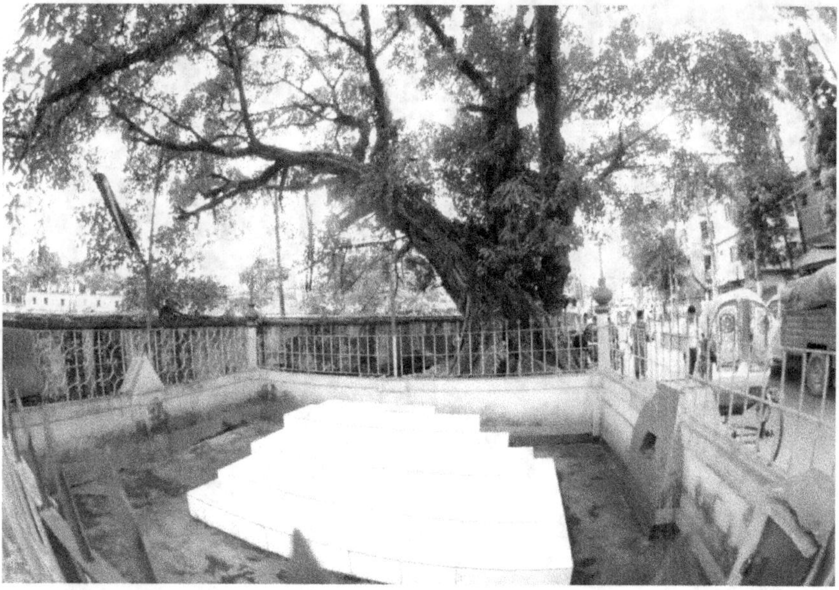

26.7.2010, 9:33:46

Etim**

a.k.a.,

Hatim Ali

Sylhet Town

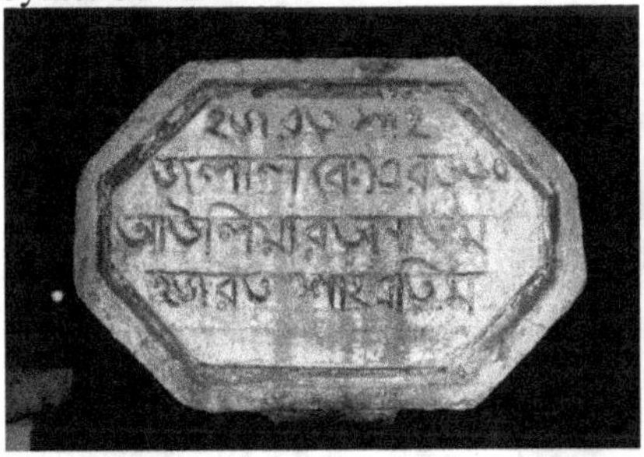

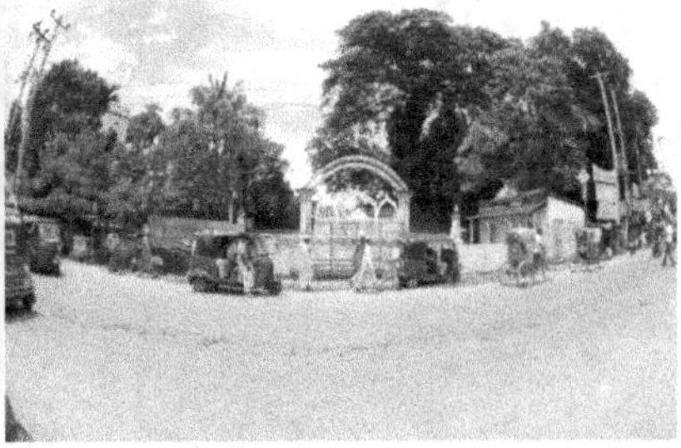

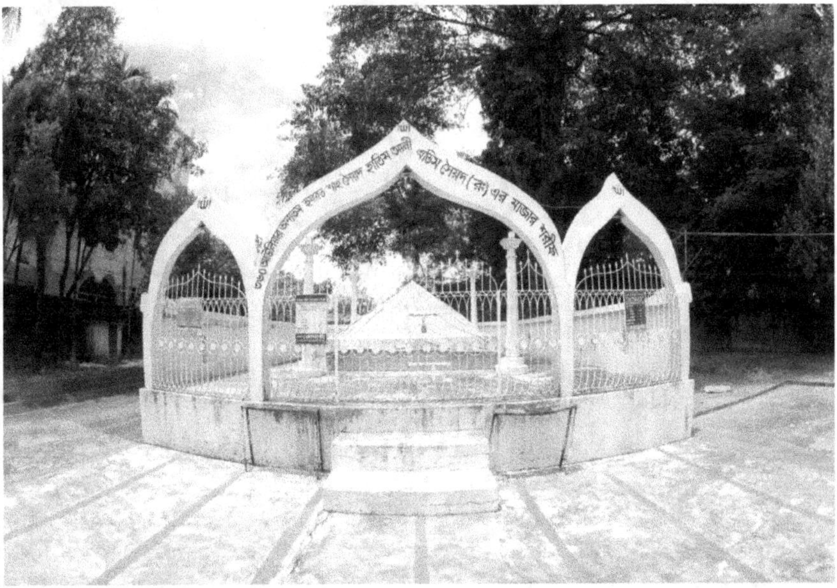

26.7.2010 19:41

This is also adjacent to the road and you can hear the hustle and bustle of the street noise. While there area was peaceful and grounding the surrounding did not give the visual peace to me.

I was please to find, visit and a confirmed sites of the 360 missionaries, I was happy that I was increasing my tally.

Mokdum Habib**

Rainagor

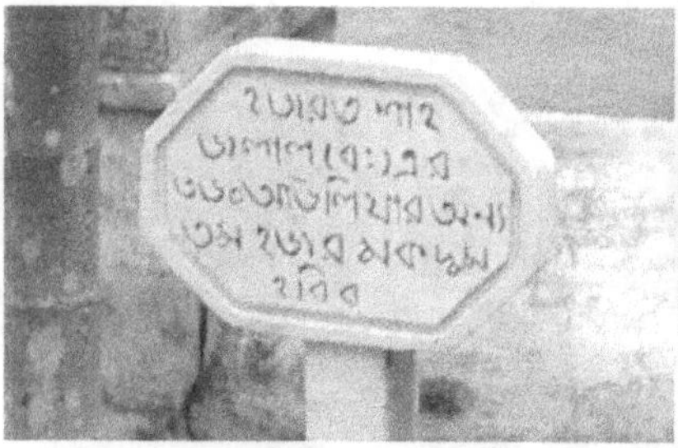
হযরত শাহ
জালাল (রঃ) এর
ওলিআউলিয়ার অন্য
তম হযরত মকদুম
হবিব

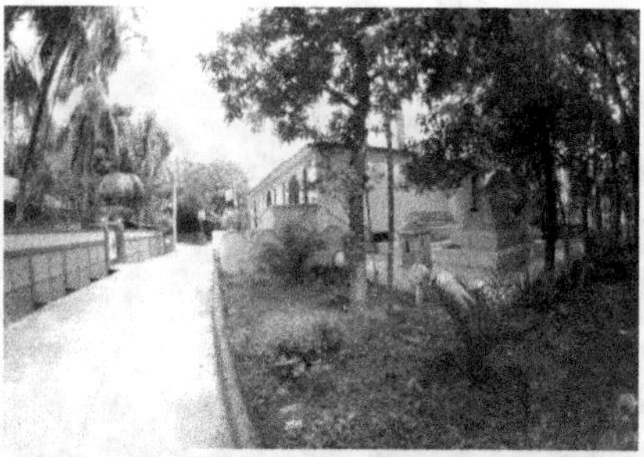

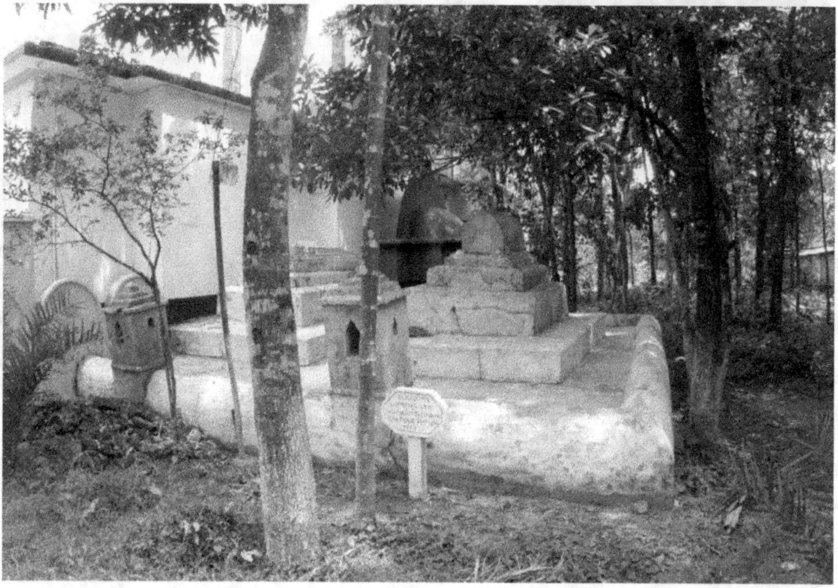

26.7.2010, 20:26:44

Mokdum Rohim Uddin**

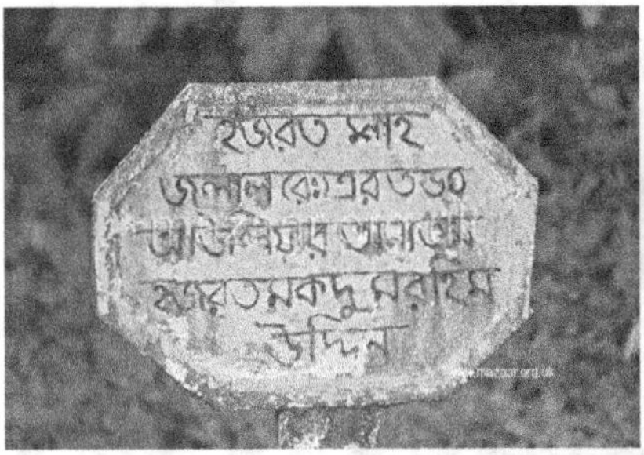
হজরত শাহ
জালাল রেঃ এর ৩৬০
আউলিয়ার অন্যতম
হজরত মকদুম রহিম
উদ্দিন

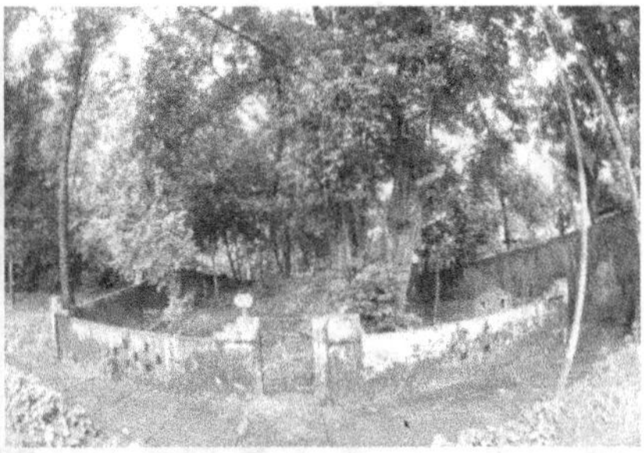

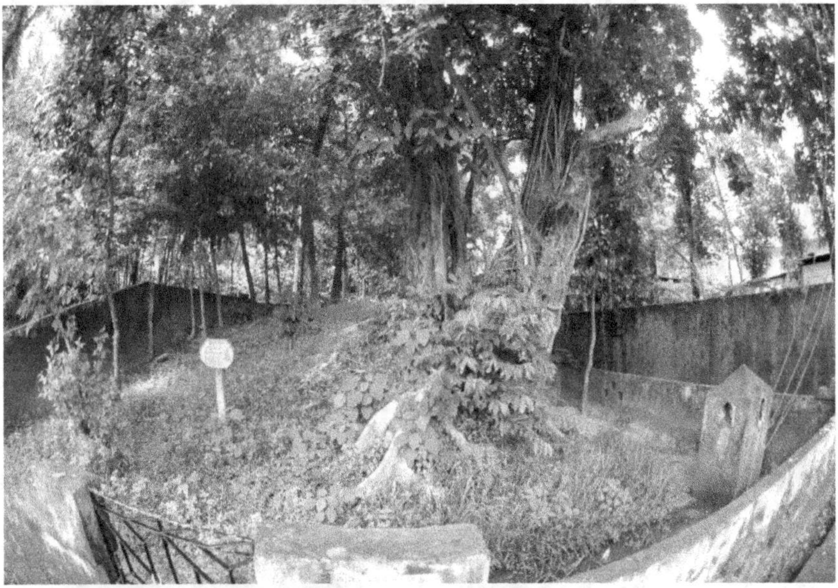

26.7.2010, 20:29:22

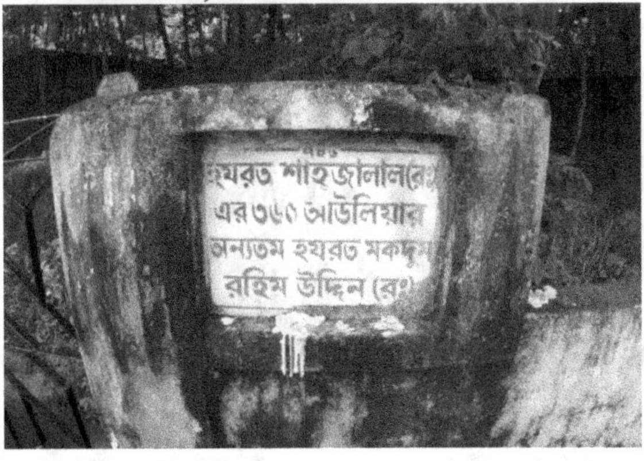
হযরত শাহজালাল রেঃ
এর ৩৬০ আউলিয়ার
অন্যতম হযরত মকদুম
রহিম উদ্দিন (রেঃ

Guleh Hushen Yemeni*

Hazrat Taleb Hushen Yemeni*

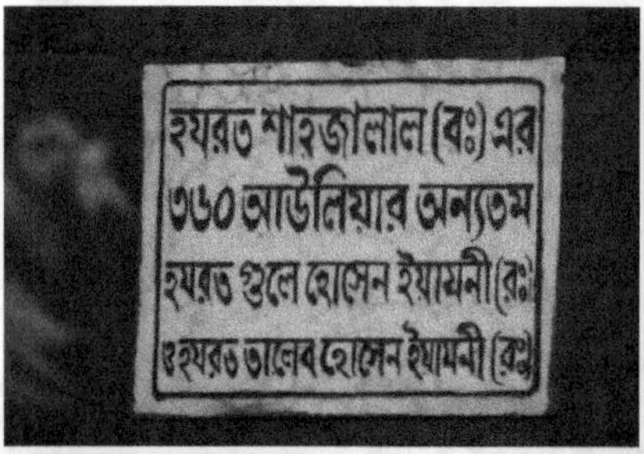
হযরত শাহজালাল (রঃ) এর
৩৬০ আউলিয়ার অন্যতম
হযরত গুলে হোসেন ইয়ামনী (রঃ)
ও হযরত তালেব হোসেন ইয়ামনী (রঃ)

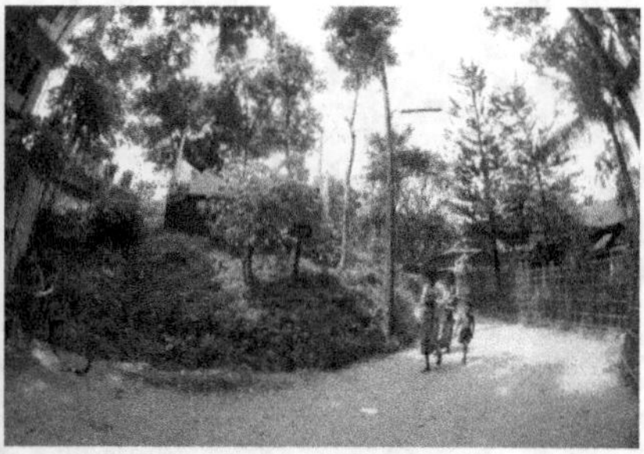

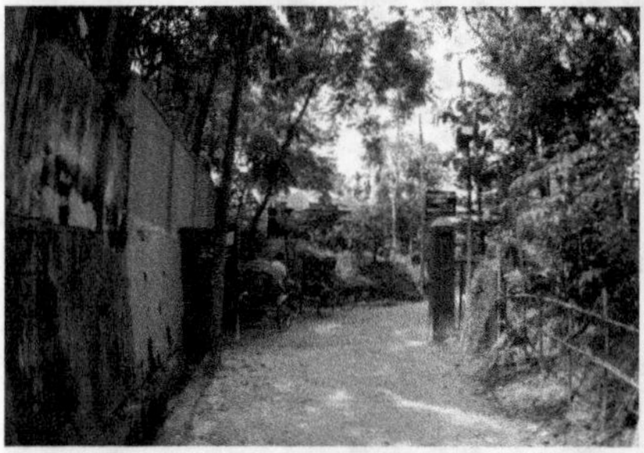

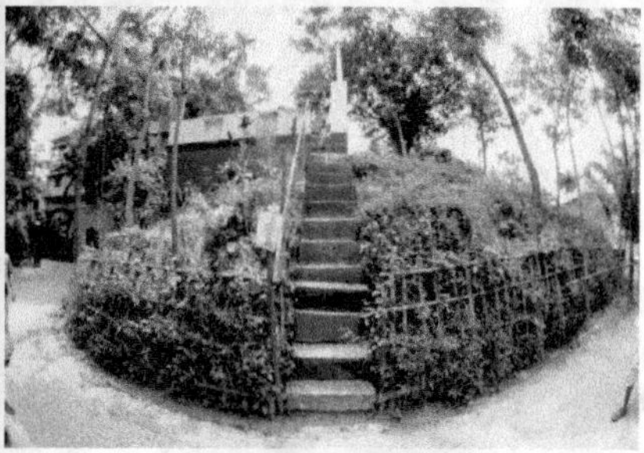

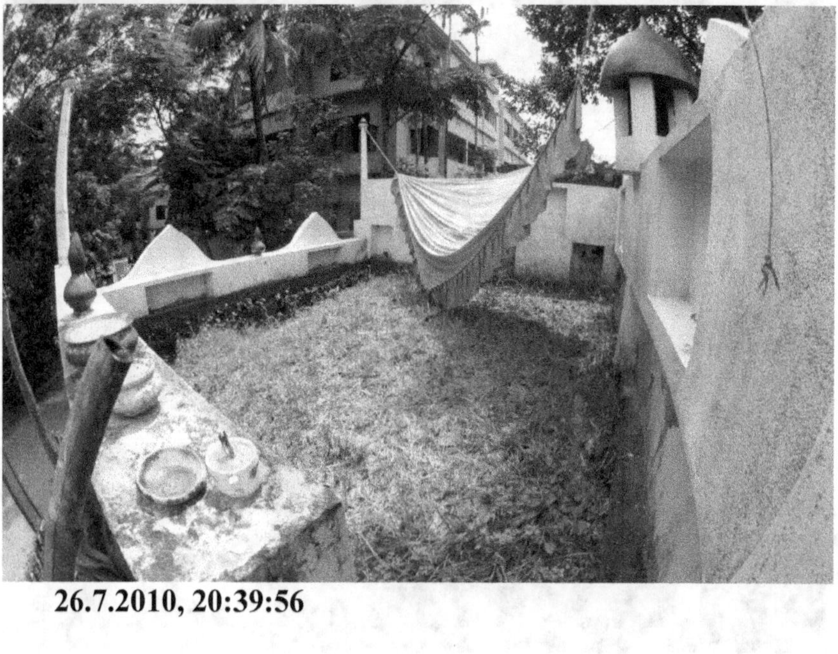

26.7.2010, 20:39:56

Shah Kolomdor

Adjacent grave to Shah Shikondor, Shikondor Pur, Mukam Bari, Poshim Gaow, Osmani Nagor, Sylhet

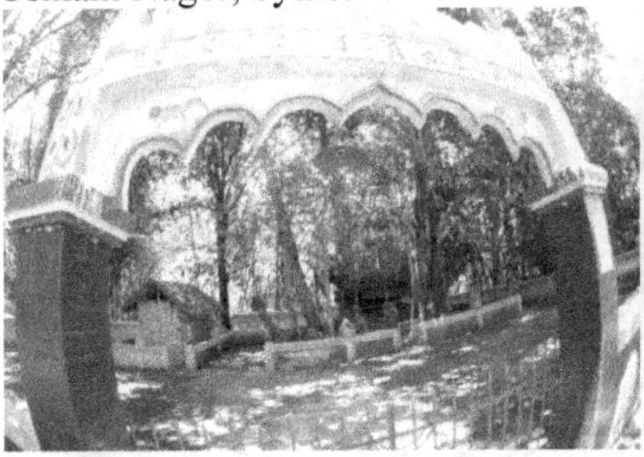
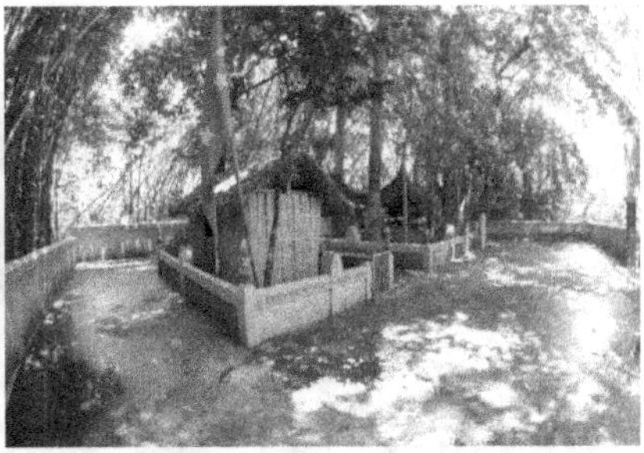
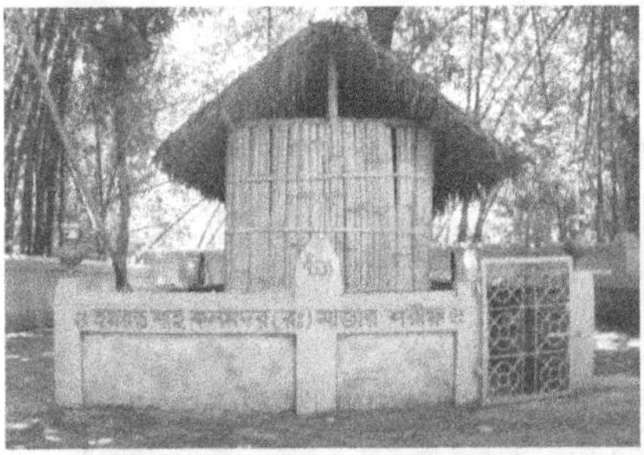
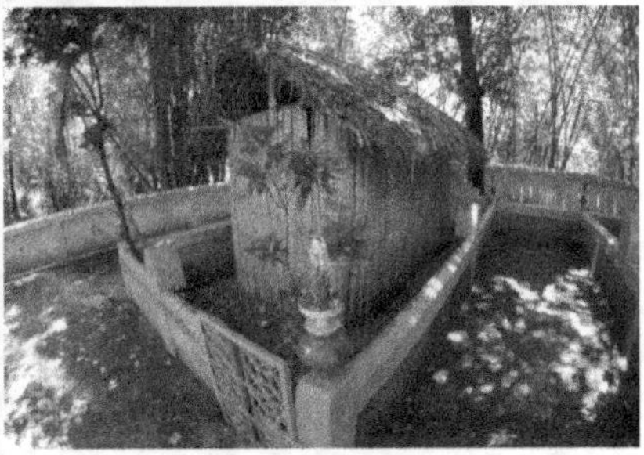
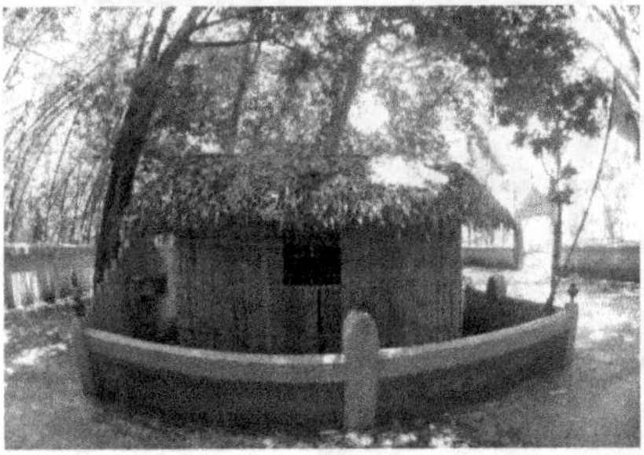
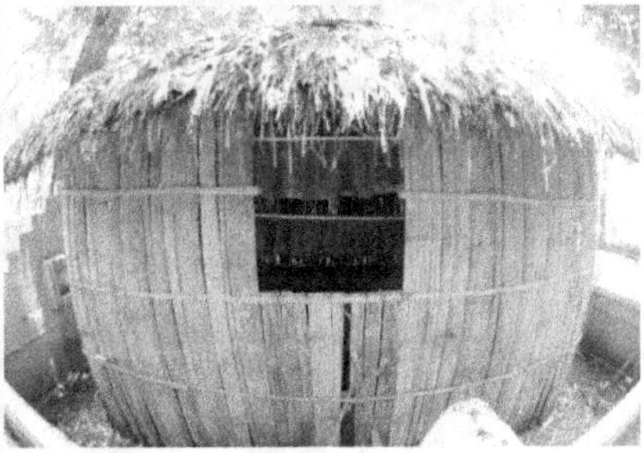
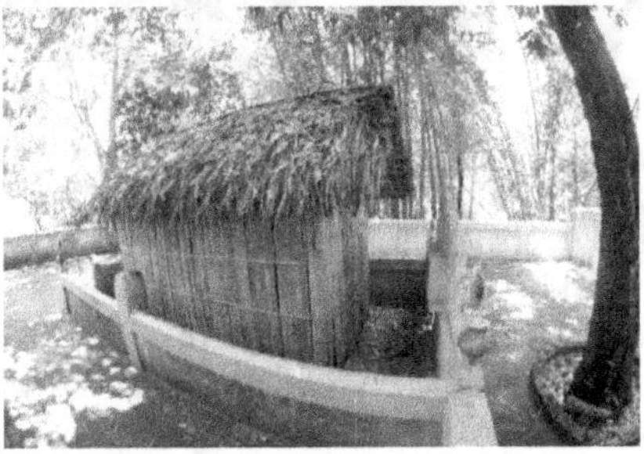

27.7.2010, 19:06:08

Shah Shikondor**

- Poschim Bari, Shikondor Pur, Osmani Nagor, Sylhet

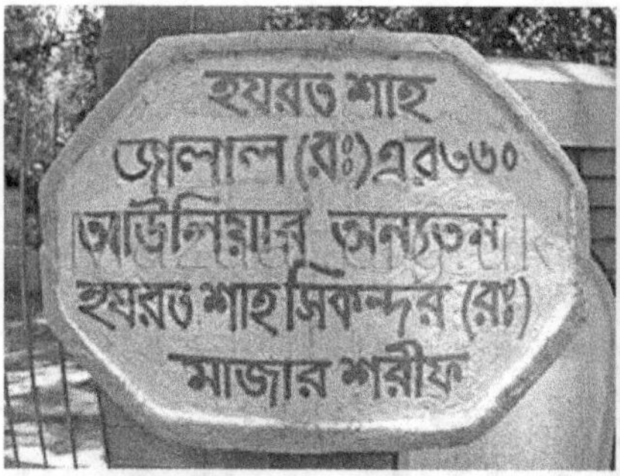
হযরত শাহ
জালাল (রঃ) এর ৩৬০
আউলিয়ার অন্যতম
হযরত শাহ সিকন্দর (রঃ)
মাজার শরীফ

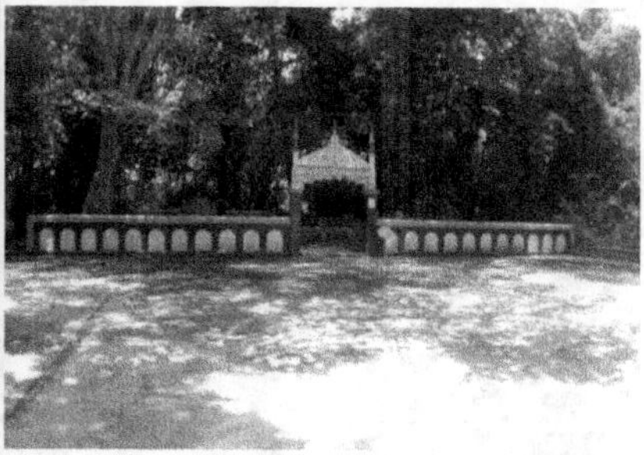

27.7.2010, 18:57

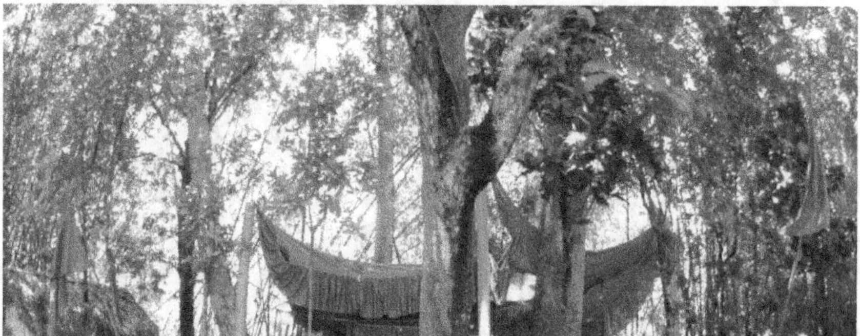

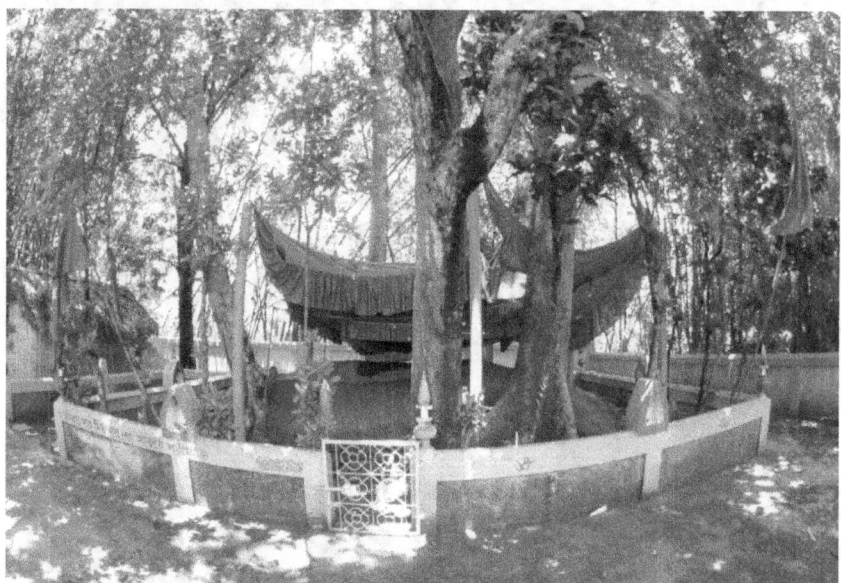

This is my mum's paternal ancestral linage. While this is my mum's side, I didn't take the same liberty. I this place provided the same tranquillity and serenity; I sat out in the yard outside the wall. These moments of tranquillity and serenity are like a dream. Little did I know what was happening to me? I will unfold that as we go along in the book. One of the other reasons was that I a child I recall my aunt, my mother's younger sister would tell us how serious the place was, so not to set a wrong foot.

Shah Sulaiman Koroni

Koronshi, Osmani Nagor, off Goala Bazaar, Sylhet.

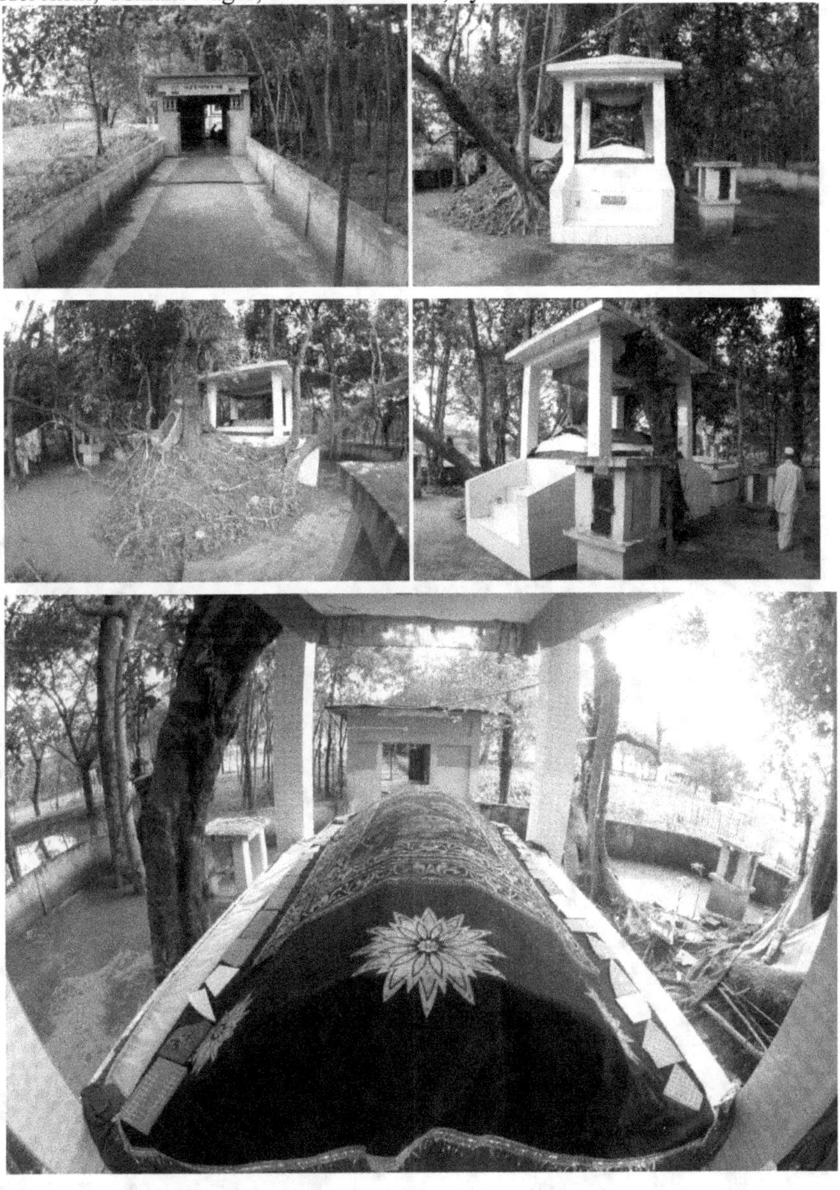

31.7.2010, 09:49:18

Mal Shaheb Kutub Uddin

Situated behind Shah Sulaiman Koroni

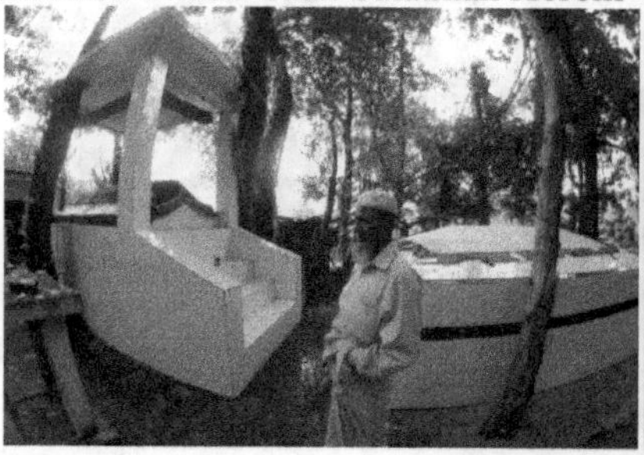

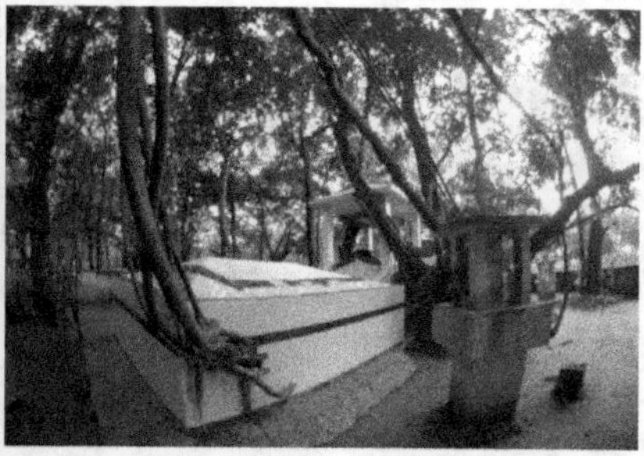

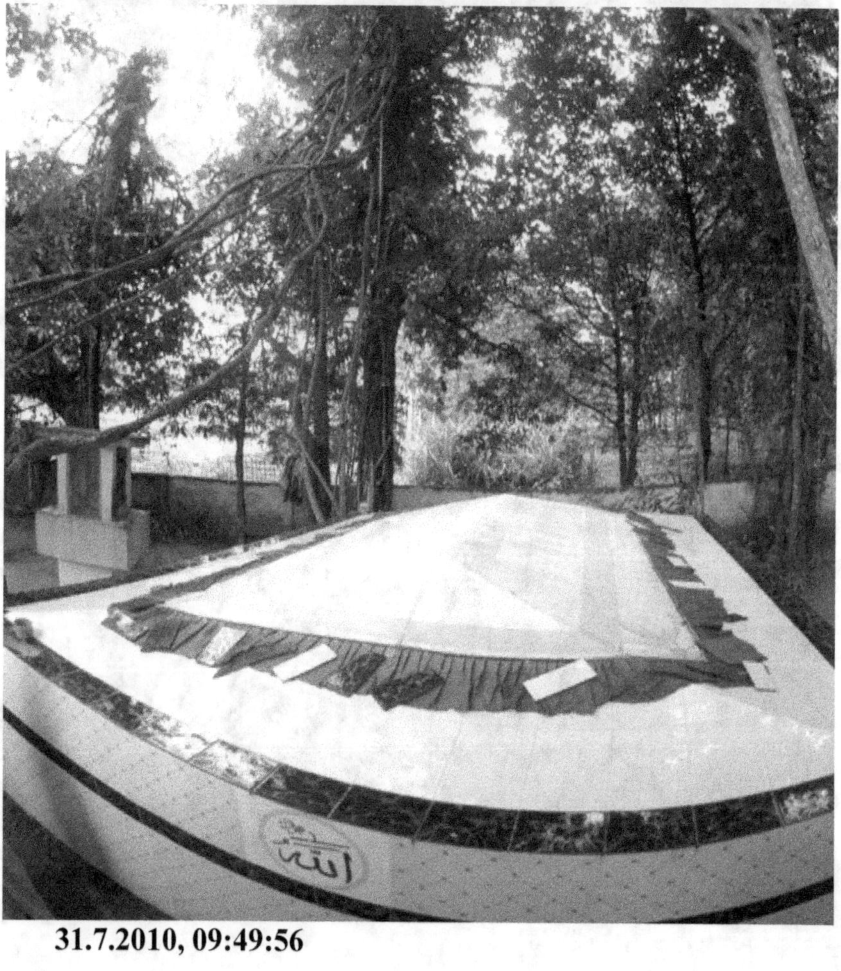

31.7.2010, 09:49:56

Shah Koronshi

Koronshi Road, Off Goala Bazar, Osmani Nagor, Sylhet

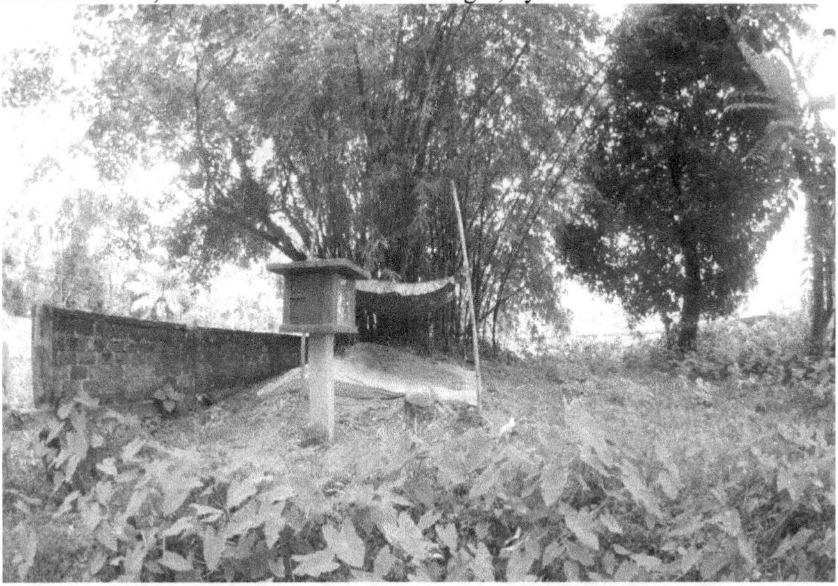

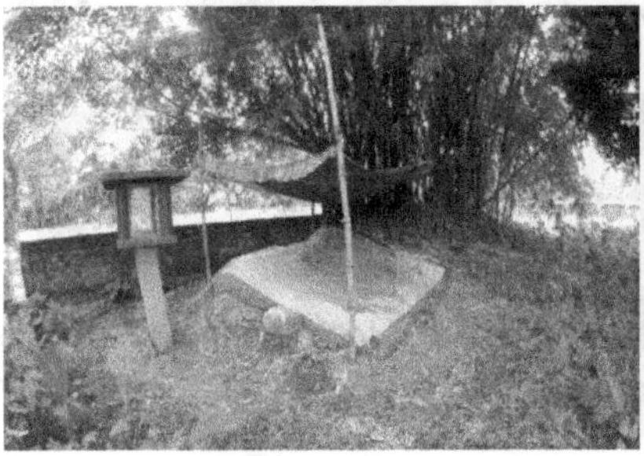

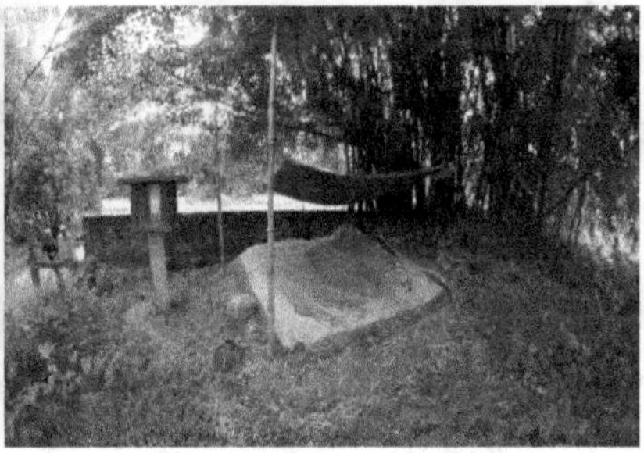

31.7.2010, 10:01:38

According to locals, this is the actual grave of Shah Koronshi, whose name the area locality is known as/ named.

Shah Konai

Shokondor Pur, Pub Gaow, Osmani Nagor, Sylhet

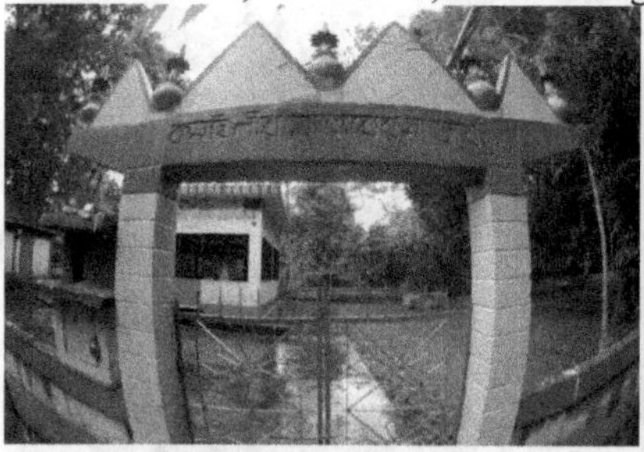

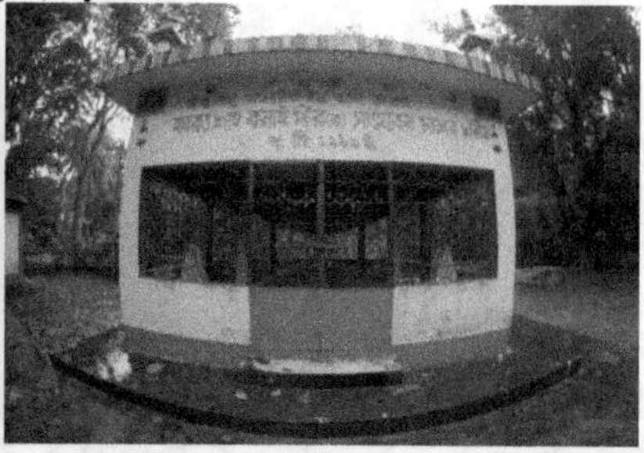

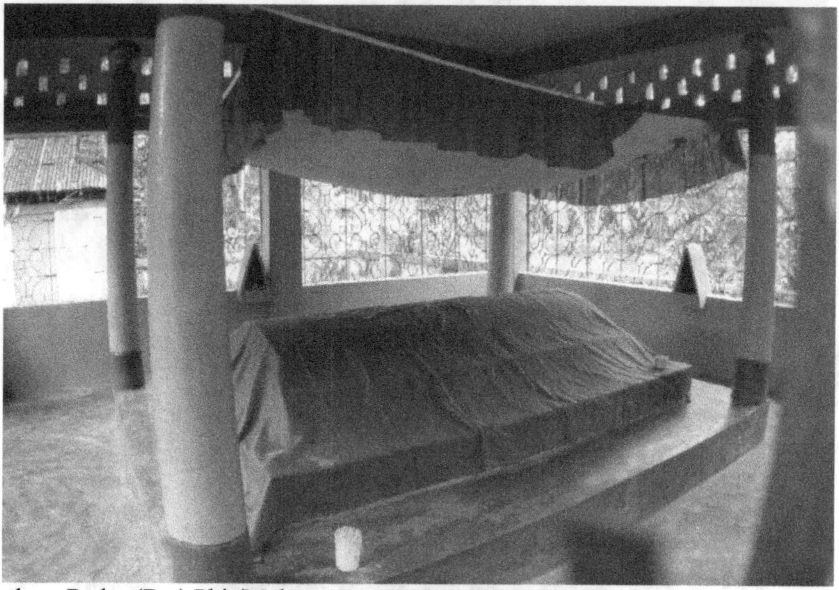

a.k.a., Badur (Bat) Phir/Mukam.

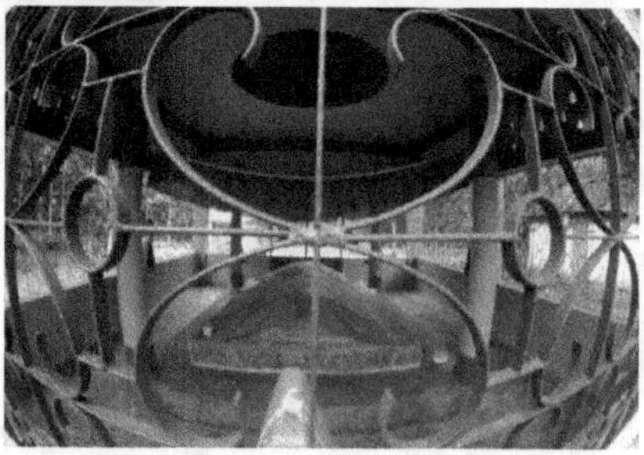

31.7.2010, 11:09:46

Shah Jalal Uddin*

Kuski Pur, Umor Pur Bazaar, Balangoinj. Sylhet (Osmani Nagor)

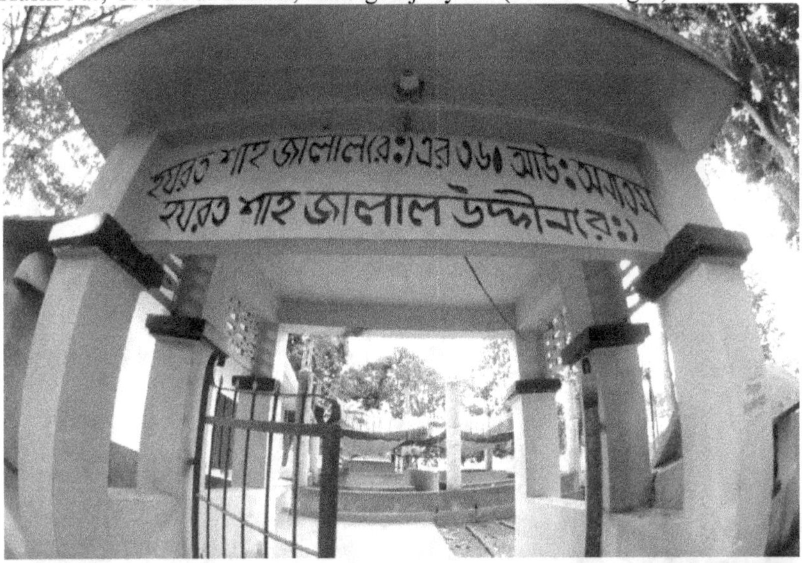
হযরত শাহ জালাল(রঃ)এর ৩৬০ আউঃ
হযরত শাহ জালাল উদ্দীন(রঃ)

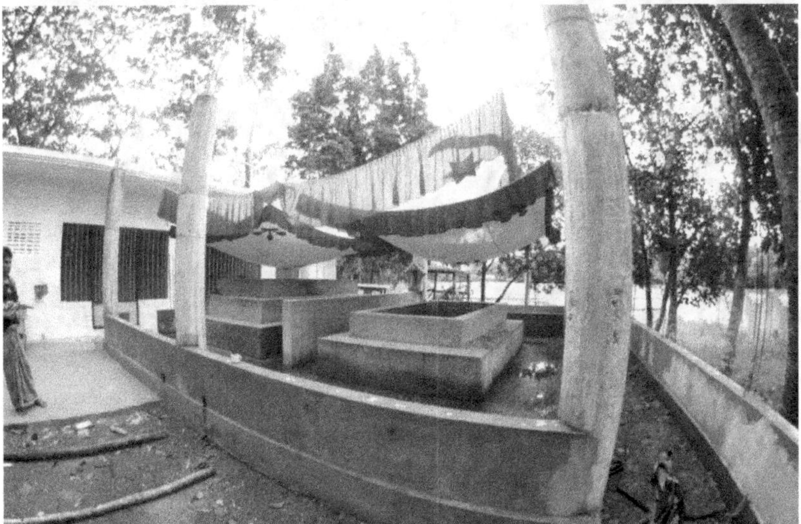

31.7.2010, 11:43:34

This place was closer to home, couple miles out, there is some investment going on, however, while there was calmness of the village lane, the aesthetics did not provide the peace I was becoming accustom too, it is possible it was a rainy dull, damp day.

Soyod Shah Damri

Iship Pur

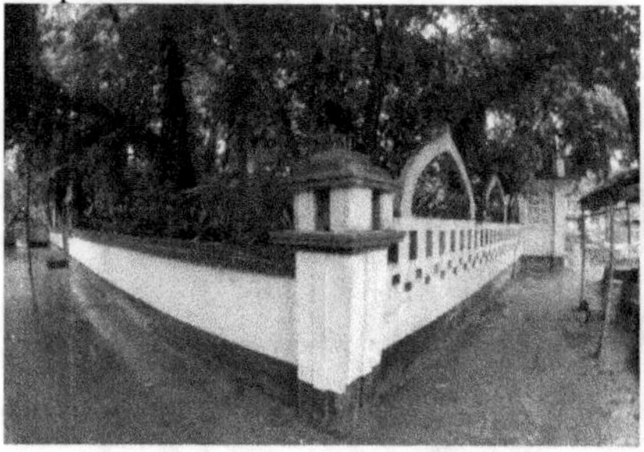

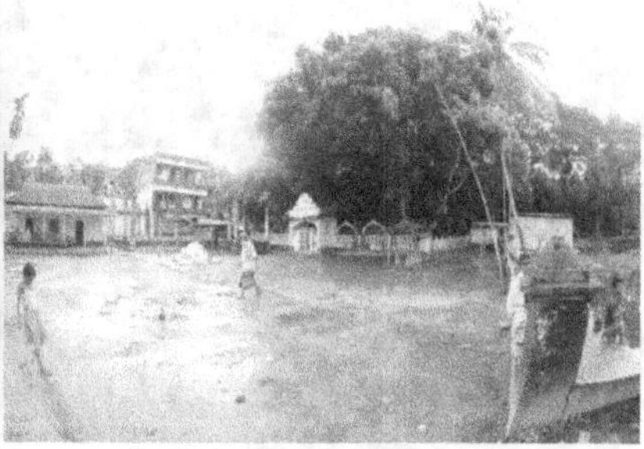

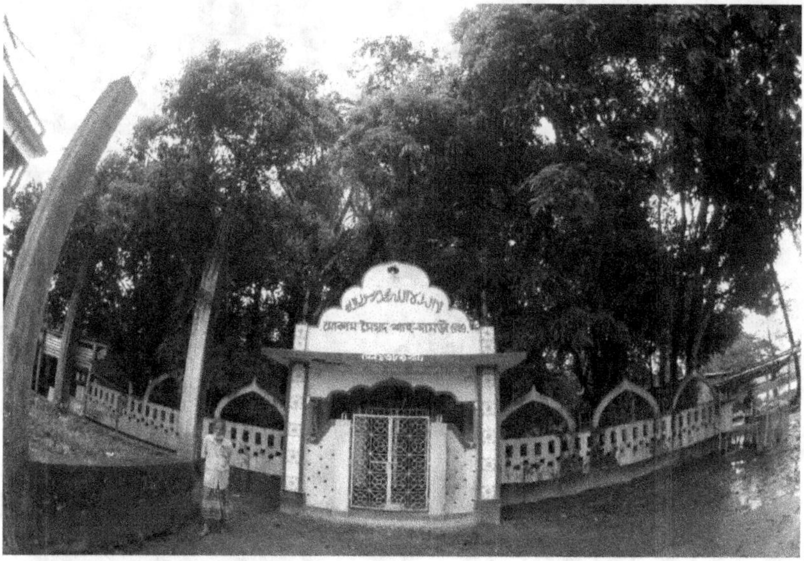

31.7.2010, 12:10:04

August 2010

Soyod Sashni Phir**

Guwaitula, Sylhet

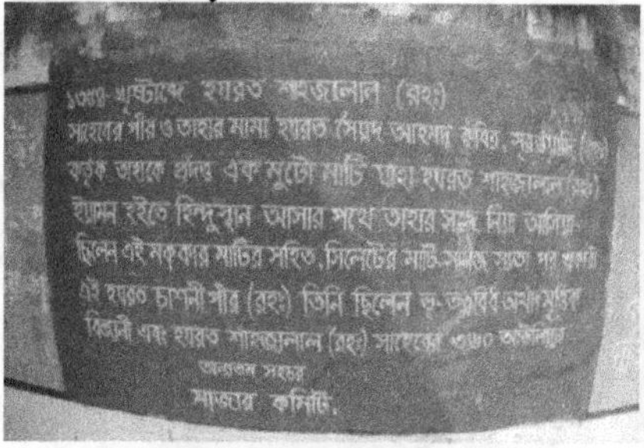

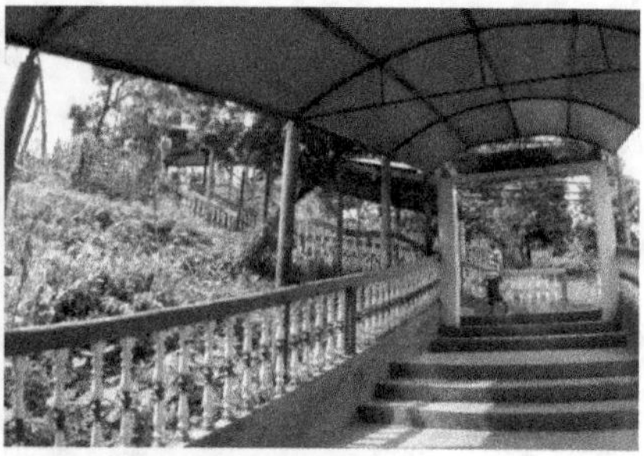

1.8.2010. 13:50:52

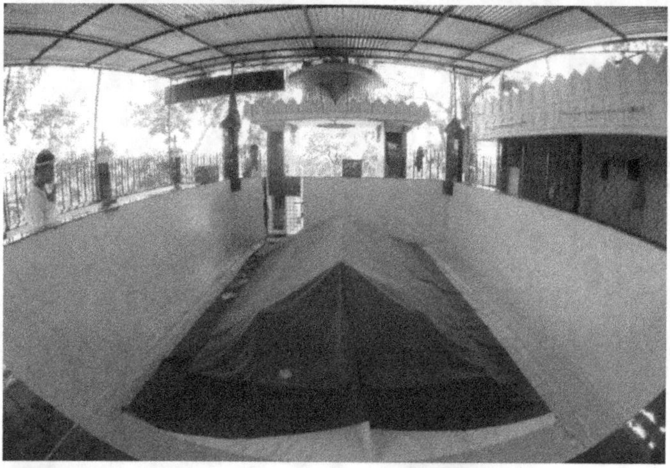

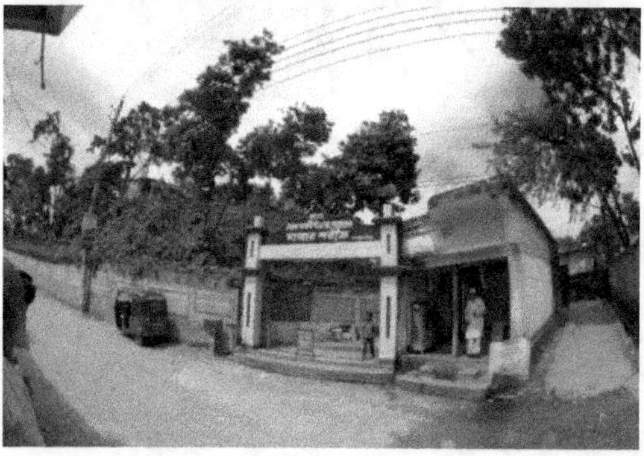

This is located in Sylhet Town, and is the most interactive experience of visiting a mazar. Here we have the Mazar of Hazrat Shah Jalal's companion who was in charge of identifying the soil, which Shah Jalal's uncle gave him to locate. And wherever that may be, that is where Shah Jalal will stop and make home.

This place also has local monkeys which interact with the visitors, visitors can also feed them, and there are shops that sell the foods to give, adding to the local economy.

Soyod Shah Moshud*

Soyod Shah Budoi

Soyod Shah Ajmoth Ullah

Soyod Shah Foteh Ullah

The area claim of these four companions of Hazrat Shah Jalal, but there were no physical signs of any graves or any other ornament.

Local, also observe a ritual of cobras drinking offerings of milk on the spot of the graves of the four. This is known as "Doodraj."

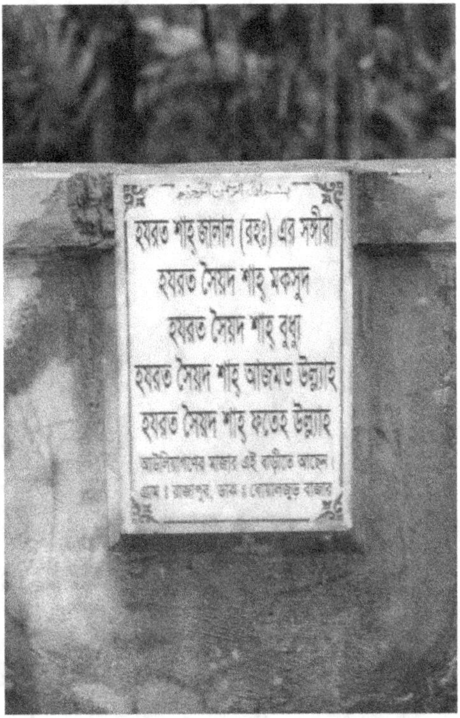
হযরত শাহ্ জালাল (রহঃ) এর সঙ্গীরা
হযরত সৈয়দ শাহ্ মকসুদ
হযরত সৈয়দ শাহ্ বুধা
হযরত সৈয়দ শাহ্ আজমত উল্লাহ
হযরত সৈয়দ শাহ্ ফতেহ উল্লাহ

j 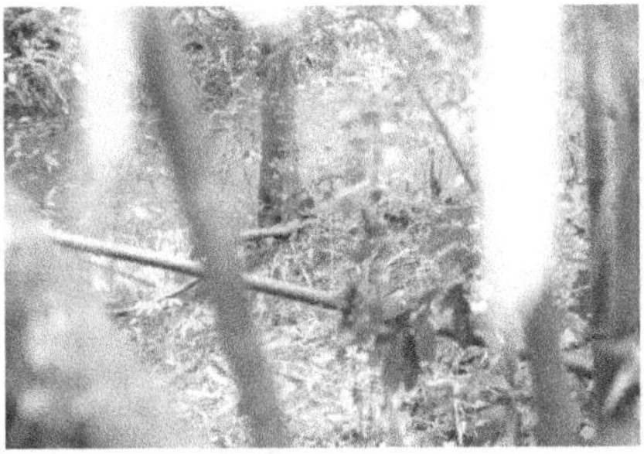

21.8.2010,

Doi Kura

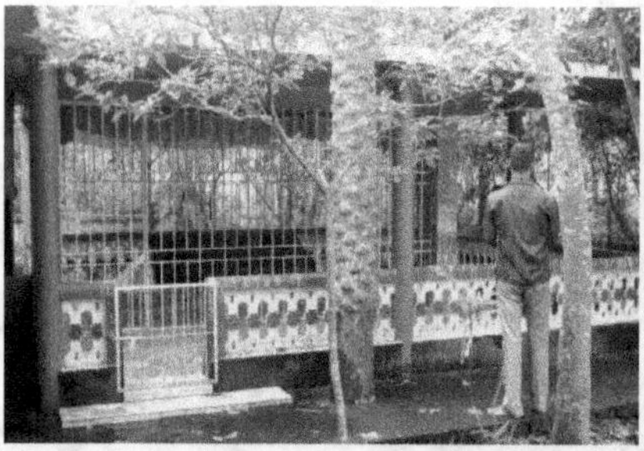

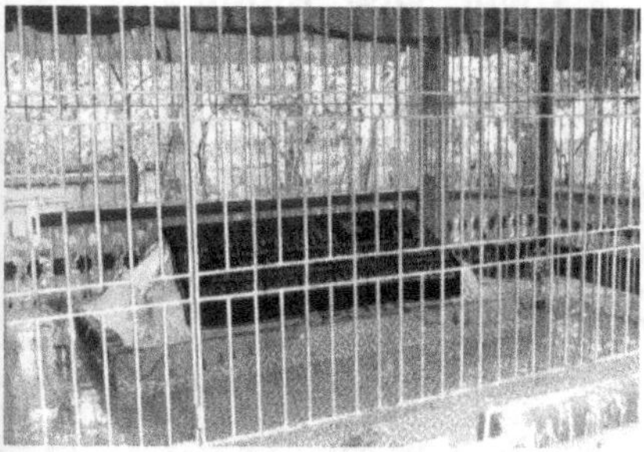

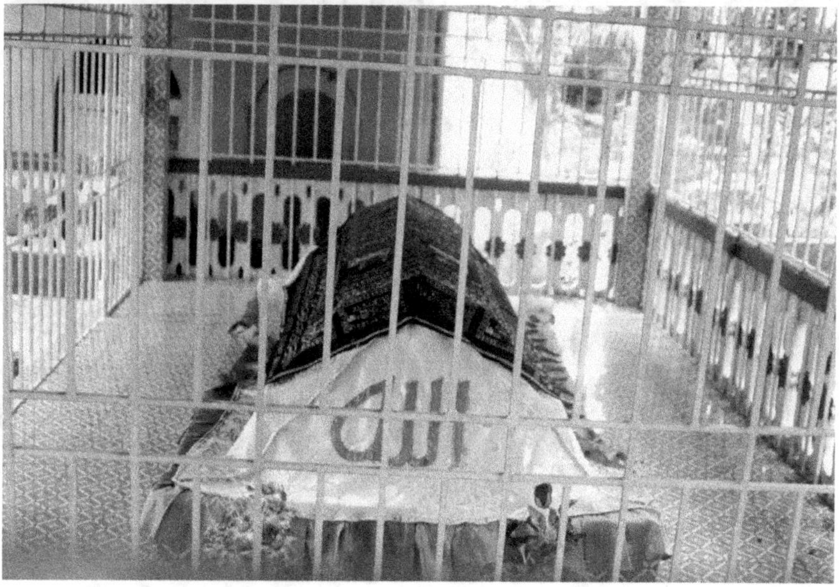

21.8.2010, 09:38:16

Shah Goali Shab

Koromshi Road, off Goala Bazaar, N2 Motorway, Osmani Nagor.

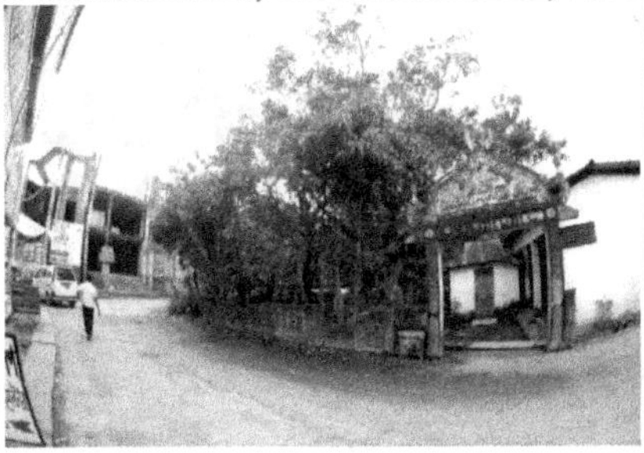

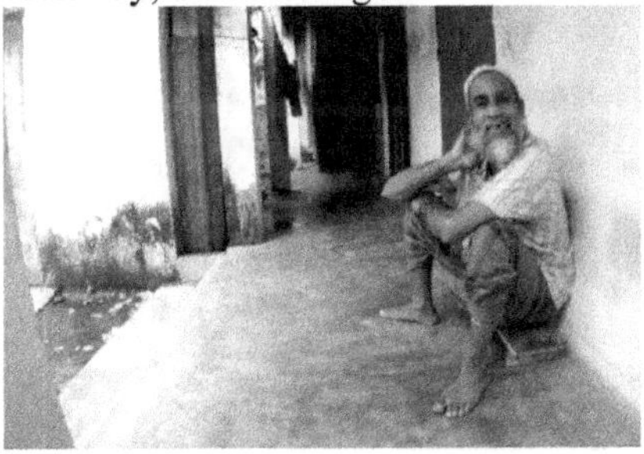

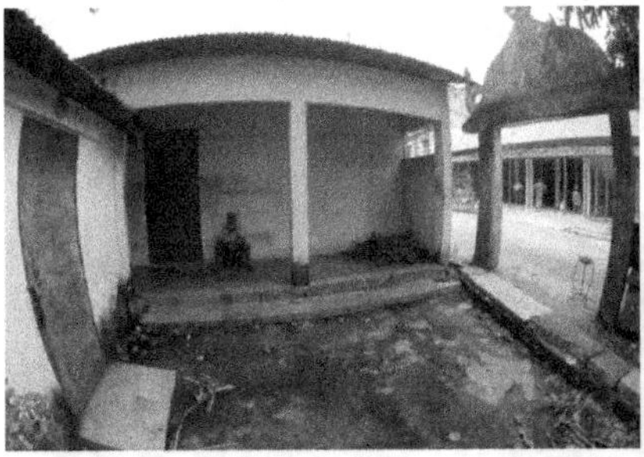

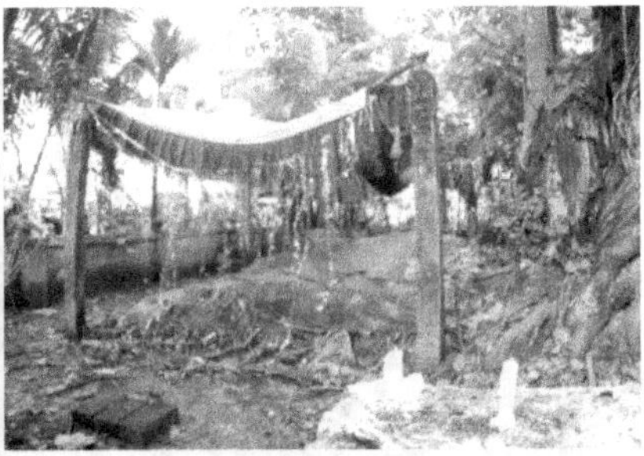

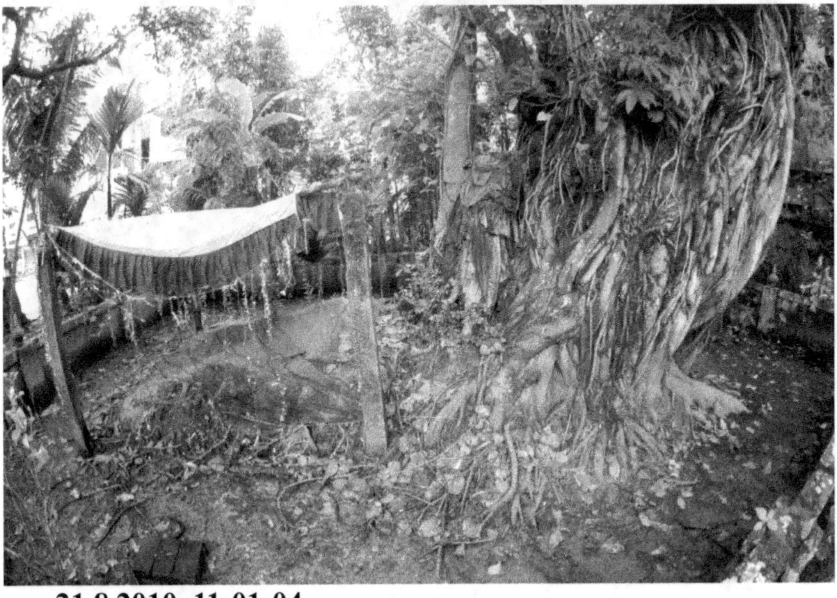

21.8.2010, 11:01:04

Not a member of the 360 group.

Shah Muktha

Tila Para, Muktar Pur, Burunga, Osmani Nagor, Sylhet

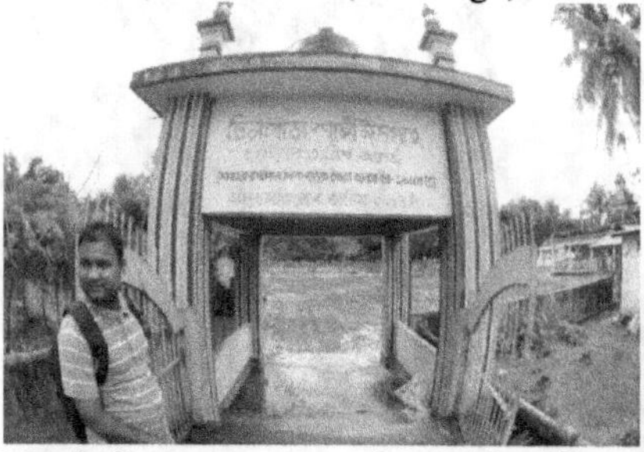
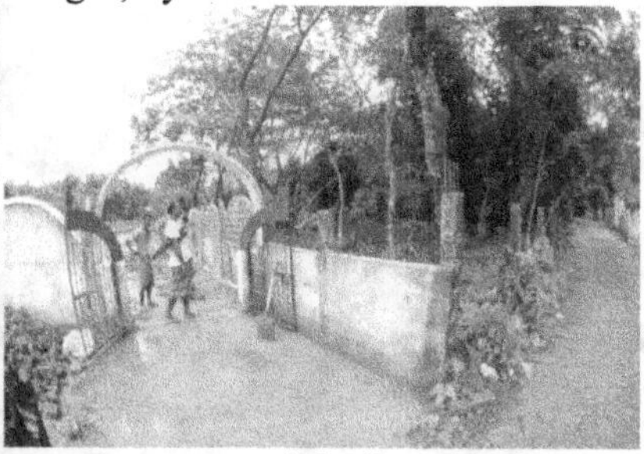

My dad's mum comes from this village area, the mosque is built on her land, and it was donated to them after she died.

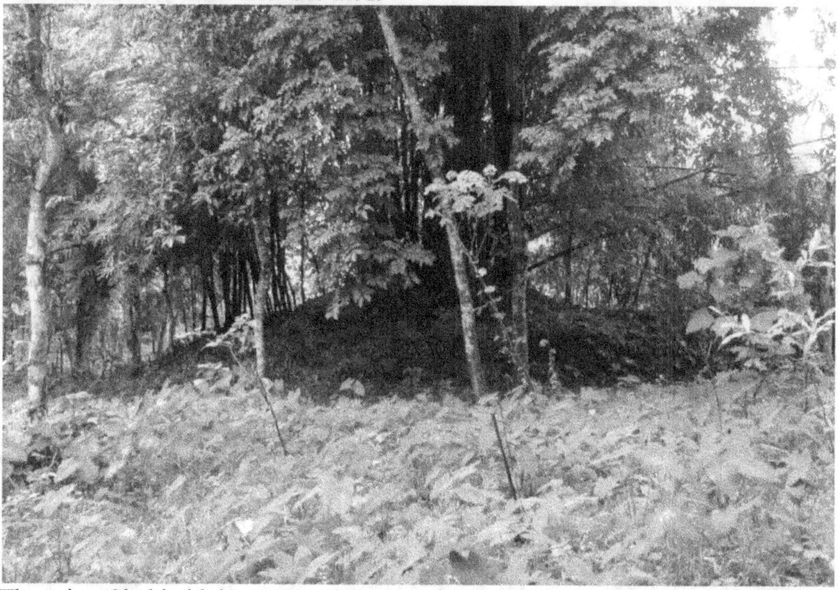

There is a Shahi eidgha next to the grave; however, the grave of Shah Muktha is just a mound, where Bamboo trees were growing out of.

While the area is names after the person and the eidgha is all concreted up, the grave has been left to the wilderness.

22.8.2010, 09:51:30

Uzir Shah

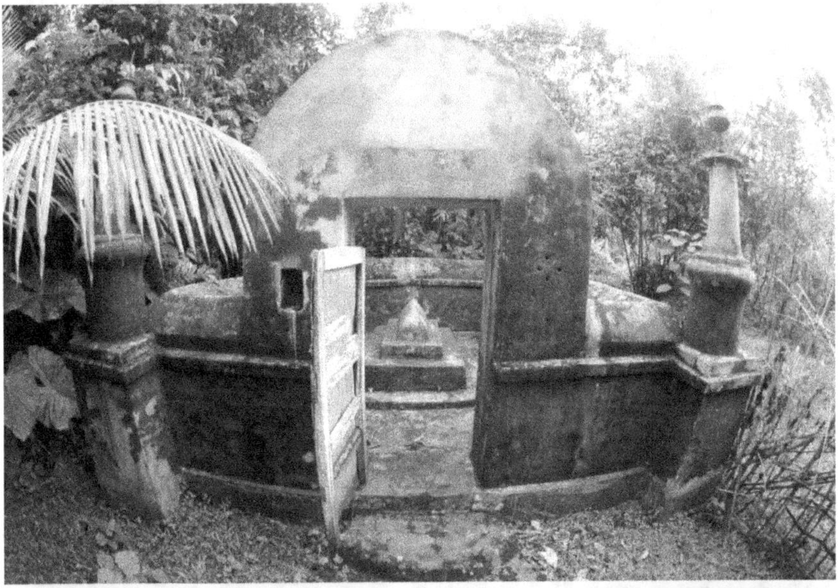

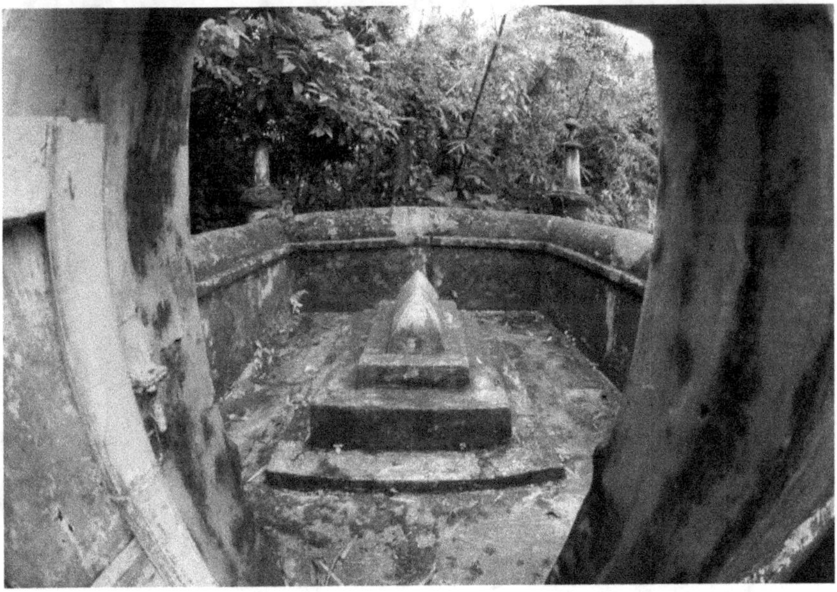

["there is a Frankenstein head, through this view"]

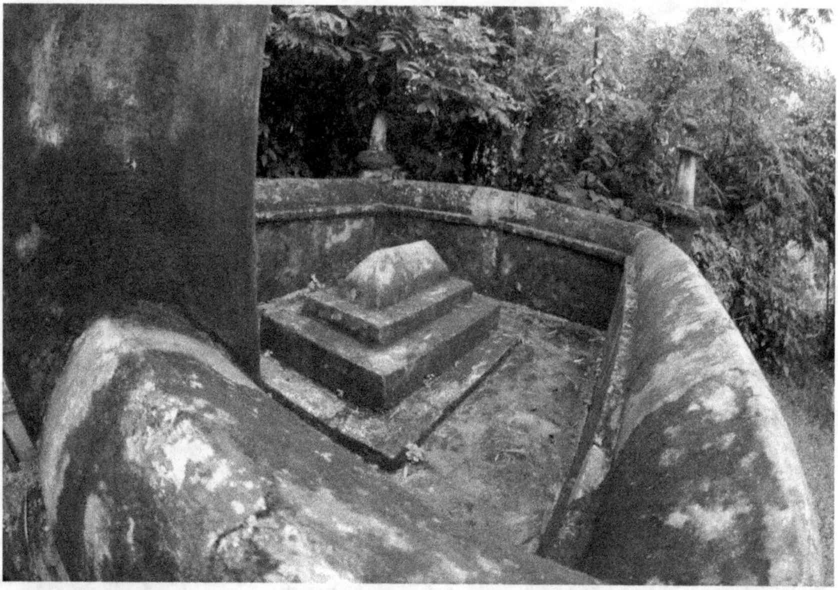

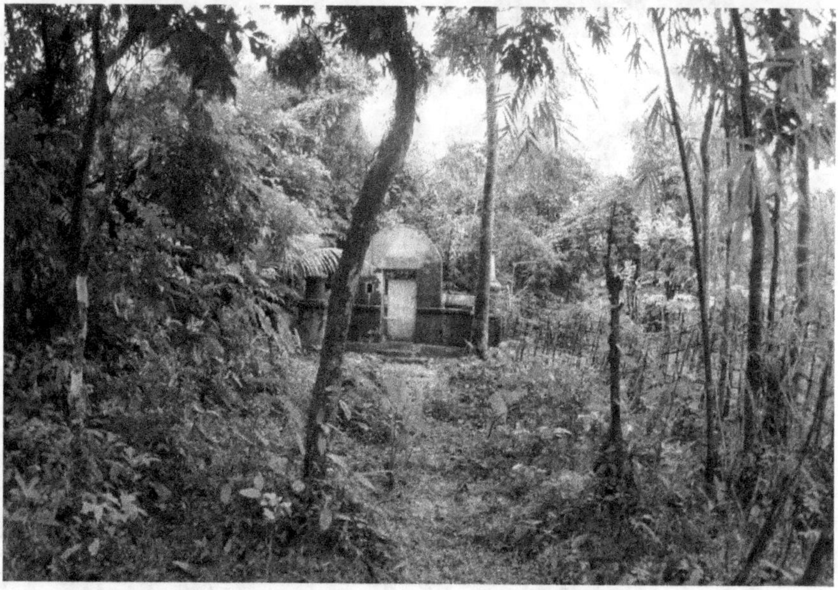

22.8.2010, 11.15.24

Deep state - surrounded by greenery, local Mukam, but not of the 360 group.

Balti Shah

On the N2 Motorway, towards Sherpur.

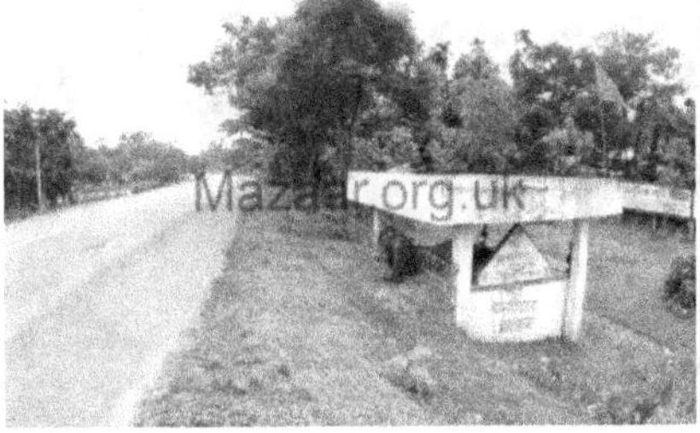
Mazaar.org.uk

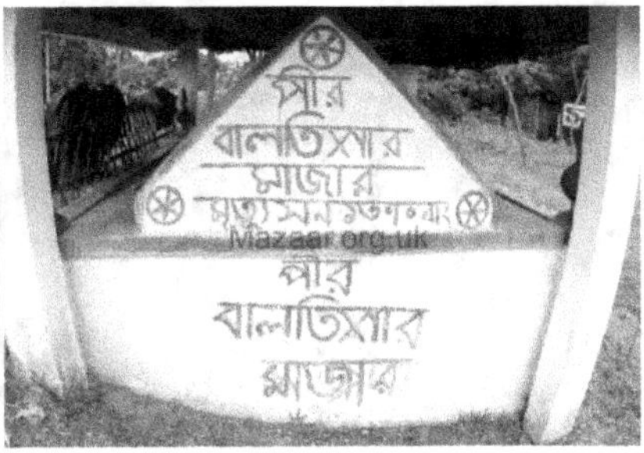
পীর
বালতিসার
মাজার
Mazaar.org.uk
পীর
বালতিসার
মাজার

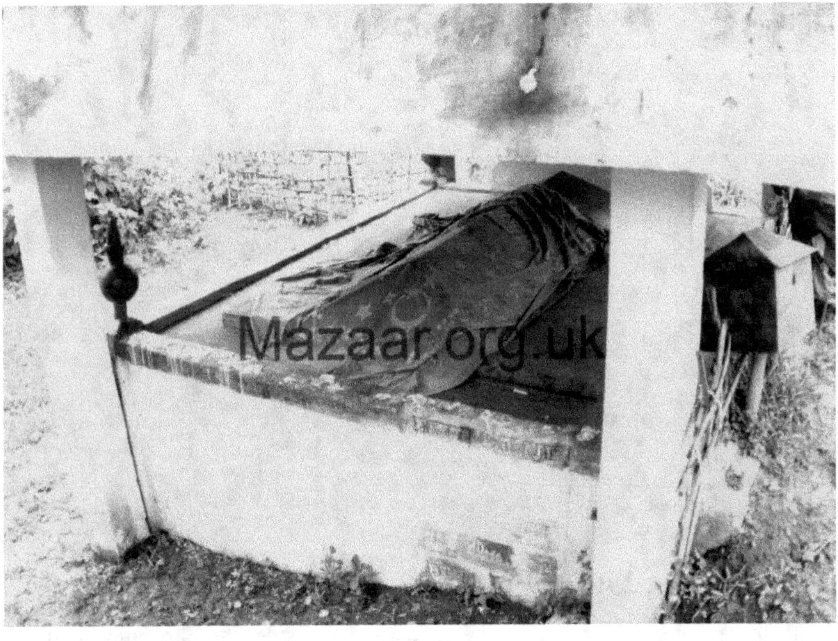
Mazaar.org.uk

22.8.2010, 19:04:20

This is not verified with an 8 sided plaque.

Hafiz Shah Ata Ullah*

Tila Para, Muktar Pur, Burunga, Osmani Nagar, Sylhet.

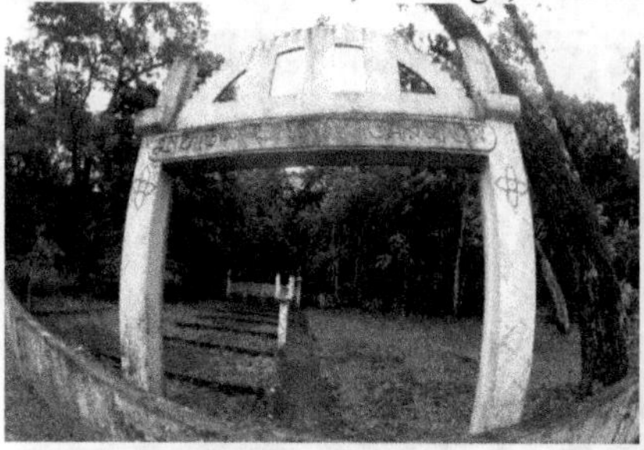

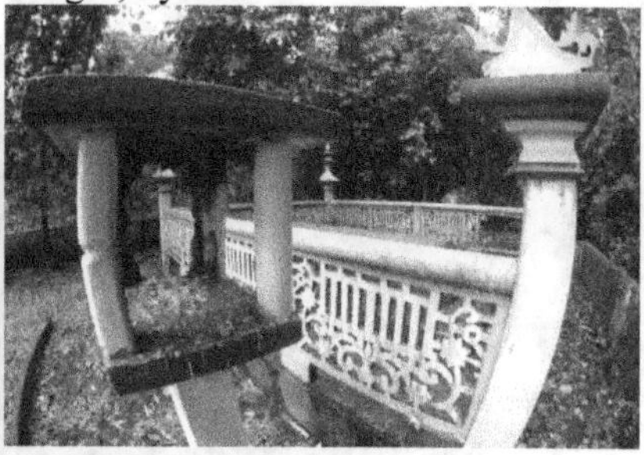

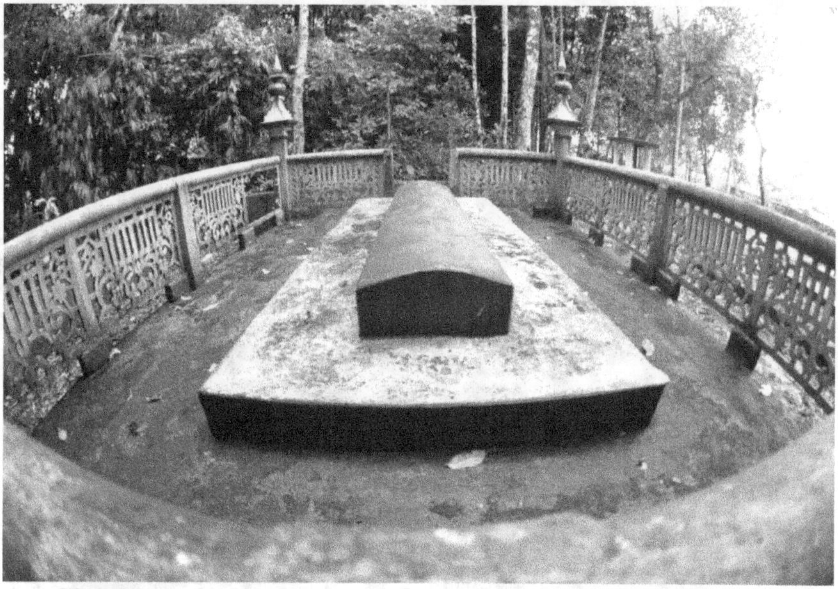

22.8.2010, 20:49:08

With these remote sites, out in the fields and wayside, they are important and relevant, but not kept as many city ones and the ones with high people traffic. What I found that Bangladesh is natural calm, serene and tranquil and depending on the way the places is looked after and maintained - aesthetically they make a difference on our perceptions and how seeing the state it is in, makes us feel, this contributes to zapping my inhibition.

Miah Roshni

Sandai Parah

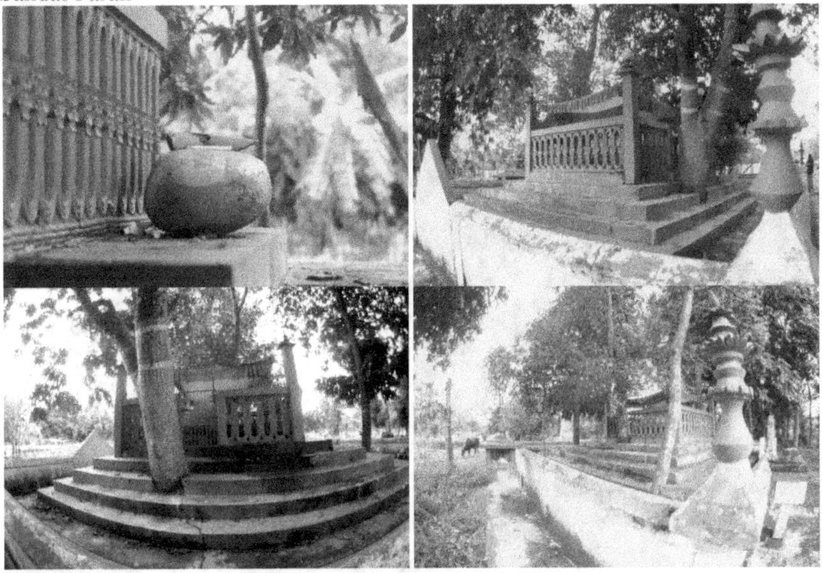

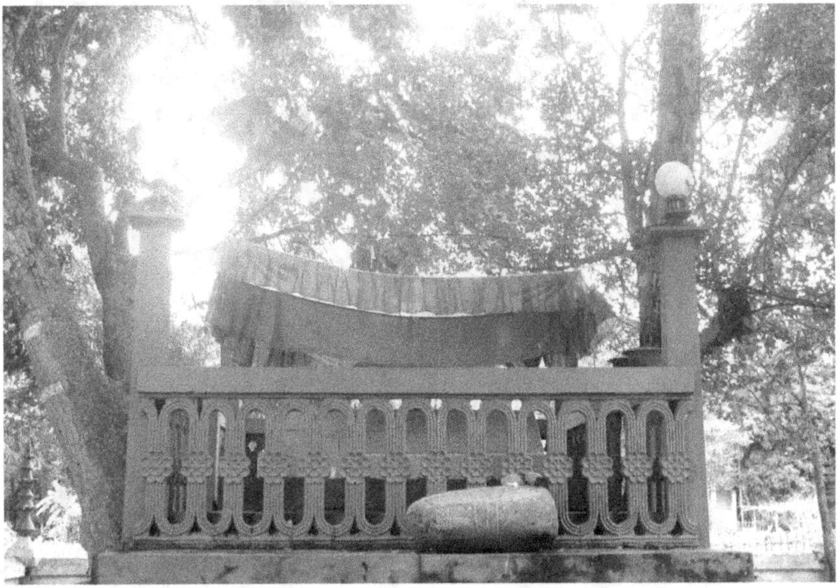

23.8.2010, 9:14:42

Shah Miah Sandai

Sandai Parah

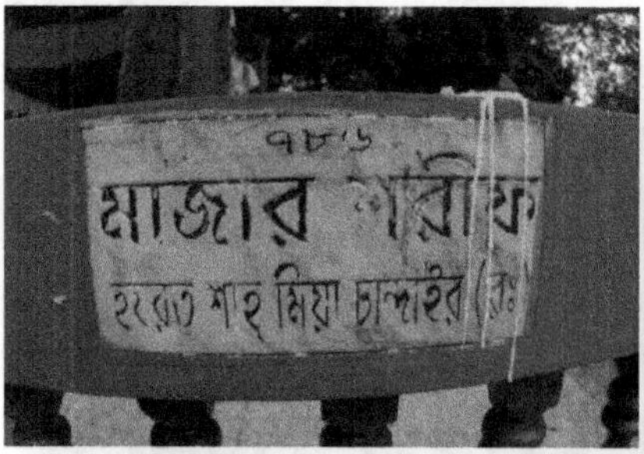
৭৮৬
মাজার শরীফ
হযরত শাহ মিয়া চান্দাইর

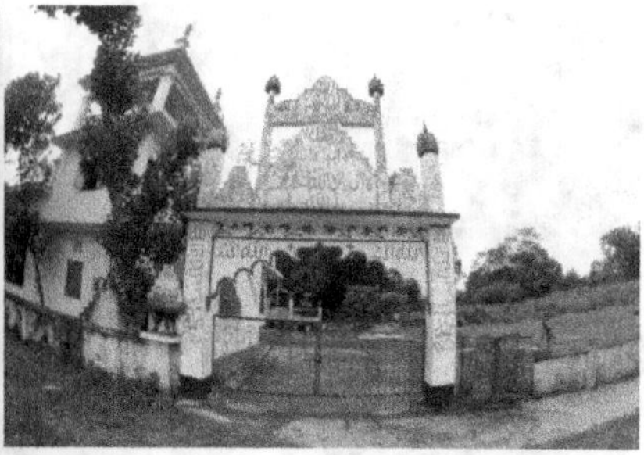

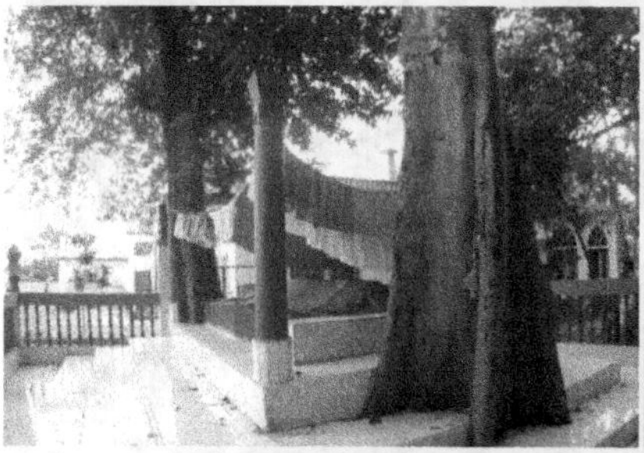

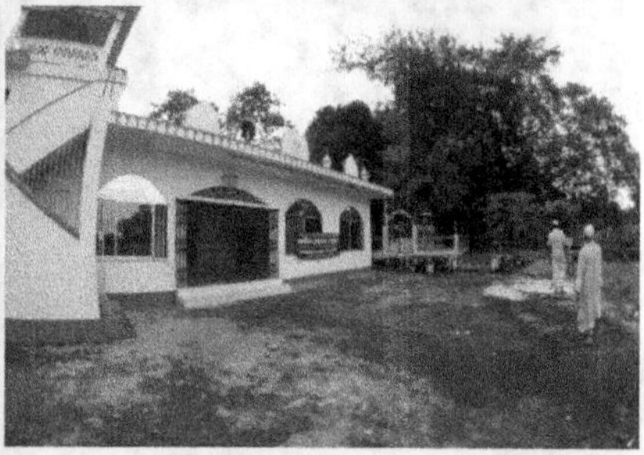

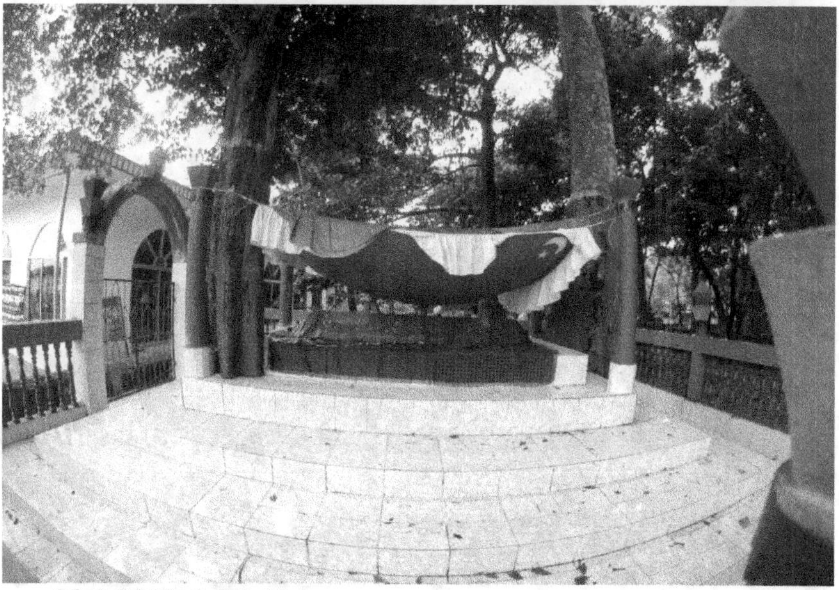

23.8.2010, 9:26:48

Shah Siddique*

Fass parah, Balagoinj

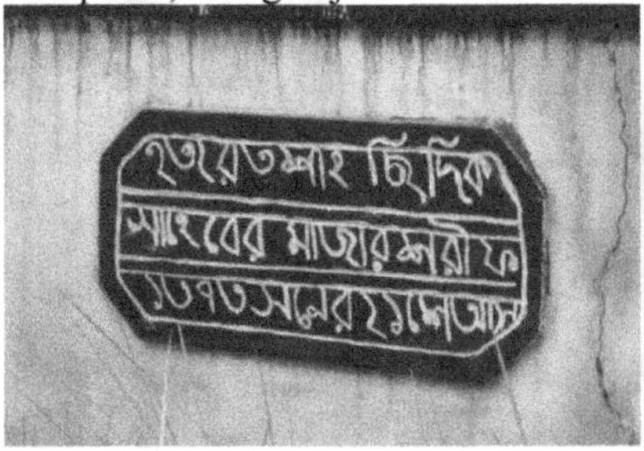
সাহেবের মাজার শরীফ
১৩৭৩ সনের

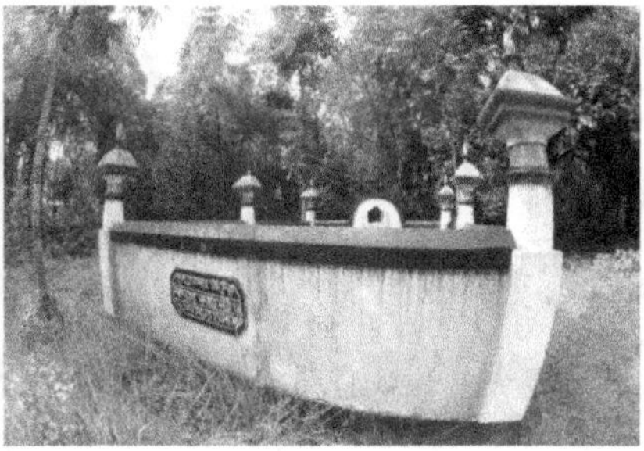

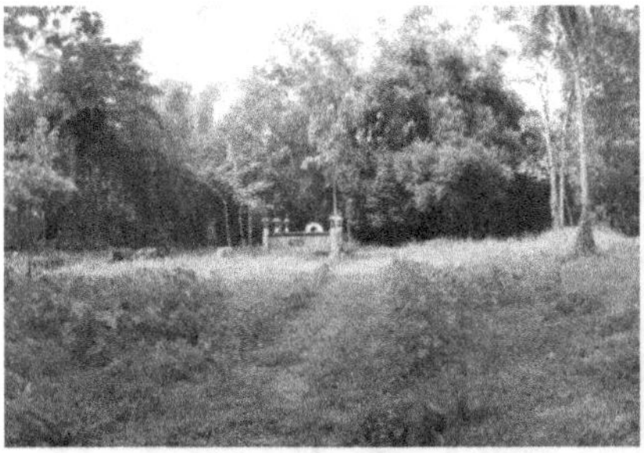

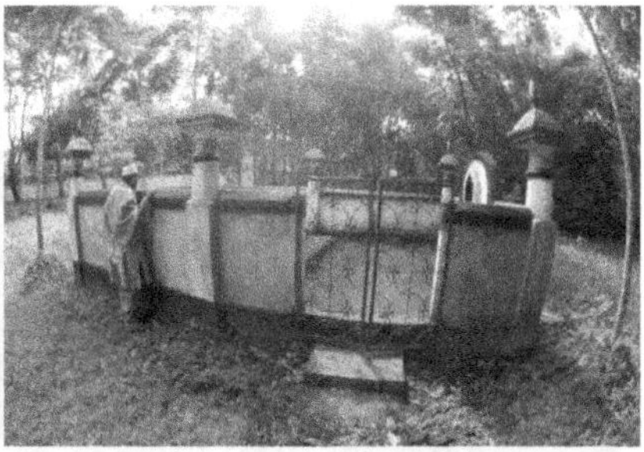

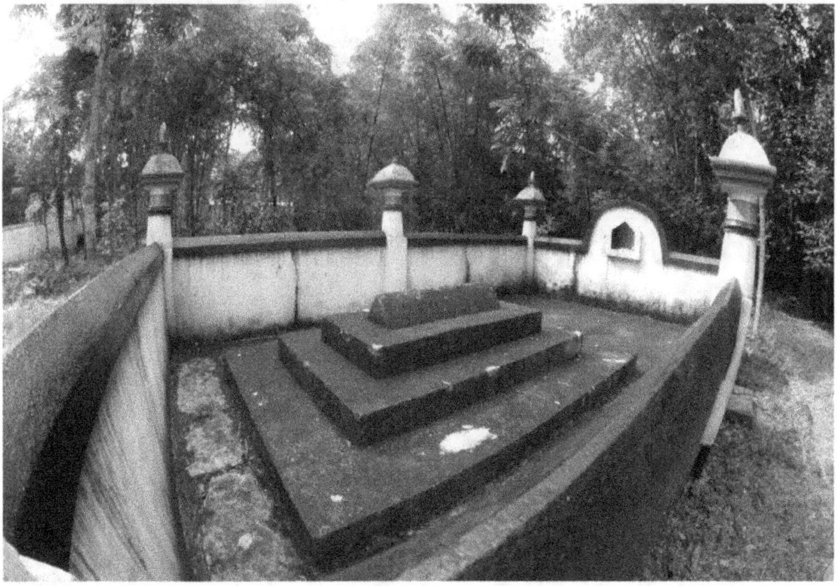

23.8.2010, 09:52:44

Fokir Moib Ullah

off Robi Dash Road, Tajpur

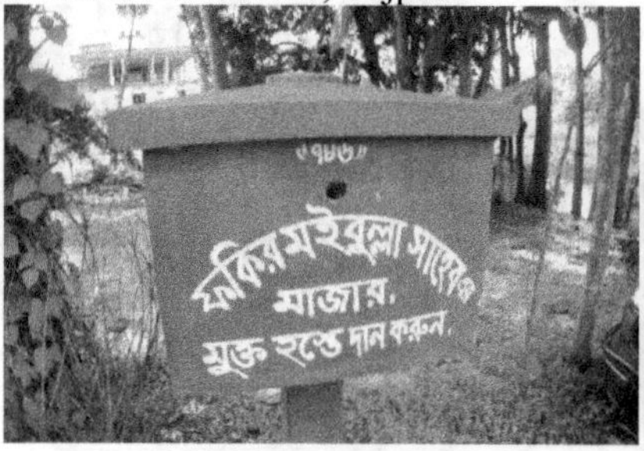
৭৮৬
ফকির মইবুল্লা সাহেবের
মাজার.
মুক্ত হস্তে দান করুন.

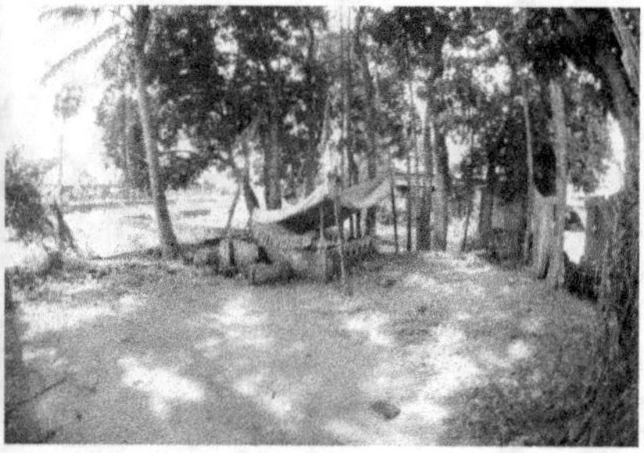

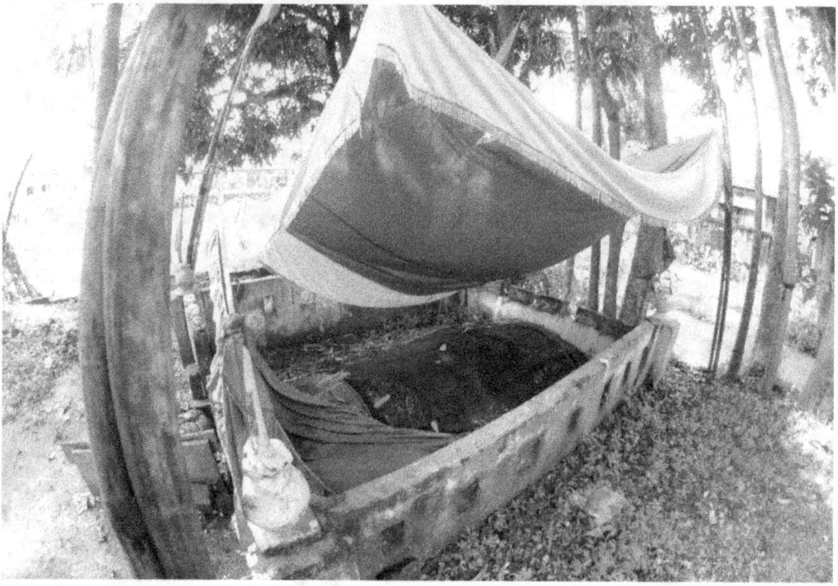

23.8.2010, 20:23:18

Dosh-all

Dosh-all, Tajpur, Balagoinj

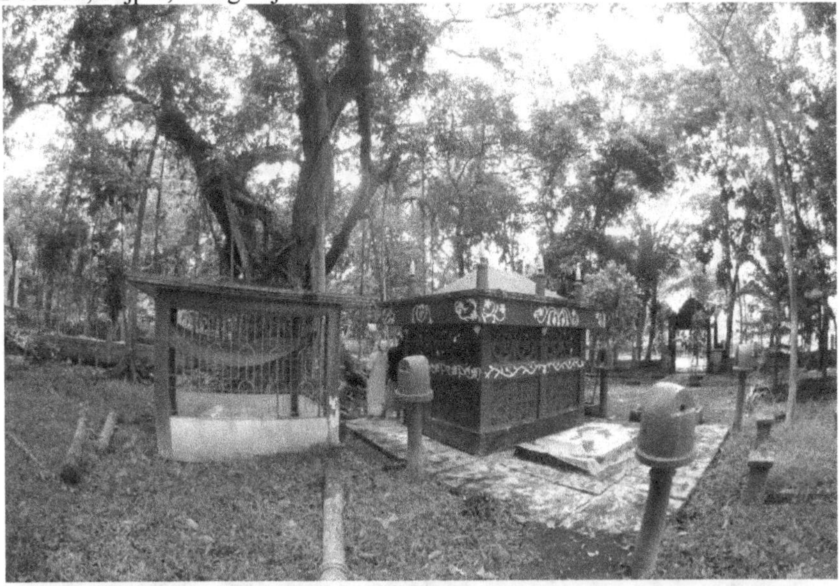

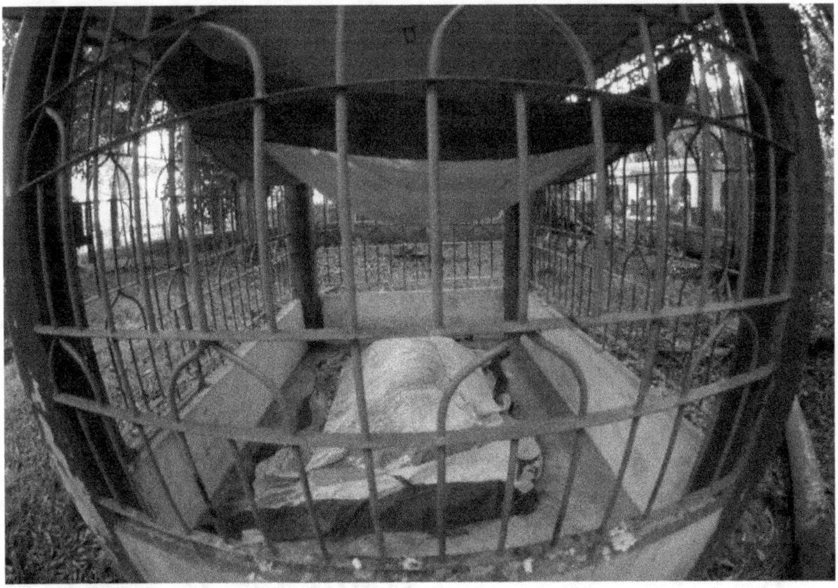

23.8.2010, 20:54:06

Shah Ajij

Dosh-all, Tajpur, Balagoinj

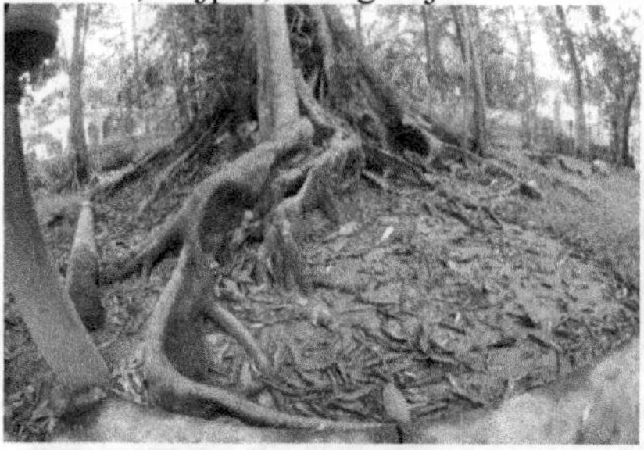
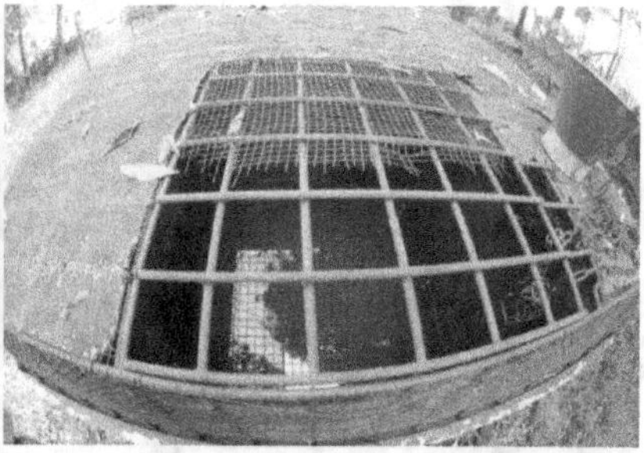
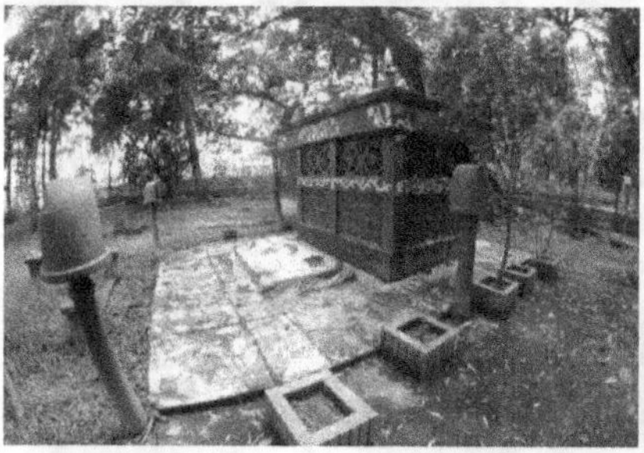
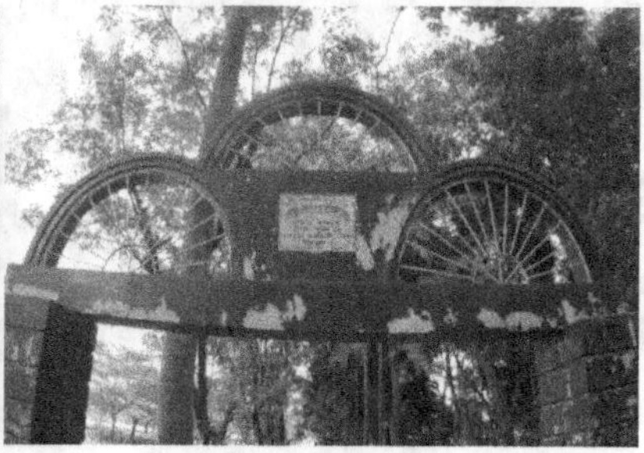
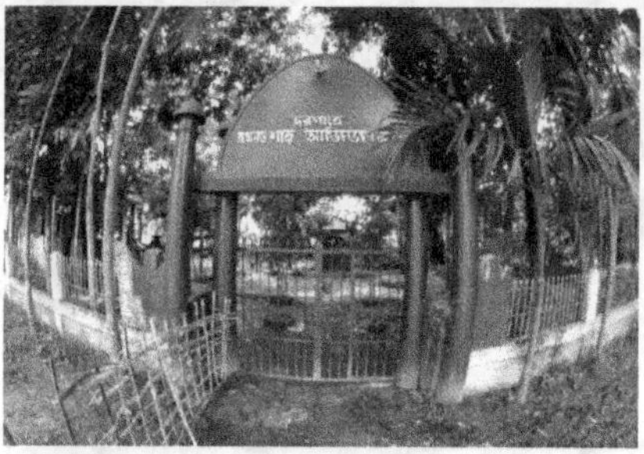
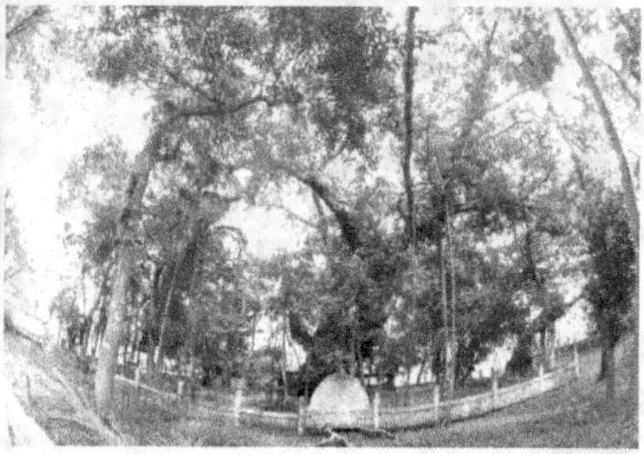
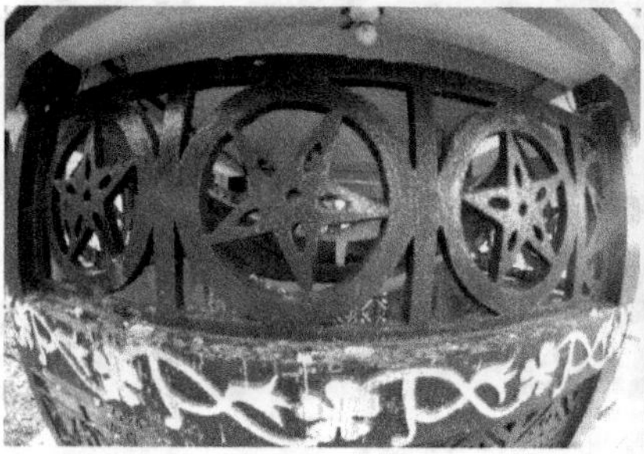
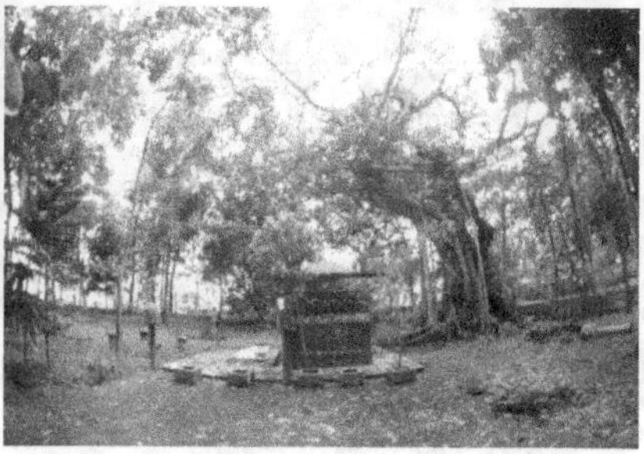

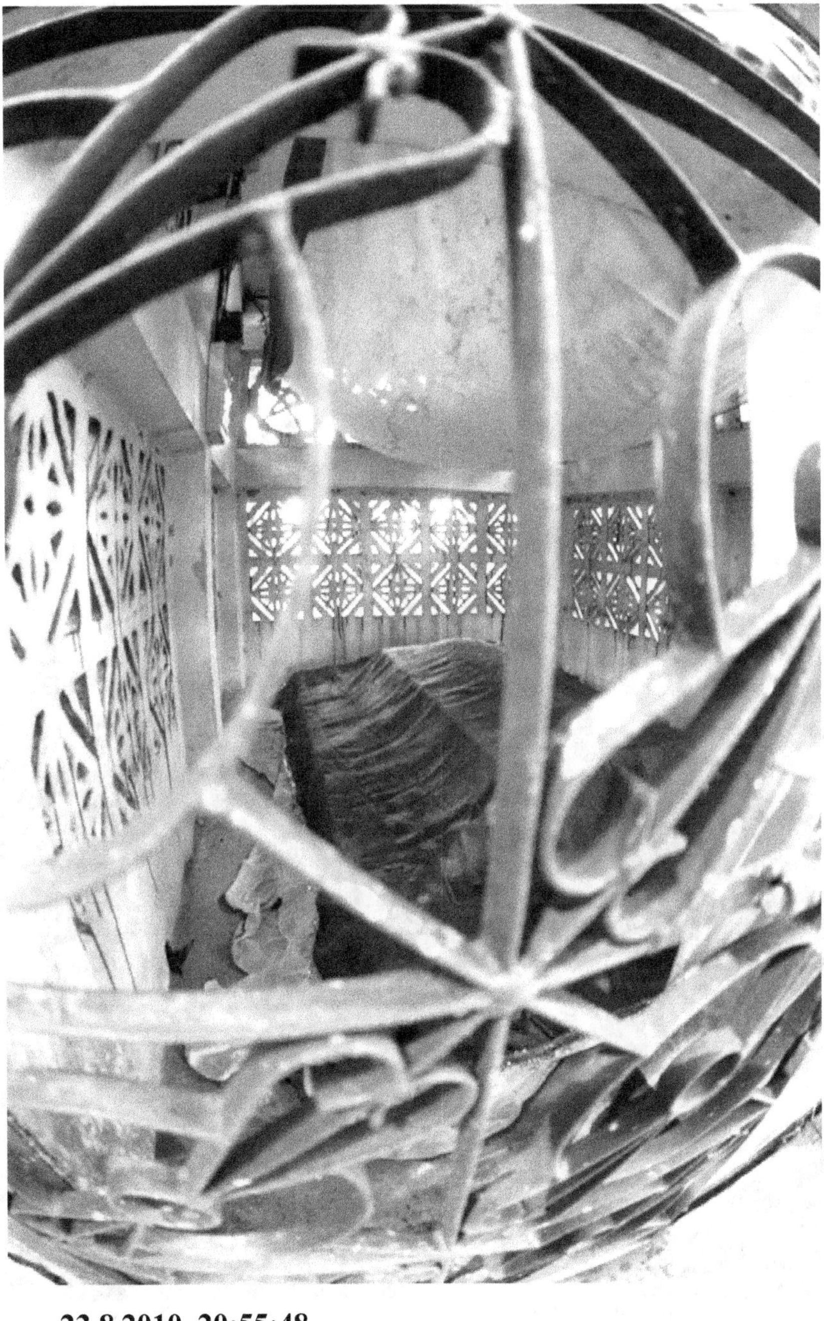

23.8.2010, 20:55:48

Shah Modon**

Tilla Ghor

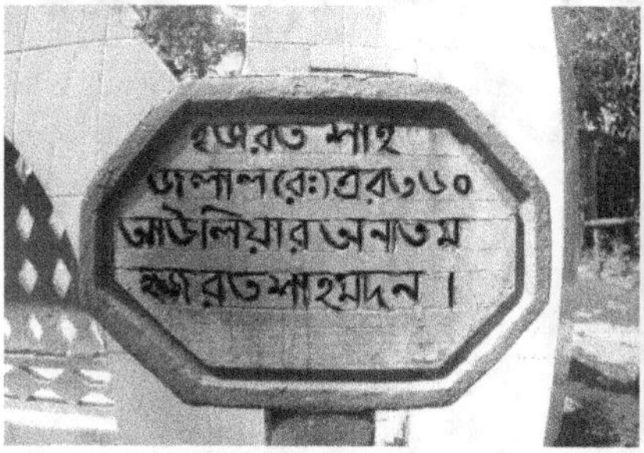
হজরত শাহ
জালাল(রেঃ)এর৩৬০
আউলিয়ার অন্যতম
হজরতশাহমদন।

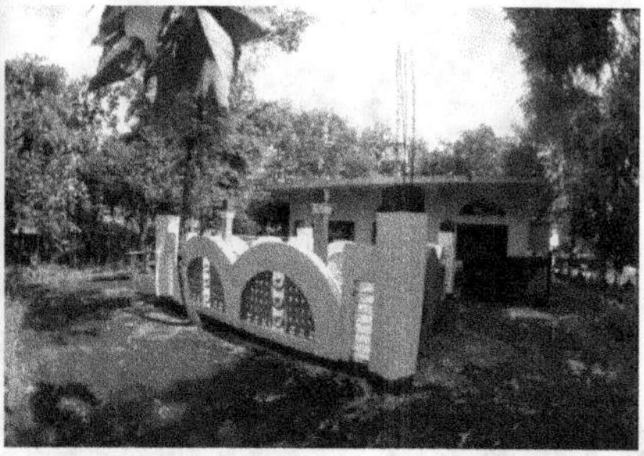

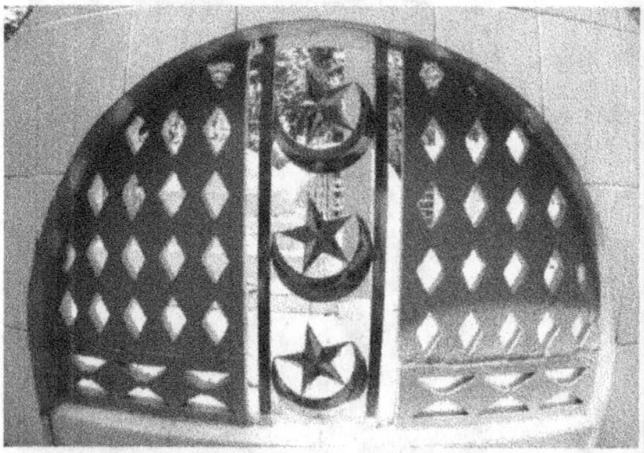

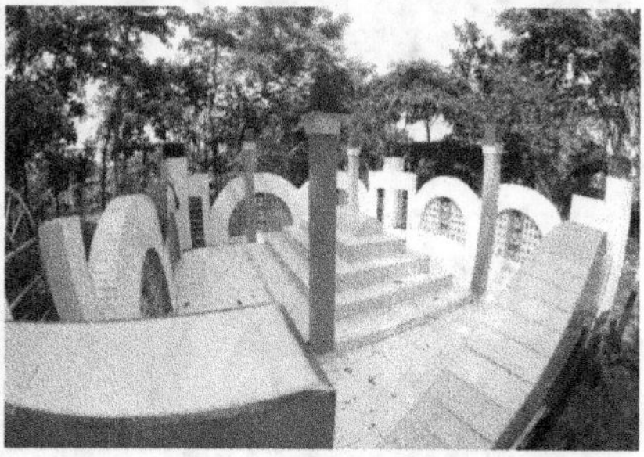

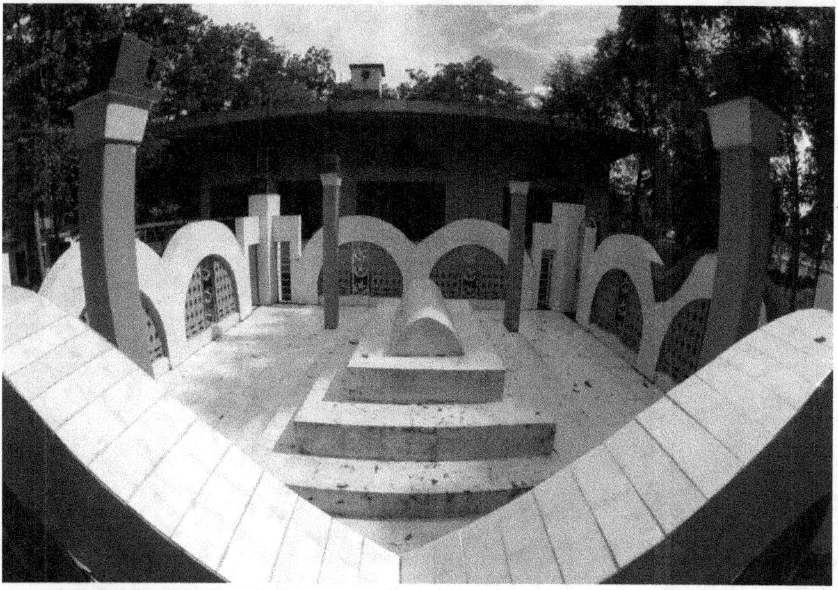

25.8.2010, 09:16:24

Toyob Soylani**

Shilam

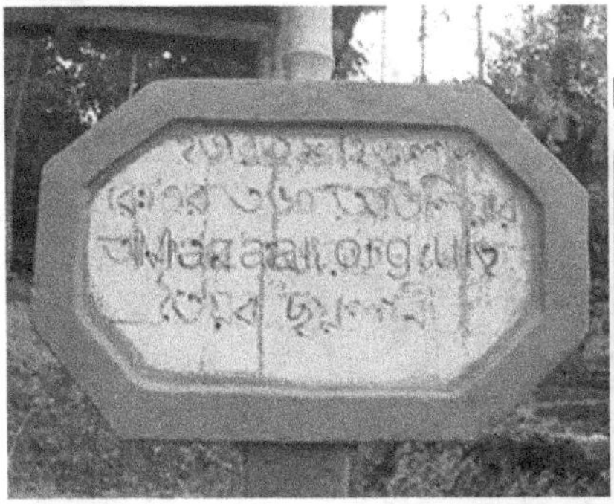
Mazaar.org.uk

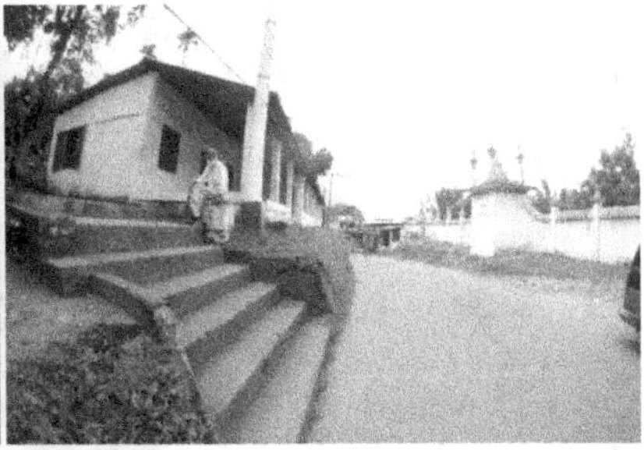

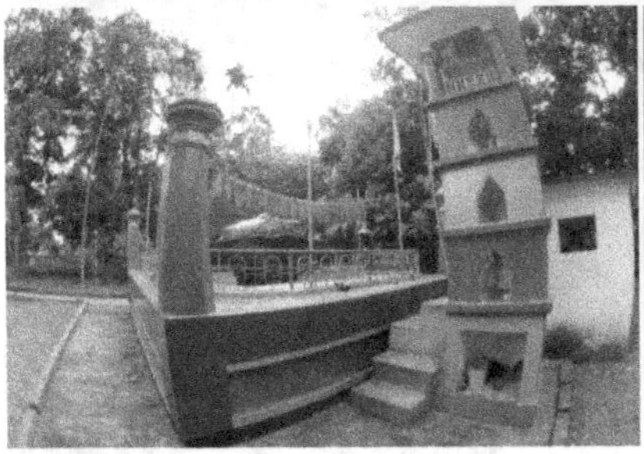

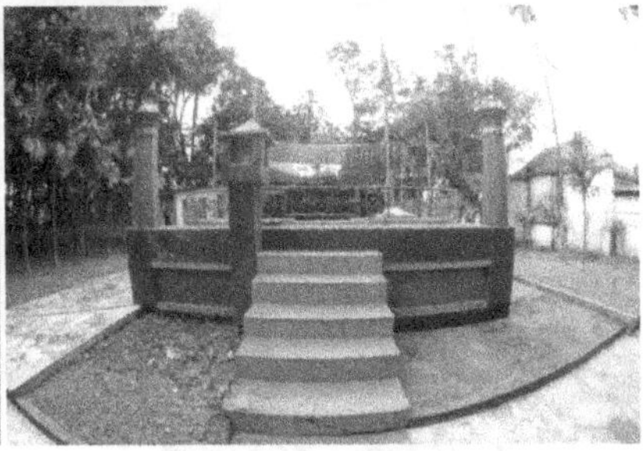

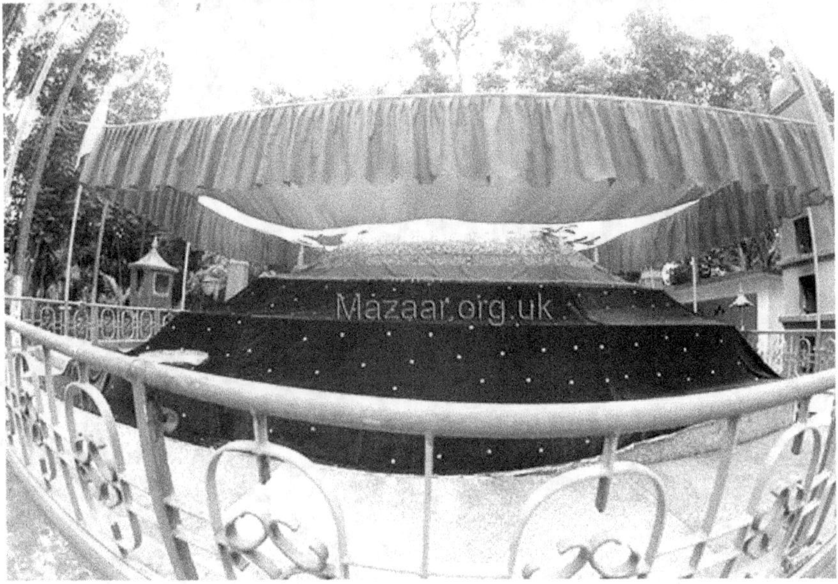
Mazaar.org.uk

25.8.2010, 10:01:08

Shodai Shuhagi

Shilam

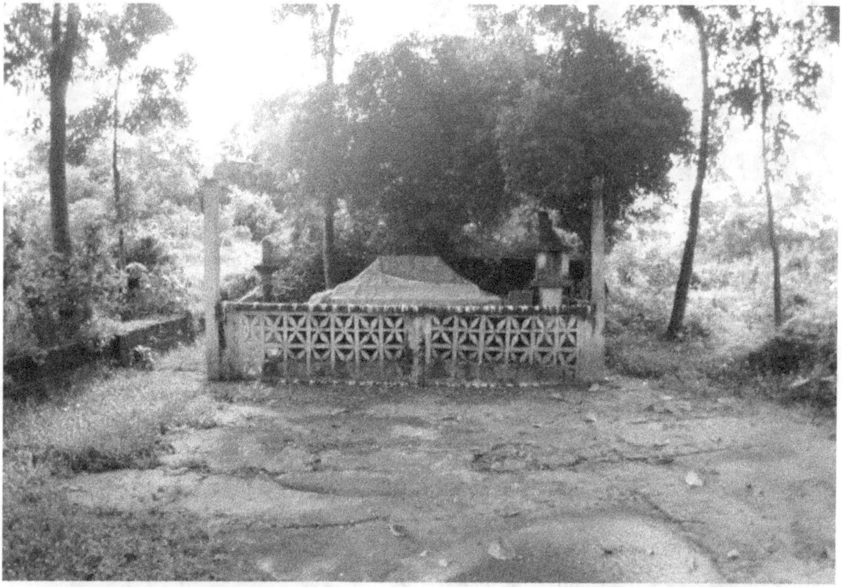

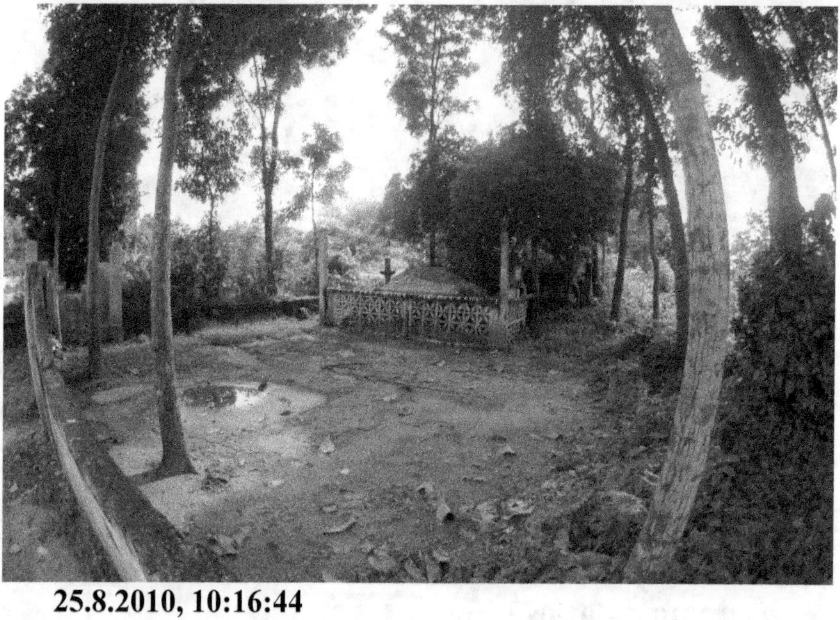

25.8.2010, 10:16:44

Shah Shikondor

Shilam

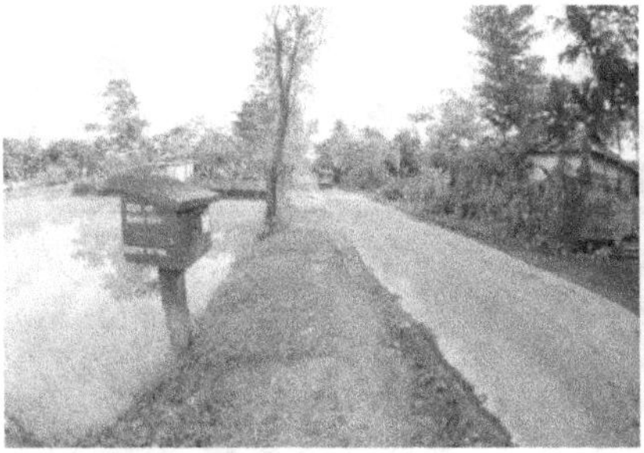

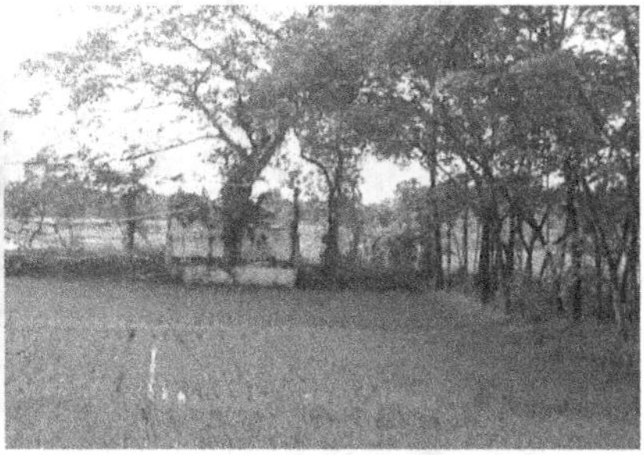

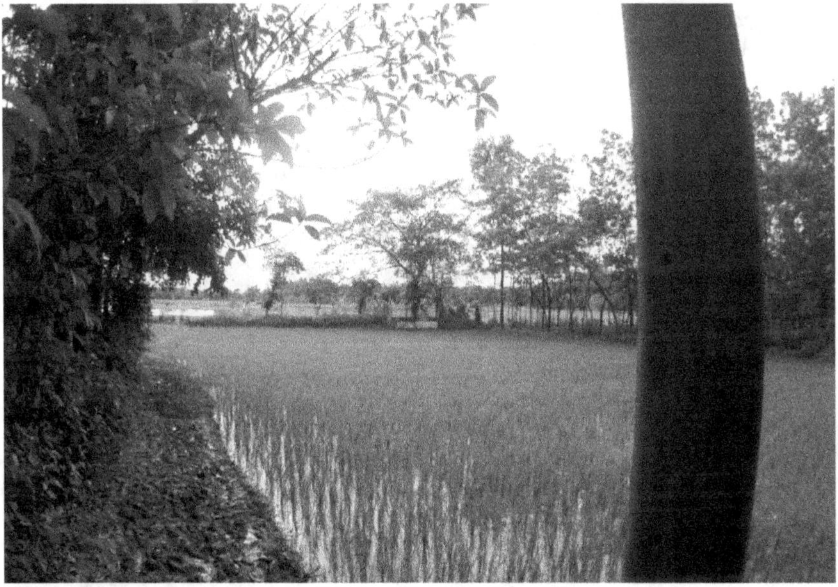

25.8.2010, 10:34:30

It was very muddy, couldn't get closer to the place, nor did I have the zoom to cover the distance.

However, this place is not verified by any 8 sided plaques.

The name of the area "Shilam," conjures up the images of Srinagar of Kashmir, romantic image, seen on films, where it is claimed to be one of the most beautiful place in the world.

Soyod Shahlal*

Soyod Muktar Shah*

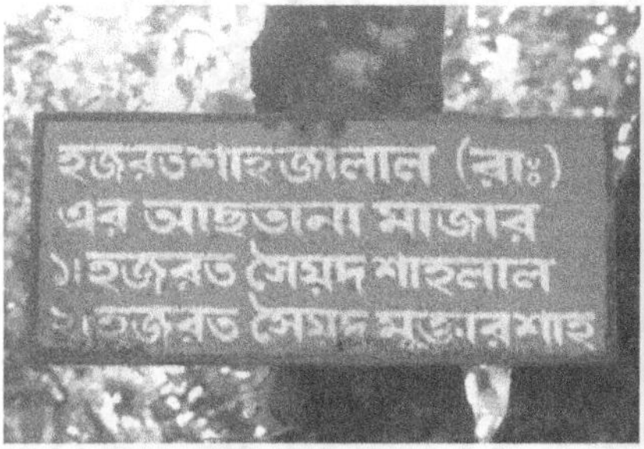
হজরতশাহজালাল (রাঃ)
এর আস্তানা মাজার
১। হজরত সৈয়দ শাহলাল
২। হজরত সৈয়দ মুক্তারশাহ

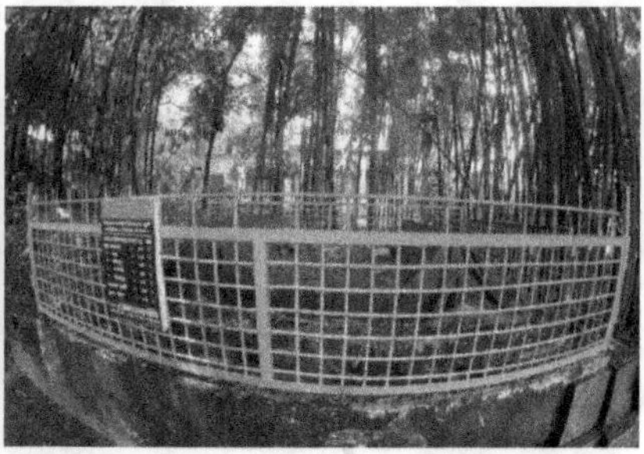

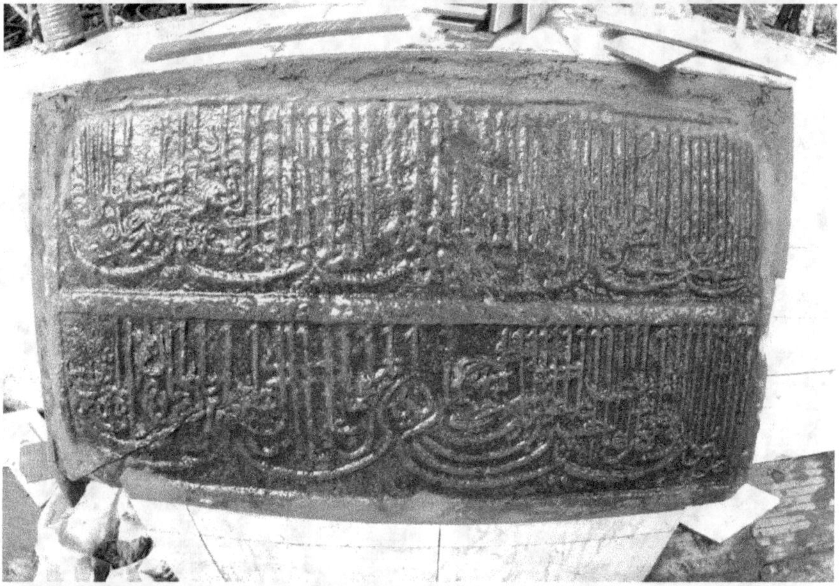

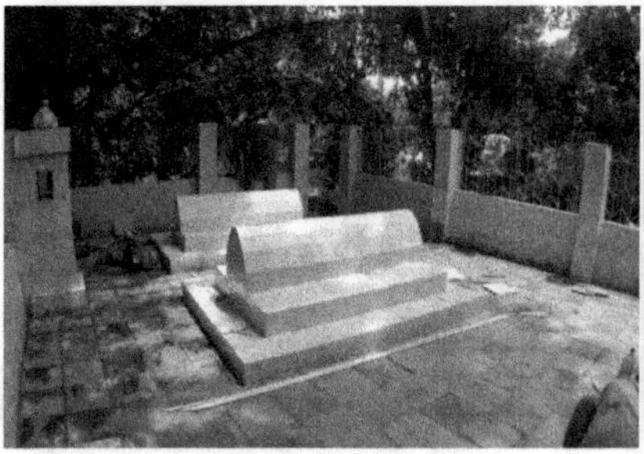

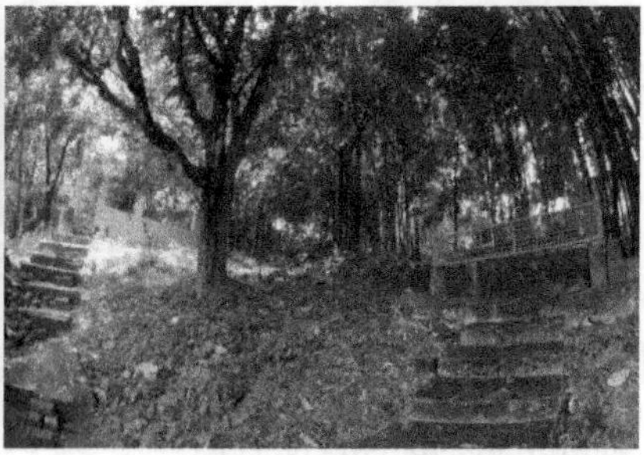

25.8.2010, 19:11:36

Kaji Jolal Uddin**

Kaji Tula, Sylhet Town

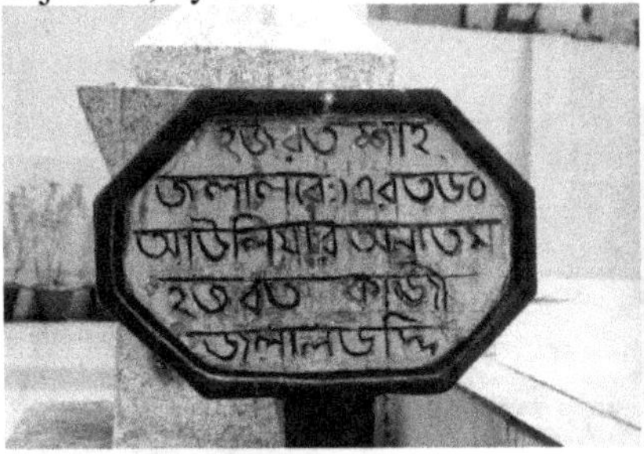

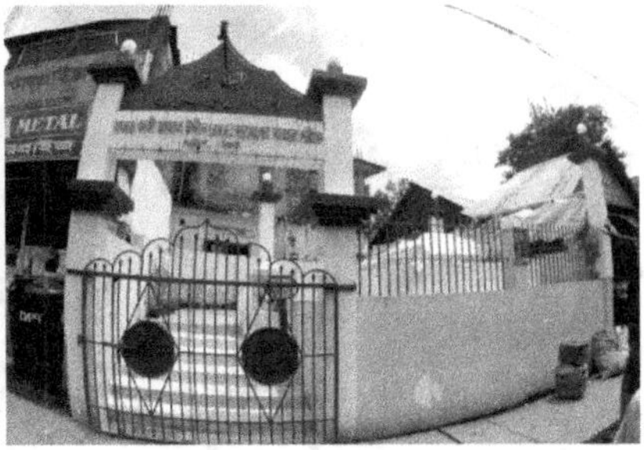

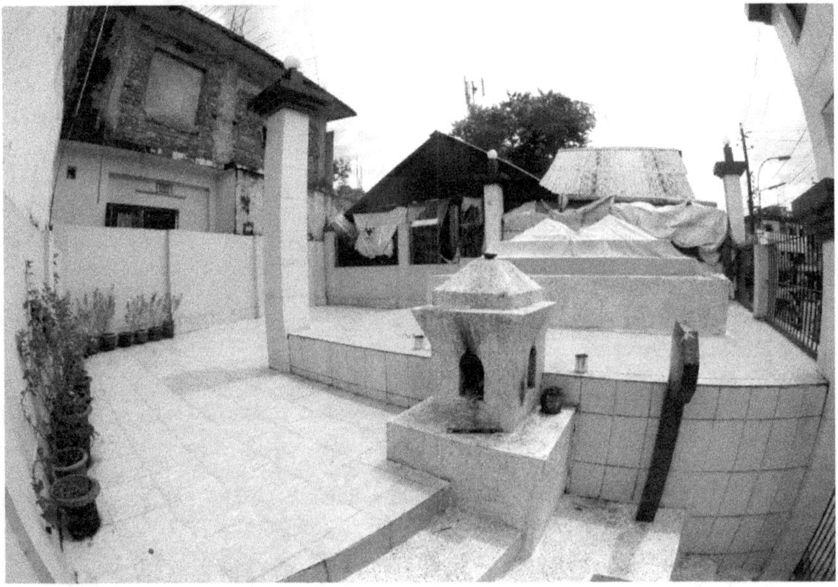

25.8.2010, 19:42:52

This place was a city place, adjacent to a road and you can hear the hustle and bustle in the distance. Walking up to it, it felt as I was walking in to a house with marble floor and wall. Each time presents and provides varying degree of sanctuary. Even though this was in the city, it preserved the peace, serenity and the tranquillity within it. You will hear me repeat this - that these places are peaceful, serene and tranquil, and I now attach, associate these descriptions to many of the mazars; and the experience of the "zapping" or quietening of the minds inhibitions. The pot of plants on the side added and homely, terrace garden feel.

Kaji Gayla Shah**

Kaji Tula, Sylhet Town

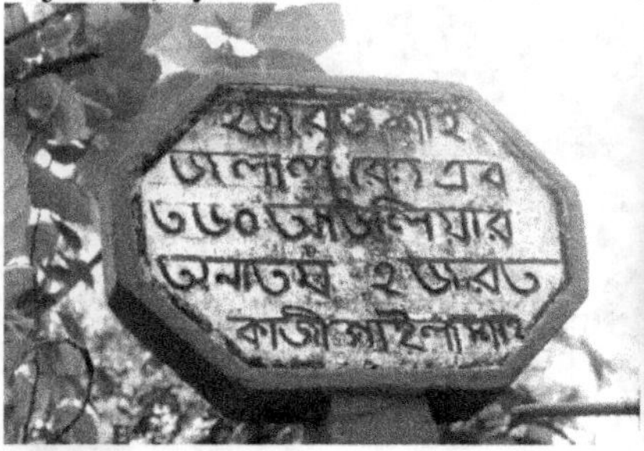
৩৬০ আউলিয়ার

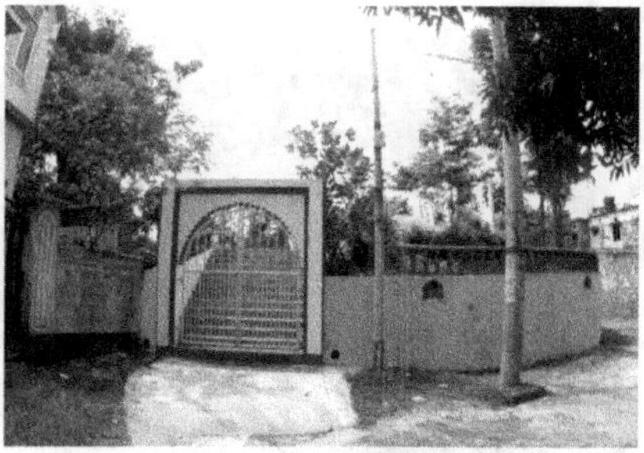

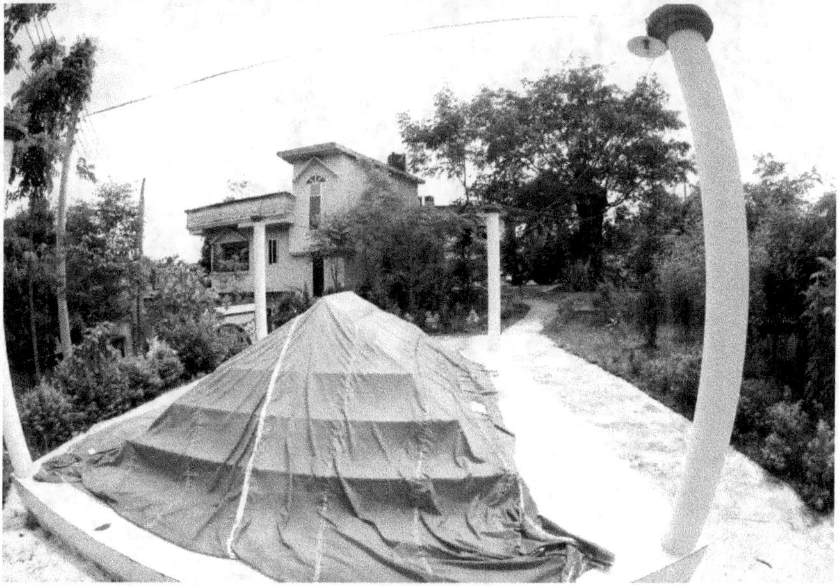

25.8.2010, 19:54:30

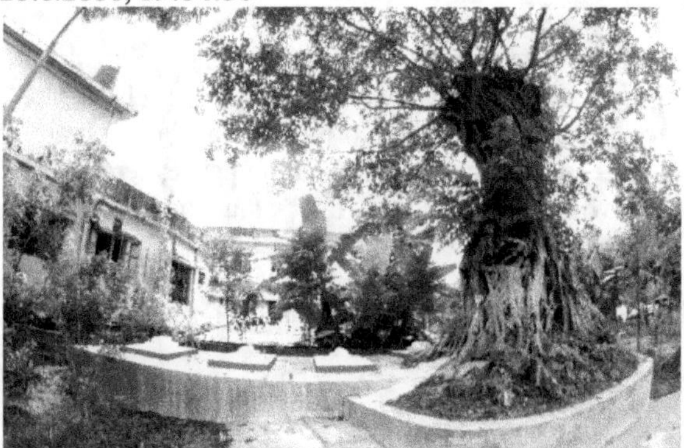

This place was a pleasant surprise, in an estate and the serenity and tranquillity engulfs you. It was under renovation and you can smell the fresh coat of paint and the concrete.

You have to go looking for this place.

Hazrat Bulbul

Noya Sorok, Sylhet

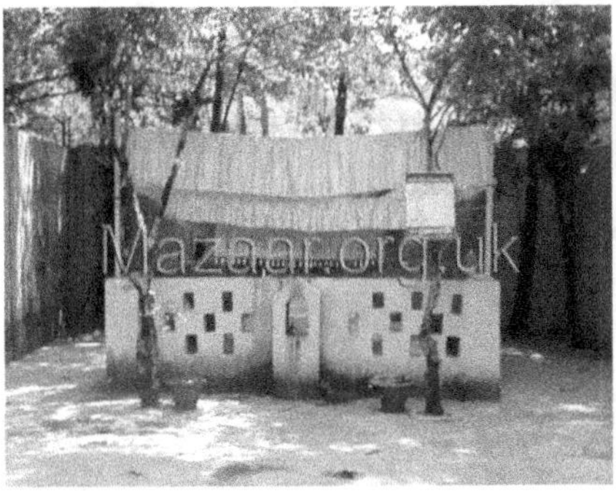
Mazaar.org.uk

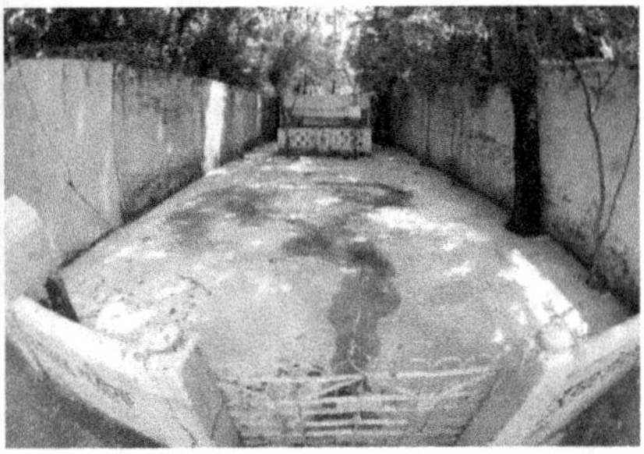

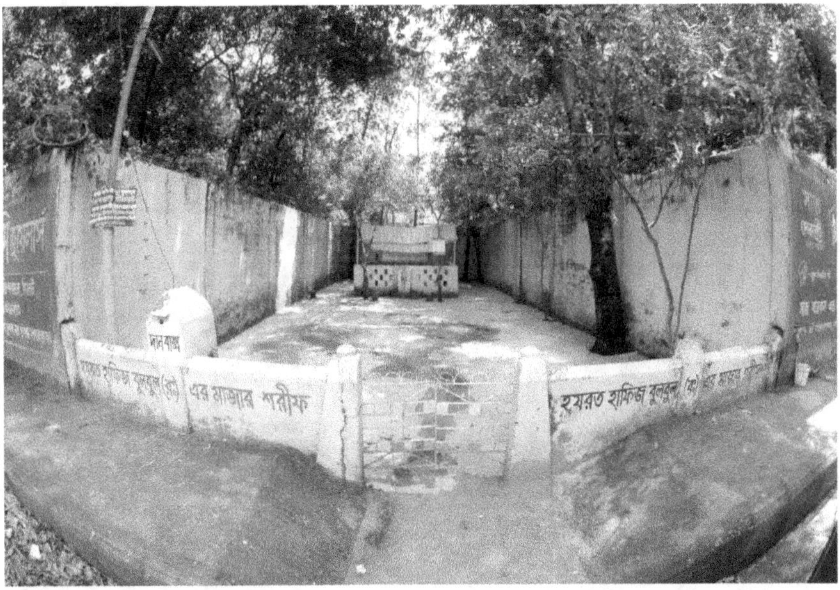

25.8.2010, 20:10:22

You can miss this place easily, walk by, it is tucked away, concealed, and at a glance you are looking at a concreted yard. It is only when you glance at the rear, which is when you realise what the place is; otherwise, to me it looked like a yard.

September 2010

Shah Kamal*

Supply Road, (by The Rai Hussain Mosque) Ambor Khana, Sylhet Town.

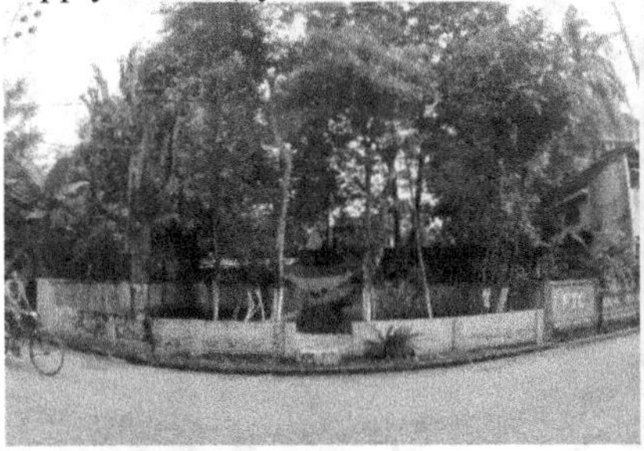

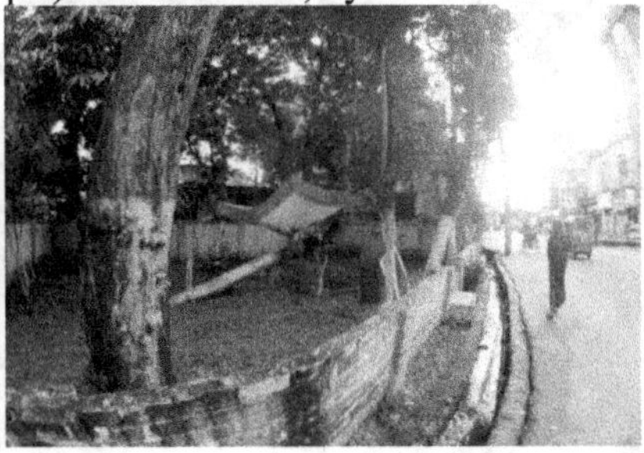

Kadim: Md Kowsar

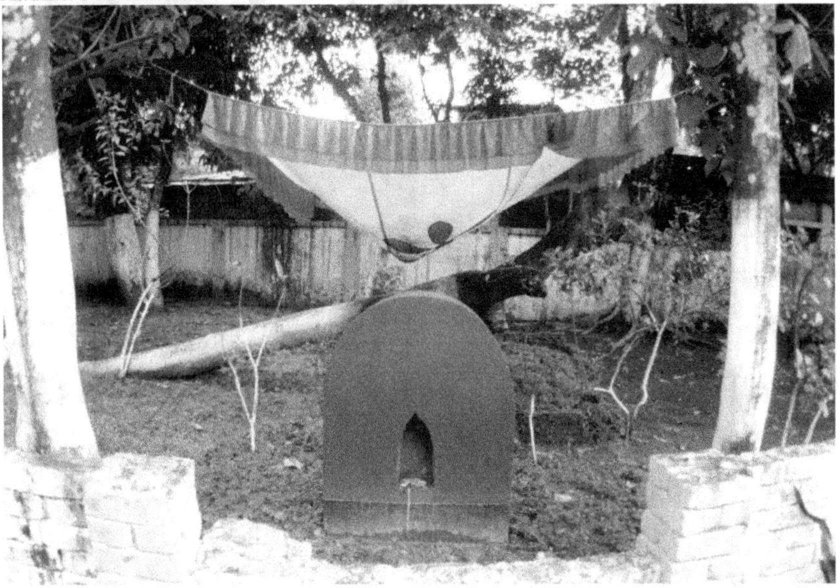

16.9.2010, 11:55:48

This site looked like a little side park/garden, but then you process what you see.

Soyod Umor Somorkandi**

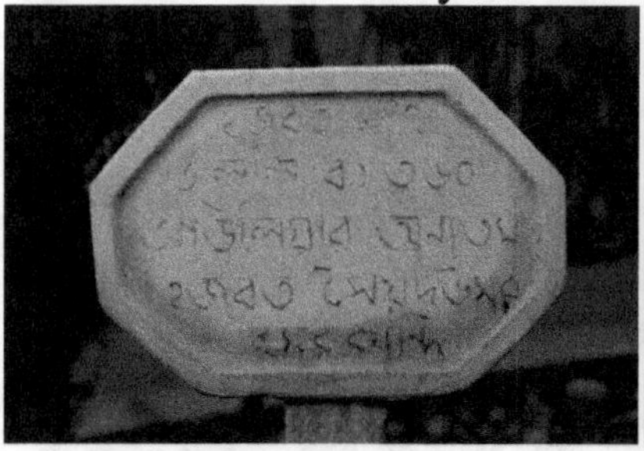

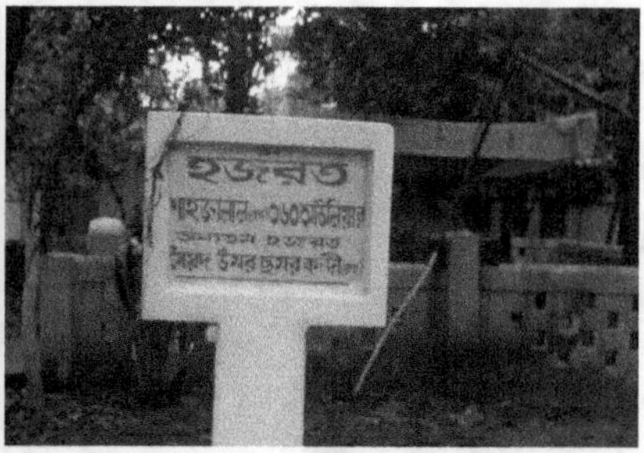
হজরত

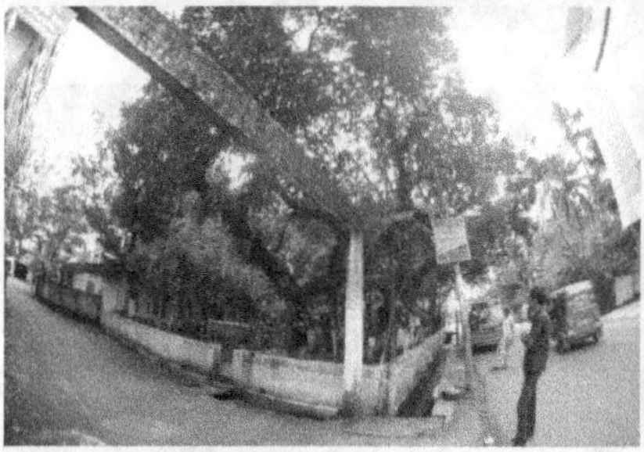

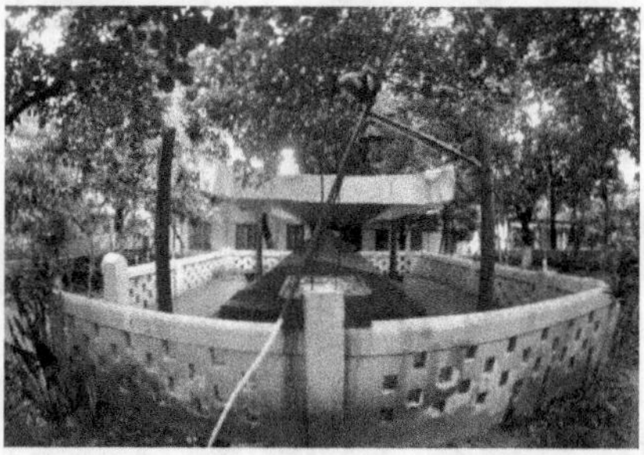

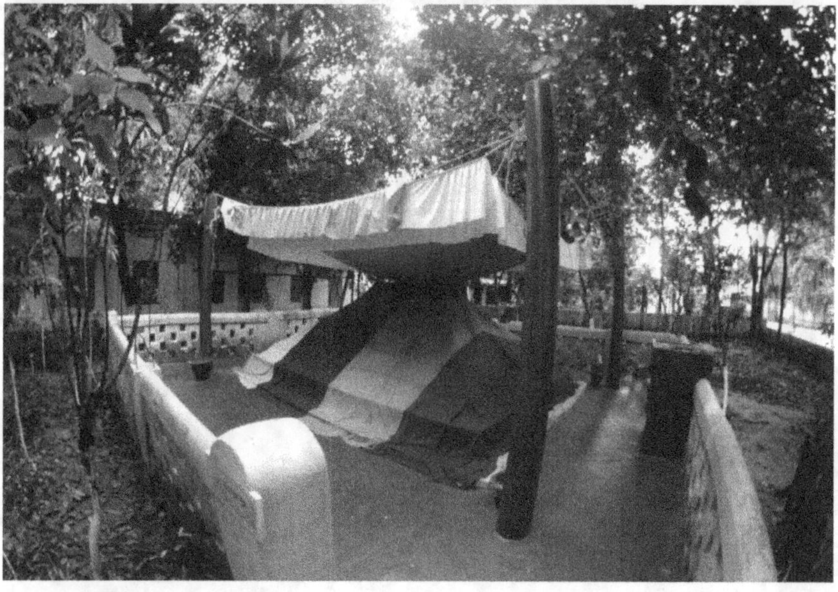

16.9.2010, 12:33:24

This was the person who was brave enough to confirm that Hazrat Shah Jalal had died and covered him up. He was close and strong companion.

Mowlana Shah Sufi Soyod Chand Ahmod Sichintja Qureshi

Dupadikir Purbo Par, Sylhet

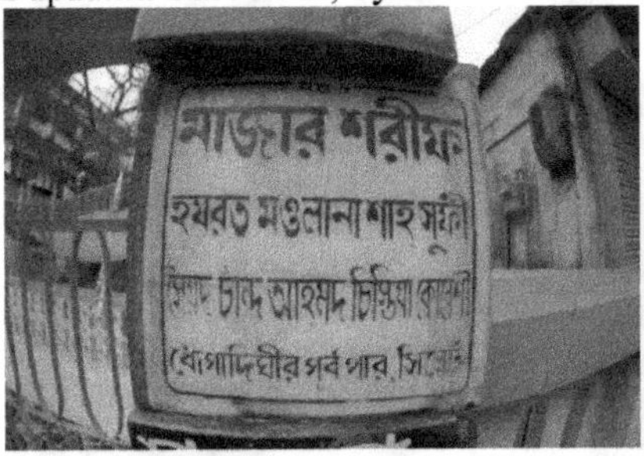
মাজার শরীফ
হযরত মওলানা শাহ সূফী

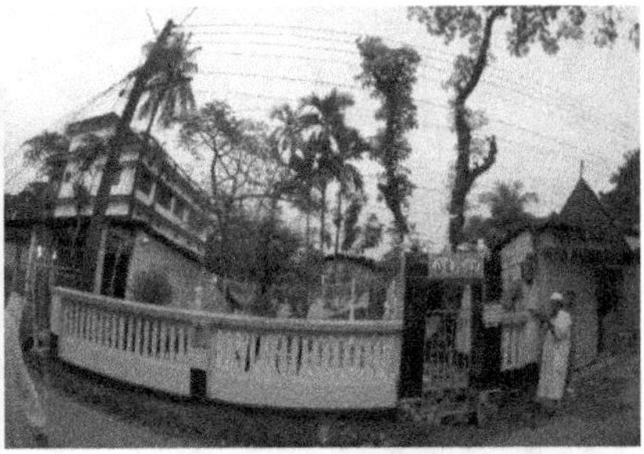

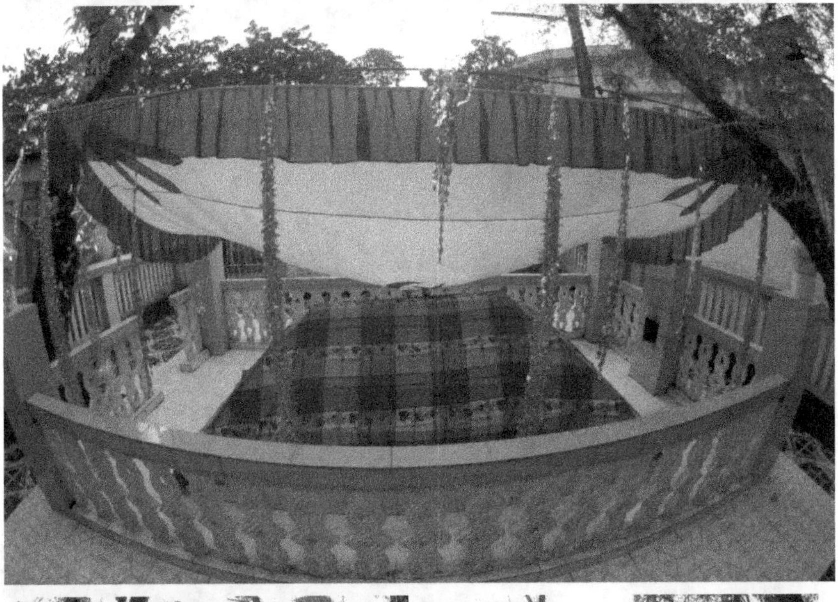

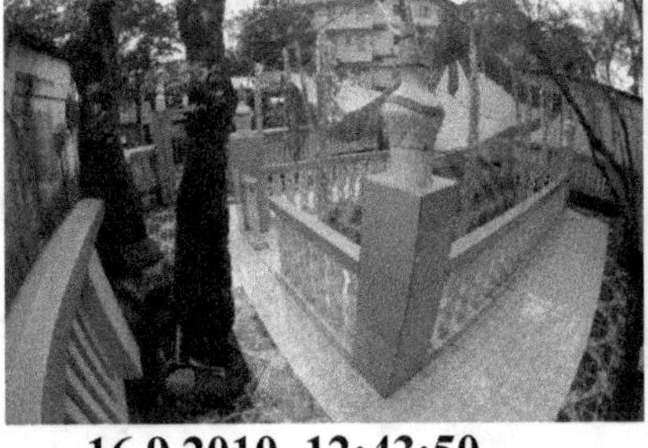

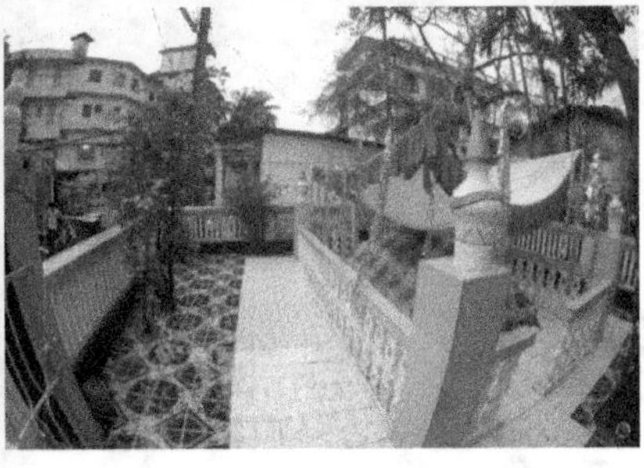

16.9.2010, 12:43:50

Dudu Shah

a.k.a.,
Mojlish Amin

Sylhet Town

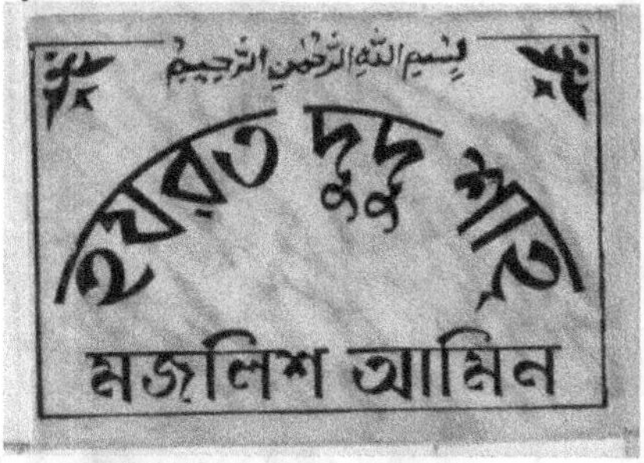
بسم الله الرحمن الرحيم
হযরত দুদু শাহ
মজলিশ আমিন

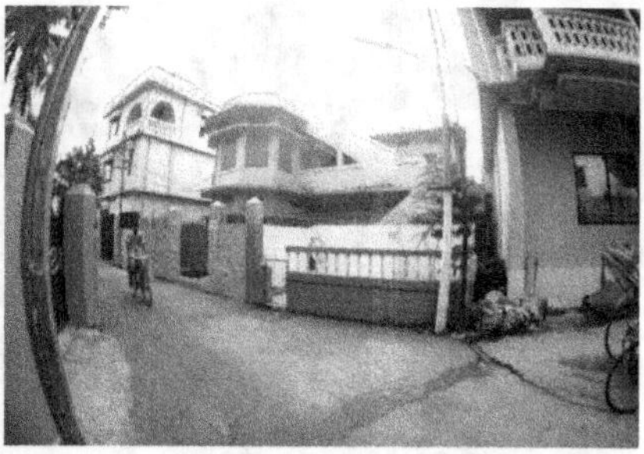

16.9.2010, 12:50:56

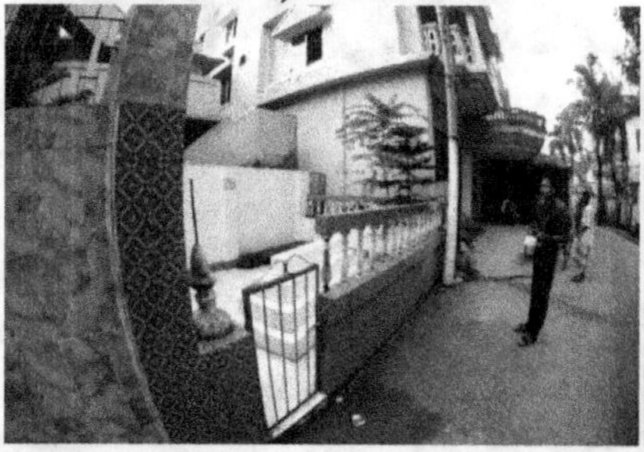

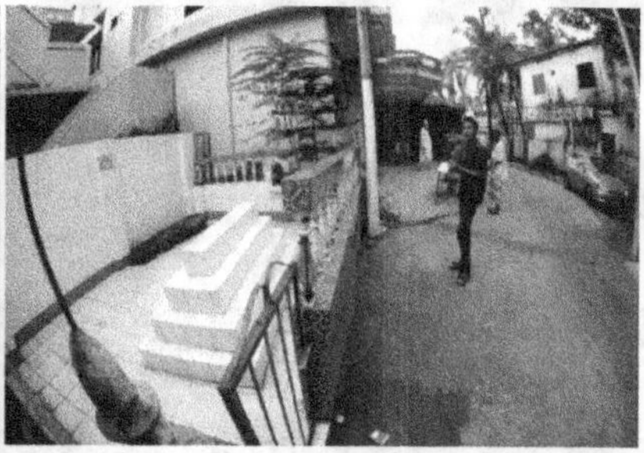

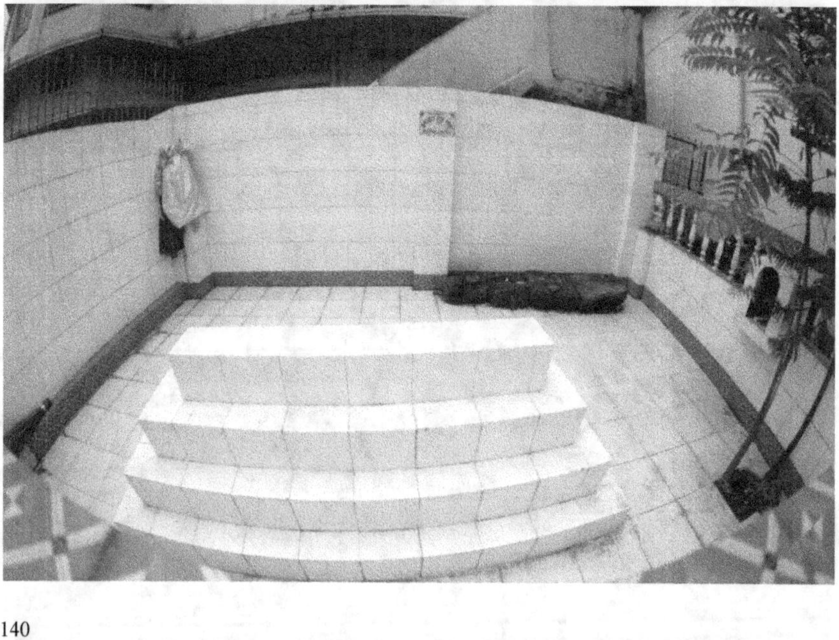

Mojlish Amin*

Sara Dikir Par

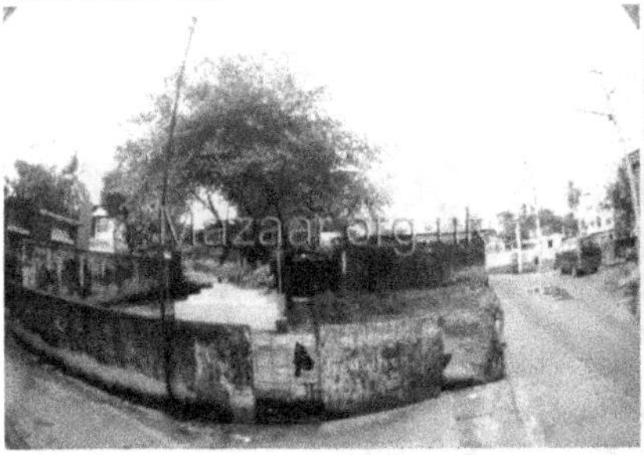
Mazaar.org.uk

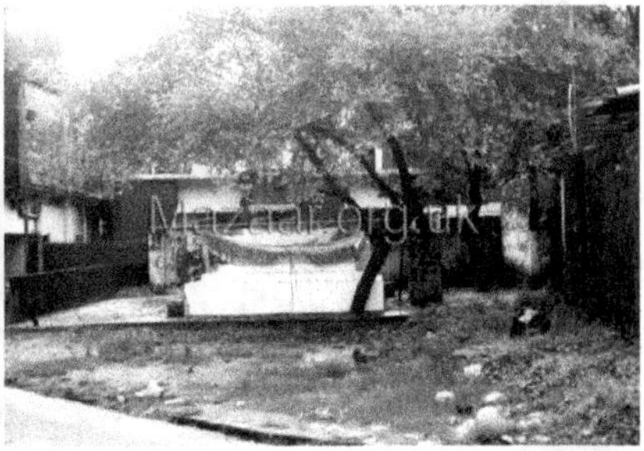
Mazaar.org.uk

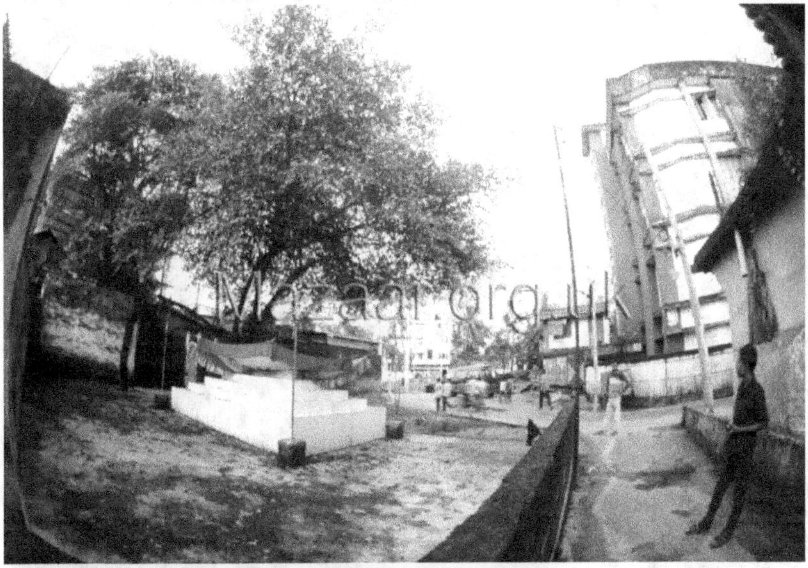
Mazaar.org.uk

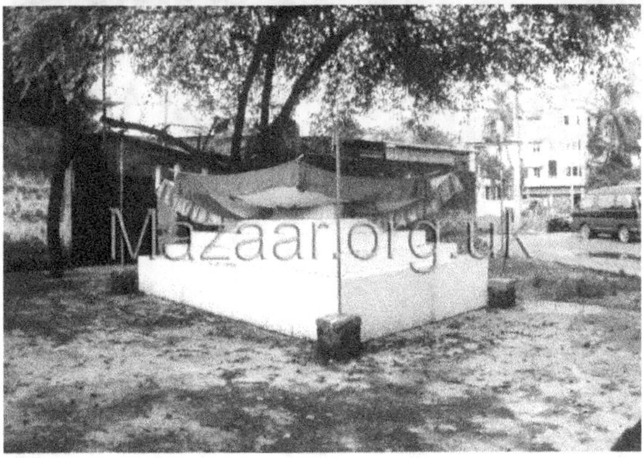
Mazaar.org.uk

As can been seen it is situated in a middle of an estate. While the whole place concreted up, it is not kept as others.

16.9.2010

Soyod Husain Shab

a.k.a.,

Gorom Phir

Sun Shadagor Bari, Shodagor Tullah, Sylhet Town.

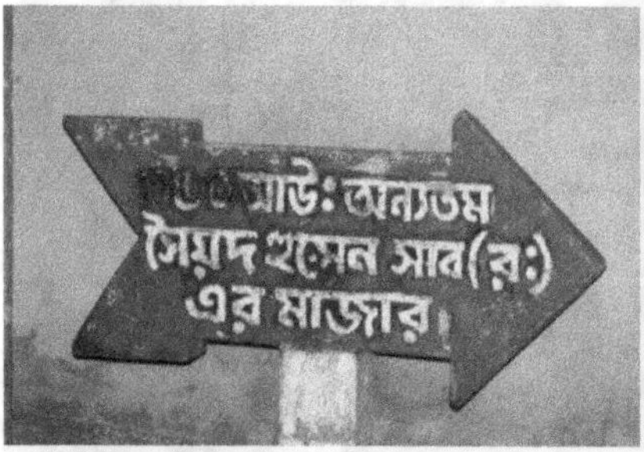
অন্যতম
সৈয়দ হুসেন সাব(র:)
এর মাজার।

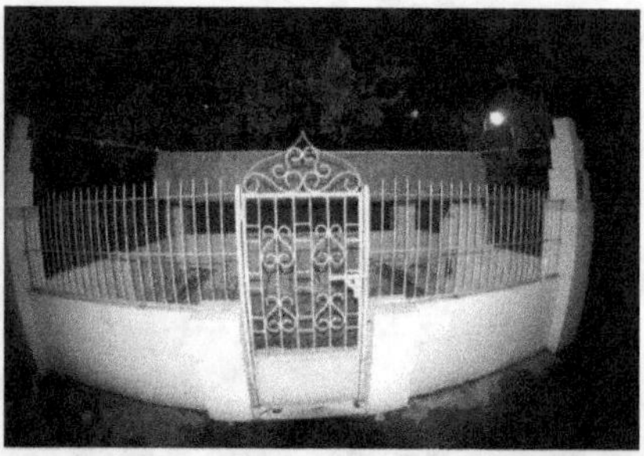

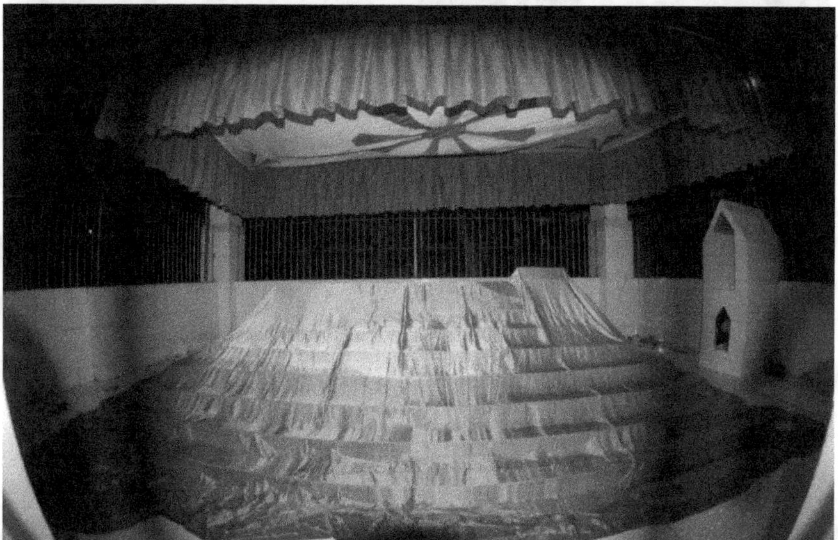

16.9.2010,

Shah Soyod Shamsuddin**

Soyod pur

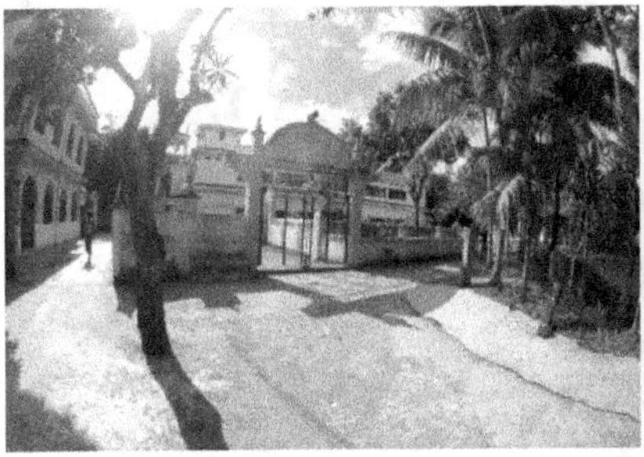
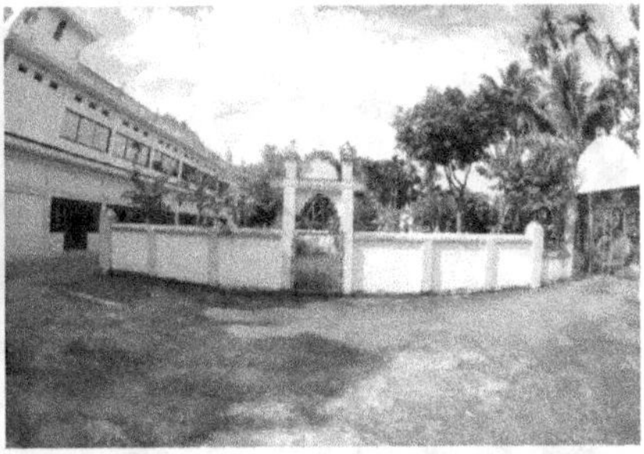
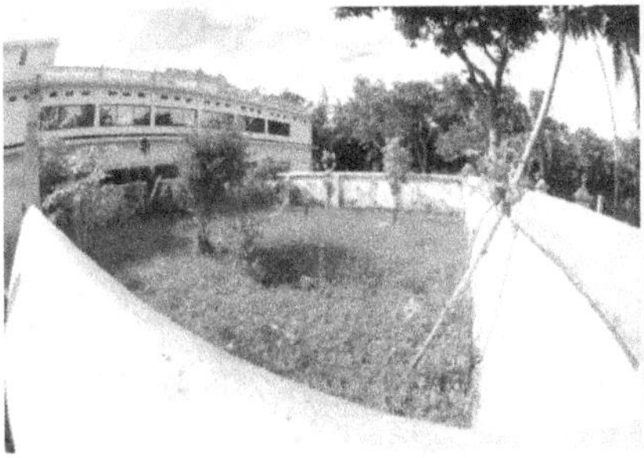
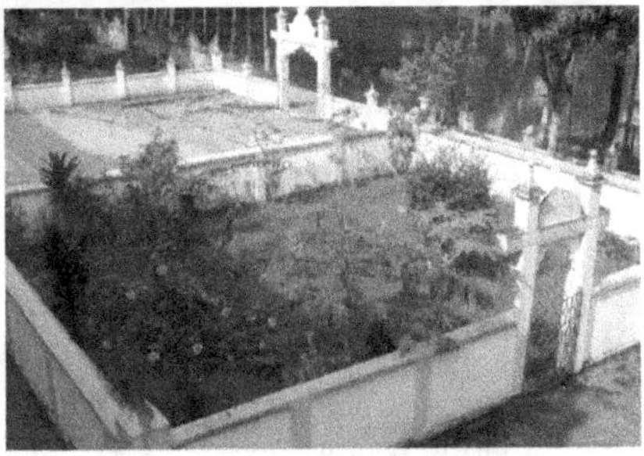

19.9.2010, 09:42:50

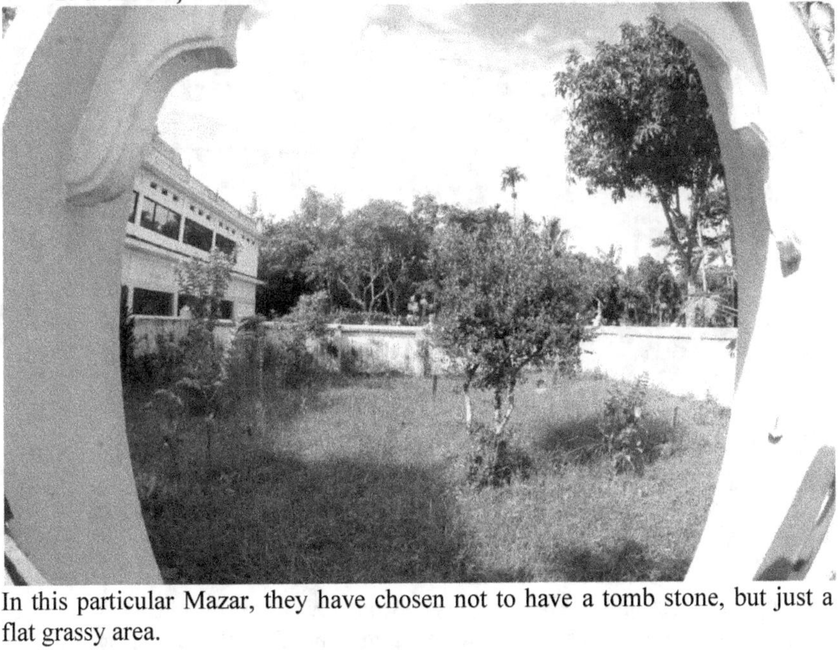

In this particular Mazar, they have chosen not to have a tomb stone, but just a flat grassy area.

Shah Kamali**

Shahar Parah,

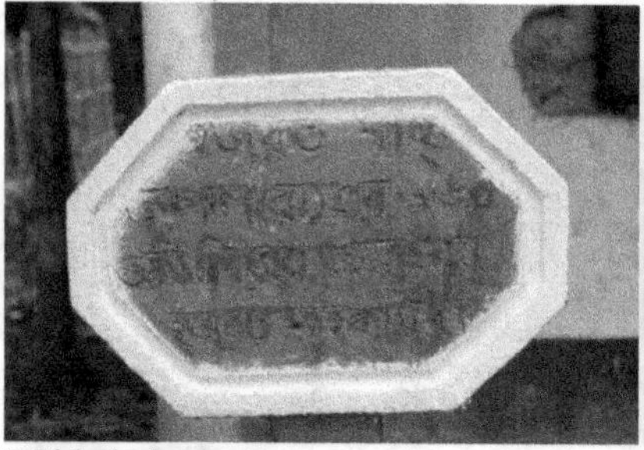

8 Sided plaque

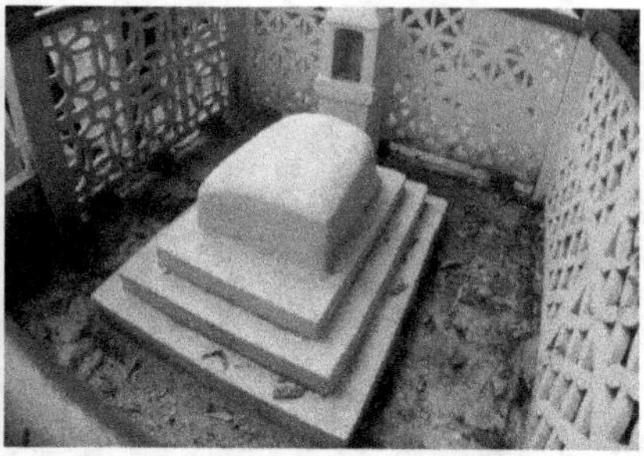

Prayer stone

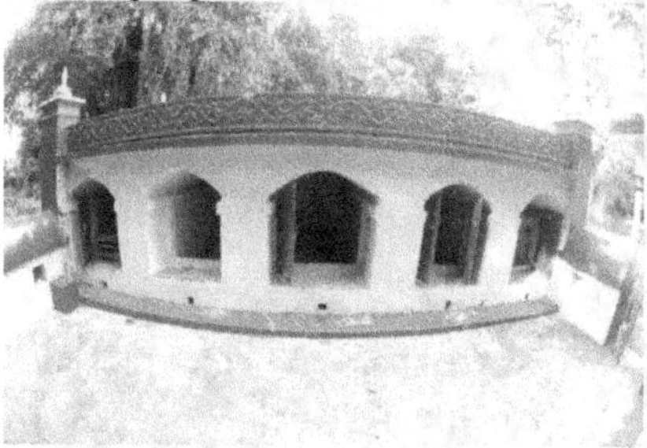

Contemplation rooms

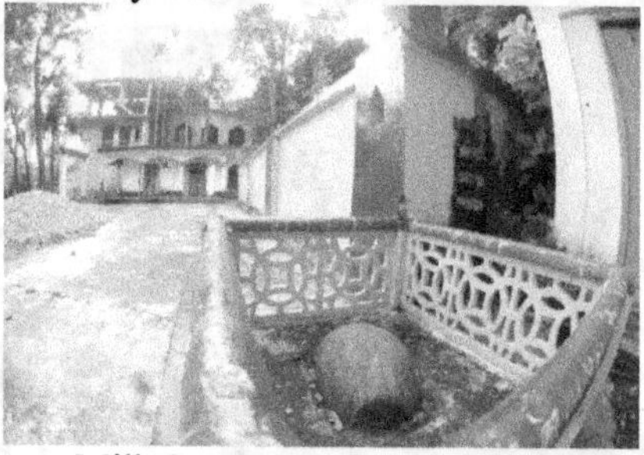

Milk Stone

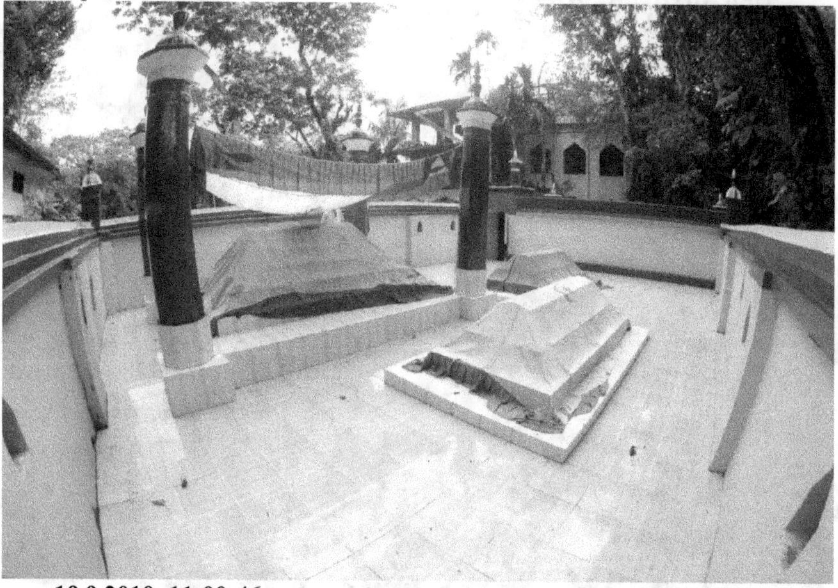

19.9.2010, 11:00:46

Tile up in white and red pillars, visually attractive, clean and well managed feeling. I was zapped there. This was my mum's mum's ancestral mazar.

Shahr Poragol Khan

In Shahar Parah,

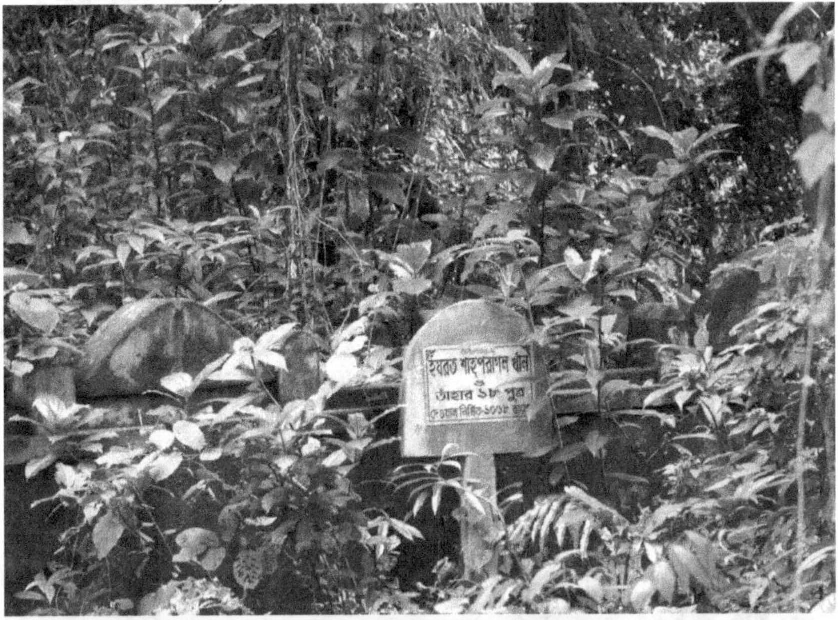

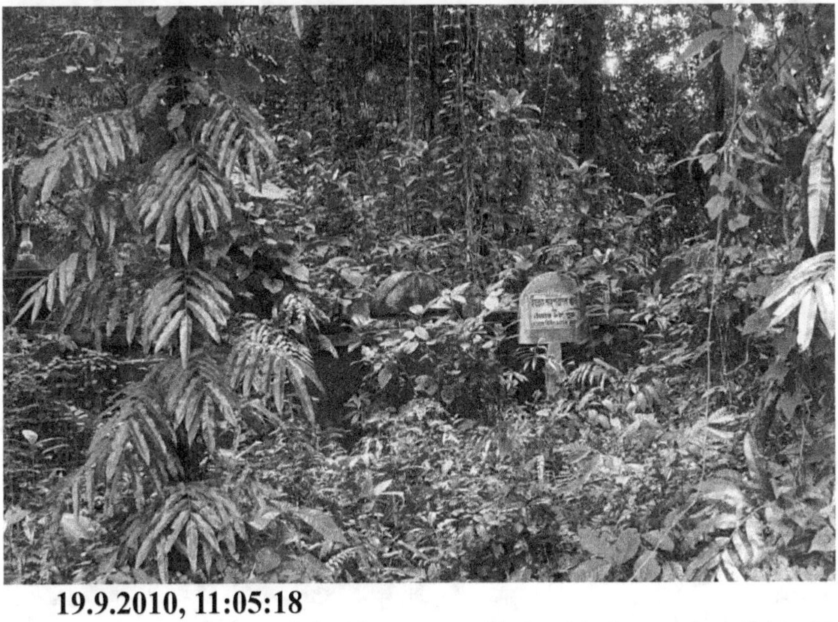

19.9.2010, 11:05:18

This is in dense foliage, and the history according to local goes, that all his 18 sons died all at once, they dropped dead.

Shah Jamal

2nd Son of Shah Kamali of Shahar Parah

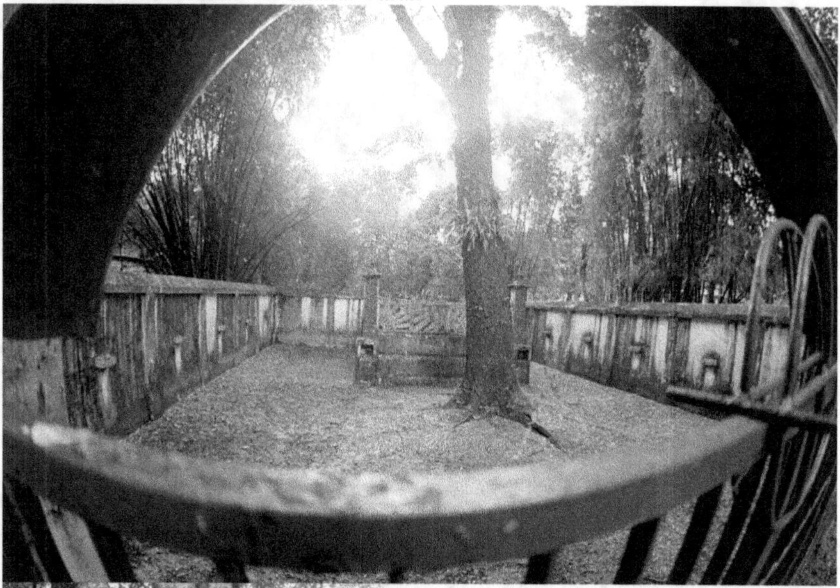

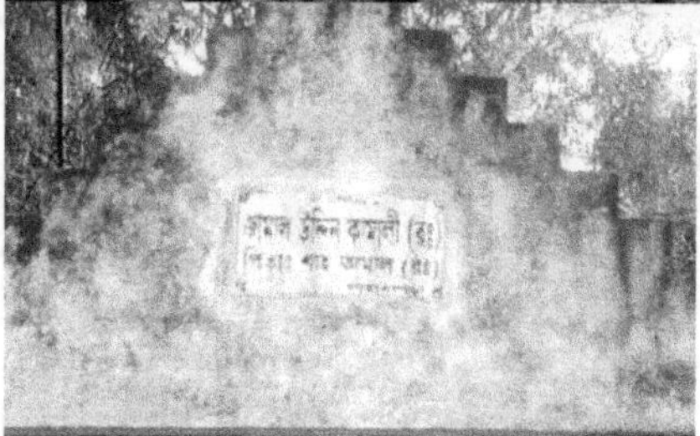

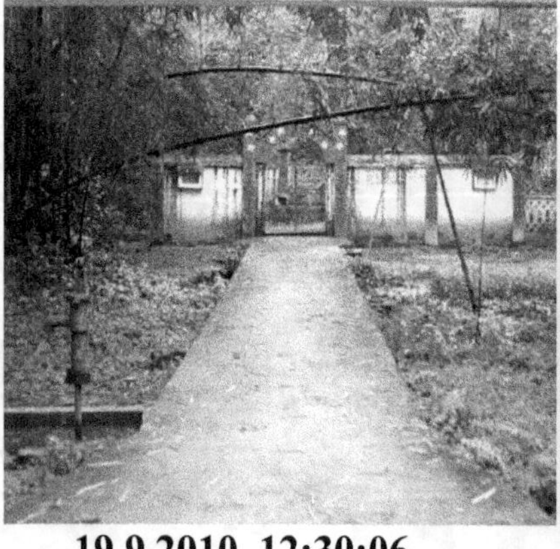

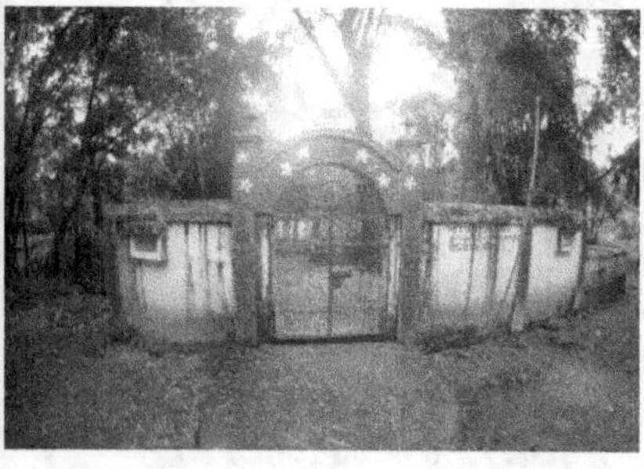

19.9.2010, 12:30:06

Shah Kala Manik*

Shahar Parah

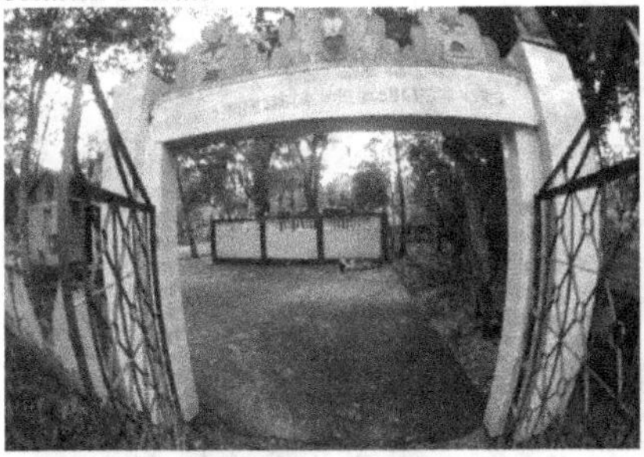

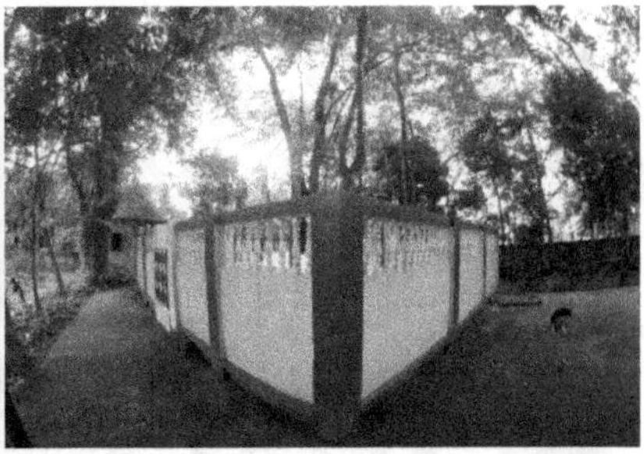

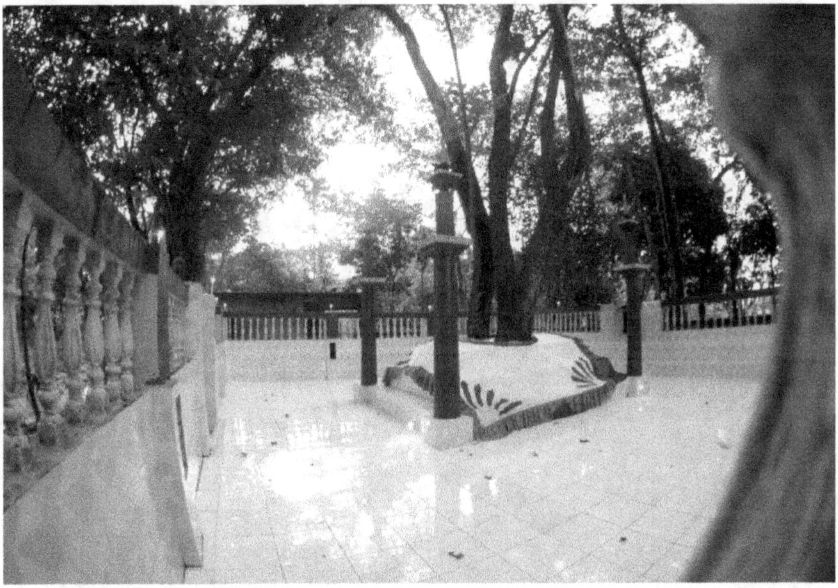

19.9.2010, 12:43:00

This was another surprise, from the outside it looks like typical site. Once you enter inner sanctum, it is all tiled up. White and light reflecting of it and also looks clean in the eye.

This site is nearby to Hazrat Shah Kamali.

Tobiz Shah

Rai Khali

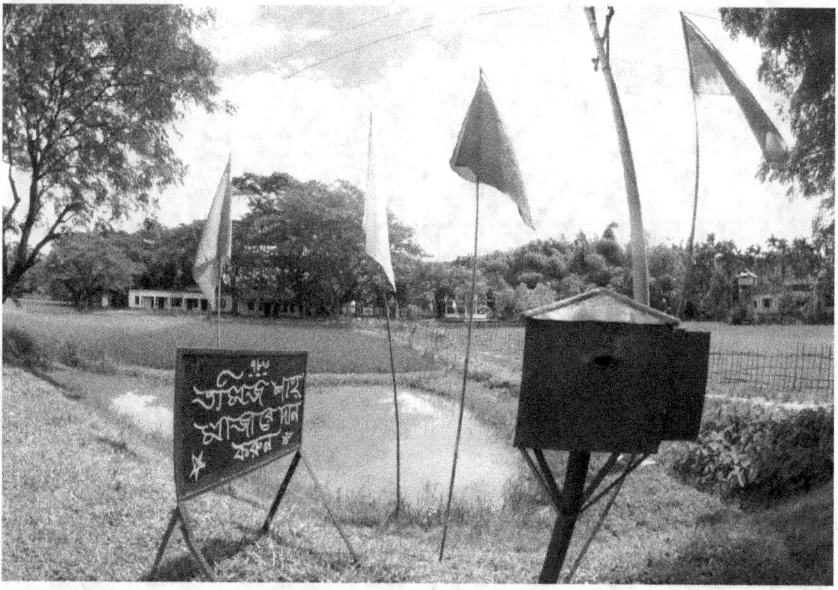
৭৮৬
তমিজ শাহ্
মাজারে দান
করুন

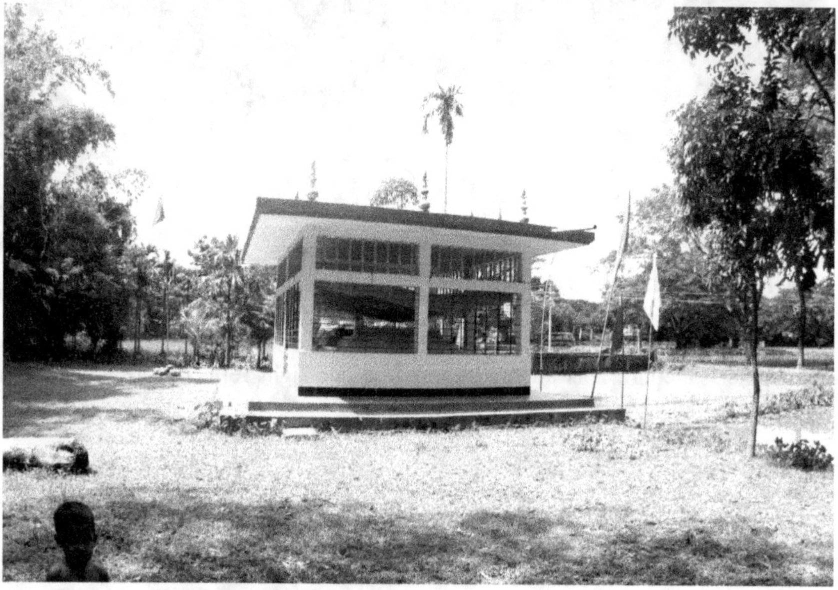

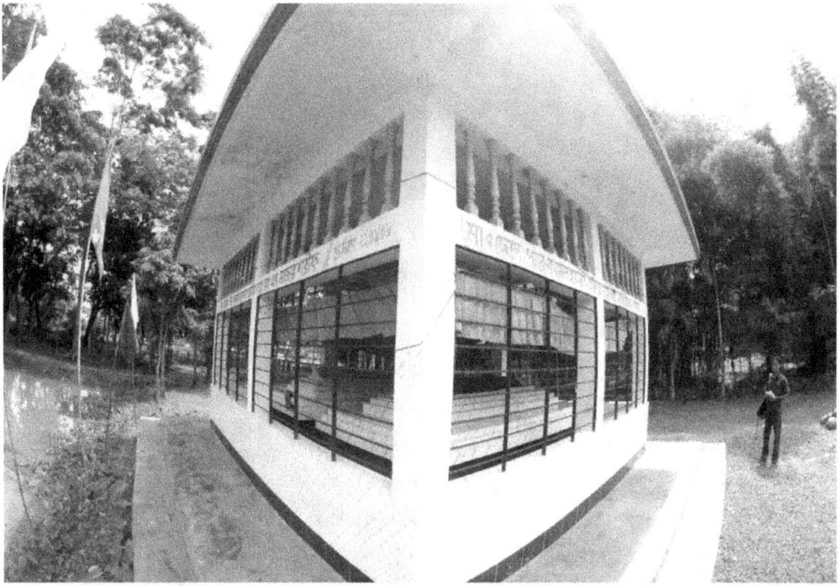

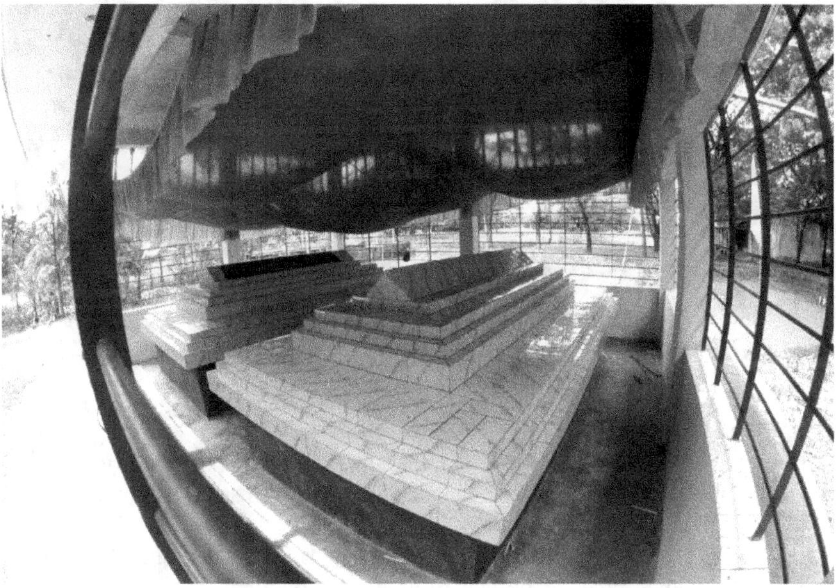

19.9.2010, 19:54:18

This isn't certified with an 8 side plaque.

Sun Borung

Sun Borung, Bishwanath

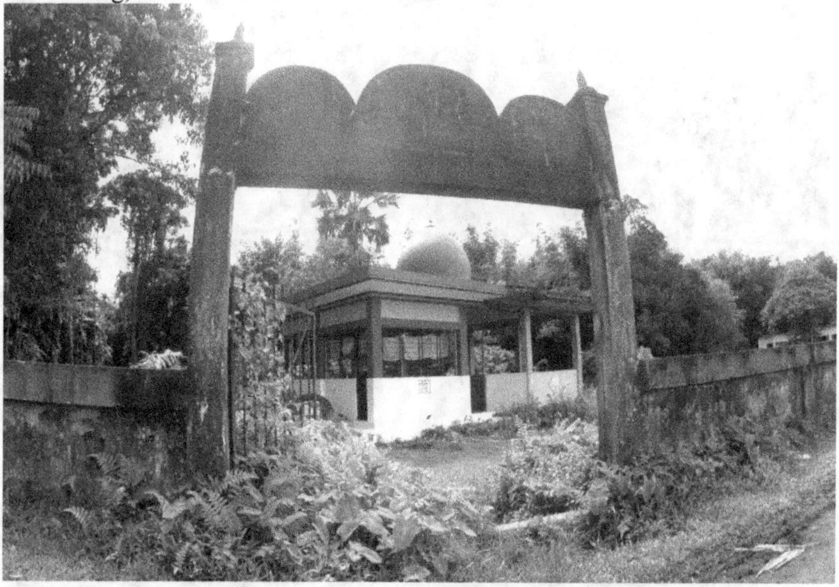

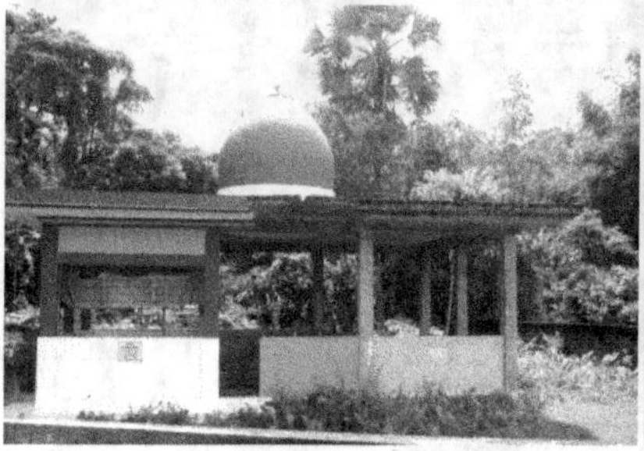

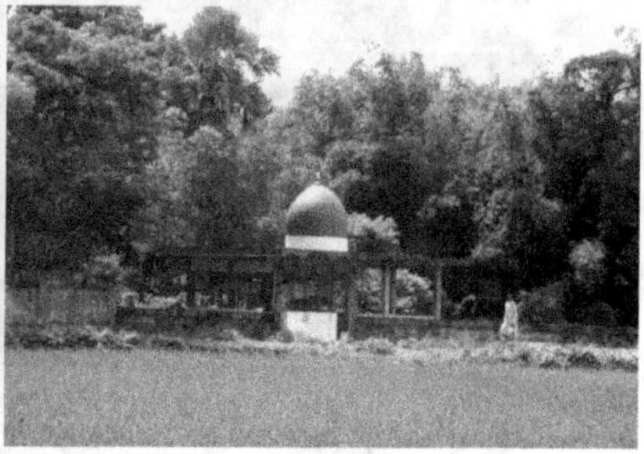

19.9.2010, 20:07:50

The locality is named after this person, for some reason this was a just a roadside, shot. I didn't go into the yard as it was overgrowing with weeds.

I didn’t feel sure or safe, unlike many others that I just went in; even the one where I got stung 6 times by hornets. It was a very painful experience.

Shah Kalu

Sun Borung, Bishwanath

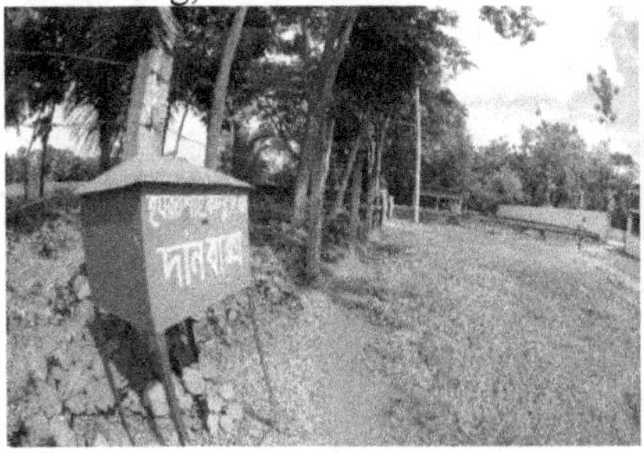

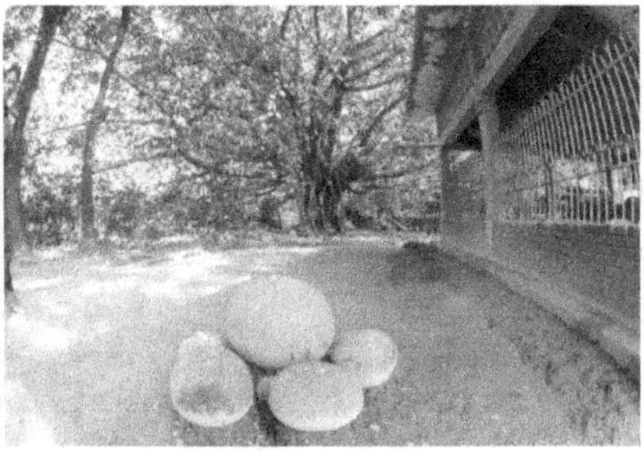

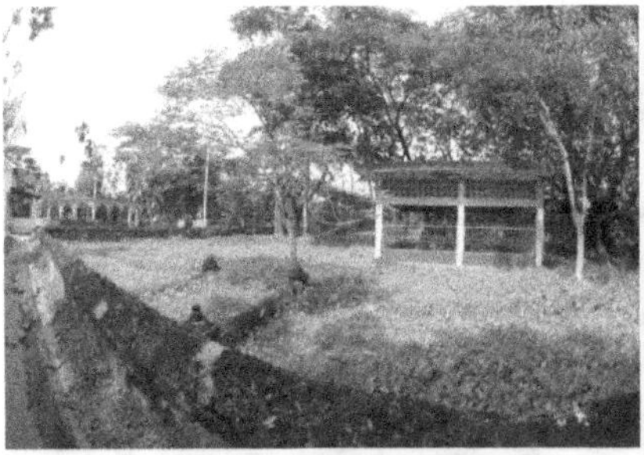

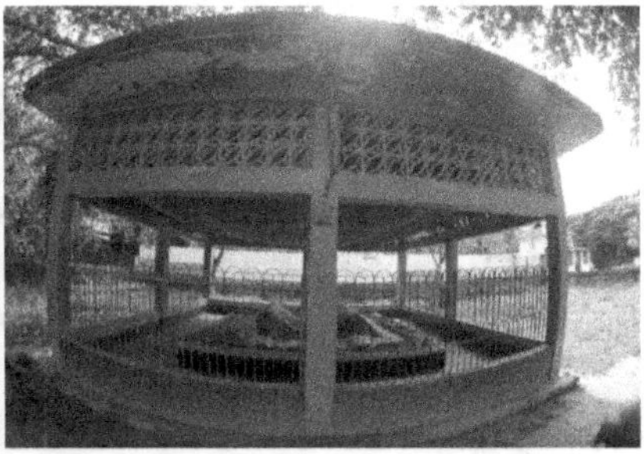

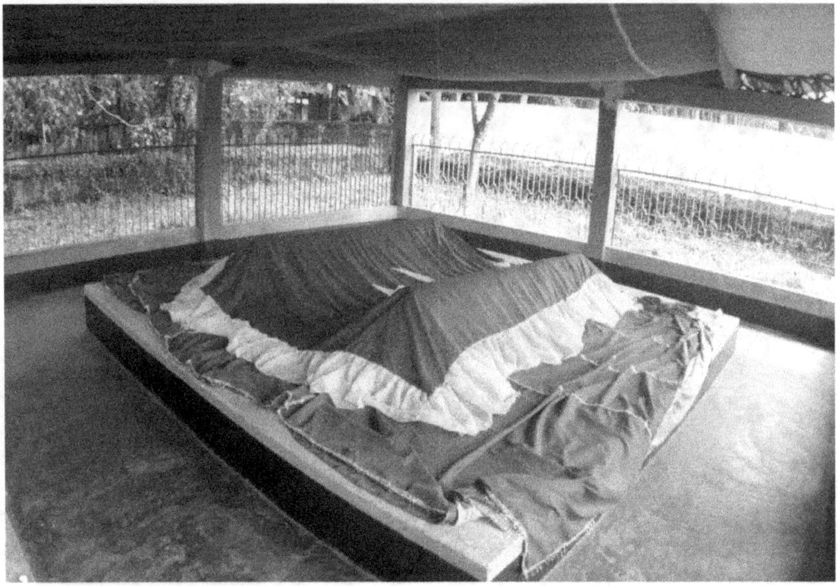

19.9.2010 20:16:14

Shah Sund

Sun Borung, Bishwanath

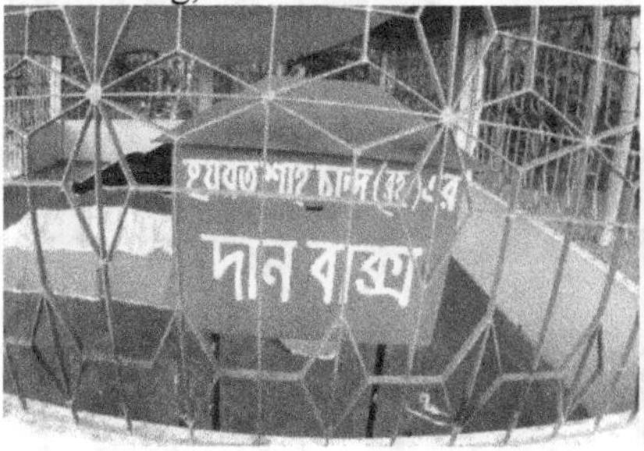
হযরত শাহ চান্দ (রহ:) এর
দান বাক্স

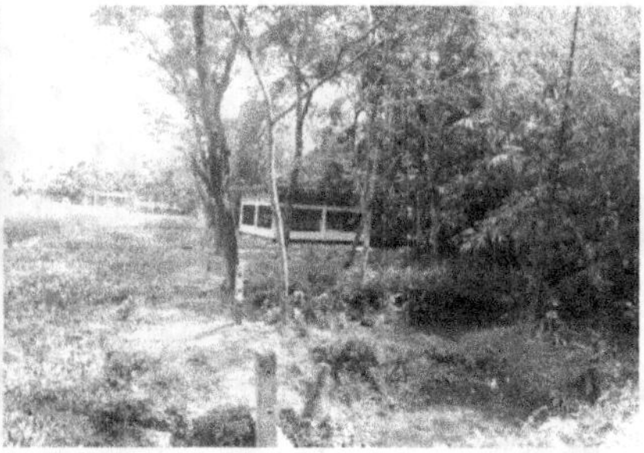

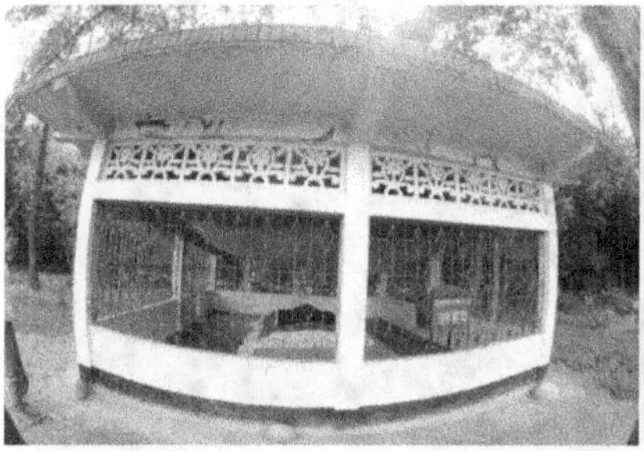

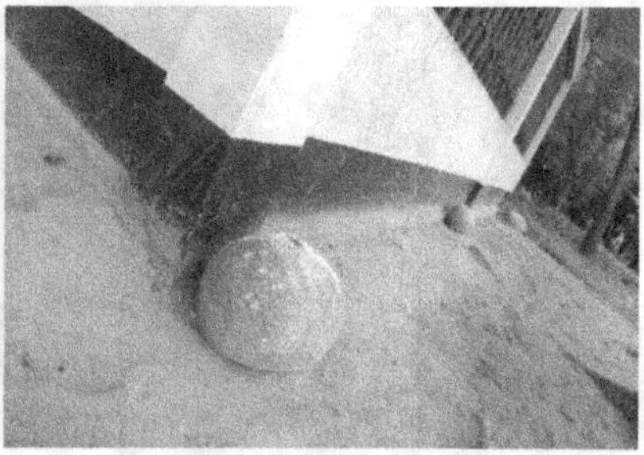

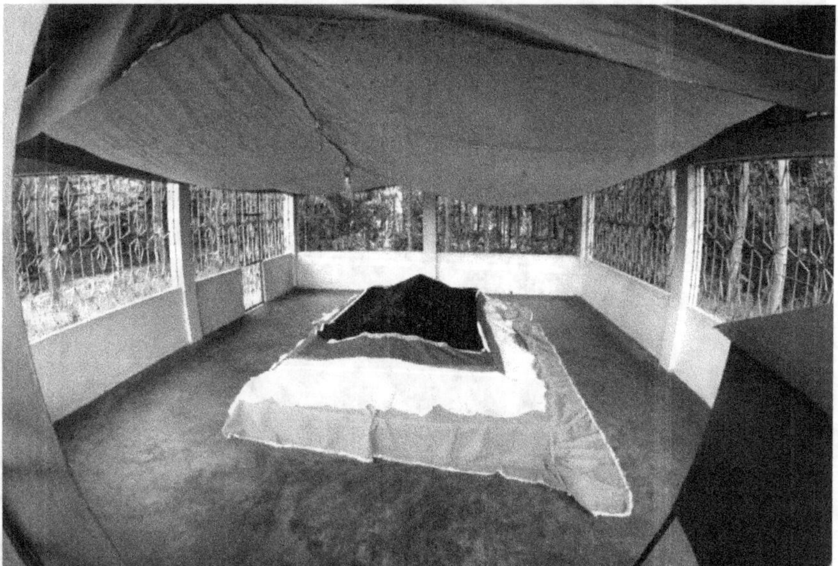

19.9.2010, 20:28:42

Shah Solim Oli

Uttar Dowrai, Jogonath Pur, Sylhet

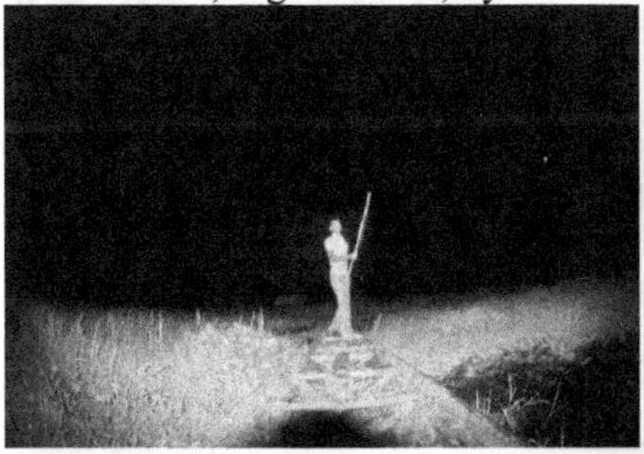

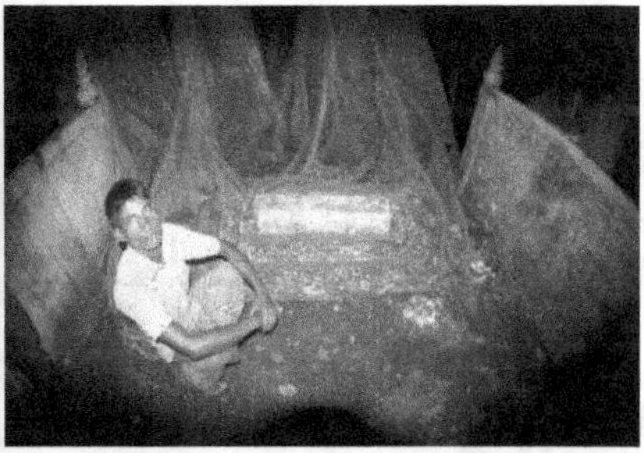

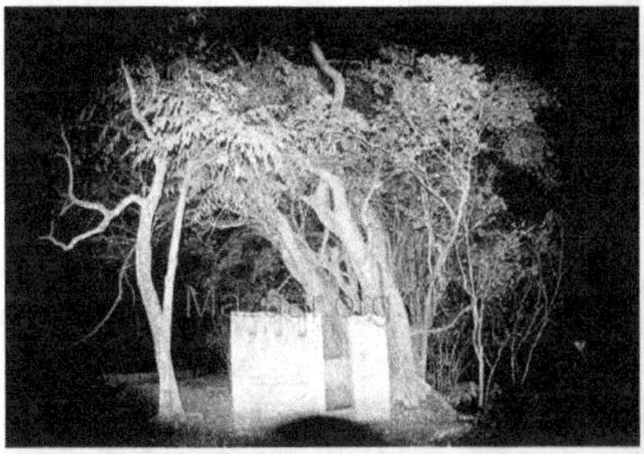

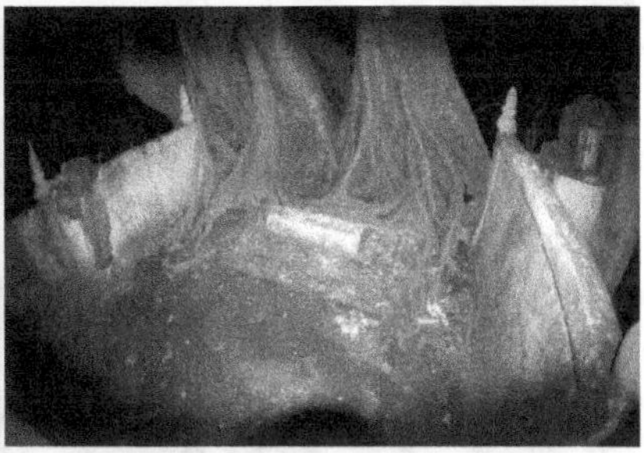

This was night time

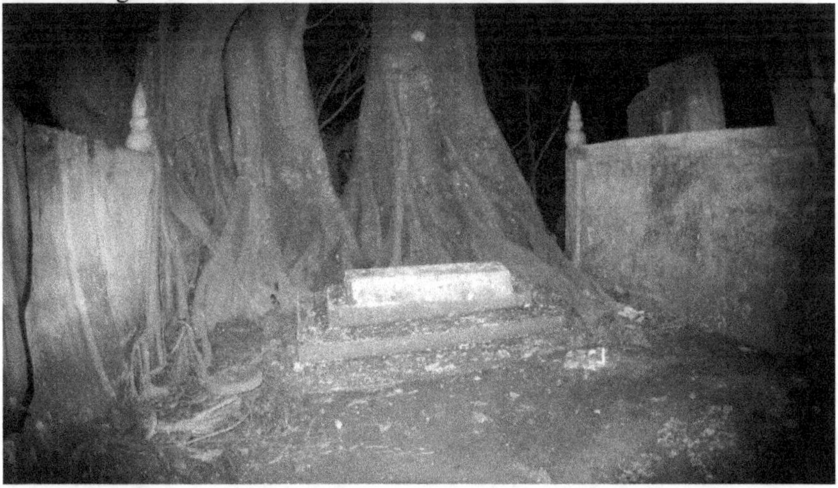

Moynur Rahman – son of the Kadim, he was very helpful. He went out of his way to get us to see the mazar, at night and in the water. He rowed the boat to the mazar. Also thanks to Abdur Rohim and his family for letting us use their boat.

19.9.2010,

Asrob Shah

Off the N2 Motorway

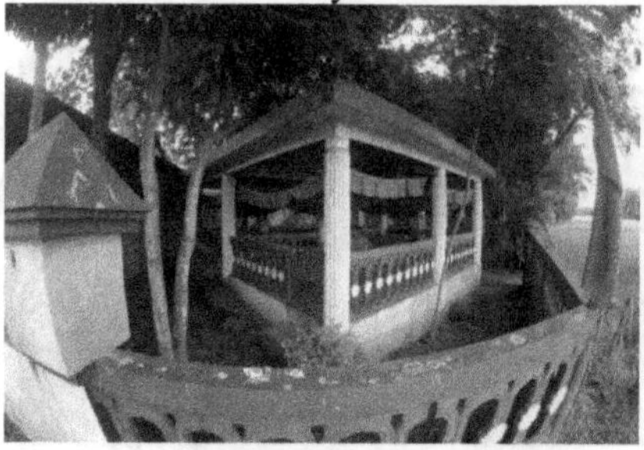

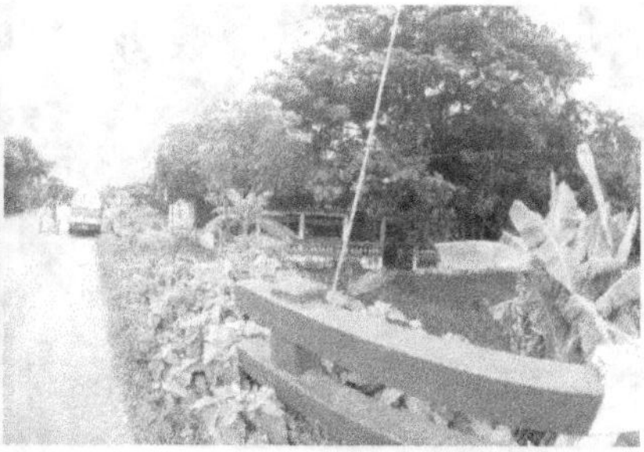

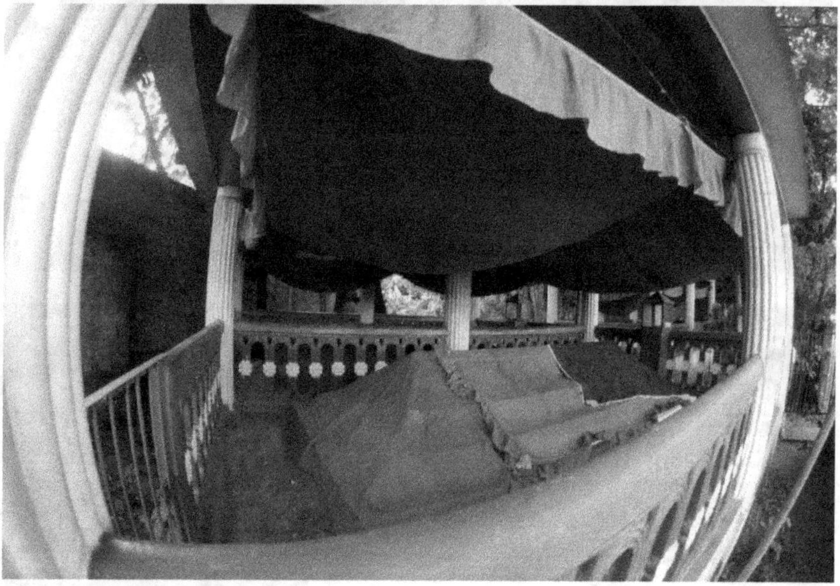

20.9.2010, 09:30:50

This was local individuals Mazar, in their garden. This wasn't far from Guala Bazar and towards Sylhet.

Shah Gorom Dewan

N2 Motorway.

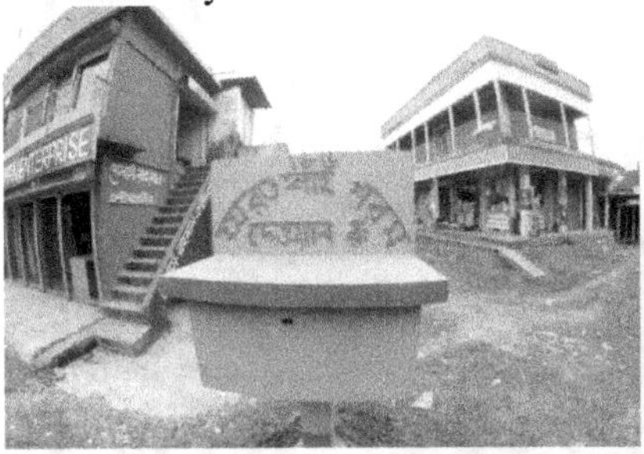

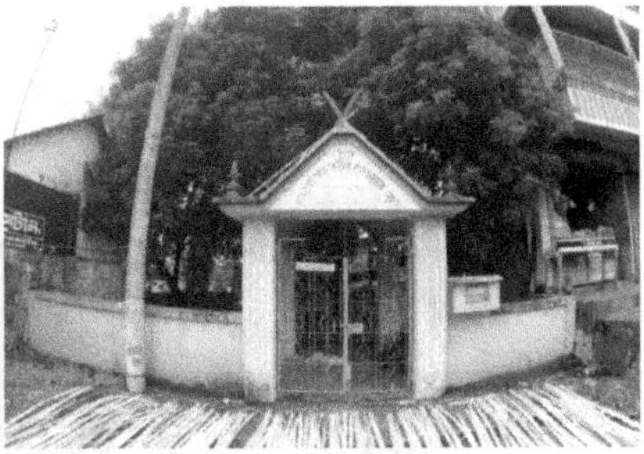

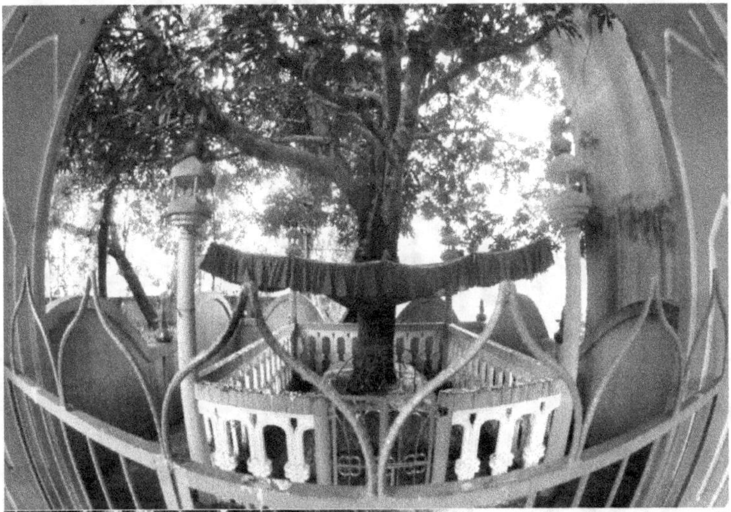

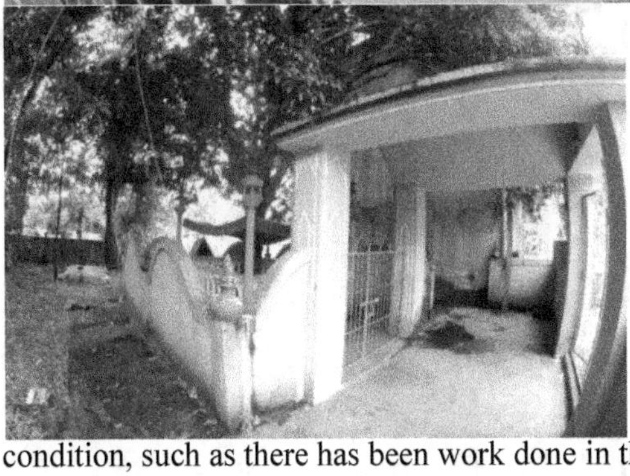

This place is on its way to Sylhet. It is a stopping point en-route for Sylhet Town off the N2 motorway. This place is a small shopping market place and the mazar is situated within the market complex.

It is built up, but not well maintained, Most of the Mazar generally are in this condition, such as there has been work done in the past, and an annual make over takes place, and the visuals change through the seasons, where you have the rotted leaves, bird droppings and candle wax, which overtime get weathers.

20.9.2010, 09:43:04

Konai Shah

a.k.a.,

Kazna Fokir

On the N2 Motorway

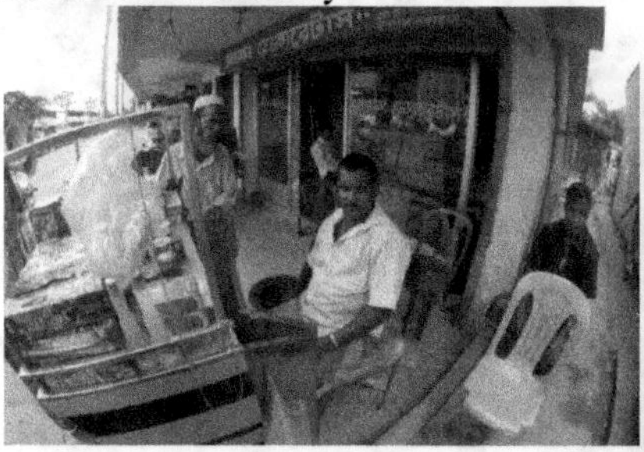

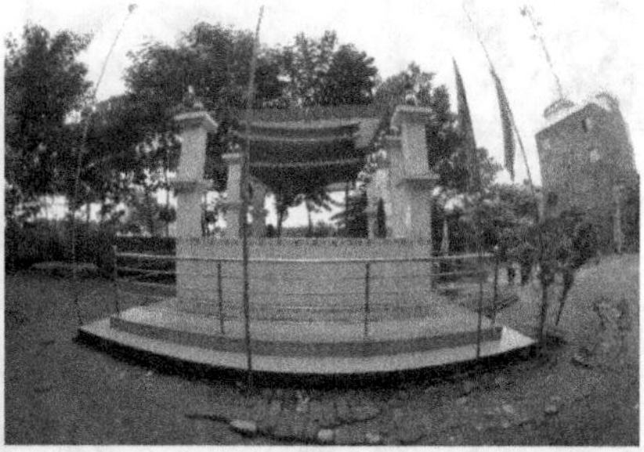

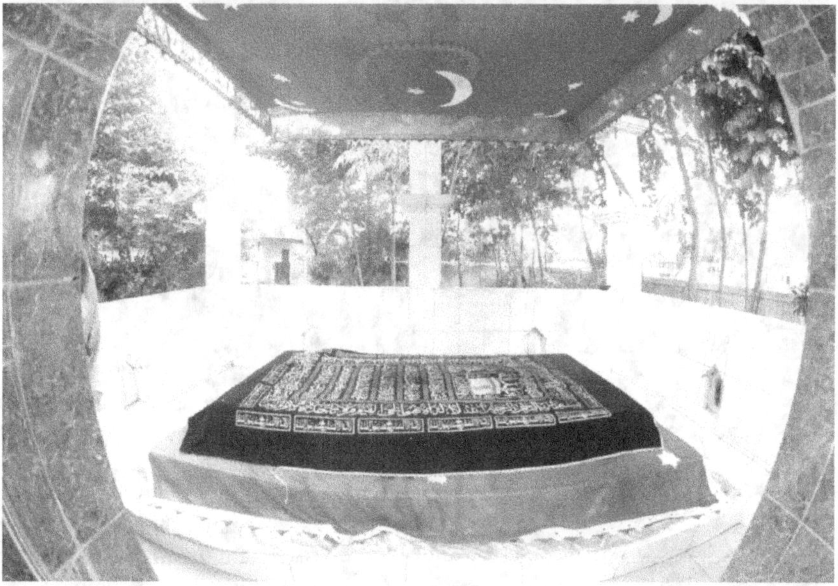

20.9.2010, 9:58:26

This person is not a member of the 306 missionaries.

Suley Shah*

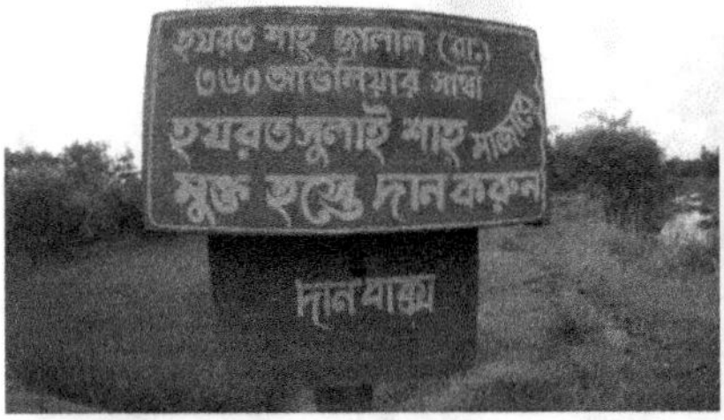
হযরত শাহ জালাল (রঃ)
৩৬০ আউলিয়ার সাথী
হযরত সুলাই শাহ মাজার
মুক্ত হস্তে দান করুন
দান বাক্স

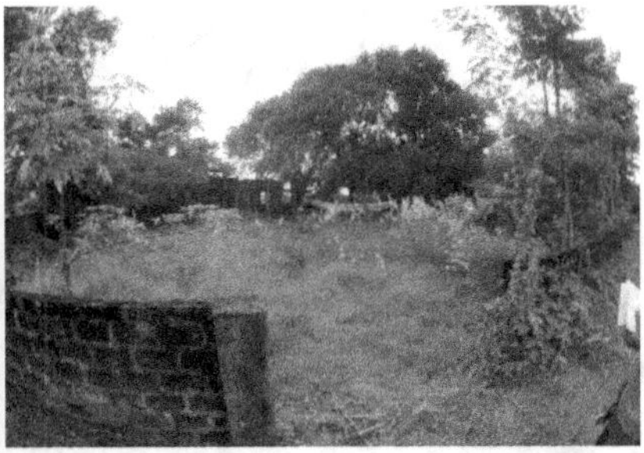

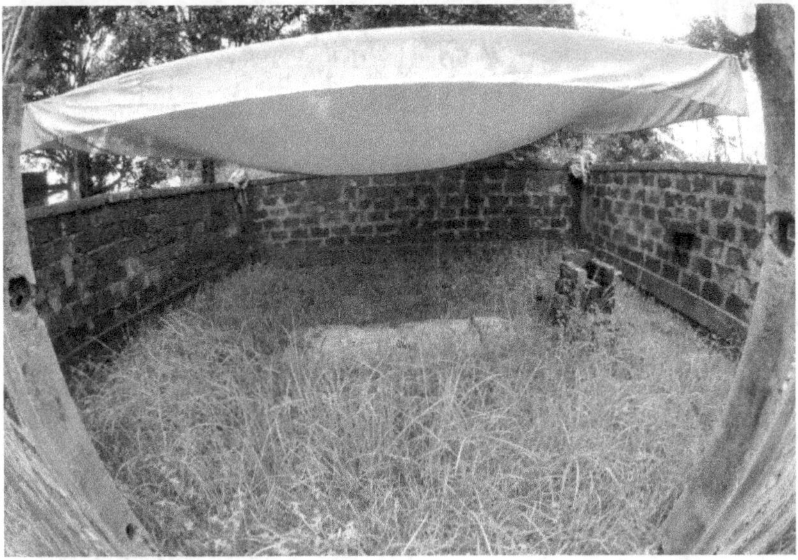

20.9.2010, 10:16:36

Having visited these places and have been witnessing the locations. I grew accustomed to what to expect. Each experience has been different and has served well. I didn't know my purpose when I begun; at the time it was madness, however, something in the mind kept pinging – it's the "method."

Little did I realise what was happening to me! The method in this madness was that I was getting strong, mentally, emotional, any concern or fear of dying disappeared, I no longer had chill, shiver, judder or miss a heartbeat when I thought about dying, meeting my maker.

I didn't know what I was doing, but the madness had a plan for me, I only realised this had happened because – as an introspective person I will contemplate and analyse things; after I returned from Dhaka, all fears and negativity disappeared.

Zinzir Shah

a.k.a.,

Nasir Husen Fokir

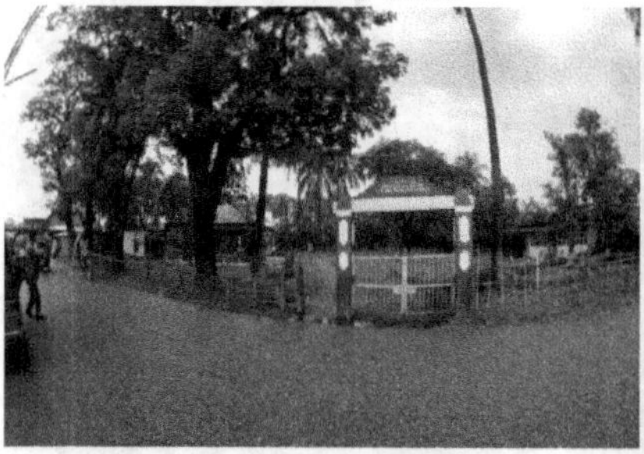

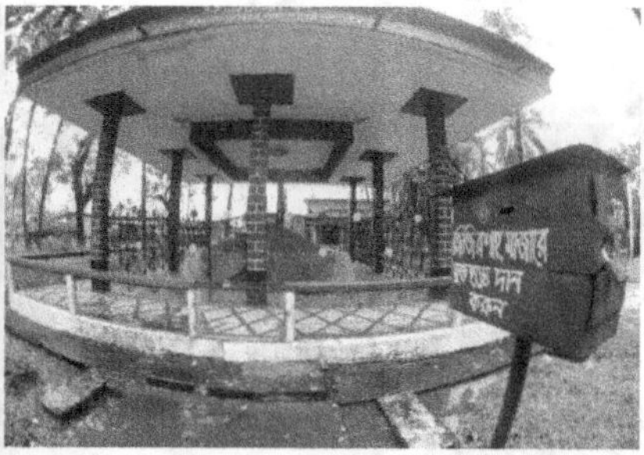

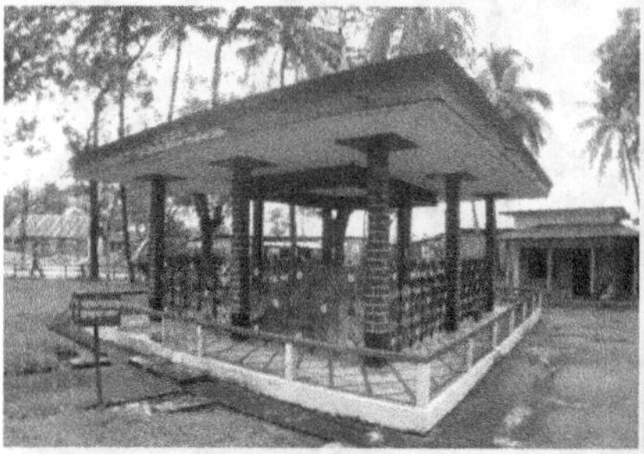

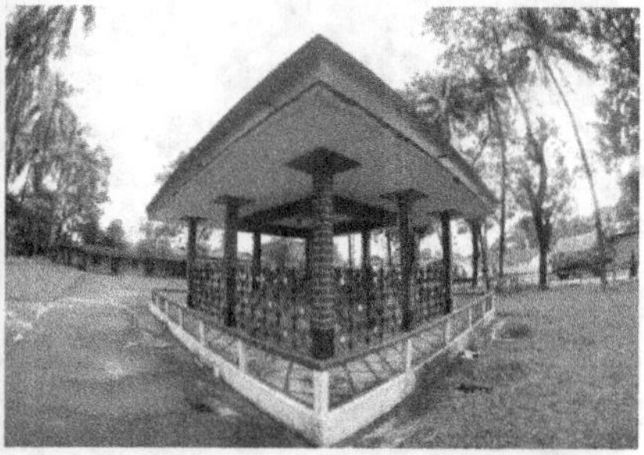

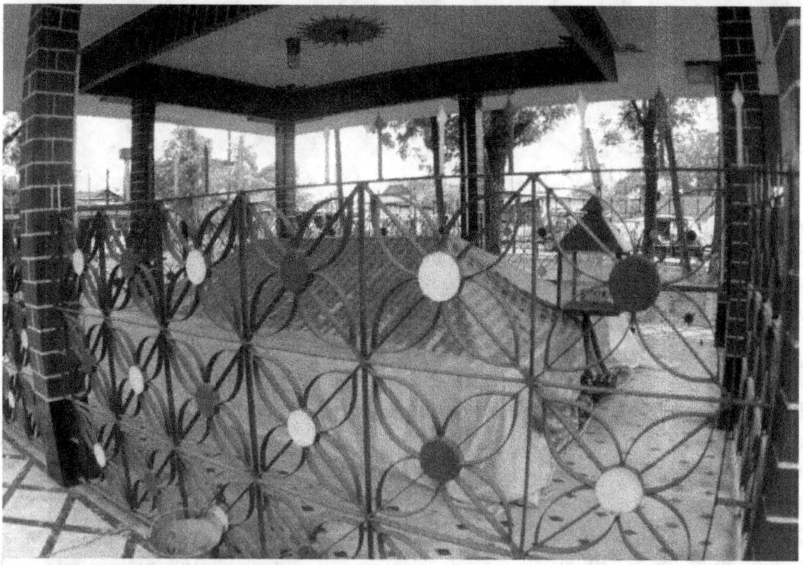

20.9.2010, 11:41:16

Shah Nur Ru

Barthokola, Sylhet

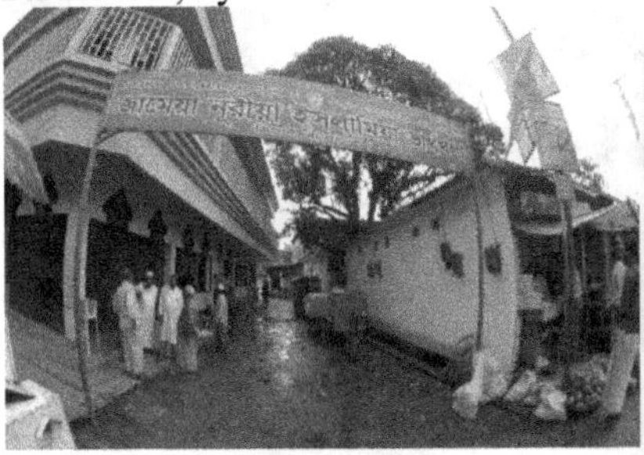

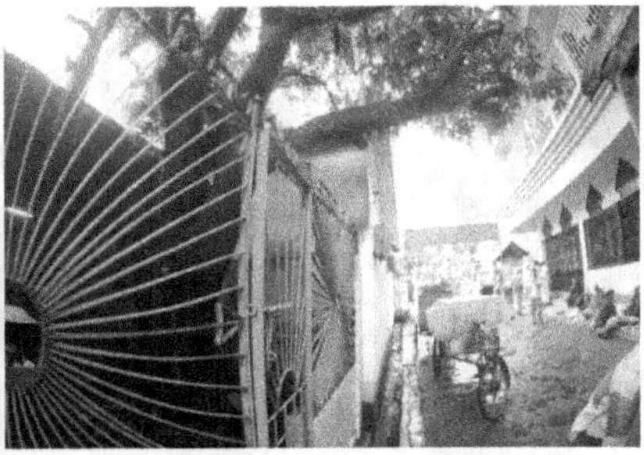

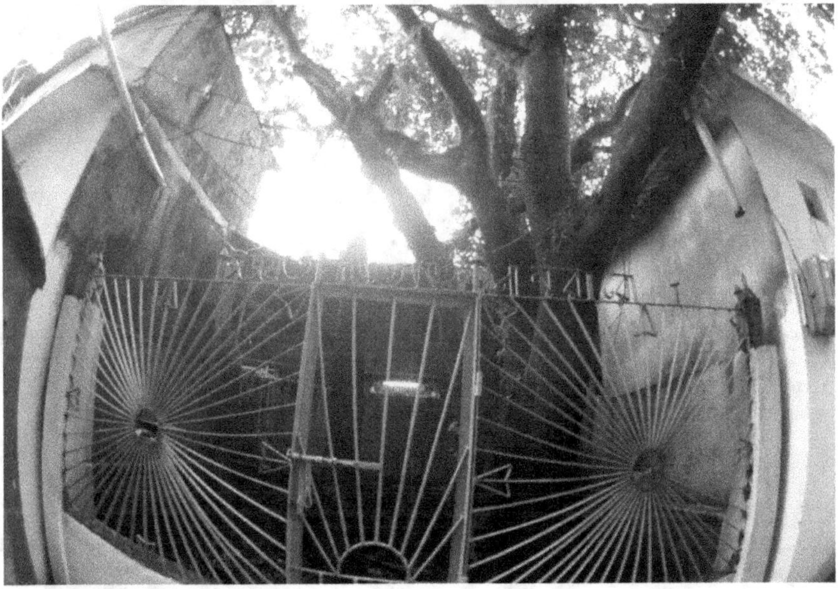

20.9.2010, 11:55:06

This place is tucked away, and visually not obvious, except the iron writing on top of the railing.

Sylhet is a Sufi mainland, even though the Middle Eastern Islam is there too, including Shia.

One thing to note and keep in mind, as it is sometimes furthest this away; is that majority of the mazar that are looked after and maintained are the family ones, the descendents piously manage them.

Gorom Dewan**

Shekh Ghat, Sylhet Town

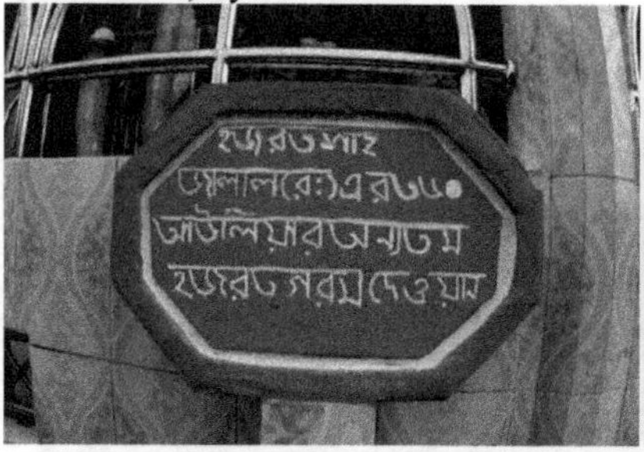
হজরত শাহ
জালাল(রঃ)এর ৩৬০
আউলিয়ার অন্যতম
হজরত গরম দেওয়ান

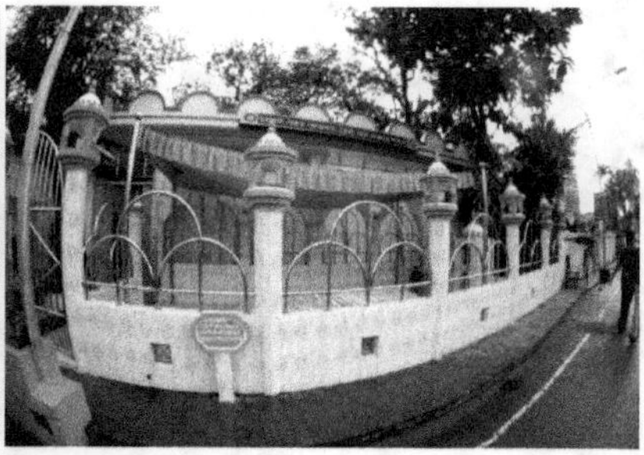

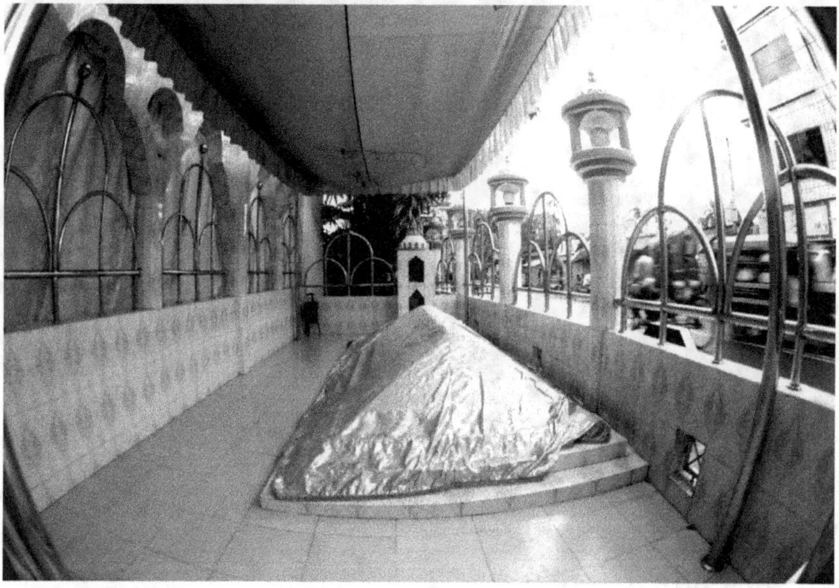

20.9.2010, 12:31

This is located on the side of the road and while it is kept and maintained, you can't avoid the street noise.

Boksh Shu Shah

Butalli, Ward 11

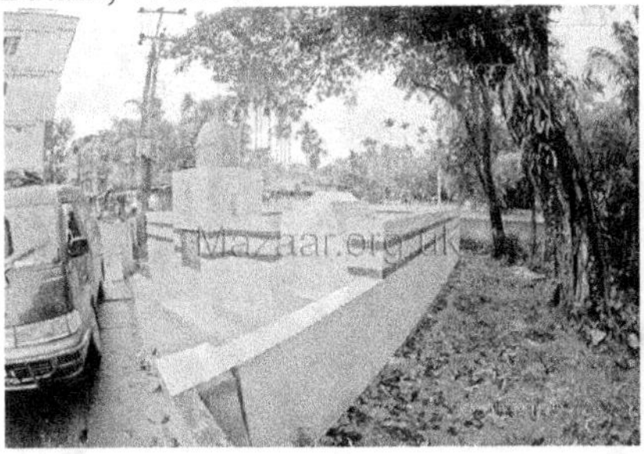
Mazaar.org.uk

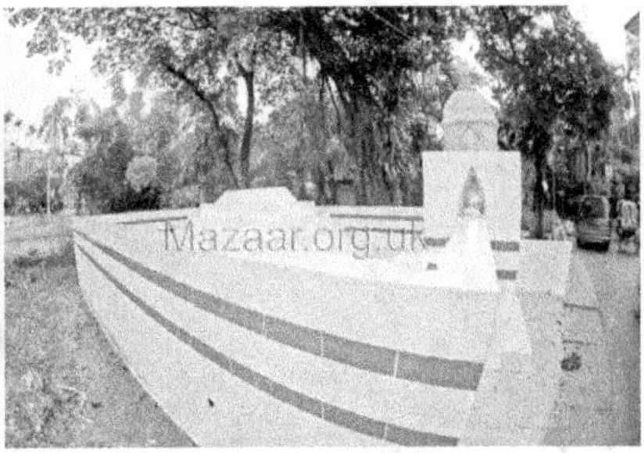
Mazaar.org.uk

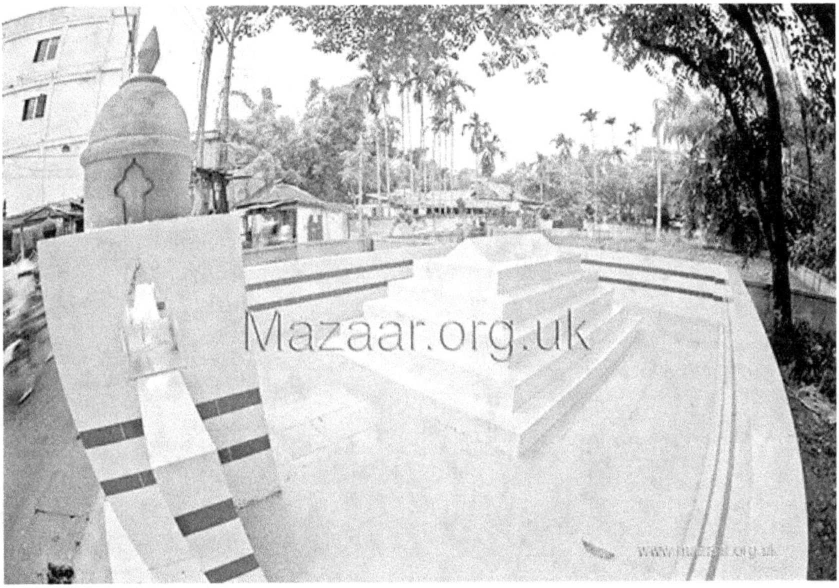
Mazaar.org.uk

20.9.2010, 12:44:36

Abu Turab**

- Jail Road - Sylhet Town.

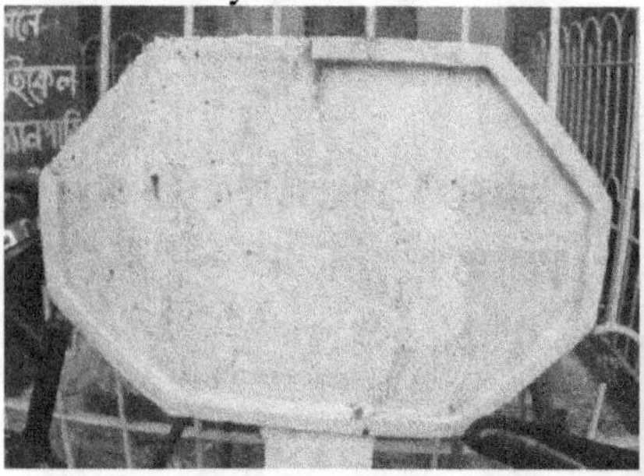

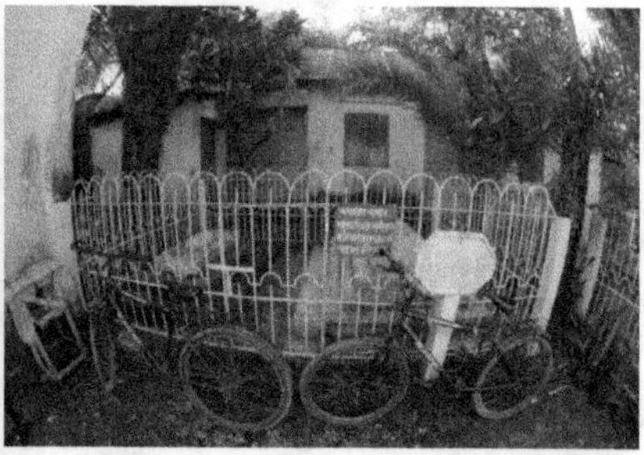

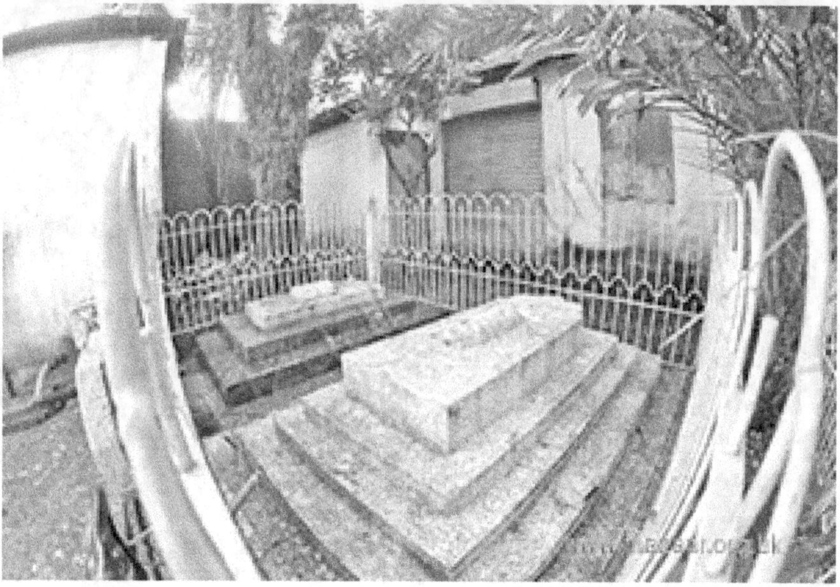

20.9.2010, 13:05

This place in Sylhet City and located inside and estate. While there was former evidence of work and care had been taken, it wasn't kept and maintained. As you can see, it looks like it is part of the garden and the place is lived in. Most secluded places in Bangladesh offer peace and tranquillity.

Shah Poran is ranked high, to second in the Mazar, as he was the nephew of Hazrat Shah Jalal. This would probably the 3rd time I visited this site in my life, twice before with other family members, this time it was on my own. This place is known as "Gorom," as in strict. The steps leading up to the inner sanctum is as always, offers and provides tranquillity and serenity.

Shah Ali Konkhar (Yemeni)

Chondittio Dorga, no.9 Doyamir, Ward 3, union, Lala bazaar.

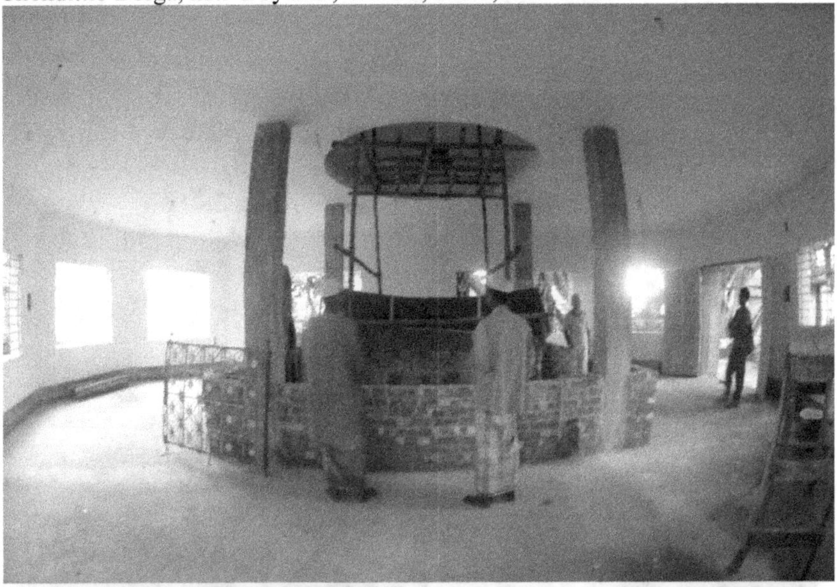

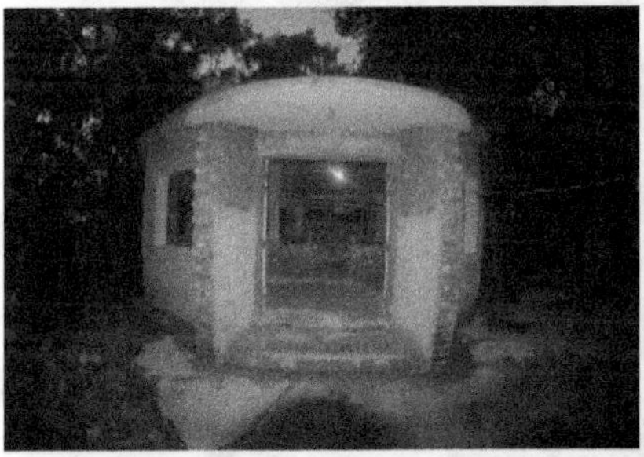

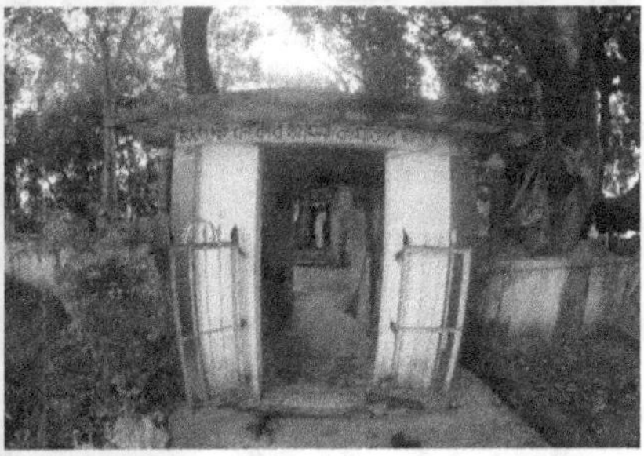

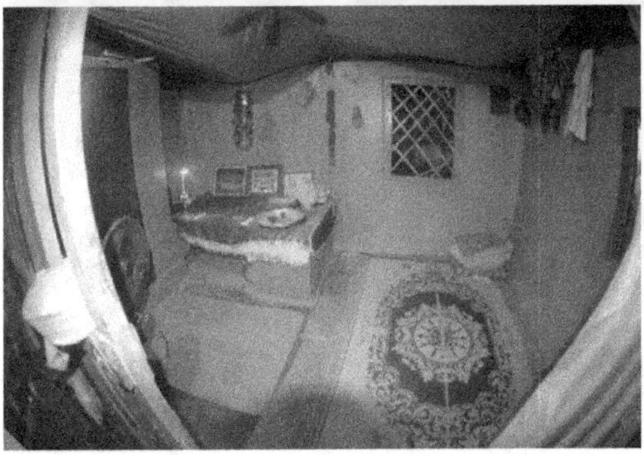

Ashon - Contemplation room

21.9.2010

Shah Ang Rahim*

Sathmile bethshundi Fokiru gaow

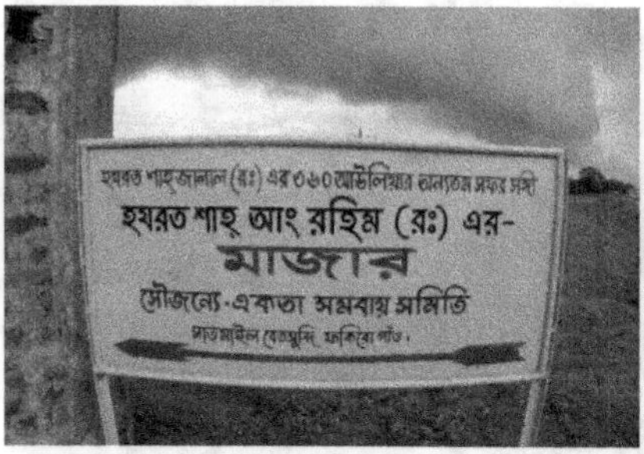
হযরত শাহ্জালাল (রঃ) এর ৩৬০ আউলিয়ার অন্যতম সফর সঙ্গী
হযরত শাহ্ আং রহিম (রঃ) এর-
মাজার
সৌজন্যে-একতা সমবায় সমিতি

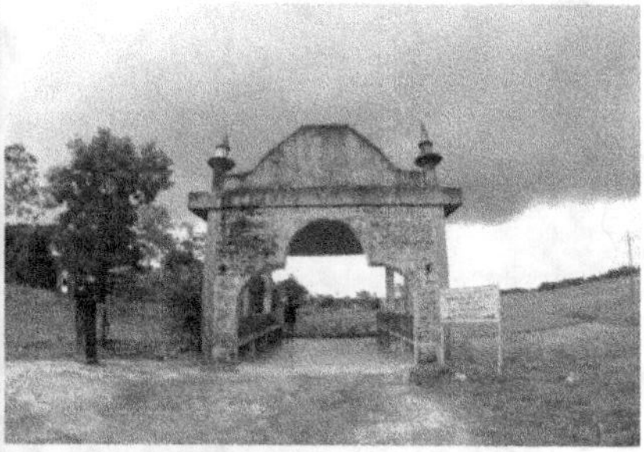

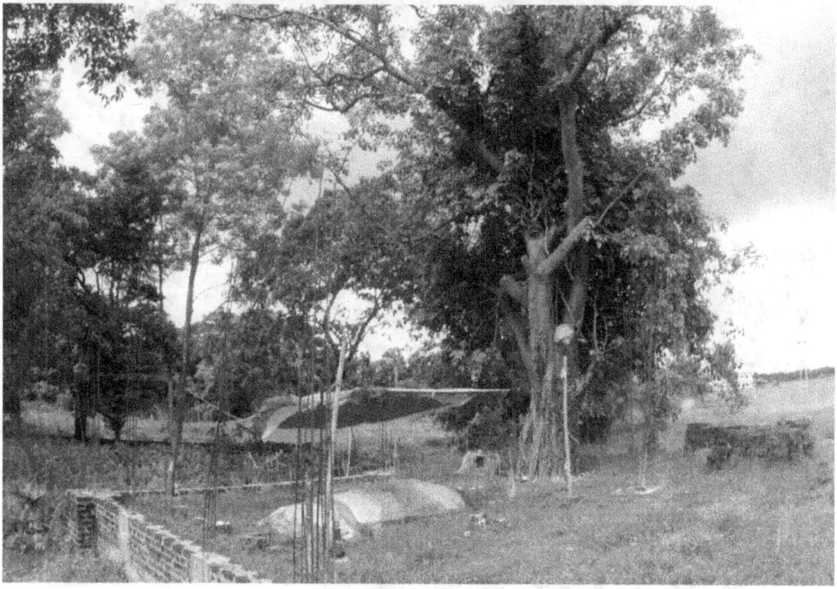

22.9.2010, 11:05:50

There is a claim on the board that this person was a member of the 360.

Shah Moin Uddin*

Shekh Parah

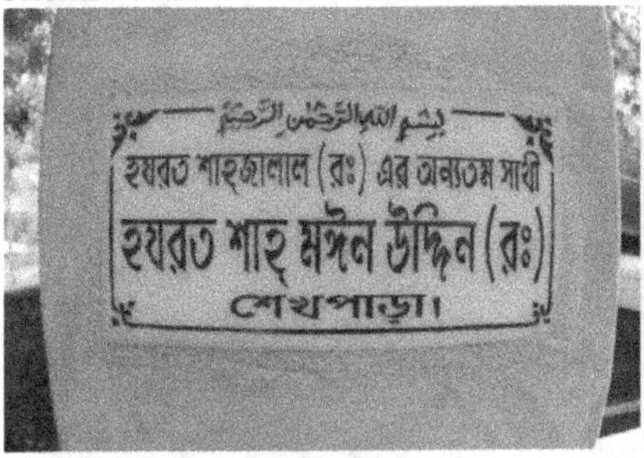
بسم الله الرحمن الرحيم
হযরত শাহজালাল (রঃ) এর অন্যতম সাথী
হযরত শাহ্ মঈন উদ্দিন (রঃ)
শেখপাড়া।

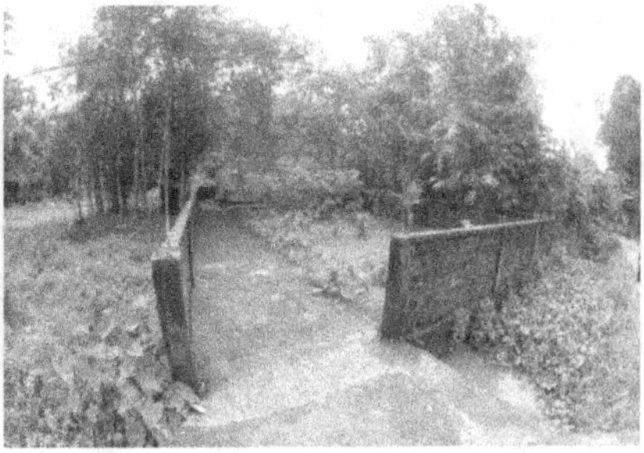

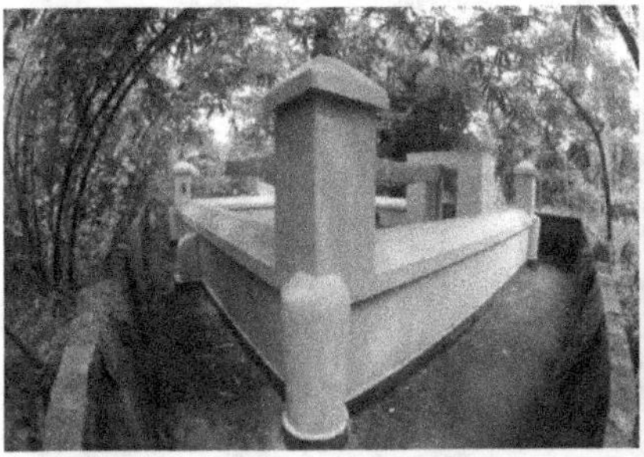

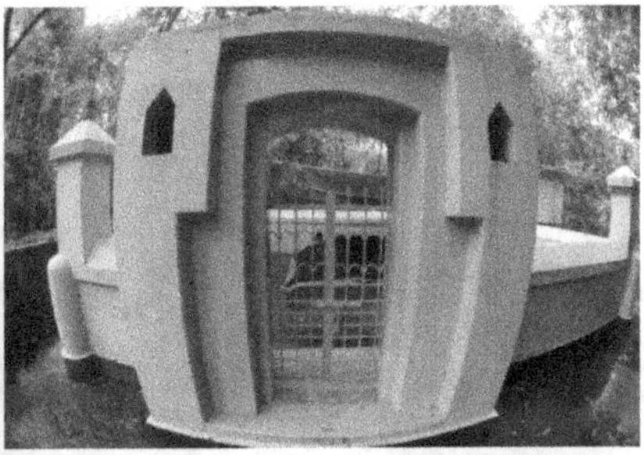

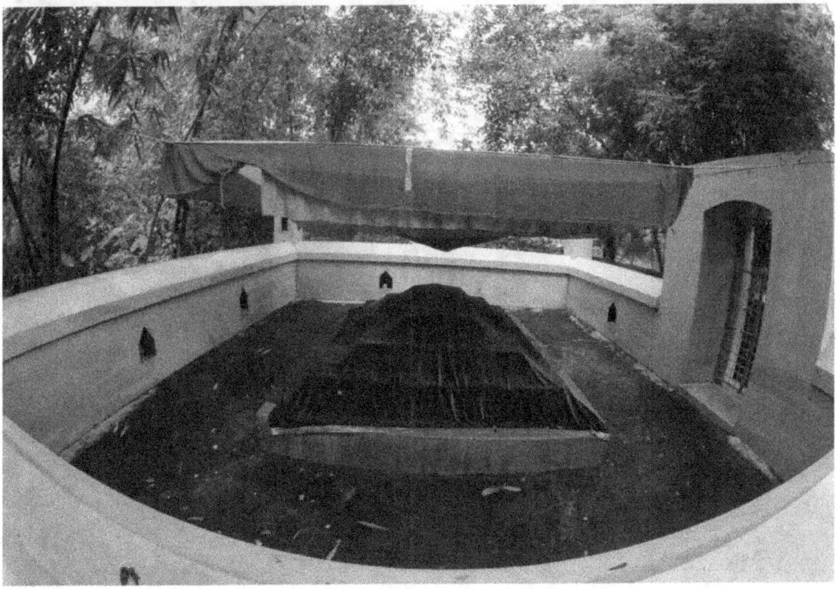

28.9.2010, 14:44:34

Shah Zia Uddin*

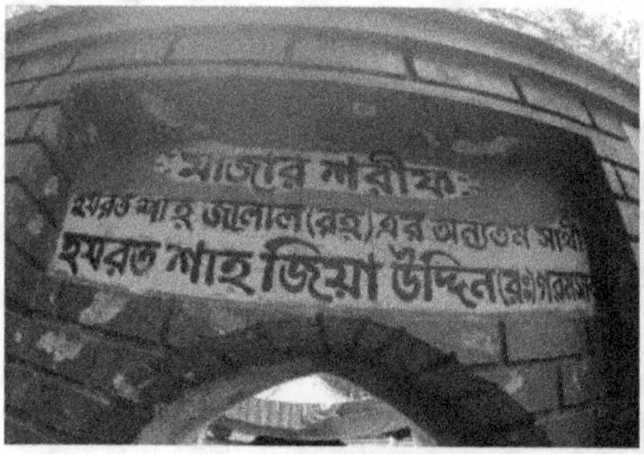
মাজার শরীফ
হযরত শাহ জালাল (রহঃ) এর অন্যতম সাথী
হযরত শাহ জিয়া উদ্দিন (রহঃ)

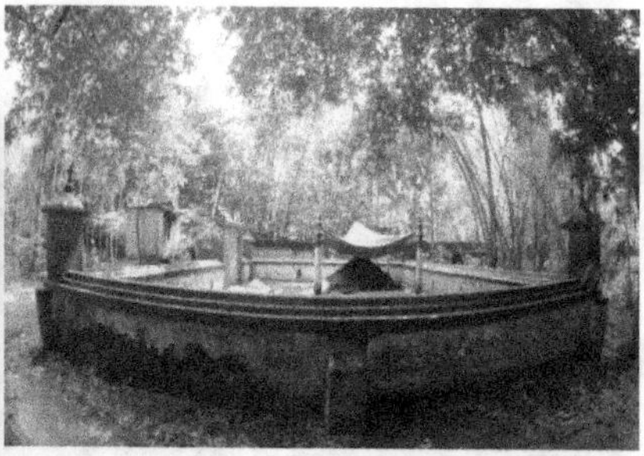

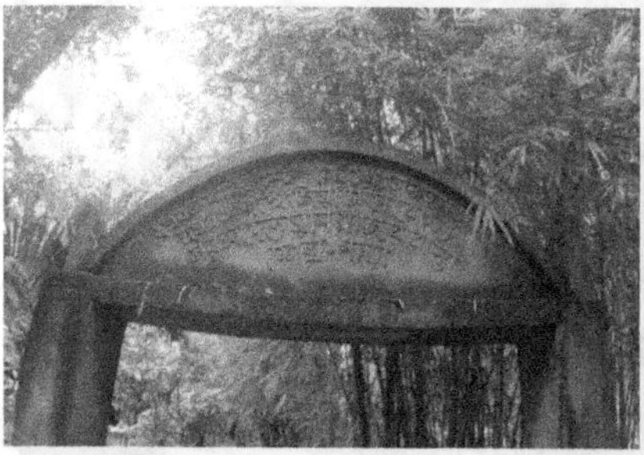

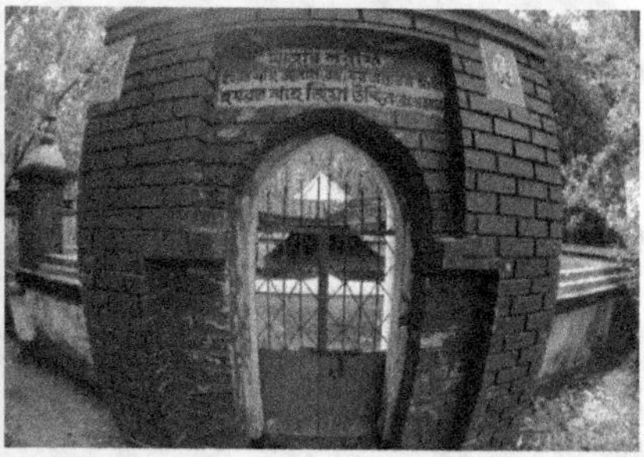

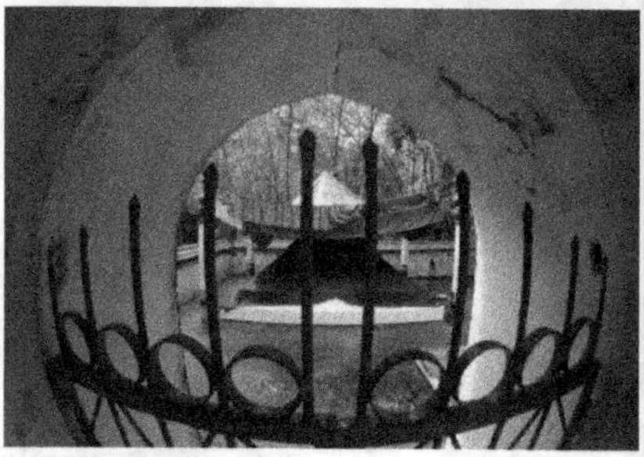

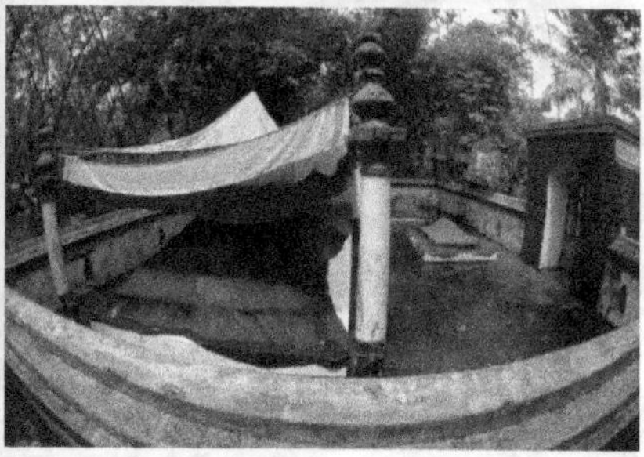

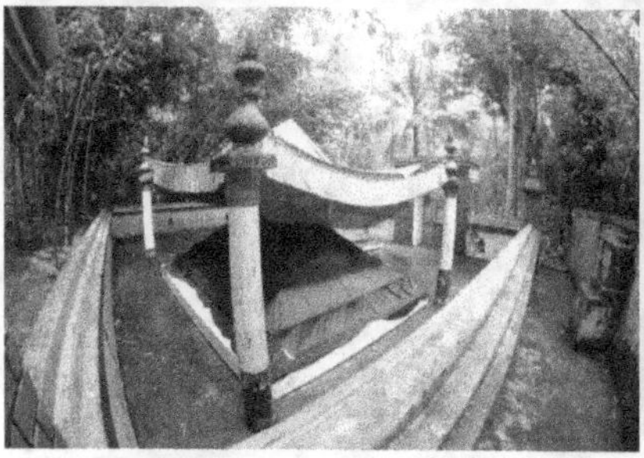

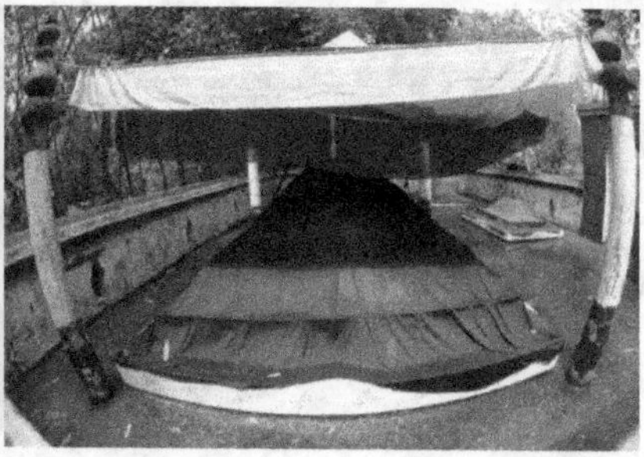

28.9.2010, 14:52:44

Shah Toki Uddin

a.k.a.,

Mohammad Toki

Shekh Para, Lukman Miar Bari, Ward 4, Jolal Pur

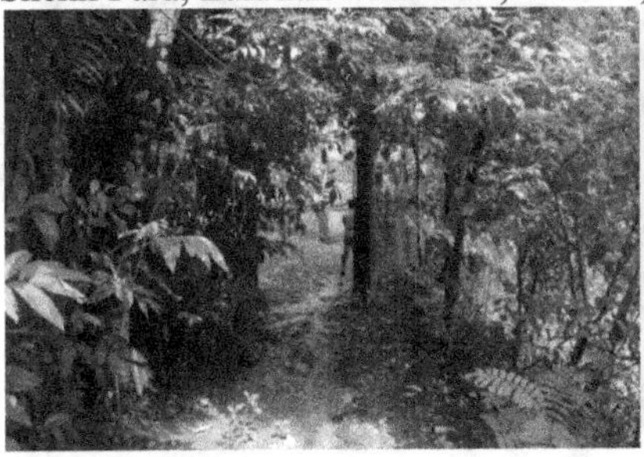

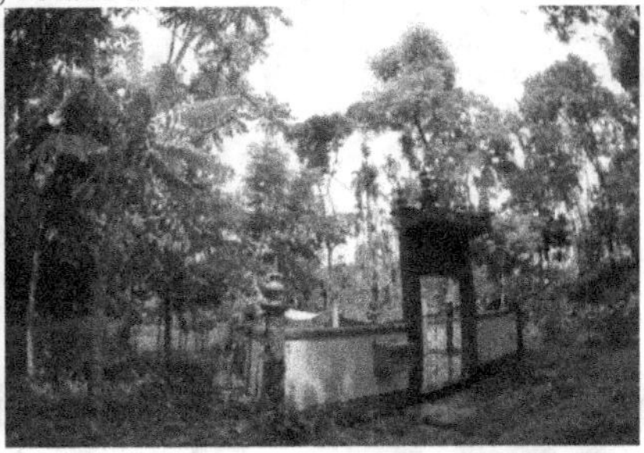

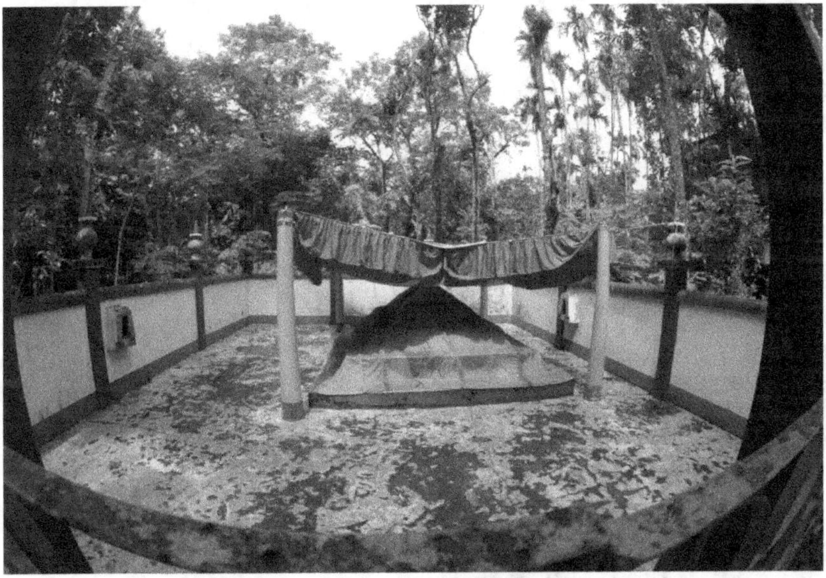

28.9.2010, 15:04:48

There were few mazar in this part of the neighbourhood. They are inside the villages and local; a tribal sense - looked after managed by a group of families.

Shah Kutub Uddin*

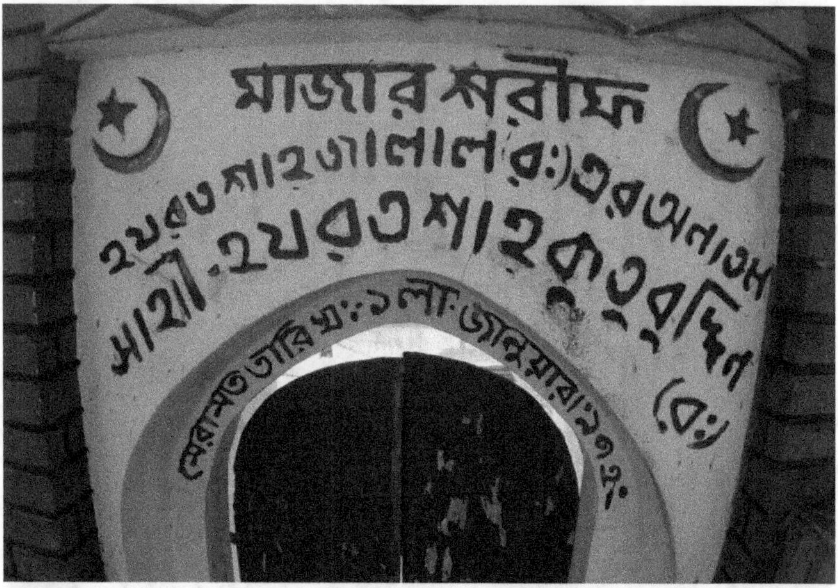
মাজার শরীফ

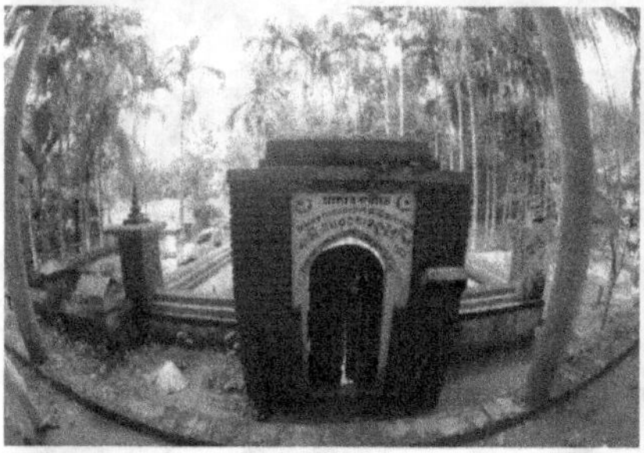

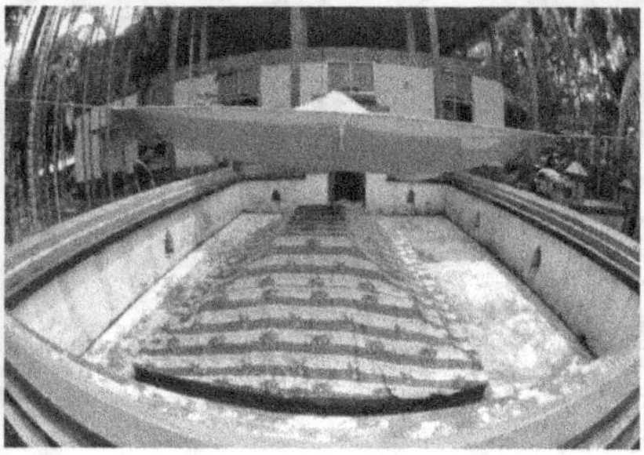

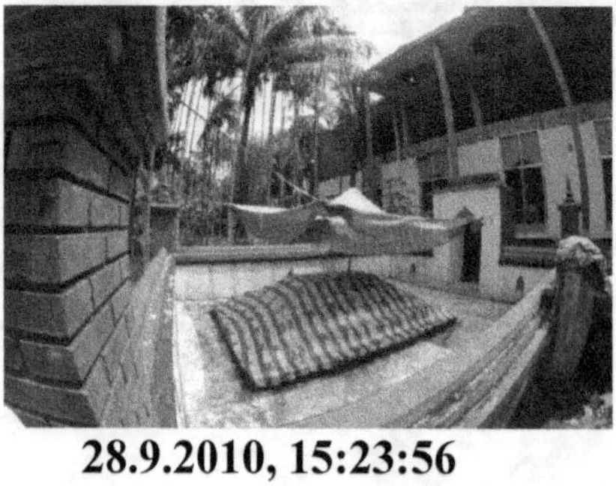

28.9.2010, 15:23:56

Shah Poilwan*

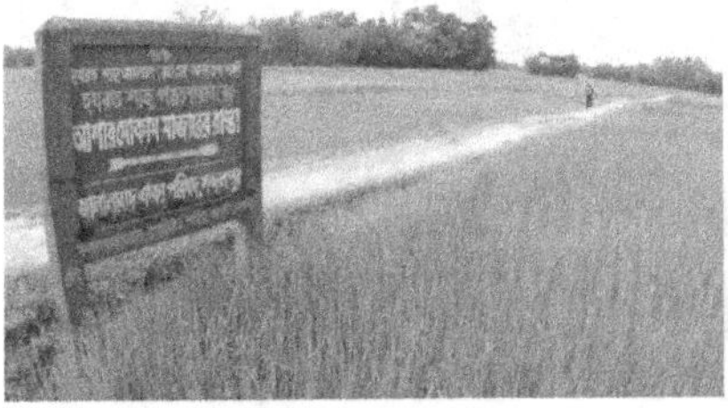

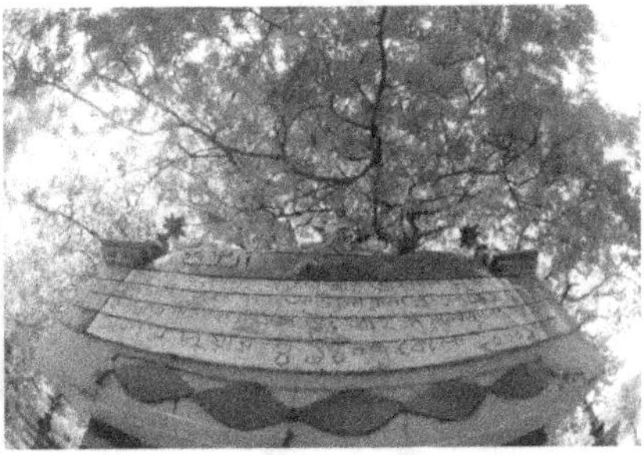

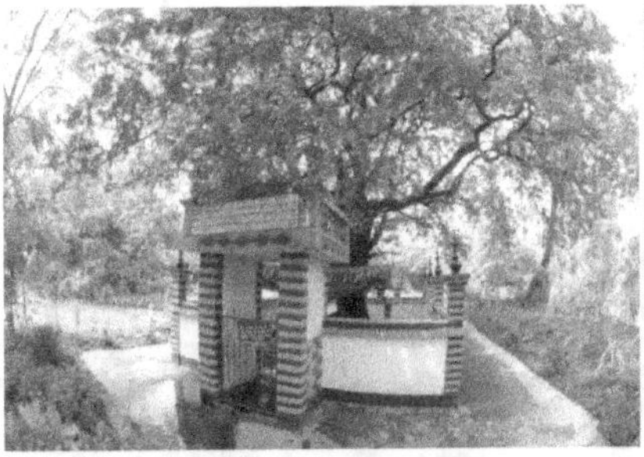

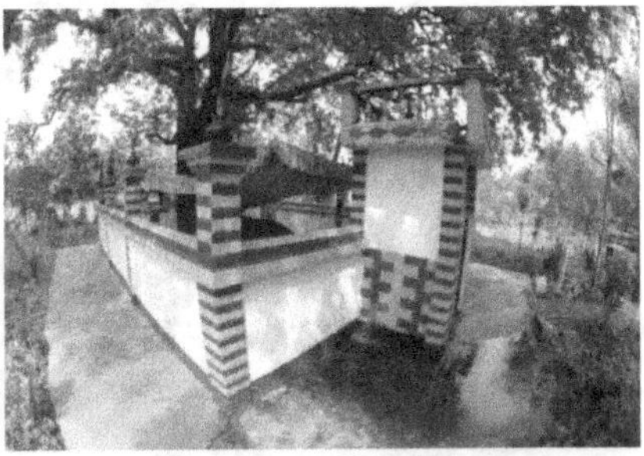

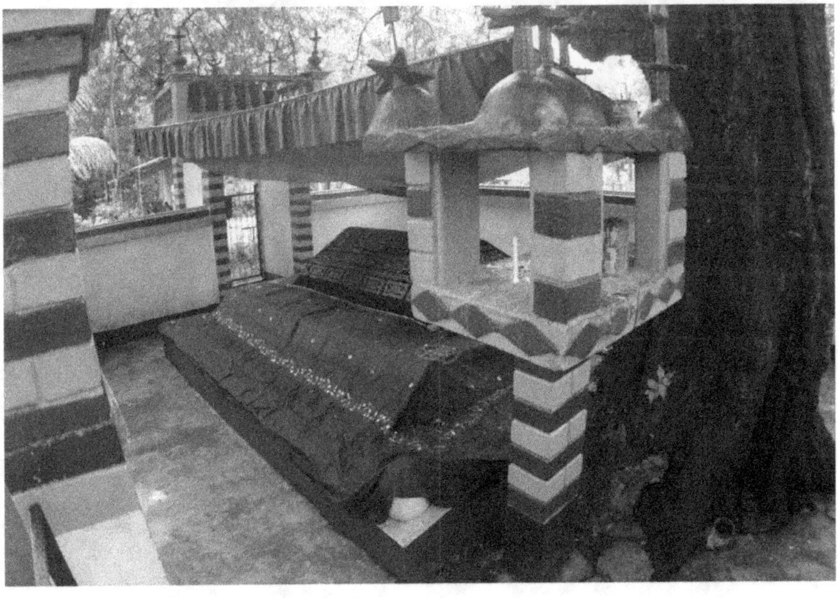

28.9.2010, 15:54:14

Kuja Shah

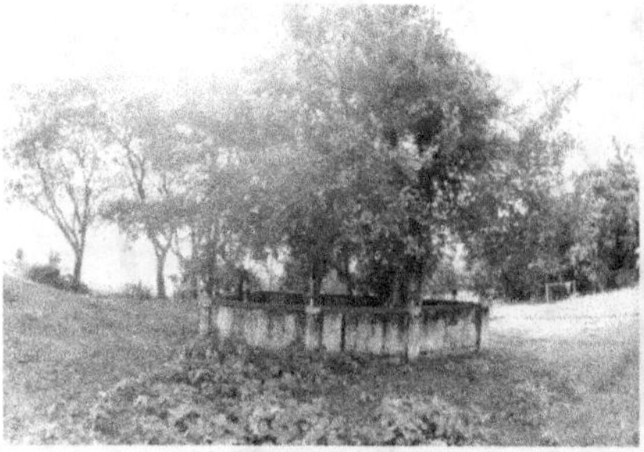

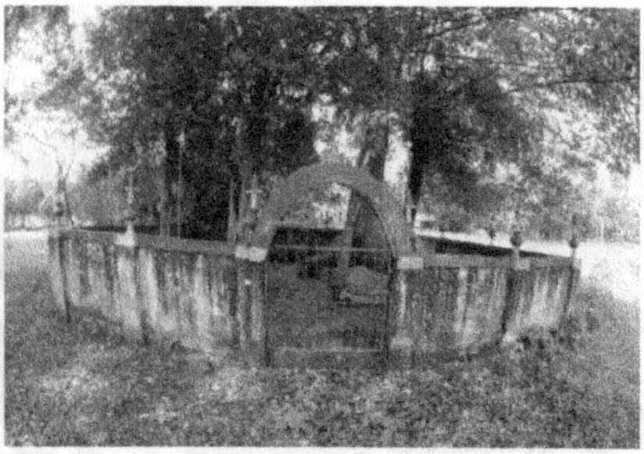

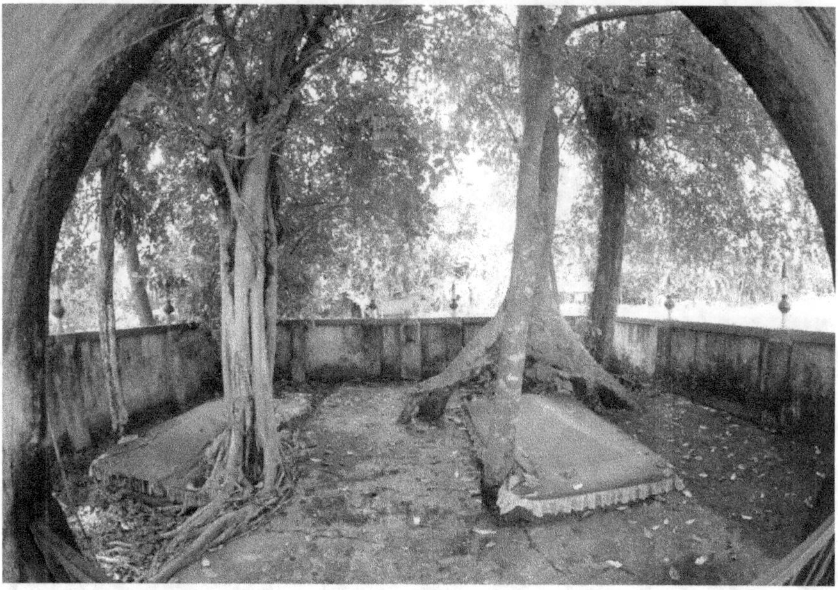

28.9.2010, 16:15:40

Manik Badsha

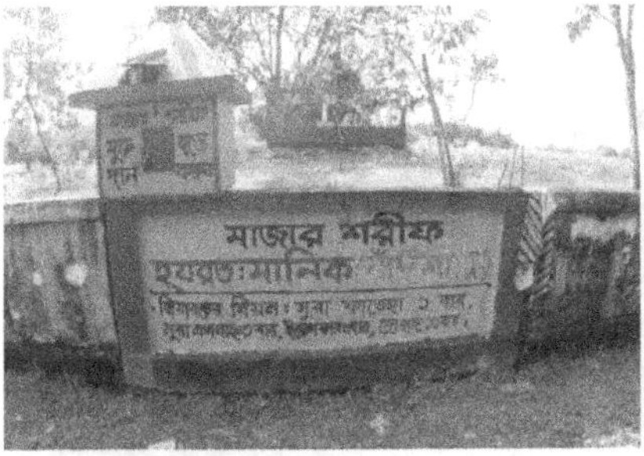
মাজার শরীফ
হযরত মানিক

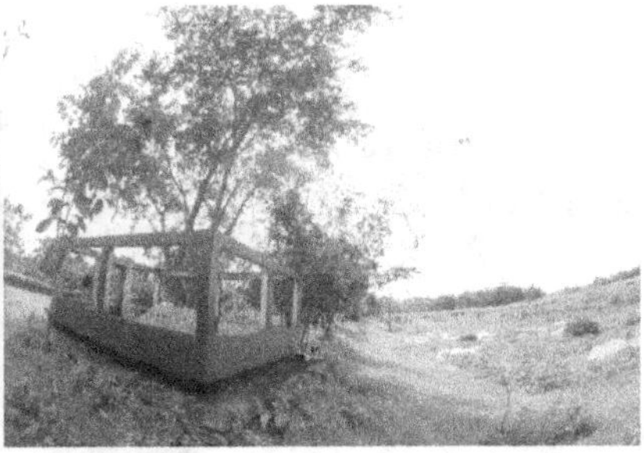

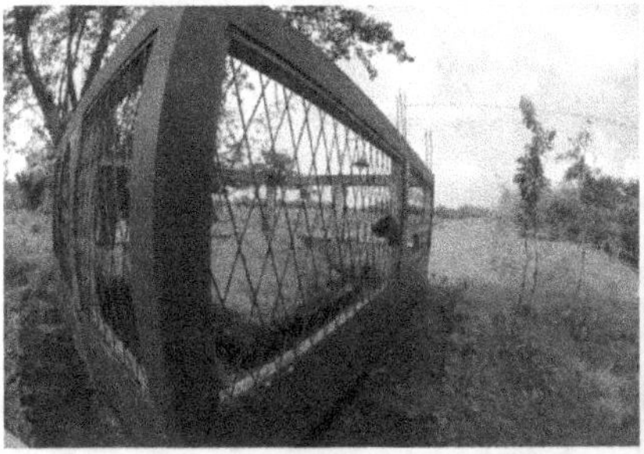

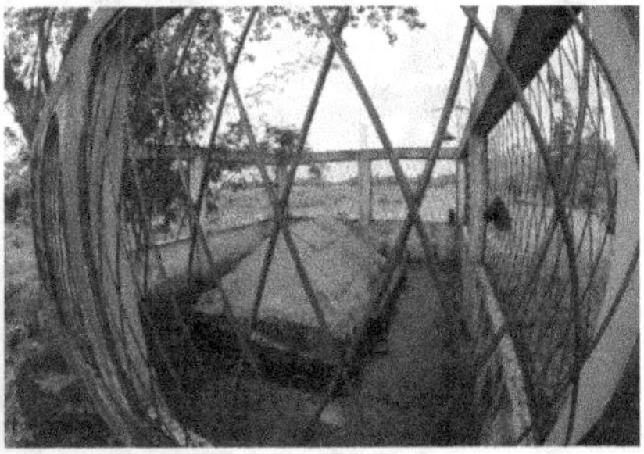

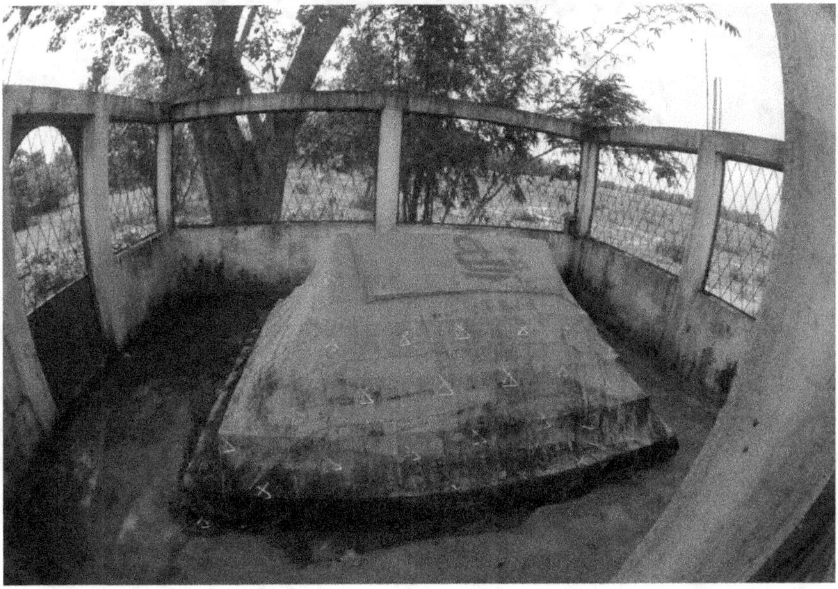

28.9.2010, 16:28:42

Kamal Shah

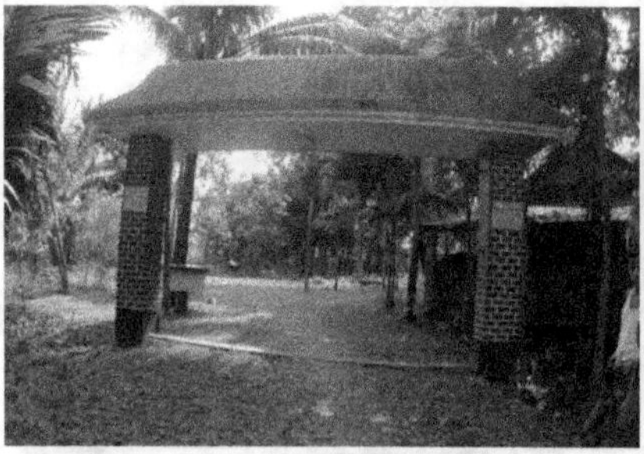

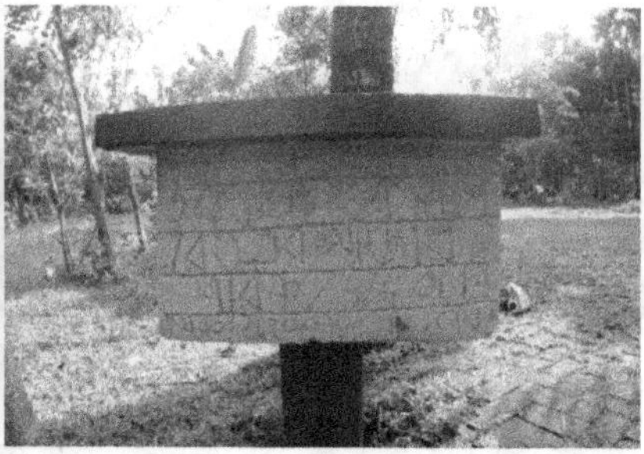

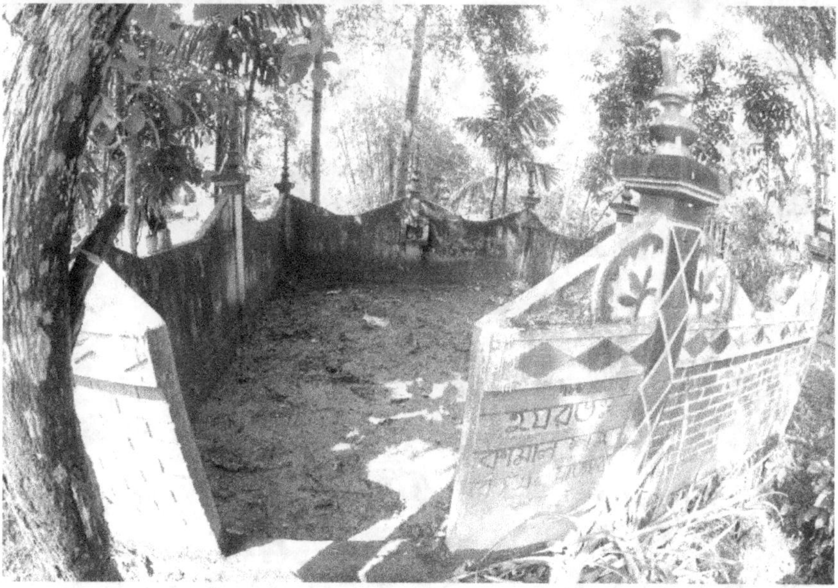

28.9.2010, 16:39:30

Rohim Uddin Ansari (Yemeni)*

Suleman Husen, Chiarman Bari, Talukdar Parah, Pub Bag, Jolal Pur.

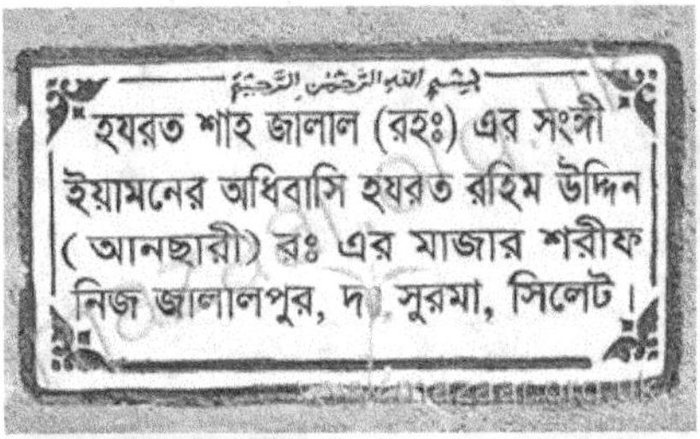
হযরত শাহ জালাল (রহঃ) এর সংঙ্গী
ইয়ামনের অধিবাসি হযরত রহিম উদ্দিন
(আনছারী) রঃ এর মাজার শরীফ
নিজ জালালপুর, দ. সুরমা, সিলেট।

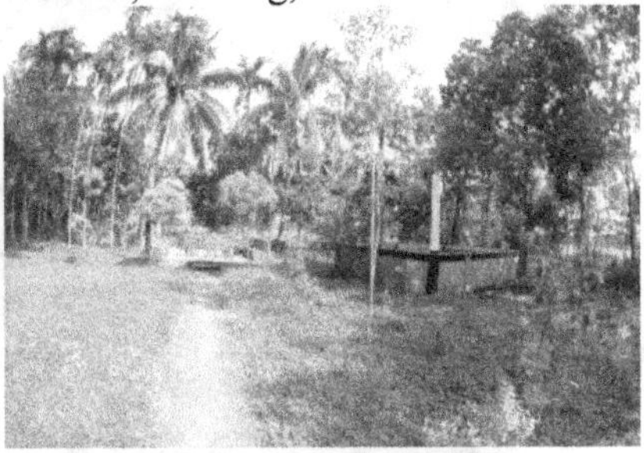

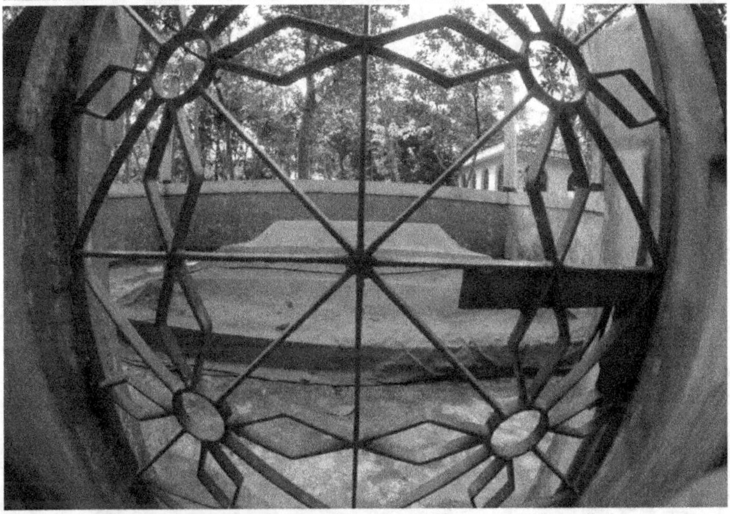

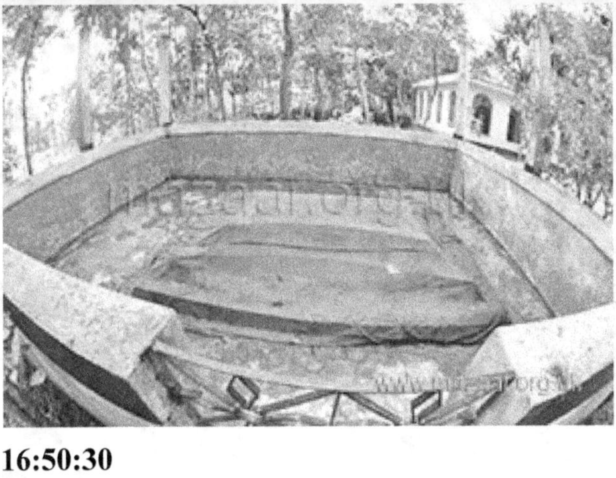

This is a village site and the mazar is concreted up but not clean as others. What I have realised, the cleaner and managed they are, you are drawn to the setting, set your mood.

28.9.2010,

16:50:30

Kotai Phir

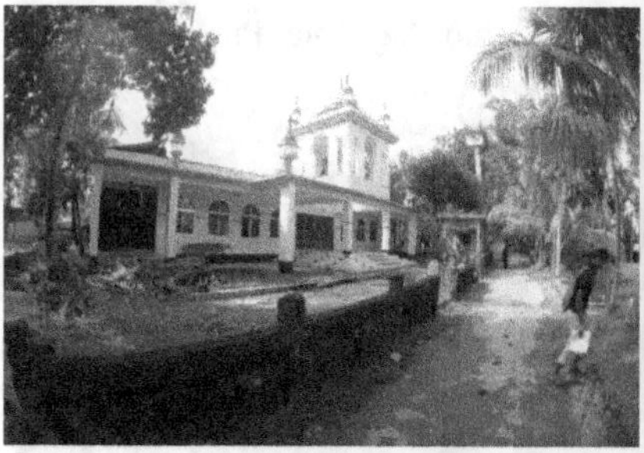
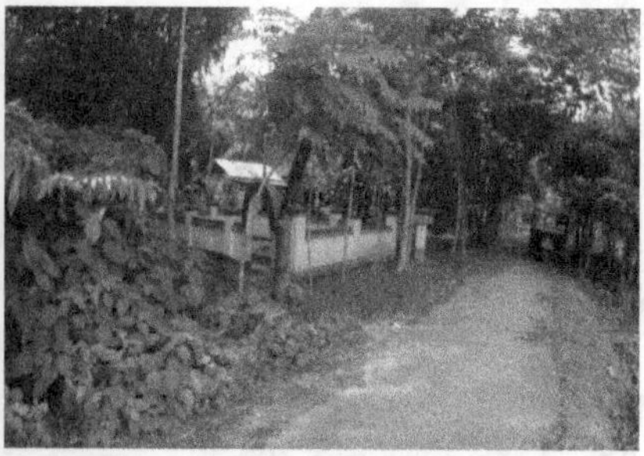
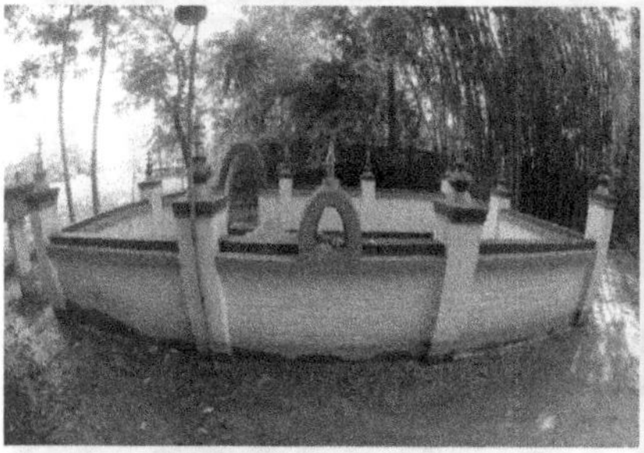
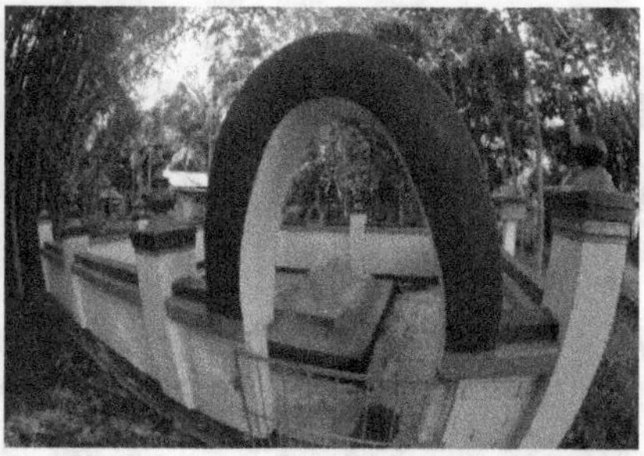
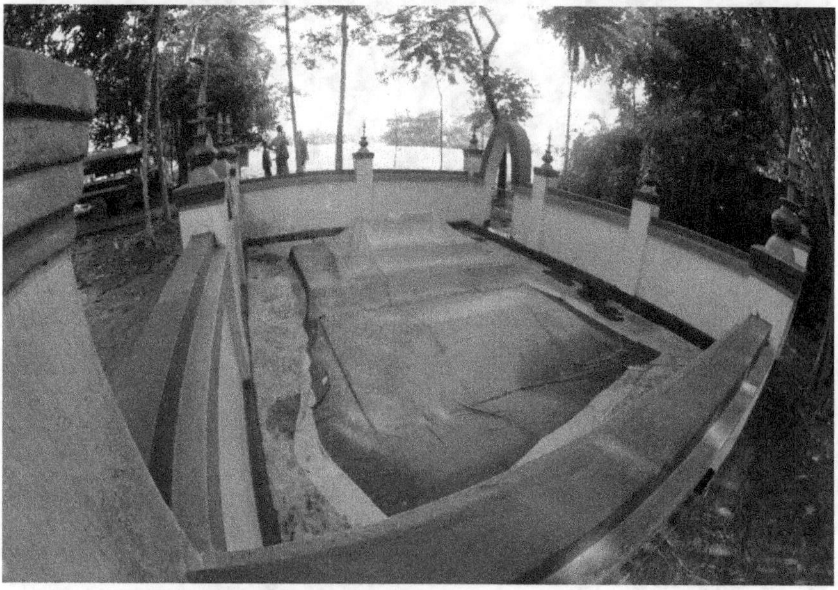

28.9.2010, 17:17:18

Soyod Ahmod Uddin

a.k.a.,

Amoy Shah

Sonar Parah,

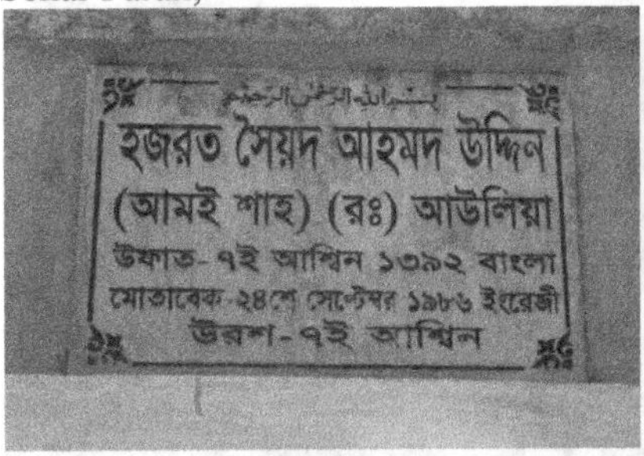
بسم الله الرحمن الرحيم
হজরত সৈয়দ আহমদ উদ্দিন
(আমই শাহ) (রঃ) আউলিয়া
উফাত-৭ই আশ্বিন ১৩৯২ বাংলা
মোতাবেক-২৪শে সেপ্টেম্বর ১৯৮৬ ইংরেজী
উরশ-৭ই আশ্বিন

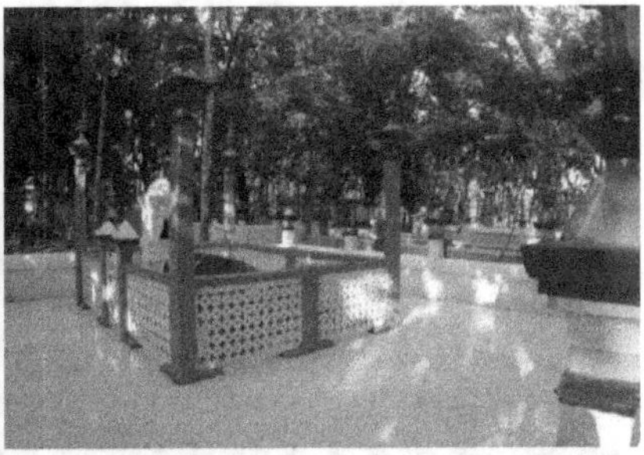

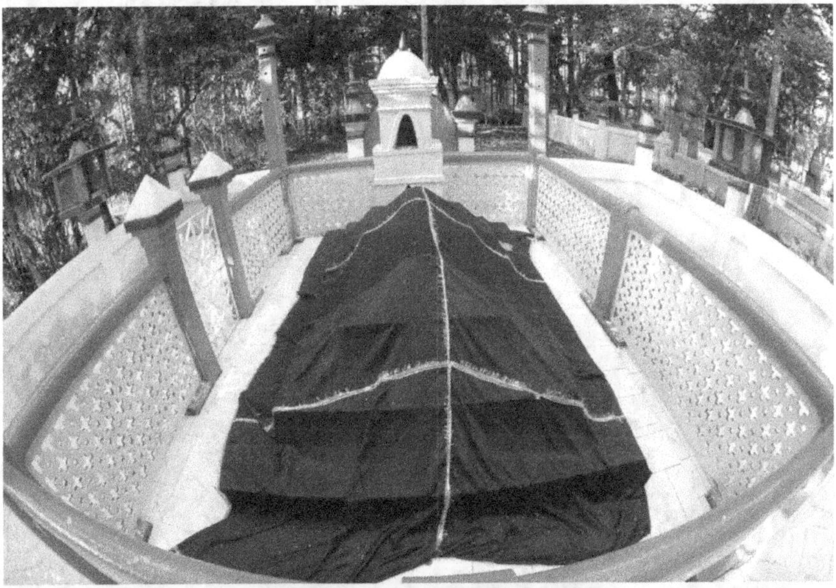

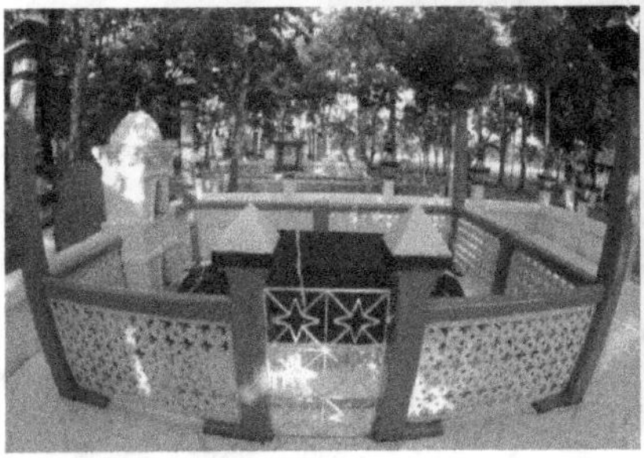

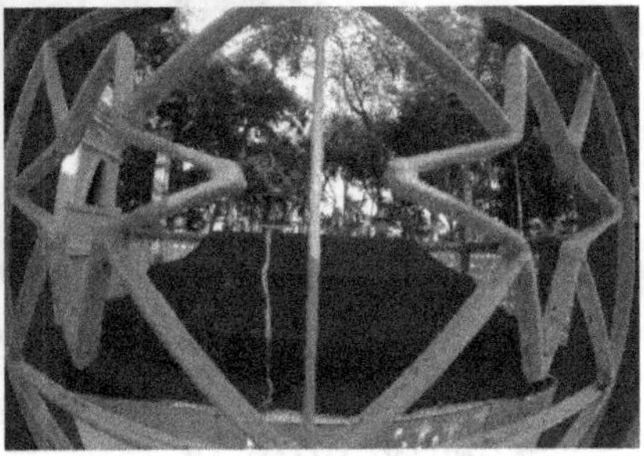

28.9.2010, 17:23:40

Shah Soyod Afjol*

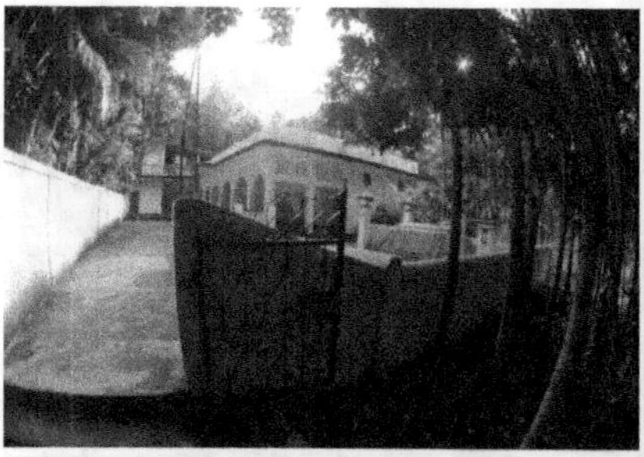

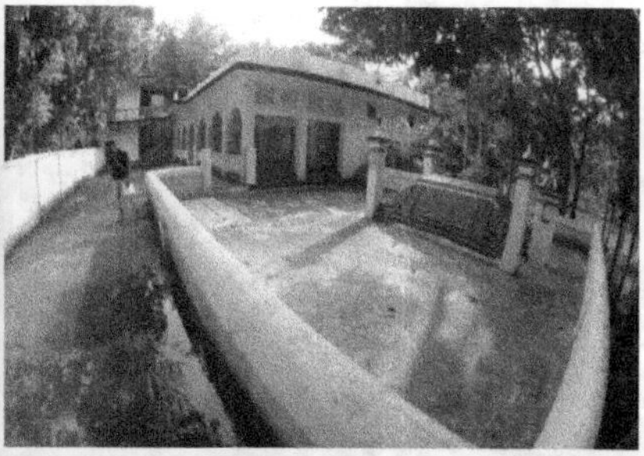

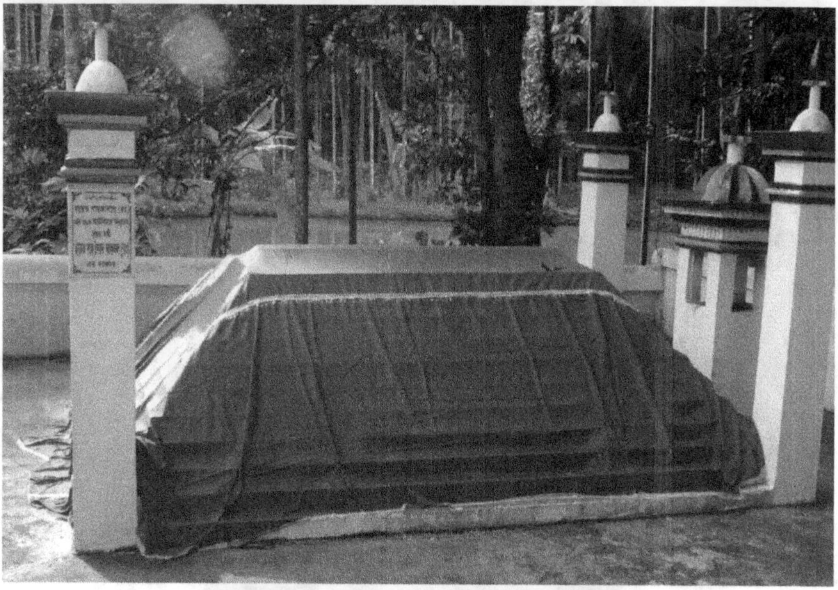

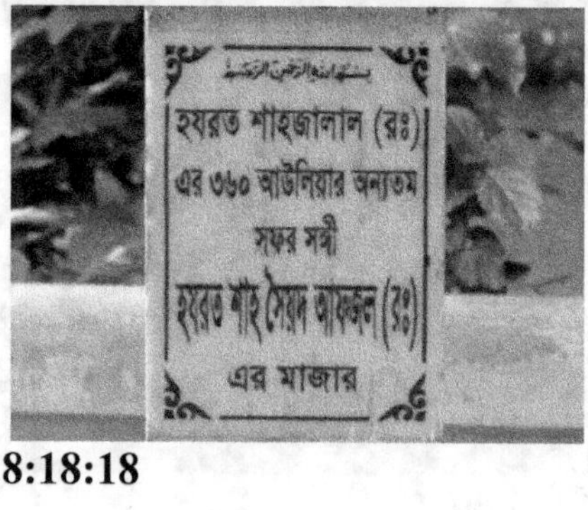
بسم الله الرحمن الرحيم
হযরত শাহজালাল (রঃ)
এর ৩৬০ আউলিয়ার অন্যতম
সফর সঙ্গী
হযরত শাহ সৈয়দ আফজল (রঃ)
এর মাজার

28.9.2010, 18:18:18

Mira Shah

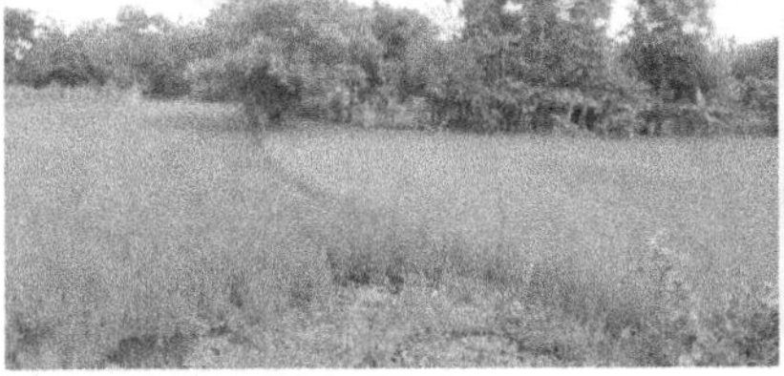

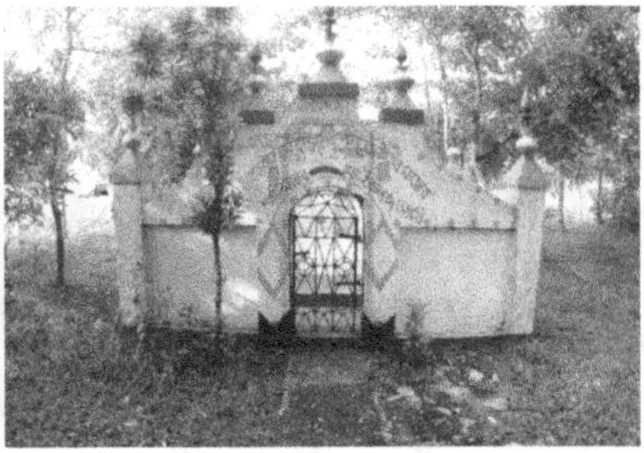

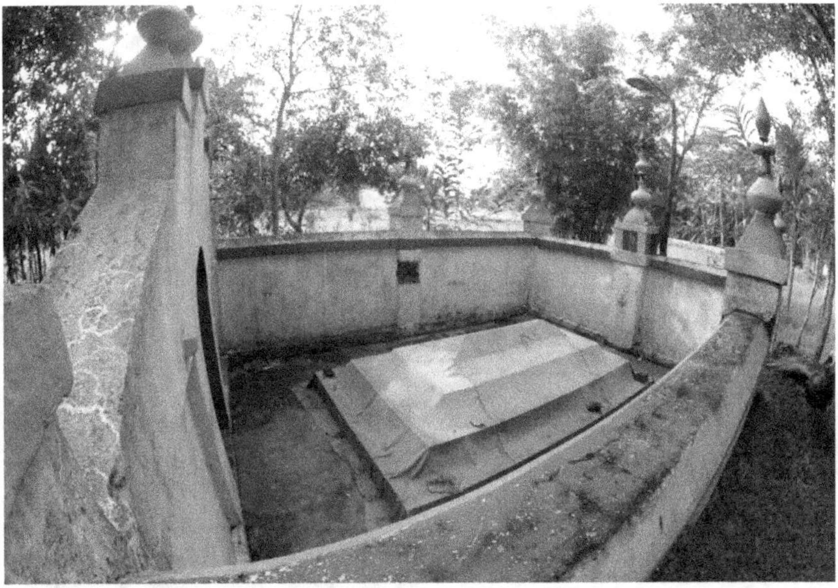

28.9.2010, 18:41:36

Phir Miah Sun Kha

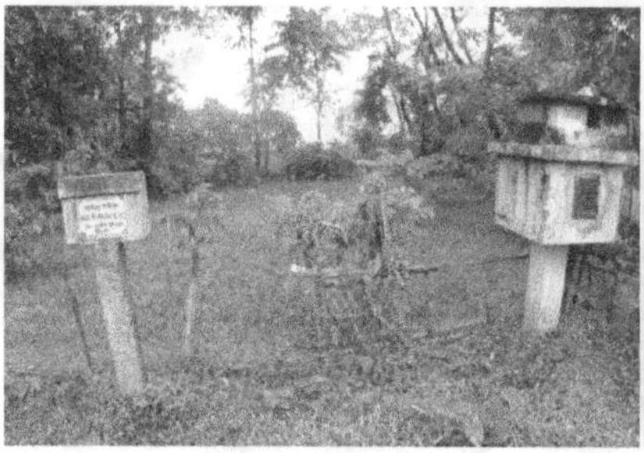

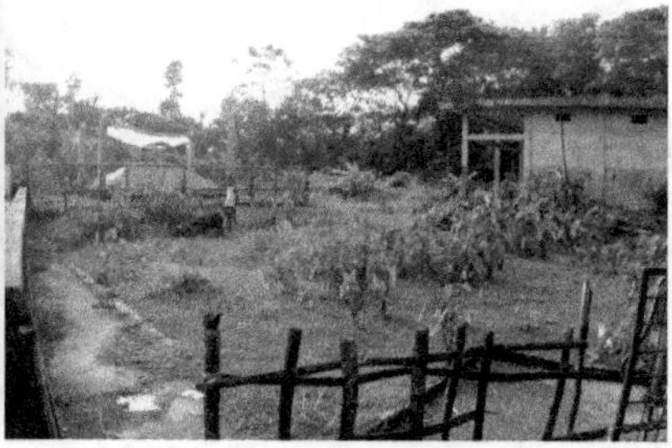

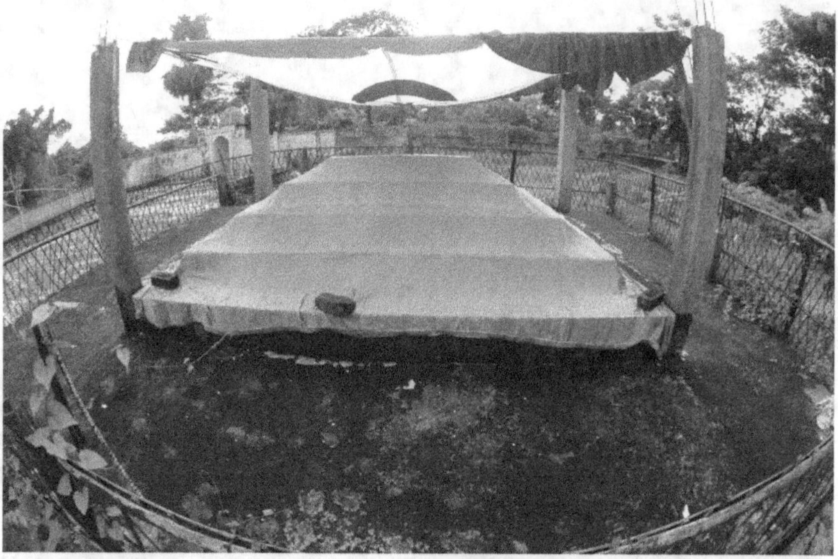

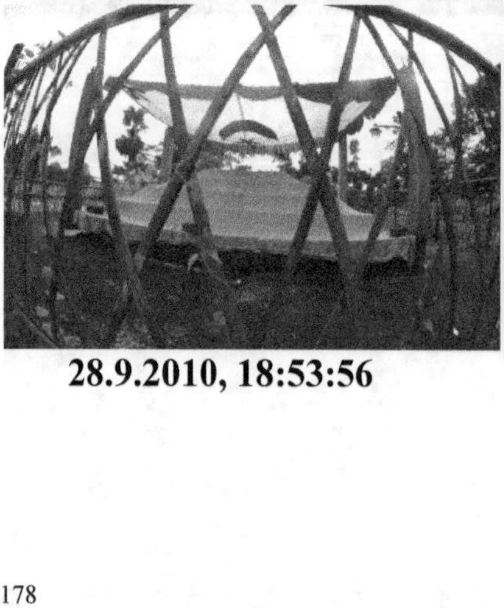

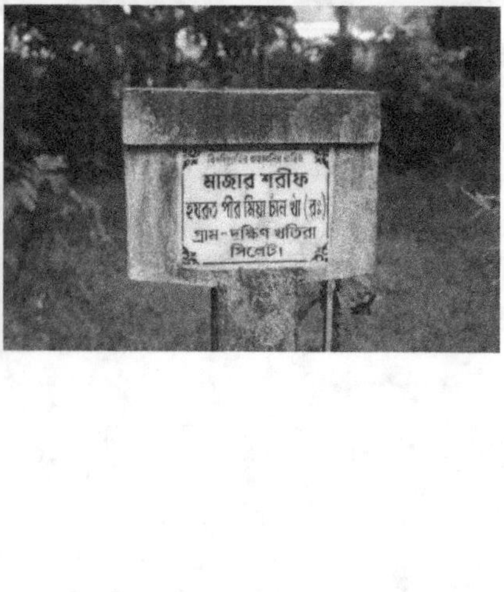
মাজার শরীফ
হযরত পীর মিয়া চান খাঁ (রঃ)
গ্রাম - দক্ষিণ খতিরা
সিলেট।

28.9.2010, 18:53:56

Soyod Komor Uddin

a.k.a.,

Kurshid Shah

Sonar Parah,

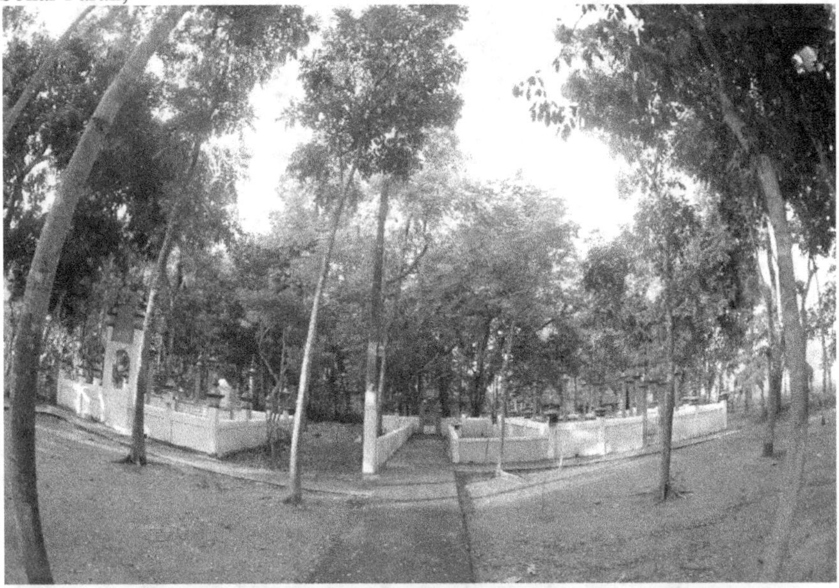

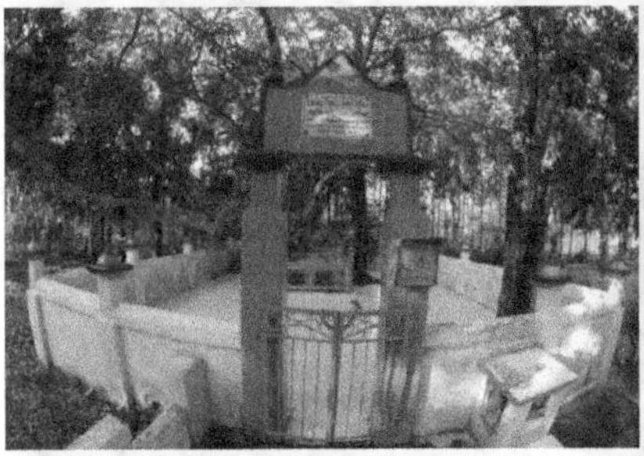

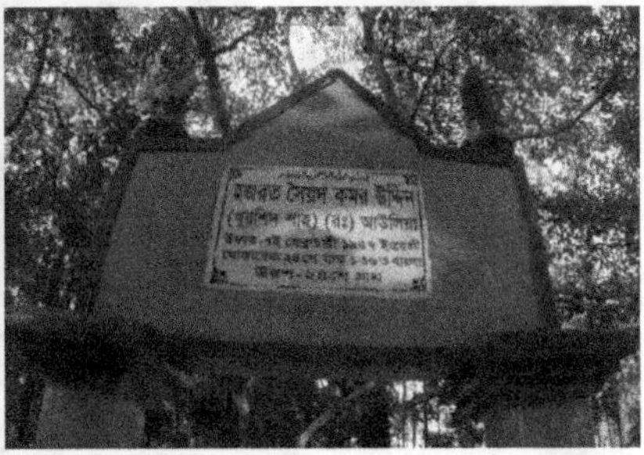

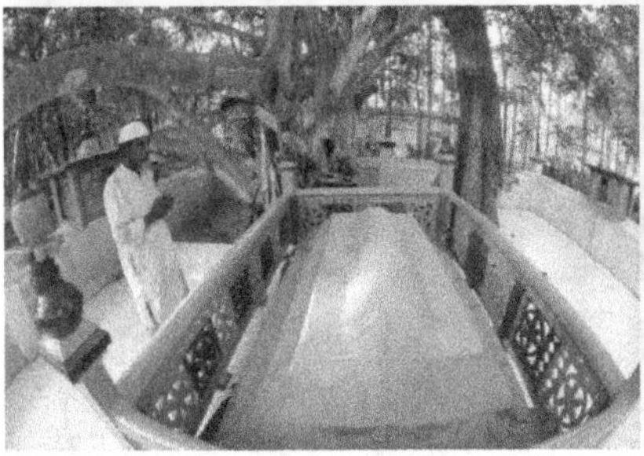

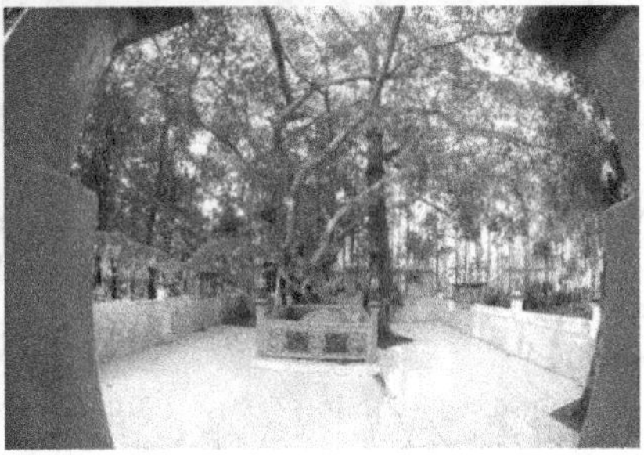

28.9.2010. 19:21:52

Soyod Sufi Uddin

Sonar Parah

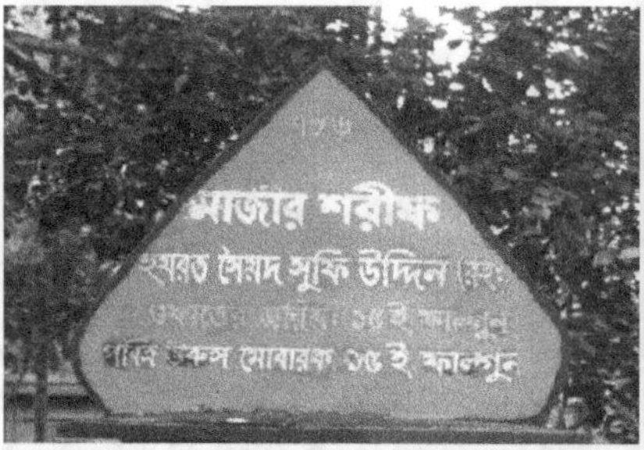
মাজার শরীফ
সৈয়দ সুফি উদ্দিন

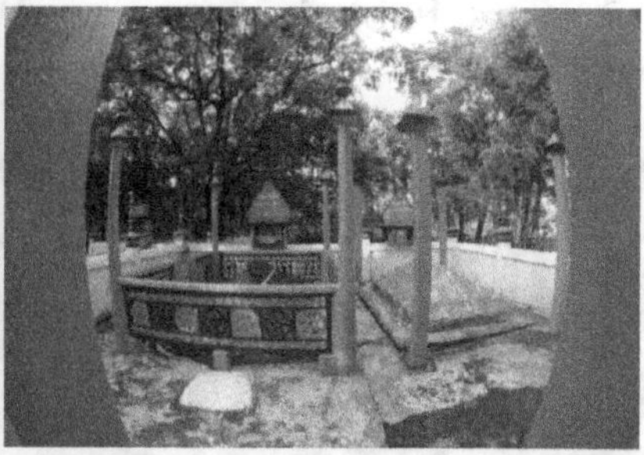

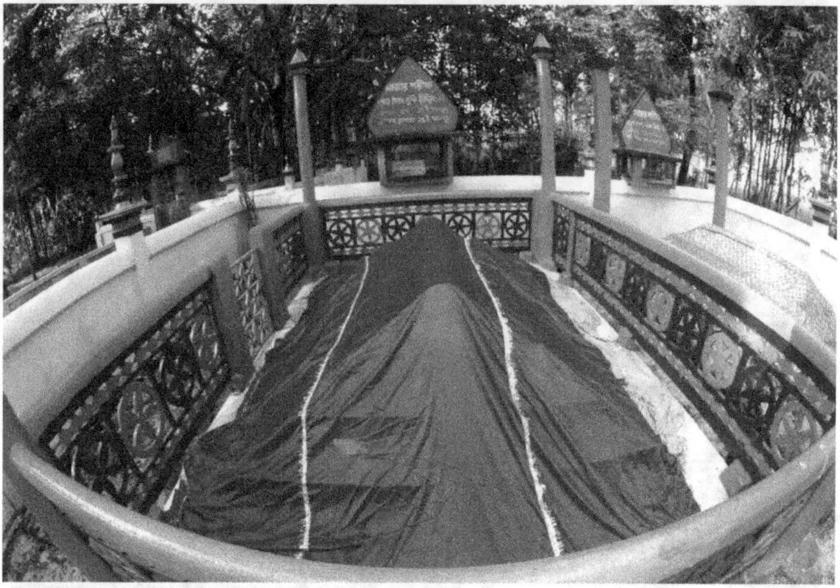

28.9.2010, 19:26:40

There are place you get total tranquillity, and then there are all different state of mind based on the setting, landscape of the Mazars.

As I was someone who went from London, health and safety is always on my psyche. That assessing was being made by visual inspections. On a raining day this are often far dramatic then on a sunny day.

Another apprehension that I had was of snakes, that there would be snakes lingering about.

Soyod Forid Uddin

Sonar Parah

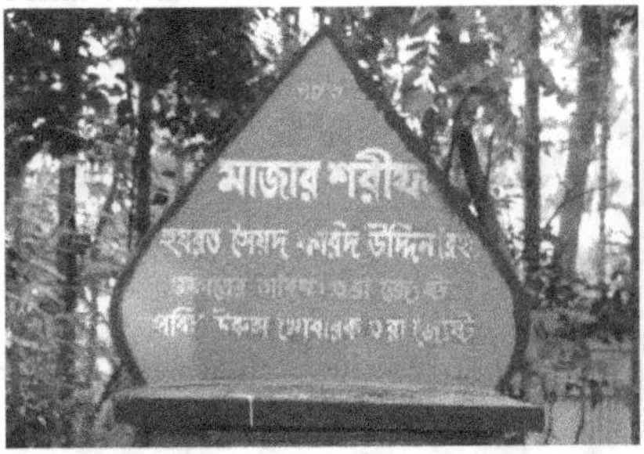
মাজার

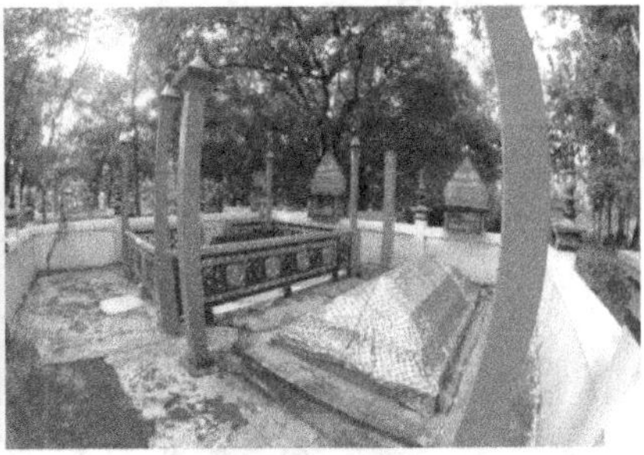

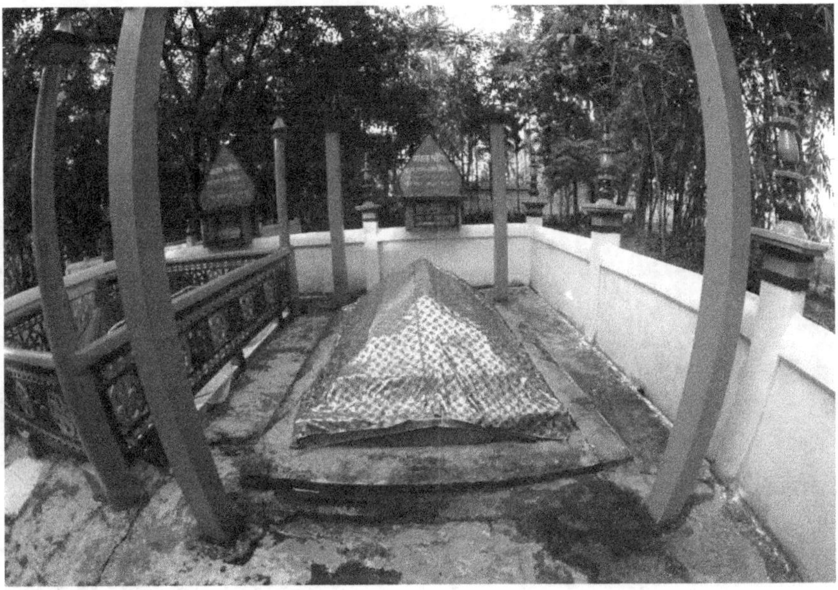

28.9.2010, 19:27:04

Well known area but not part of the 360 missionaries.

Shah Sobuj Ali

Shilam Road

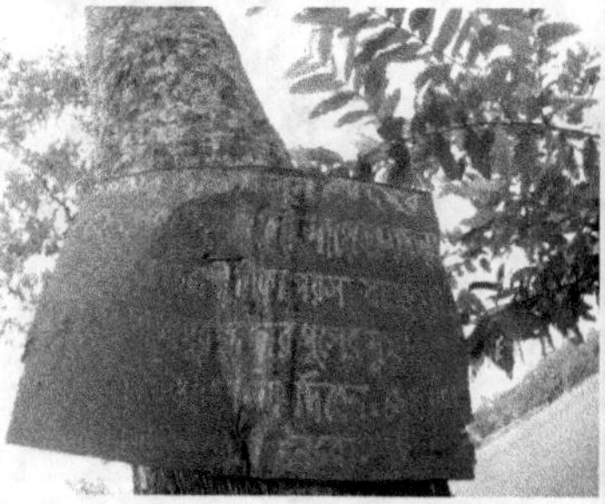

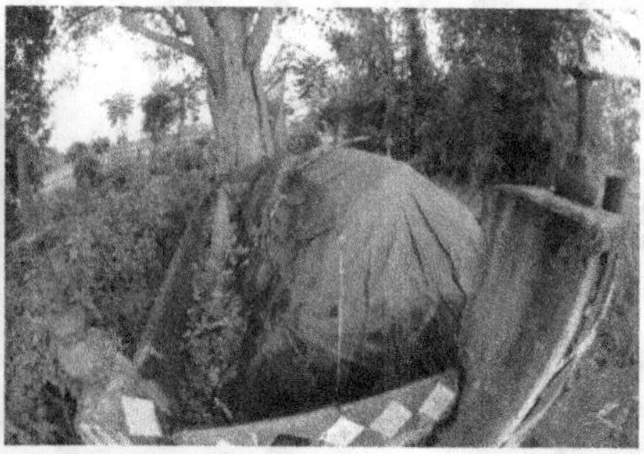

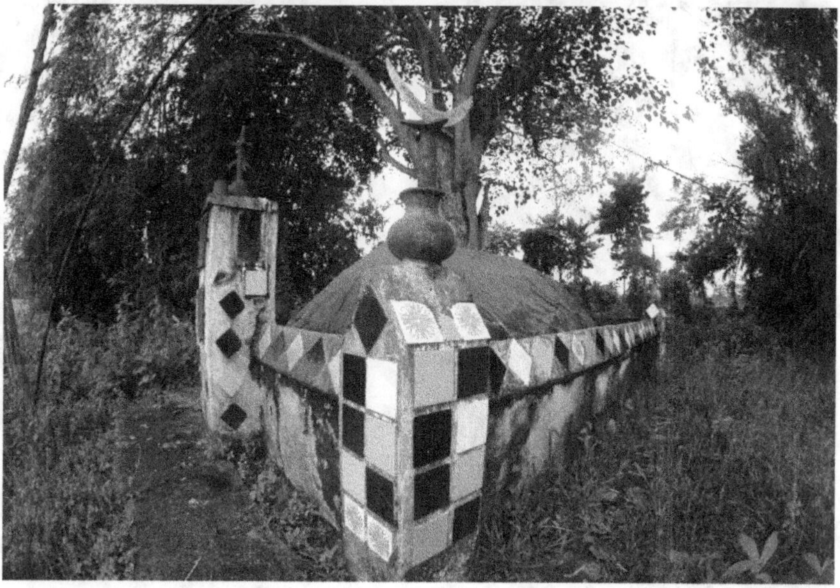

28.9.2010, 20:01:34

This was off the beaten tracks, but was visible from the main road. The mosaic tiles, like harlequin, caught my eyes.

Bibir Mukam

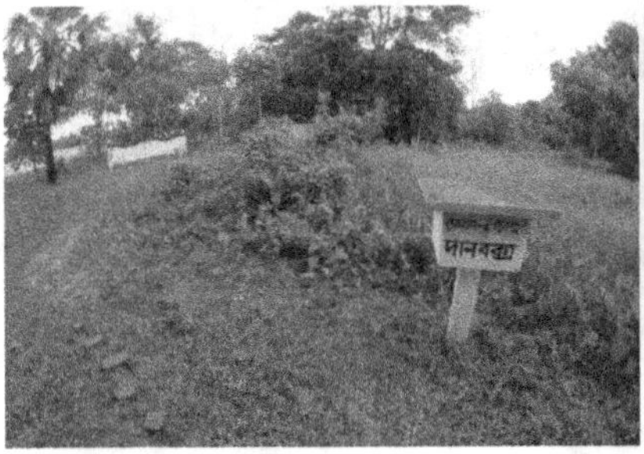

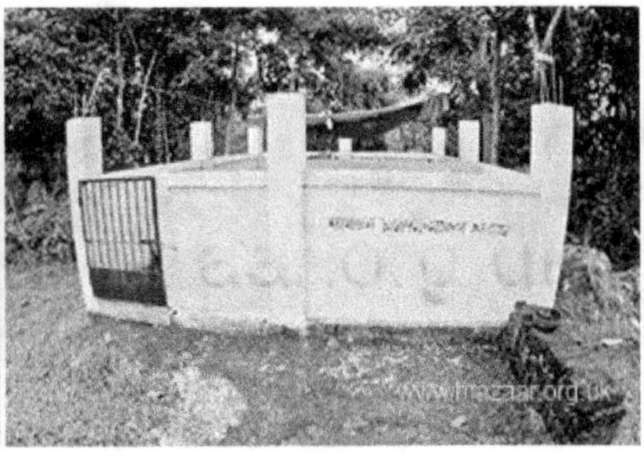
www.mazaar.org.uk

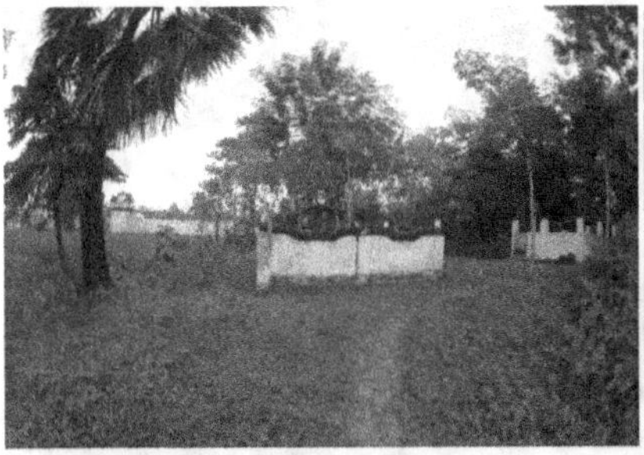

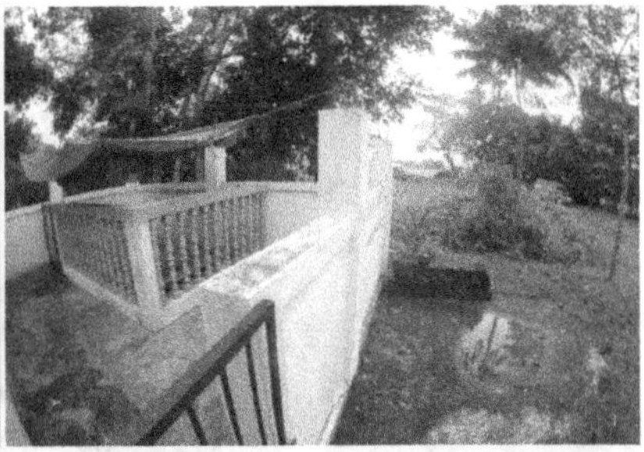

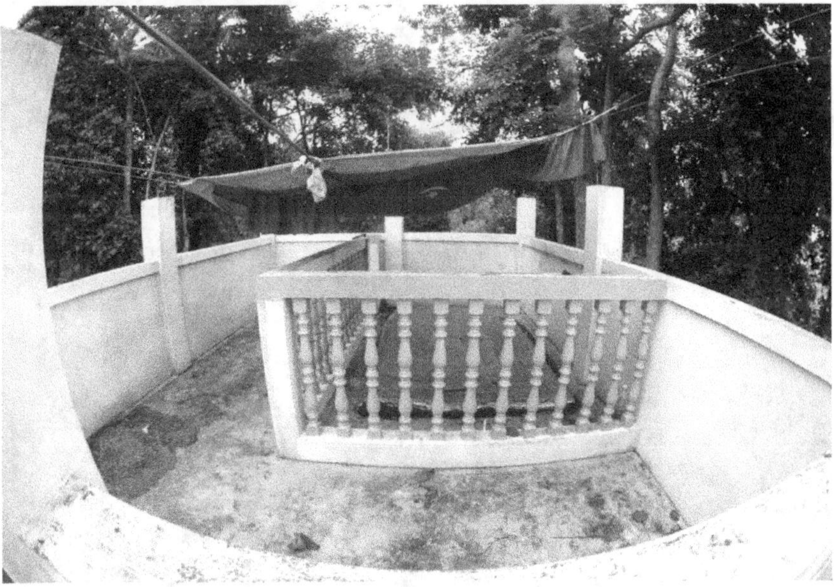

28.9.2010, 20:08:24

Shajan Ali*

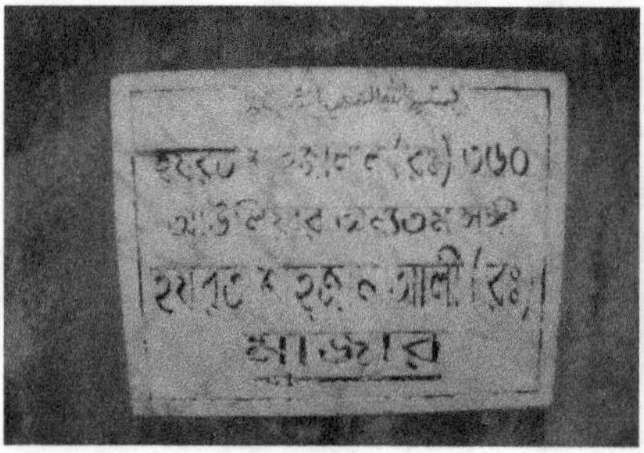

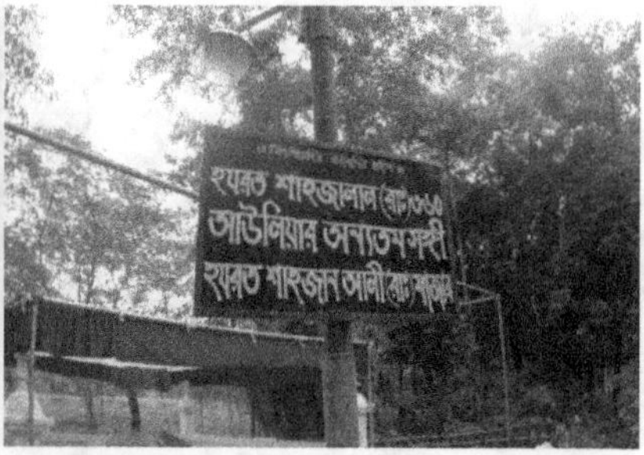
হযরত শাহজালাল (রঃ) ৩৬০
আউলিয়ার অন্যতম সঙ্গী
হযরত শাহজান আলী (রঃ)

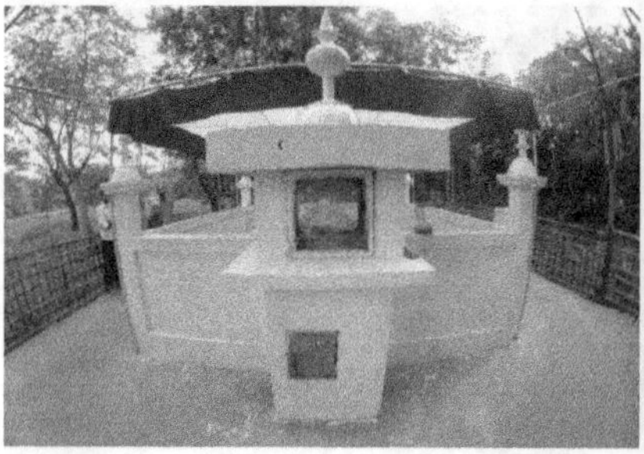

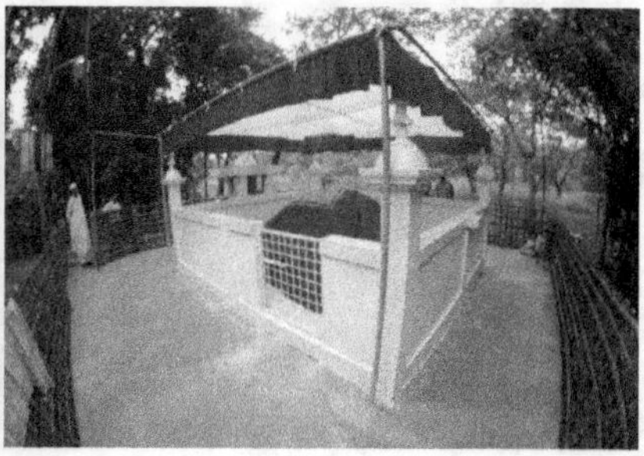

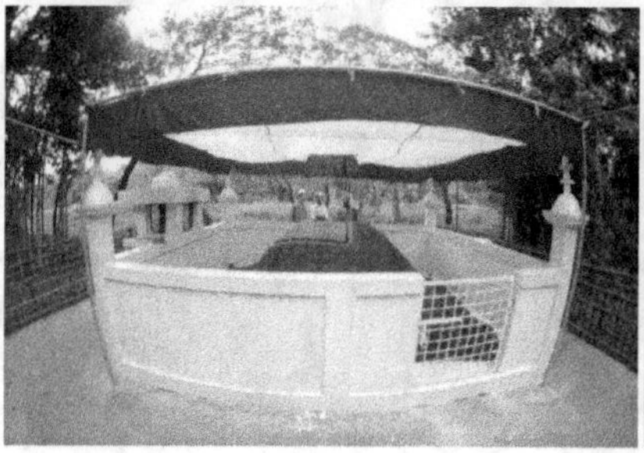

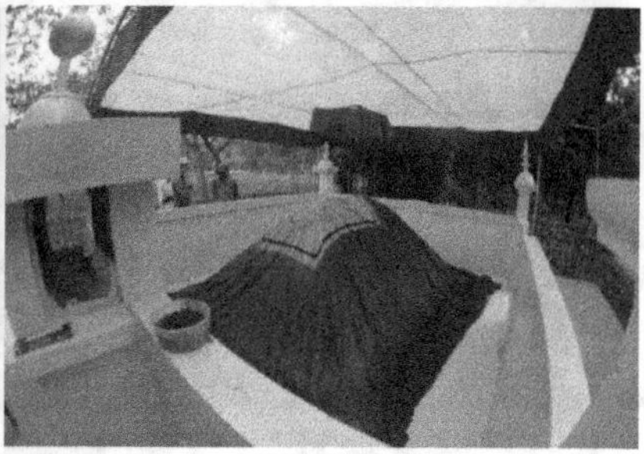

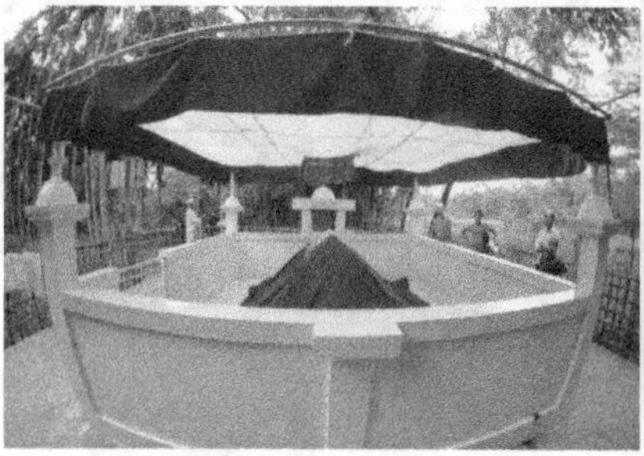

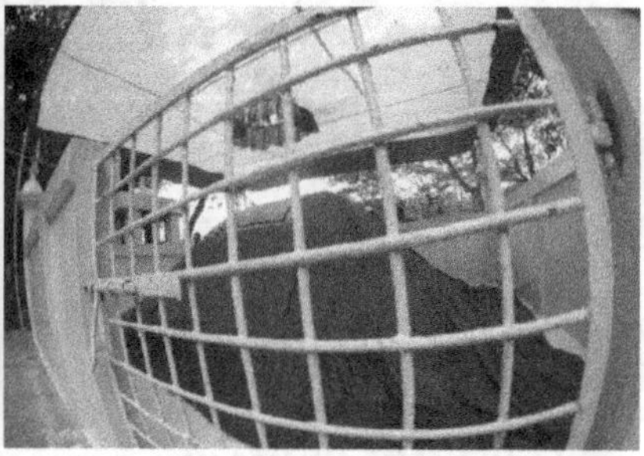

28.9.2010, 20:54:38

Sheik Nowab Ali

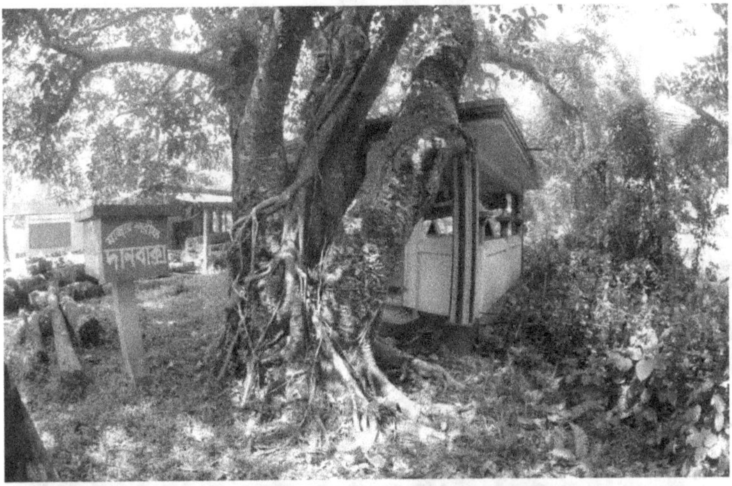

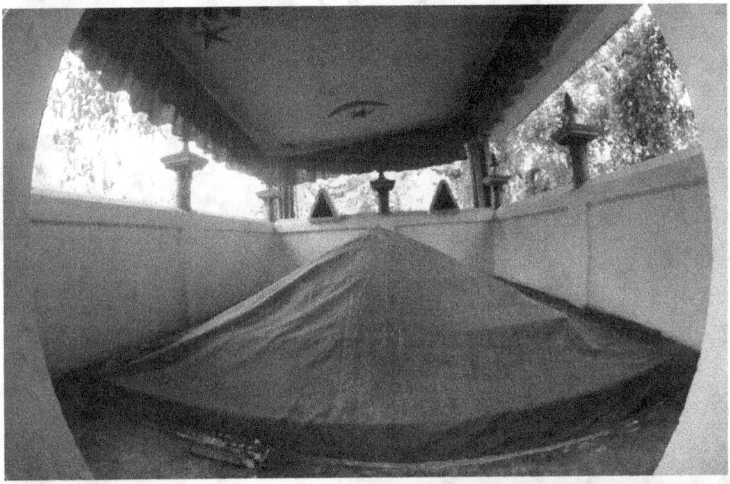

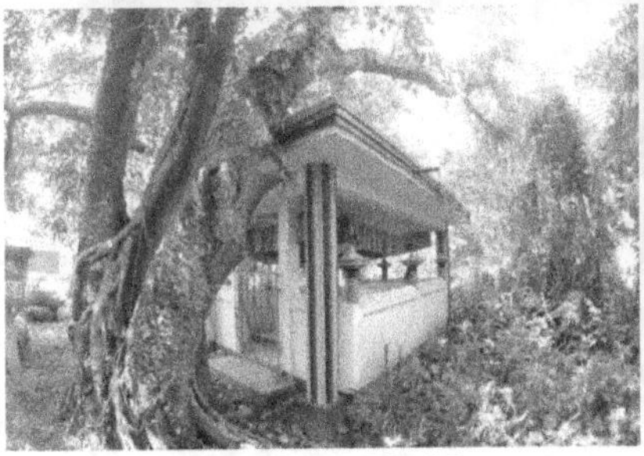

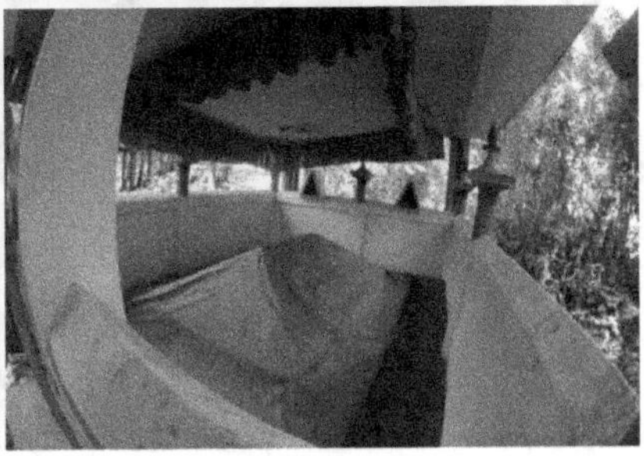

29.9.2010, 14:59:02

Shah Shayok Forid Ansari**

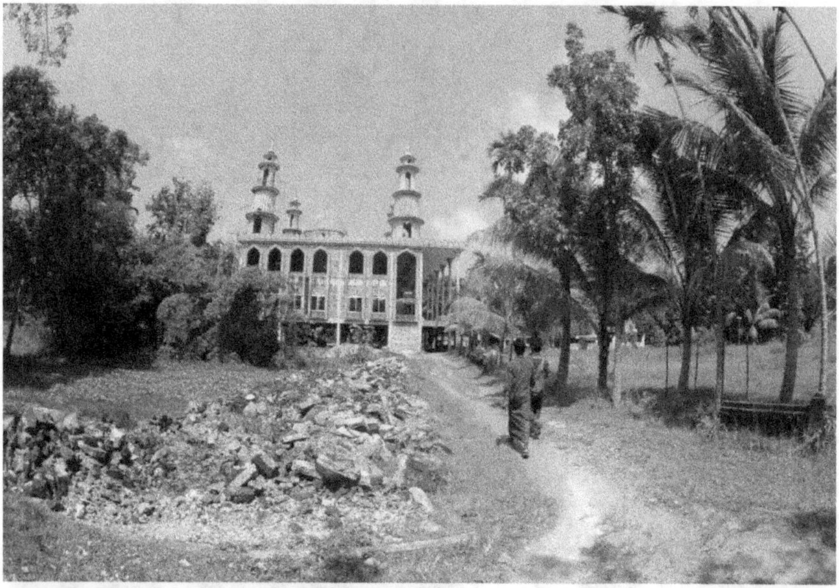

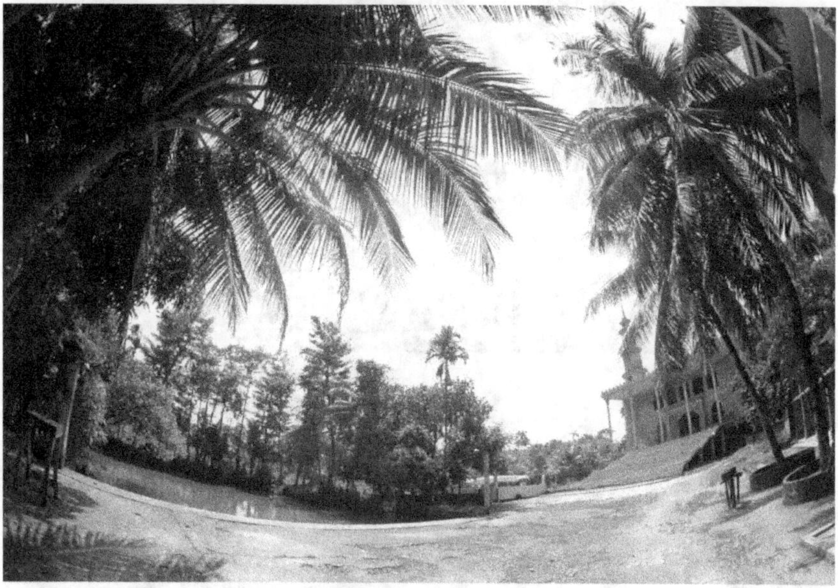

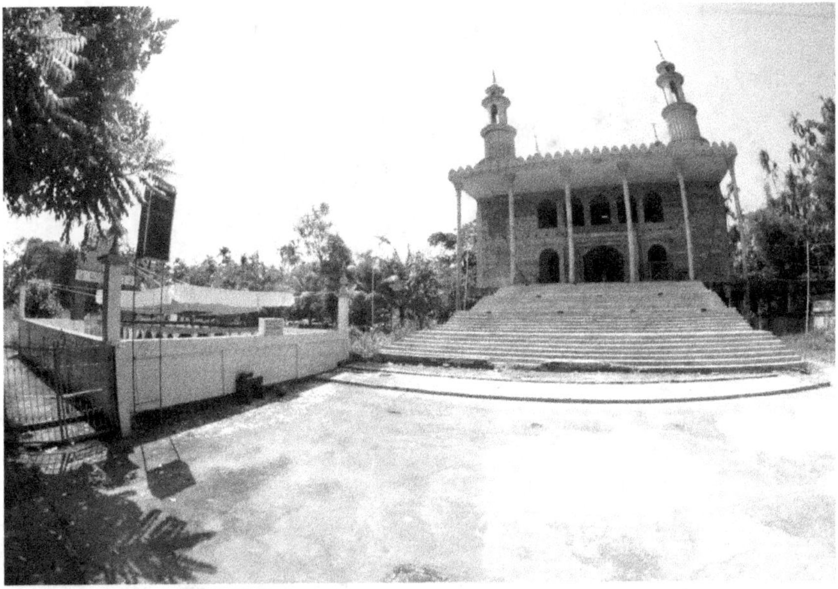

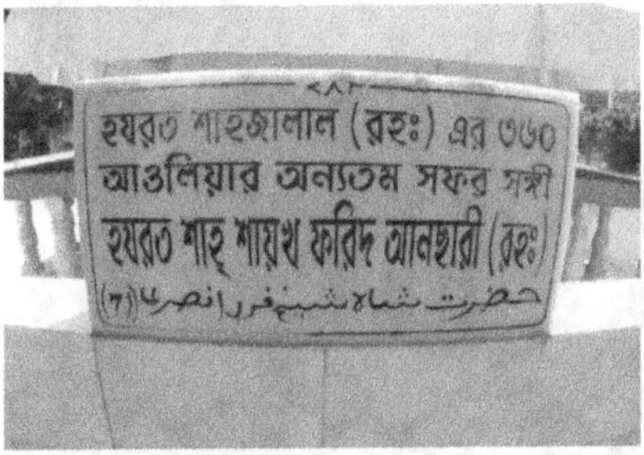
হযরত শাহজালাল (রহঃ) এর ৩৬০
আওলিয়ার অন্যতম সফর সঙ্গী
হযরত শাহ্ শায়খ ফরিদ আনছারী (রহঃ)

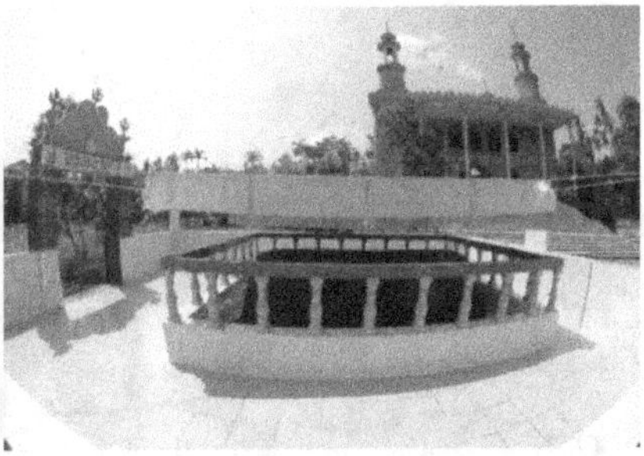

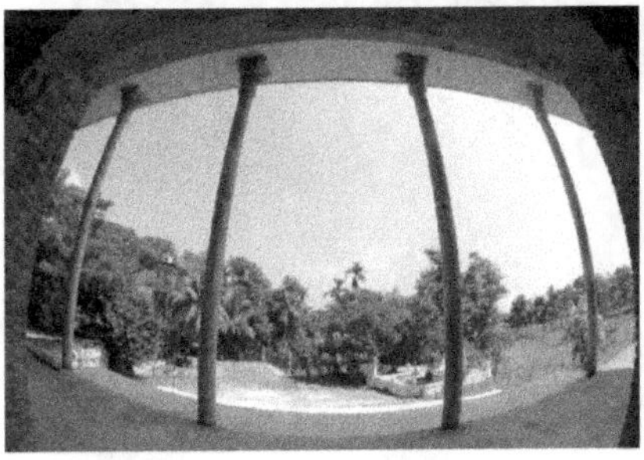

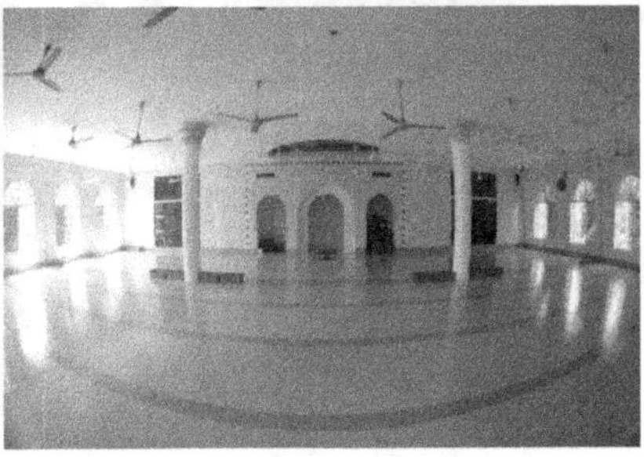

29.9.2010, 15:29:00

Shah Moulovi Sufi Shahen Kajim

Additto Pur, (Boro Bari) Sylhet Town

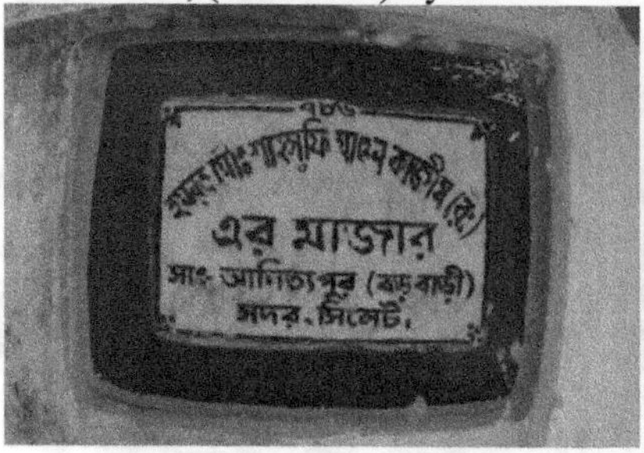
এর মাজার
সাং- আদিত্যপুর (বড়বাড়ী)
সদর. সিলেট।

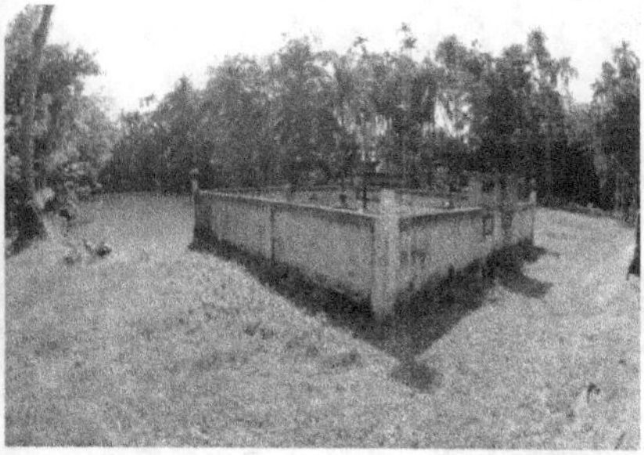

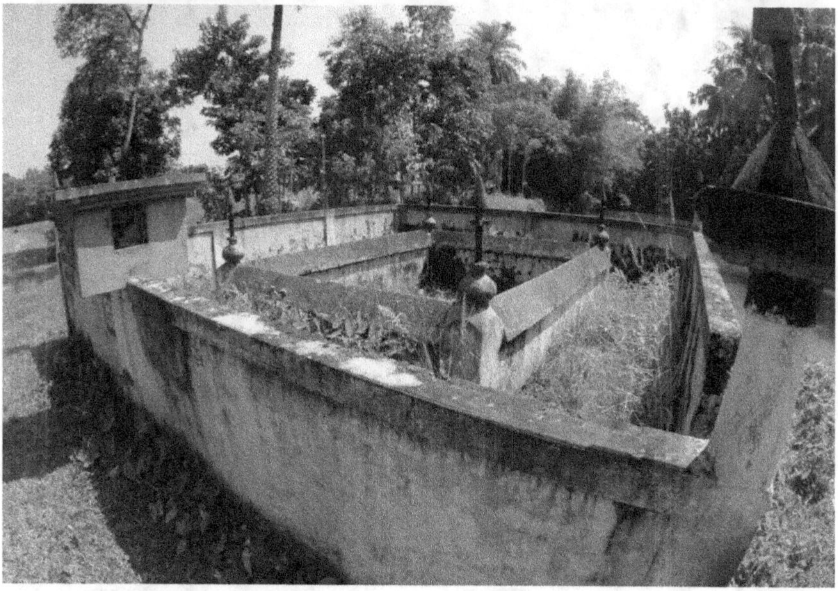

29.9.2010, 15:50:38

Monnan Shah

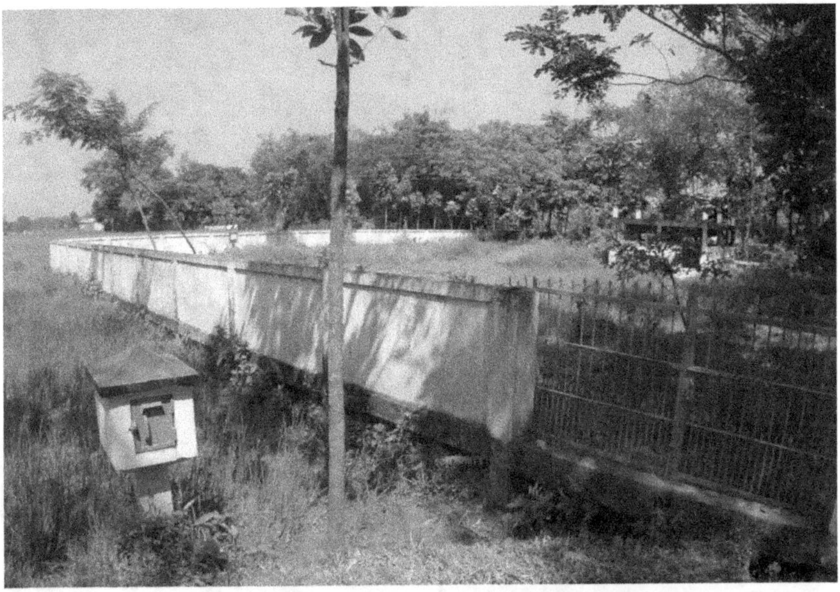

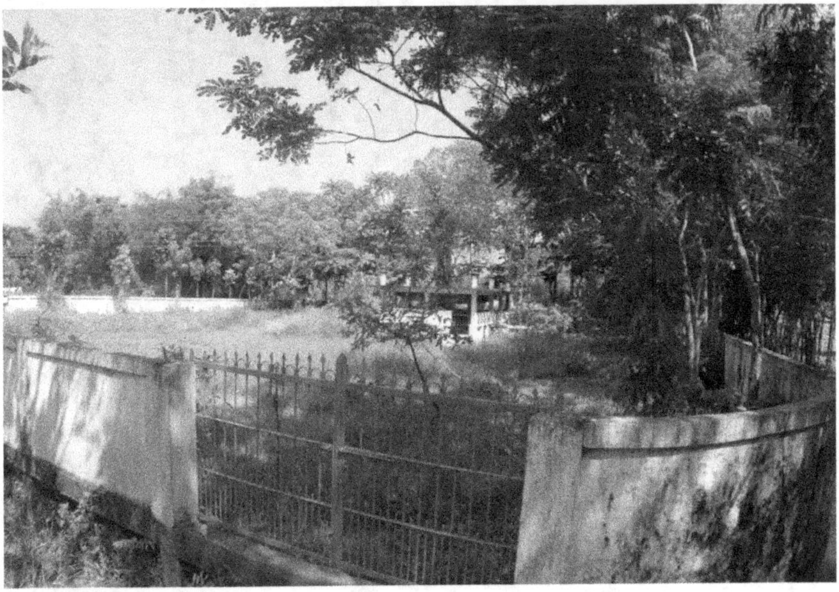

Site was inaccessible

29.9.2010, 16:04:38

Shah Kidur*

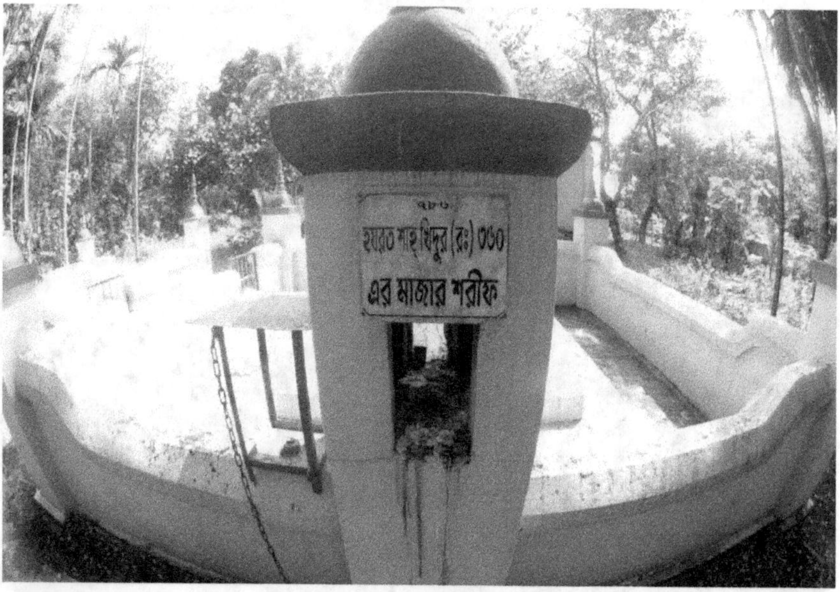
৭৮৬
হযরত শাহ খিদুর (রঃ) ৩৬০
এর মাজার শরীফ

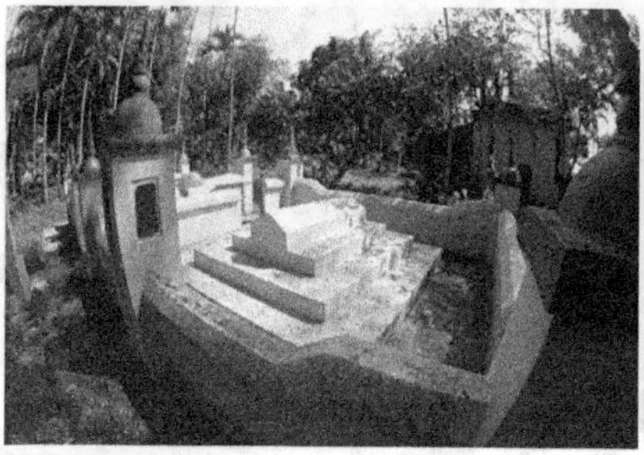

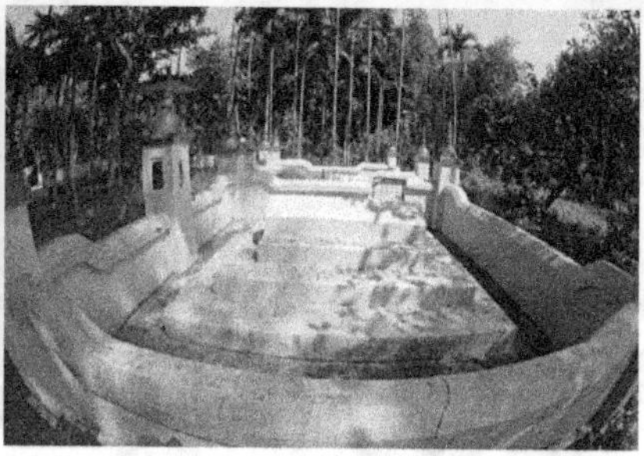

29.9.2010, 16:10:12

There is a claim on the plaque that he has some significance to the 360 missionaries.

Shah Imam Boksh

This grave is adjacent to Shah Kidur.

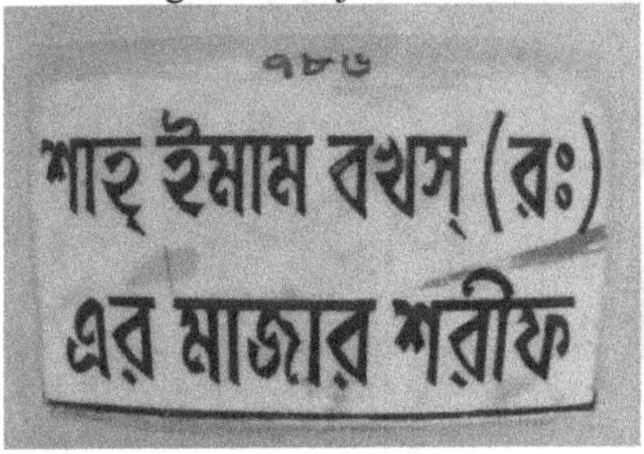
৭৮৩
শাহ্ ইমাম বখস্ (রঃ)
এর মাজার শরীফ

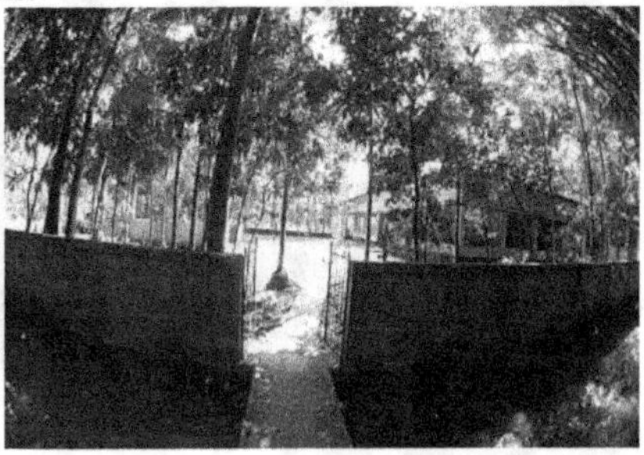

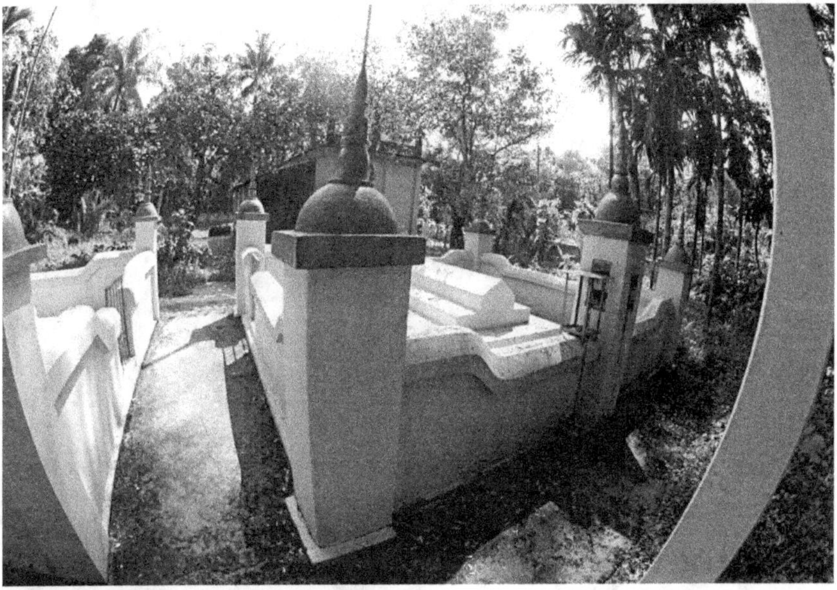

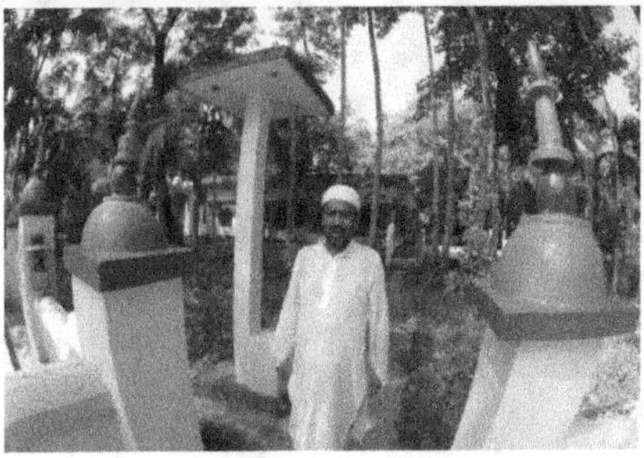

29.9.2010, 16:12:40

Qari Sheik Shah Osman Uddin*

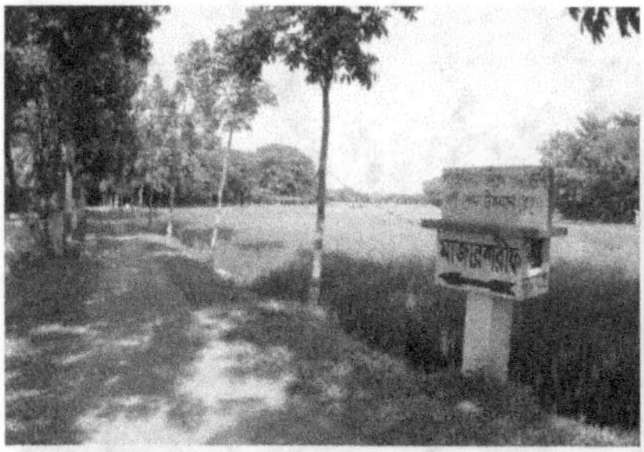

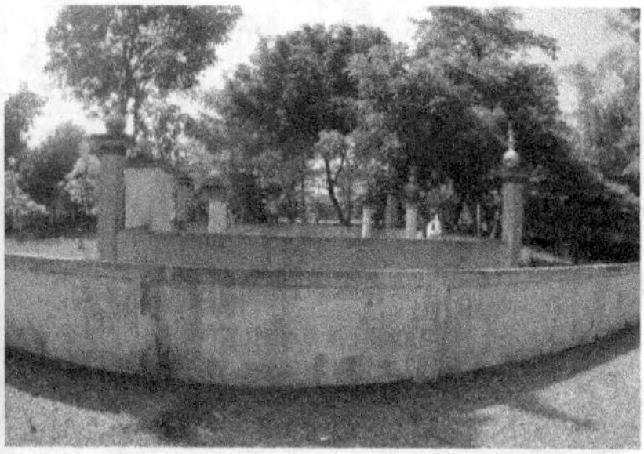

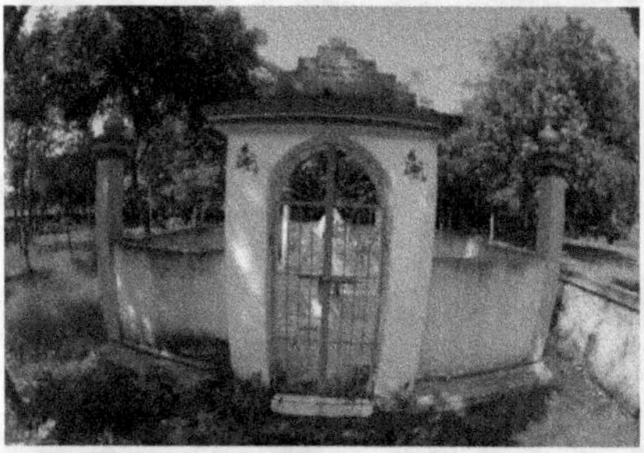

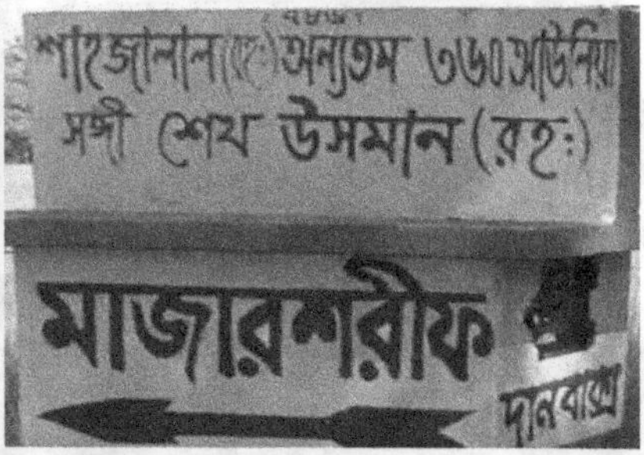
শাহজালাল(রঃ) অন্যতম ৩৬০ আউলিয়া
সঙ্গী শেখ উসমান (রহঃ)
মাজারশরীফ
দানবাক্স

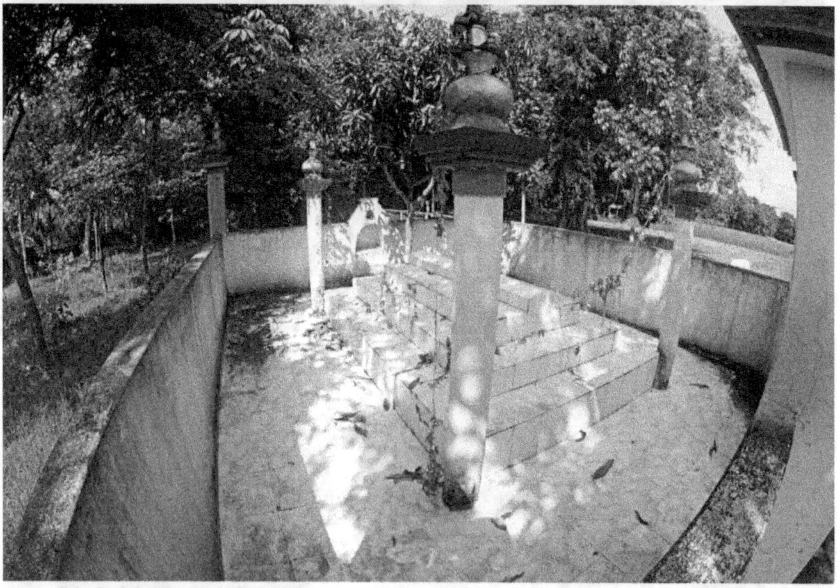

29.9.2010, 16:37:38

There is claim of being part of the 360 missionaries, but there is no 8 sided plaque verifying it. Then again it cannot be claimed willy-nilly, it will be met with scrutiny

Shah Batauk*

Bagerkola, Sylhet

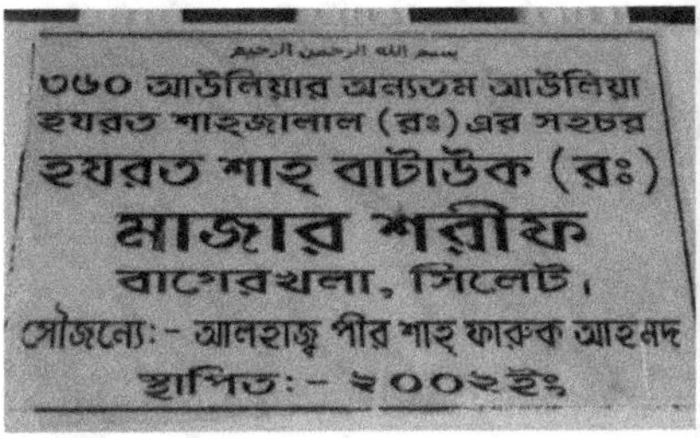
بسم الله الرحمن الرحيم
৩৬০ আউলিয়ার অন্যতম আউলিয়া
হযরত শাহজালাল (রঃ) এর সহচর
হযরত শাহ্ বাটাউক (রঃ)
মাজার শরীফ
বাগেরখলা, সিলেট।
সৌজন্যে:- আলহাজ্ব পীর শাহ্ ফারুক আহমদ
স্থাপিত:- ২০০২ইং

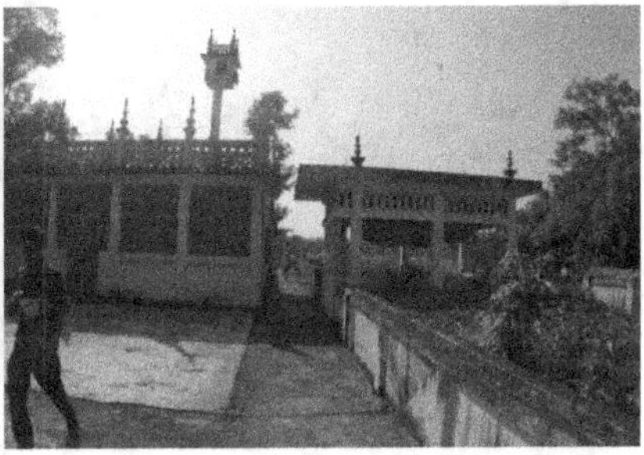

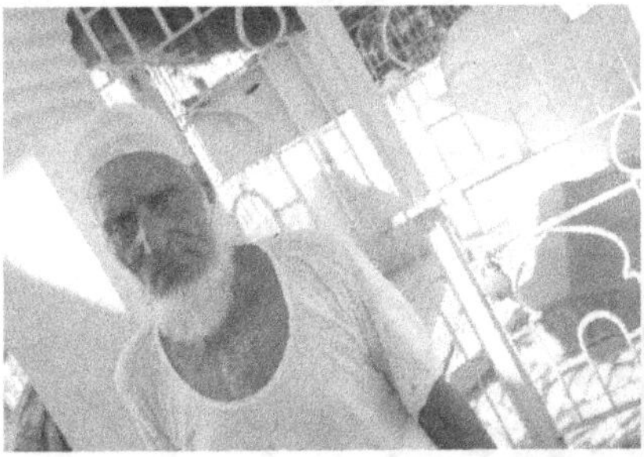

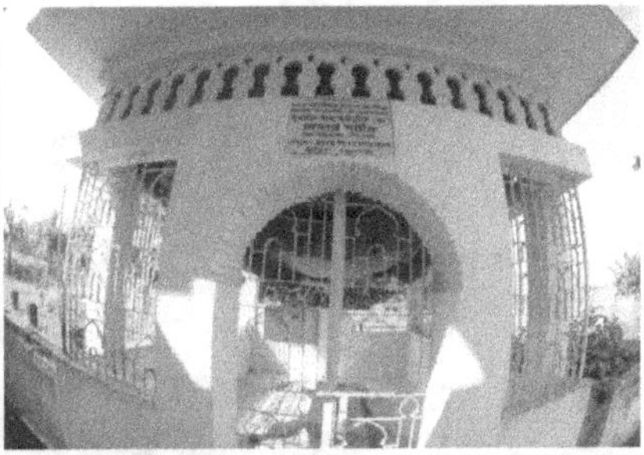

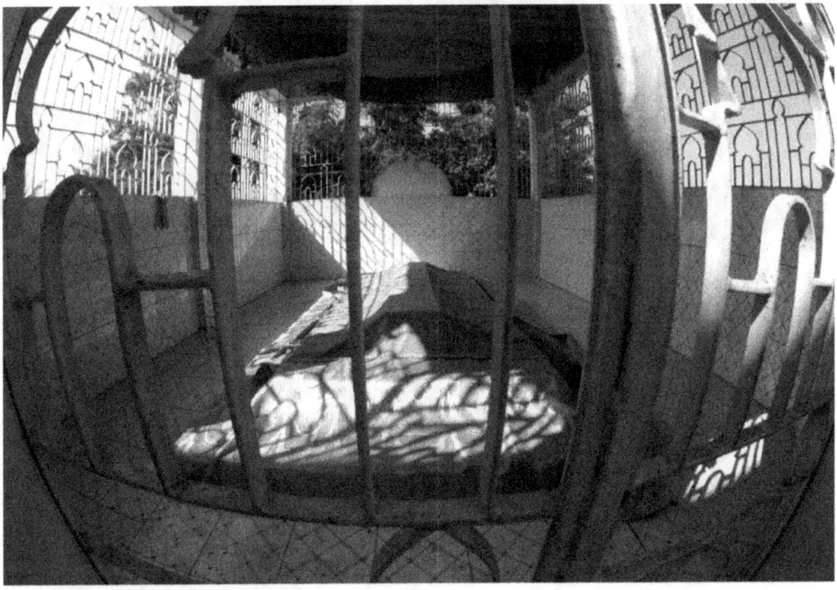

29.9.2010, 17:20:46

There is a claim of being part of the 360 group.

Phir Mohammod Abdul Malik

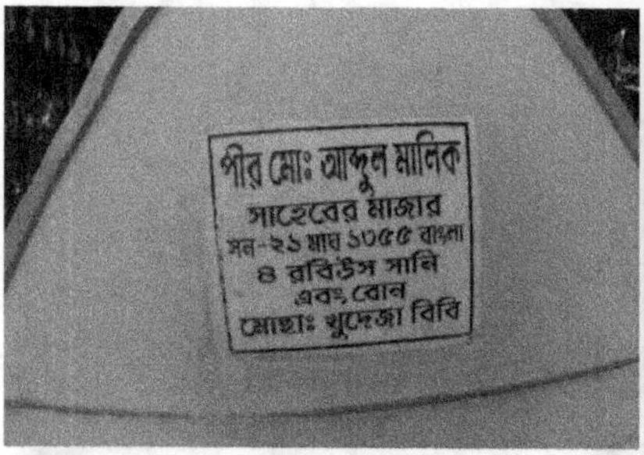
পীর মোঃ আব্দুল মালিক
সাহেবের মাজার
সন-২১ মাঘ ১৩৫৫ বাংলা
৪ রবিউস সানি
এবং বোন
মোছাঃ খুদেজা বিবি

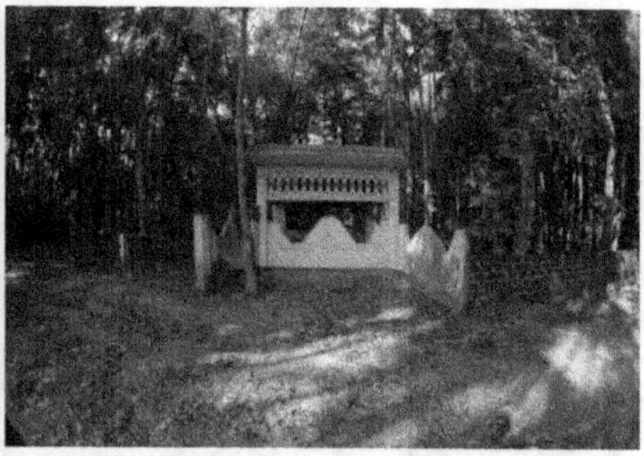

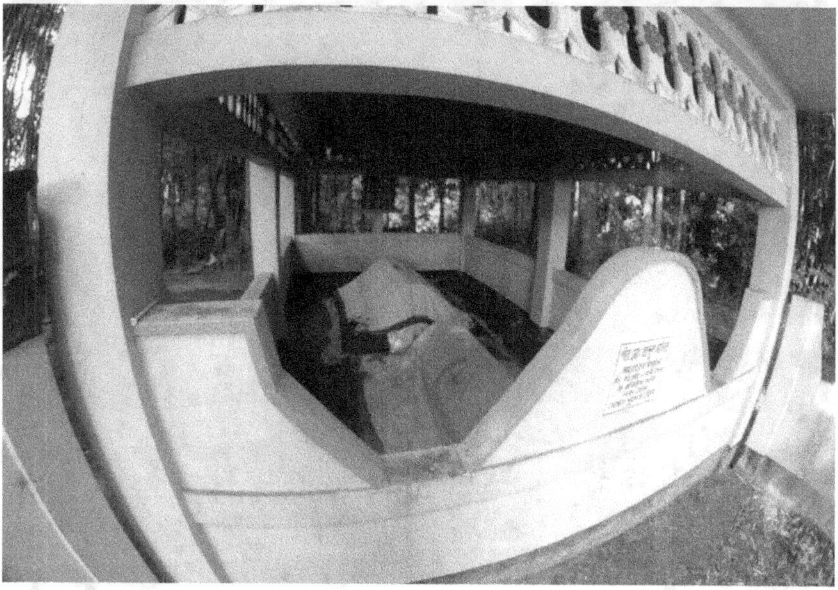

29.9.2010, 18:09:08

Shah Sikandar*

Lala Bazar

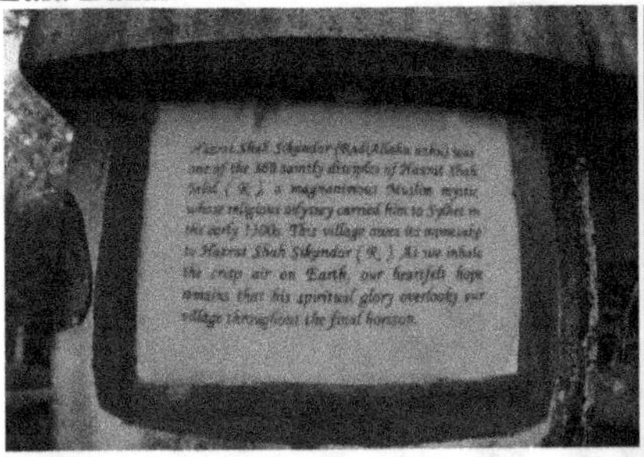

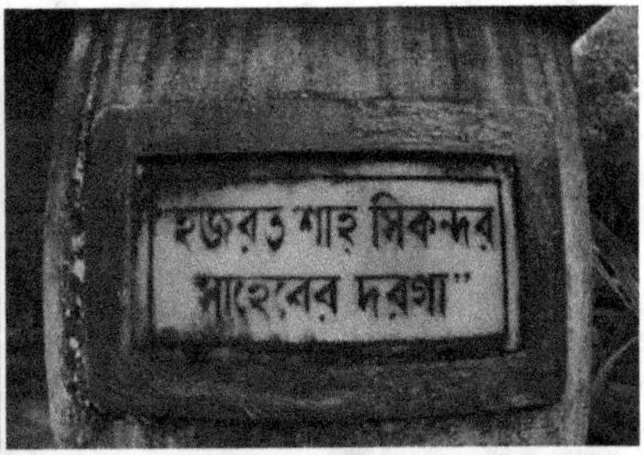
"হজরত শাহ সিকন্দর
সাহেবের দরগা"

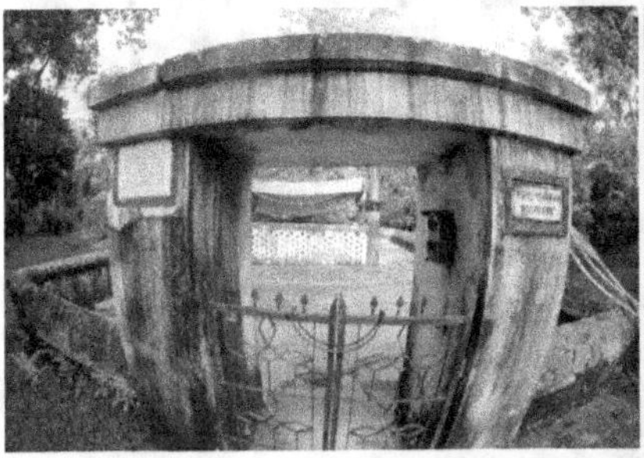

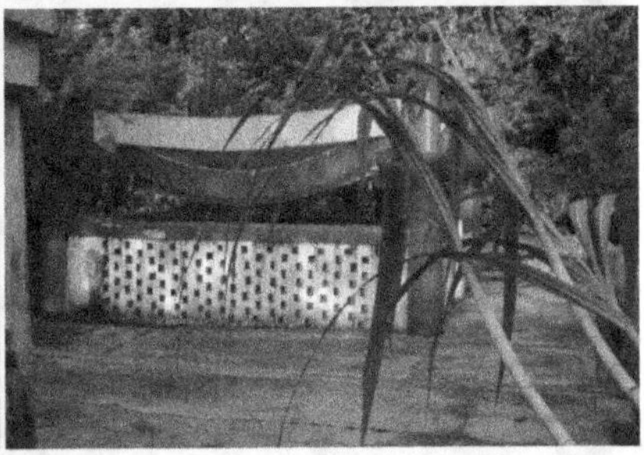

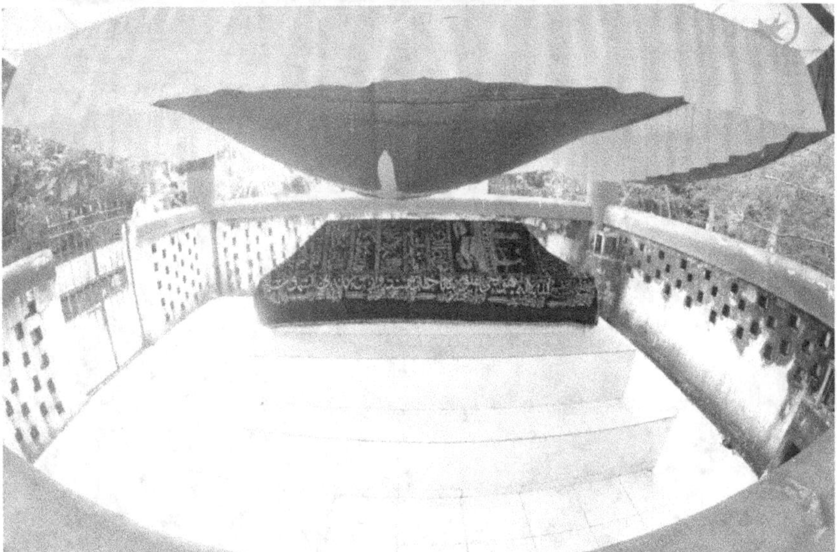

29.9.2010, 19:10:22

Sultan Monir Uddin Yemeni

Katadiya, Dorga Lama, Lala Bazar, Dokkin Surma, Sylhet

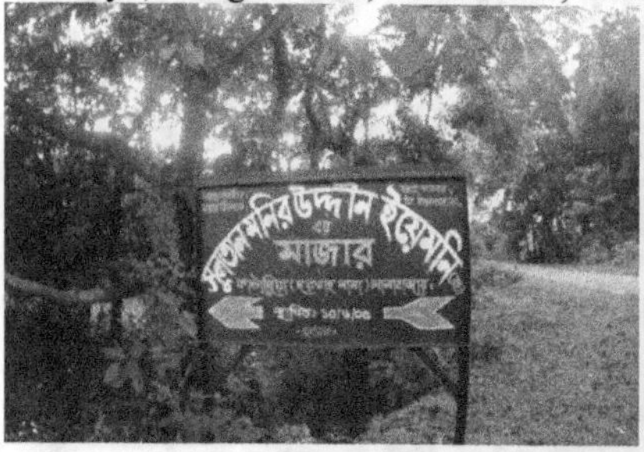
মাজার

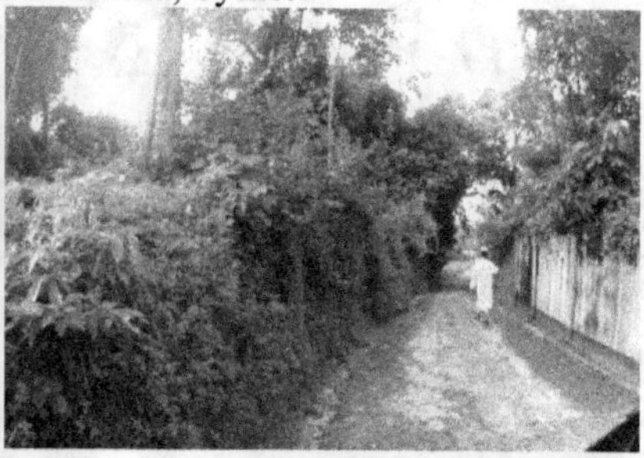

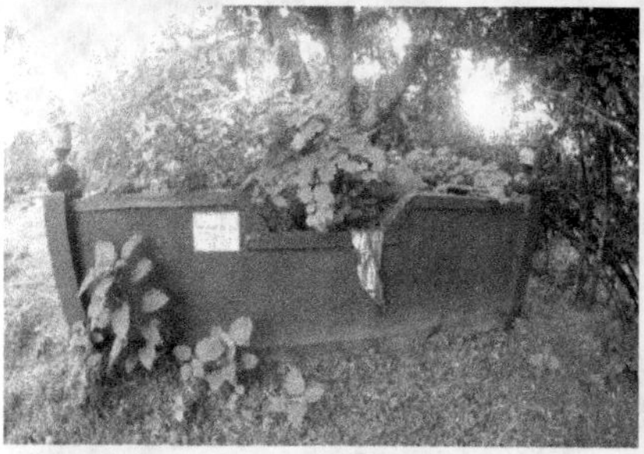

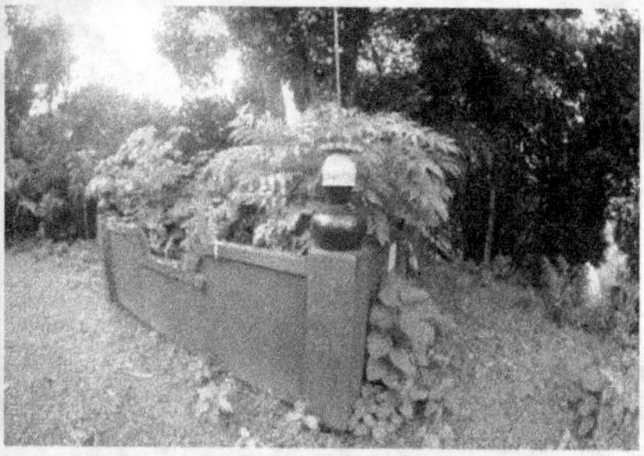

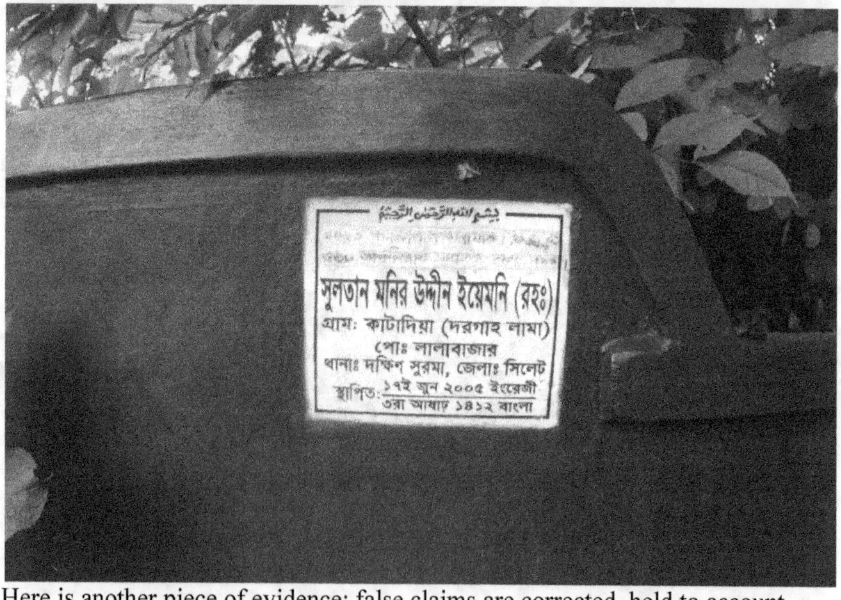
بِسْمِ اللّٰهِ الرَّحْمٰنِ الرَّحِيْمِ
সুলতান মনির উদ্দীন ইয়েমনি (রহঃ)
গ্রাম: কাটাদিয়া (দরগাহ লামা)
পোঃ লালাবাজার
থানাঃ দক্ষিণ সুরমা, জেলাঃ সিলেট
স্থাপিত: ১৭ই জুন ২০০৫ ইংরেজী
৩রা আষাঢ় ১৪১২ বাংলা

Here is another piece of evidence; false claims are corrected, held to account.

29.9.2010, 19:38:04

Bu Ali*

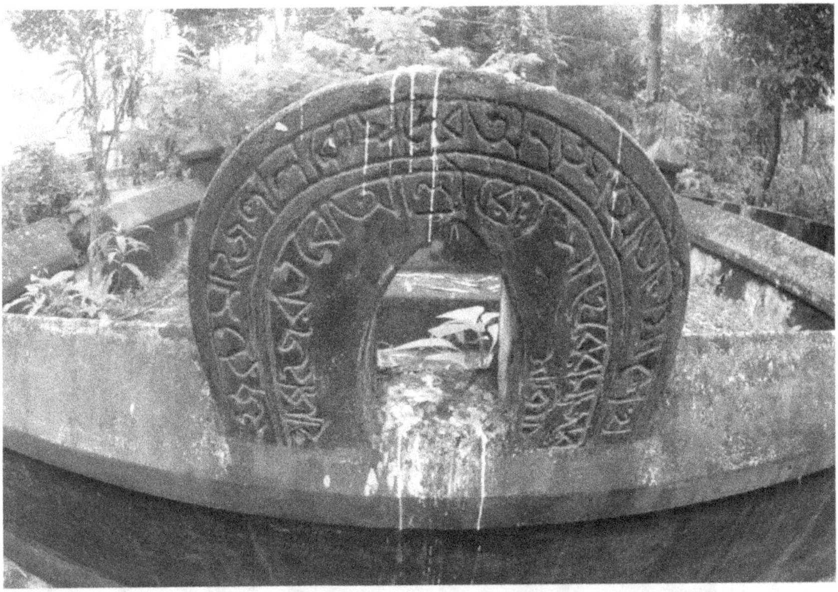

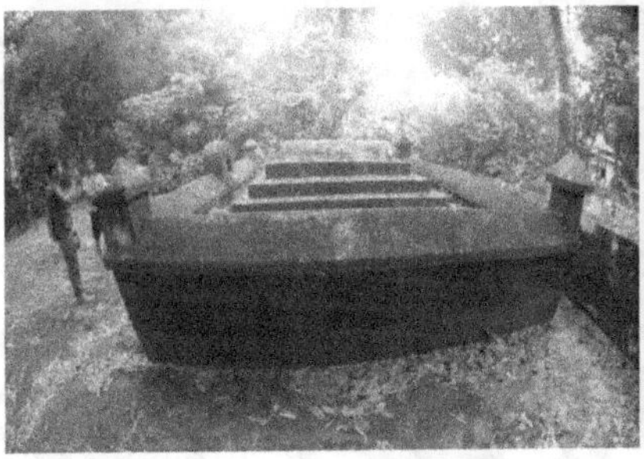

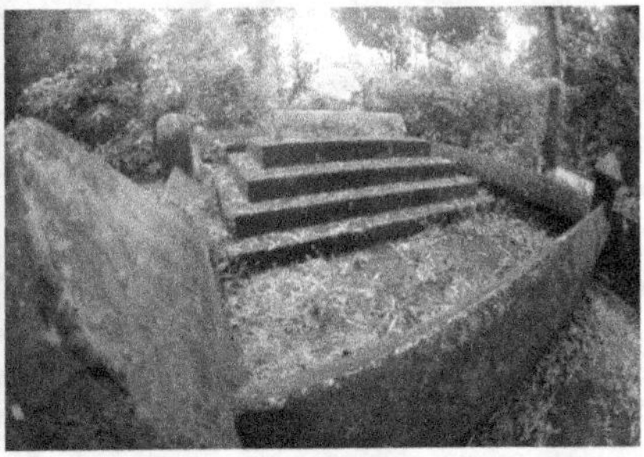

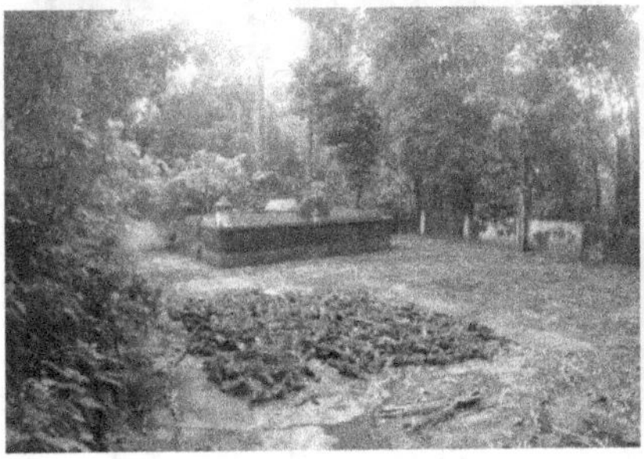

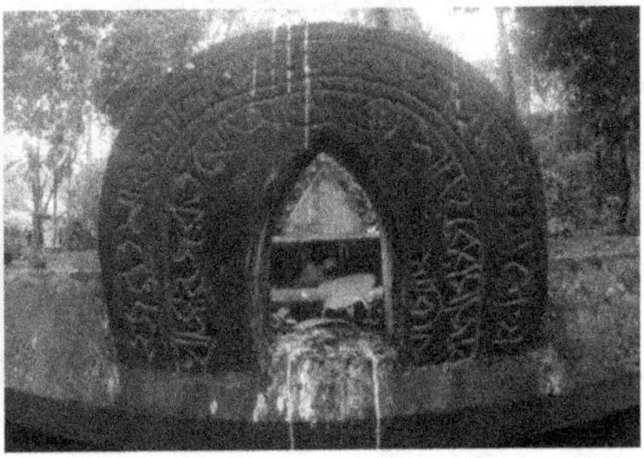

29.9.2010, 19:57:58

Soyod Sofor Ali

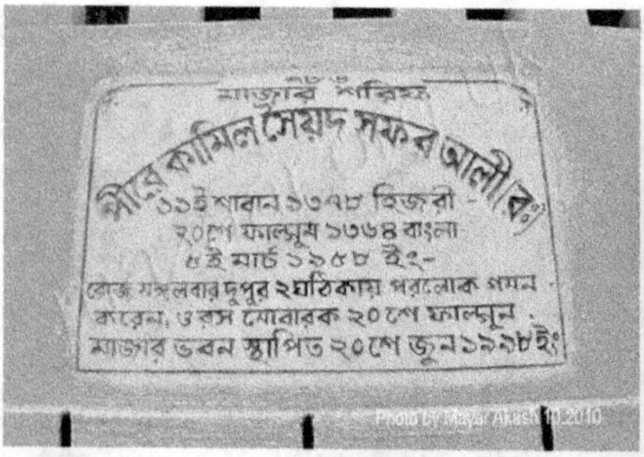
মাজার শরিফ
পীরে কামিল সৈয়দ সফর আলী (রঃ)
১১ই শাবান ১৩৭৮ হিজরী -
২০শে ফাল্গুন ১৩৬৪ বাংলা
মার্চ ১৯৫৮ ইং-
রোজ মঙ্গলবার দুপুর ২ঘটিকায় পরলোক গমন
করেন, ওরস মোবারক ২০শে ফাল্গুন
মাজার ভবন স্থাপিত ২০শে জুন১৯৯৮ইং
Photo by Mayar Akash 10.2010

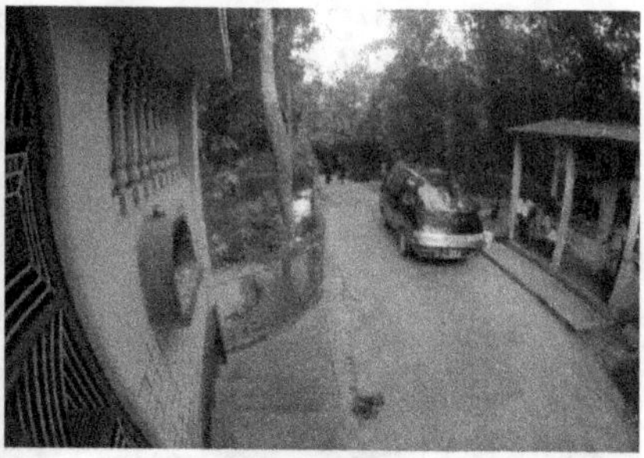

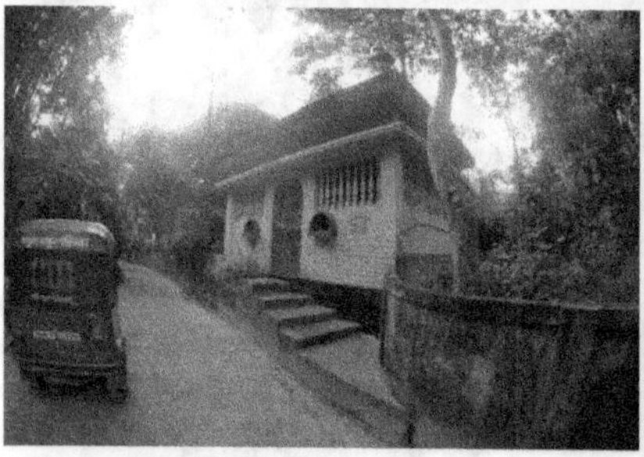

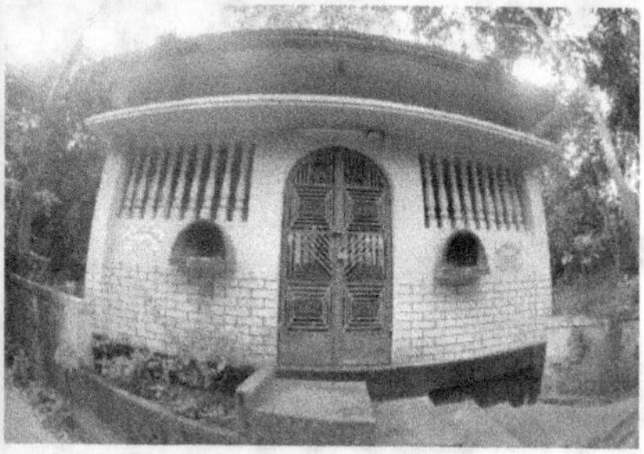

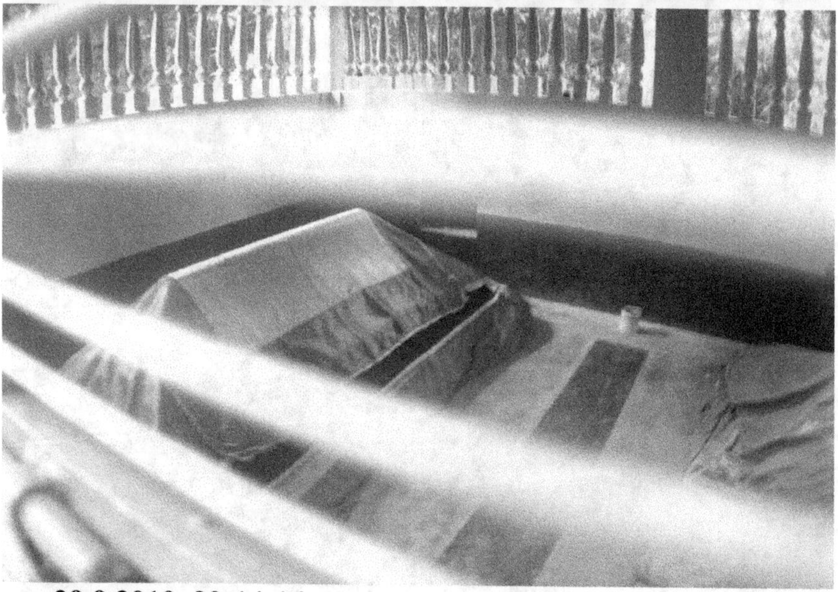

29.9.2010, 20:14:16

This was a stopover on our return journey.

Makdum Jafor Gojonbi**

Mohammod Pur

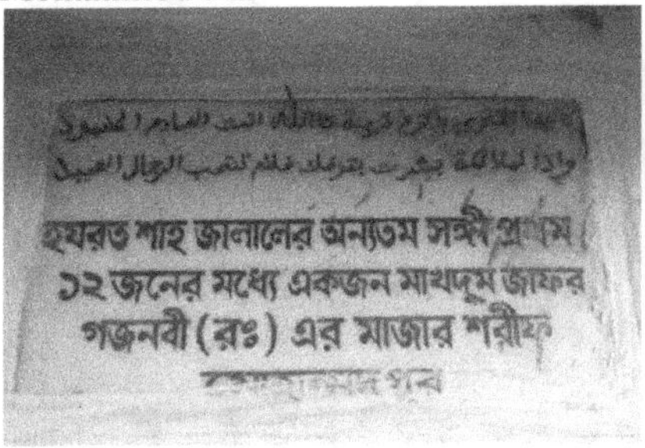
হযরত শাহ জালালের অন্যতম সঙ্গী
১২ জনের মধ্যে একজন মাখদুম জাফর
গজনবী (রঃ) এর মাজার শরীফ

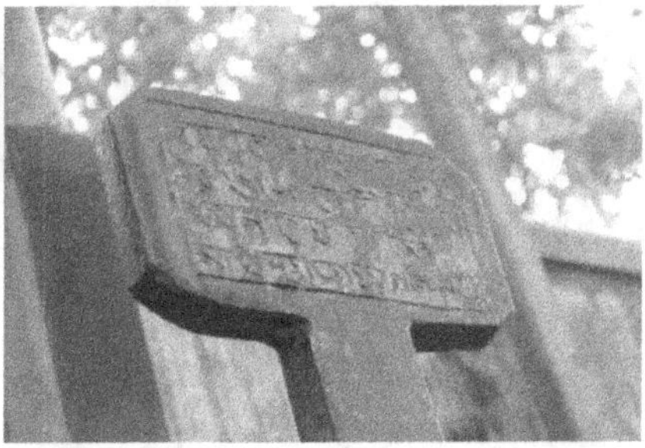

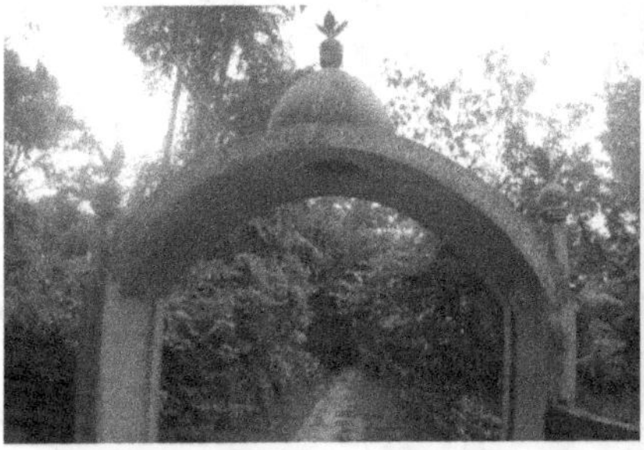

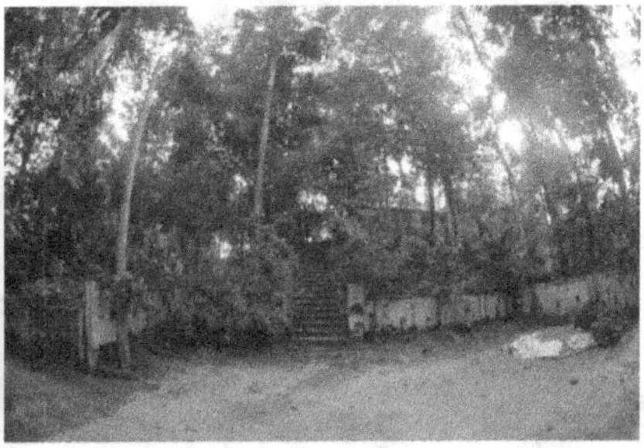

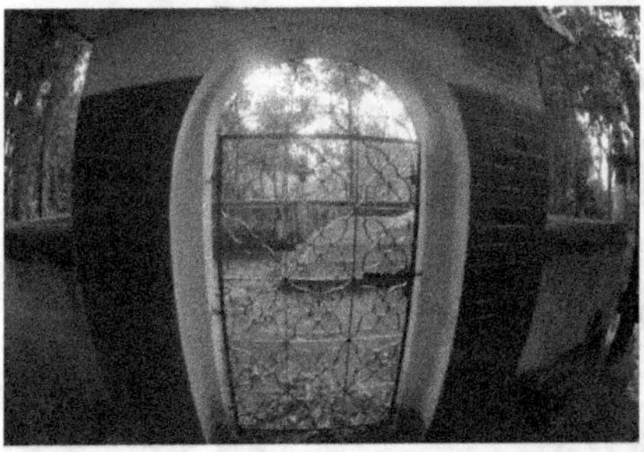

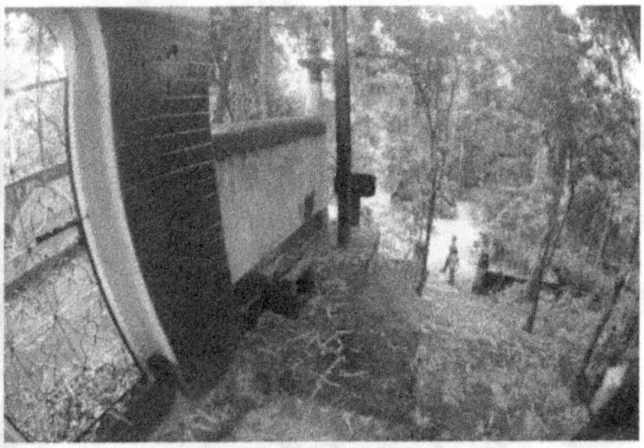

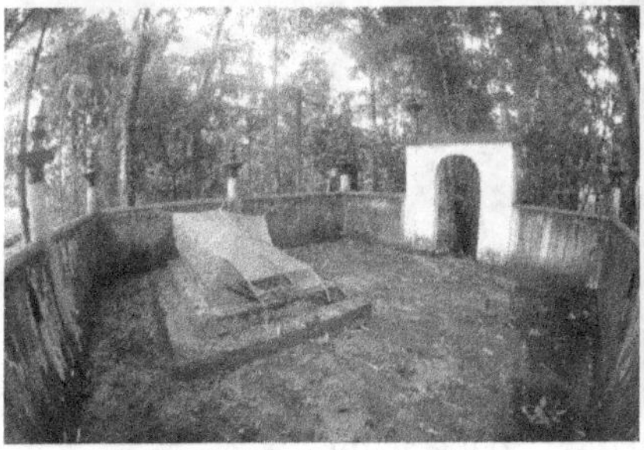

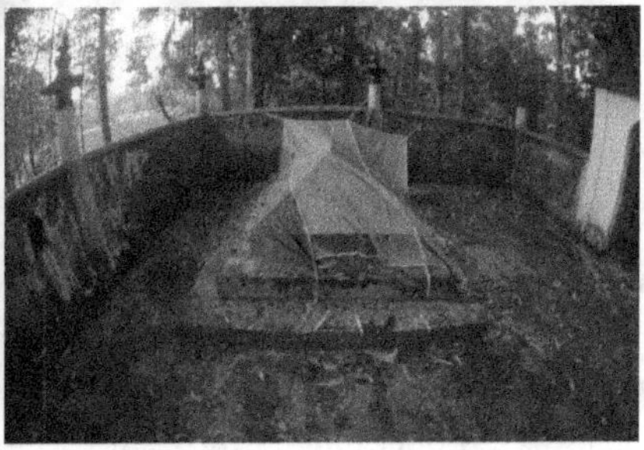

29.9.2010, 20:25:46

Soyod Shah Badsha

Tilla Mawon (Mohammod) Pur

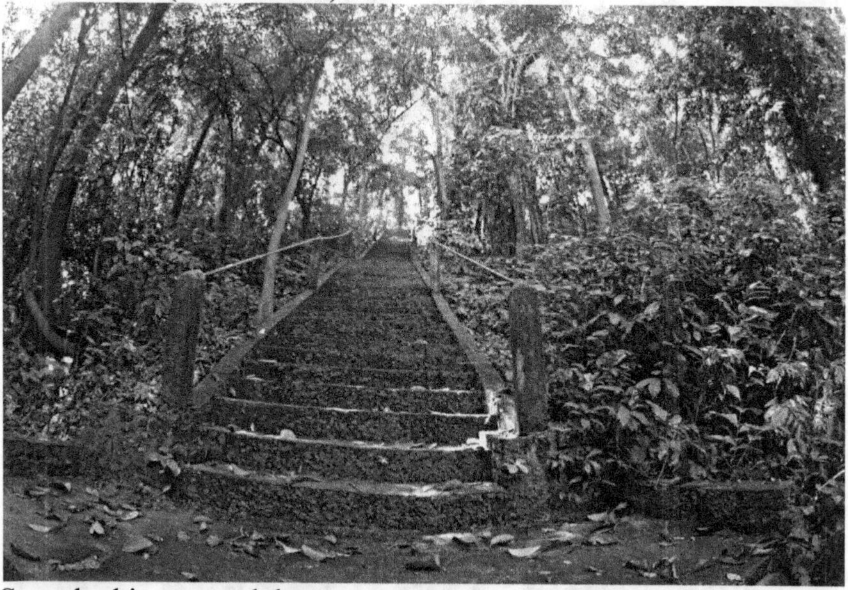

Steps looking up and down

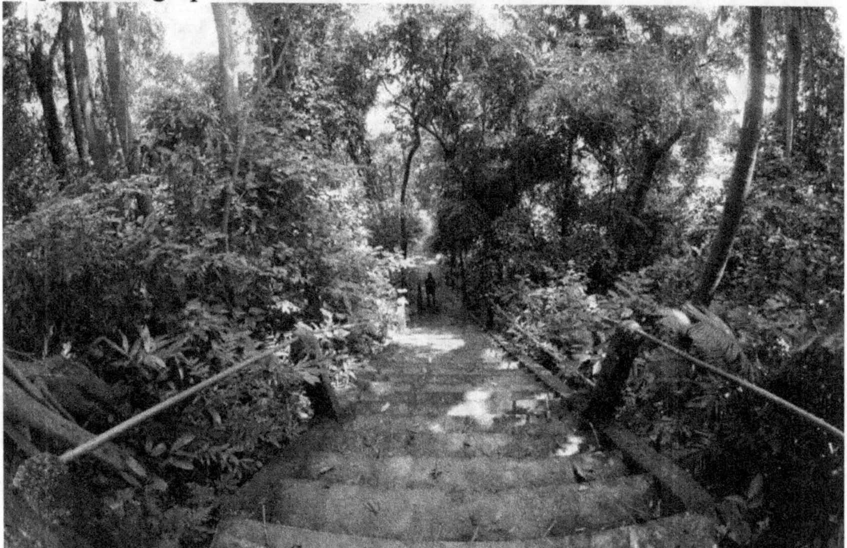

This was a proper jungle Mazar; it was up these stairs on top.

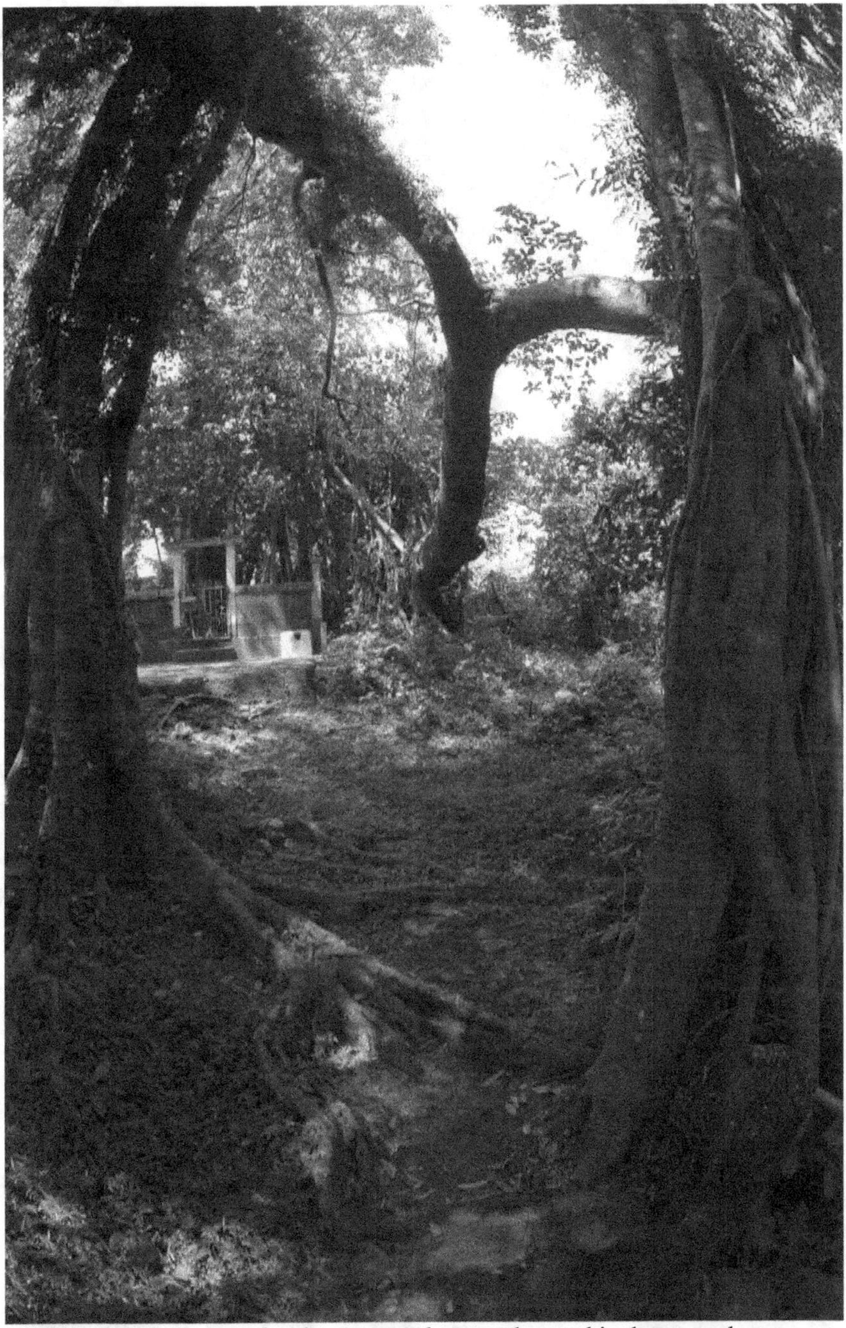

Overgrown that the branches have come down and rooted in the ground.

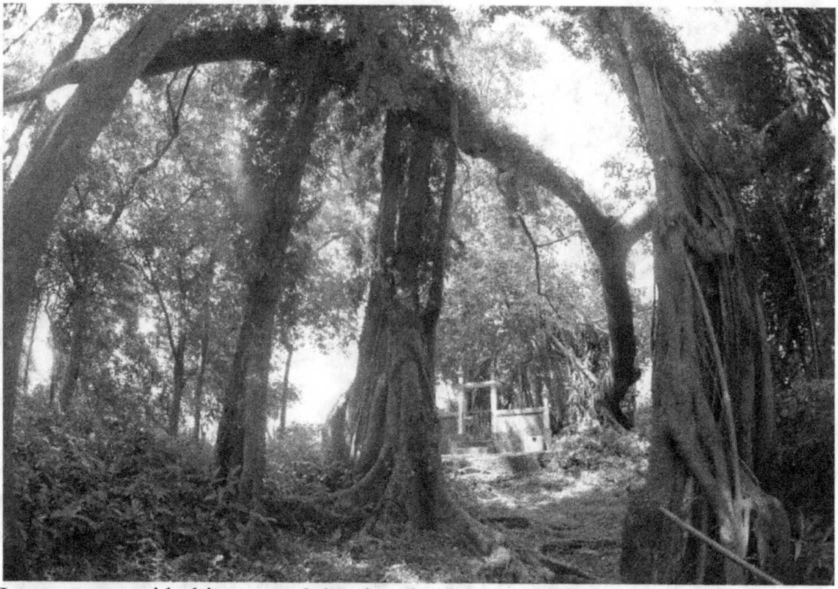

I was at awe with this tree and the site, the sheer size of the tree engulfs you.

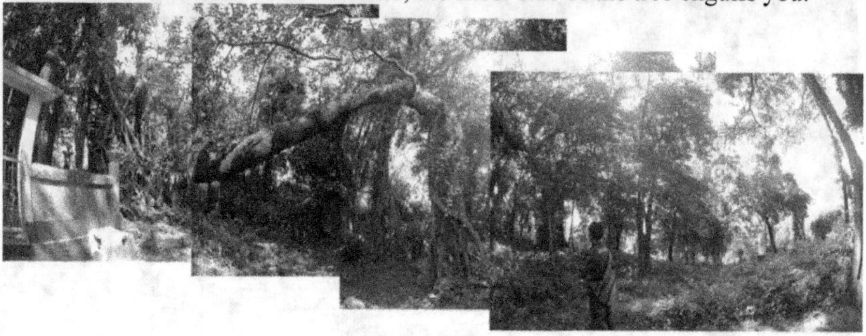

320 degree view

A panoramic image created from multiple images taken to give the sense the tree and how it has grown and spread around. The panoramic down not do justice to the scale

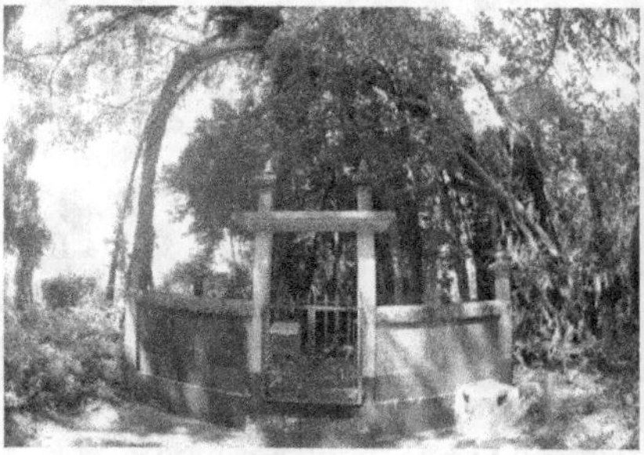

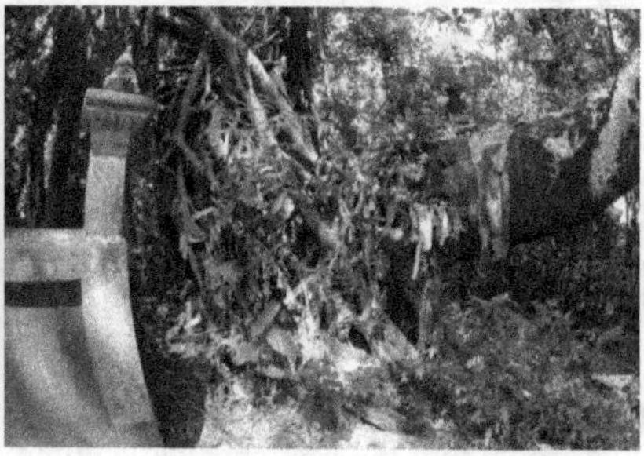

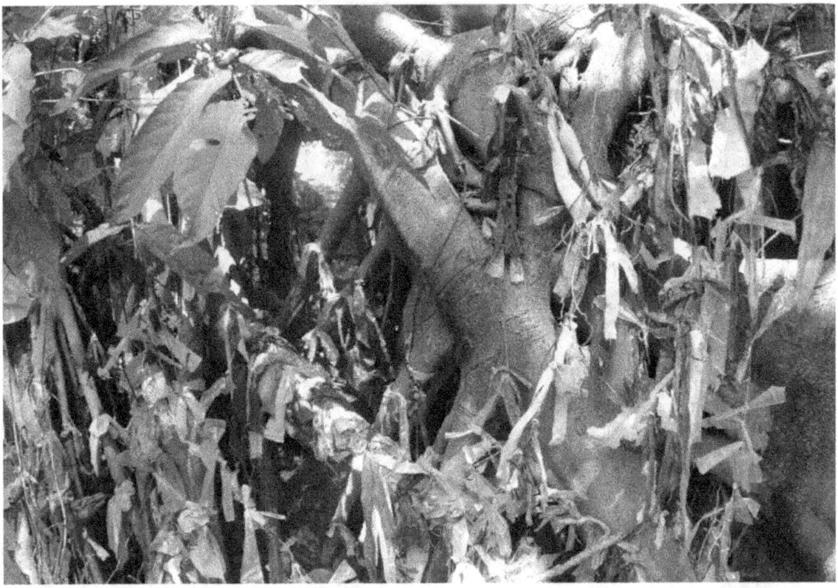

Ribbons tied on the tree trunk and the gate.

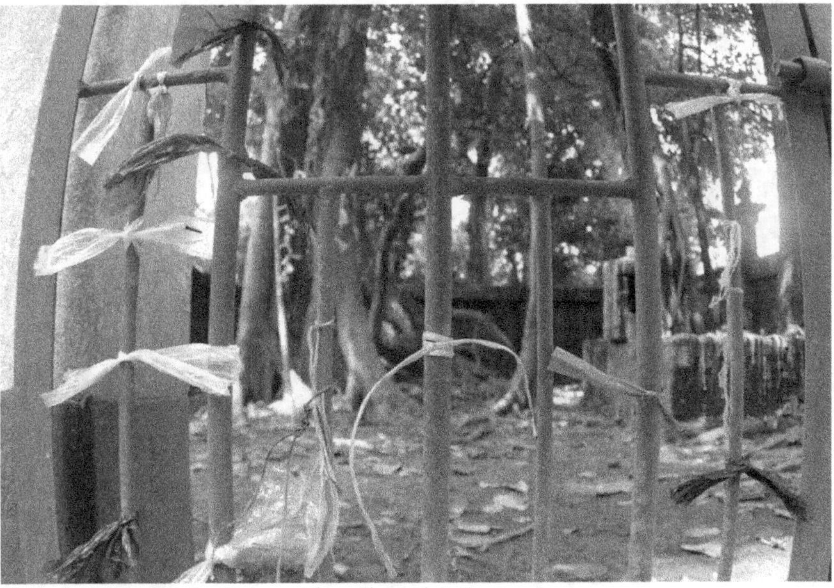

This place was by far the most jungliest place!

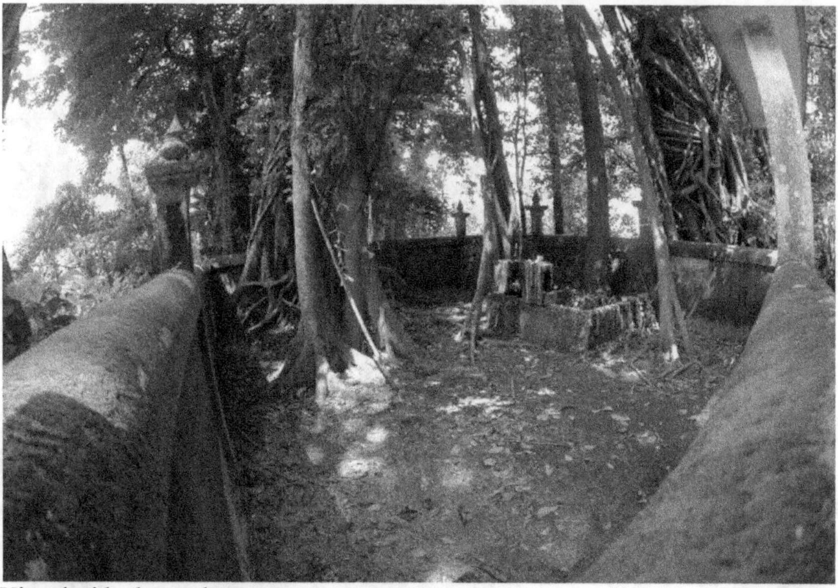

View inside the enclosure

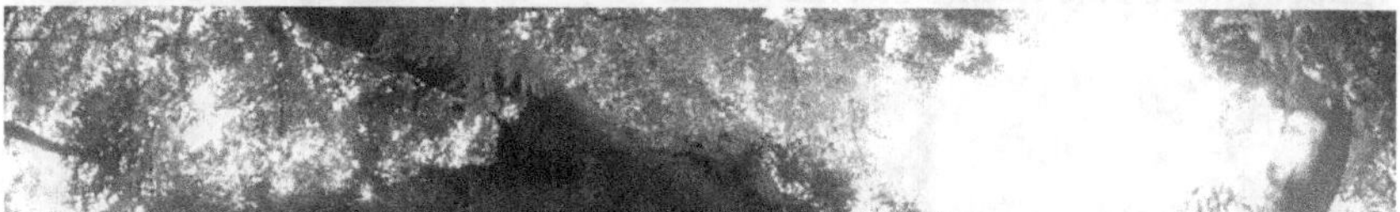

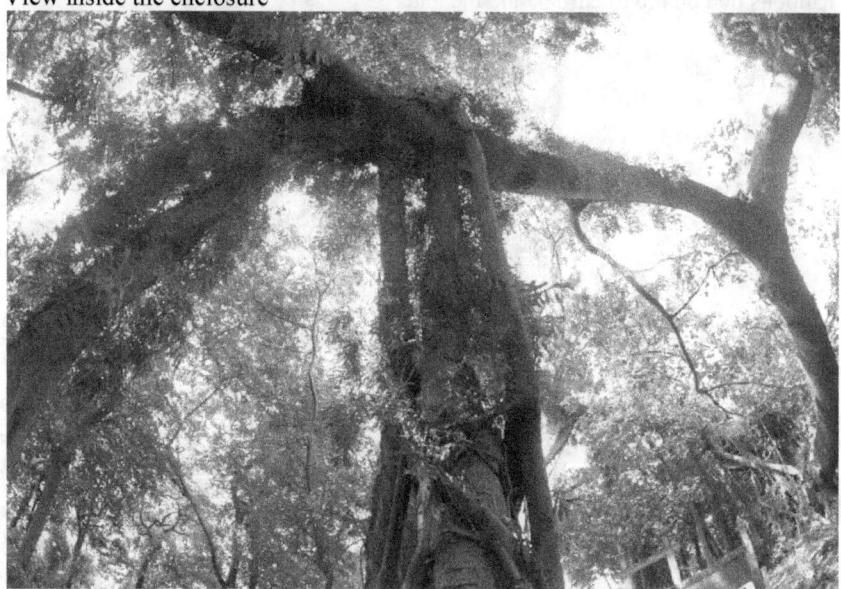

Here we see the branch size and how it has butted the main trunk of the tree.

30.9.2010, 10:50:06

Shah Bikom*

Nurpur Mukam Bari, Fensugoinj

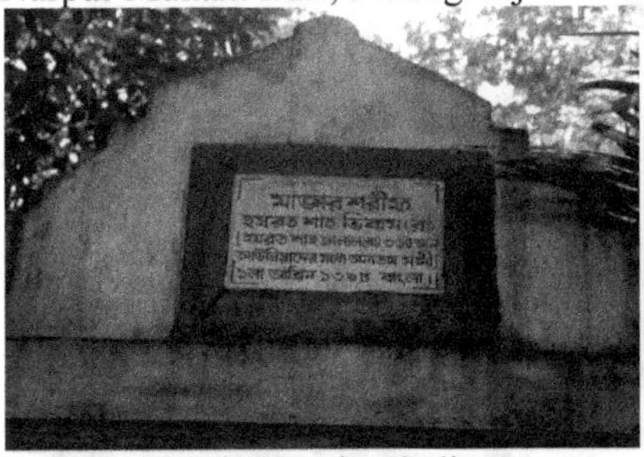

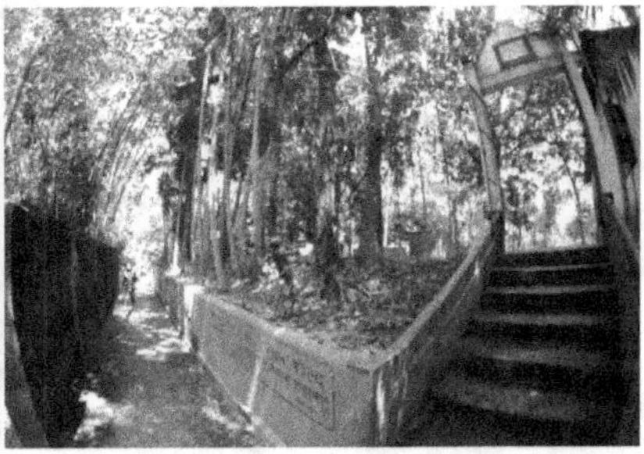

Kadim: Abdal Hussain Shelim

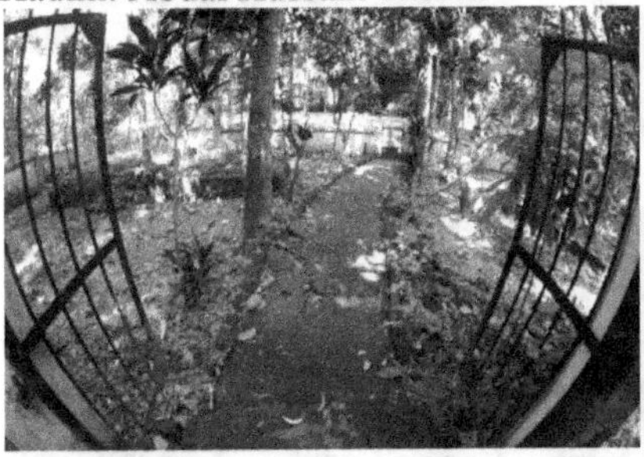

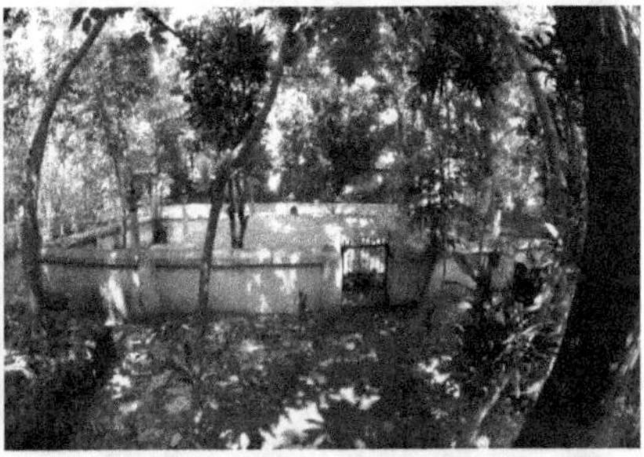

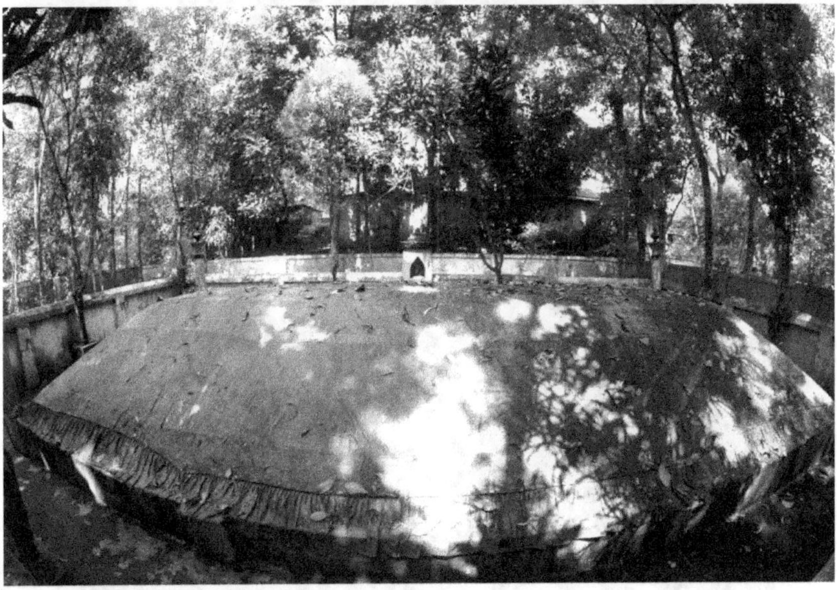

30.9.2010, 12:19:44

There is a claim of being part of the 360 group.

Lal Mostan Phir

Shang Forid Pur, Inda Nagor, Fensu Goinj

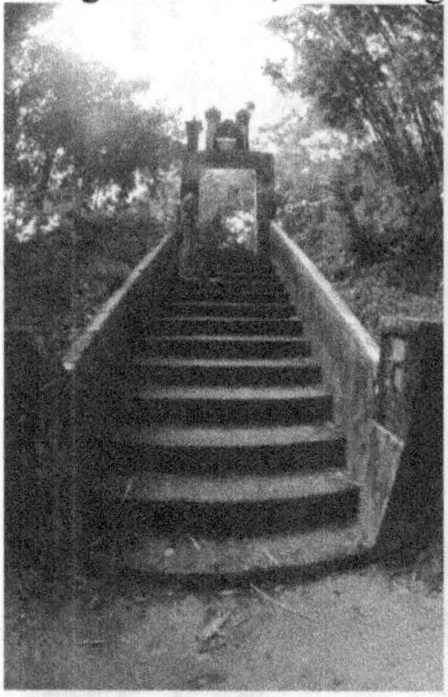

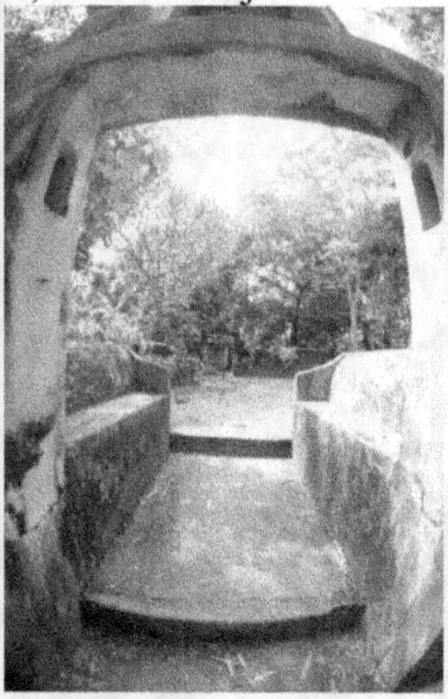

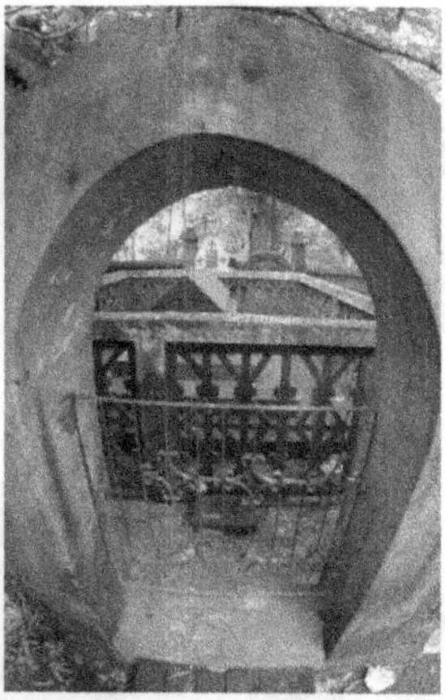

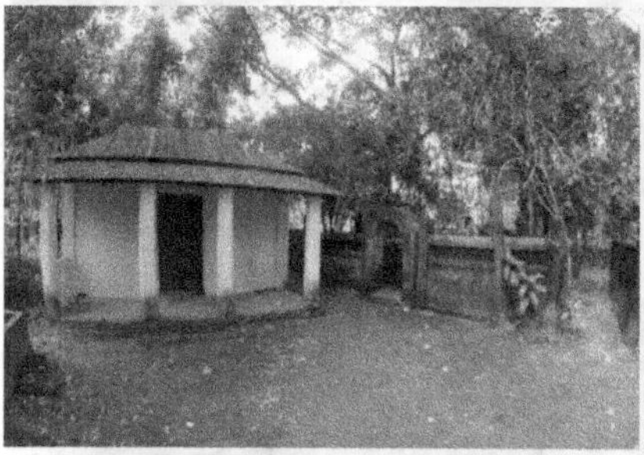

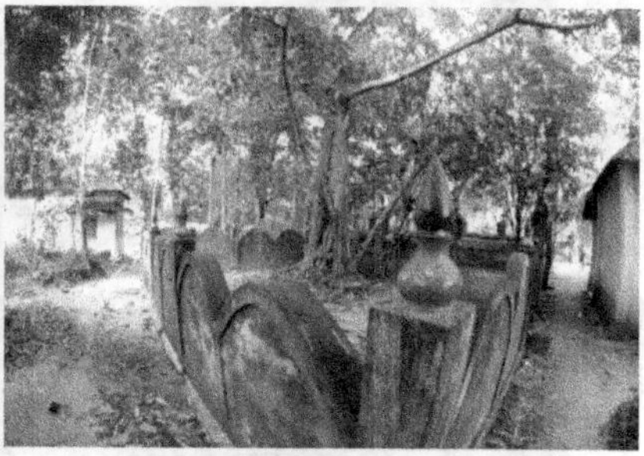

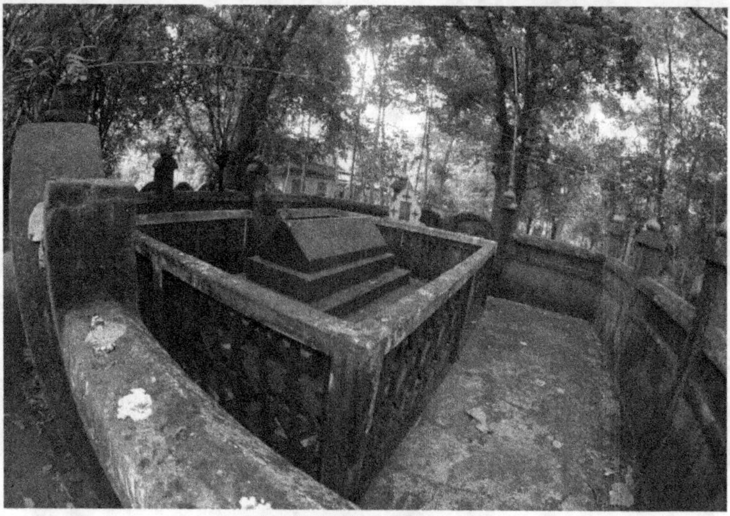

30.9.2010, 13:02:58

Mahjam Shah

Ina nogar, Kosua Bore, BIDC, Fensugoinj

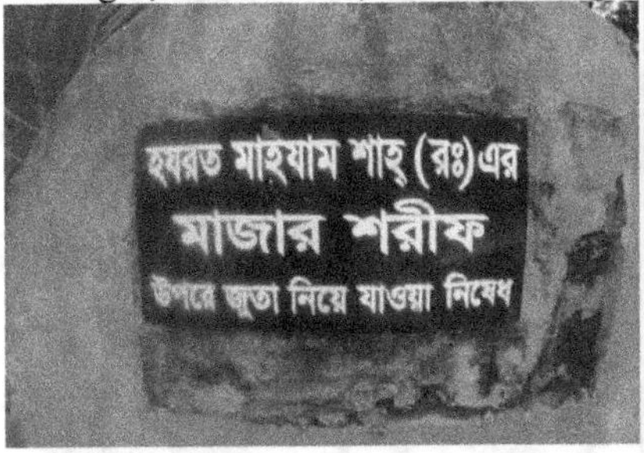
হযরত মাহ্যাম শাহ্ (রঃ)এর
মাজার শরীফ
উপরে জুতা নিয়ে যাওয়া নিষেধ

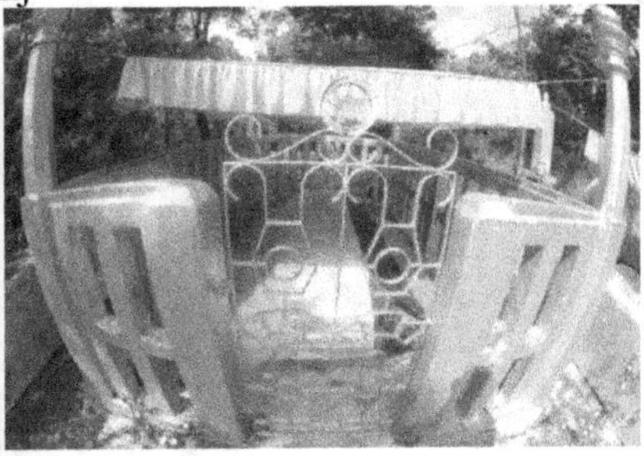

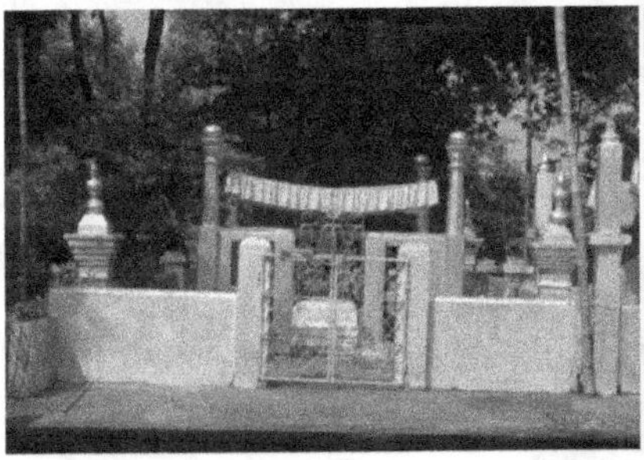

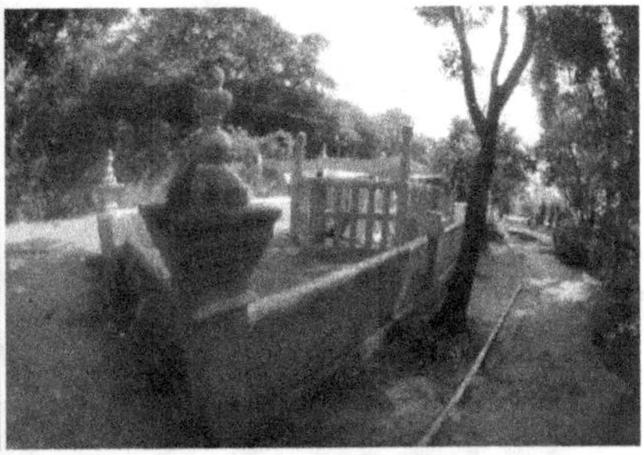

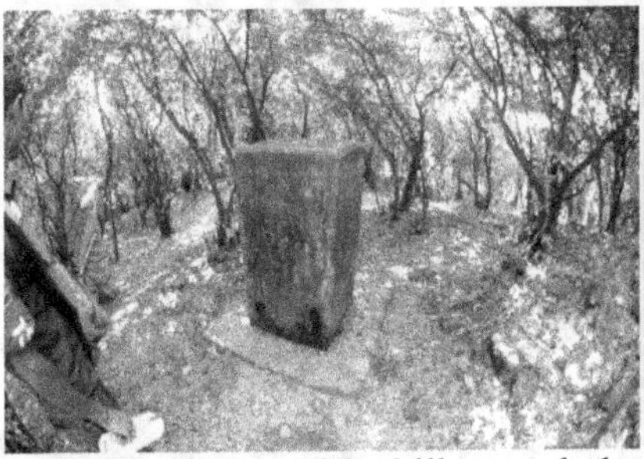

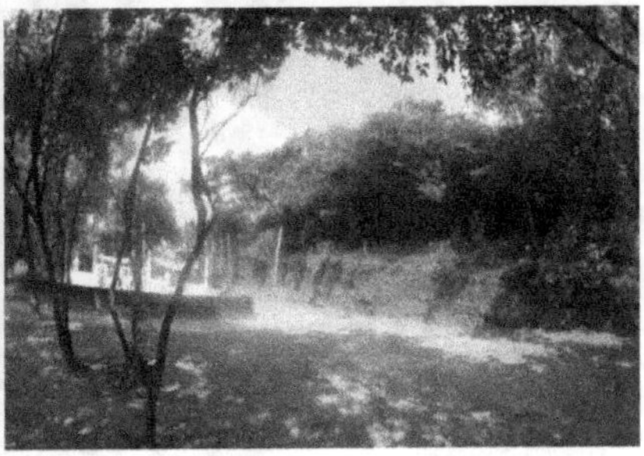

A pillar at the top of the hill to mark the spot where the palace was.

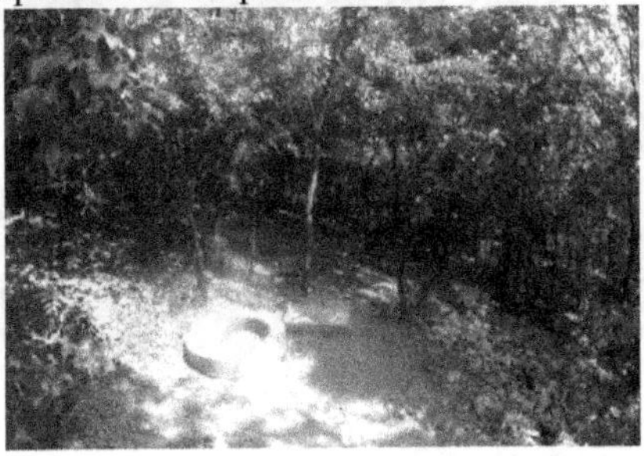

Local devotee, Shamsun Nehar assisted us. She lead us up to the 7 kings doulot area (not clear of the story) She took us to the feeding section of the “bhaggs” (tigers). It is said that the foxes that roam and feed on the foods left are “bhaggs (Tigers)” in disguise; who in turn are disguised of the Auwliya it is said.

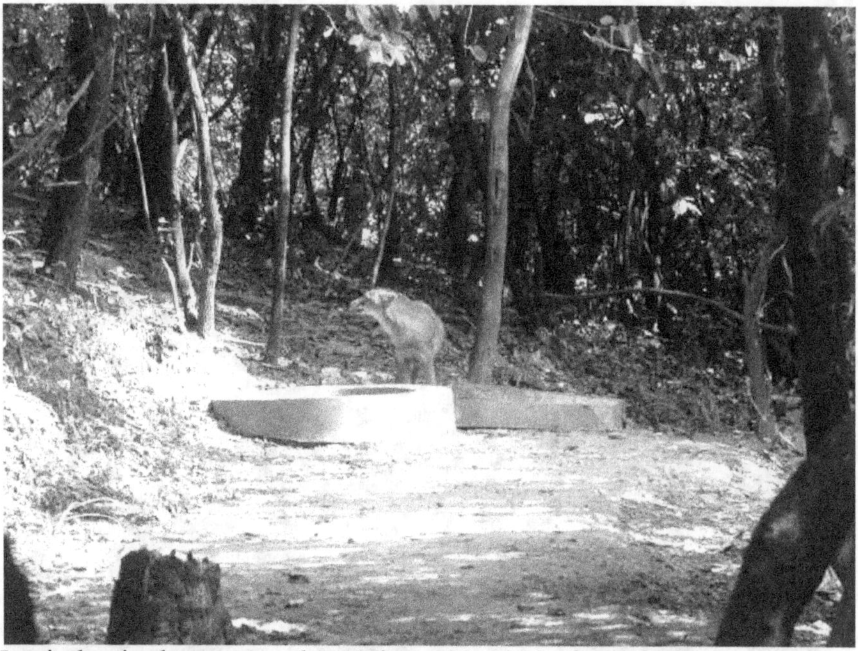

I waited patiently to capture these "Tiger spirits" in the form of a fox.

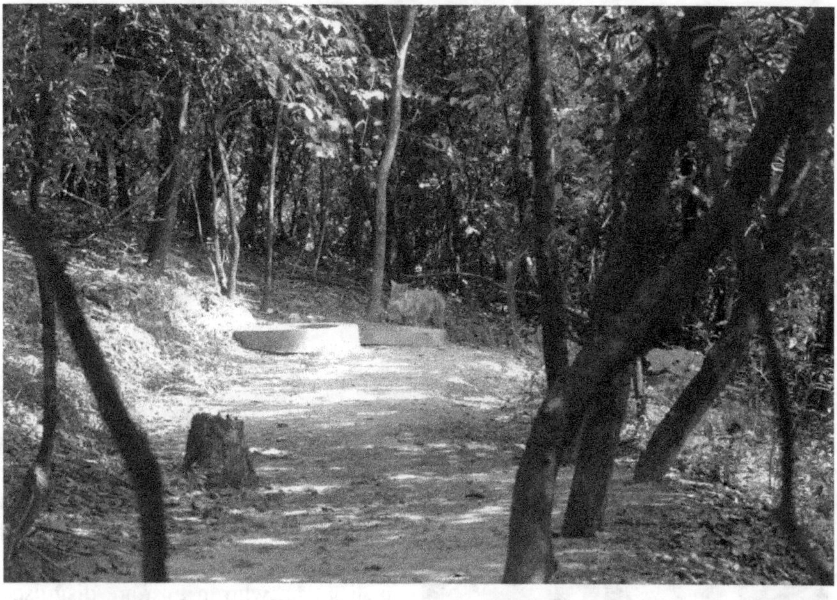

30.9.2010, 13:58:32

Shah Kutub Uddin

Monipuri Teabagan, Mize Gaow, Fensugoinj, Ward 3

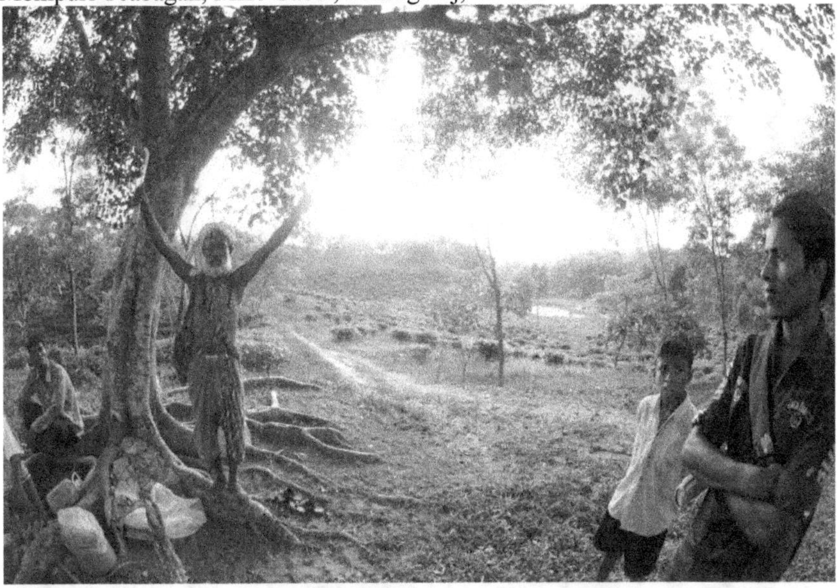

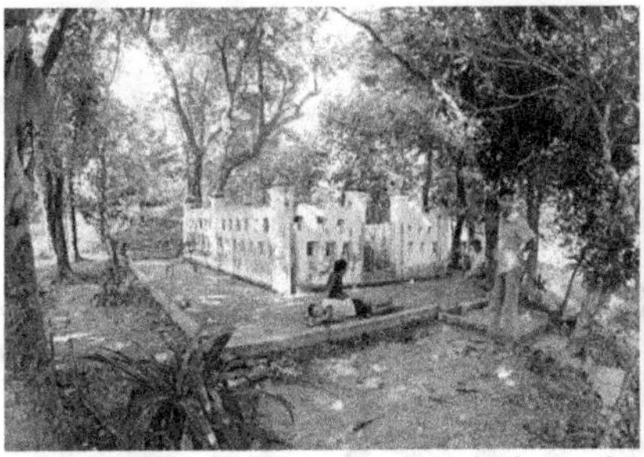

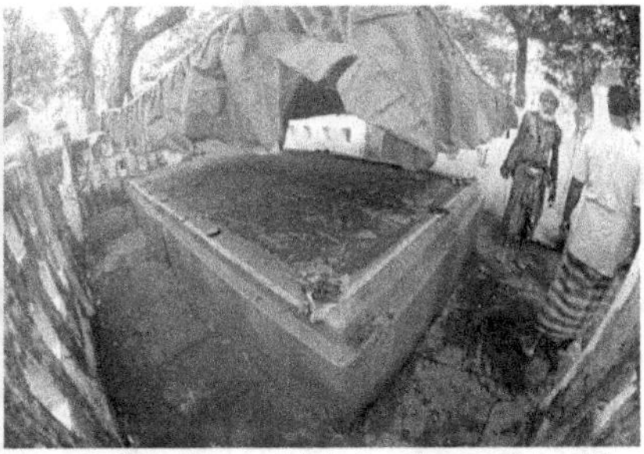

Surprisingly there were people in and around the site, which is situated inside a tea estate. There were people chilling out, sleeping beside the tomb stone.

30.9.2010, 14:44:46

Shah Junaid Malum Gujrati**

(Malum = Knowledgeable, Intelligent), No.1 Union, Rajpur, Fensugoinj Rail Station, Fensugoinj, Ward 7.

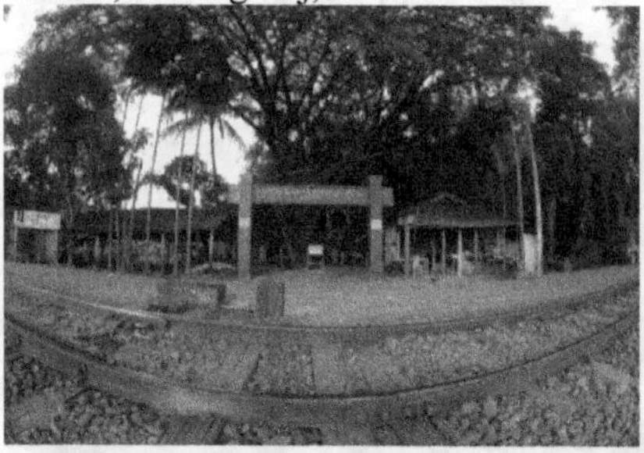

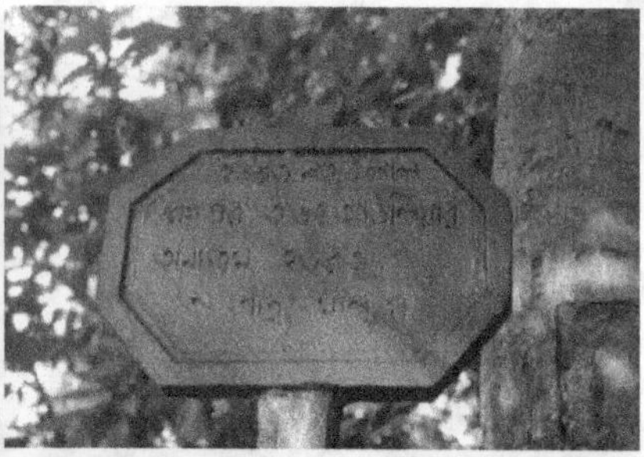

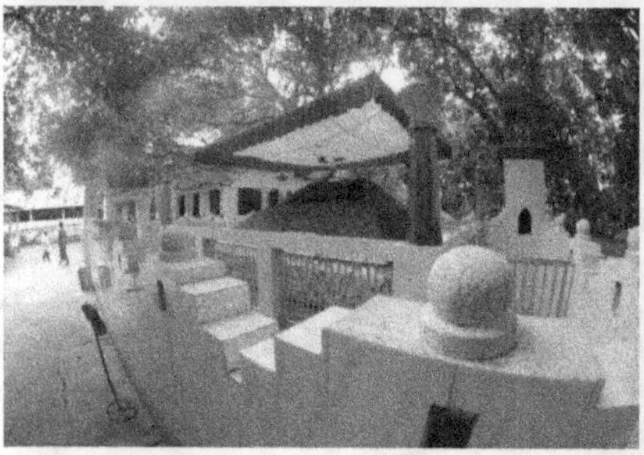

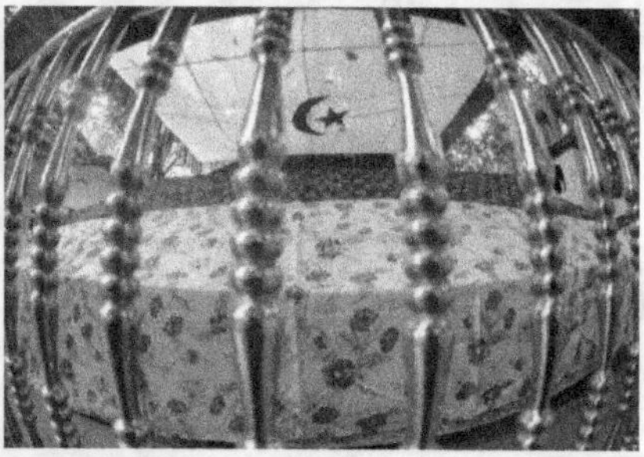

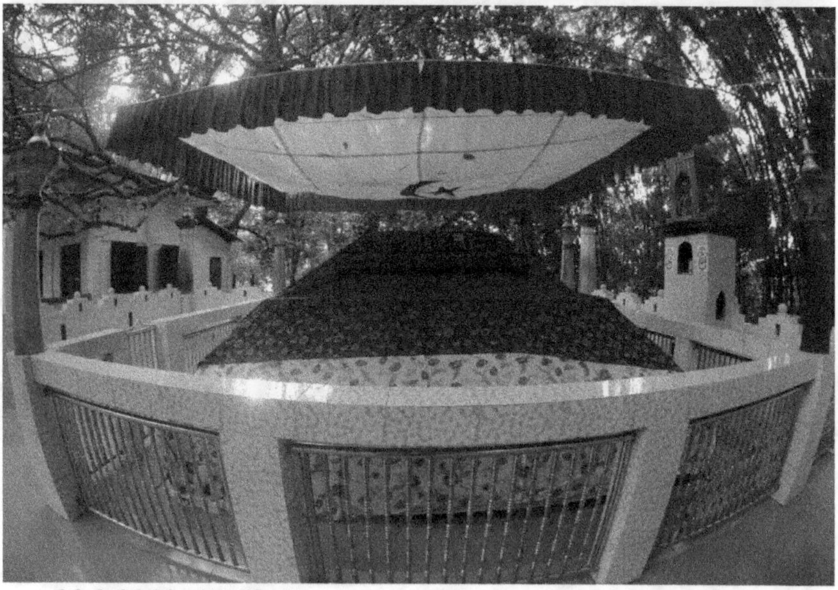

30.9.2010, 15:48:42

Shah Shohor Ullah

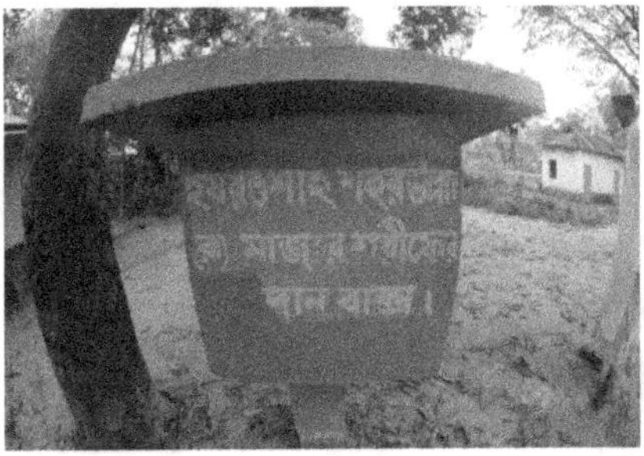

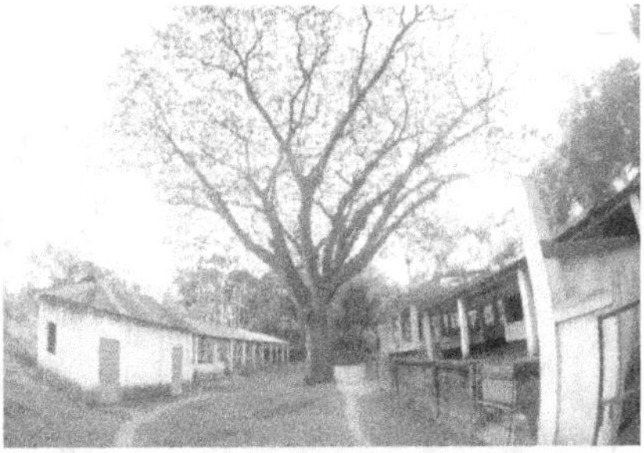

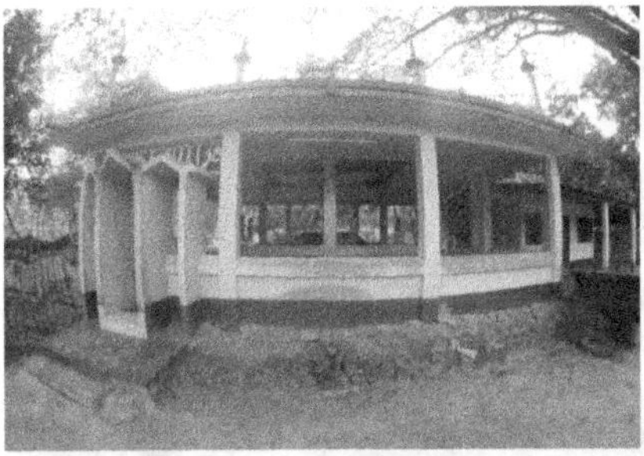

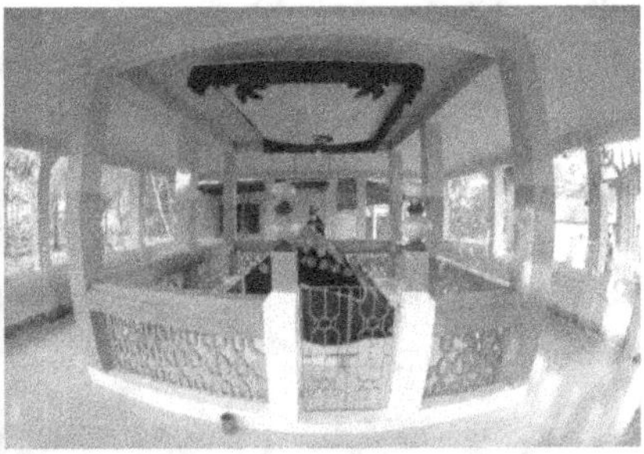

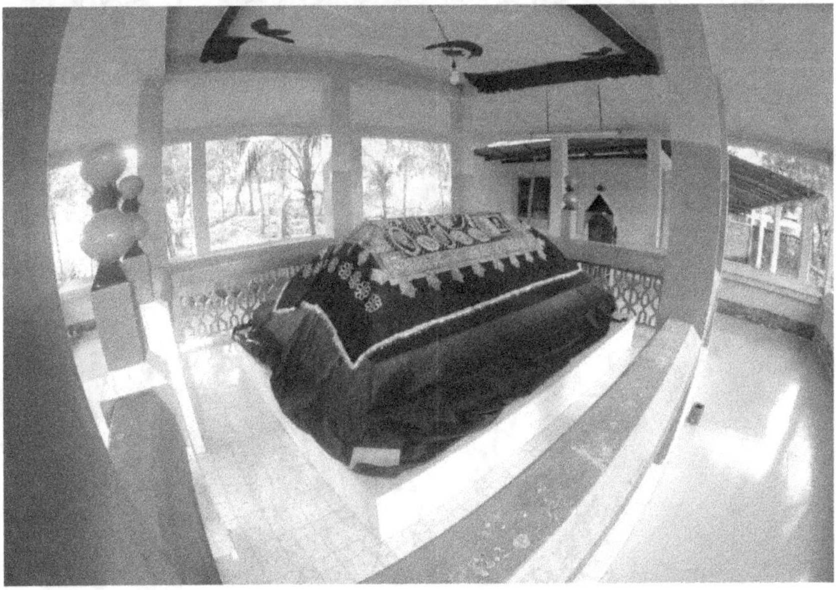

30.9.2010, 16:51:30

Shah Soyod Ali

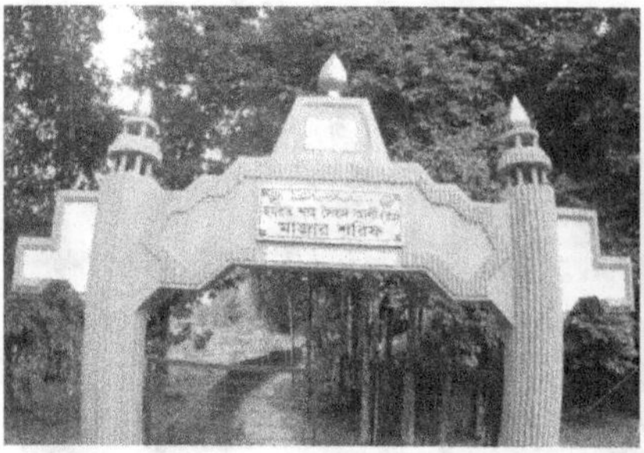

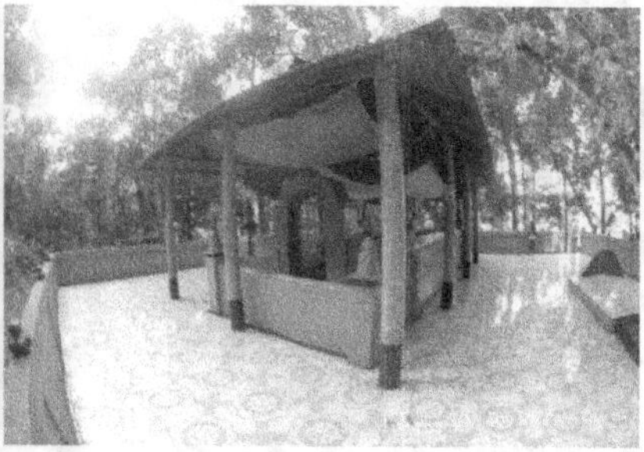

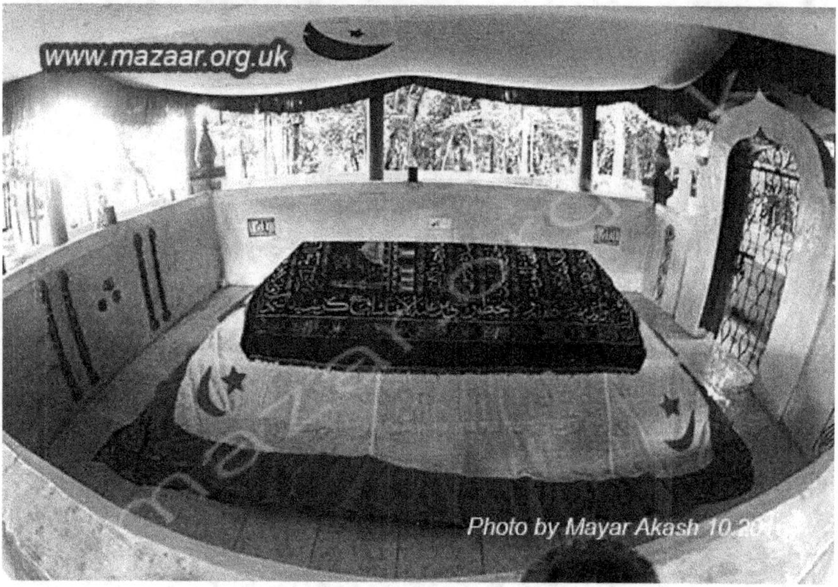
www.mazaar.org.uk
Photo by Mayar Akash

30.9.2010, 17:33:32

October 2010

Shah Abdul Goffur Khan

a.k.a., Sola Shah (Sola = sack)
He was a kadim for Shah Ali Konkar Mazar. He was a descendent of Isha Khan and came from Mymensingh. He became a hermit and lived inside the tree trunk.

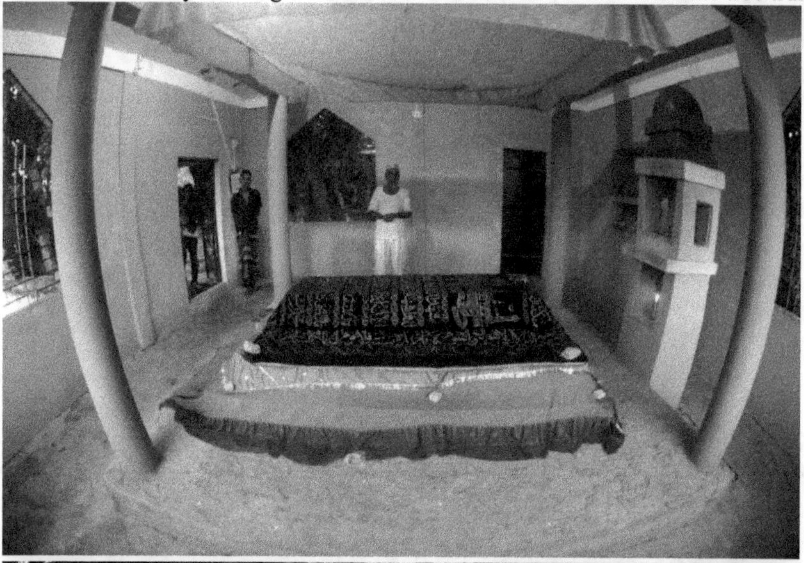

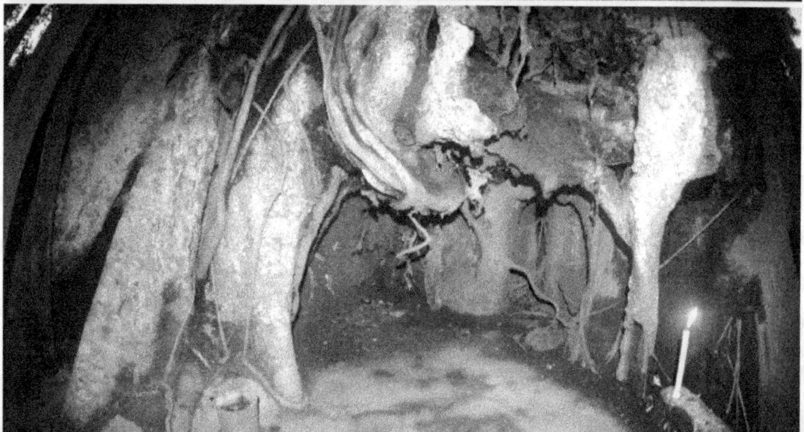

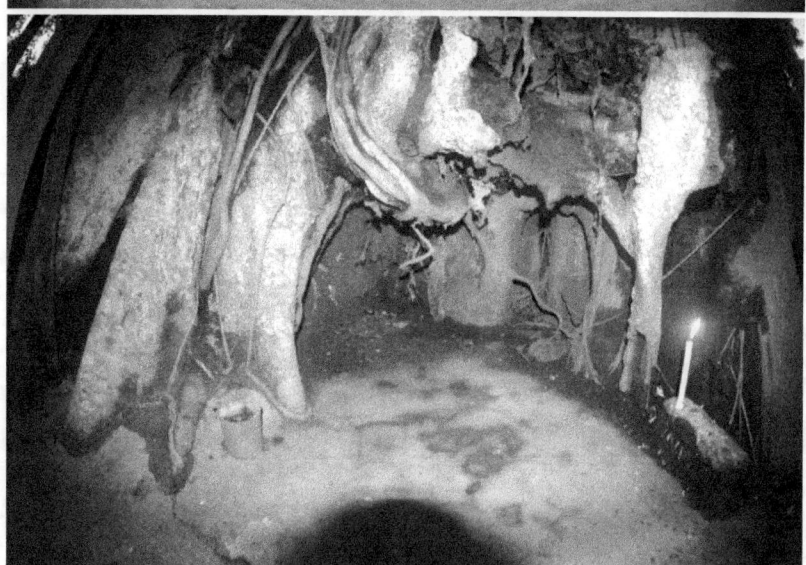

1.10.2010, 21:39:36

Maulana Shah Monaullah

Bawon Pur, Bishwanath, no. 6 union, Sylhet

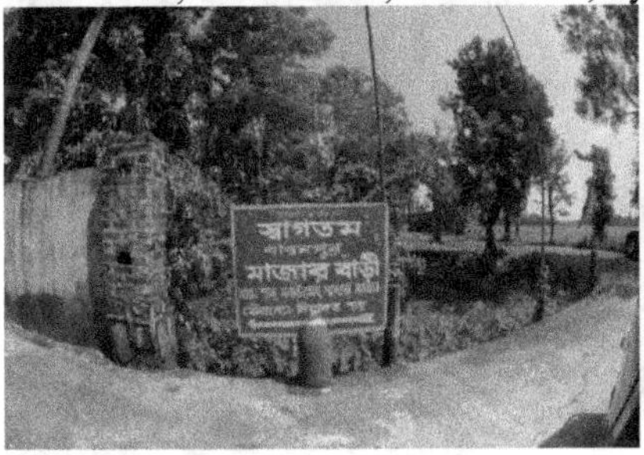
স্বাগতম
মাজার বাড়ী

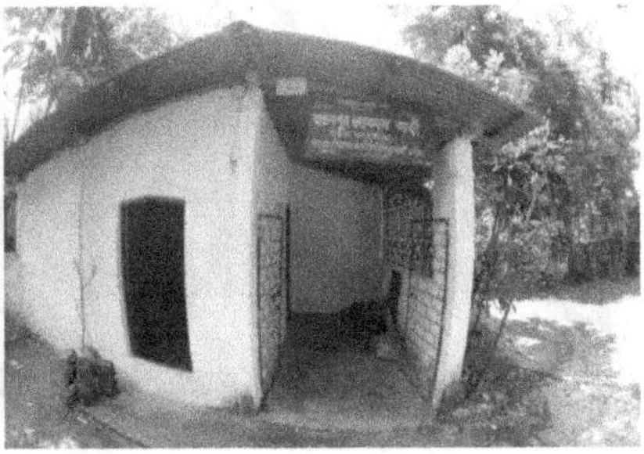

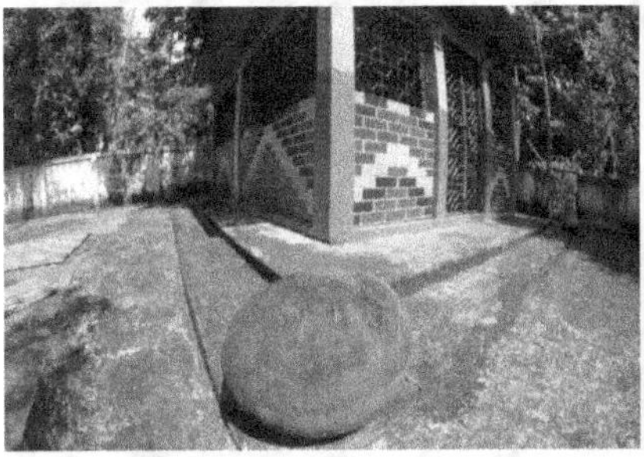

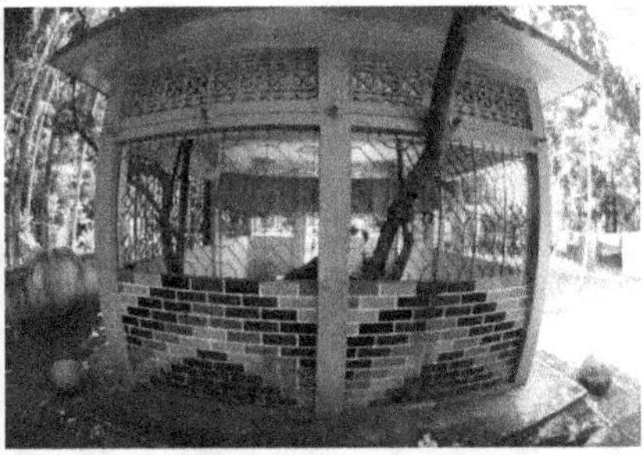

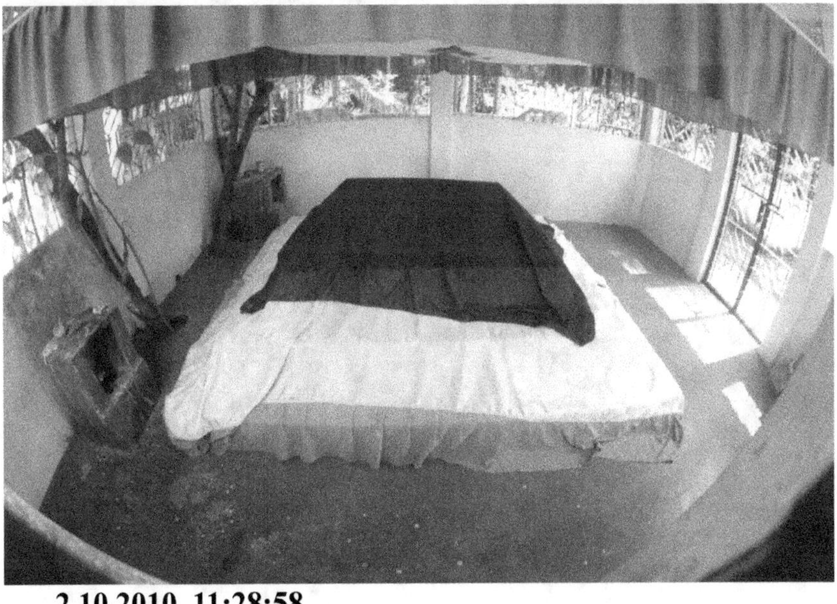

2.10.2010, 11:28:58

Kazi Kondokar

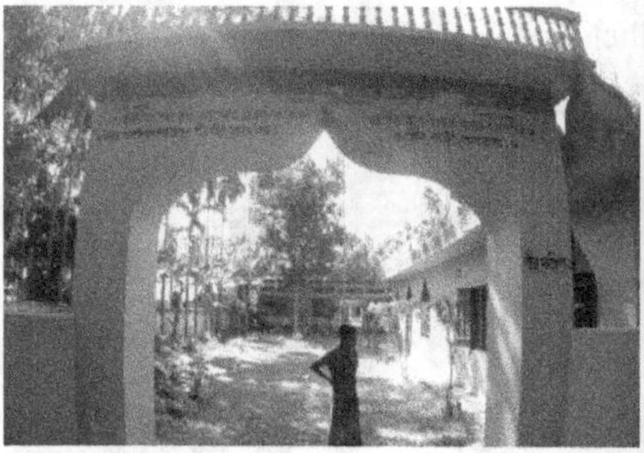

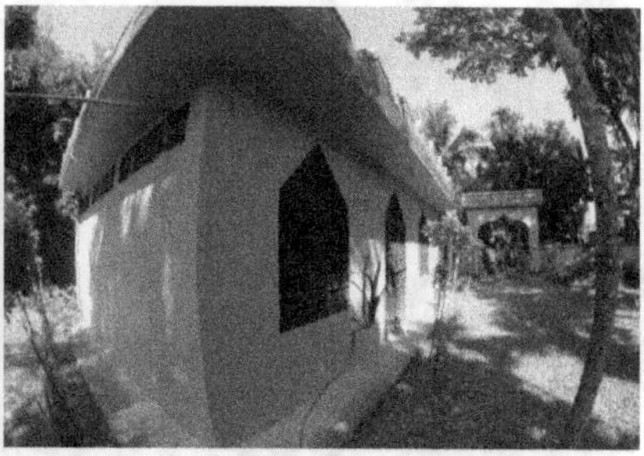

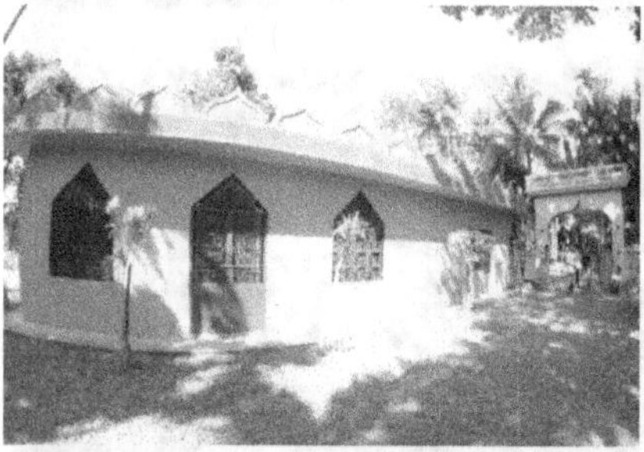

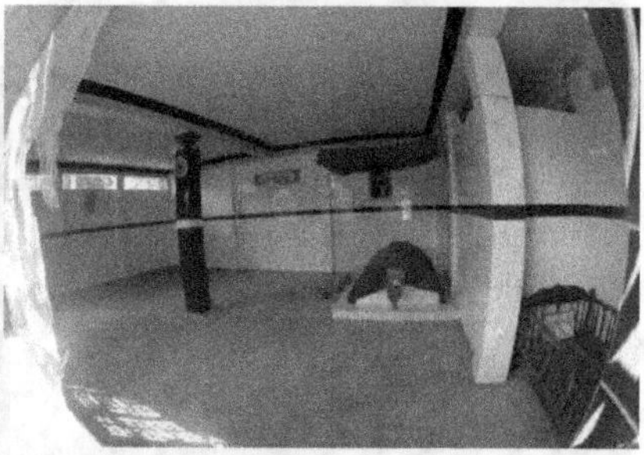

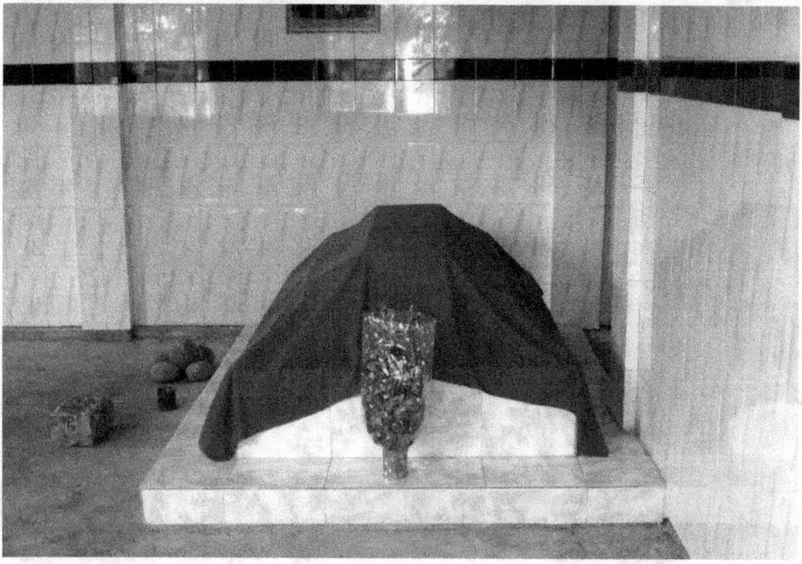

2.10.2010, 14:02:20

Kazi Umor Kondokar**

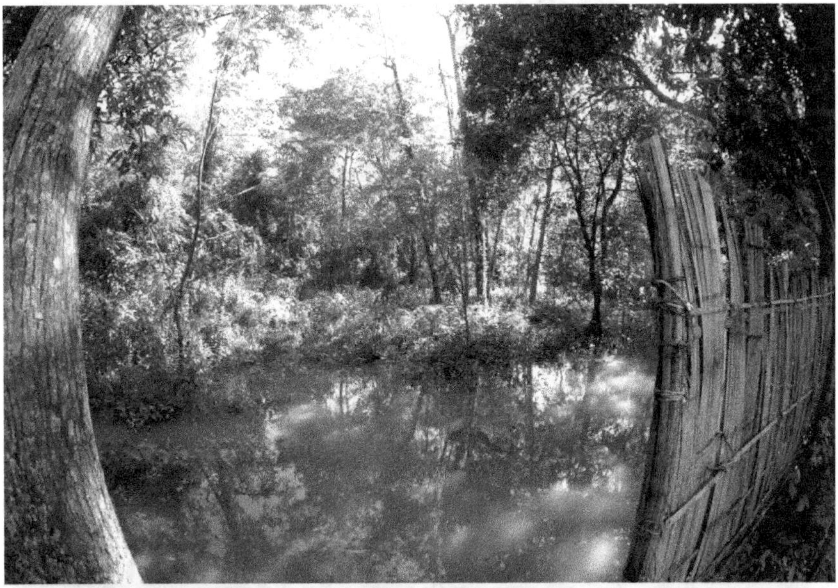

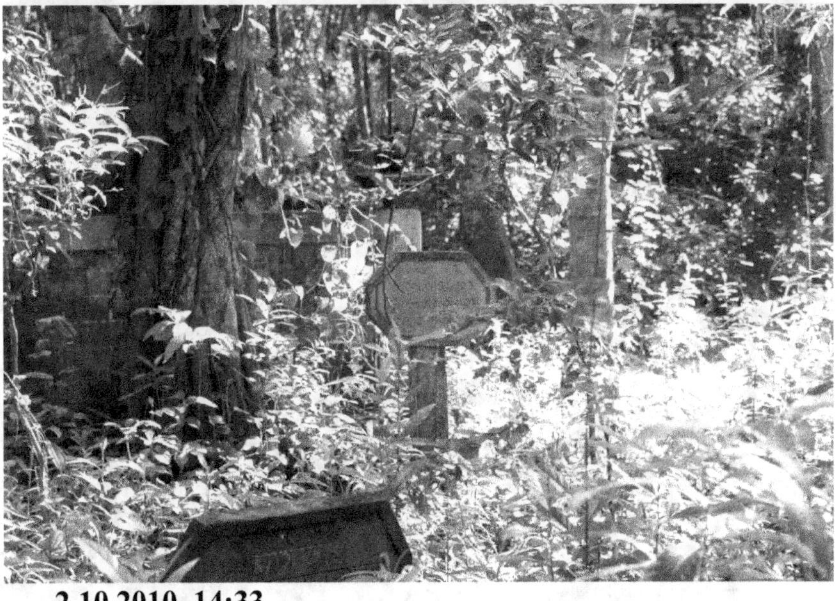

2.10.2010, 14:33

This was situated in a swamp, however, clearly marked with 8 sided sign. This was truly a jungle venture. It is fallen away side, where the water rises when t rains and not much investment has gone to the maintenance side, it is a reflection on the Kadim and the descendents.

Kutub Shah

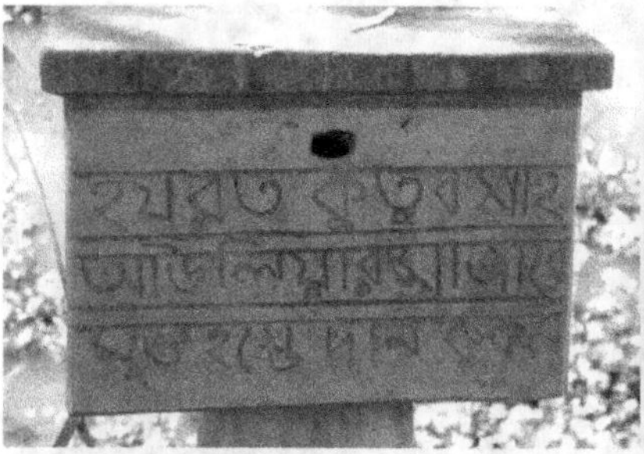
হযরত কুতুব শাহ
আউলিয়ার মাজার

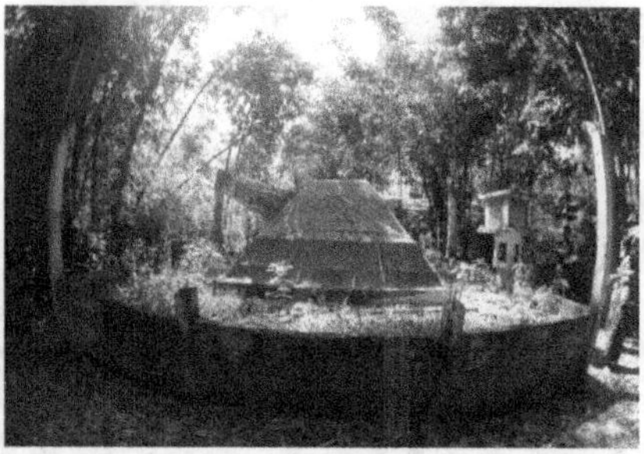

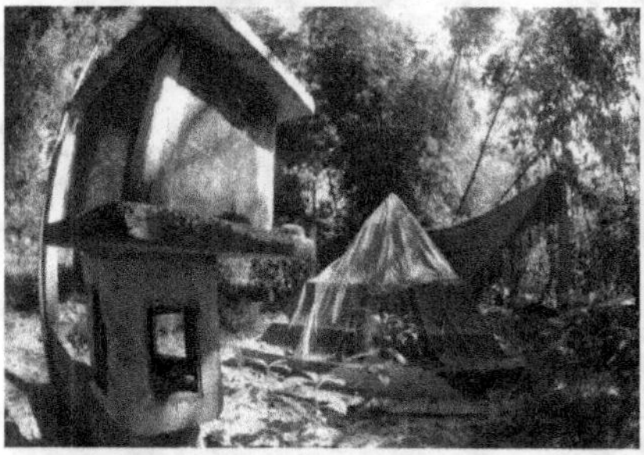

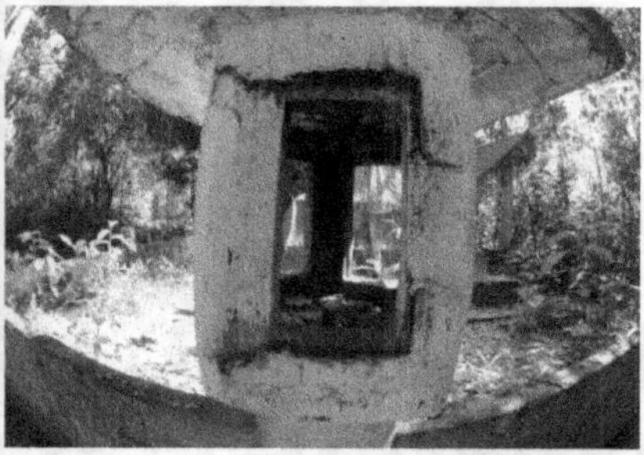

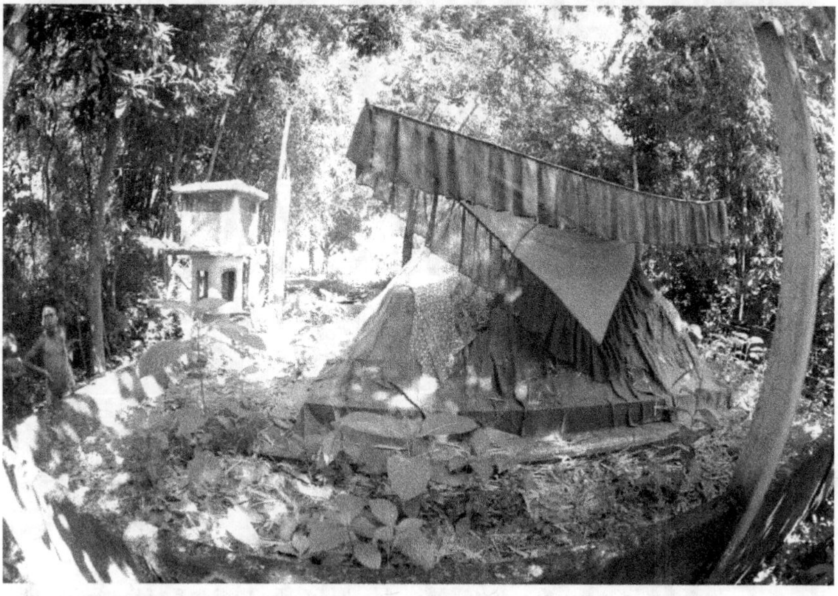

2.10.2010, 13:38:40

Shah Jamal

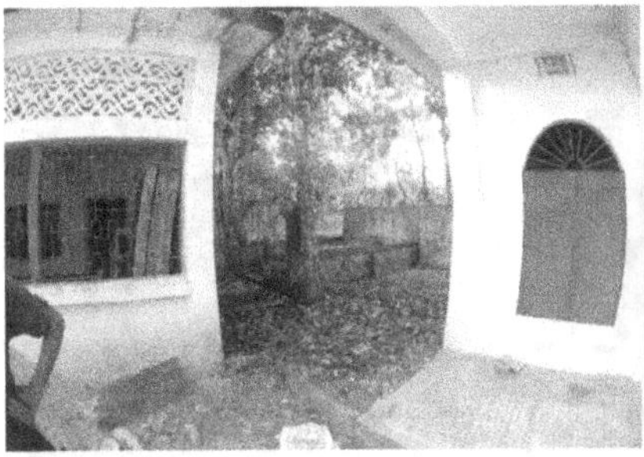

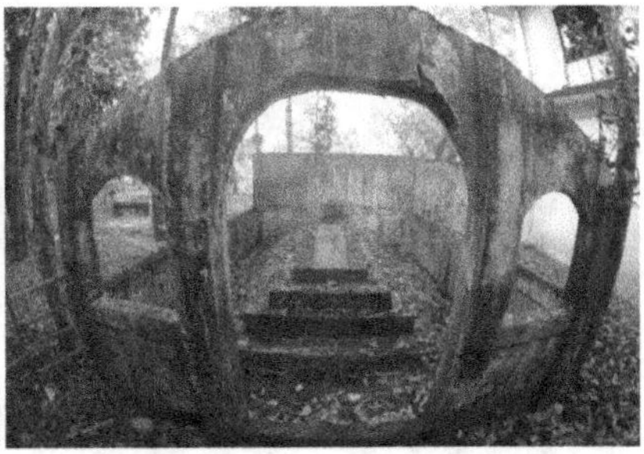

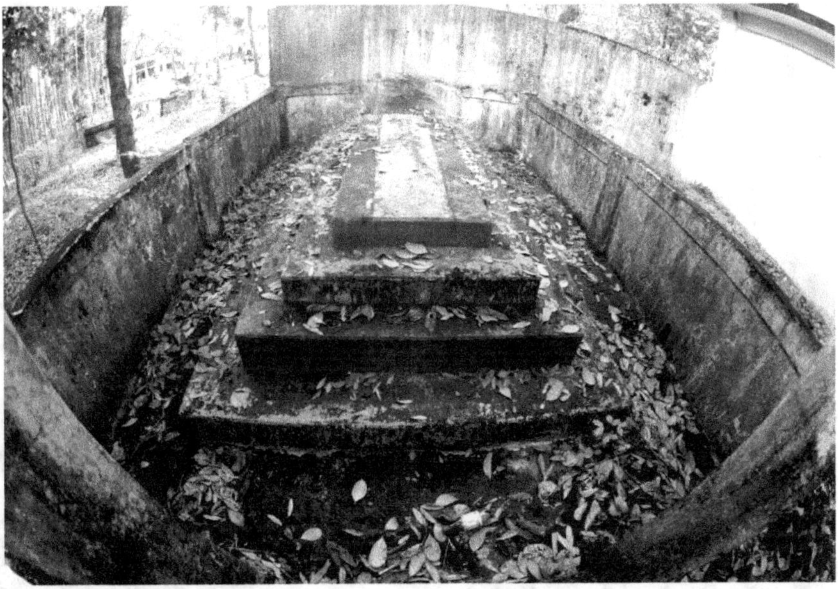

2.10.2010, 15:48:16

The Mazars that are not looked after or managed are the ones who have moved away from the Sufi way and accepted the Middle Eastern Islam, or the descendents have just passed away.

Sheik Auwliya

This space is shared by two graves.

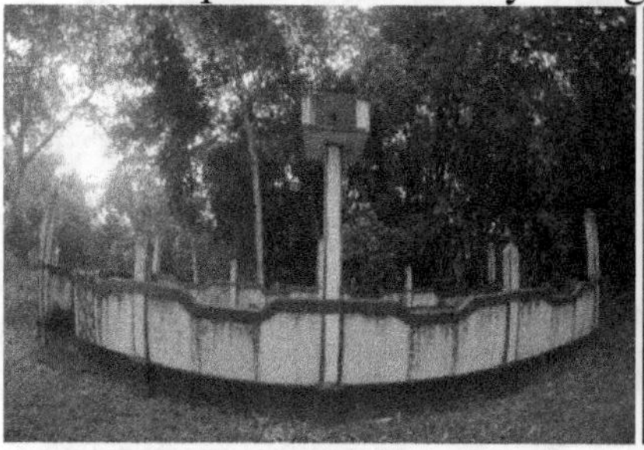

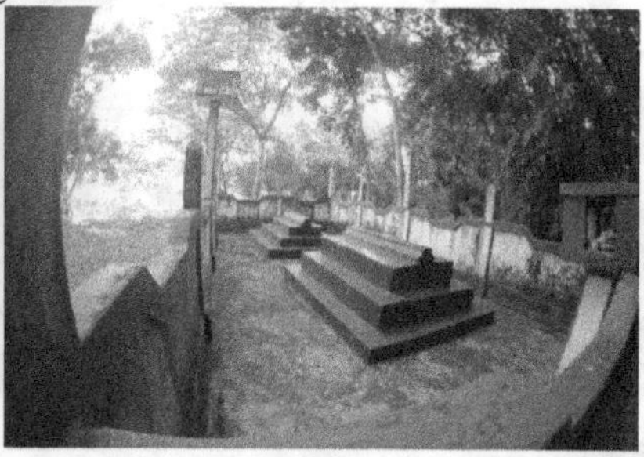

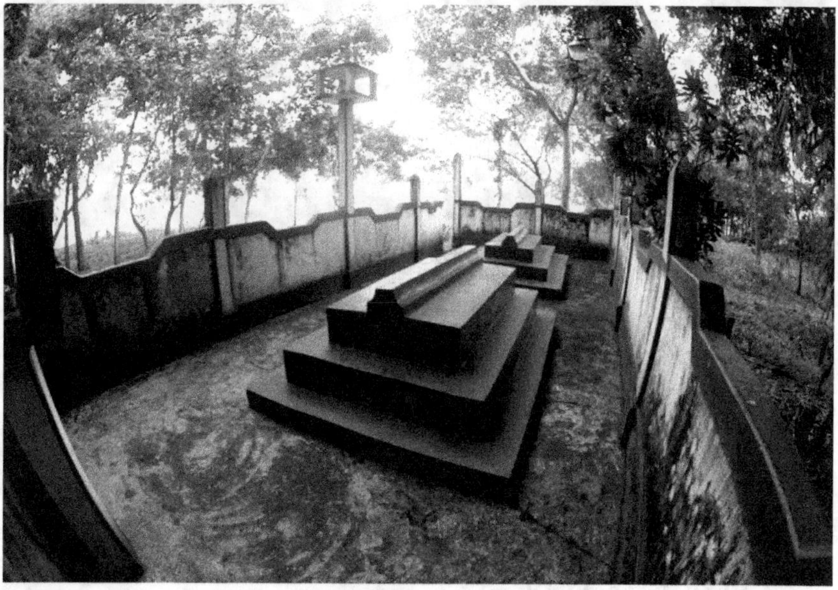

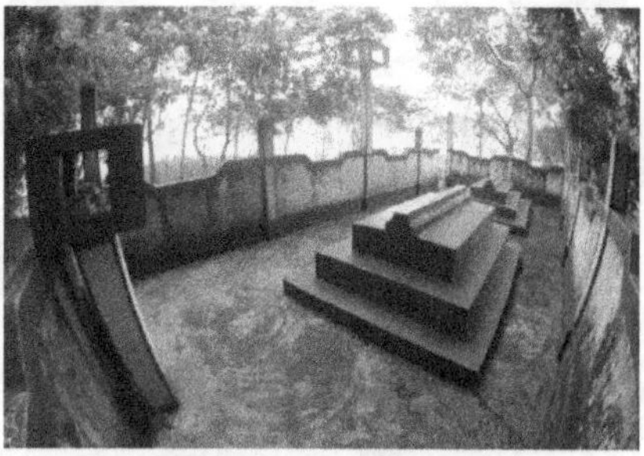

2.10.2010, 16:43:34

Sheik Chand

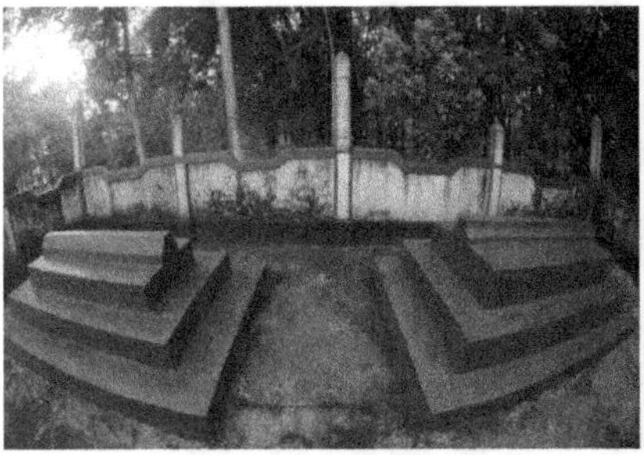

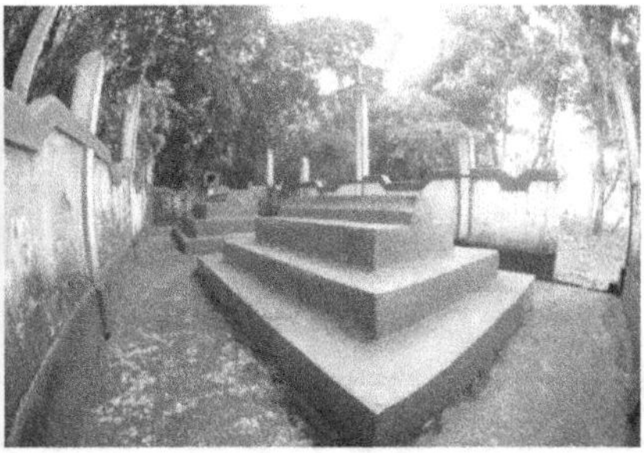

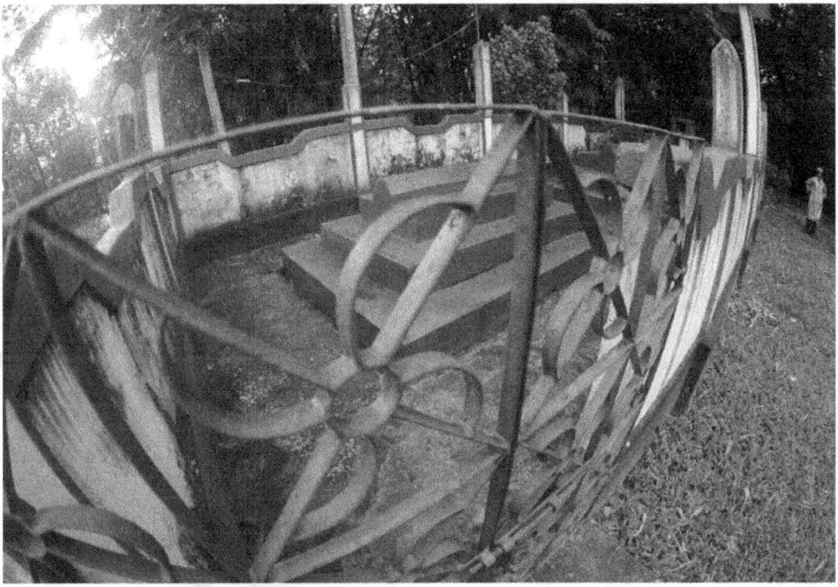

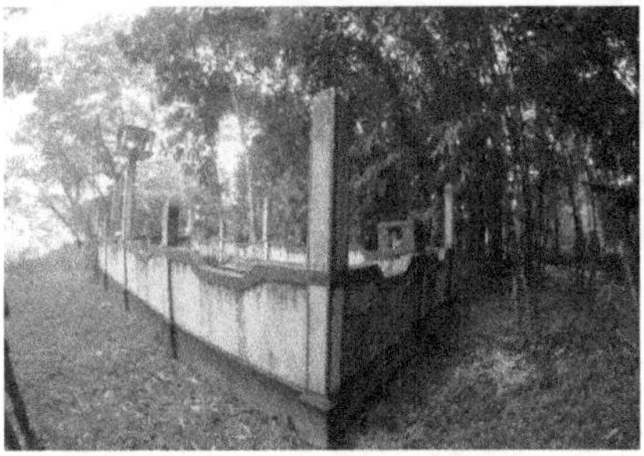

2.10.2010, 16:44:14

Shah Sufu Masim Shah

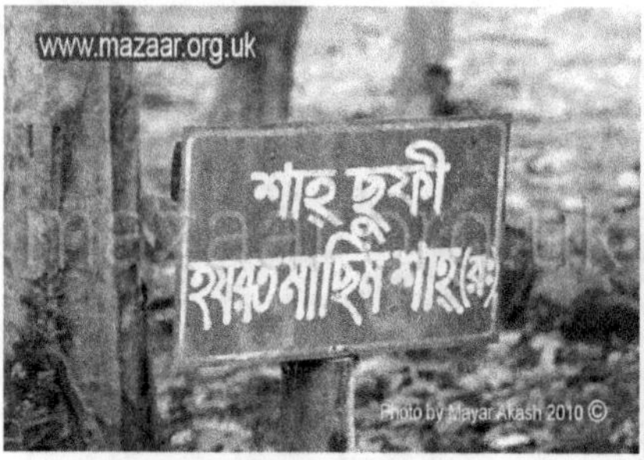
www.mazaar.org.uk
শাহ ছুফী
হযরত মাছিম শাহ (রঃ)
Photo by Mayar Akash 2010 ©

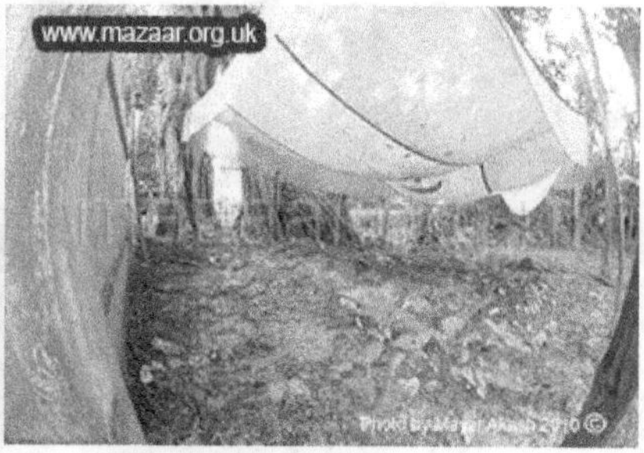
www.mazaar.org.uk
Photo by Mayar Akash 2010 ©

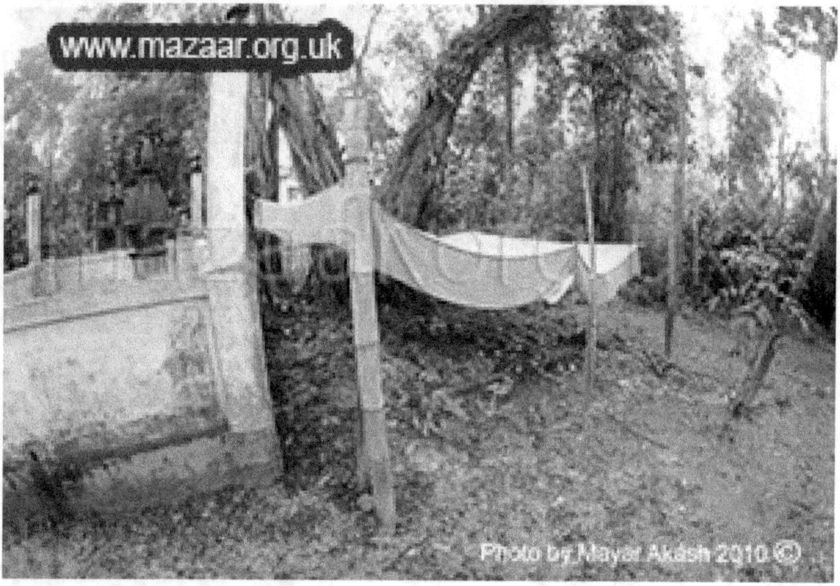
www.mazaar.org.uk
Photo by Mayar Akash 2010 ©

2.10.2010, 16:59:50

These were truly 100% jungle. I was apprehensive; I was thinking a snake might just pop out. The area was wet and damp, on reflection; I must say I was a nutter getting to this place.

Shah Sufi Najim Shah

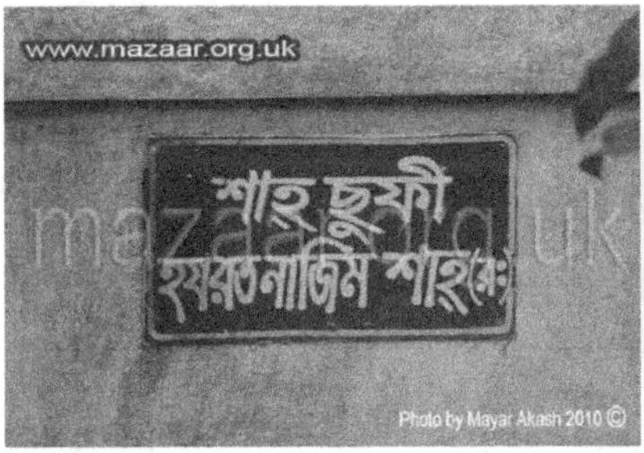
www.mazaar.org.uk
শাহ্ ছুফী
হযরত নাজিম শাহ্(রেঃ
Photo by Mayar Akash 2010 ©

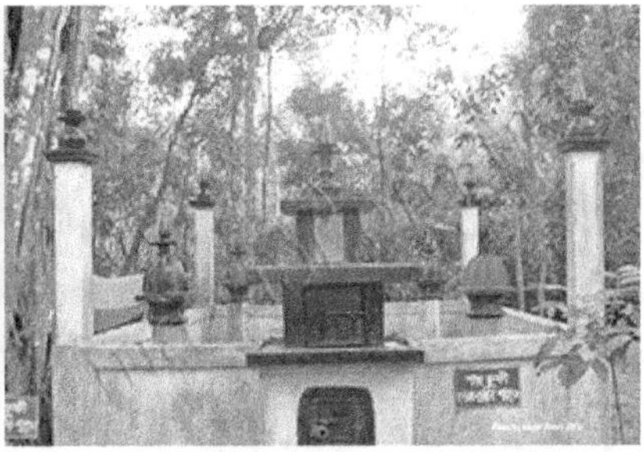

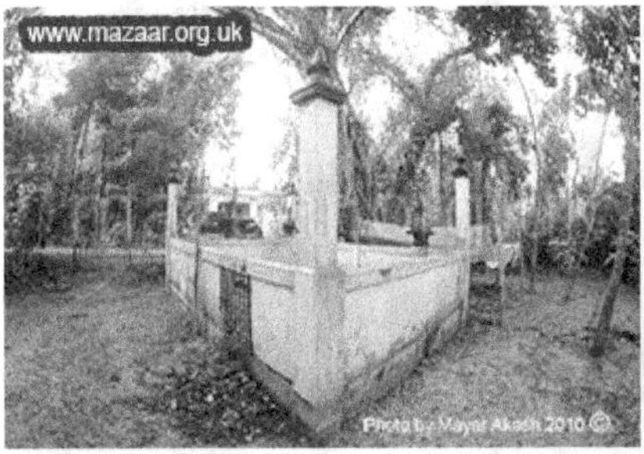
www.mazaar.org.uk
Photo by Mayar Akash 2010 ©

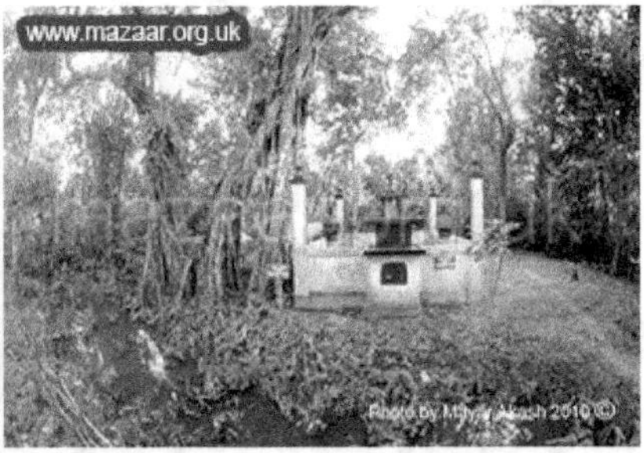
www.mazaar.org.uk
Photo by Mayar Akash 2010 ©

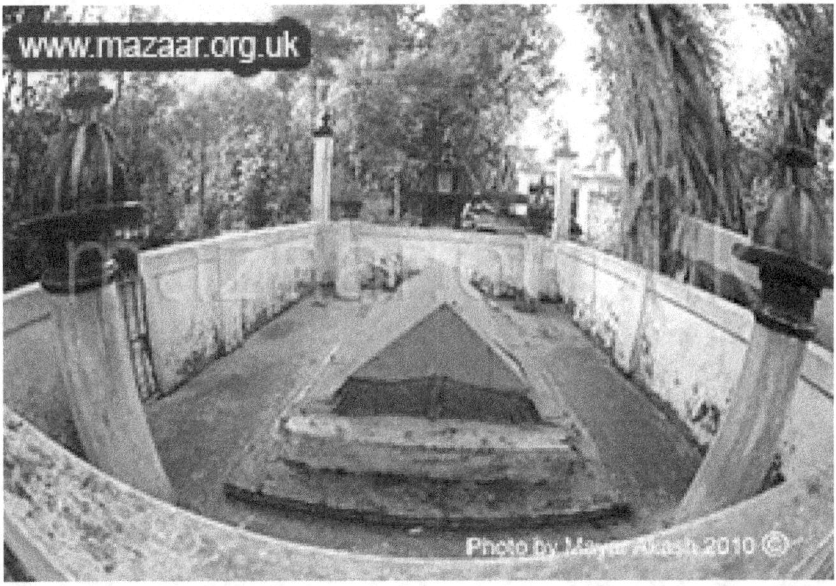
www.mazaar.org.uk
Photo by Mayar Akash 2010 ©

2.10.2010, 16:59:30

Shah Sufu - Hanif Shah

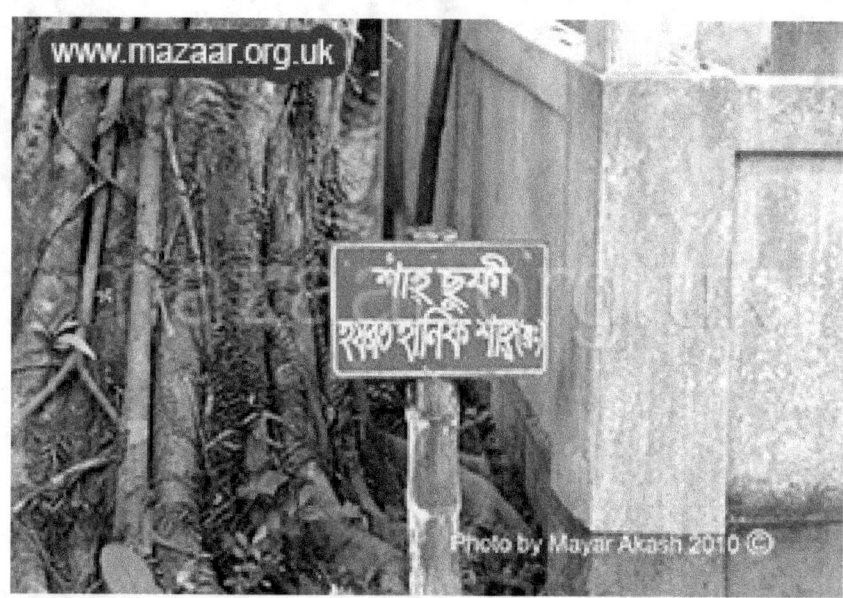

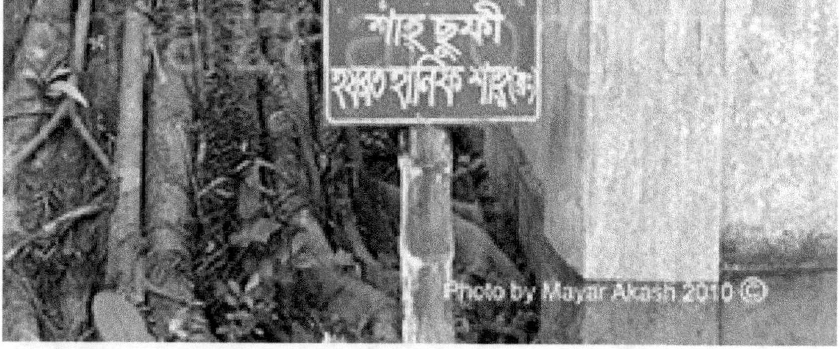
www.mazaar.org.uk
শাহ ছুফী
Photo by Mayar Akash 2010 ©

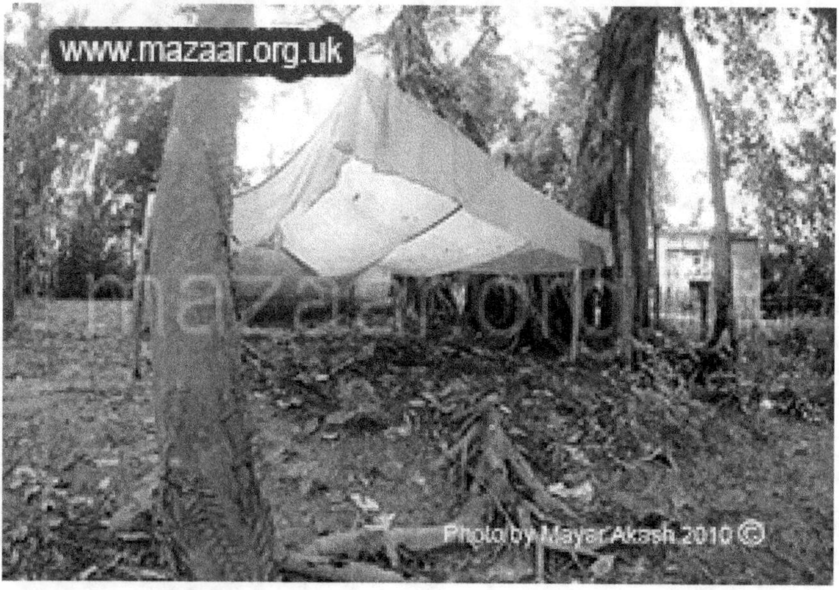
www.mazaar.org.uk
Photo by Mayar Akash 2010 ©

2.10.2010, 17:00:00

Soyod Kutub*

a.k.a.,

Soyod Jalal

Gram: Bangi, Shilam, Sylhet

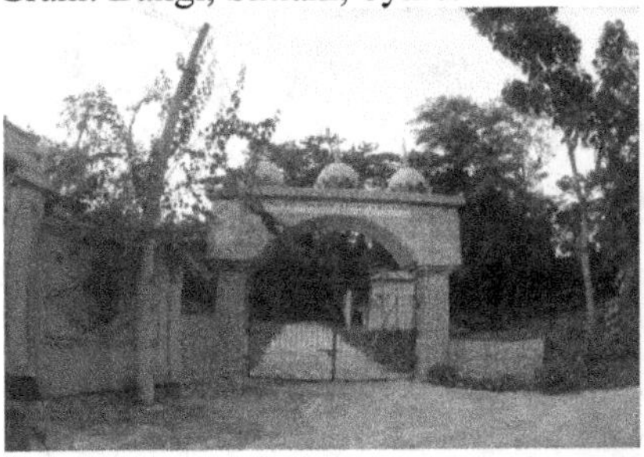

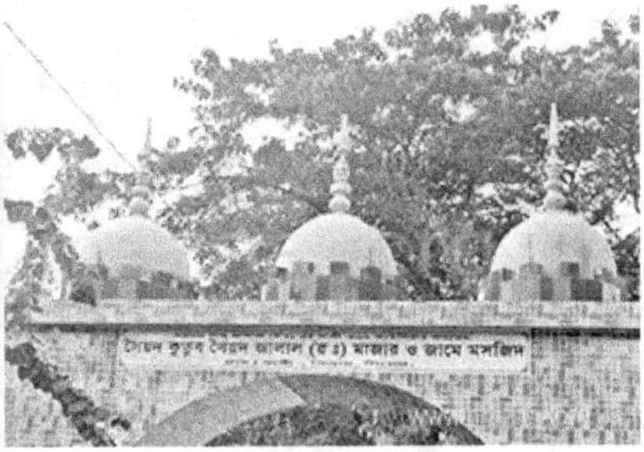
সৈয়দ কুতুব সৈয়দ জালাল (রঃ) মাজার ও জামে মসজিদ

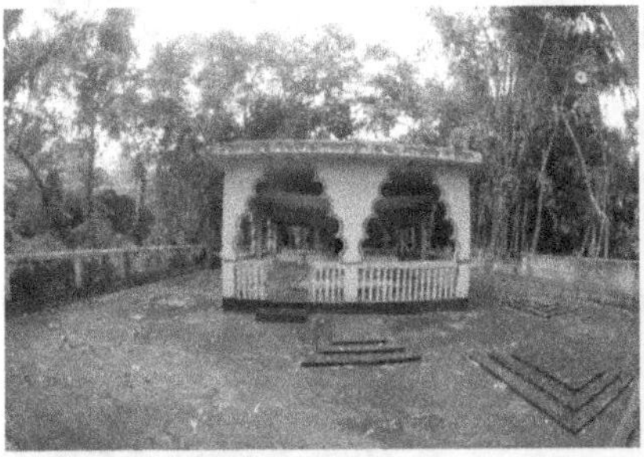

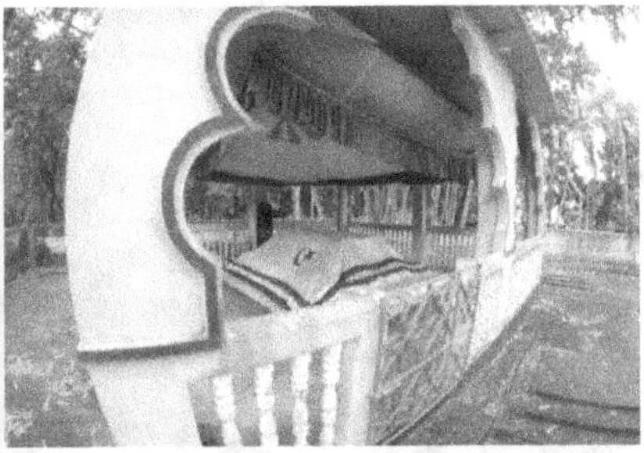

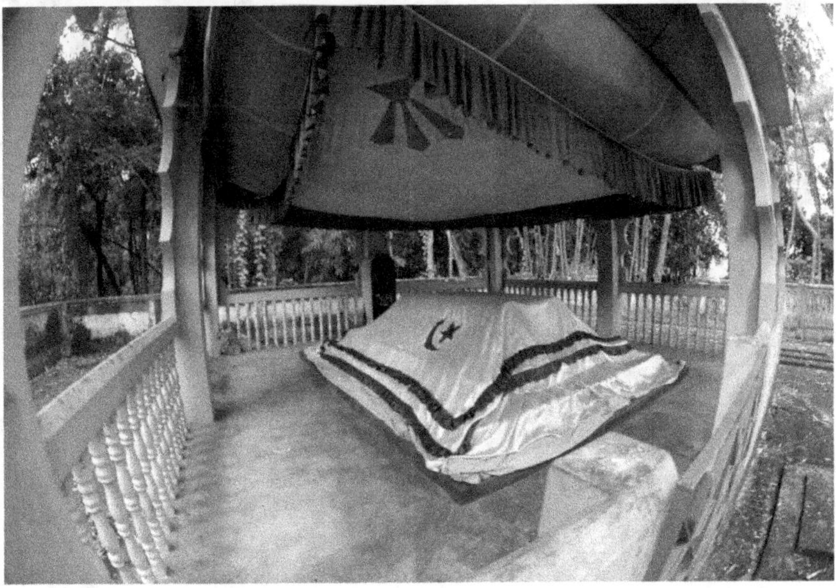

2.10.2010, 17:23:58

Dilbor Shah

Gorom Tolla

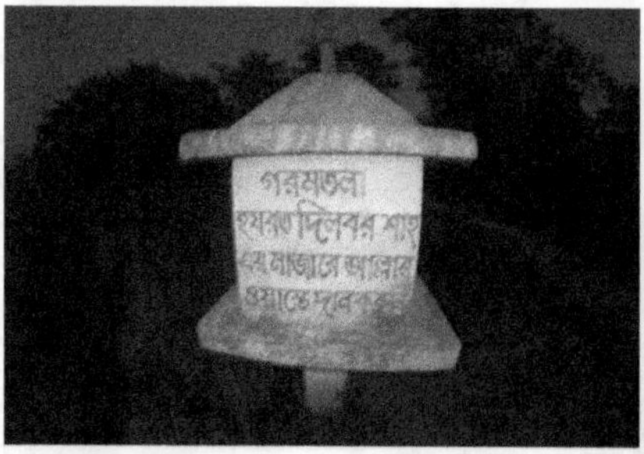
গরমতলা

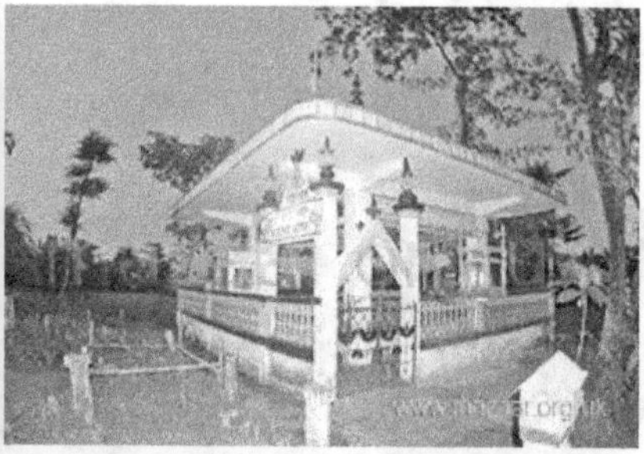

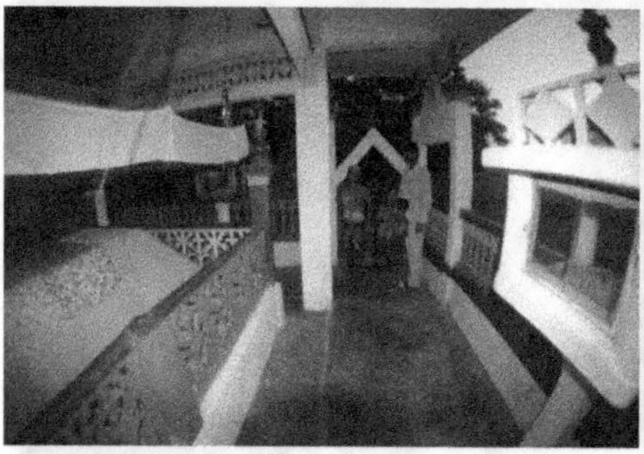

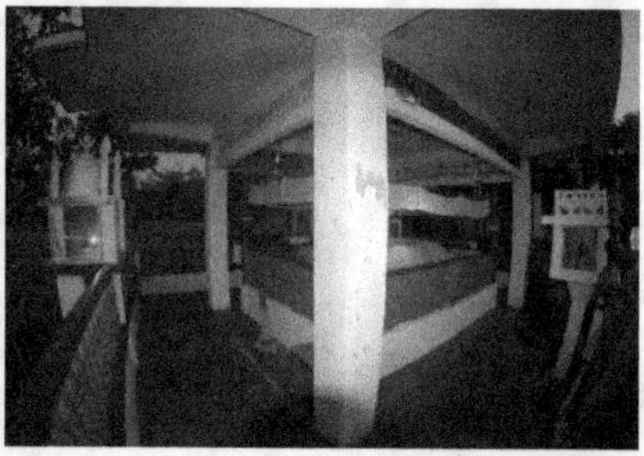

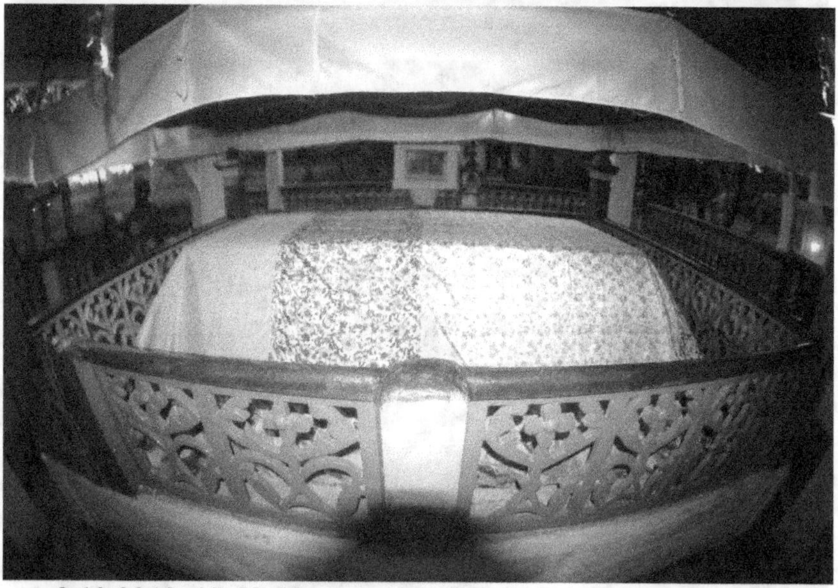

2.10.2010, 17:52:28

Dowr Baksh Kotib

or

Feson Shah

a.k.a., Hafiz Fosih
Boro Fesi, ward 3, Jogonath pur, no.8, Asher Kandi Union.

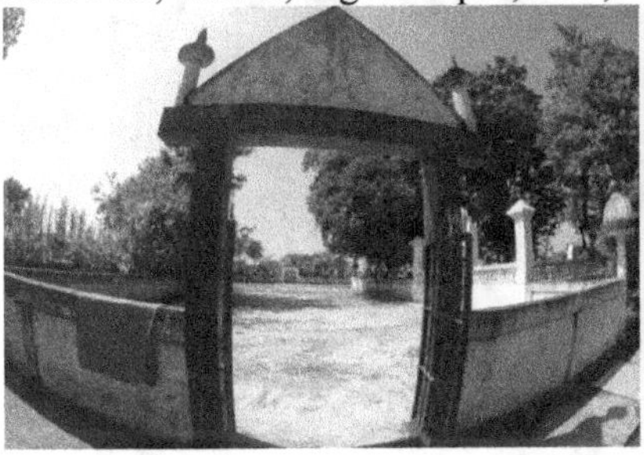

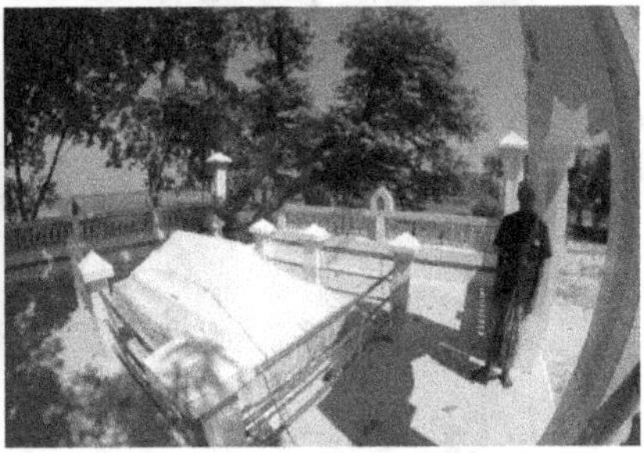

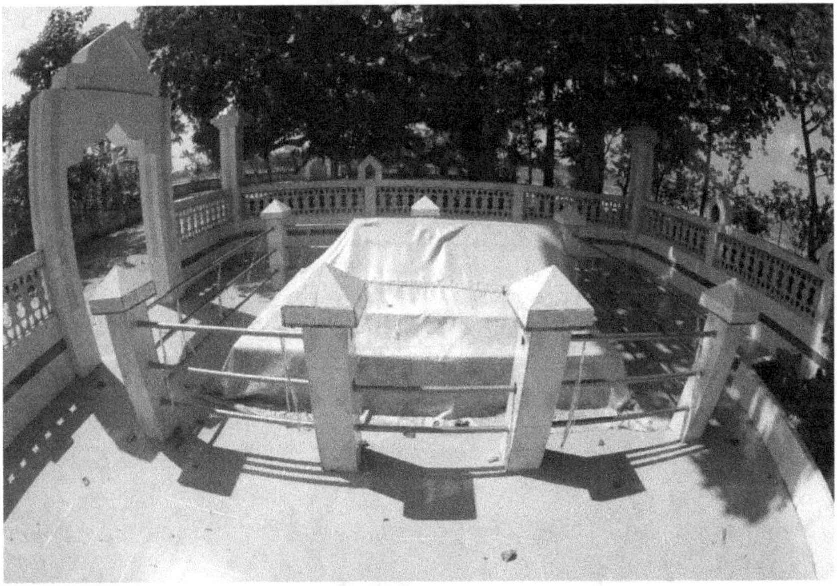

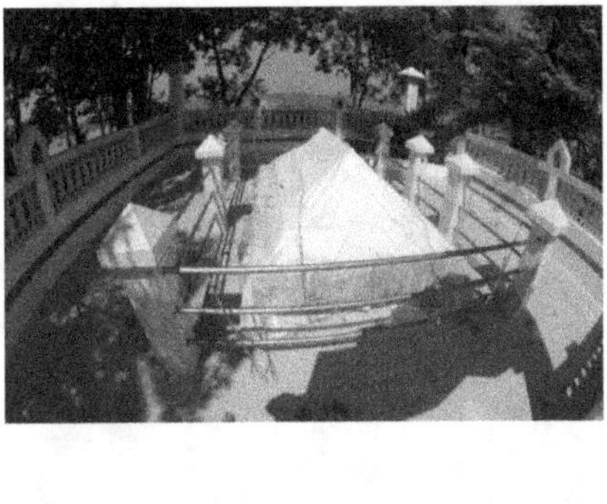

There is an ongoing dispute with the mazar listed below

Name:
H. Hafiz Fosih?
a.k.a.,
H. Feson Shah?

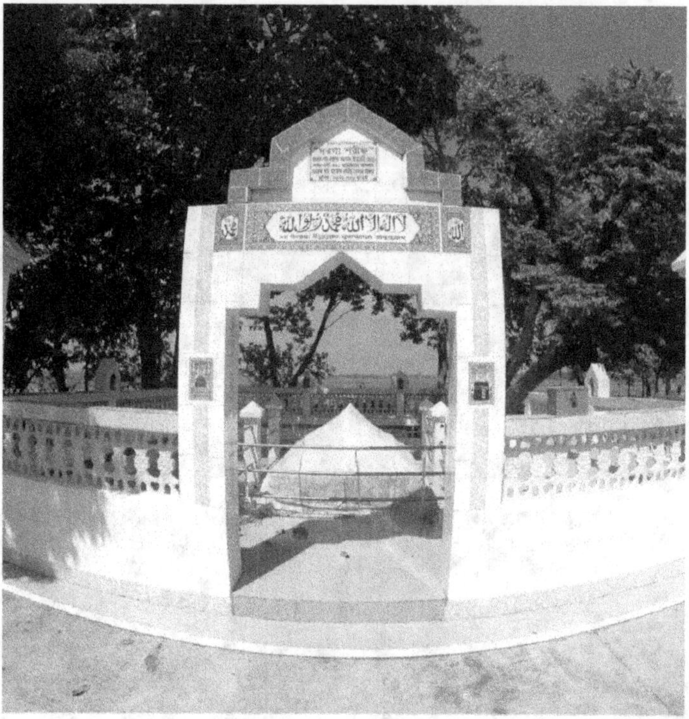

Address:
Boro Fesi, Ward: 3
Jogonath Pur
No. 8 Asher Kandi Union

Kadim:
Md Ustar Miah

Notes:
There has been a dispute and legal challenges between "Dowrai Boxs" Mazar and "Feson Shah" Mazar.

Dowrai claim that it is the mazar of Dowrai Boxs. Dowrai lost the legal challenges and now the mazar rest with Feson Shah a.k.a., Hafiz Fosih.

Note 2:
Fesi is also pronounced as "hesi"

3.10.2010, 12:37:06

Dowr Boksh Koti's Ashon*

Shah Arzu Miahr Bari, Son of Late Shah Abdur Rob
Poschim Parah (Ati)' Dowrai/Dasorai, Ward: 3, No. 5 Asher Kandi Union, Shunamgoinj

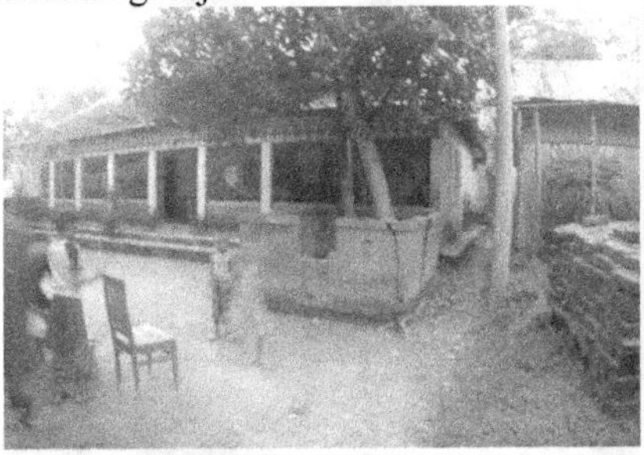
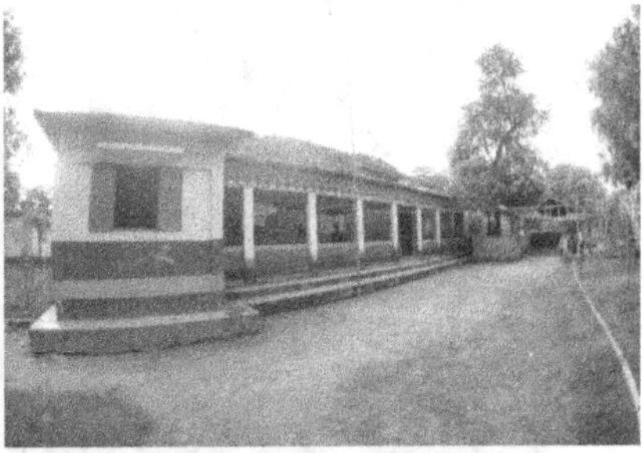
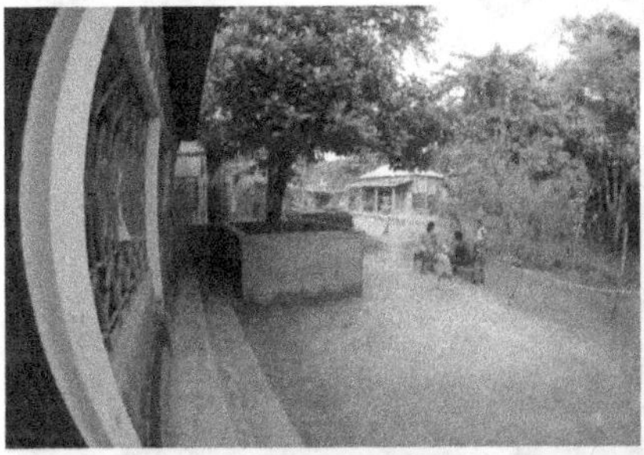
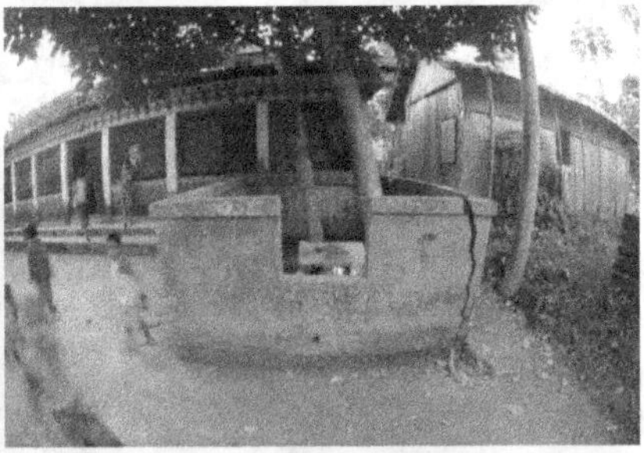
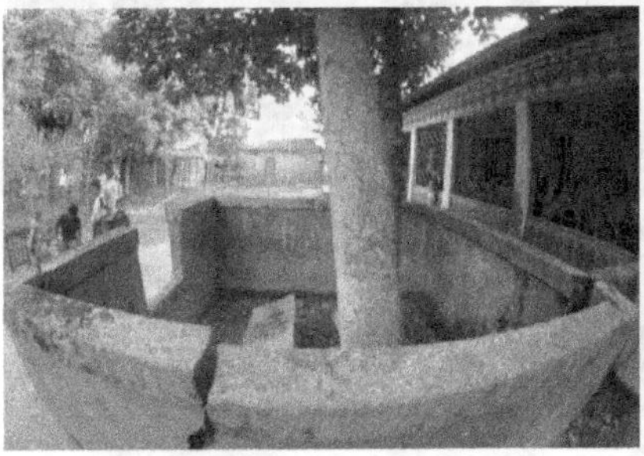
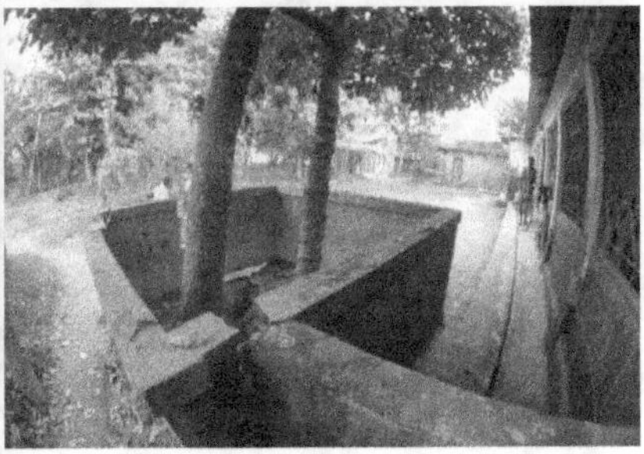

3.10.2010, 17:34:58

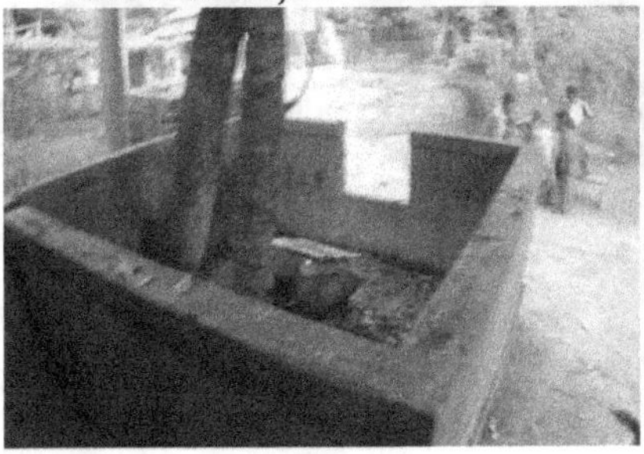
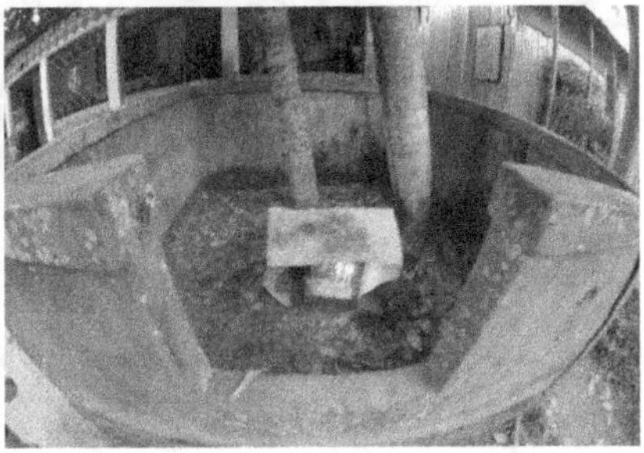

Kirti Shah*

Patantullah Tea Garden

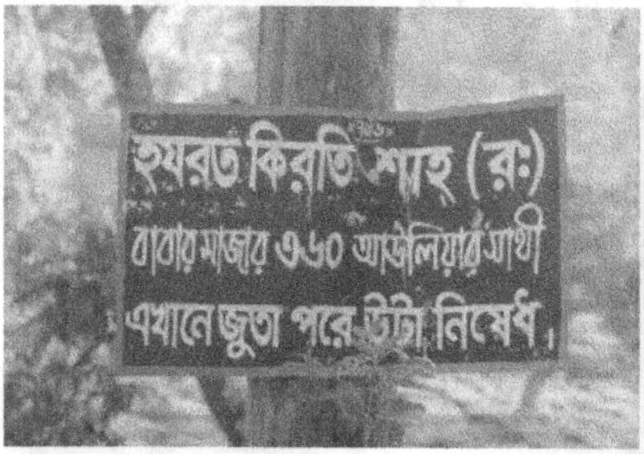
হযরত কিরতি শাহ (রঃ)
বাবার মাজার ৩৬০ আউলিয়ার সাথী
এখানে জুতা পরে উঠা নিষেধ।

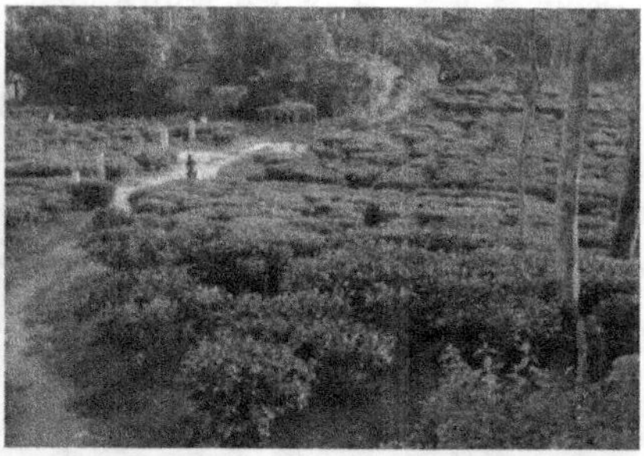

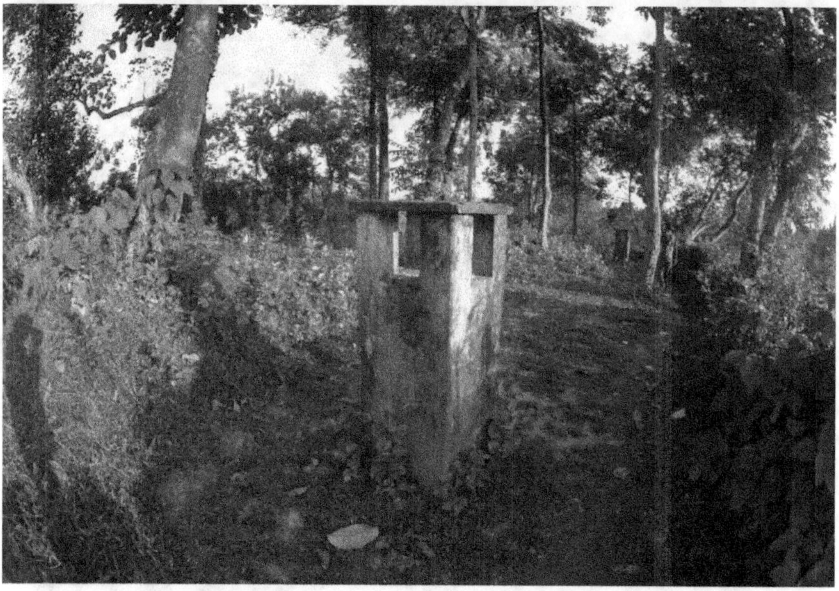

4.10.2010, 16:43:50

Of many of the Mazar, this one claims that this person was a member of the 360 missionaries, but there are no official markings, nor is there anything of significance or of reverence. Very basic and baron.

Gazi Doulot Shah*

Hajji Parah, Tarapur Tea Garden, Tukor Bazar Union, Ward 7, Sylhet Town

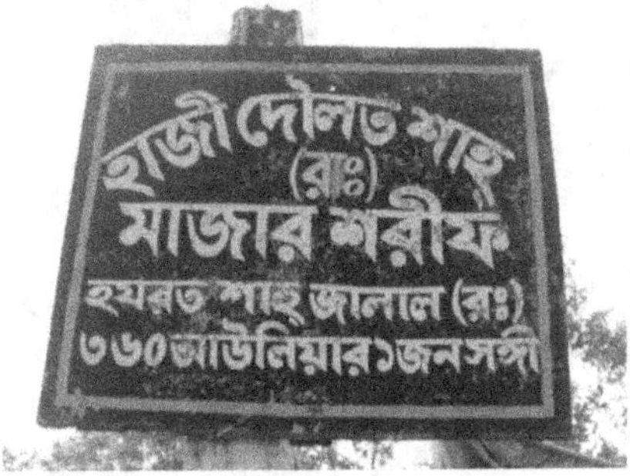
হাজী দৌলত শাহ্
(রাঃ)
মাজার শরীফ
হযরত শাহ্ জালাল (রঃ)
৩৬০ আউলিয়ার ১জন সঙ্গী

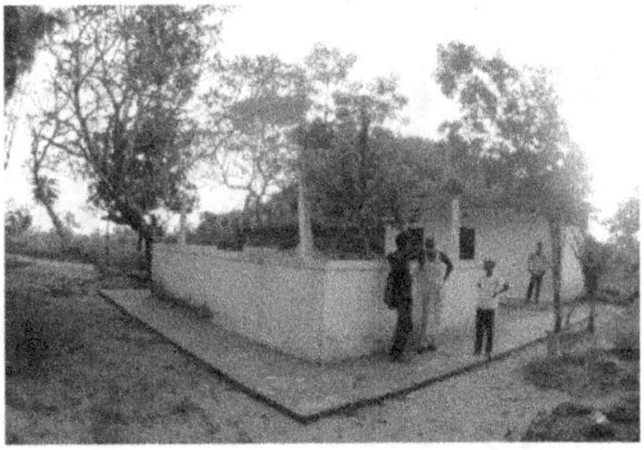

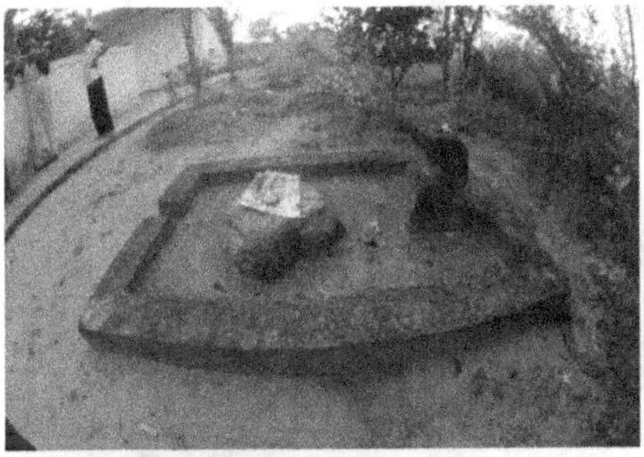

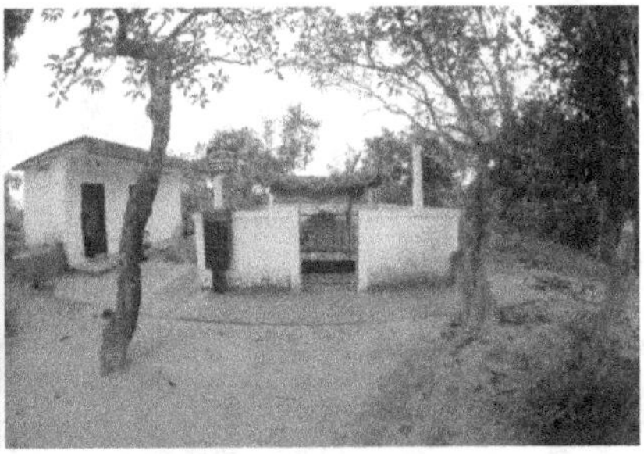

4.10.2010, 17:08:24

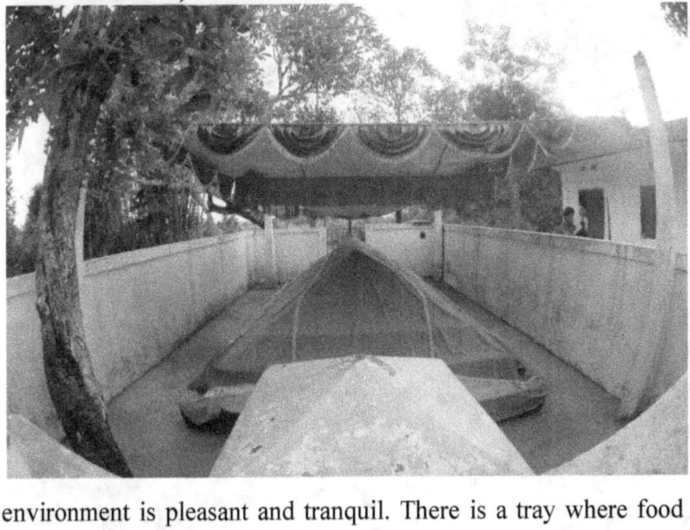

The Mazar is situated inside the tea Garden, on top of a hill. The road mud/sand tracks, there is a steep climb up. The Mazar is maintained and looked after. The environment is pleasant and tranquil. There is a tray where food is left for the "bhaggs" (Tigers)

Shahi Gorom Dewan Mohon Jalal*

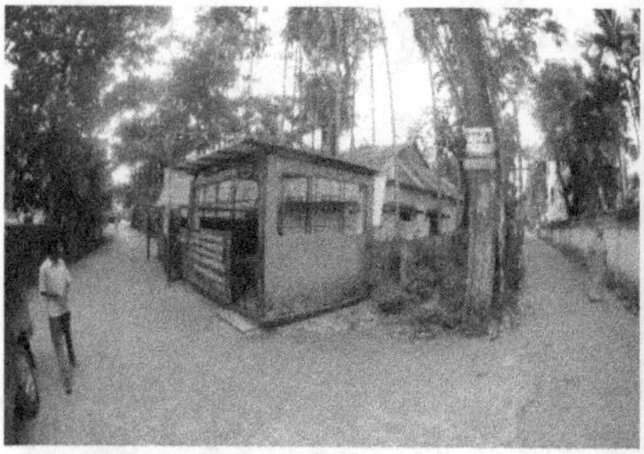

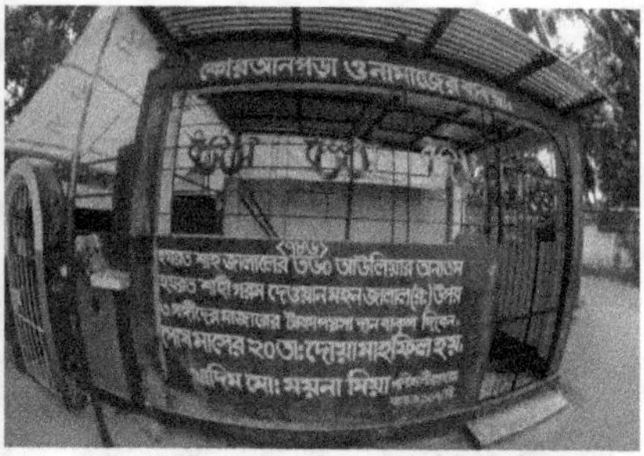

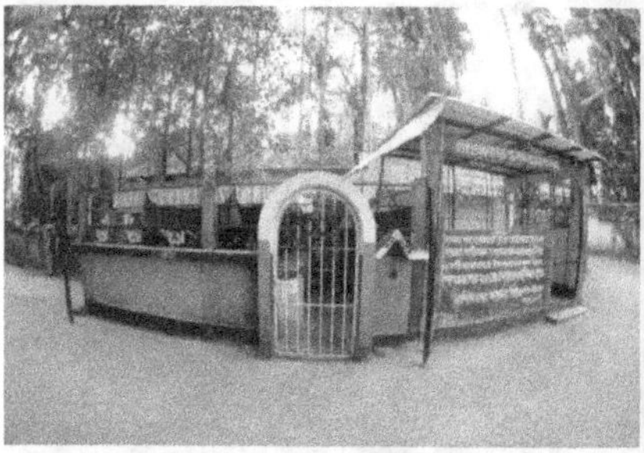

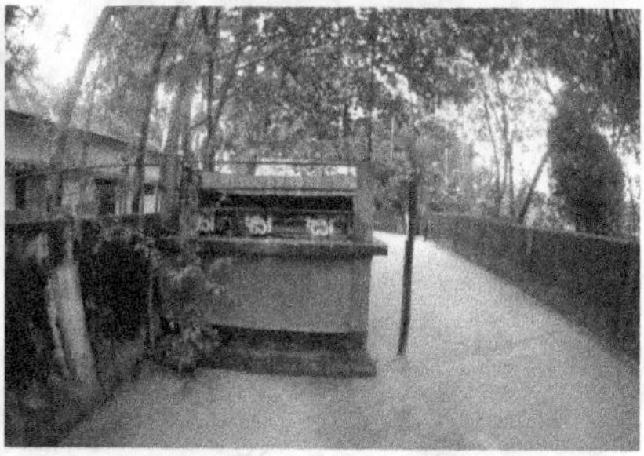

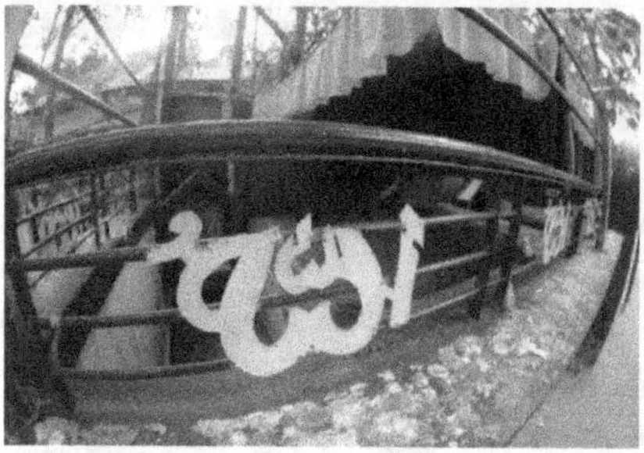

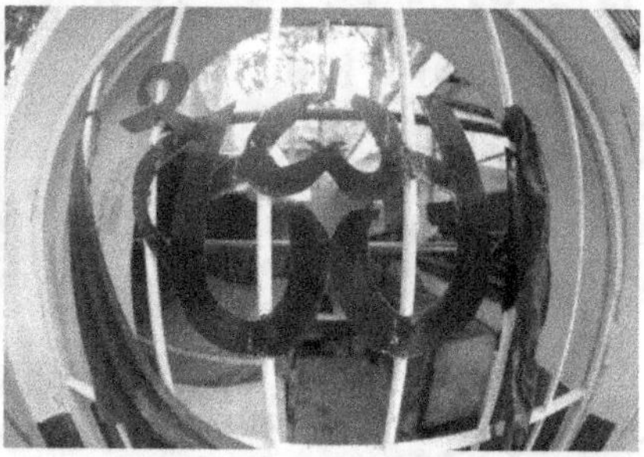

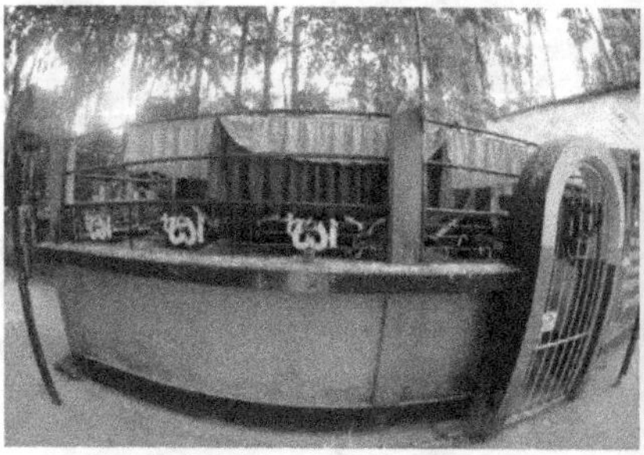

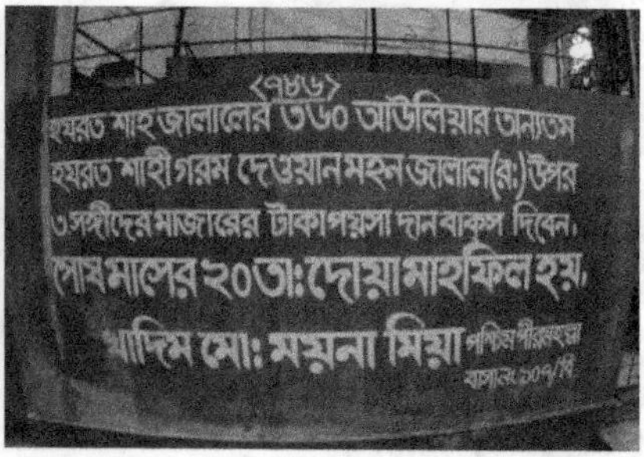

<৭৮৬>
হযরত শাহ জালালের ৩৬০ আউলিয়ার অন্যতম
হযরত শাহী গরম দেওয়ান মহন জালাল(রঃ) উপর
ও সঙ্গীদের মাজারের টাকাপয়সা দান বাক্স দিবেন।
পোষ মাসের ২০তাঃ দোয়া মাহফিল হয়।
খাদিম মোঃ ময়না মিয়া

5.10.2010, 15:55:20

Soyod Umor Faruk*

Soyod Mugni, Majumdari, Sylhet

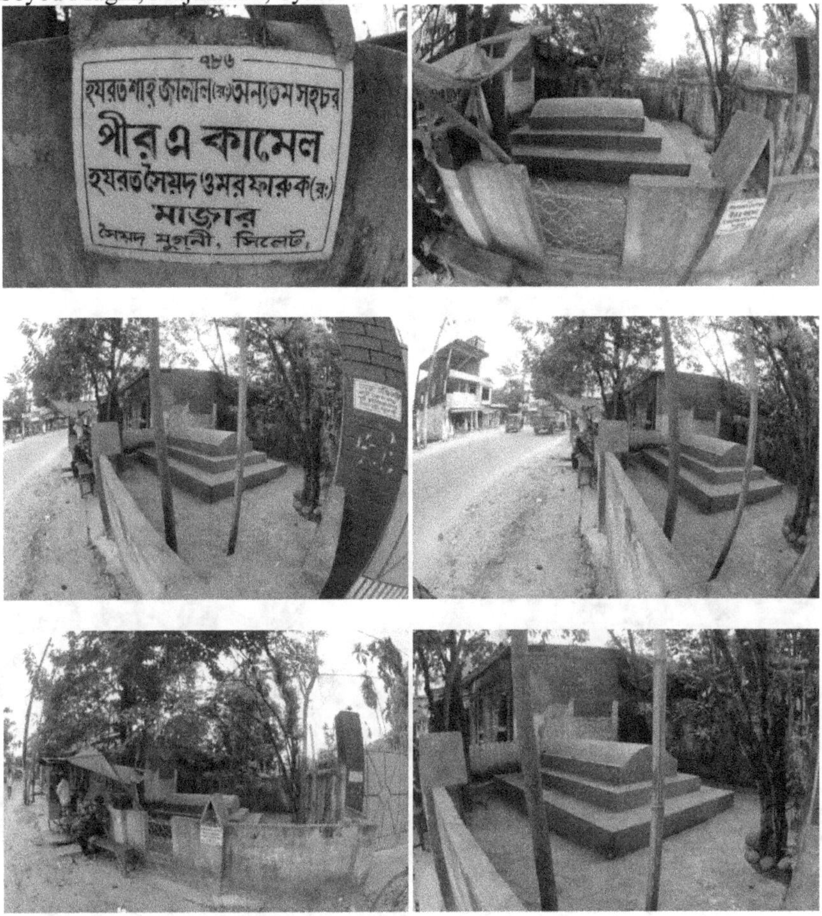
৭৮৬
হযরত শাহ্ জালাল (রহ:) অন্যতম সহচর
পীর এ কামেল
হযরত সৈয়দ ওমর ফারুক (র:)
মাজার
সৈয়দ মুগনী, সিলেট,

5.10.2010, 13:43:14

"Conditions and the weather at the Mazars shaped the way you felt"

Sath Phirer Mazar

Majumdar Bari, Majumdari, Ward 4, Sylhet Town

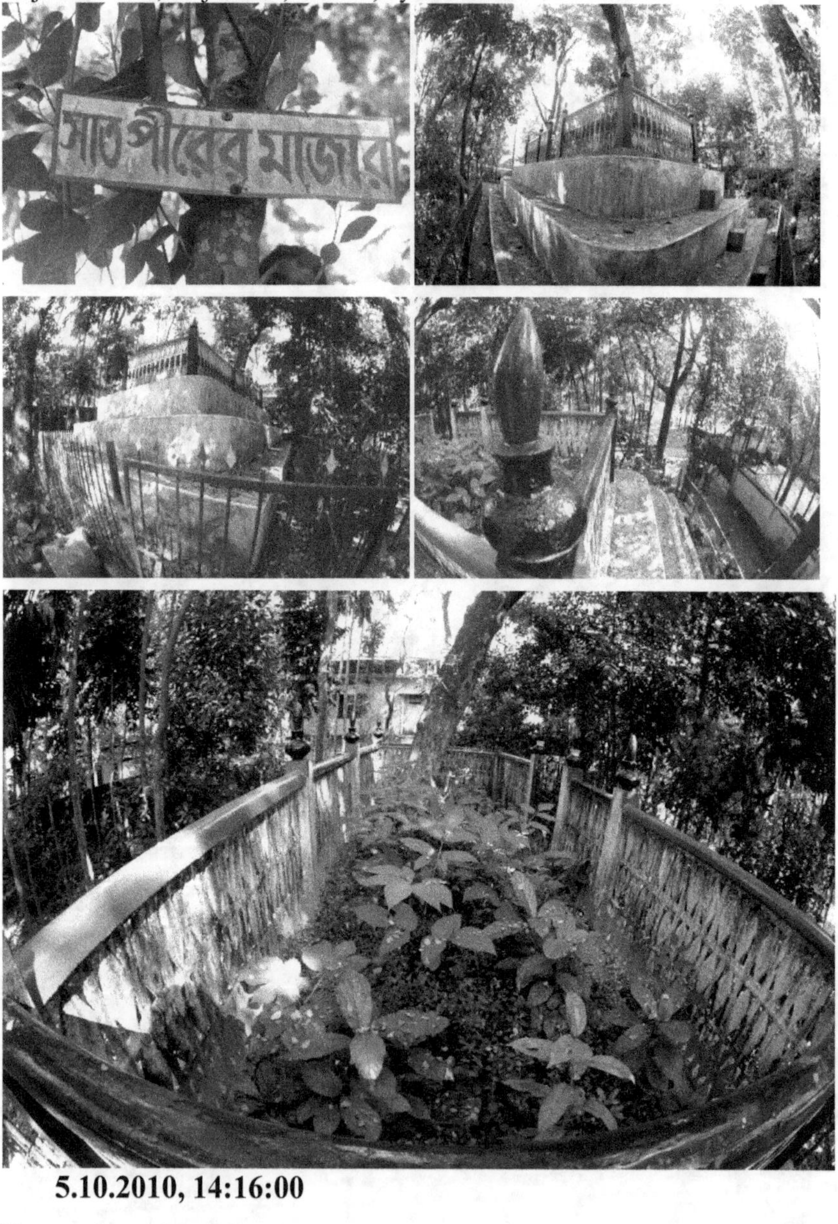
সাতপীরের মাজার

5.10.2010, 14:16:00

Not members of the 360 group.

Shah Mulogtulagi

Shah Tulshi

Soyod Bari Rasta, Lesu bagan, Purbo Phir Moholla, property 28, ward 6, Sylhet Town

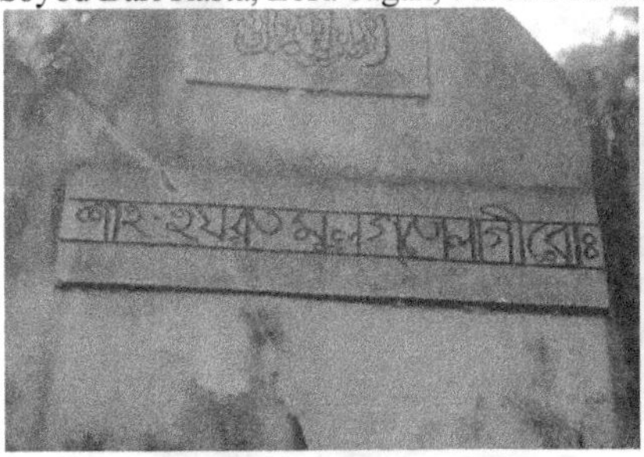

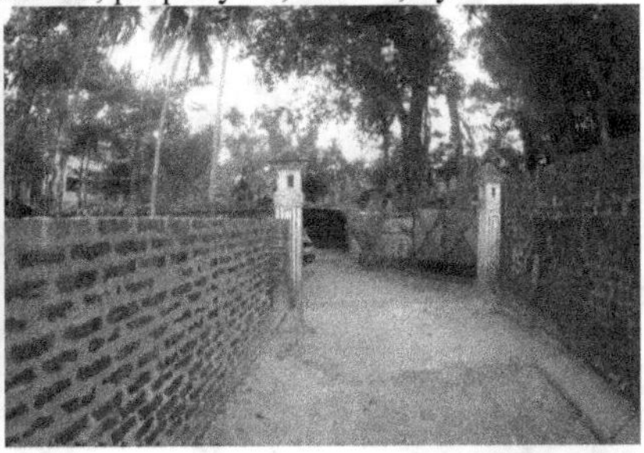

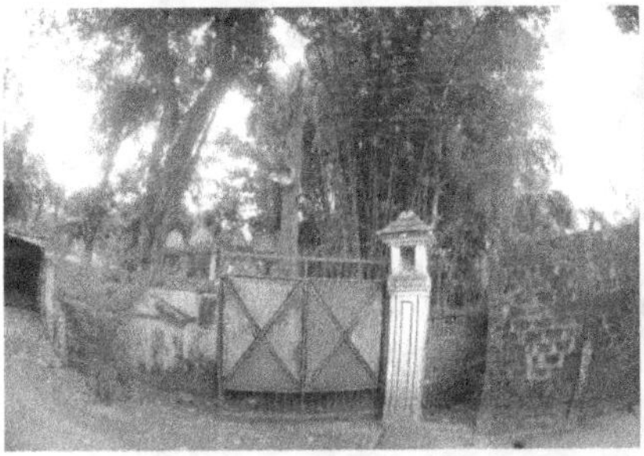

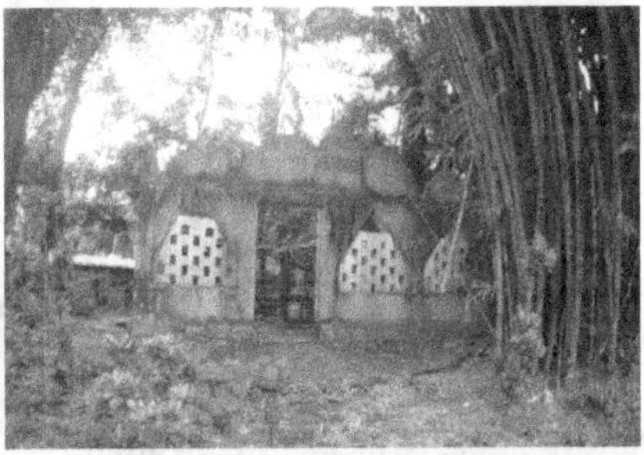

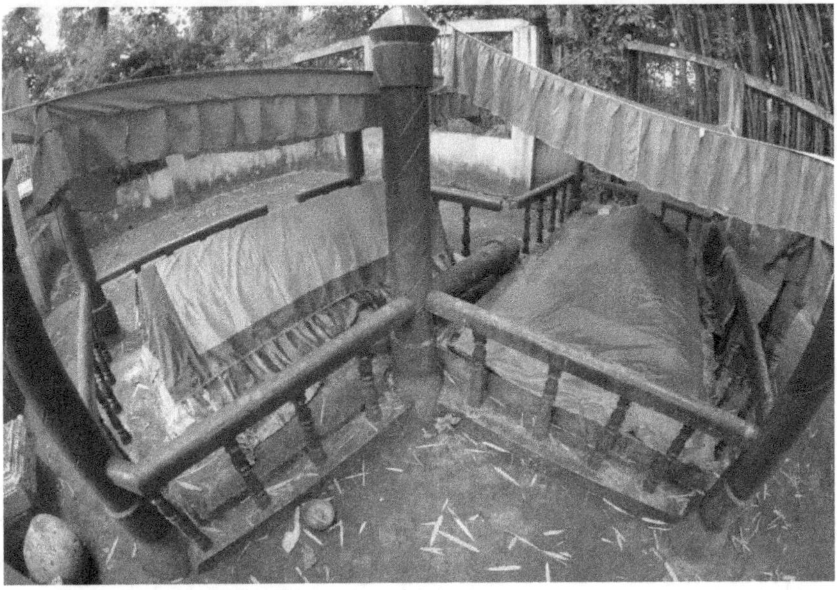

5.10.2010, 15:41:10

Akol Kua

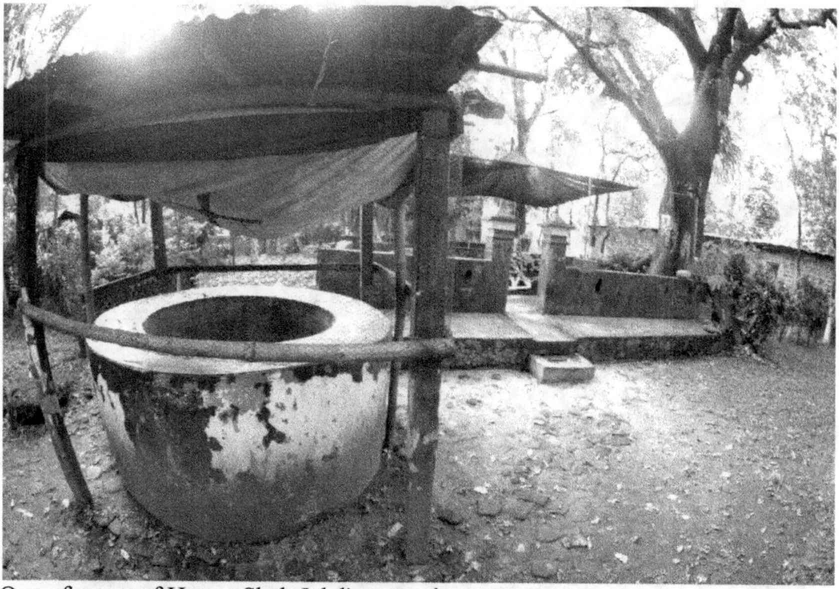

One of many of Hazrat Shah Jalal's campsites.
Phir Moholla, Sylhet Town, Ward 6.

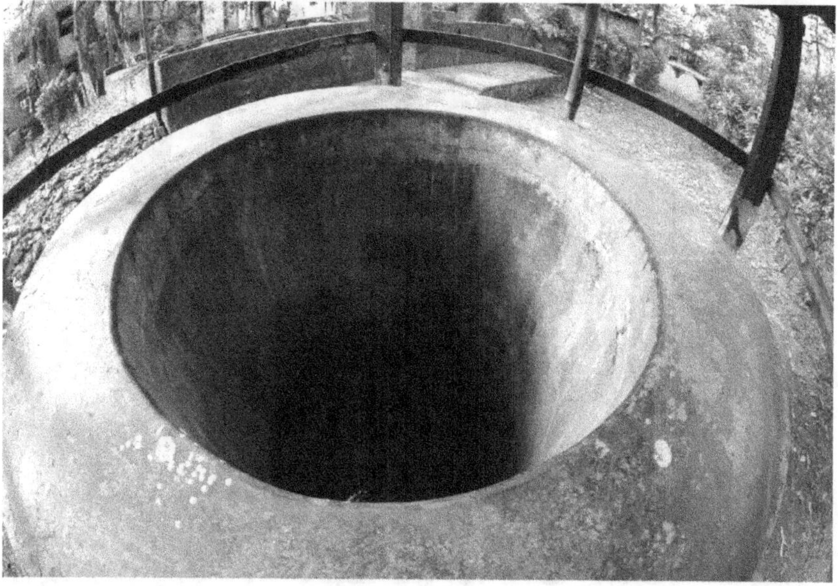

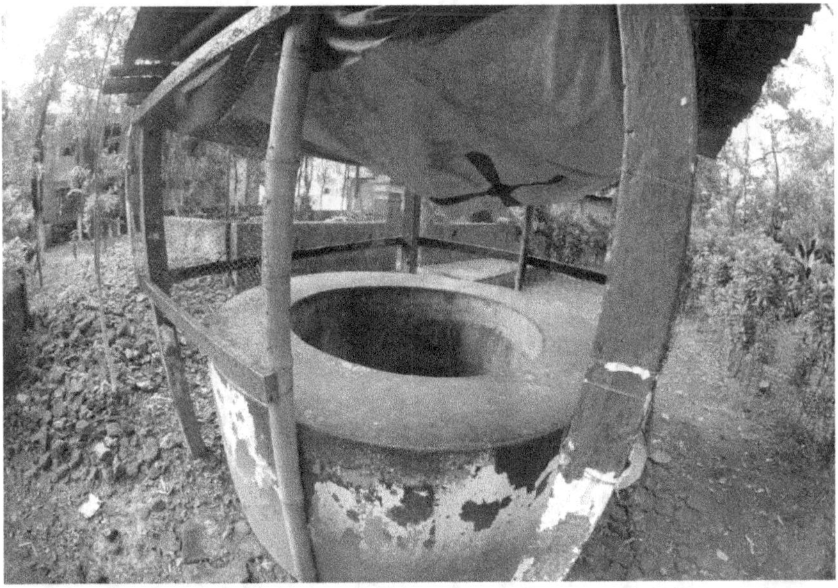

5.10.2010, 15:05:08

Shah Shundor**

No.8 Union, Mukamergul, Kadim Nagor, Shodor, Sylhet

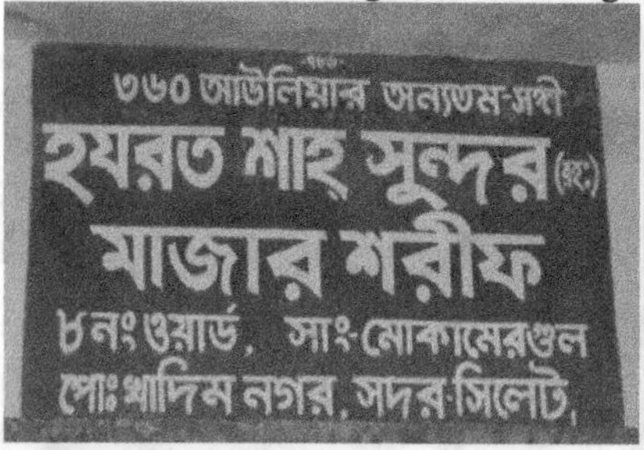
৩৬০ আউলিয়ার অন্যতম-সঙ্গী
হযরত শাহ সুন্দর (রহঃ)
মাজার শরীফ
৮নং ওয়ার্ড, সাং-মোকামেরগুল
পোঃ খাদিম নগর, সদর-সিলেট,

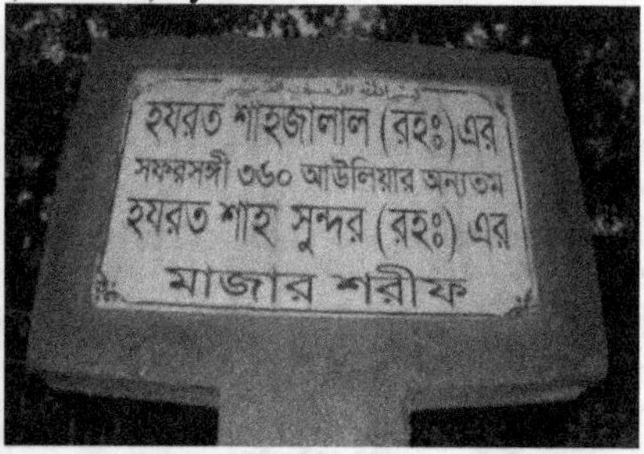
হযরত শাহজালাল (রহঃ) এর
সফরসঙ্গী ৩৬০ আউলিয়ার অন্যতম
হযরত শাহ সুন্দর (রহঃ) এর
মাজার শরীফ

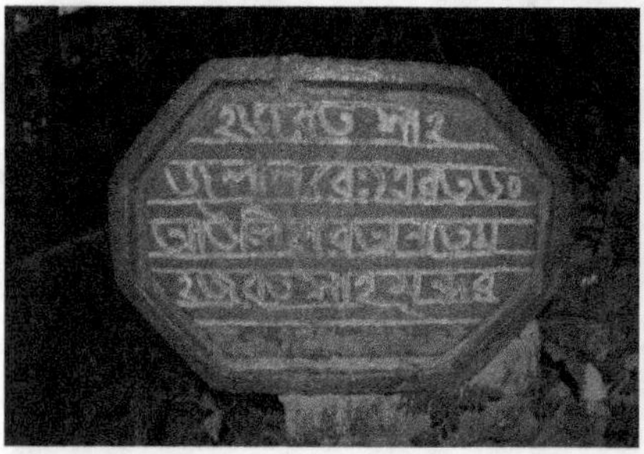

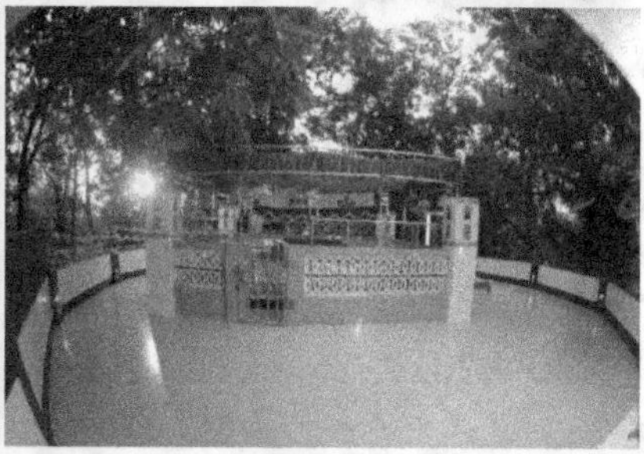

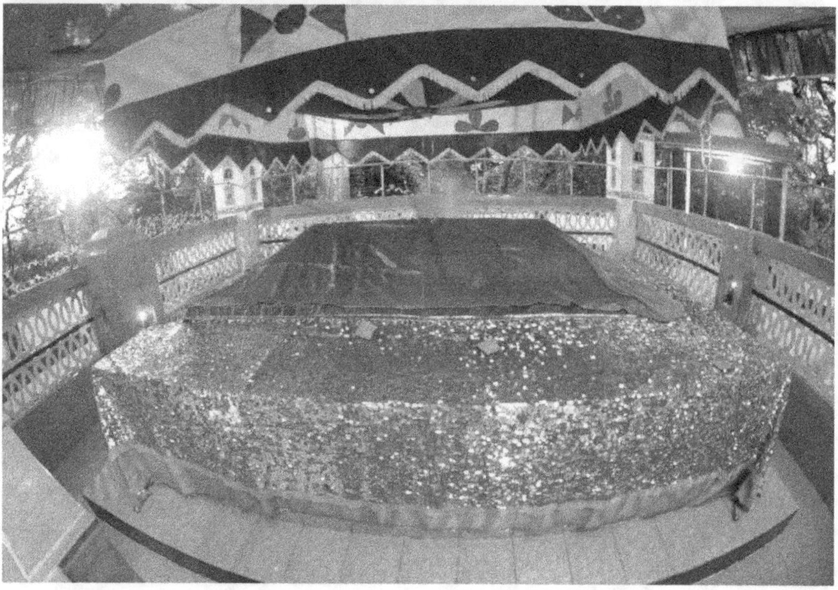

5.10.2010, 17:30:58

Char Gulali

Soyod Mugni Road, Majumdar / Kashdobir, Ward 6, Sylhet town

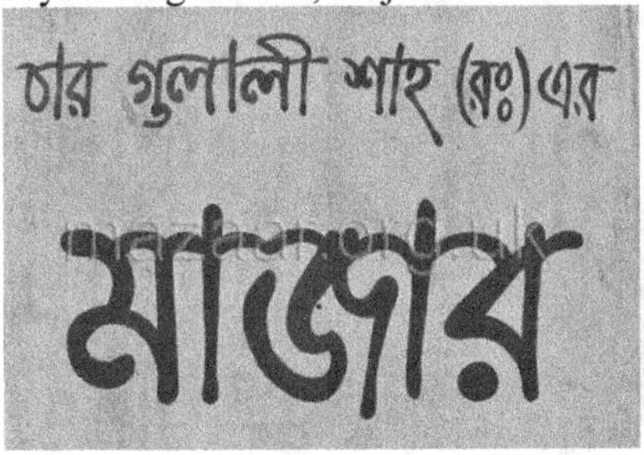
চার গুলালী শাহ (রঃ)এর
মাজার

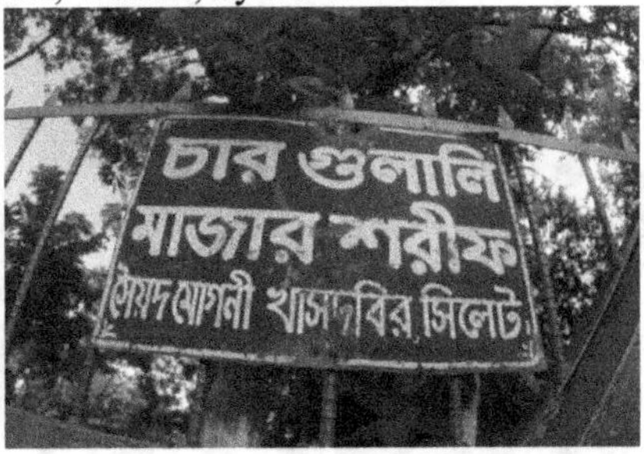
চার গুলালি
মাজার শরীফ
সৈয়দ মোগনী খাসদবির,সিলেট

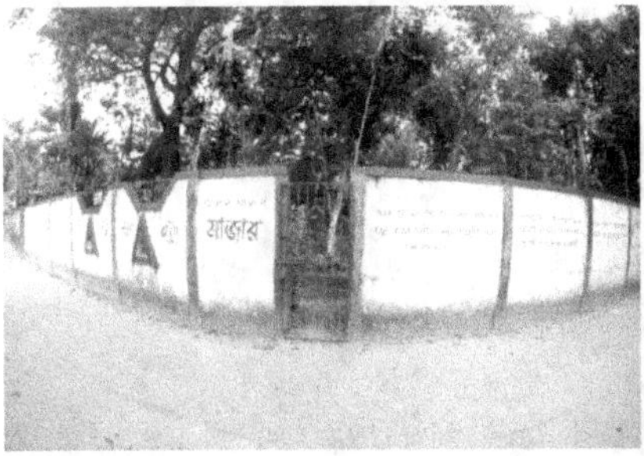

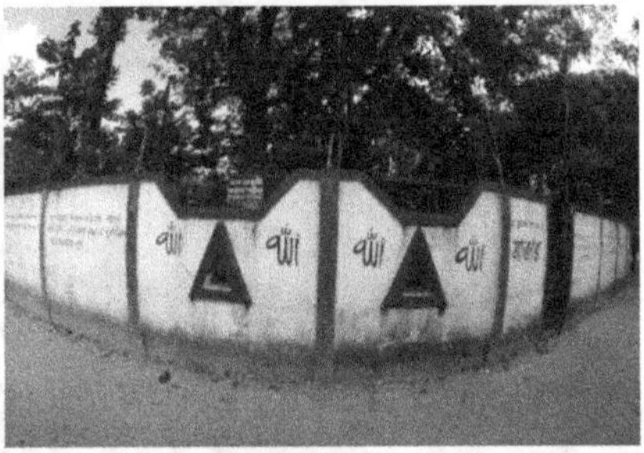

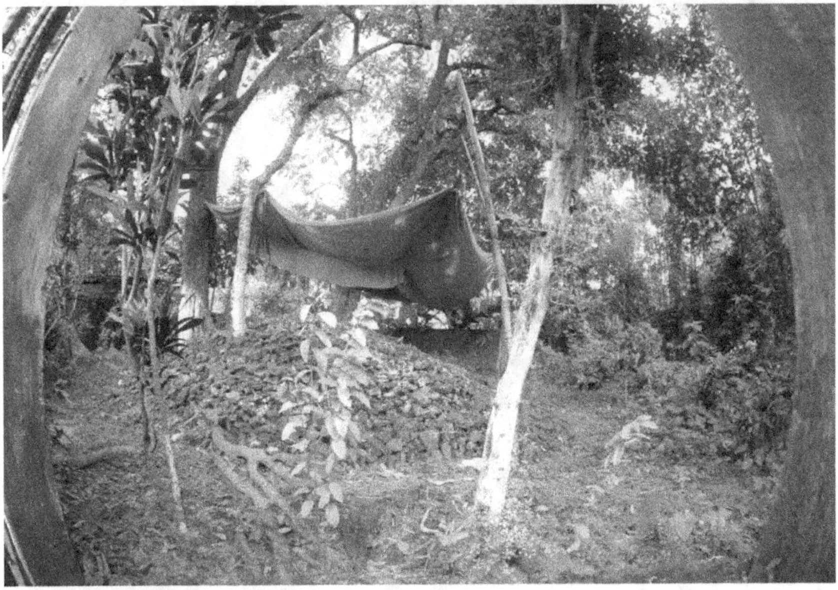

5.10.2010, 13:56:40

There are 4 people here, the site was inaccessible.

Shah Alom*

Shah Ali

Phir Moholla, Ward 6, Sylhet Town

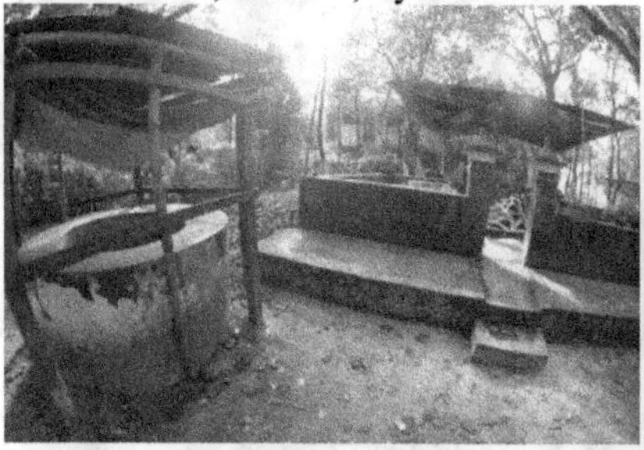

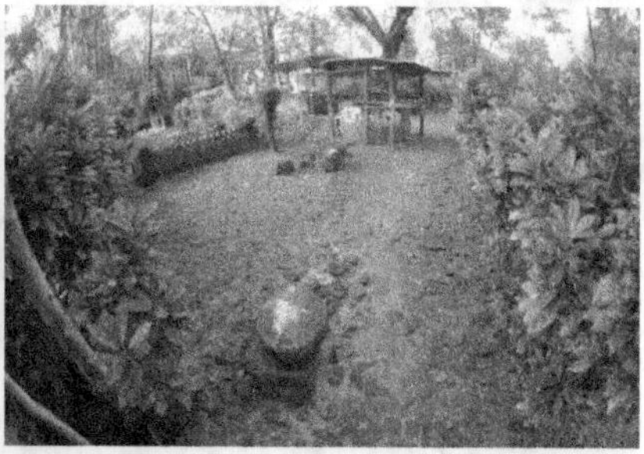

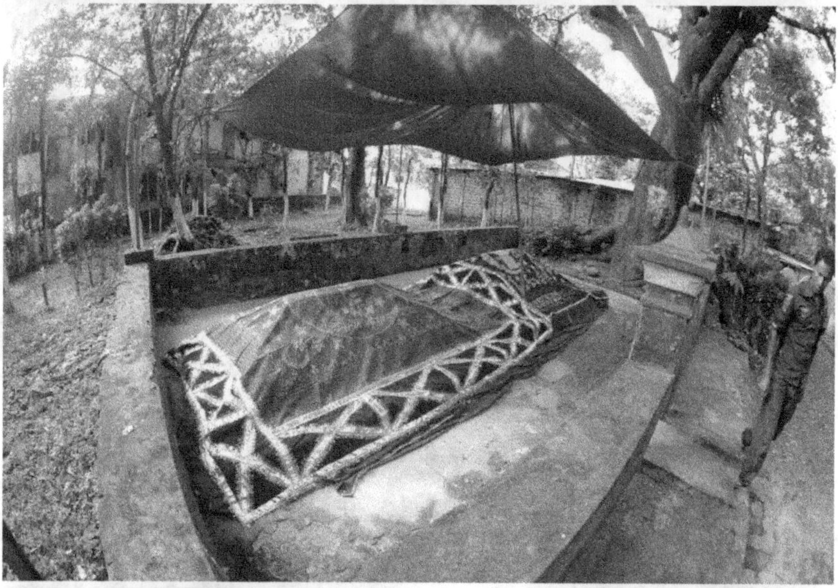

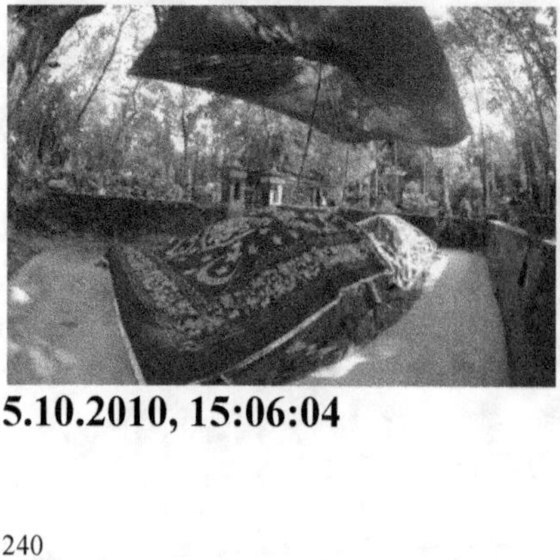

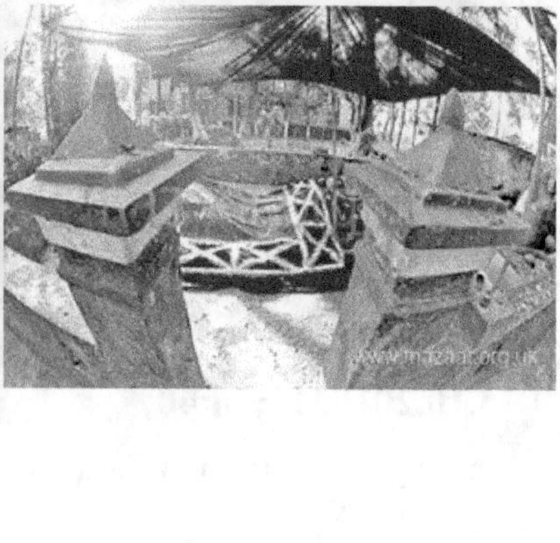
www.mazaar.org.uk

5.10.2010, 15:06:04

Ambor Shah

Soyod Miar Colony, Ambor Khana, Ward 4, Sylhet Town

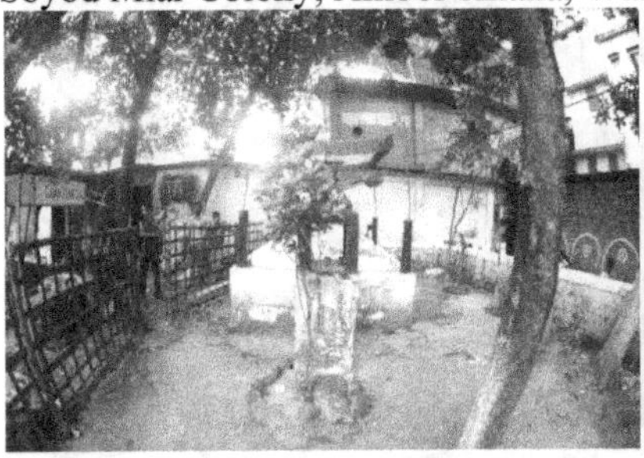

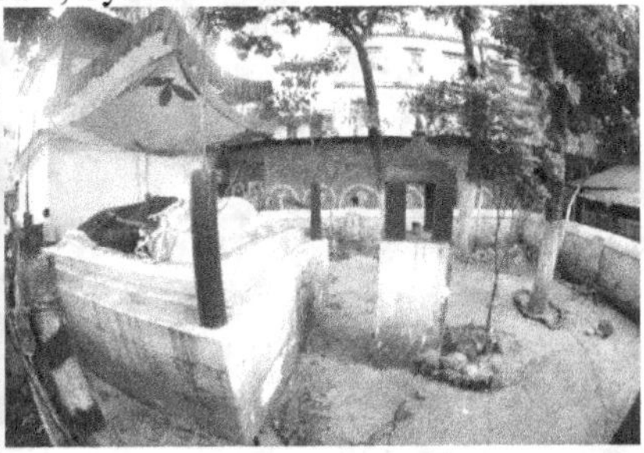

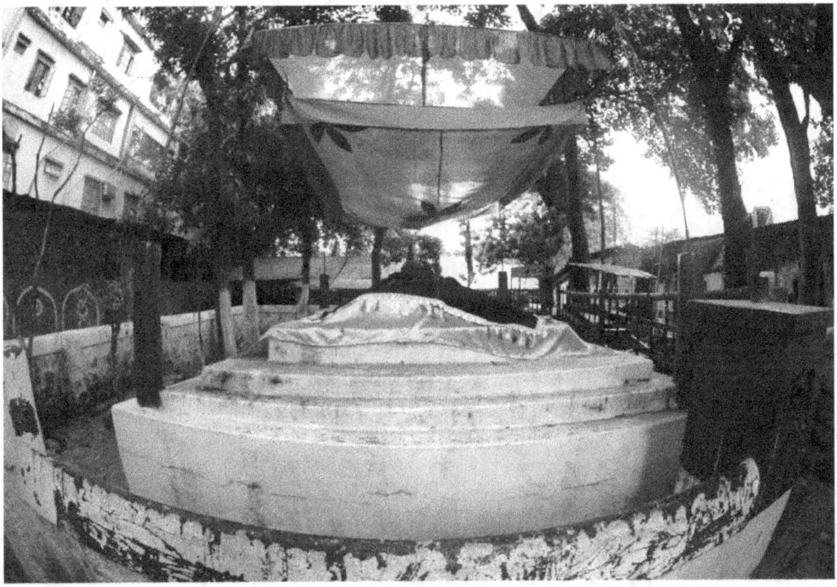

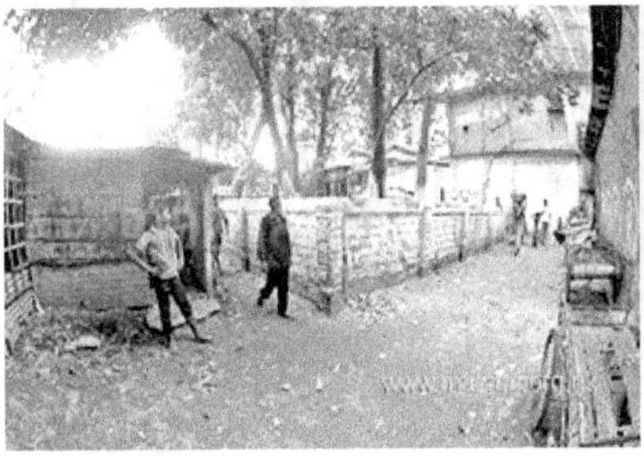

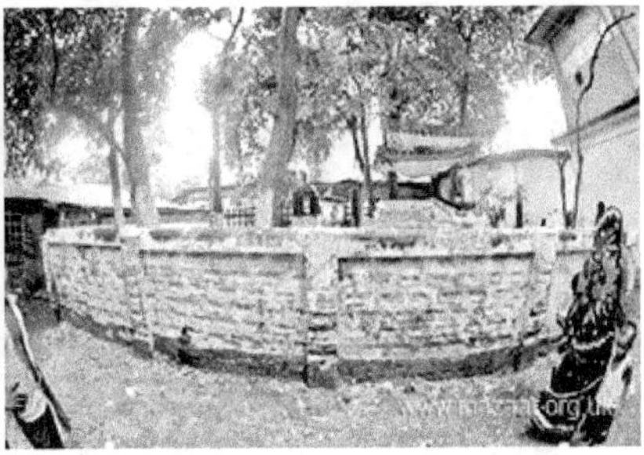

5.10.2010, 16:19:00

This place is tucked away, off the beaten tracks.

Shah Forid Rowshan Serag**

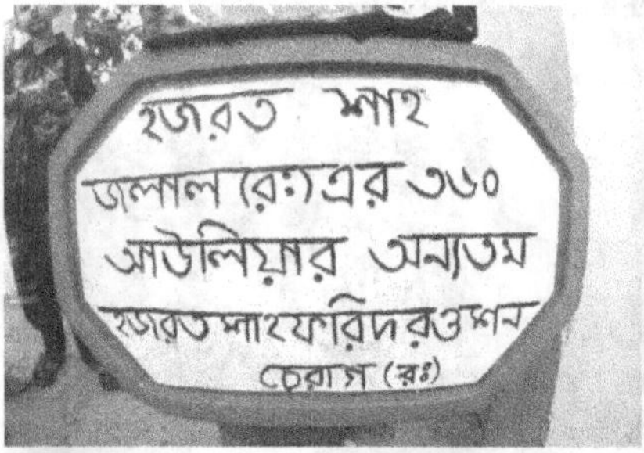
হজরত শাহ
জালাল (রঃ) এর ৩৬০
আউলিয়ার অন্যতম
হজরত শাহ ফরিদ রওশন
চেরাগ (রঃ)

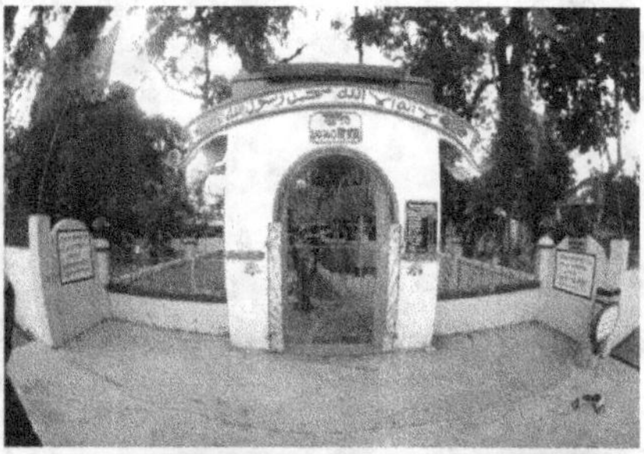

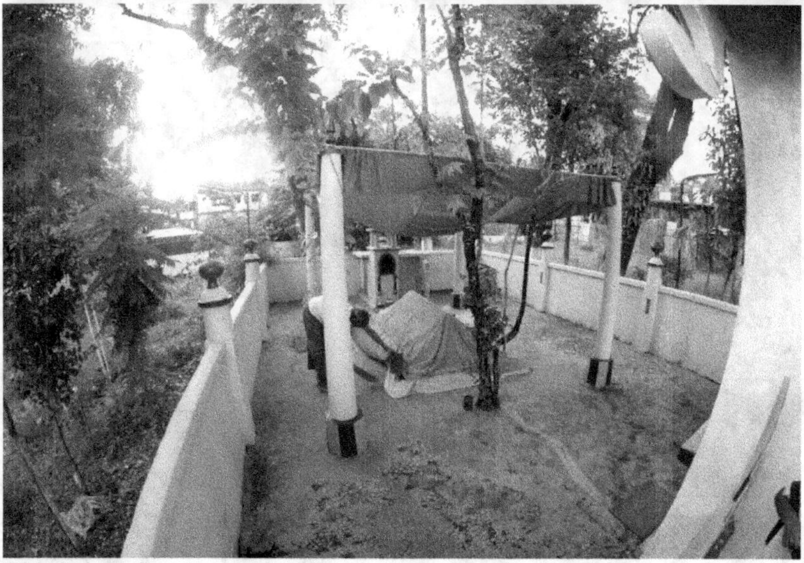

This is in Sylhet Town, the place is well maintained, and is situated on the side of the street. It is easy to get to.

The Sylhet council have paid for much improvements of this Mazar.

5.10.2010, 16:07:14

Shah Sufi Soyod Jahan*

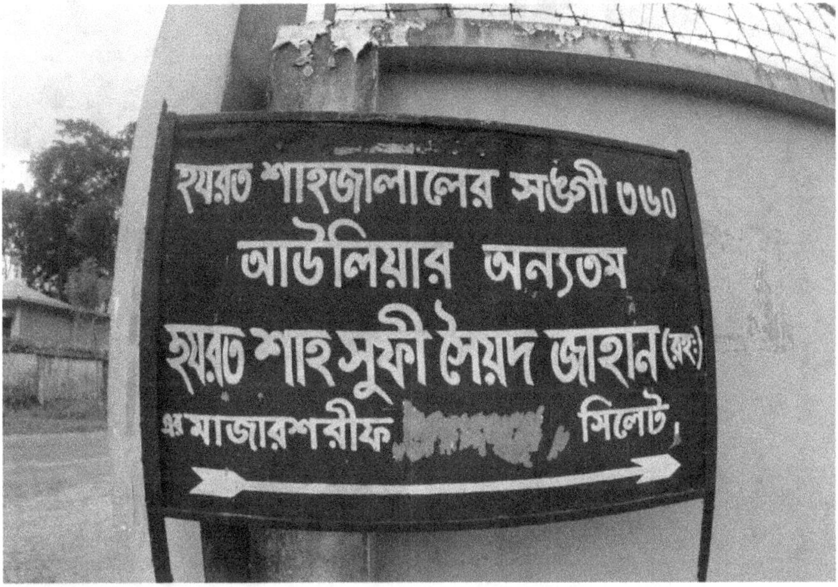
হযরত শাহজালালের সঙ্গী ৩৬০
আউলিয়ার অন্যতম
হযরত শাহ সুফী সৈয়দ জাহান (রহঃ)
মাজারশরীফ
সিলেট

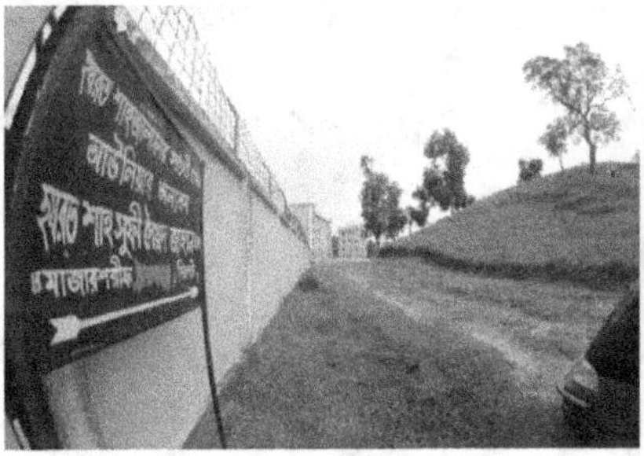

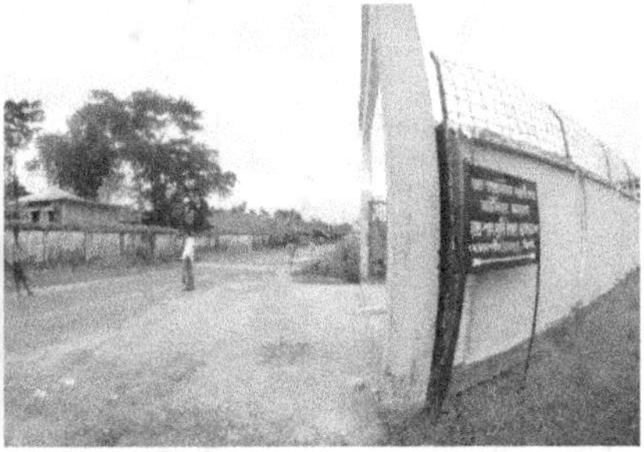

5.10.2010, 16:40

This was just a sign directing to the mazar, but we didn't get to it.

Dewan Shah

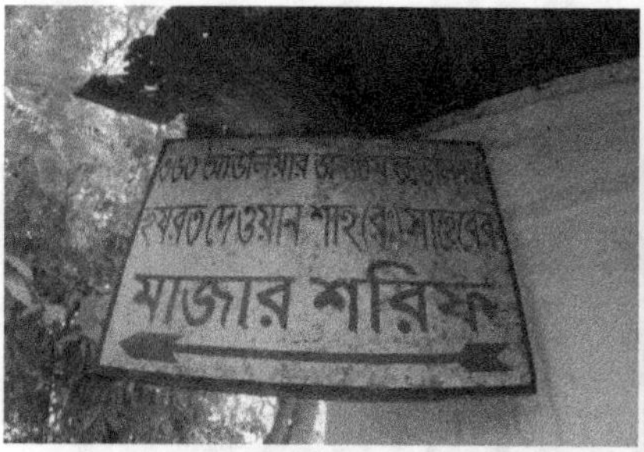
হযরত দেওয়ান শাহ (রঃ) সাহেবের
মাজার শরিফ

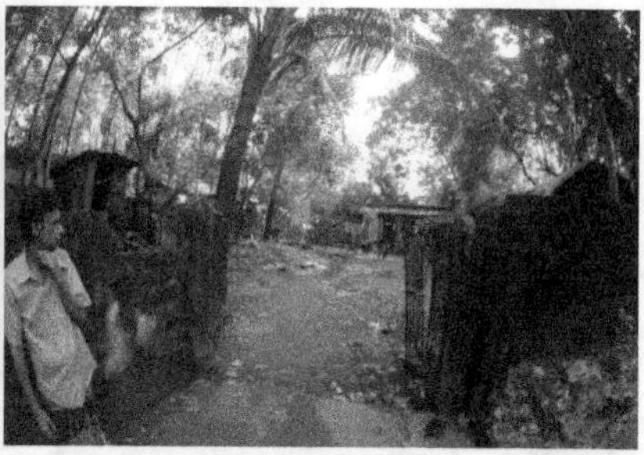

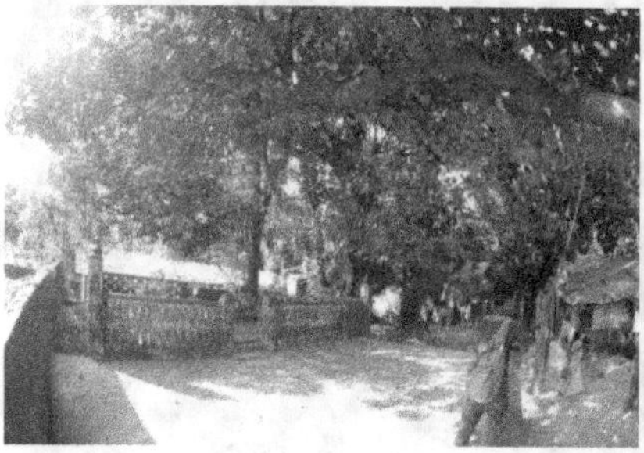

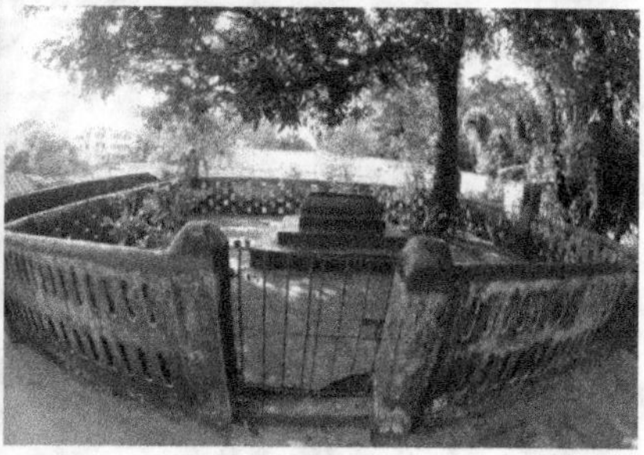

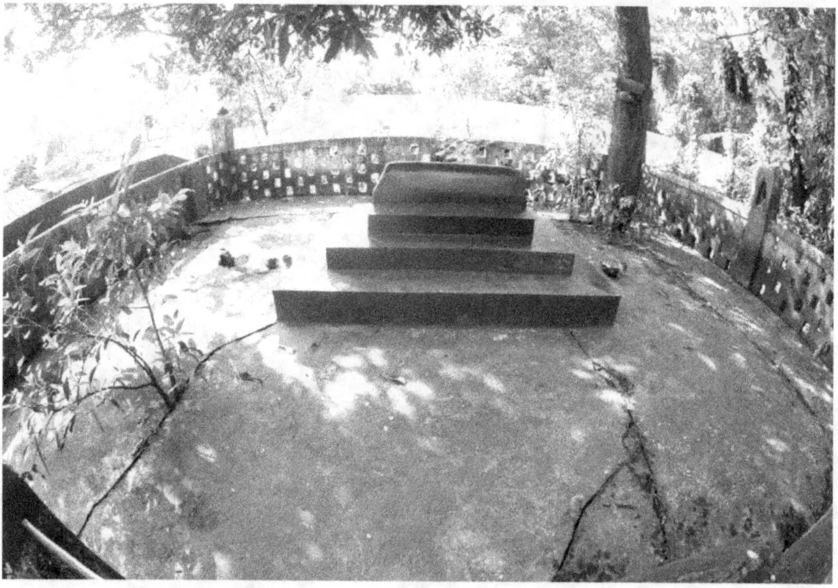

5.10.2010, 14:40:56

Shah Suleman Gazi

Kashdobir, Chowkidikhir, Sylhet Town

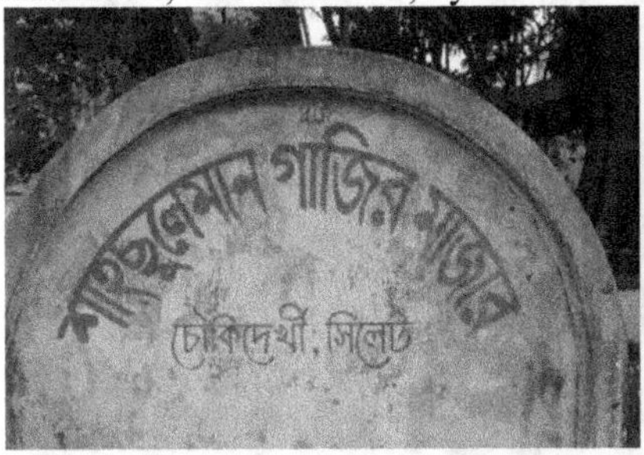
চৌকিদেখী, সিলেট

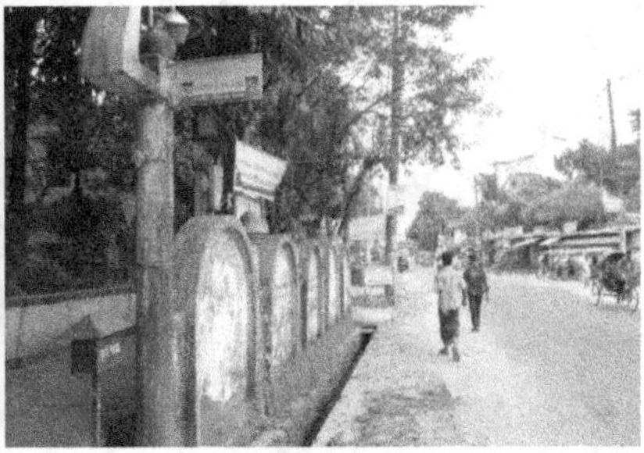

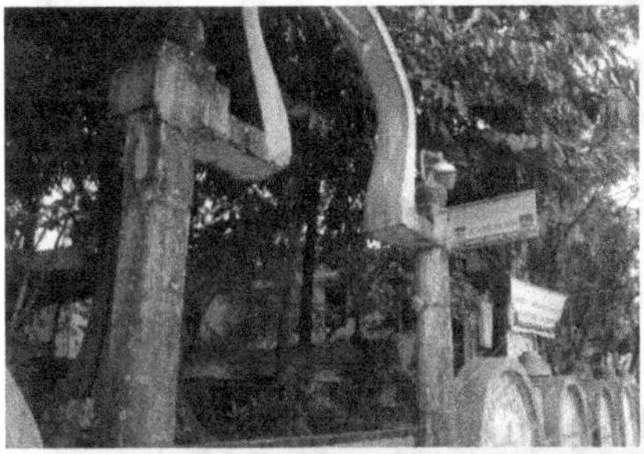

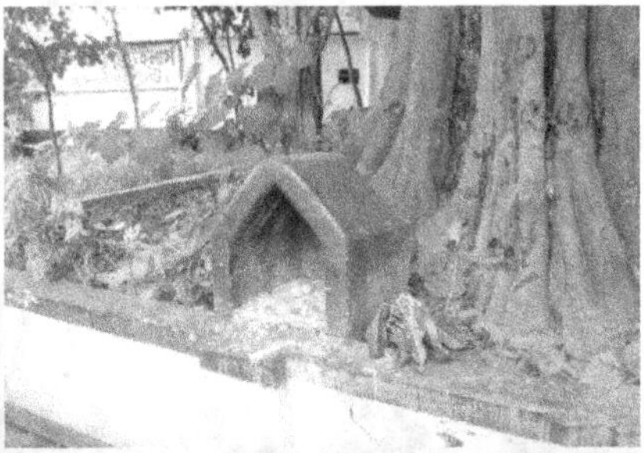

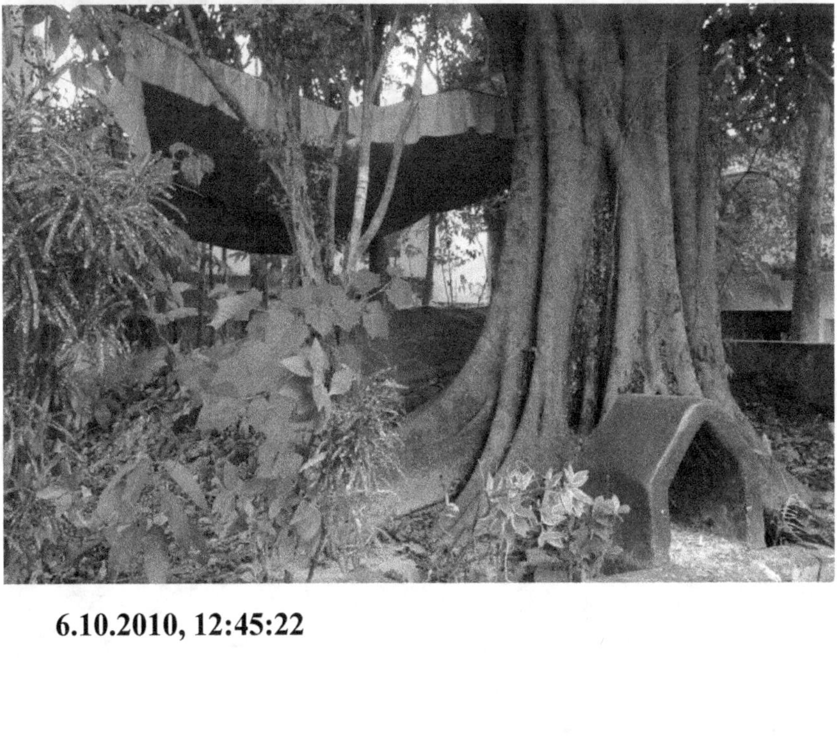

6.10.2010, 12:45:22

Gazi Shah Shamsuddin Bihari**

Att Ghor, Mazar Para, Jogonath Pur Road, Shunamgoinj (no.3 Mirpur Union)

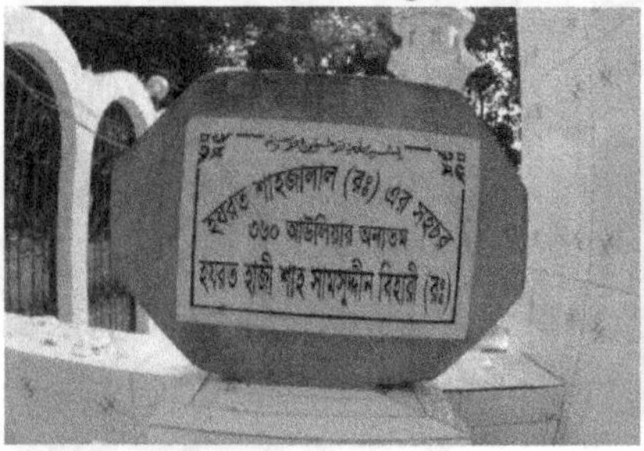
হযরত শাহজালাল (রঃ) এর সহচর
৩৬০ আউলিয়ার অন্যতম
হযরত গাজী শাহ সামসুদ্দীন বিহারী (রঃ)

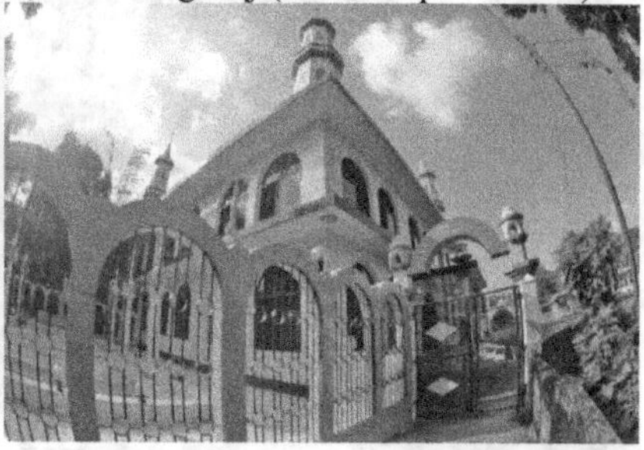

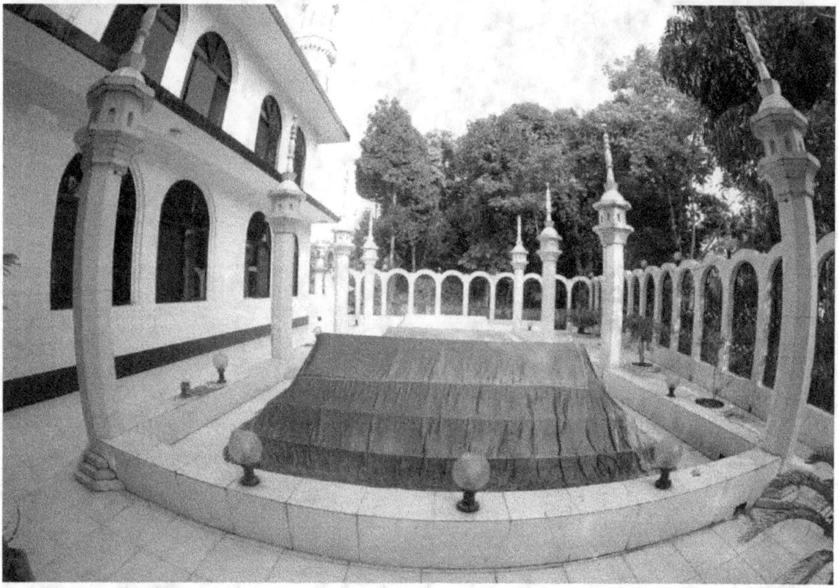

10.10.2010

This is located inside a village. The place was very tranquil as these places are in the village. It was a large complex, very well kept and maintained.

Shah Jalal Yemeni***

Dorga gate, Sylhet Town

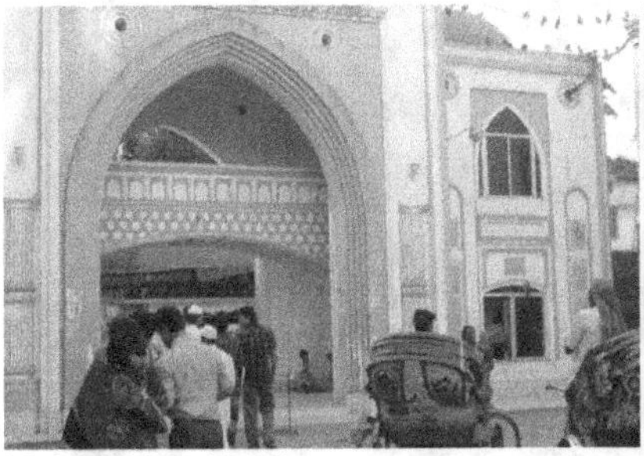

13.10.2010, 16:21

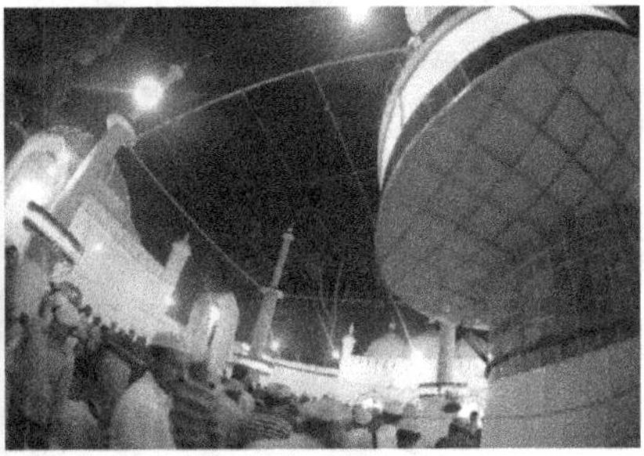

27.10.2010, 21:20

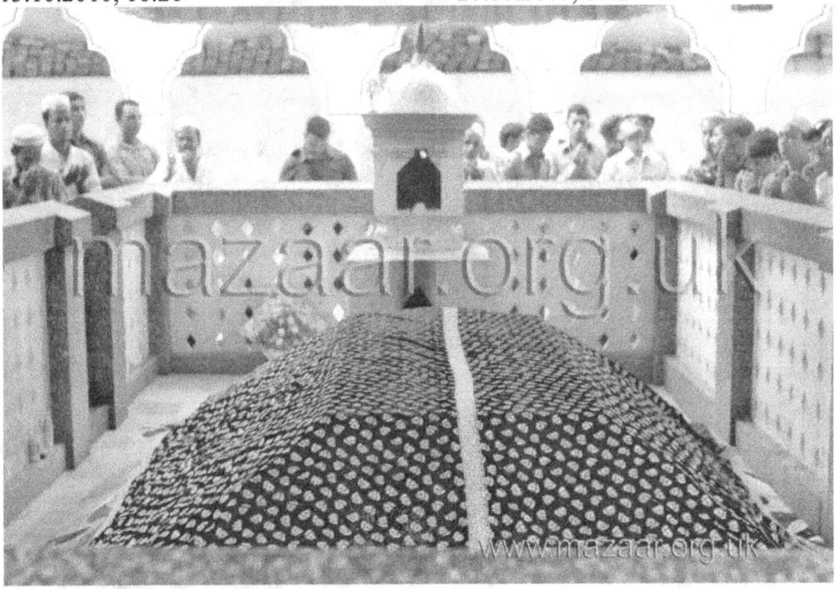
mazaar.org.uk
www.mazaar.org.uk

13.10.2010, 16:40

Now that I had visited my own ancestral mazars, the next place was the Dorga, Where Hazrat Shah Jalal was. This were all Sylhetis travelling from UK and abroad visit and pay their respects. I too went there few times and contemplate. While the outside courtyard in serene and tranquil, visually it is busy as people congregate and pass through. In the inner section where the mazar is - in is serene and tranquil and any anxiety, inhibitions, they get zapped. I had total peace and stillness in my mind, my thoughts stopped, my senses took over, ears heard the silence, just the nature, my nose took in the fragrance from the incense sticks and the aromas from the rose water and the touch marble floor by my feet grounded me and the atmosphere in that square just blanketed me.

Babeh Doulot*

a.k.a., Bibi Doil

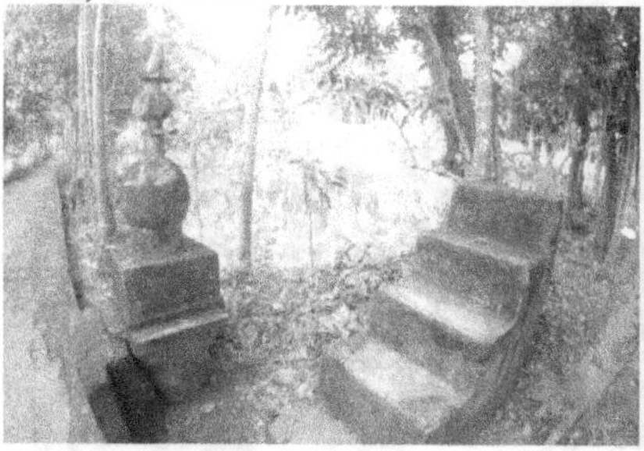

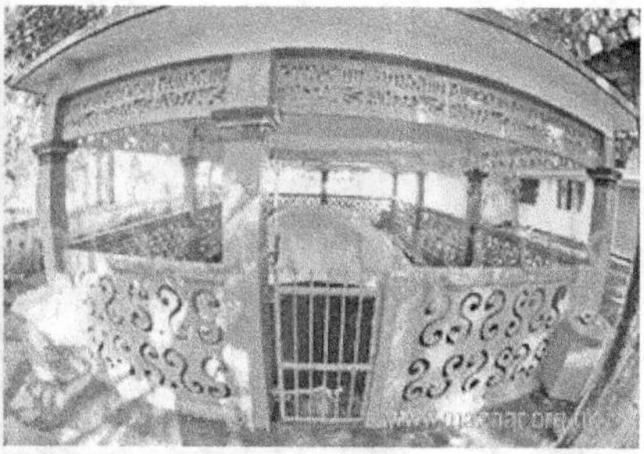

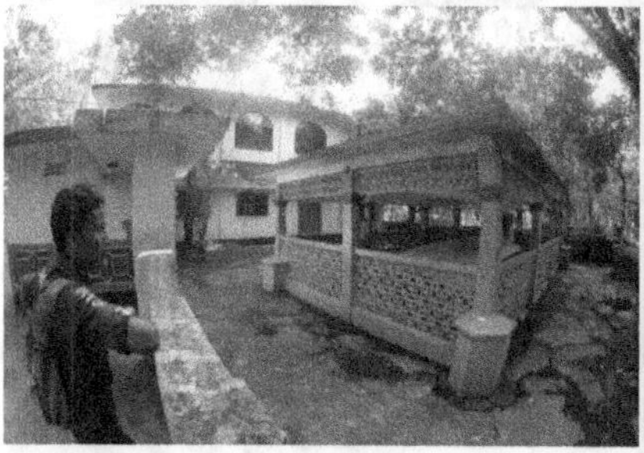

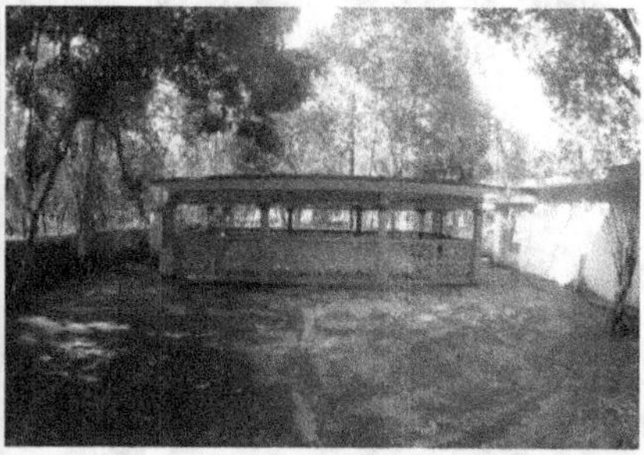

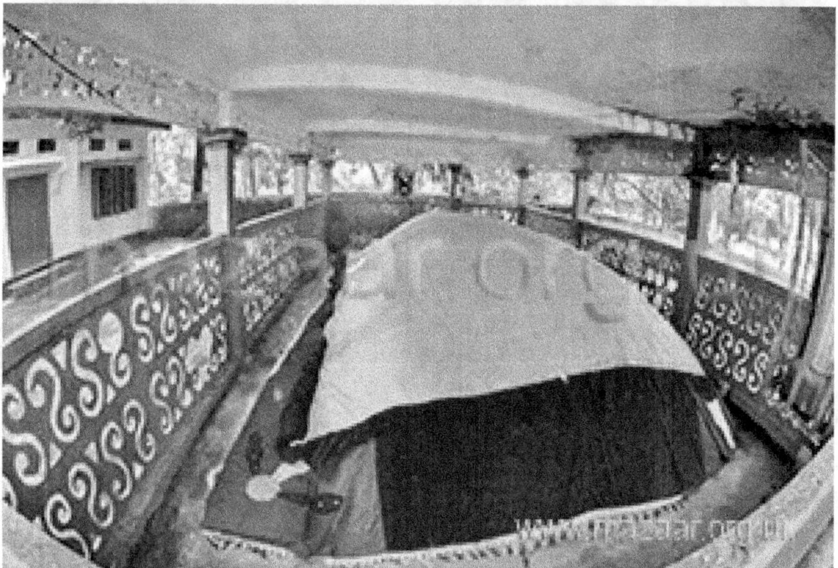

16.10.2010, 12:03:50

Mir Mohi Uddin

Abdit Parah, Fokir Parah, Lala bazar.

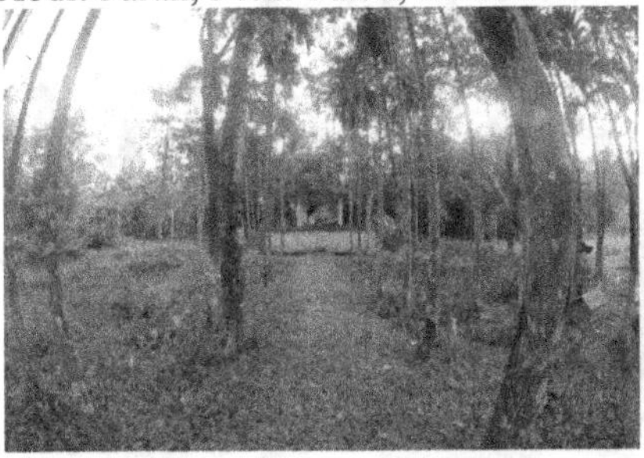

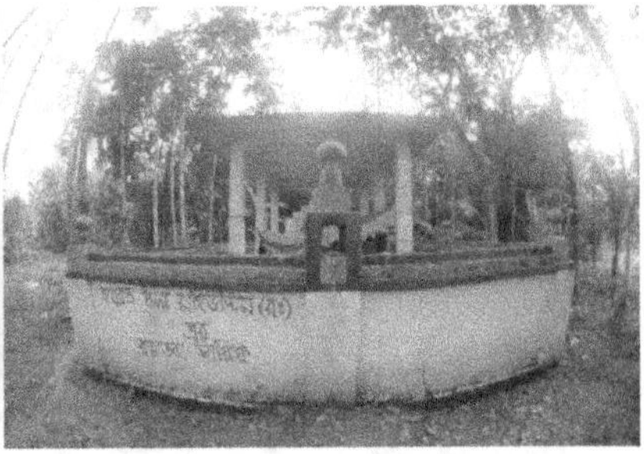

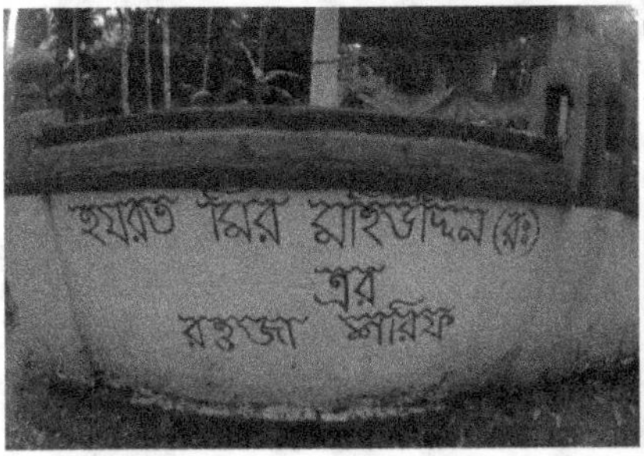
হযরত মির মাহিউদ্দিন (রঃ)
এর
রওজা শারিফ

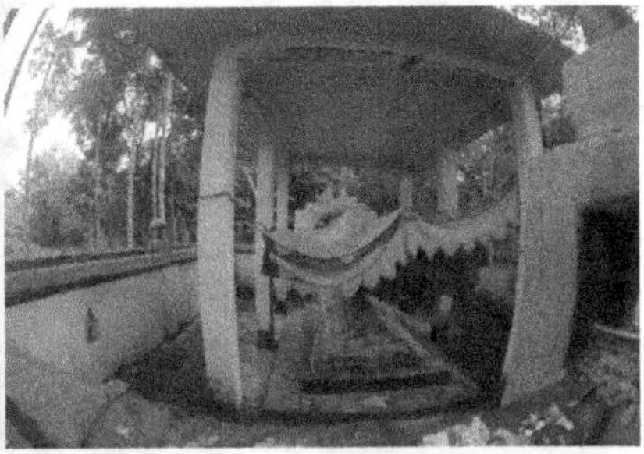

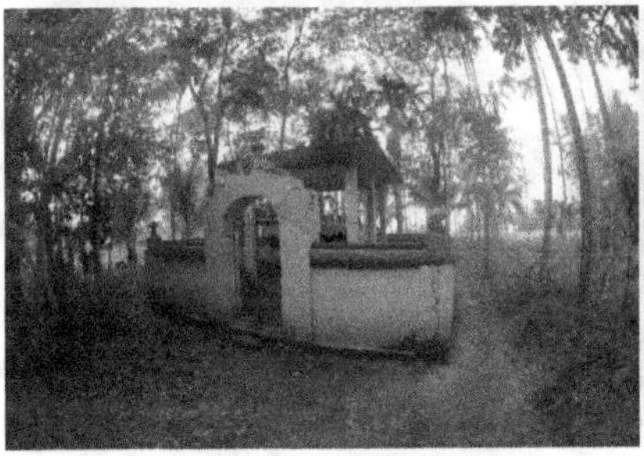

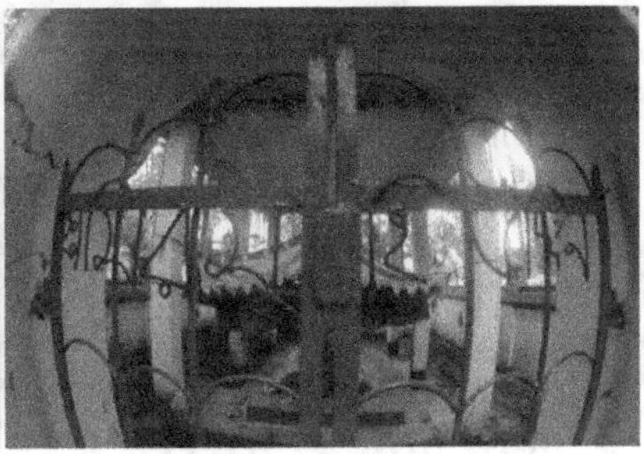

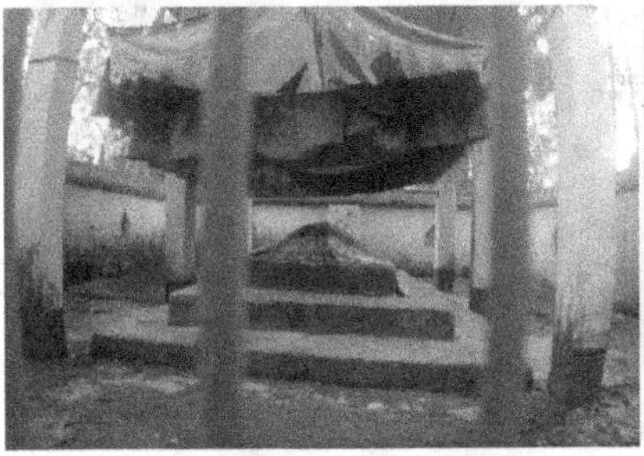

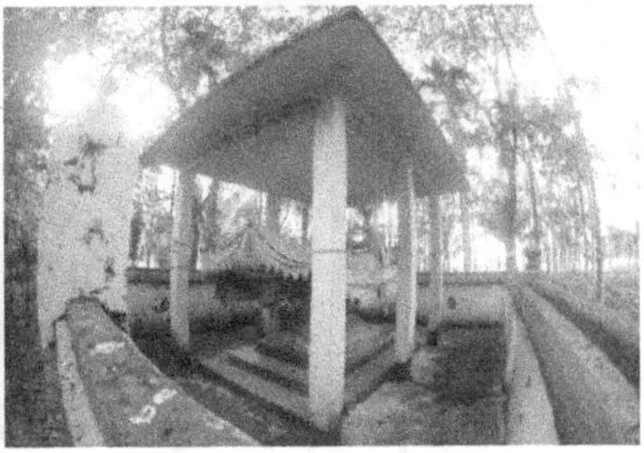

17.10.2010, 12:06:25

Etim Phir

Etim Goinj,

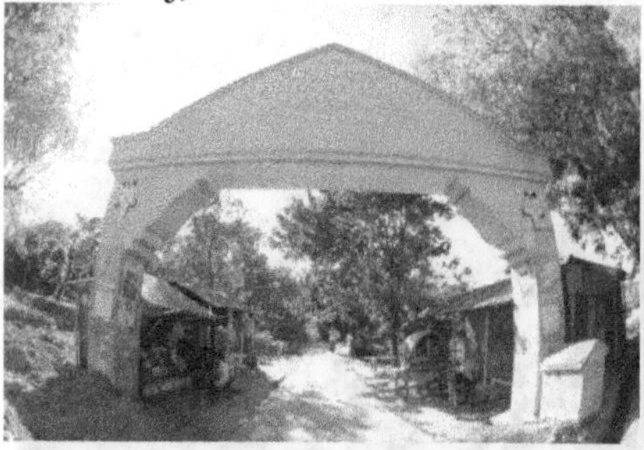

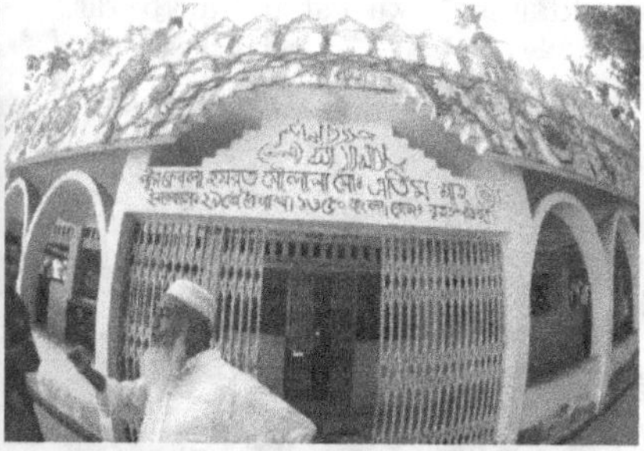

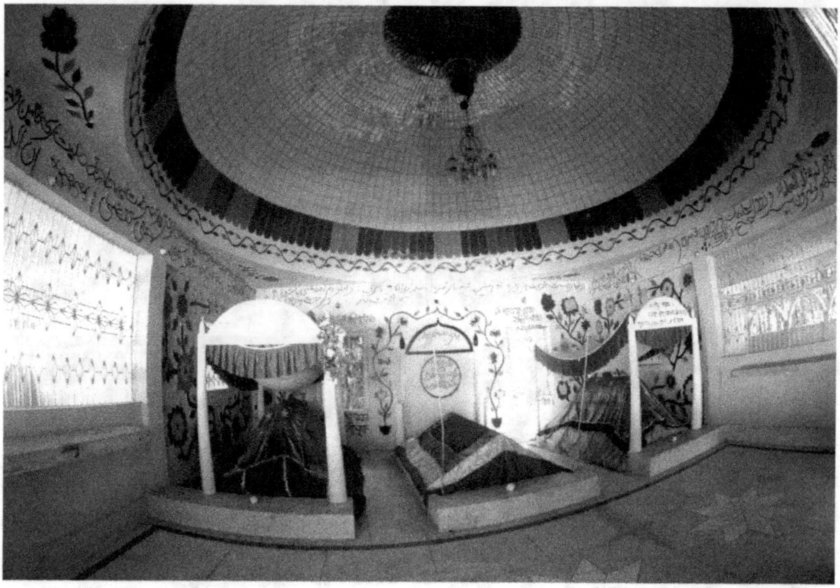

20.10.2010, 14:04:34

This place was very ornate and kept well; they are not of the Shah Jalal's era.

Kotali Shah

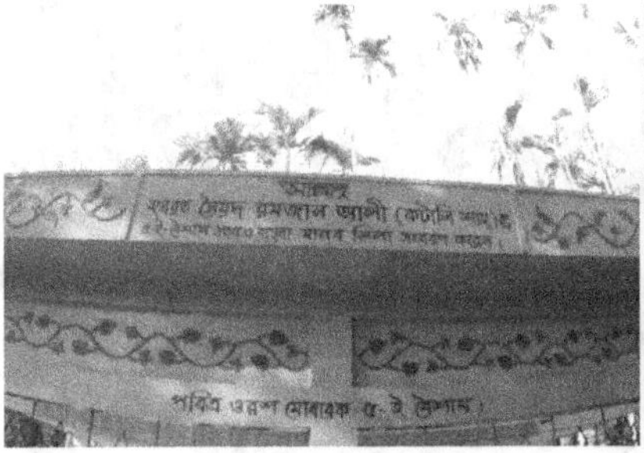

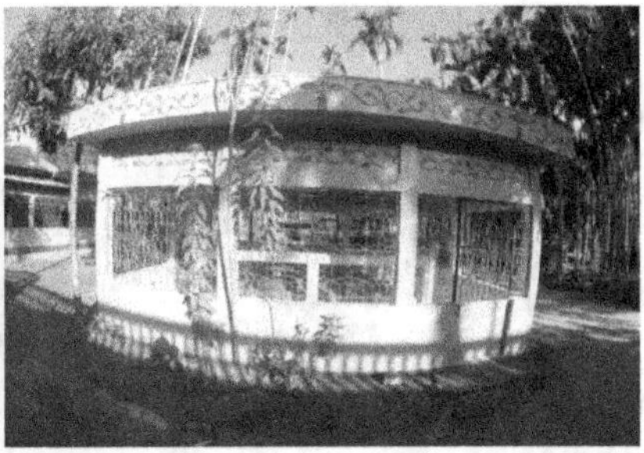

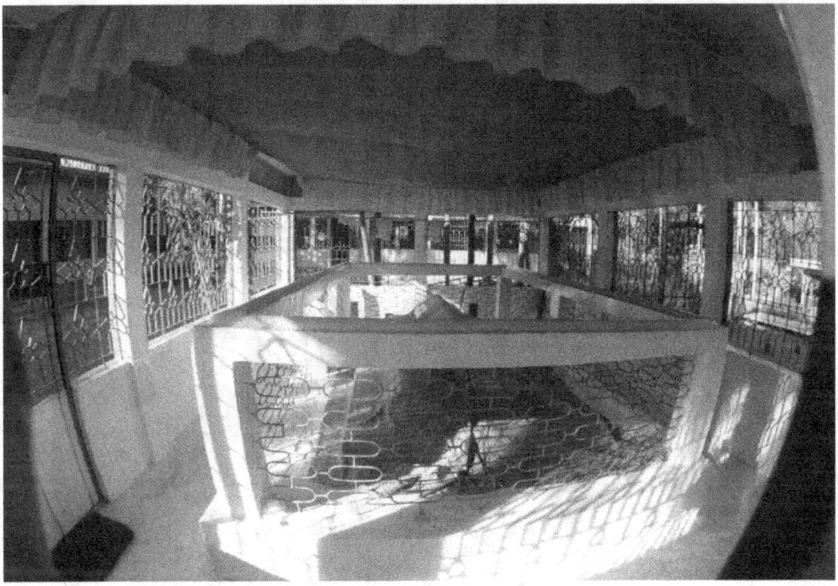

20.10.2010, 15:24:00

Soyod Shah Ajman Ali

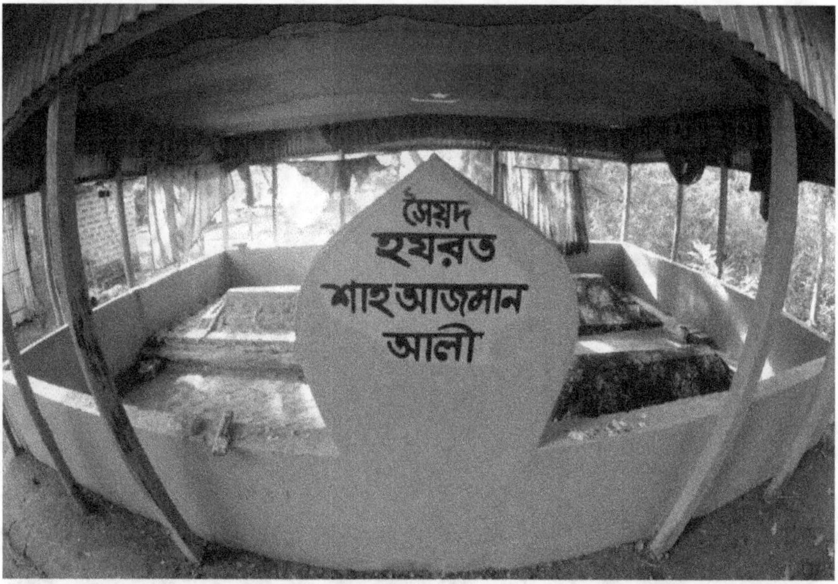
সৈয়দ
হযরত
শাহ আজমান
আলী

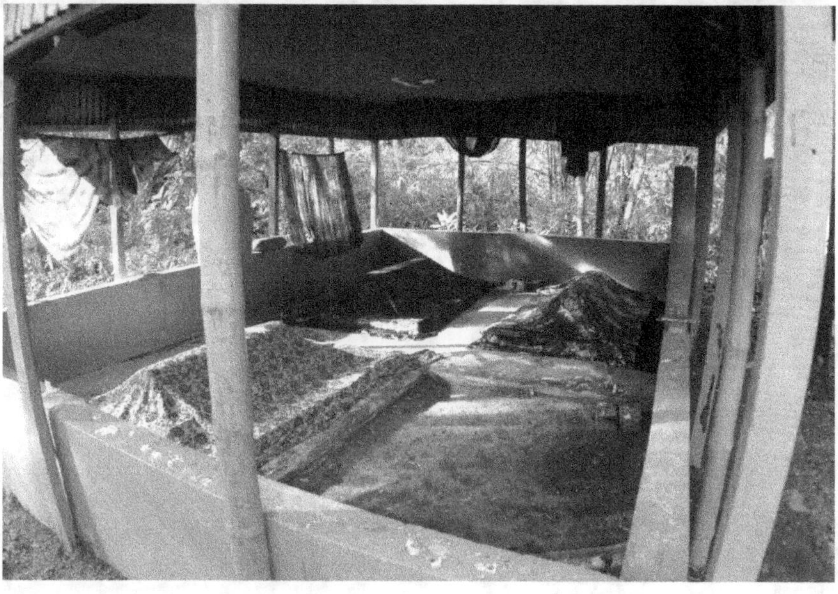

20.10.2010, 15:27:10

Soyod Shodor Qureshi

Hobigonj

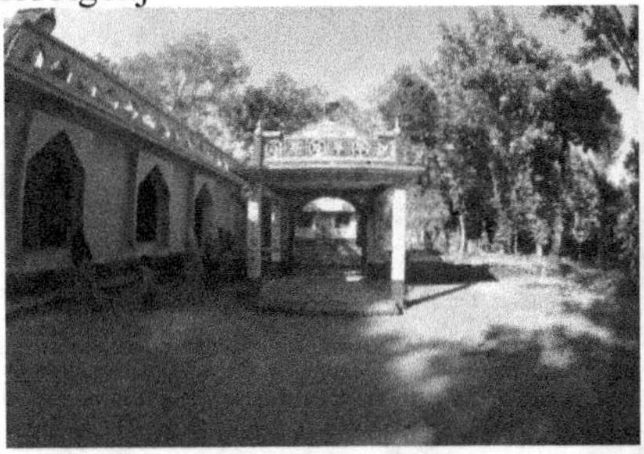

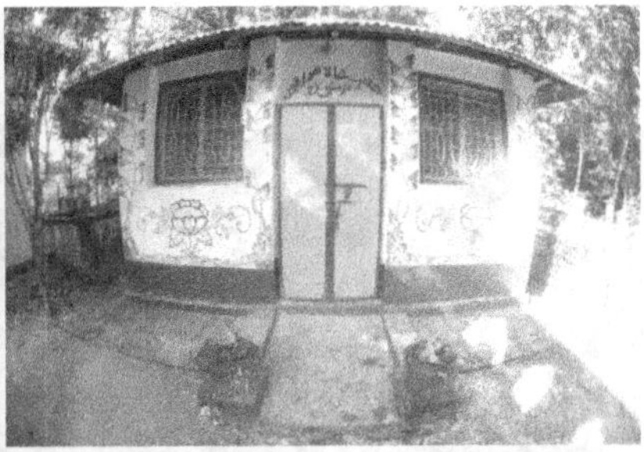

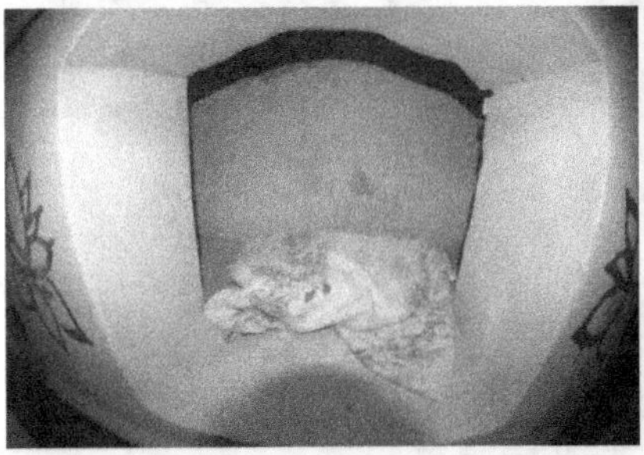

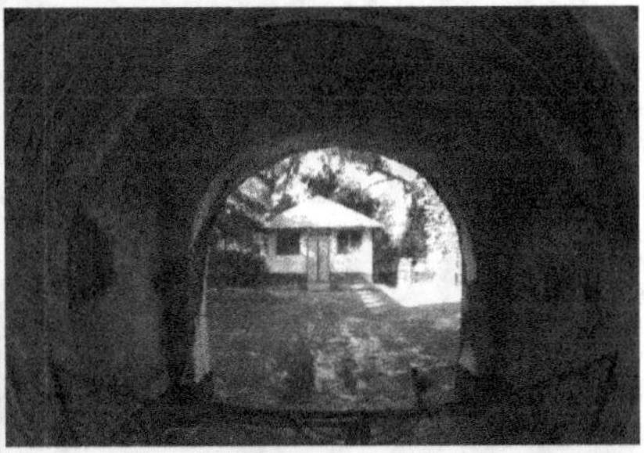

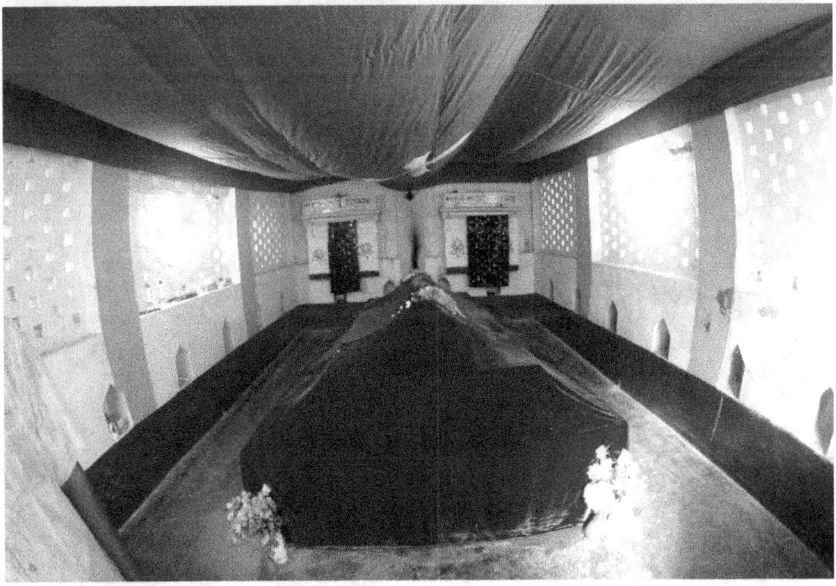

20.10.2010, 14:49:42

Samri Mukam

Osmani Nagar

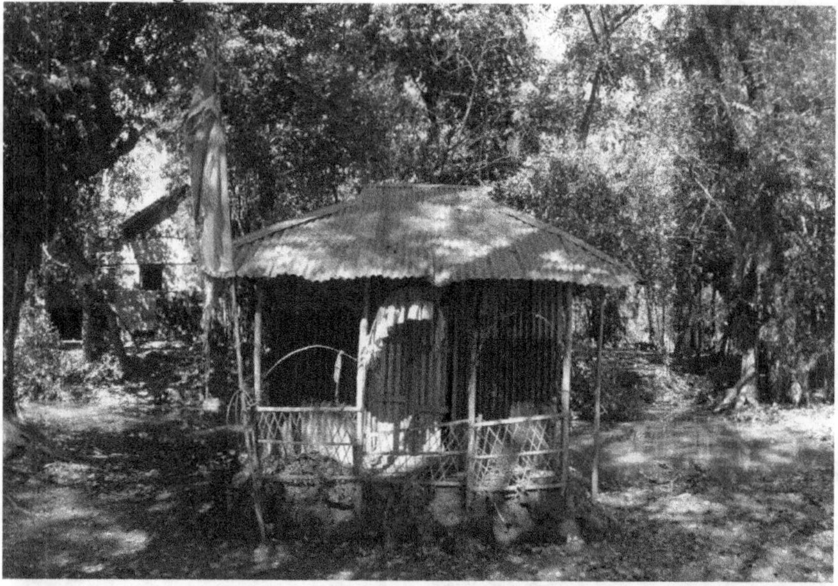

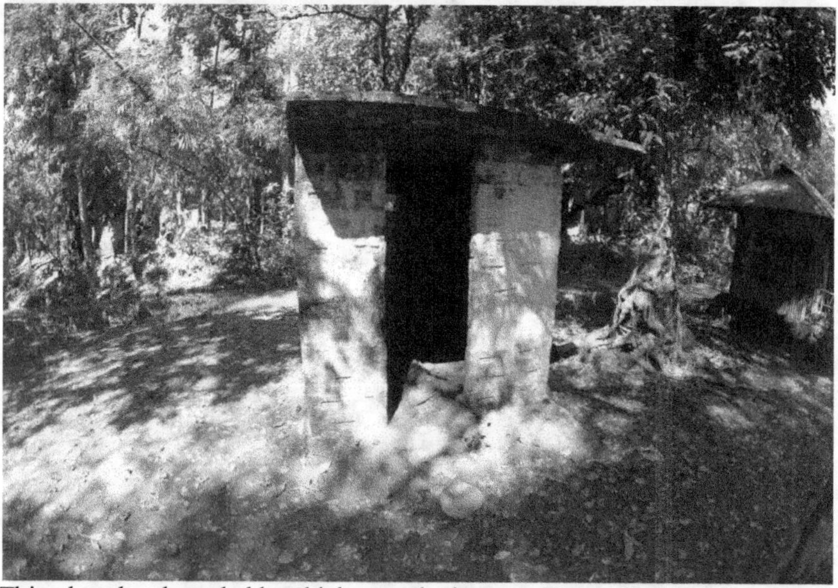

This place has been held to high regards, because Hazrat Shah Jalal's convoy stopped there, where is laid his skin/hide on the ground and prayed, with the other missionaries with him, it would most probably that he led the prayer, jamat.

The hut is where he laid the hide and did his prayer; it has been preserved for centuries now.

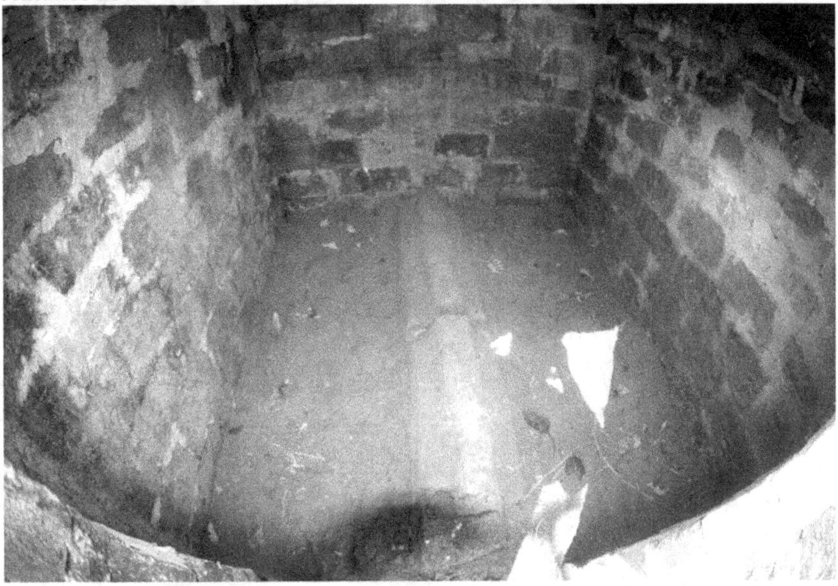

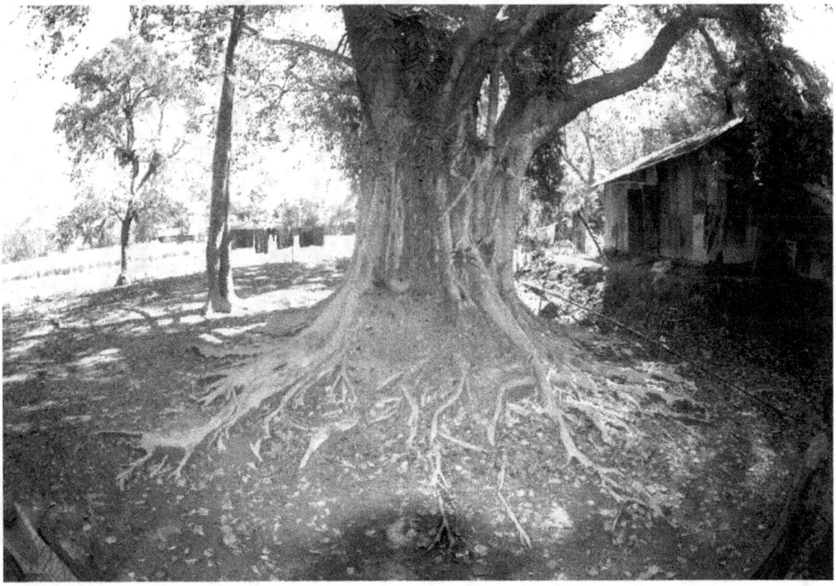

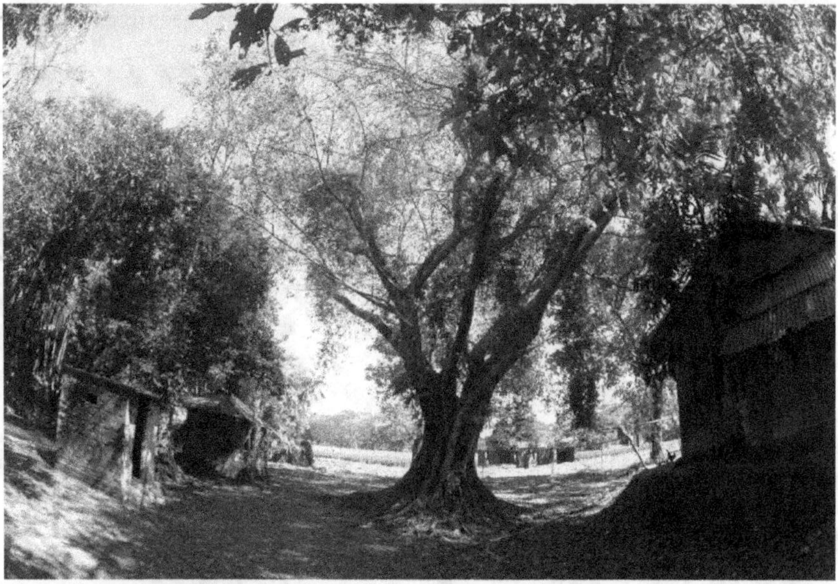

They all congregated in the "Utaan" (Yard), around the tree,

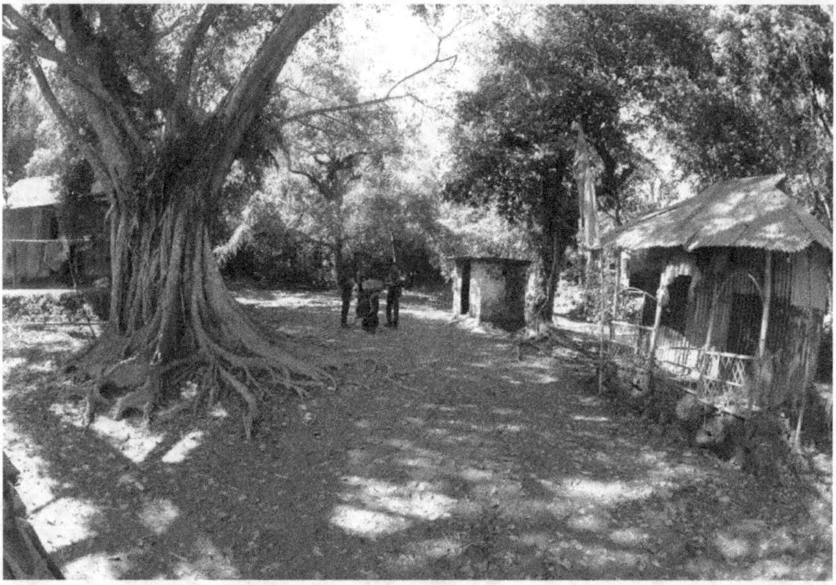

20.10.2010, 13:00:20

Soyod Shah Taj Uddin

Tajpur, Aurogor Pur, Osmani Nagor, Sylhet

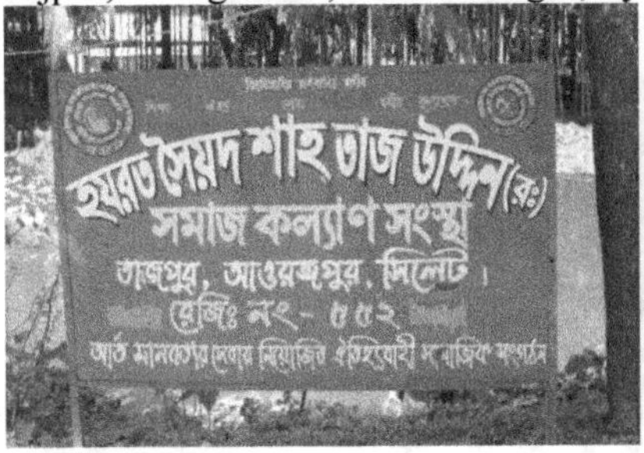
হযরত সৈয়দ শাহ তাজ উদ্দিন (রঃ)
সমাজ কল্যাণ সংস্থা
তাজপুর, আওরঙ্গপুর, সিলেট।
রেজিঃ নং- ৫৫২

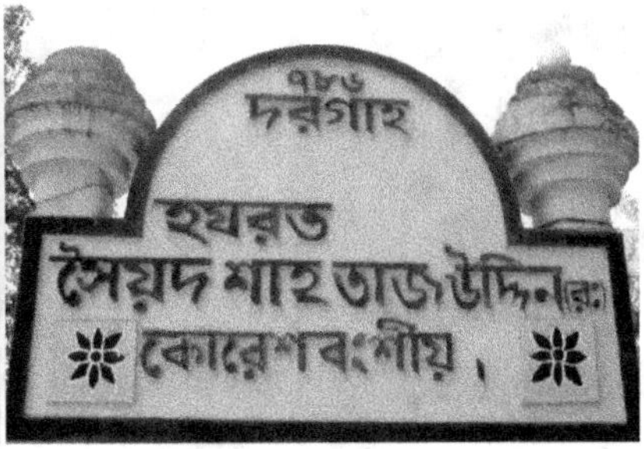
৭৮৬
দরগাহ
হযরত
সৈয়দ শাহ তাজউদ্দিন (রঃ)
কোরেশবংশীয়।

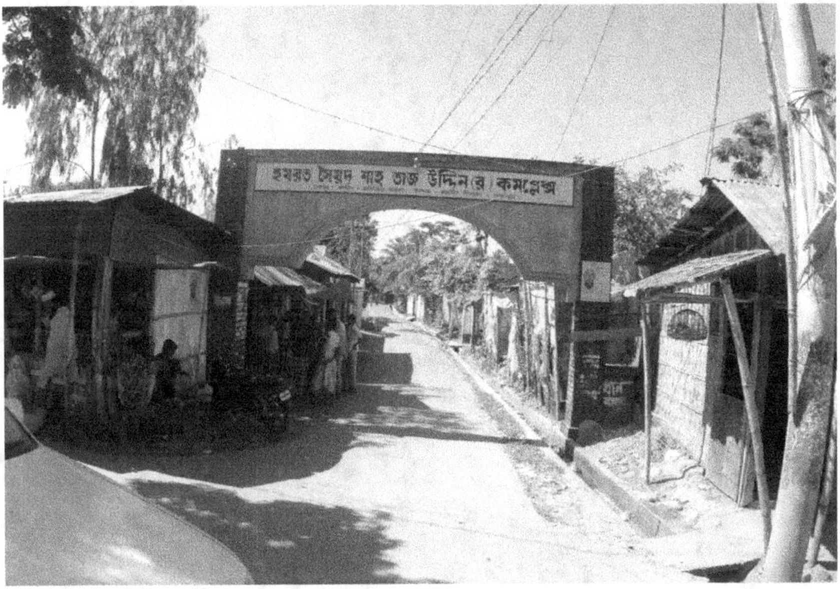
হযরত সৈয়দ শাহ তাজ উদ্দিন (র) কমপ্লেক্স

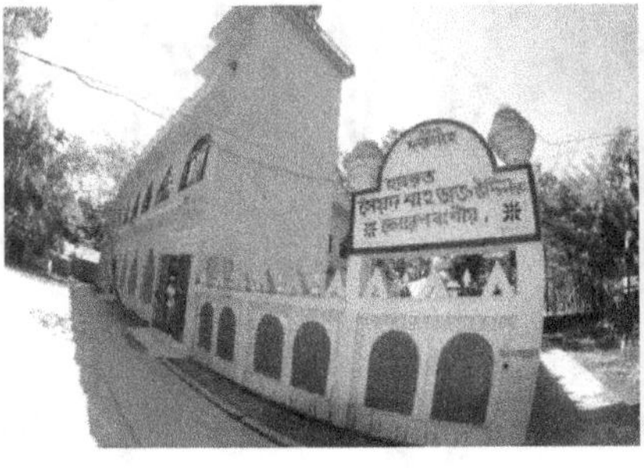

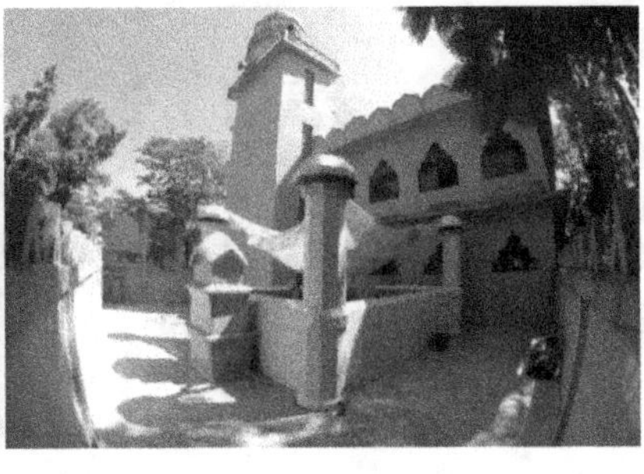

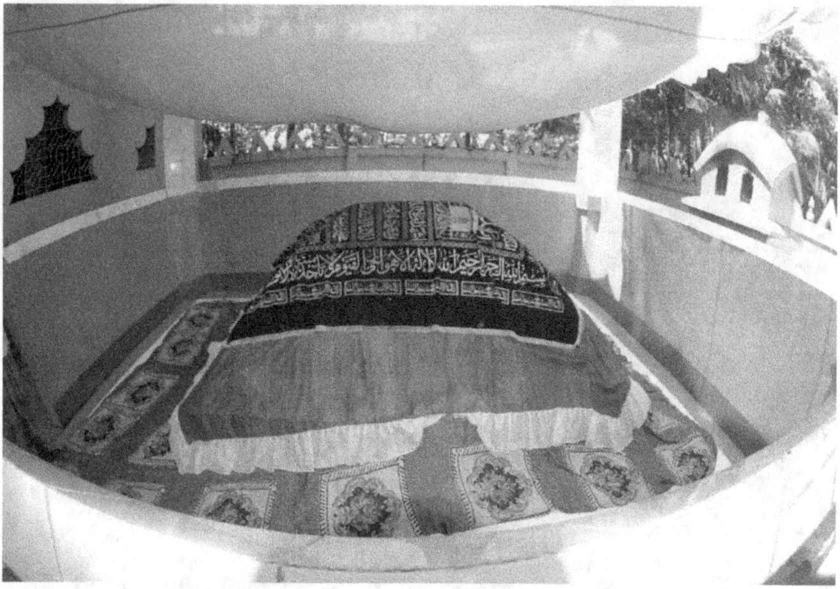

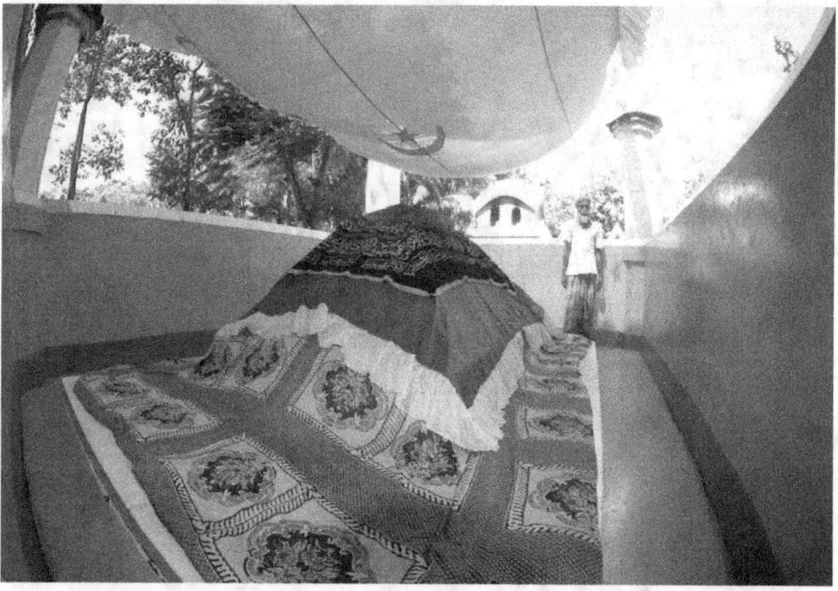

20.10.2010, 12:27:58

Sufi Soyod Jahan*

Soyod Pur, Sylhet

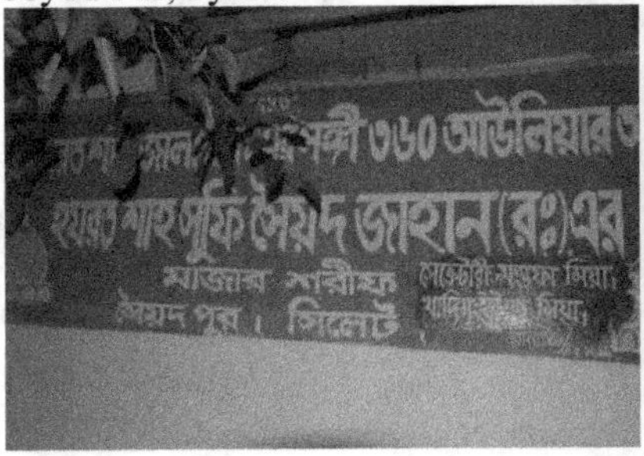
৩৬০ আউলিয়ার
শাহ সুফি সৈয়দ জাহান (রঃ) এর
মাজার শরীফ
সৈয়দ পুর। সিলেট

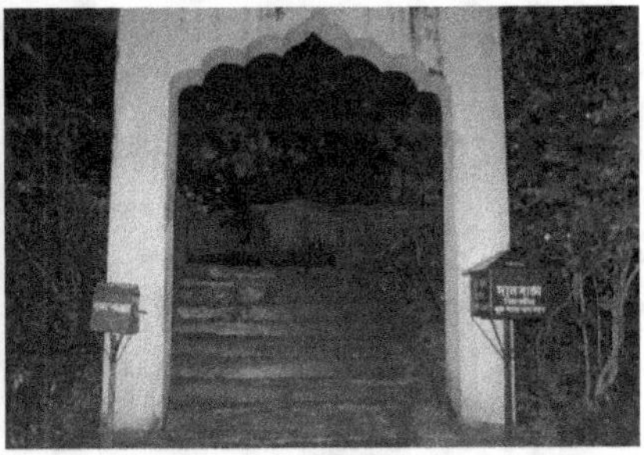

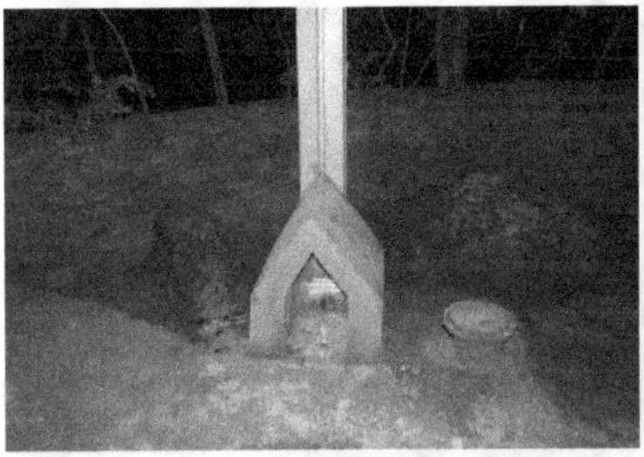

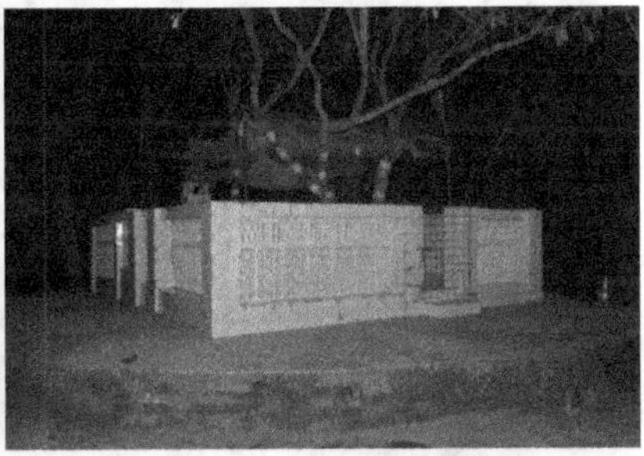

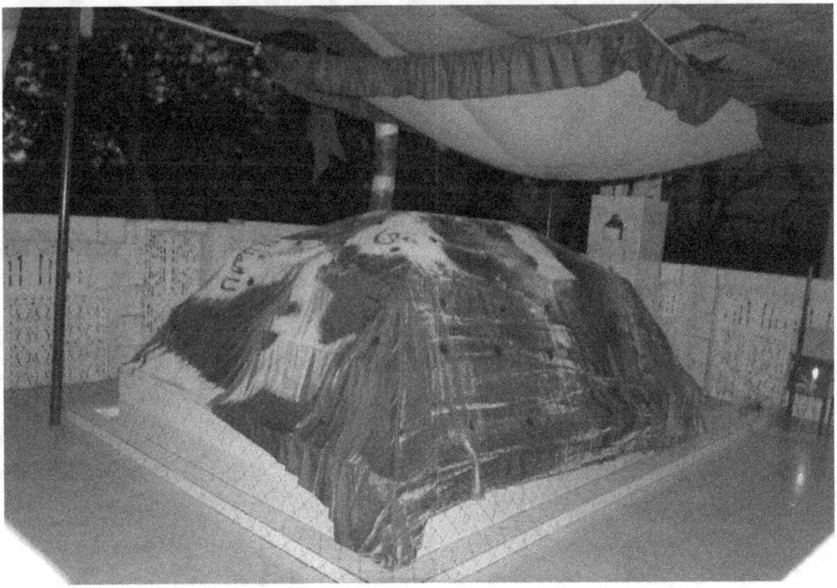

A remote place, perched on top of hill, you have o get there by foot.

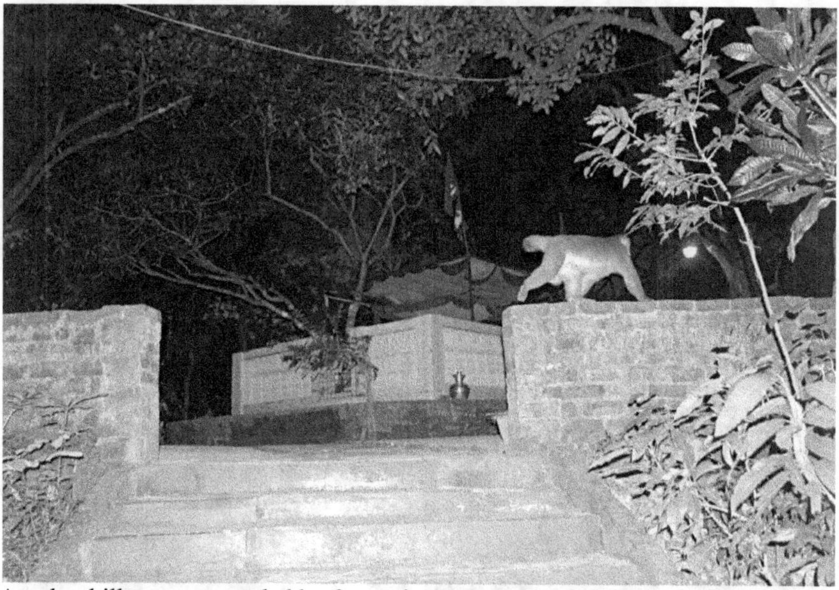

Another hill top, surrounded by forest, just managed to catch a monkey, dash by.

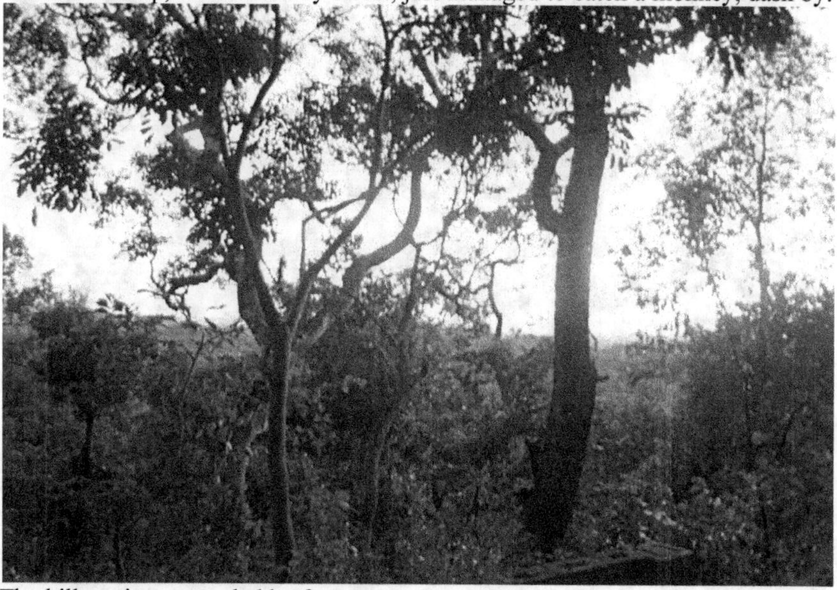

The hill top is surrounded by forestry.

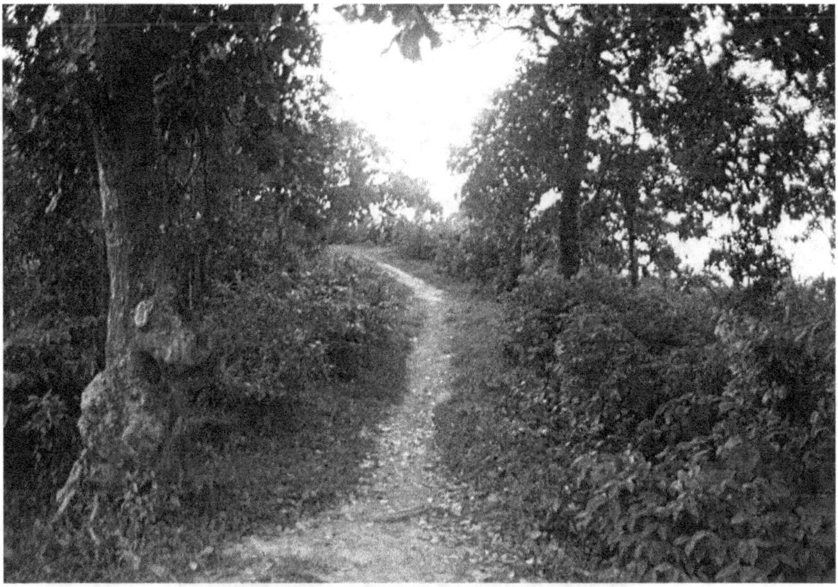

Here are parts of the pathway to and out of the Mazar.

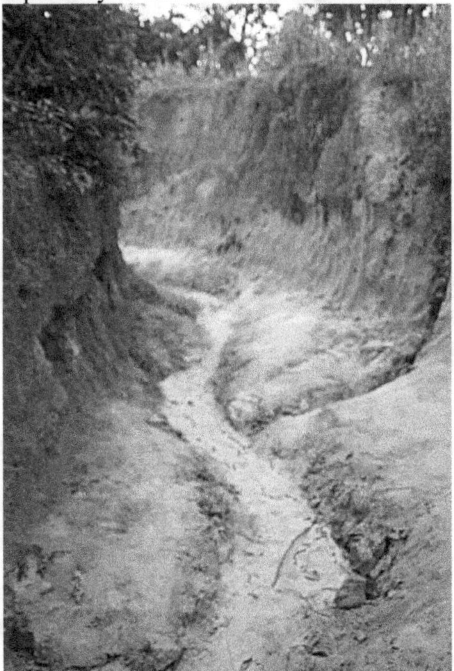

21.10.2010, 17:26:24

Shah Jalal's 1 Brick Mosque

One brick Mosque, Sylhet

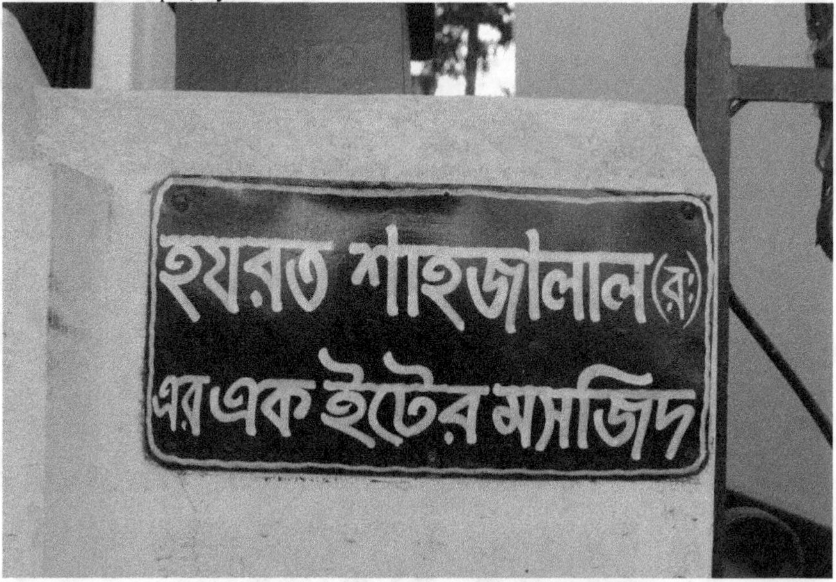
হযরত শাহজালাল(রঃ)
এর এক ইটের মসজিদ

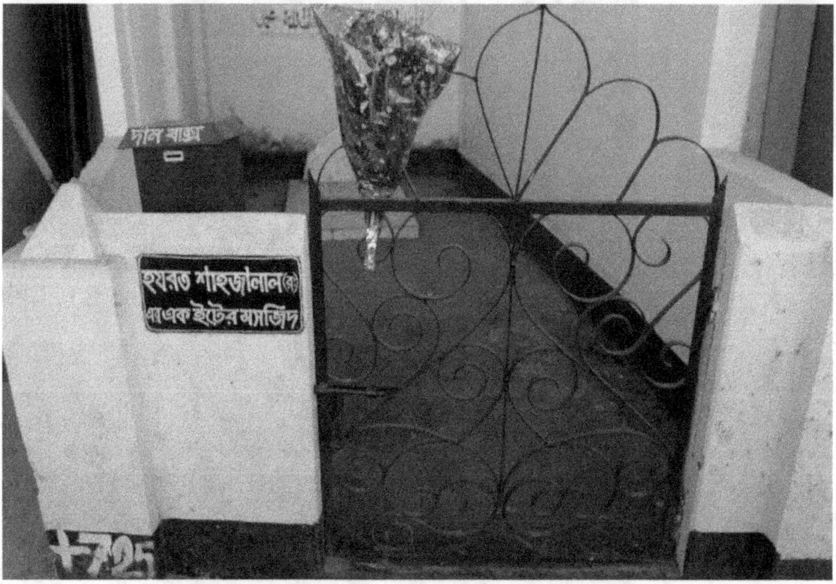
হযরত শাহজালাল(রঃ)
এর এক ইটের মসজিদ

21.10.2010, 15:38:08

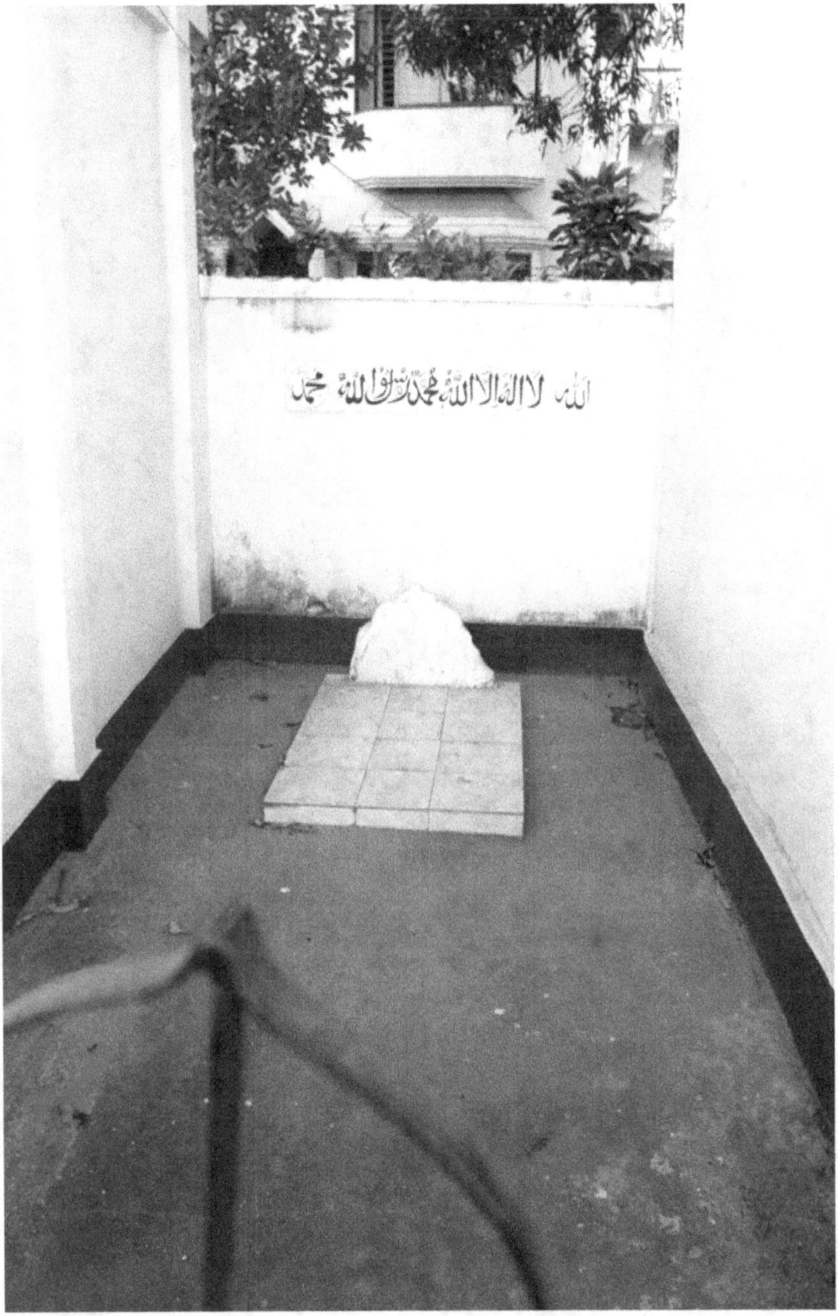

Jamal Kamal

Rainagor, Doji Parah

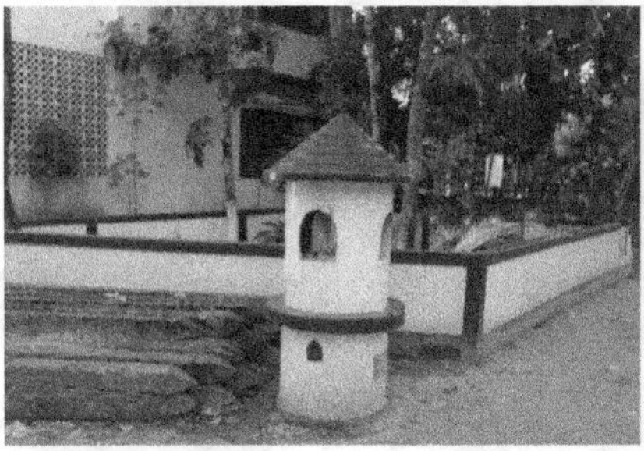

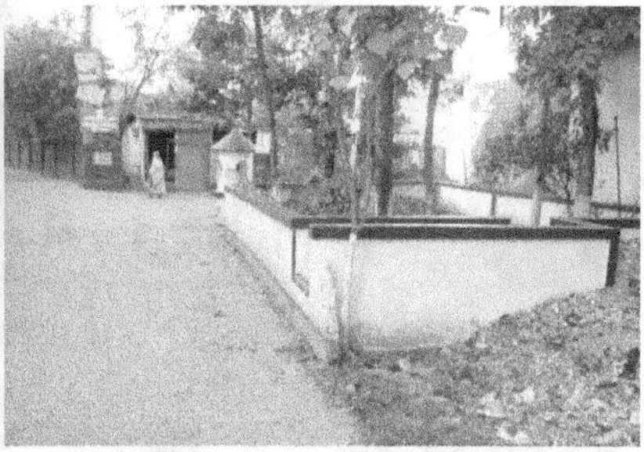

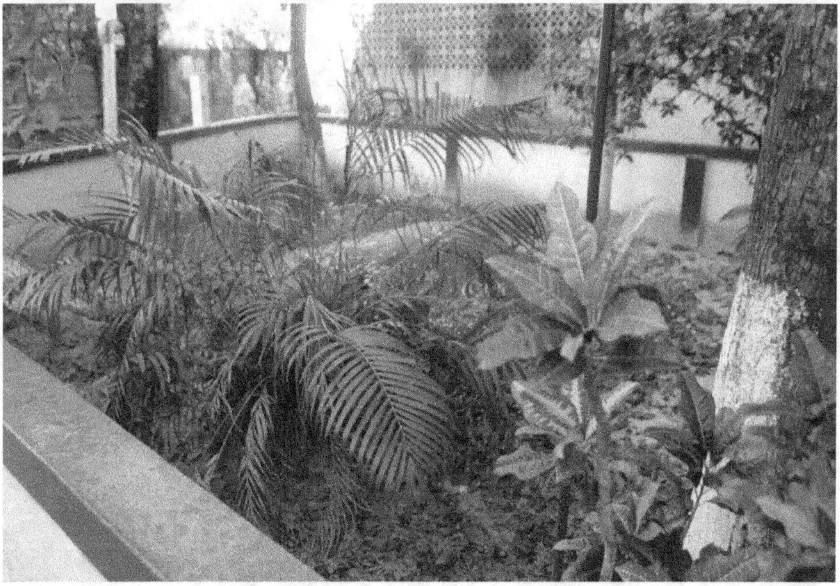

21.10.2010, 16:01:20

This not credited with the 8 sided plaque.

Labioth

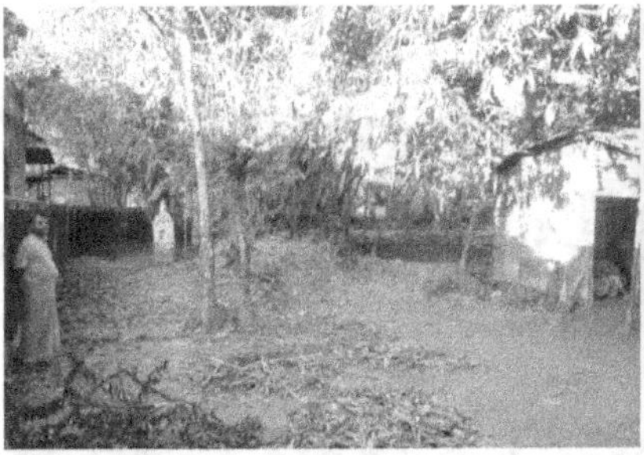

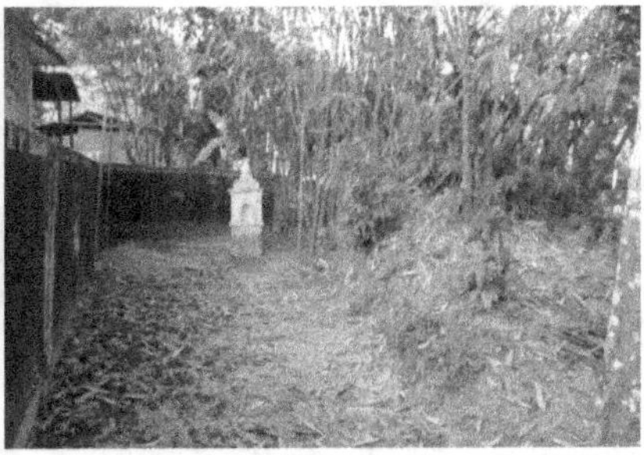

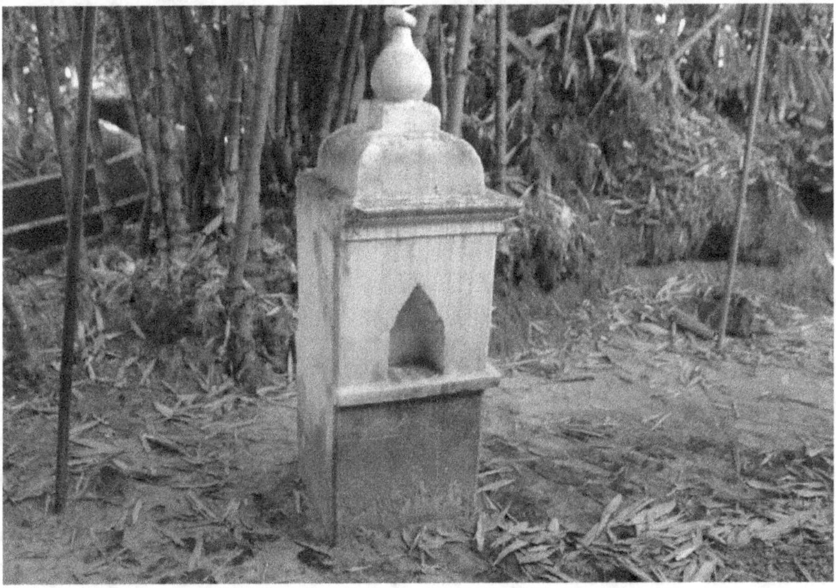

21.10.2010, 16:16:08

This not credited with the 8 sided plaque.

This was situated within a bari complex, needed local chaperoning to get there. Once there, it wasn't like anything I have seen and the site was marked by this pillar with a candle burning space.

Phir Forhan Shah

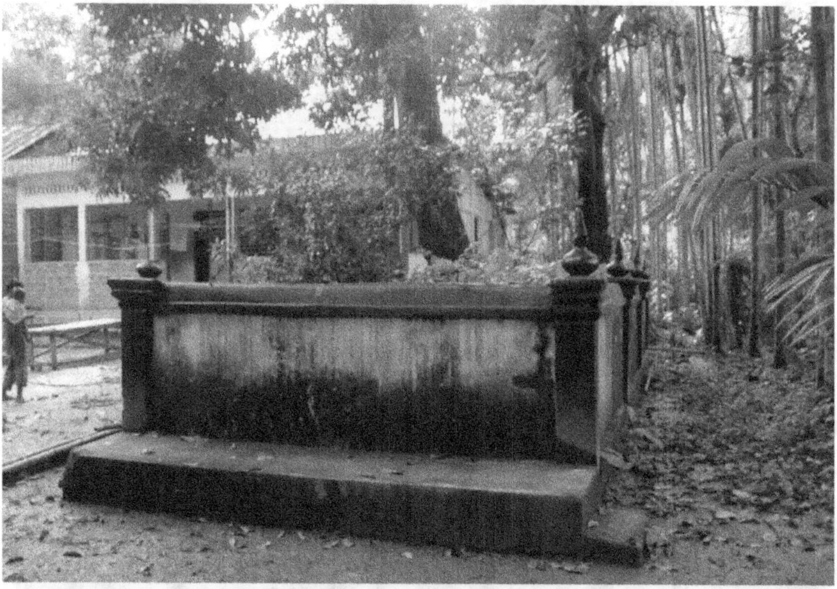

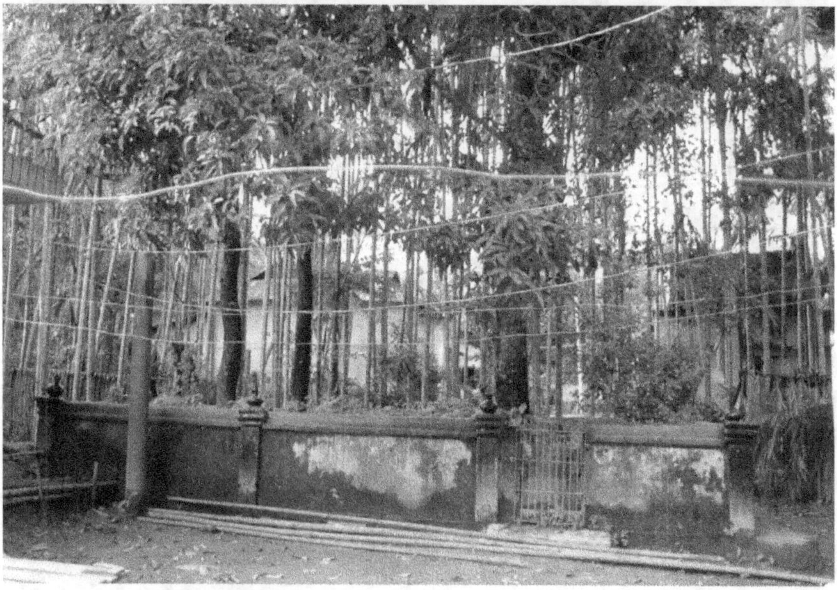

22.10.2010, 16:08:47

Not a member of the 360 missionaries.

Rosul Boksh

Fokir Parah, Shunathitha

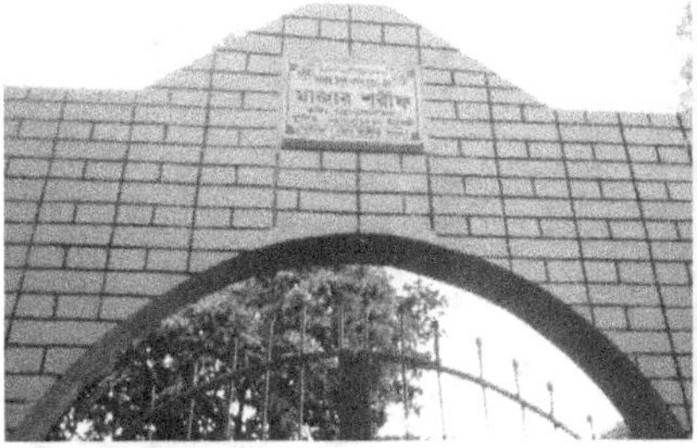
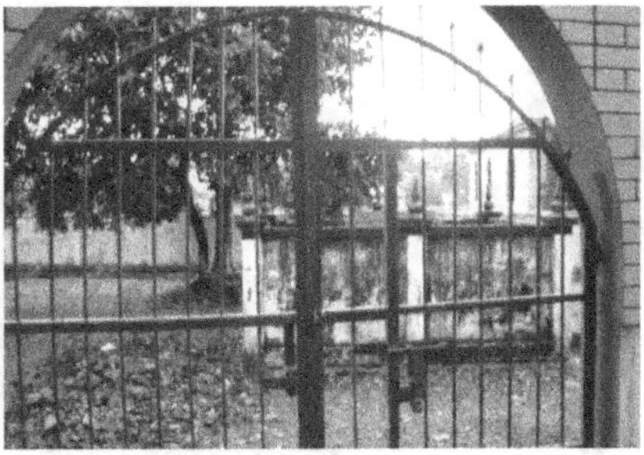
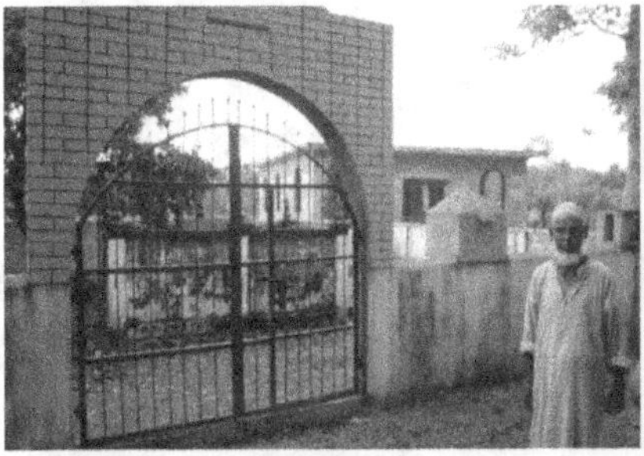
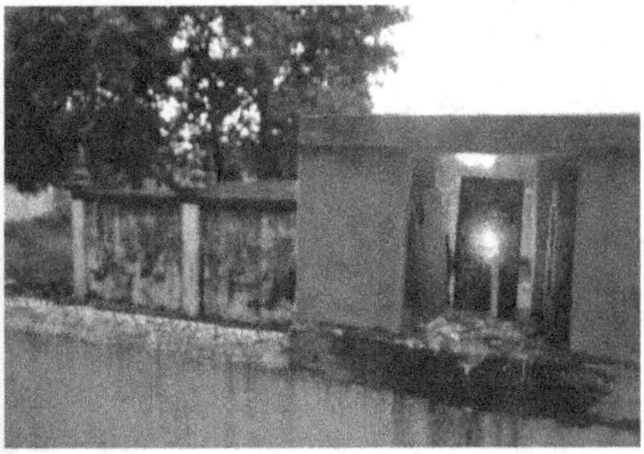
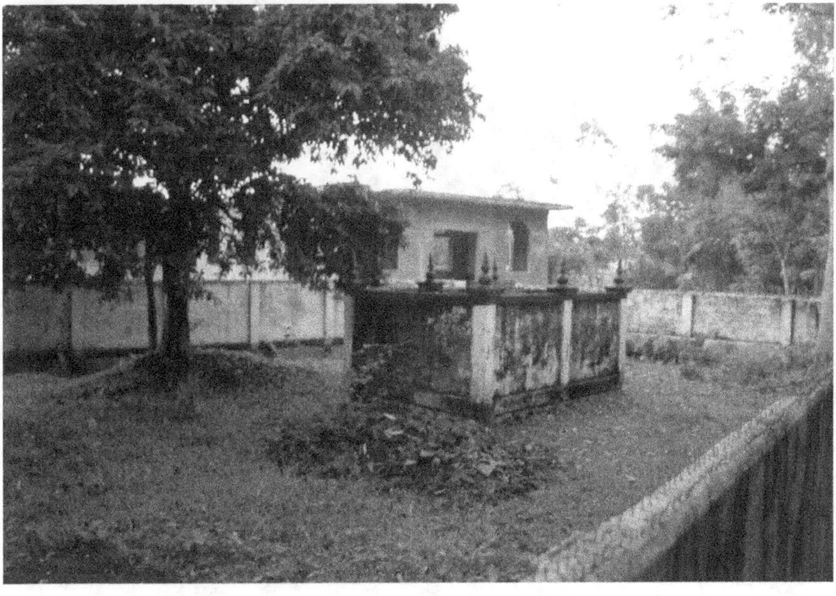

22.10.2010, 17:10:52

Not a member of the 360 group.

Lorai Shah

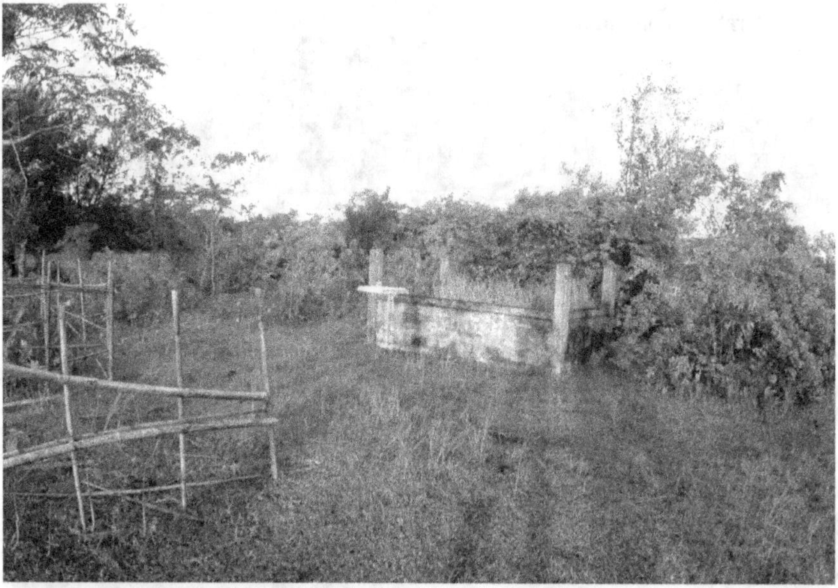

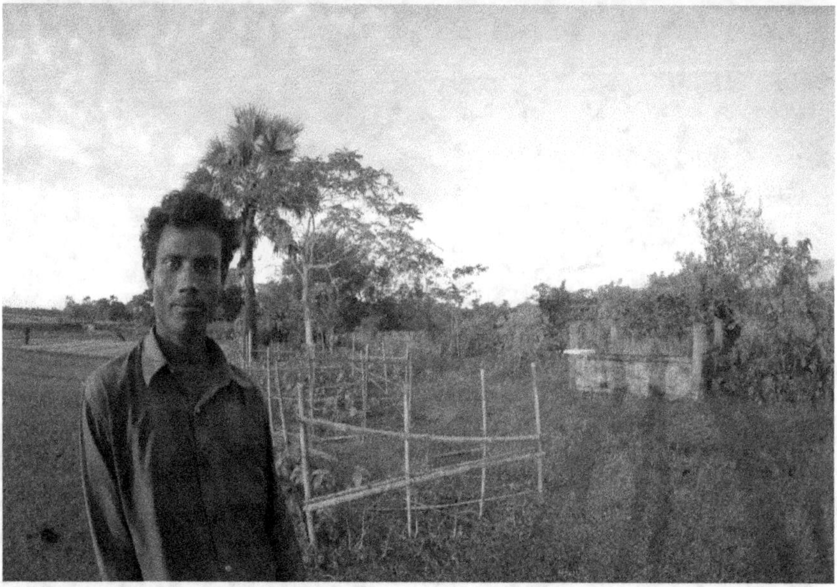

22.10.2010, 16:52:04

This was situated amongst fields, it wasn't anything like I was expecting.

Fass Phir**

Zinda Bazaar, Sylhet Town

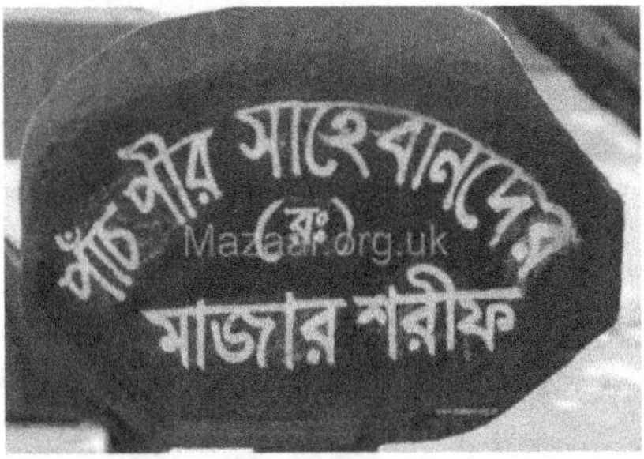
পাঁচ পীর সাহেবানদের
(রঃ)
মাজার শরীফ
Mazaar.org.uk

Abdul Mutalib**
Ahmod Shah**
Ajom Shah**
Sultan Shah**
Zia Uddin**

24.10.2010 17:1

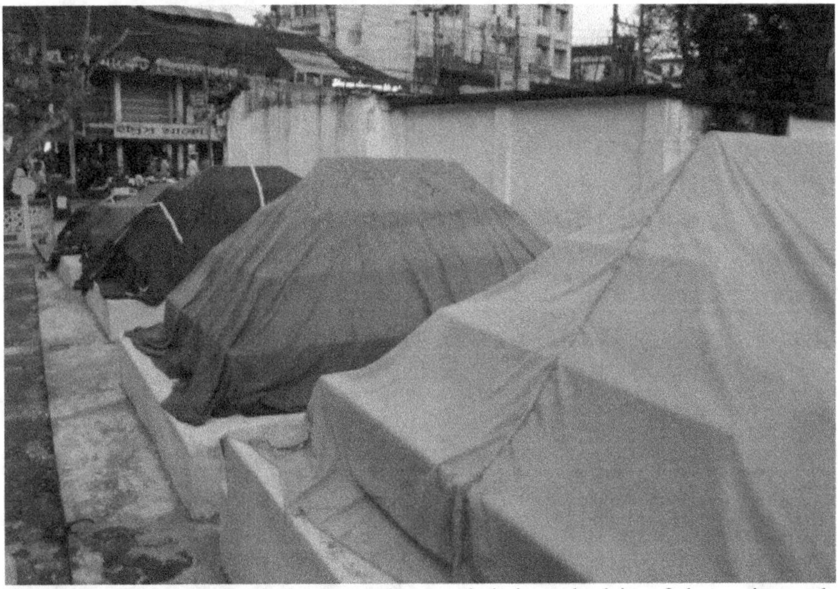

This is located on a lively busy market road; it is tucked in of the main road. This place in not far from the Dorga and it houses 5 people from the 360 missionaries.

The graves are not named in the order of the graves, so if the Kadim is there, then you can ask him.

Zinda Phir**

Zinda Bazaar - named after this Phir, Sylhet town

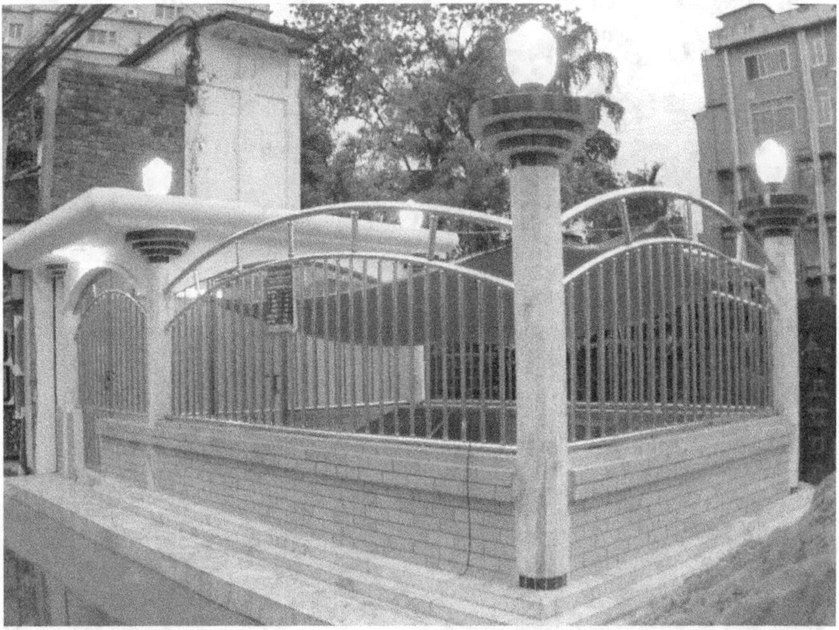

1.8.2010, 16:03:28

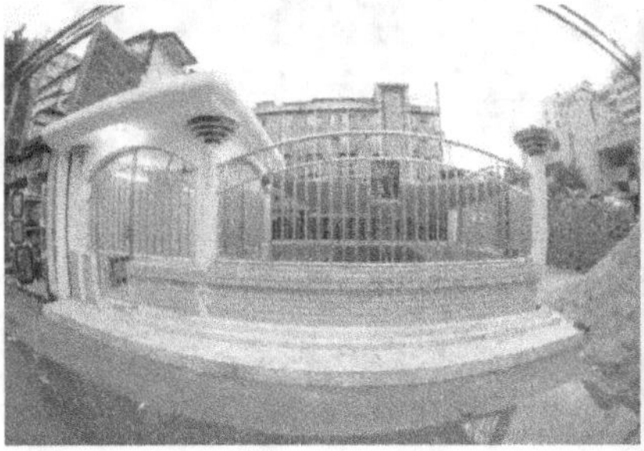

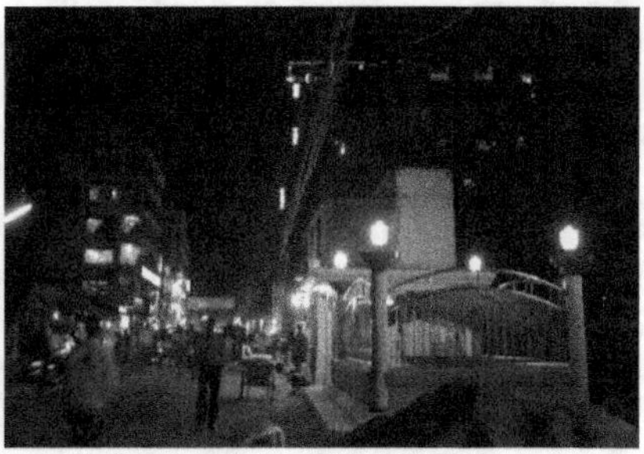

24.10.2010, 19:13:12

This is located in Zinda Bazar, on the main road.

Baha Uddin**

a.k.a., Shah Putala
Badeshor, Gulapgoinj

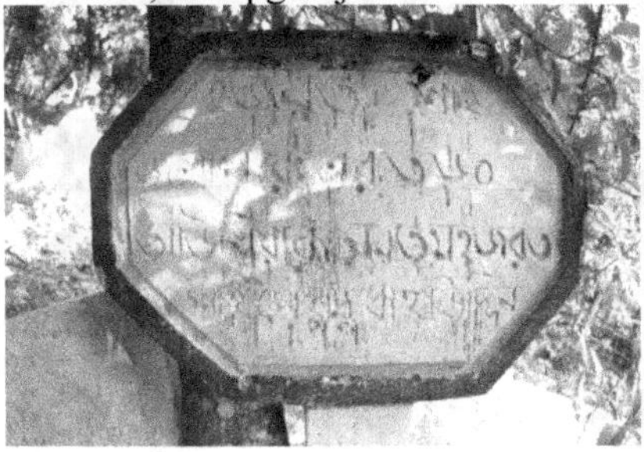

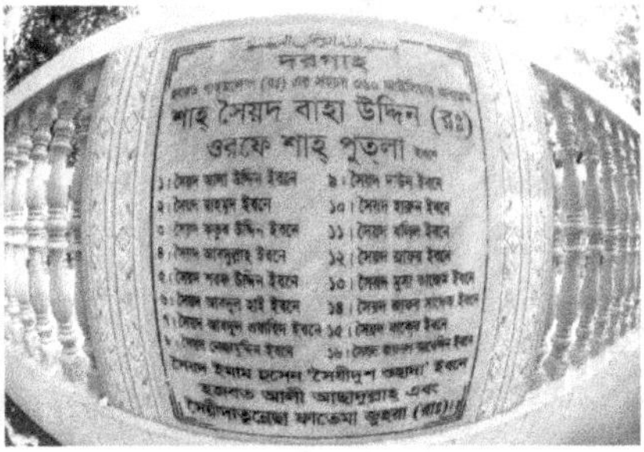
দরগাহ
শাহ্ সৈয়দ বাহা উদ্দিন (রঃ)
ওরফে শাহ্ পুতলা

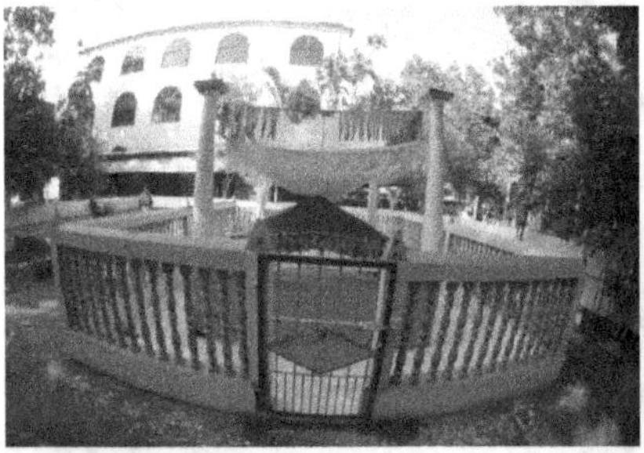

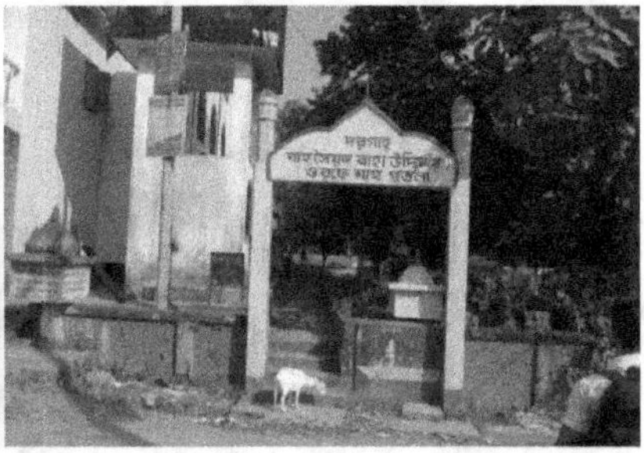

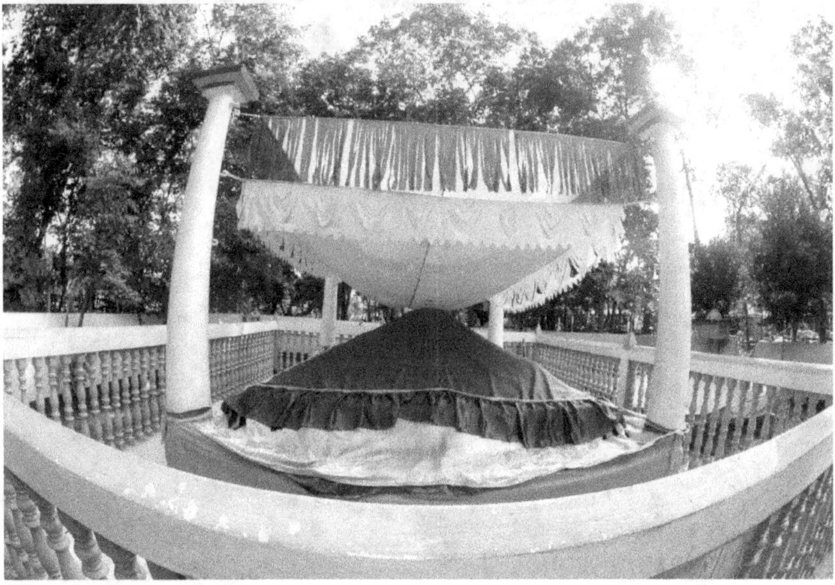

25.10.2010, 13:19:32

Shah Taj Moni

Shah Gous

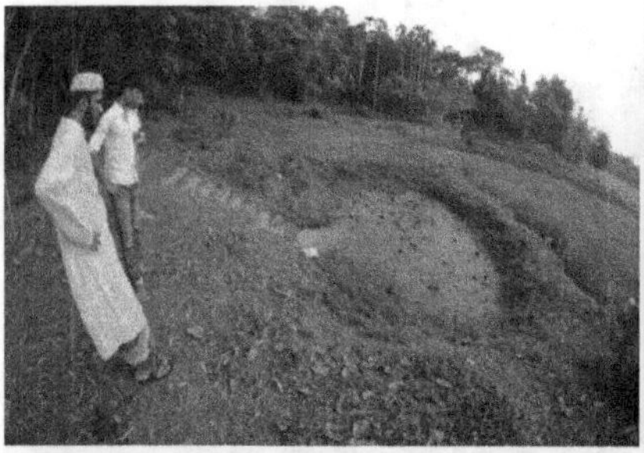

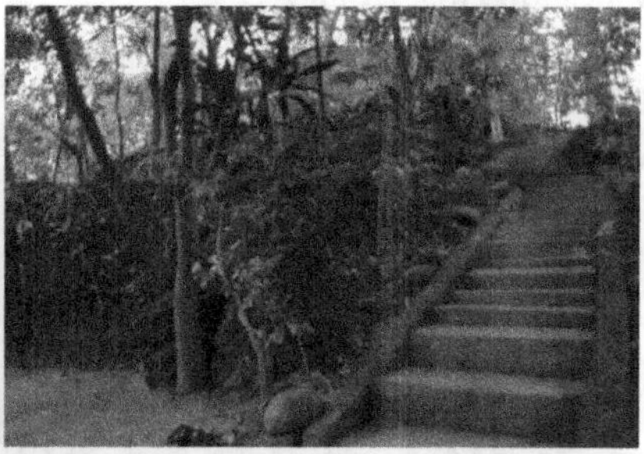

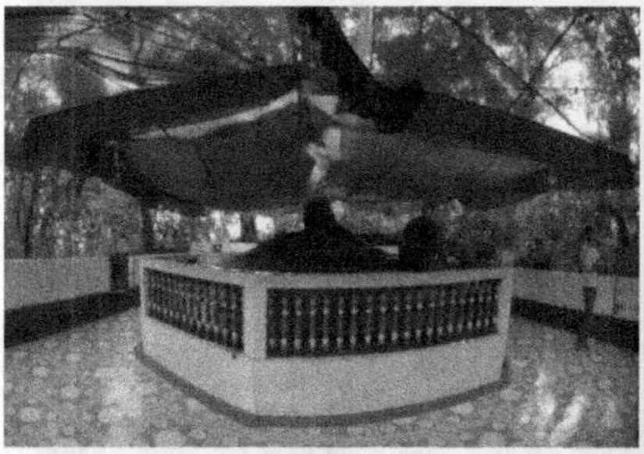

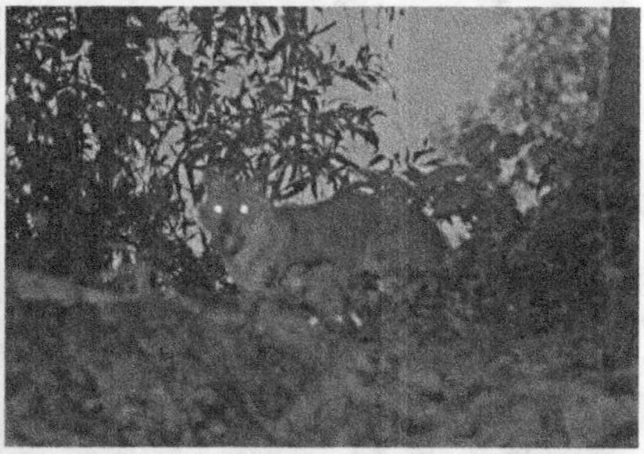

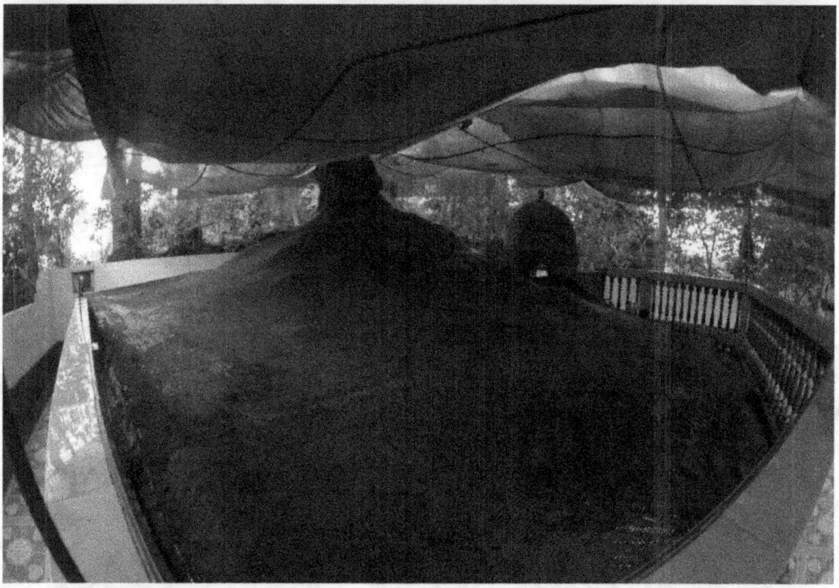

25.10.2010, 15:59:06

This place high up and also has a legend of Tigers spirit come in a guise of a fox.

Boro Phir

Gulapgoinj

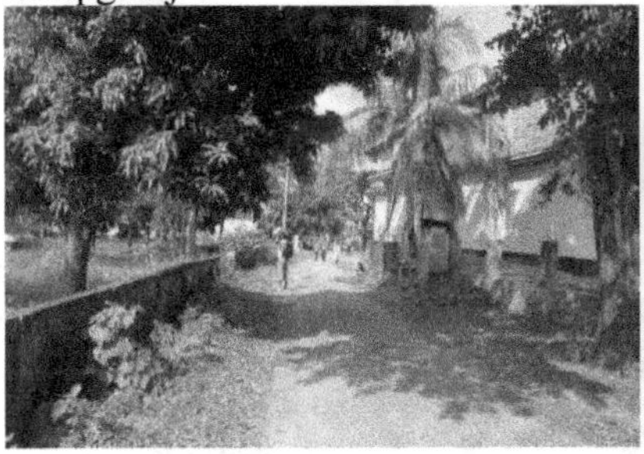

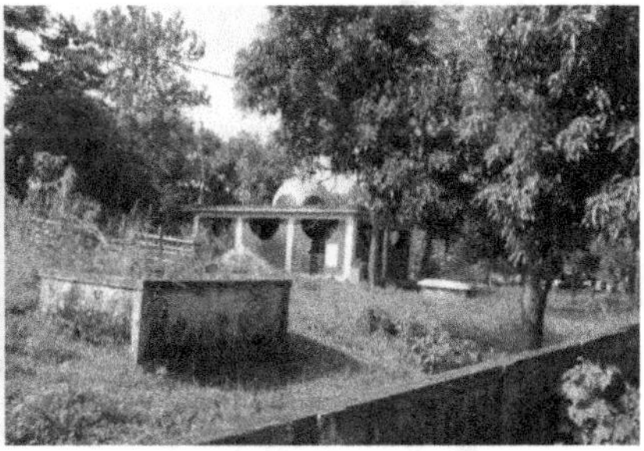

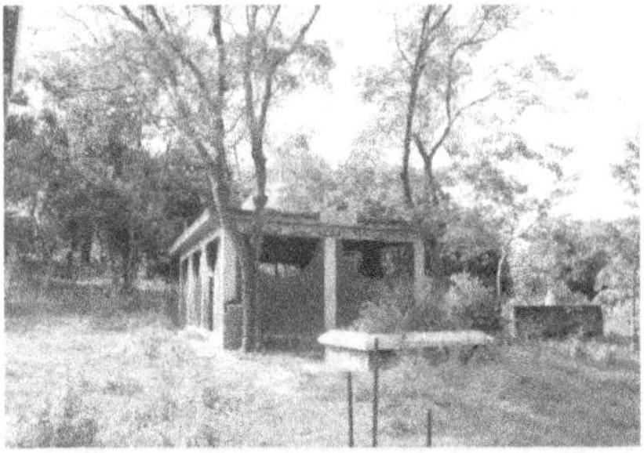

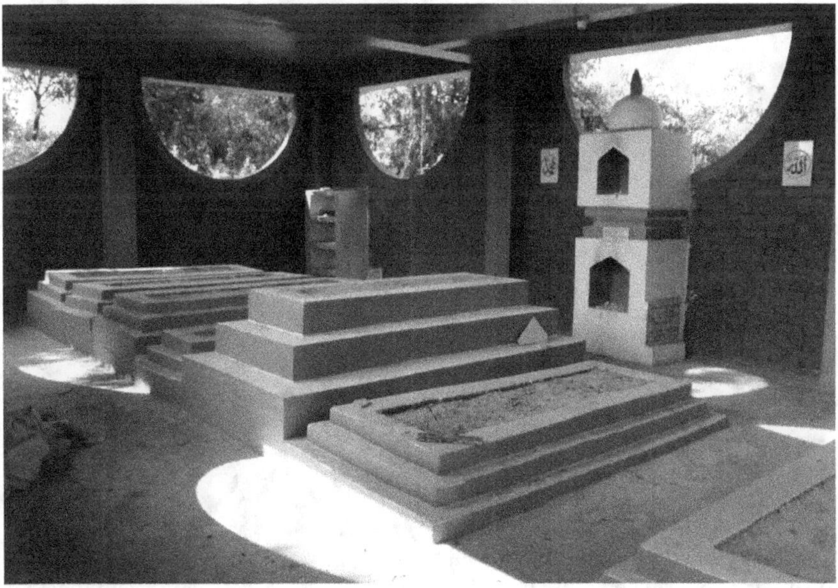

25.10.2010, 12:27:24

Shah Miraphing

a.k.a.,

Mirer Fir

Phir Mir

Dawker Gul, Rohimia madrasha, Kanai ghat, Sylhet

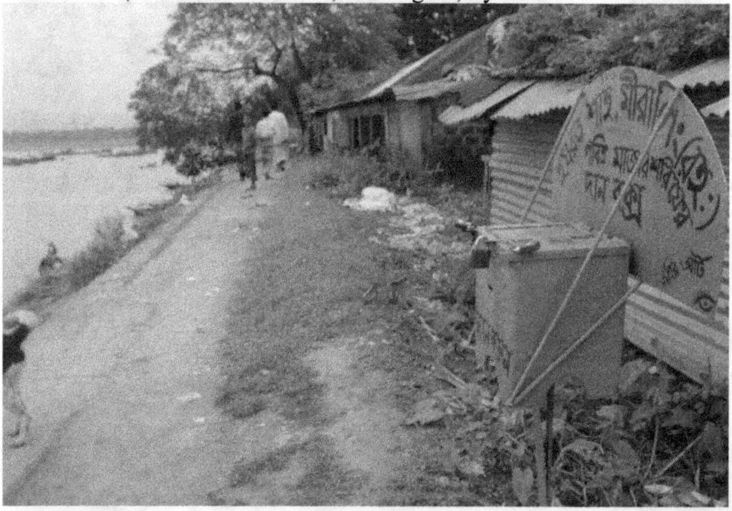

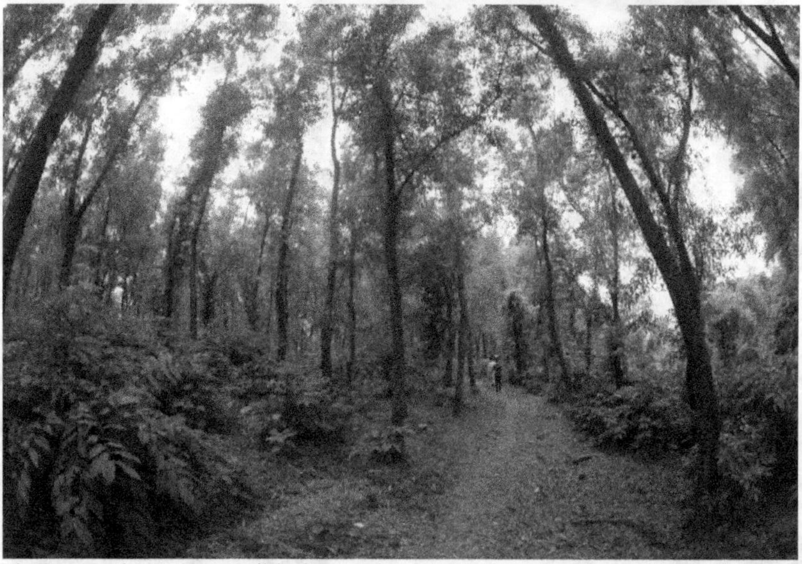

The mazar is not accessible by road yet. From Kanai Ghat Bazaar we took a boat/ferry to Dawker Gul. It took about an hour to get to the jetty/docking station. We had to travel down the Luba River a tributary of the mountain waters from India. The mazar borders about 1-1/2 miles from India.

From the dock at a bazaar known as Noya bazaar we walked to the mazar. It was fair walk to the foot of the hill. It was a good trek up the hill and through a forest and then out in an opening on the top.

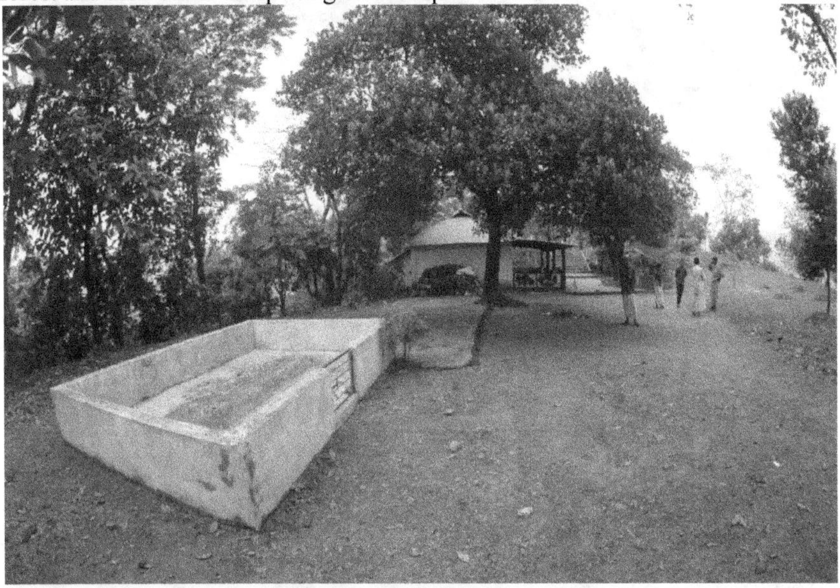

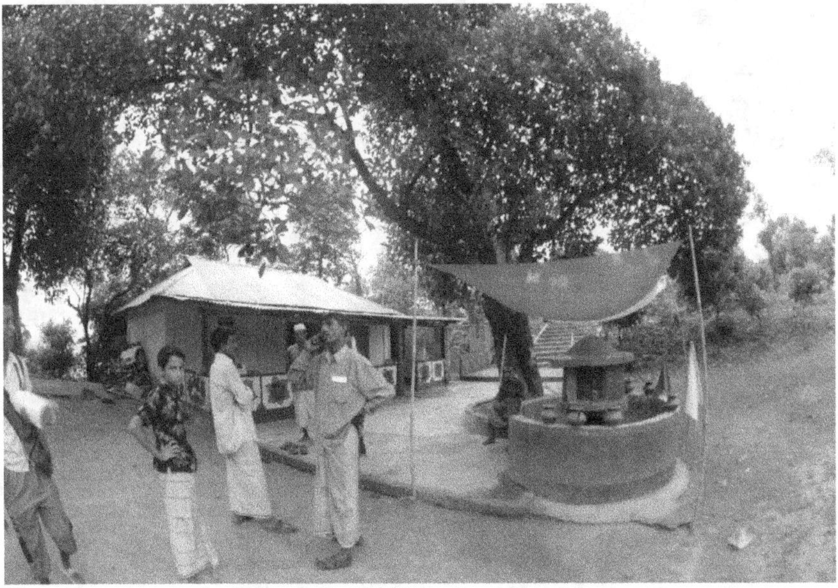

There is was water facilities, toilet facilities (basic) and prayer rooms.

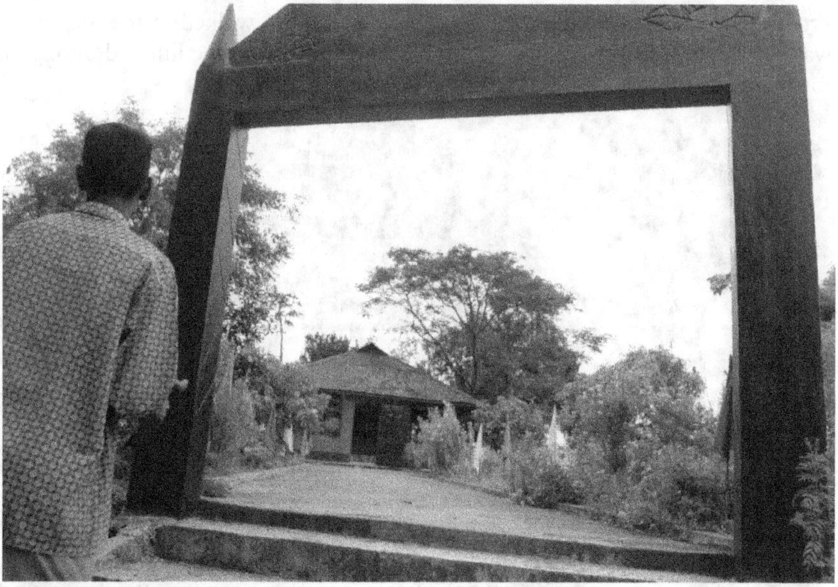

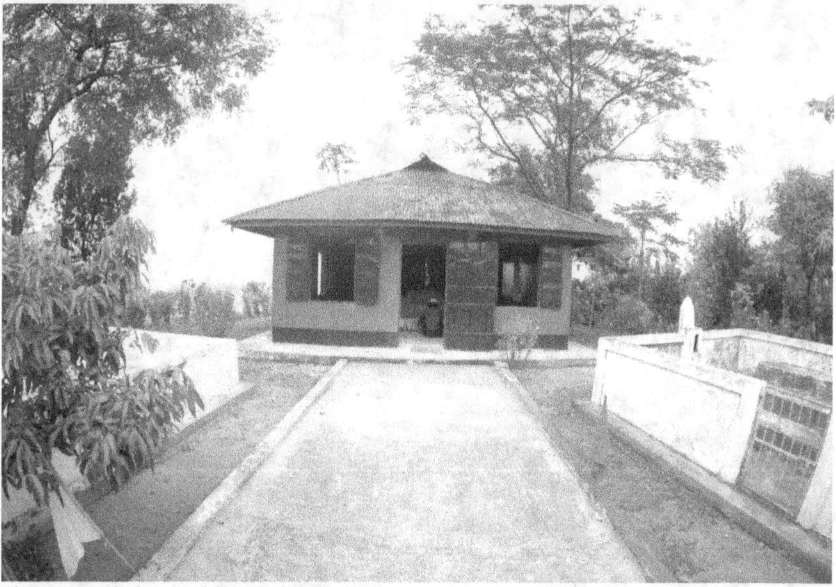

The mazar is housed in a brick built hut.

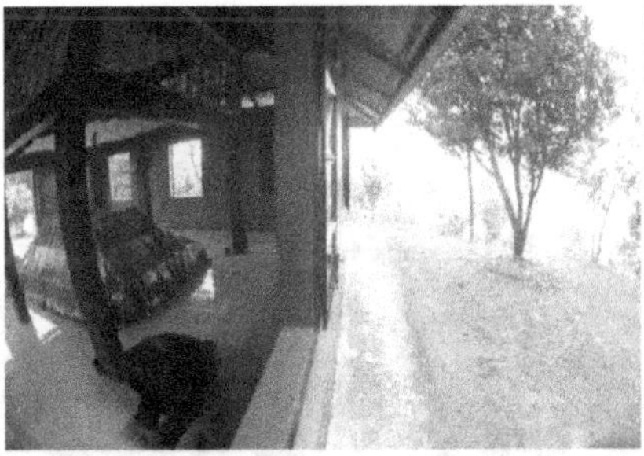

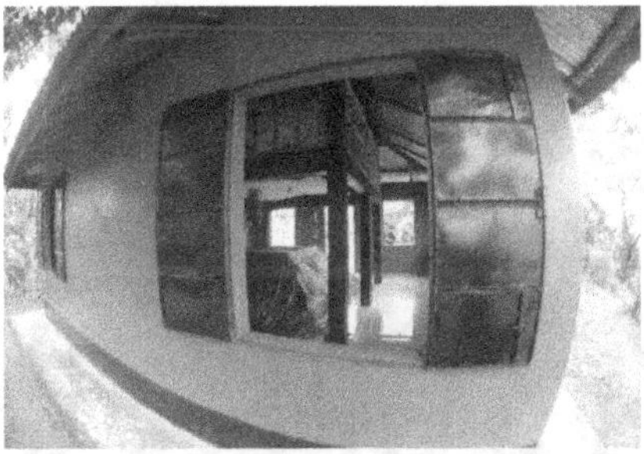

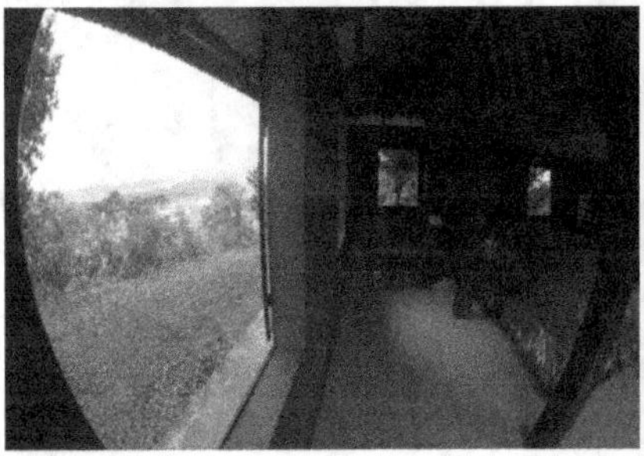

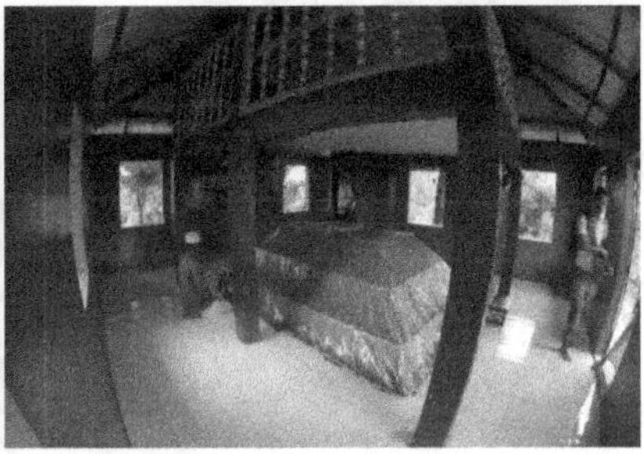

The mazar overlooks the Lubna River and the mountains that border India. It's a awe inspiring view.

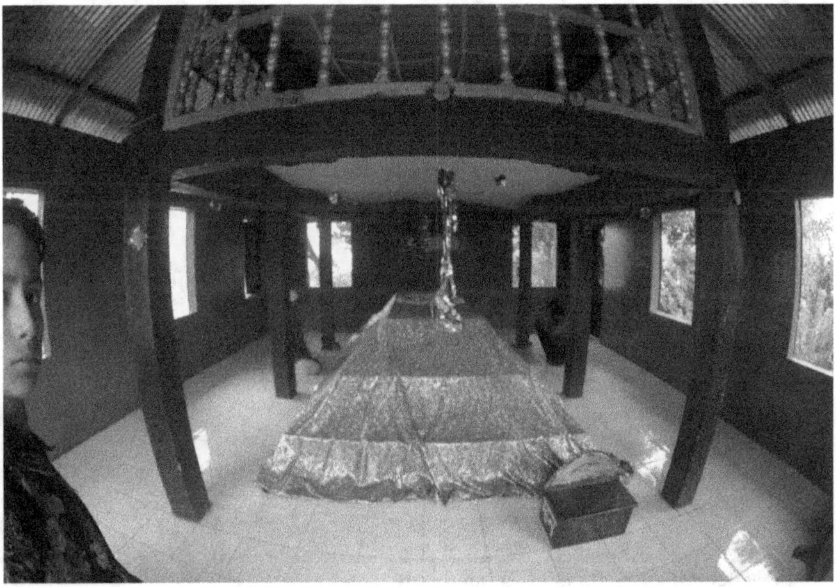

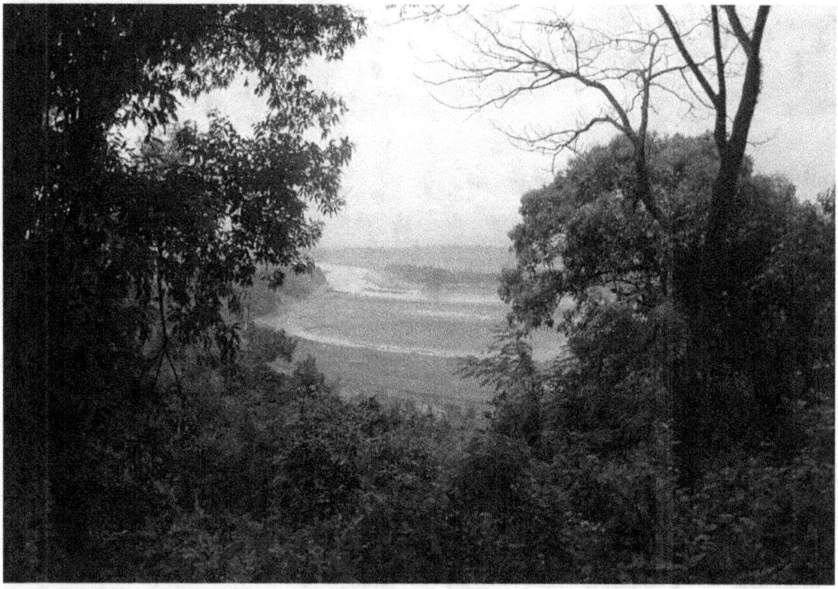

View from the top is simply breath taking, what a piece of real estate! I was looking down to the Lubna River and the boarder of India.

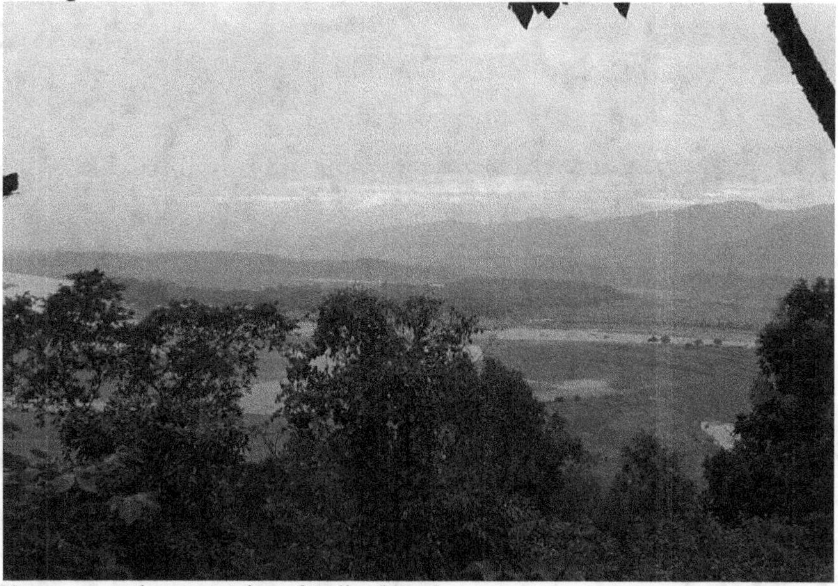

You can see the mountains of Indian boarder.

26.10.2010, 15:22:26

Shah Zada Sheikh Ali**

(Prince of Yemen) Beside Hazrat Shah Jalal Mazar, Dorga Gate, Sylhet Town.

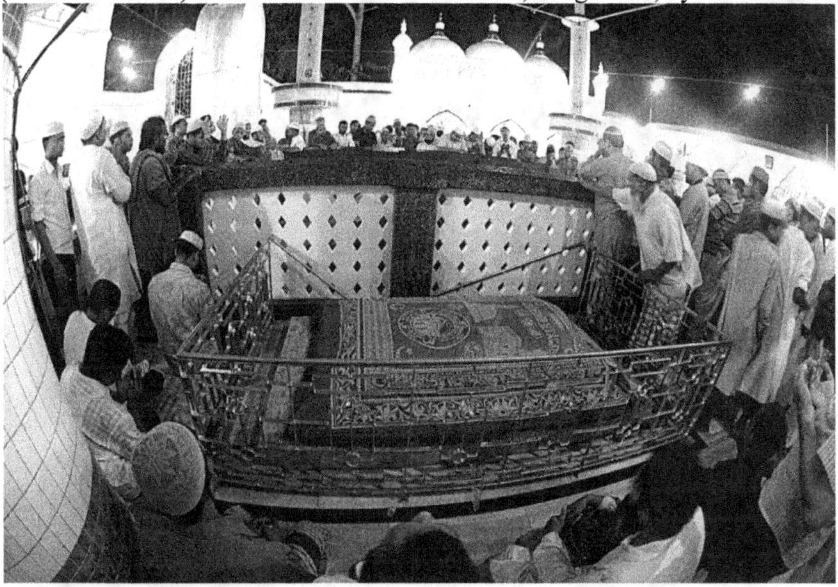

27.10.2010, 21:15

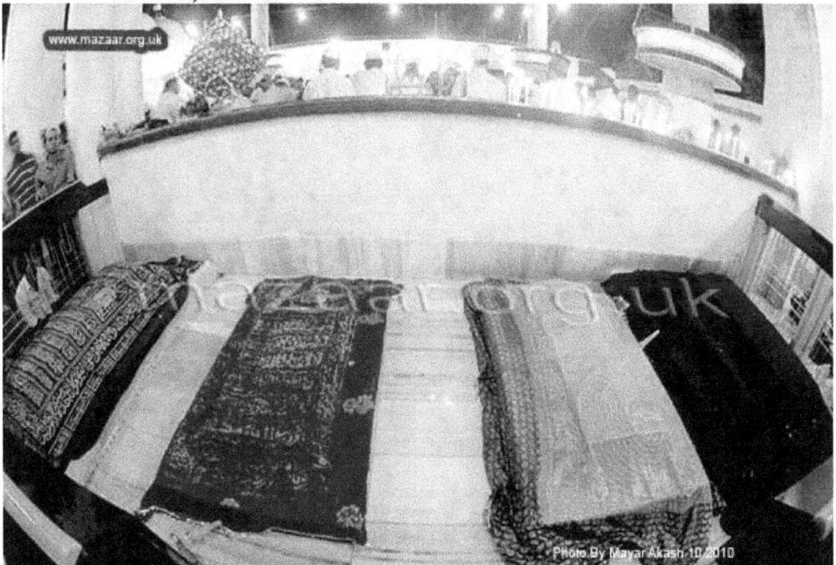
www.mazaar.org.uk
Photo By Mayar Akash 10/2010

27.10.2010, 20:49

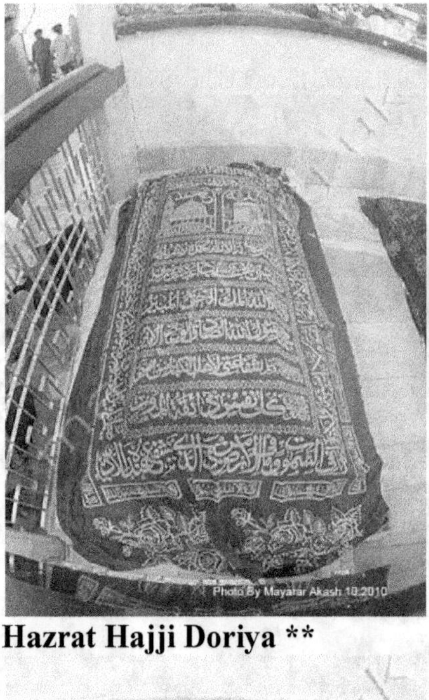
Photo By Mayarar Akash 10.2010

Hazrat Hajji Doriya **

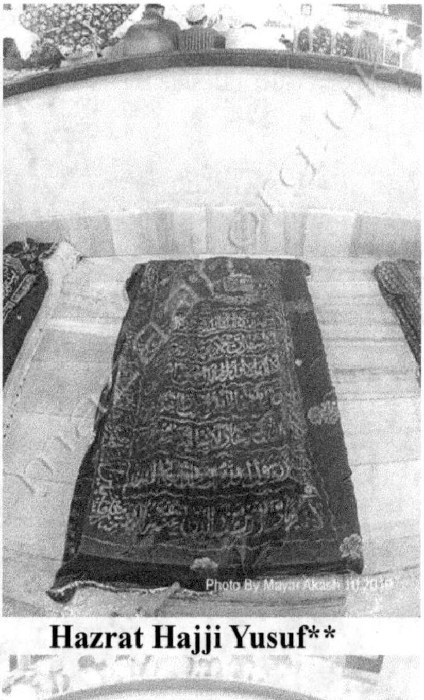
Photo By Mayar Akash 10.2010

Hazrat Hajji Yusuf**

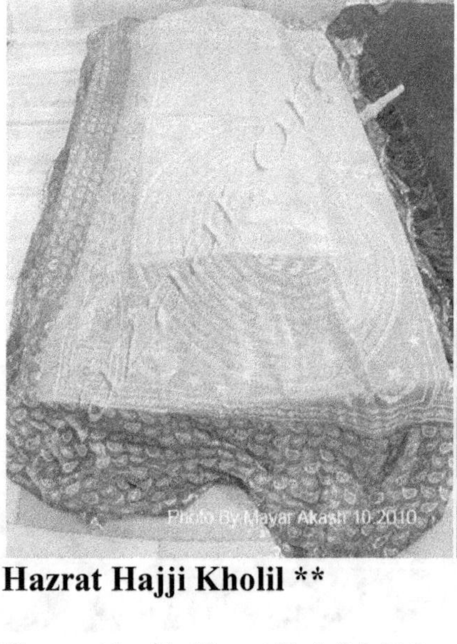
Photo By Mayar Akash 10.2010

Hazrat Hajji Kholil **

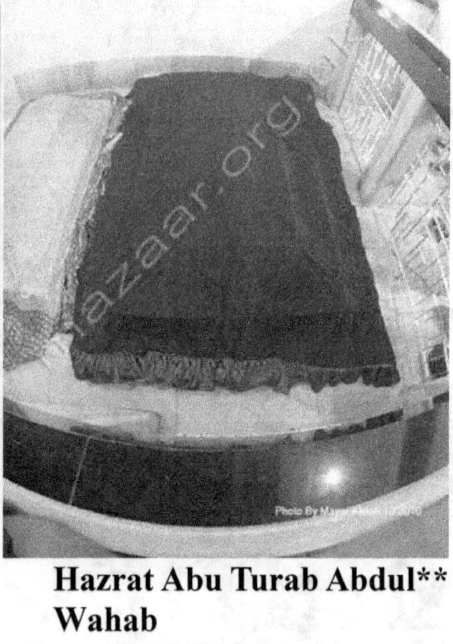

Hazrat Abu Turab Abdul Wahab**

They rest beside Hazrat Shah Jalal Mazar, Dorga Gate Sylhet Town.

Moju Shah

In the Dorga, side street, Sylhet town

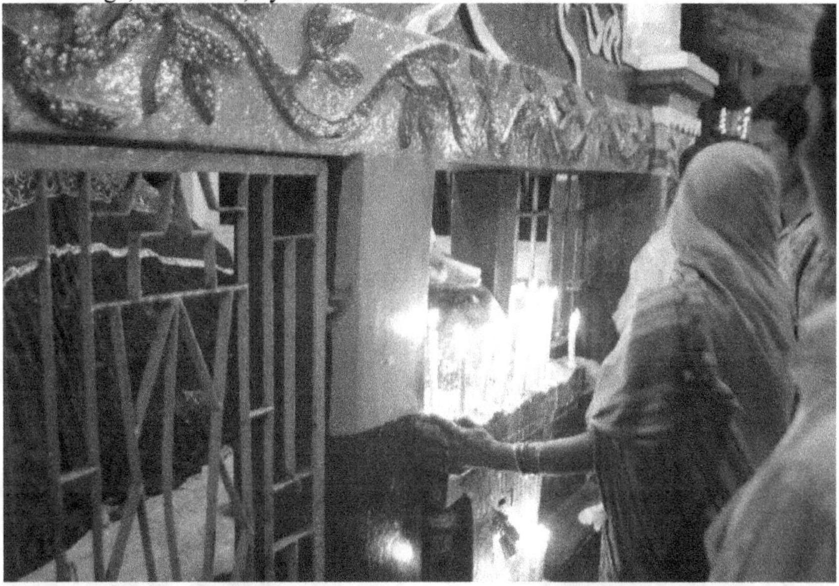

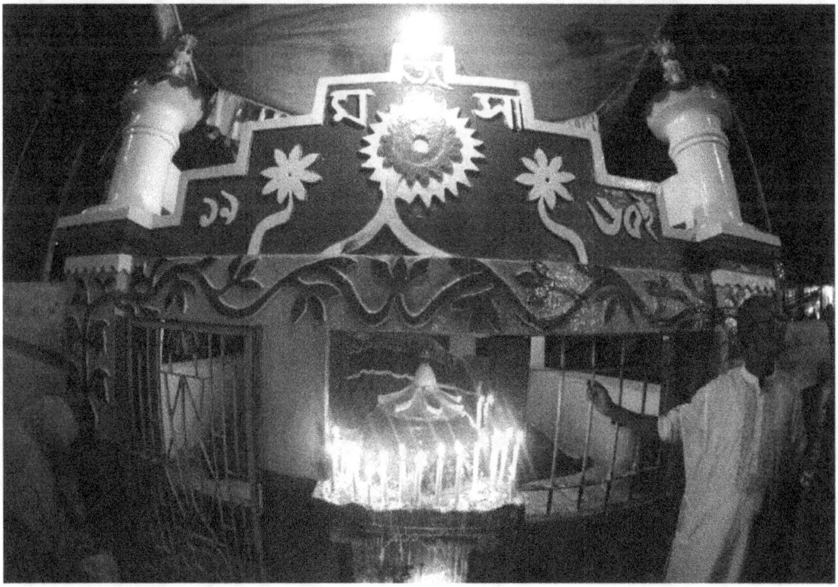

27.10.2010, 18:33:04

Fokir Jibai Kha

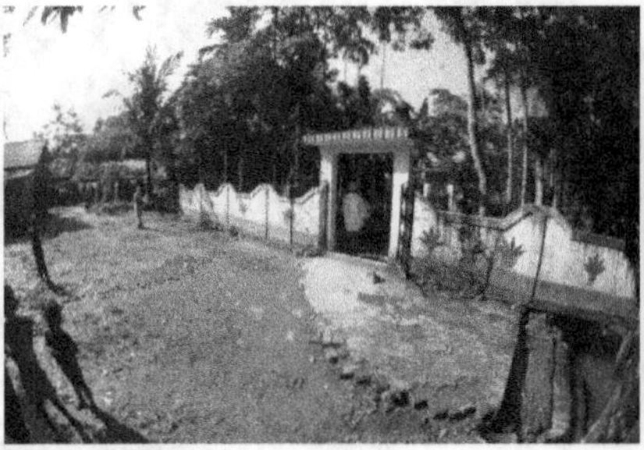

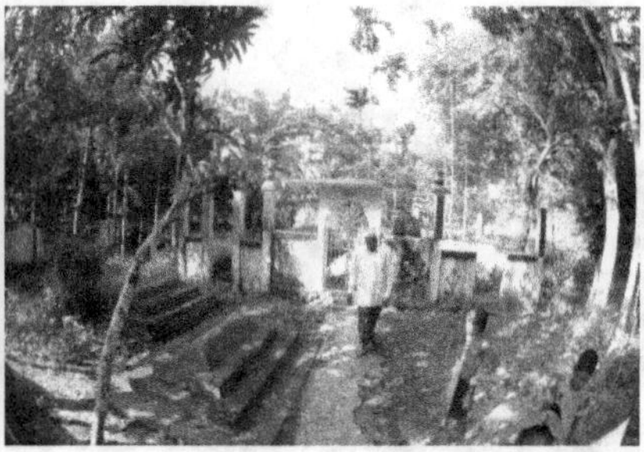

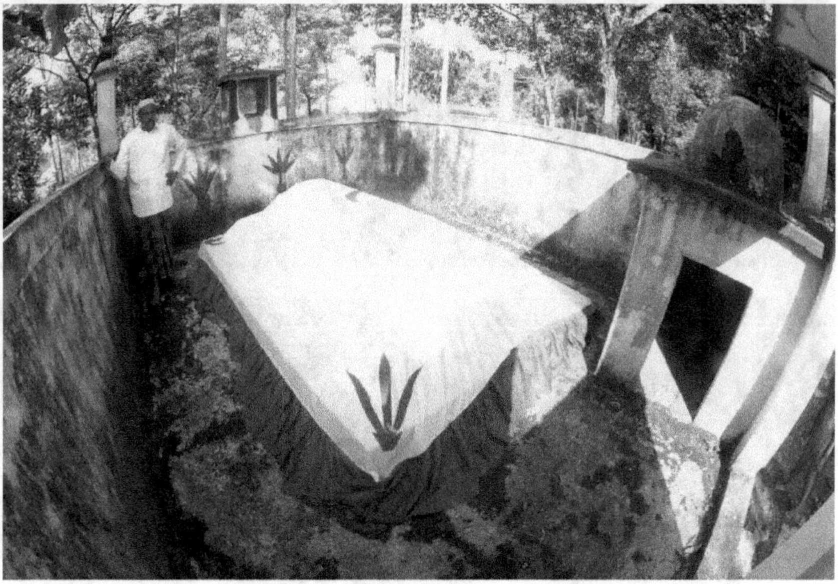

29.10.2010, 17:48:44

November 2010

Shi-a Panjathan Mazar

Bawon Gaow, Chairman bari, Osmani Nagor

We have now come to the Shia section of Bangladesh. Separate to the Sufism and the 360 Auwliyas of Hazrat Shah Jalal.

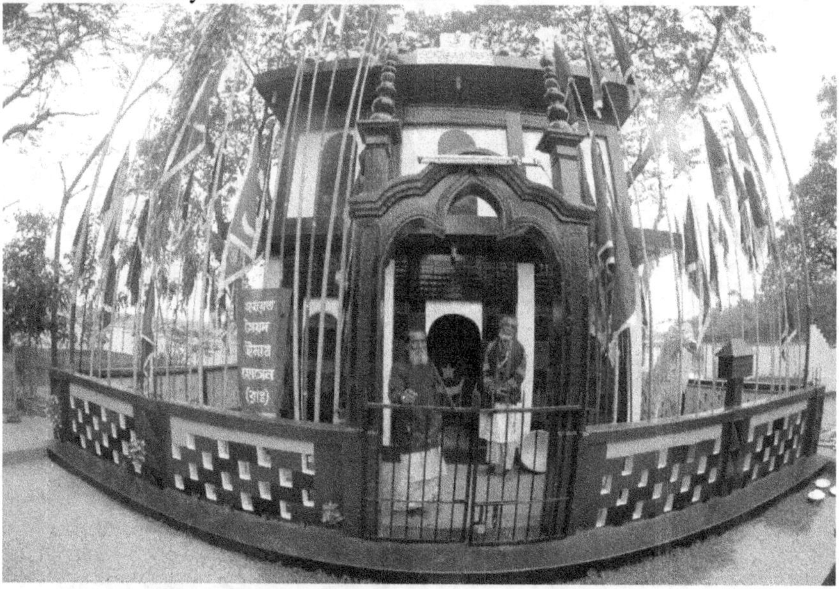

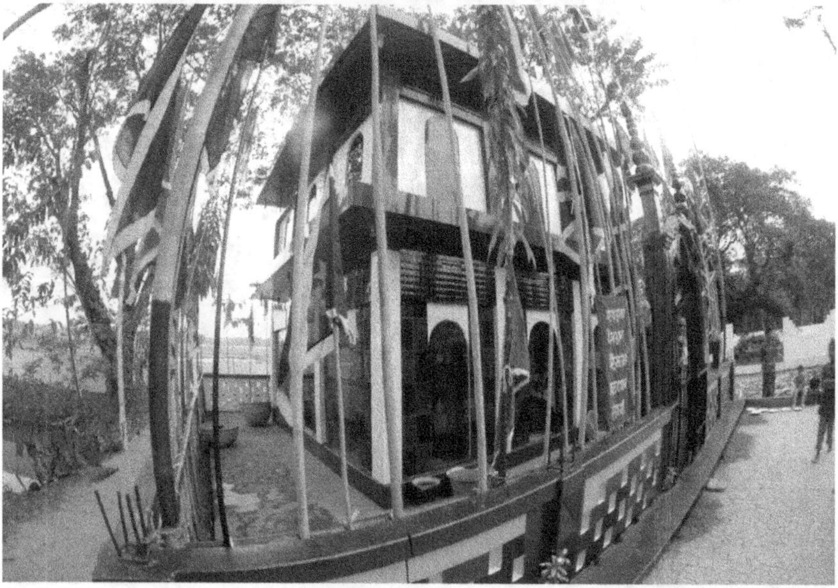

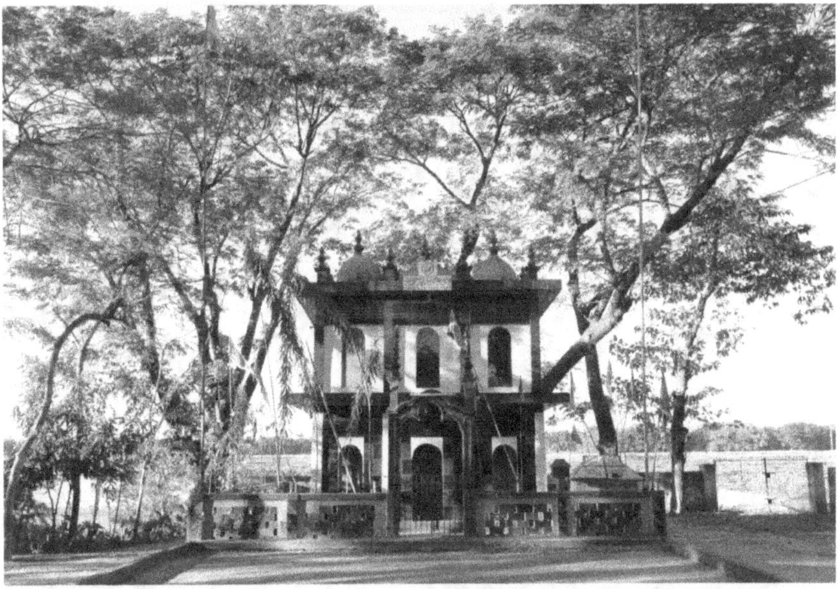

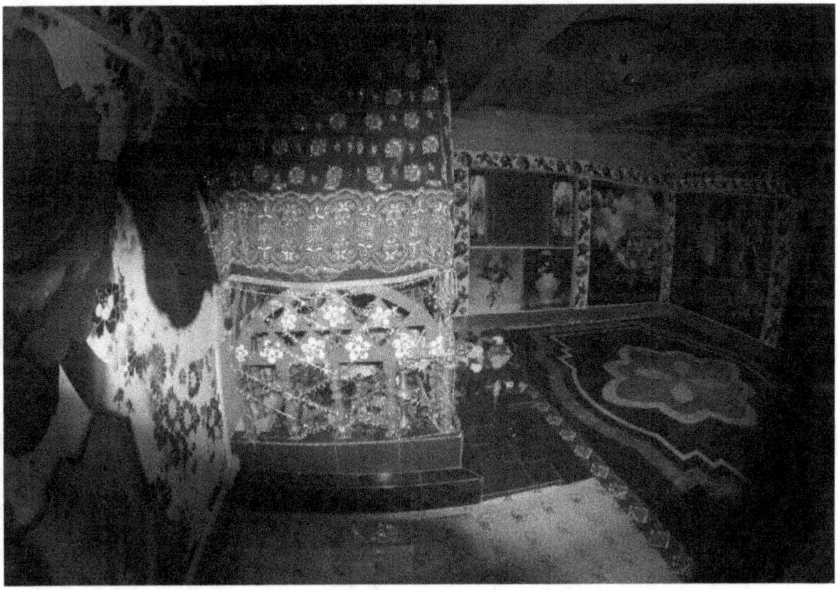

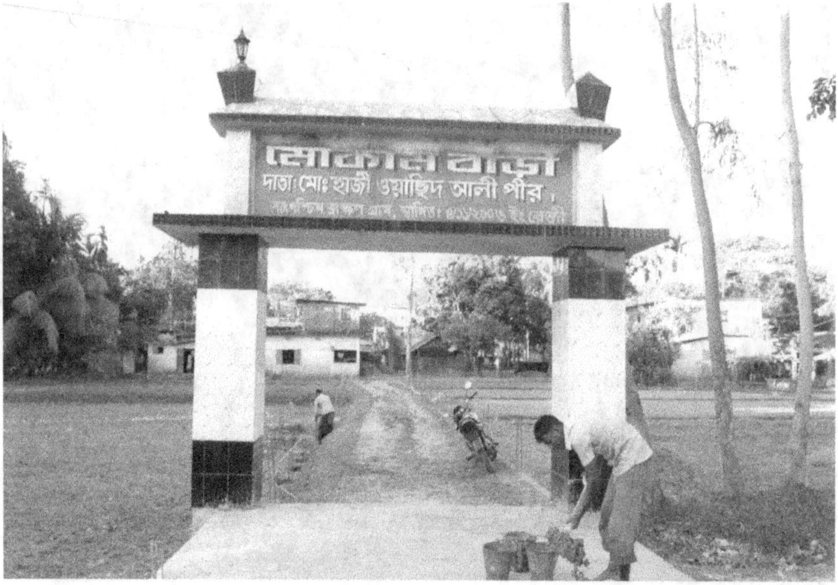
দাতা: মোঃ হাজী ওয়াছিদ আলী পীর ,

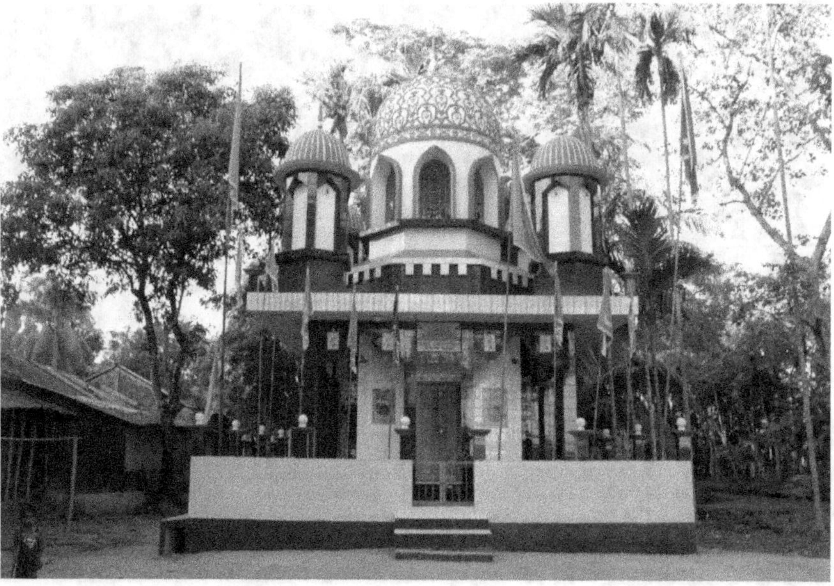

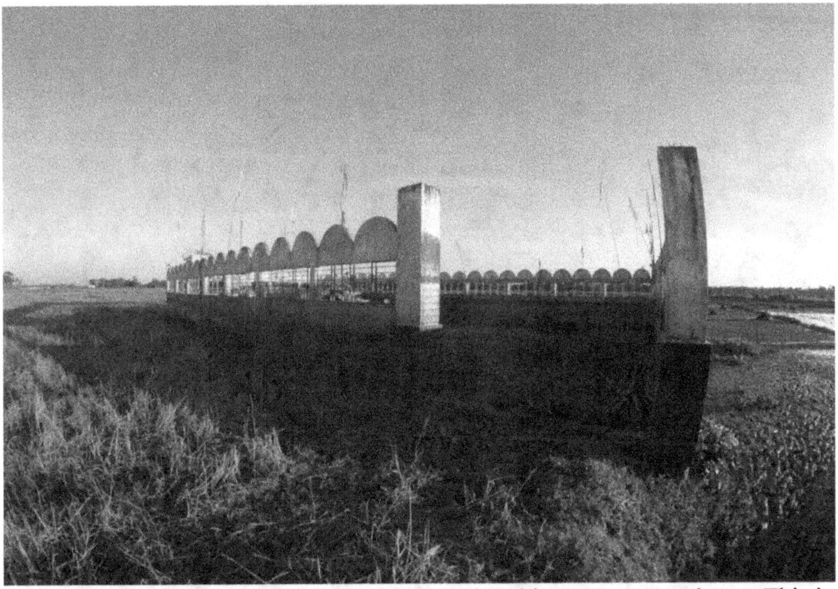

Korballar mat. This is the battle field, where the Shia pageantry ends up. This is a high walled enclosure in the middle of paddy fields.

8.11.2010, 16:34:00

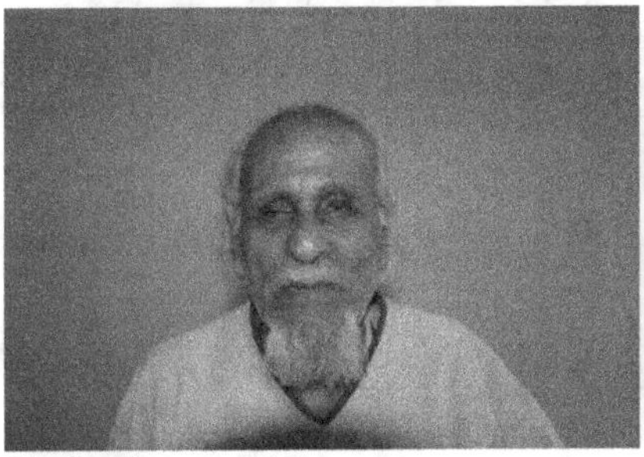

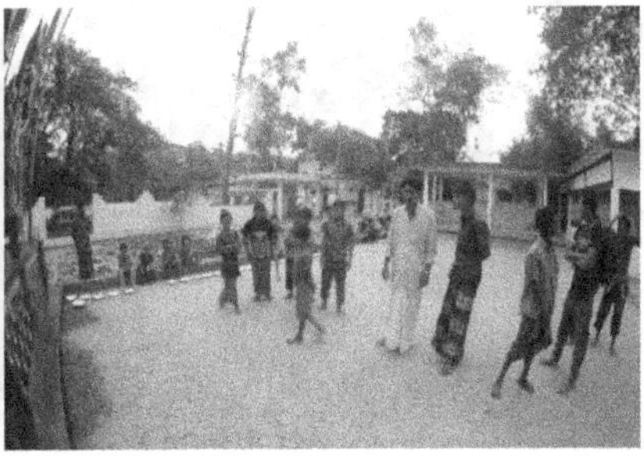

The leader.

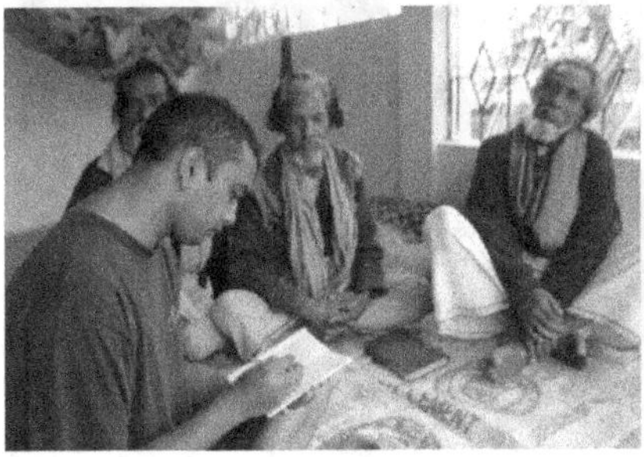

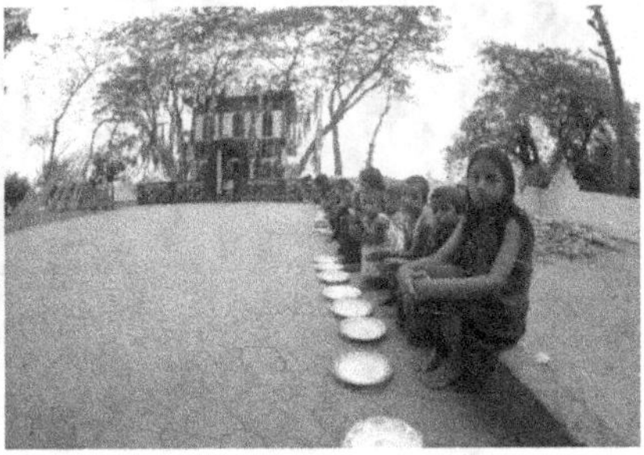

Shah Soli Shah

Osmani Nagor

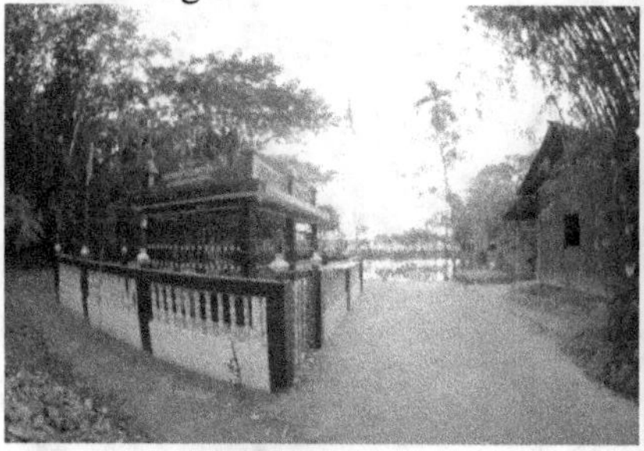

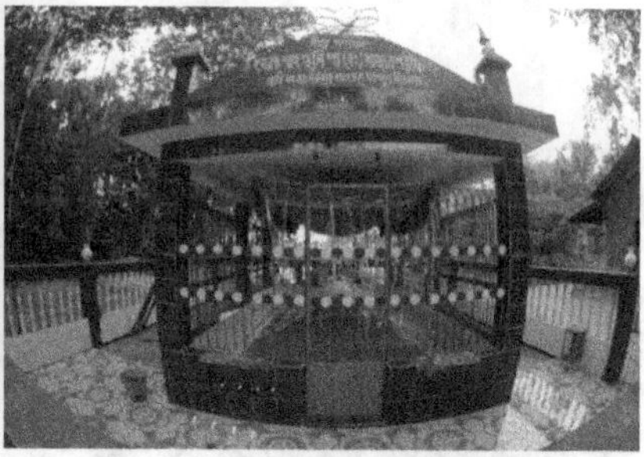

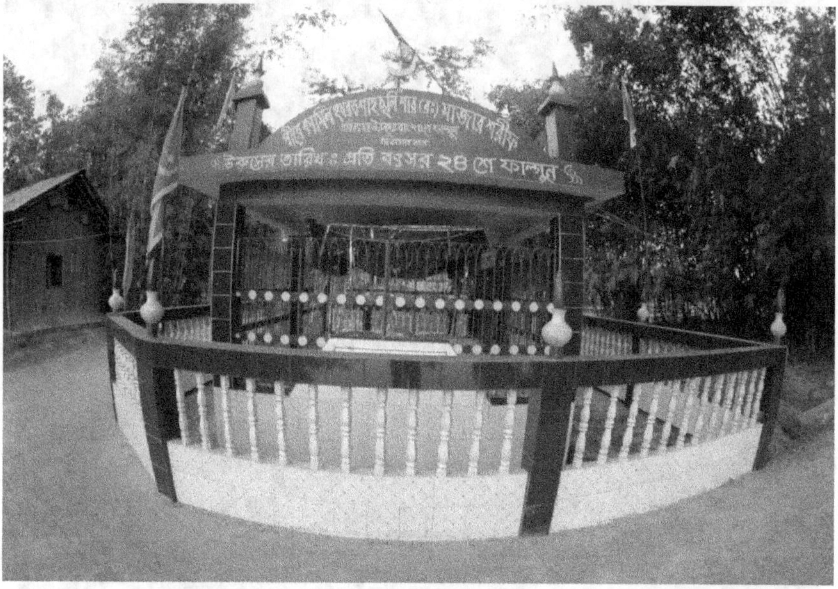
উরসের তারিখঃ প্রতি বৎসর ২৪ শে ফাল্গুন

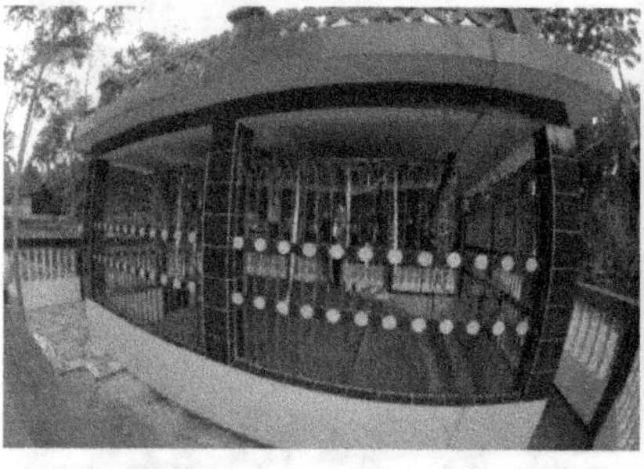

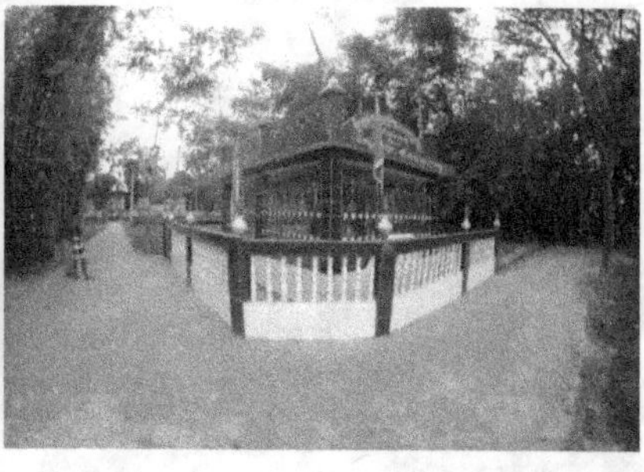

8.11.2010, 16:40

December 2010

Madari Shah

Dowrail, Dhaka Dokkin, Sylhet

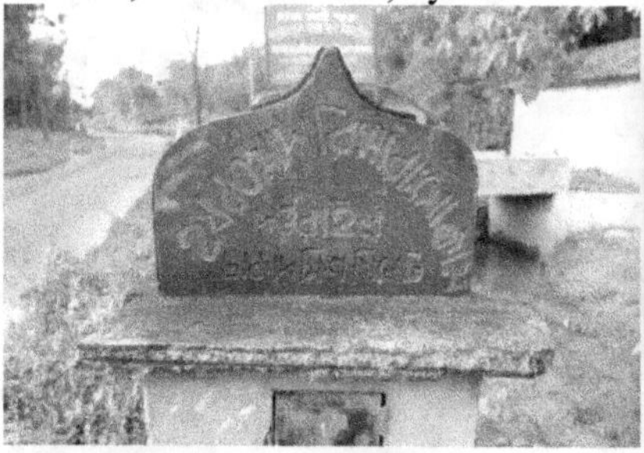

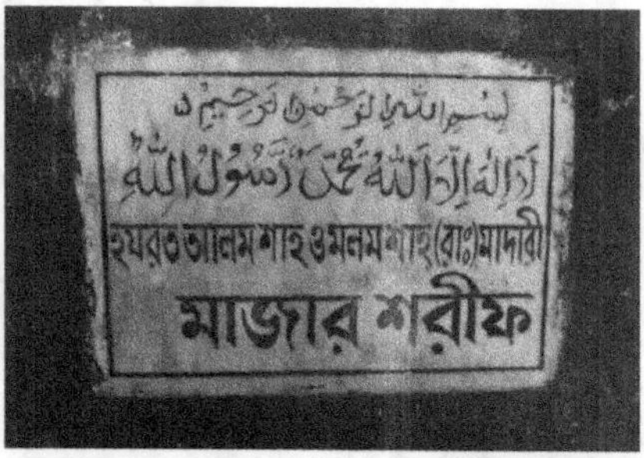
بسم الله الرحمن الرحيم
لا اله الا الله محمد رسول الله
হযরত আলম শাহ ও মলম শাহ (রাঃ) মাদারী
মাজার শরীফ

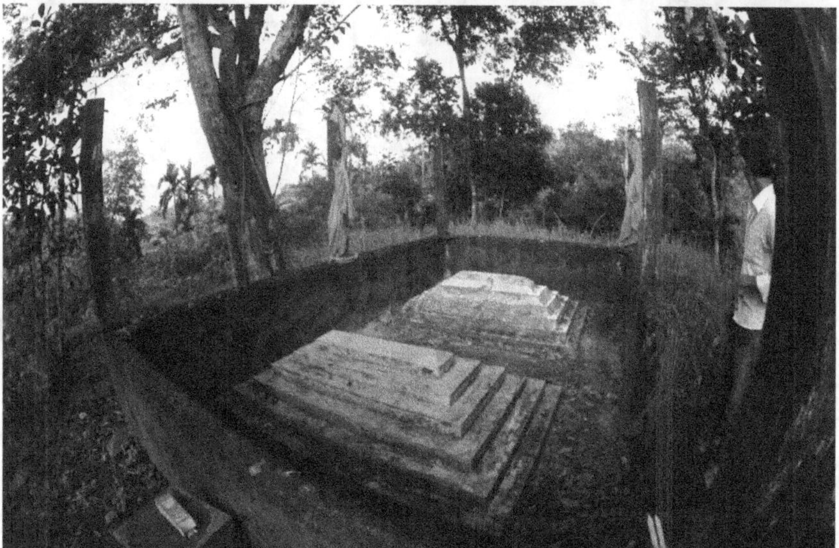

10.12.2010, 20:39:45

Modu Shudon*

Stadium Gate, Sylhet Town

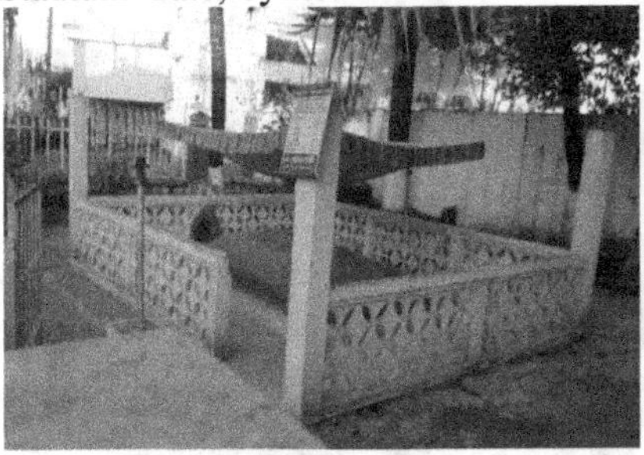

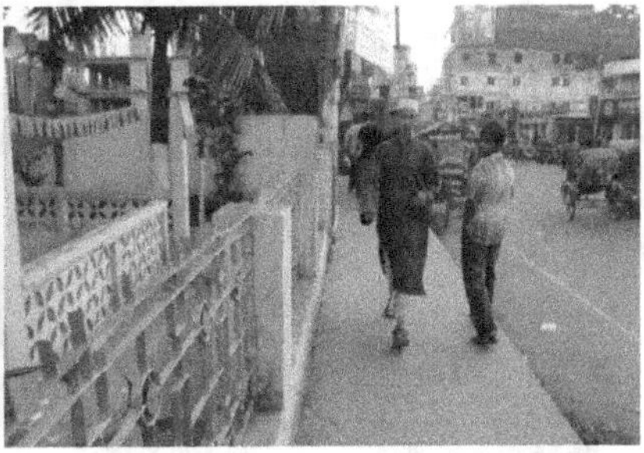

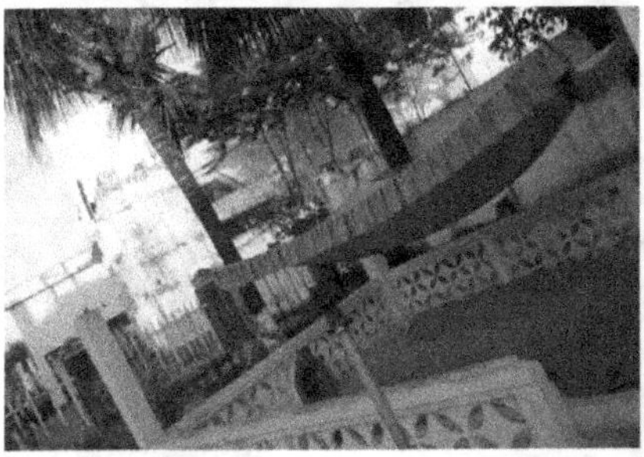

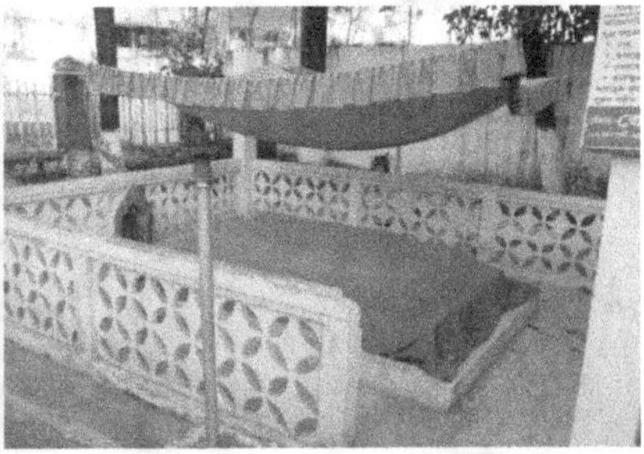

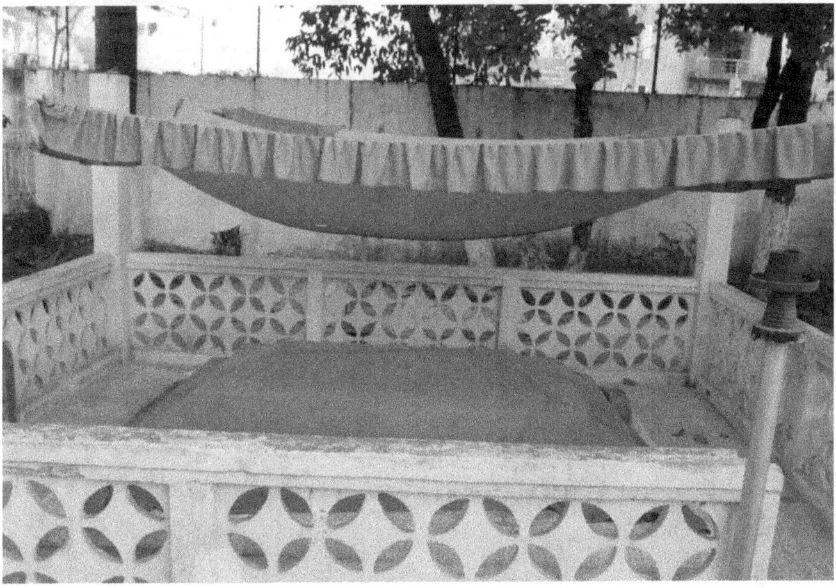

21.12.2010, 16:20:12

Jumma at Dorga

Dorga

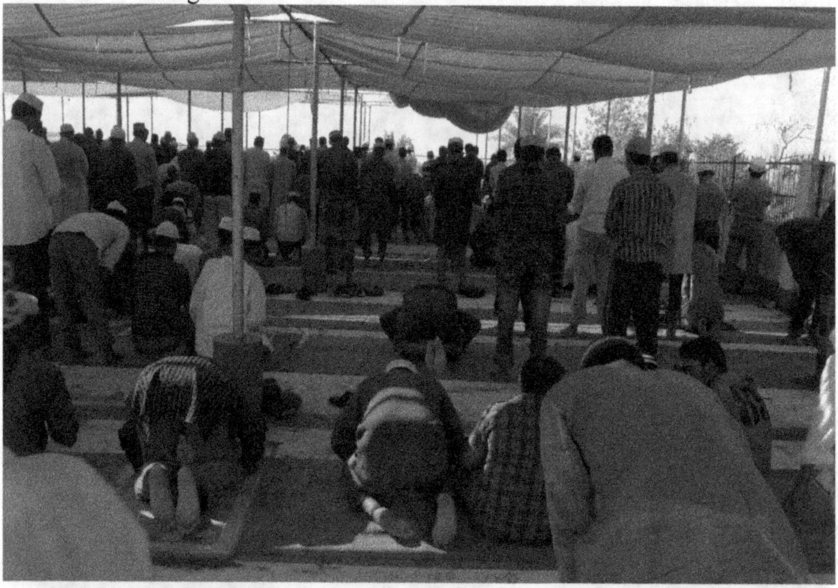

24.12.2010, 13:15.

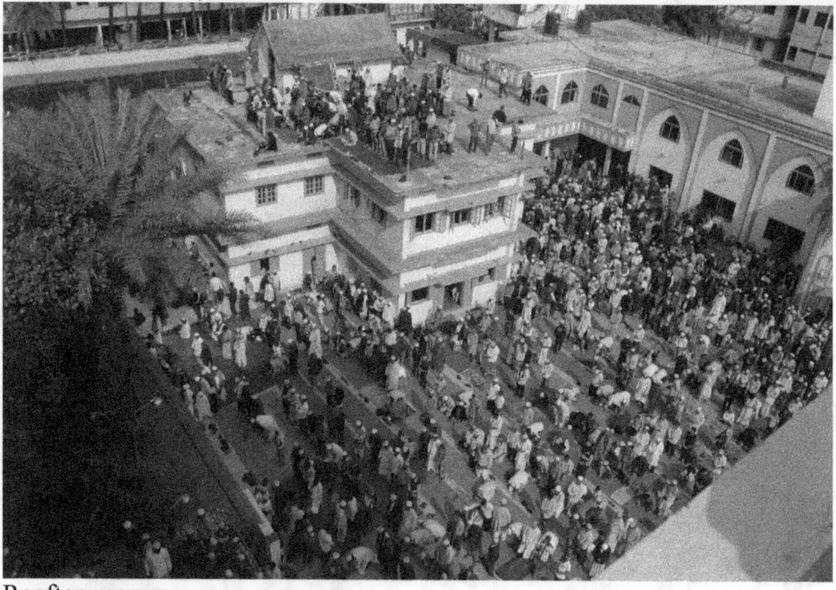

Rooftop prayers.

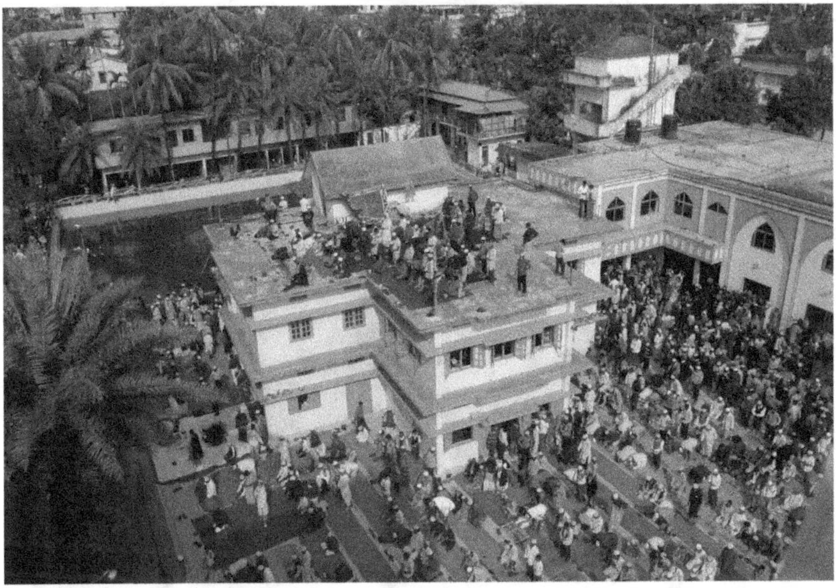

Looking down to the forecourt

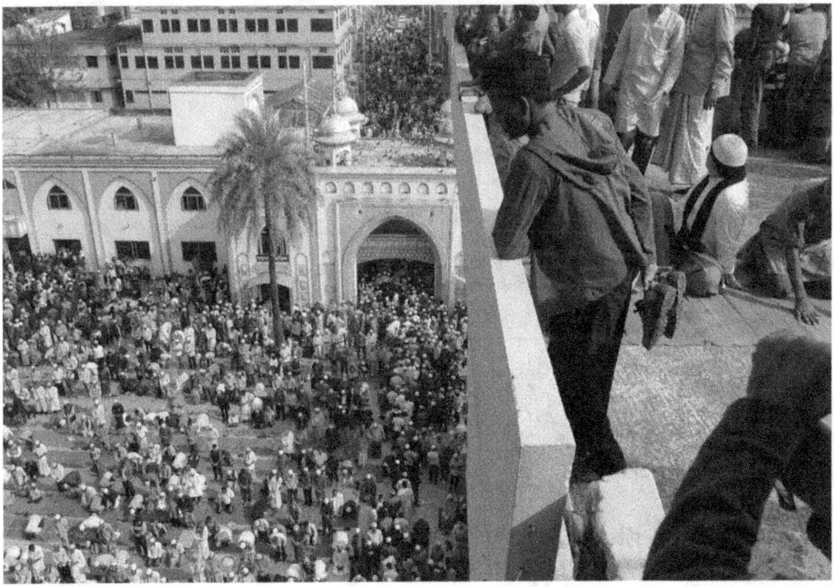

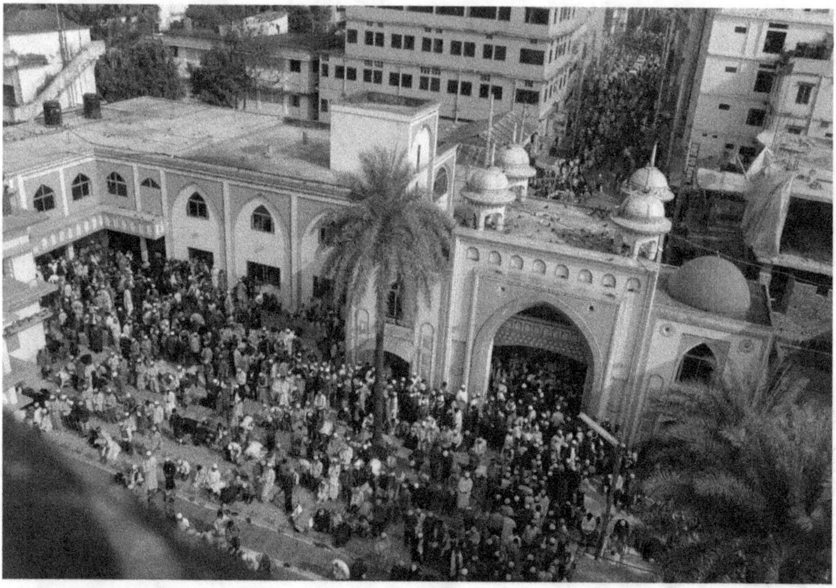

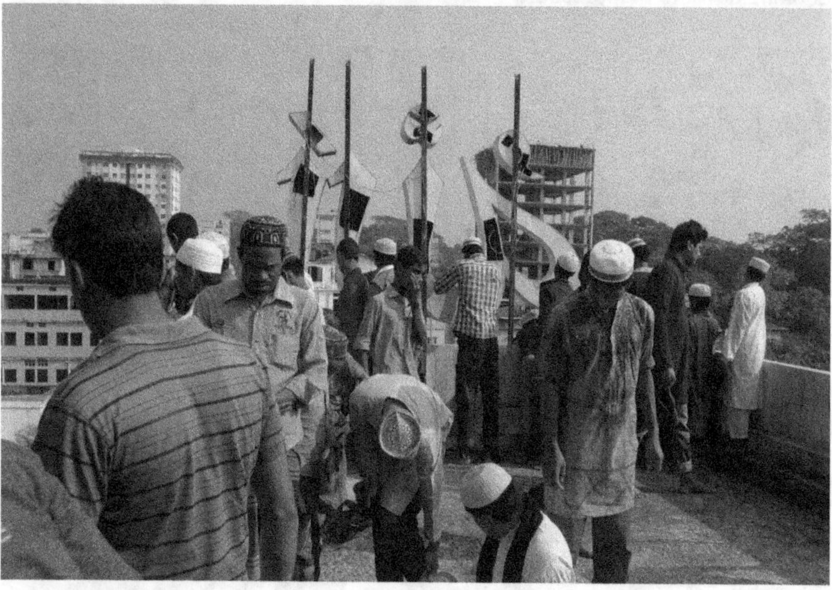

Looking at the back of the Allahu sign.

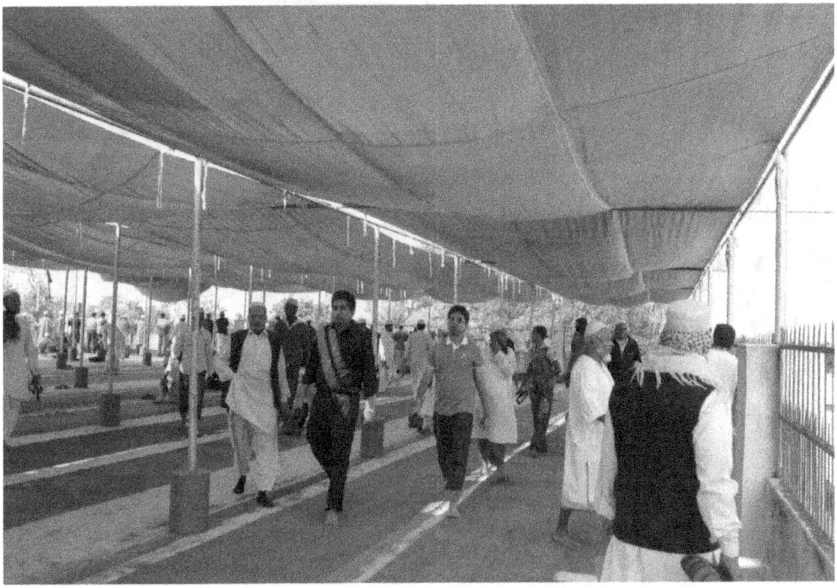

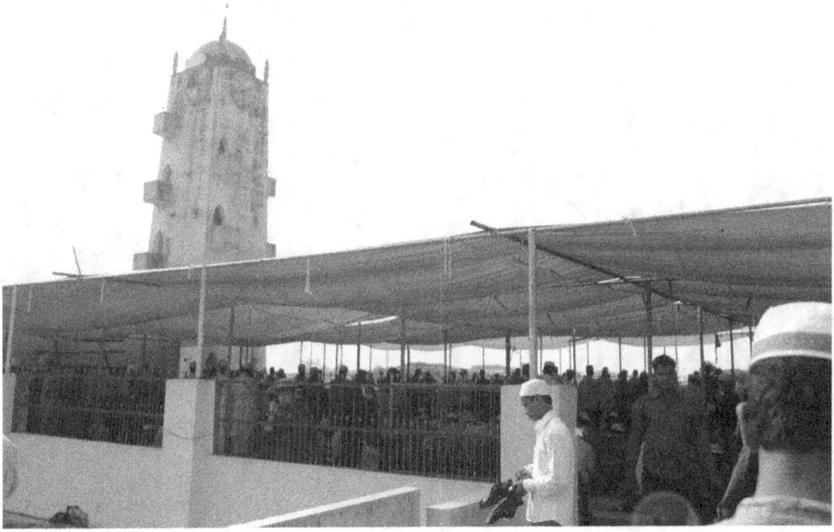

On rooftop of the mosque, facing the clock tower/minaret

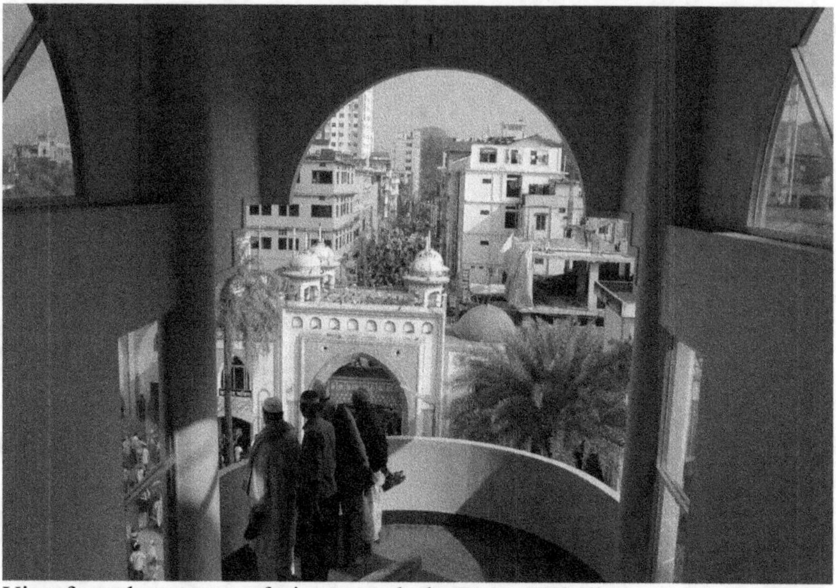

View from the top steps, facing towards the Dorga Moholla

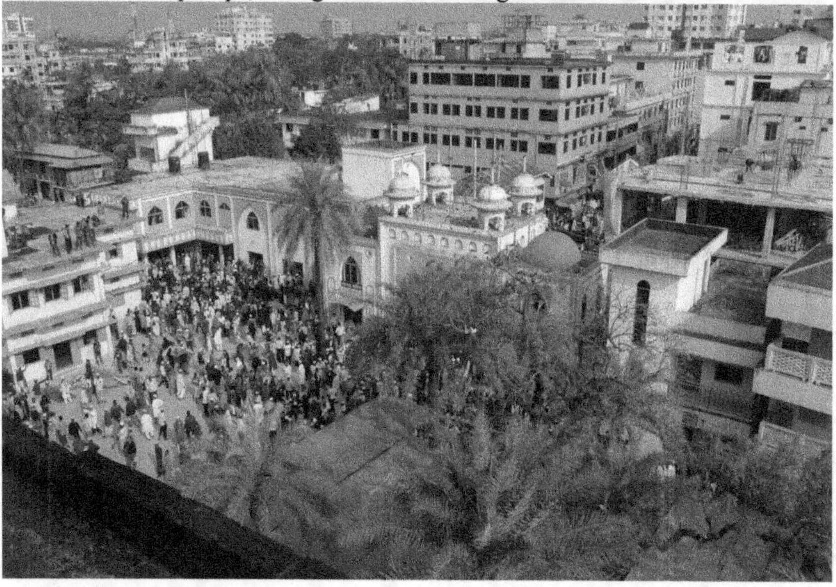

24.12.2010, 13:34

January 2011

Kaza Shah Solim

Singsha Pur, Purbo Parah, Mukam Mosque, Satok, (Koitok Rd off Shunamgoinj Road)

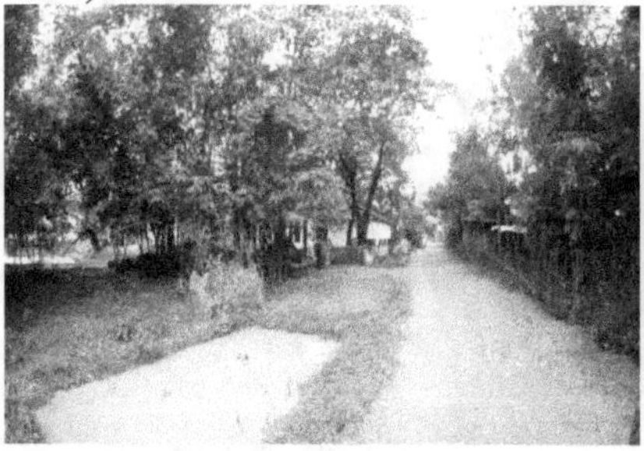

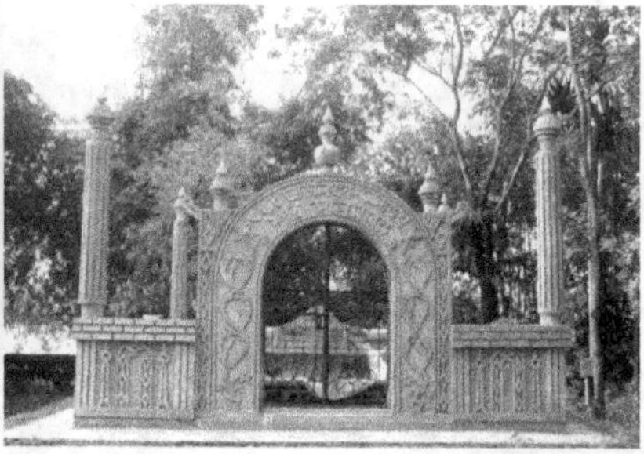

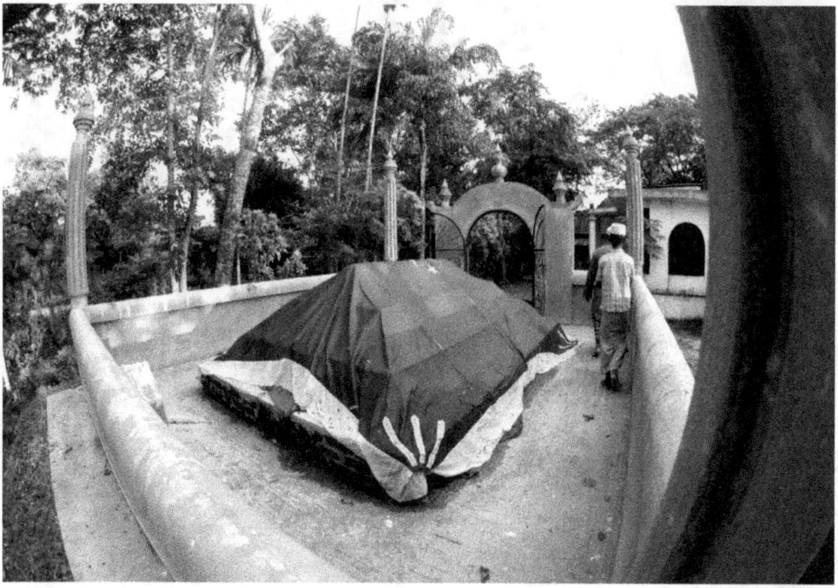

1.1.2011, 11:31:

This was a journey and half, as were many others. This place was in Satok, Shunamgoinj district.

It was in a village setting and as with village setting the Mazar is off the beaten tracks, which means you have to walk through either private land, homes and mosques. With site, they were renovated it.

For because of the work was going on and not the finished item, I didn't feel the 100% of the zapping.

Soyod Shah Yusuf Iraqi*

Soyod Gaow, Shab Bari, Satok, Koitok Road, off Shunamgoinj Road.

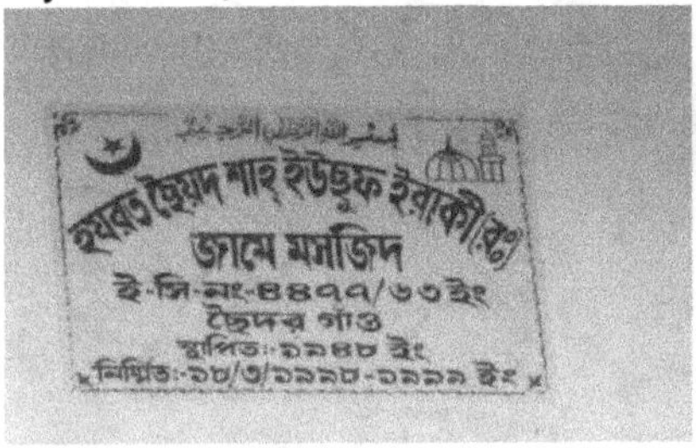
হযরত ছৈয়দ শাহ্ ইউছুফ ইরাকী (রঃ)
জামে মসজিদ
ই-সি-নং-৪৪৭৭/৬৩ ইং
ছৈদর গাঁও
স্থাপিত: ১১৪৮ ইং
নির্মিত: ১৮/৩/১৯৯৮-১৯৯৯ ইং

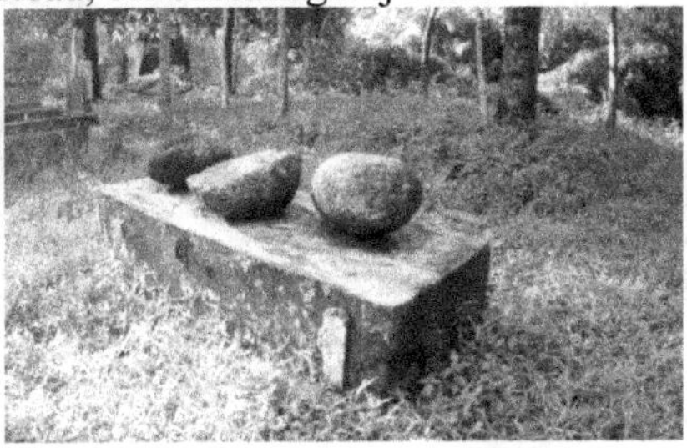

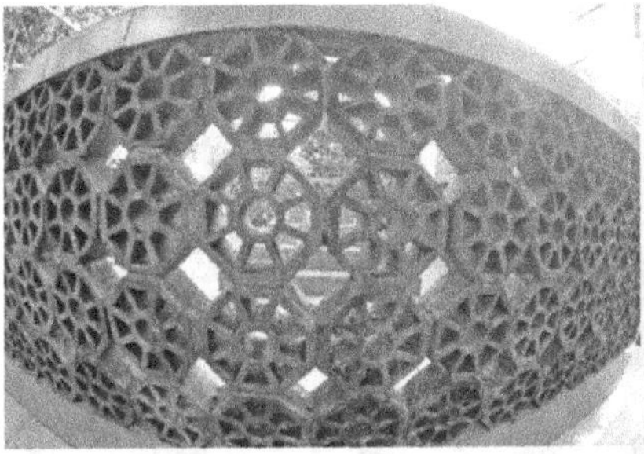

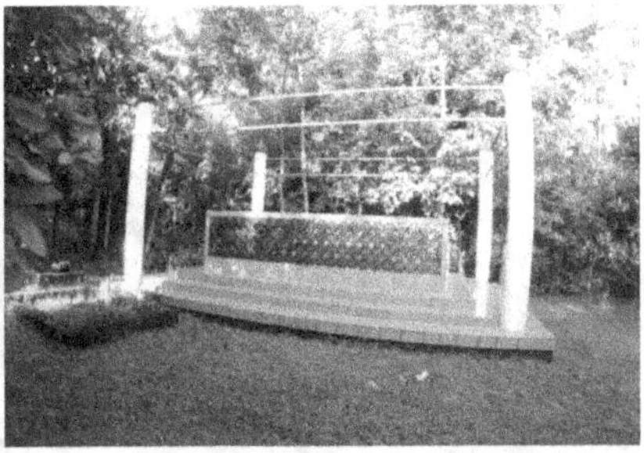

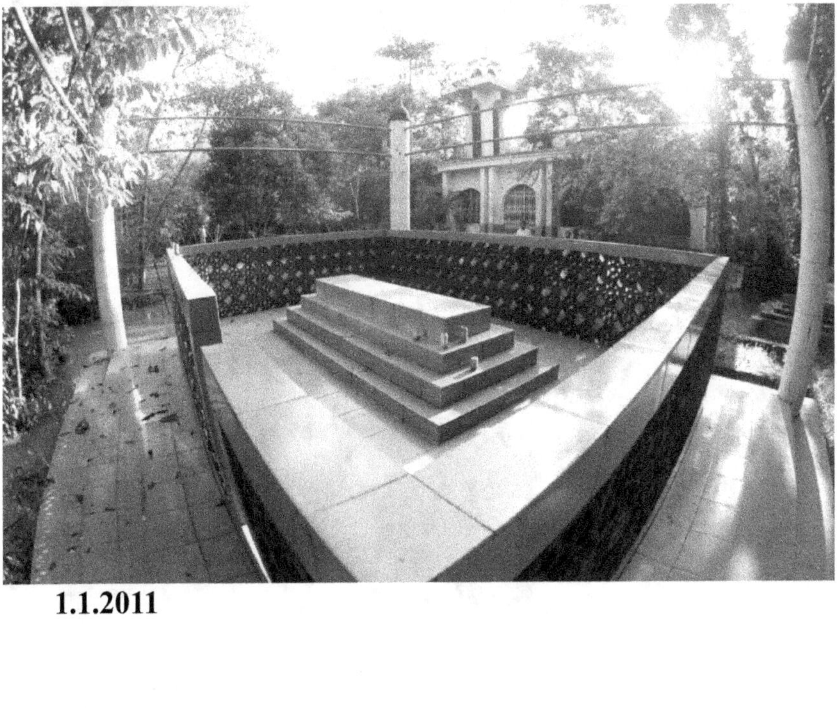

1.1.2011

Moulovi Soyod Shah

Abu Mohammod Taher Bagdadi

Soyod Gaow, Shab Bari, Satok, Koitok Road, off Shunamgoinj Road. 19.6.1327

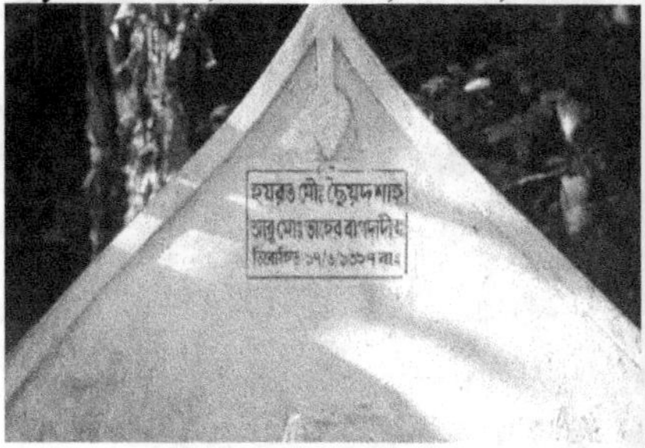
হযরত মৌঃ ছৈয়দ শাহ
আবু মোঃ তাহের বাগদাদীঃ

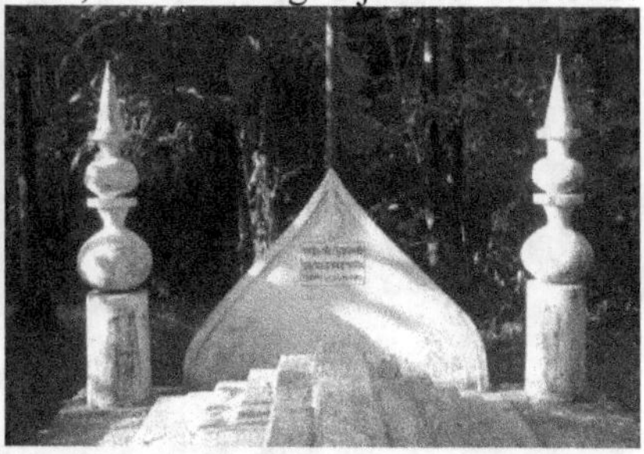

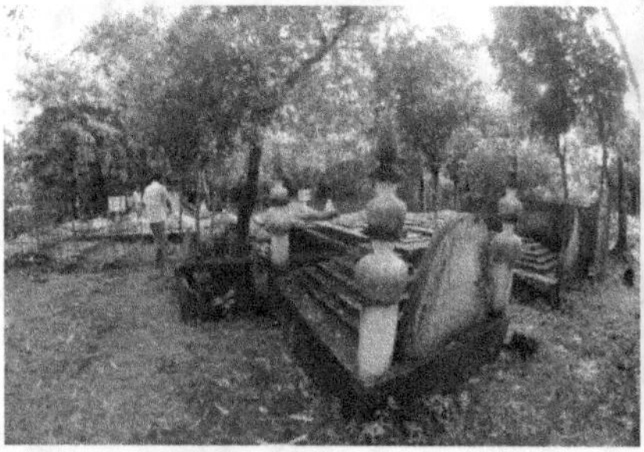

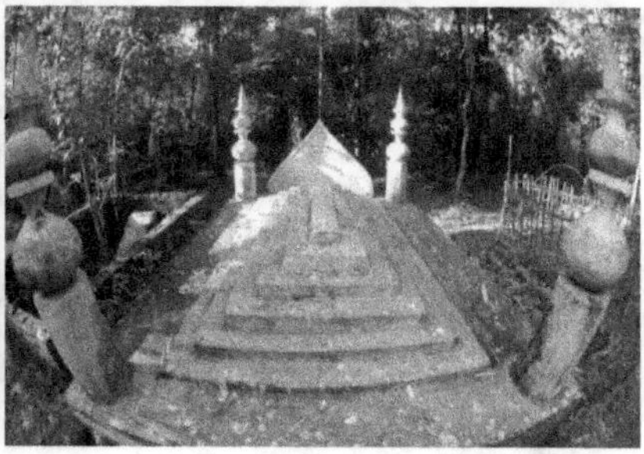

1.1.2011.

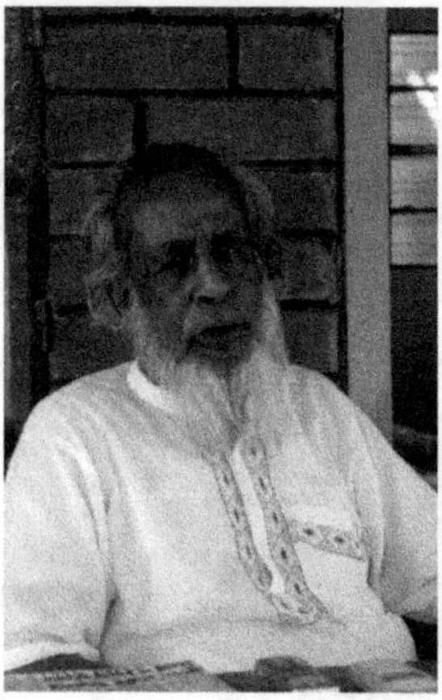

Soyod Mosud Ali, He's direct descendent, who is about 12/14 generation down.

It was intriguing to find another grave from an earlier date.

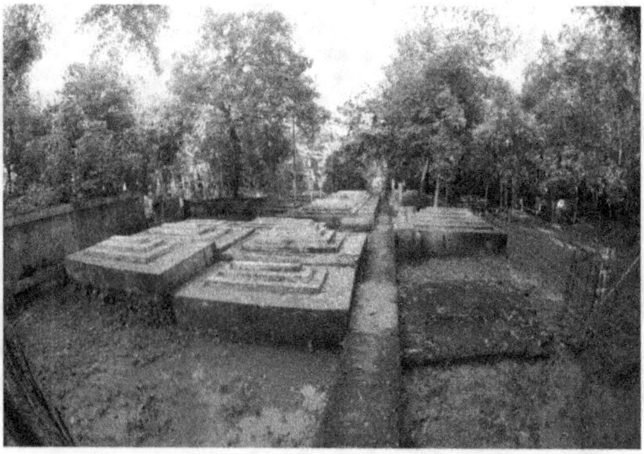

Soyod Korim Dad Rumi

Nuwarai, Nuwarai Bazar, Satok town, Shunamgoinj

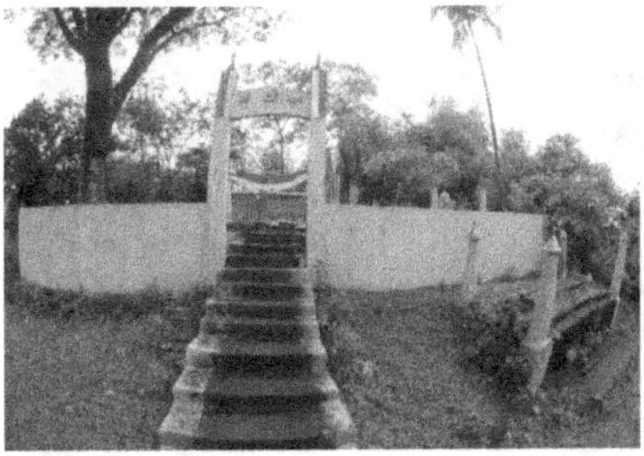

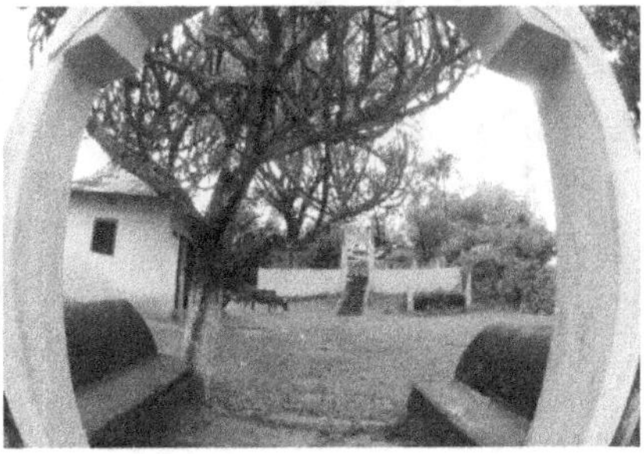

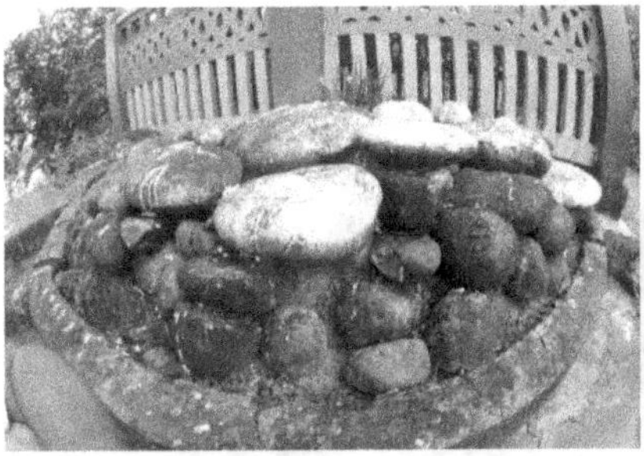

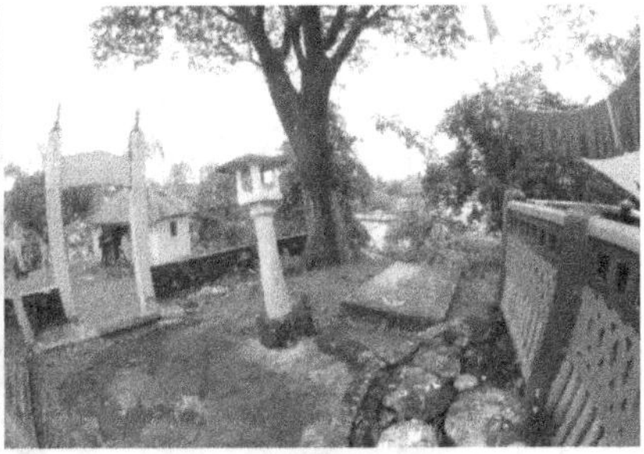

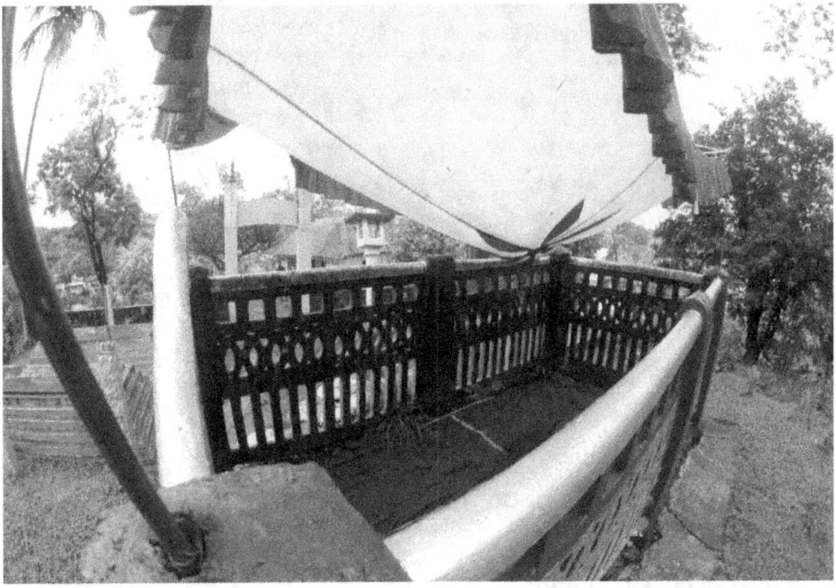

1.1.2011, 16:01:44

Hazrat Sultan Shah Arfin*

Ashon =Camp, Satok Cement Factory Complex, Fokir Tilla.

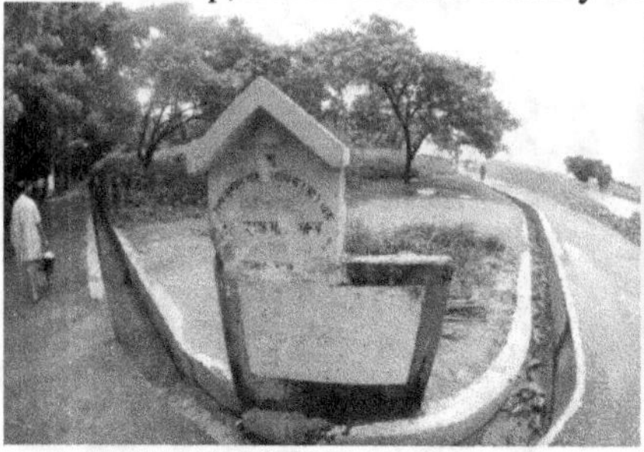

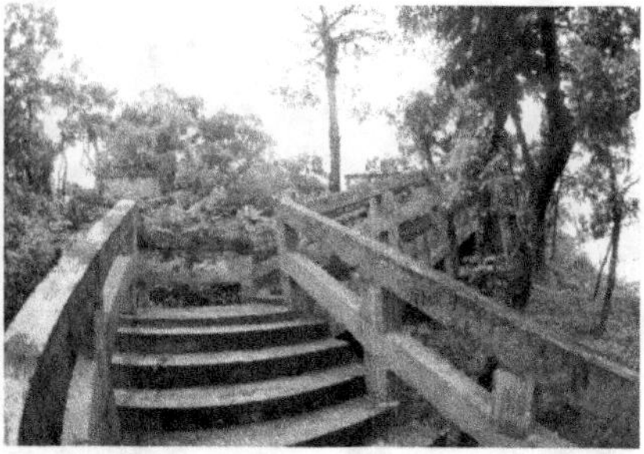

He is not buried here.

Modur Ali Shah Moslan

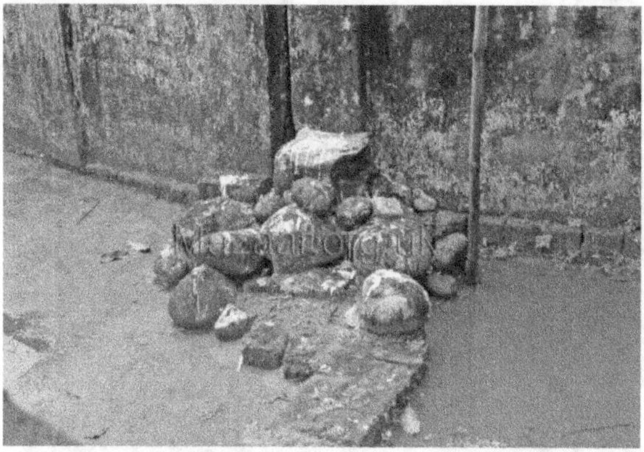

This was on one of the long journeys, and to get to the place was a trek. But it had to be done as Arfin was one of the 360 missionary. I must say early on this quest, I didn't understand and wasn't able to make the distinction between a mazar and an Ashon.

Mazar is the burial place and Ashon is their camp site.

While this is Arfin's camp, this is not his grave site

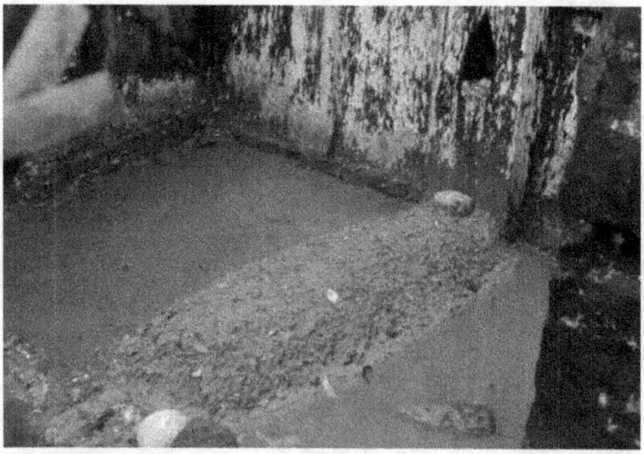

Zarali Shah

1.1.2011, 16:37:06

Durbin Shah

Durbin Tillah, Satok Cement Factory Complex, Abashik Area 4, Satok

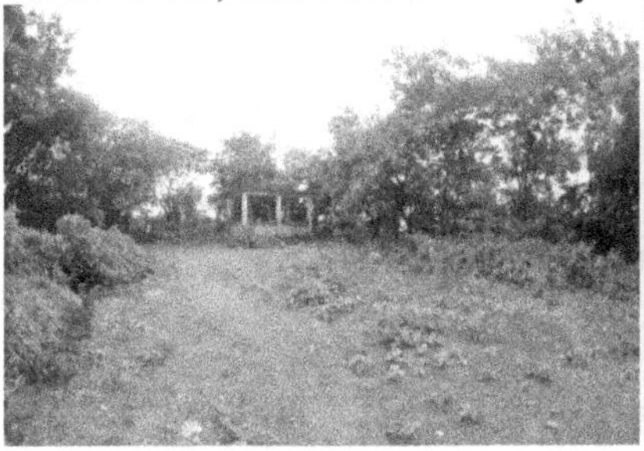
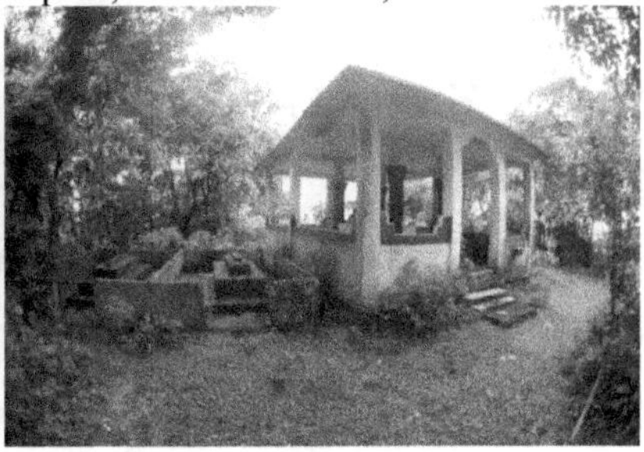

1.1.2011, 17:13:52

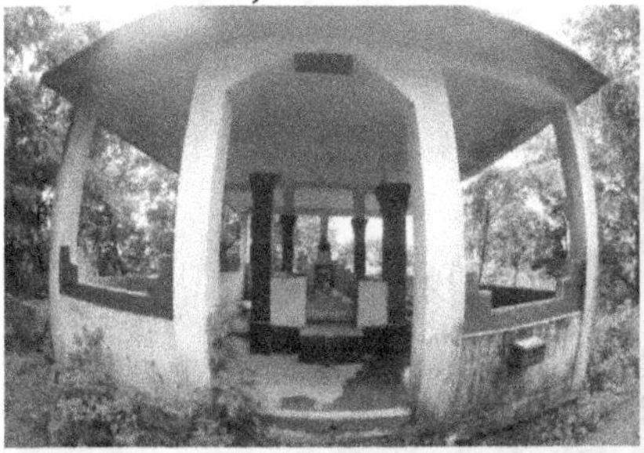
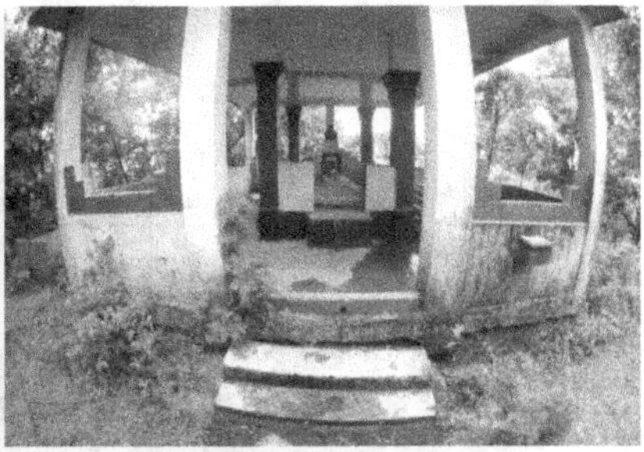
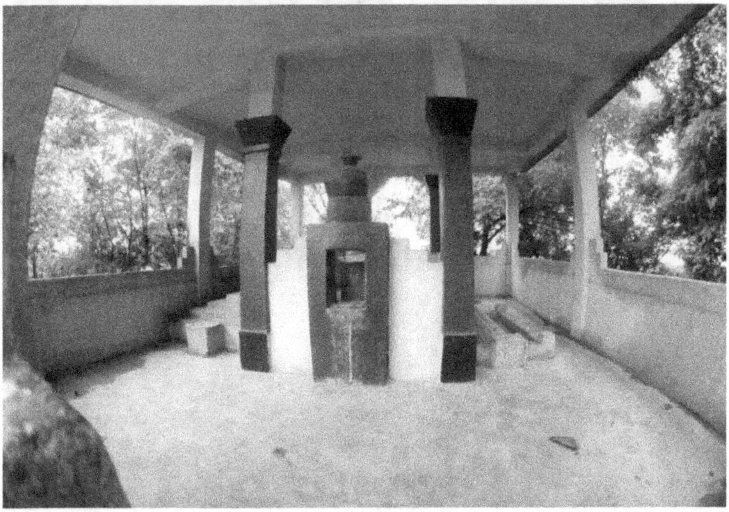

From Satok bazaar you have to take a boat and cross the river by boat to Nuwarai Bazar., Need to park your vehicle somewhere in Satok town.

Ferry cost 1tk per person. There are no directions sign to the mazar; you have to ask the locals for direction.

Md Asmin Shah Fokir

Satok, Shunamgoinj

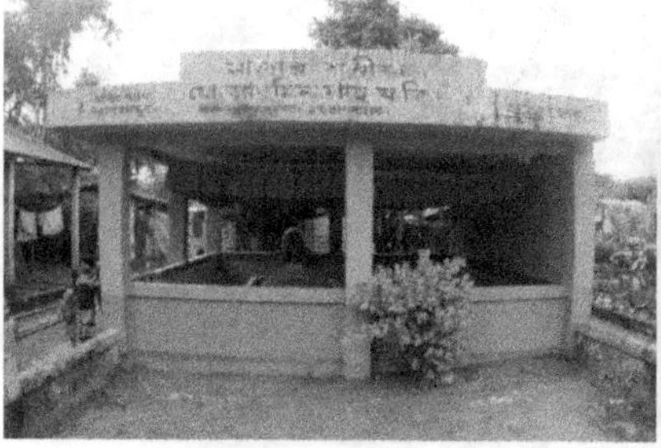

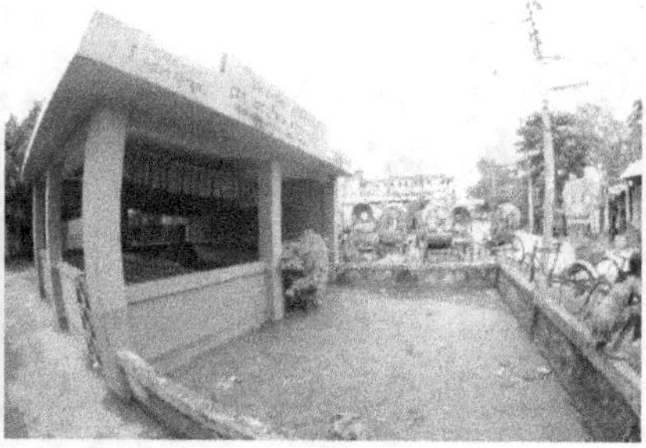

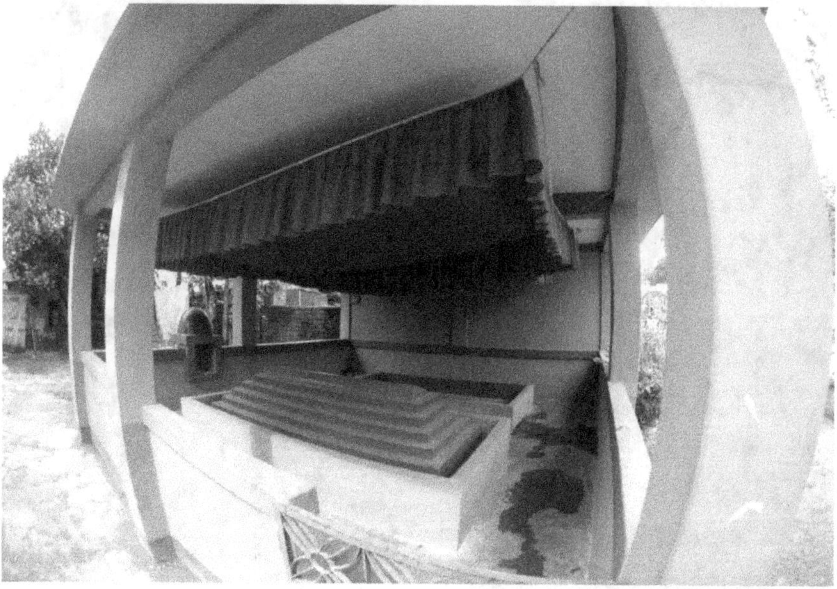

1.1.2011, 18:39:34

Mullah Mubarak Shah

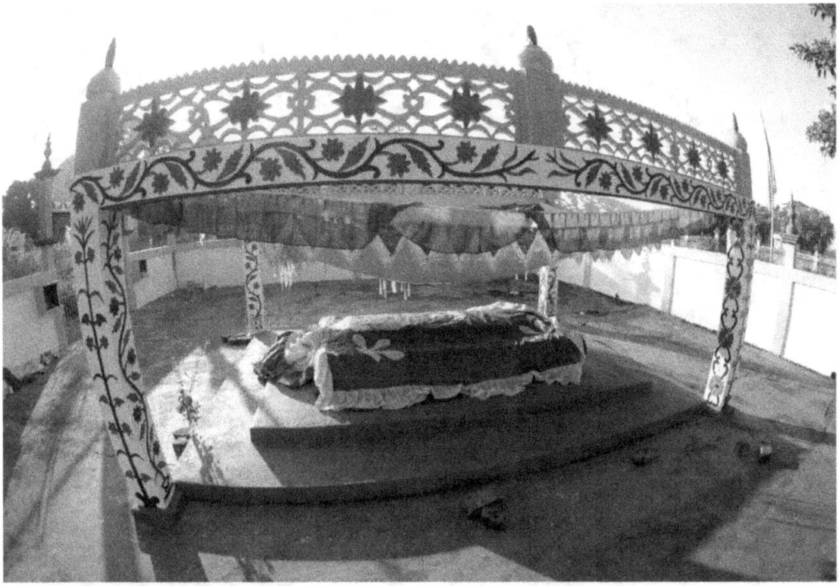

8.1.2011, 16:08

This is my paternal ancestral linage. This was the first place I went and did my salaam. For me this place provided me the serenity and tranquillity. Because this was my paternal ancestral Mazar, I have a long contemplation and spoke to Shah Mullah Mubarak Shab. I was so in the sereneness that I laid down beside the grave and closed my eyes 20-30 minutes. I had no fear, as I only ended up in Bangladeshi because of the Wegener's Granulomatosis and rare vasculitus disease, which was an auto immune disorder; there was no cure and one that, at the time had a life span of up to 4 years. So, I felt at home and I rested as a submission of my body to further soak up the moment.

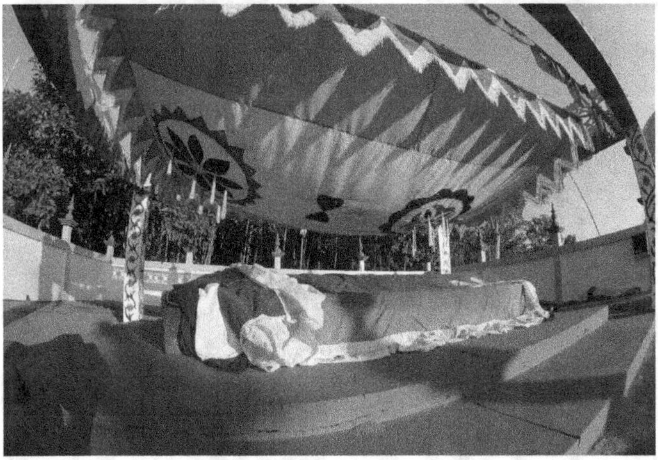

Soyod Shah Mustafa

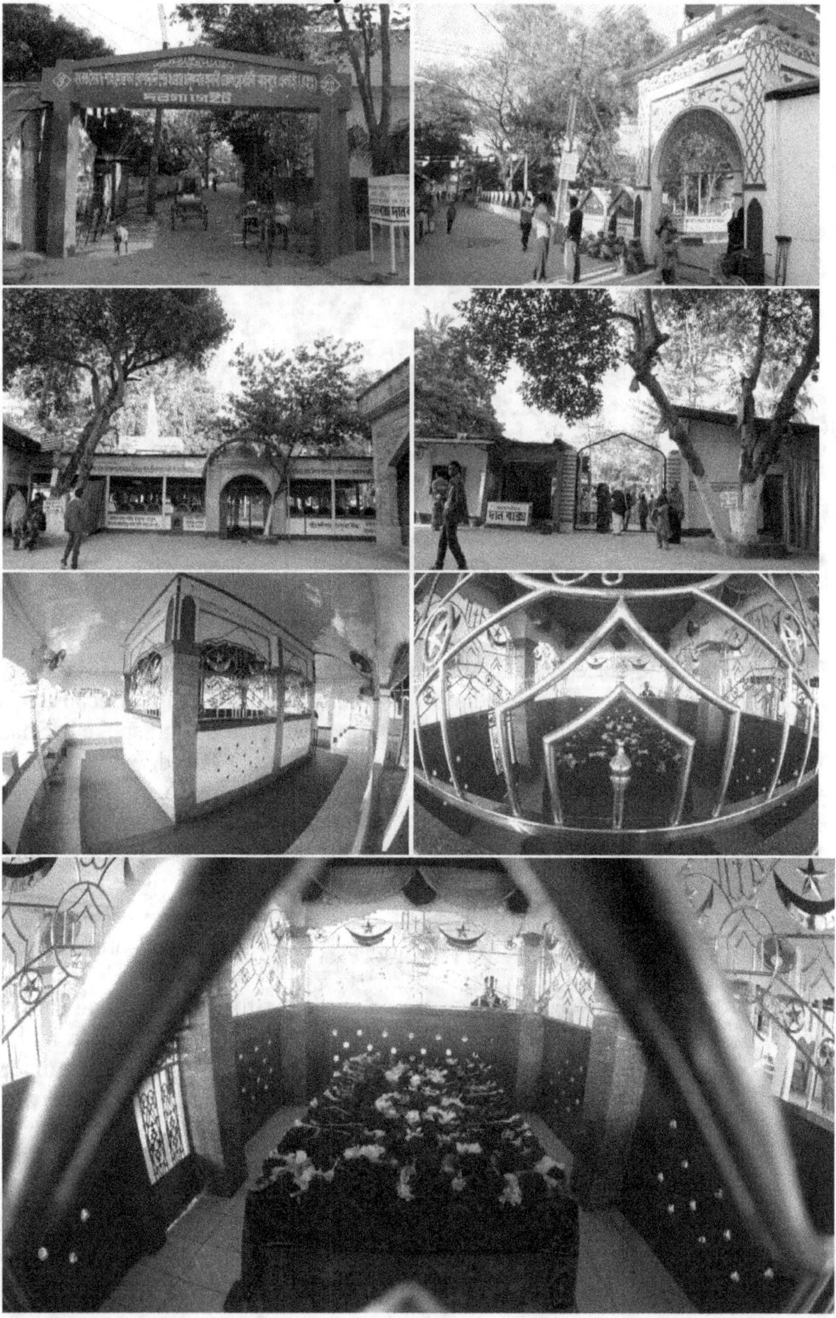

28.1.2011, 16:05

Soyod Shah Ismail Bagdadi

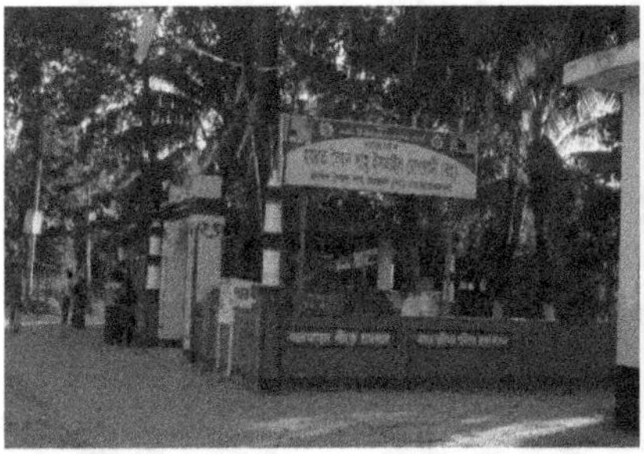

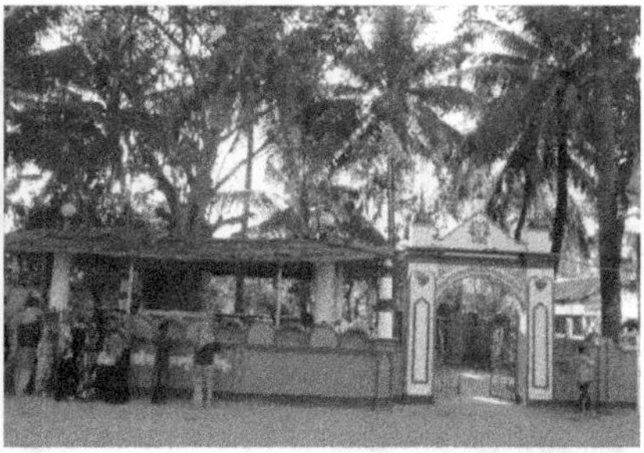

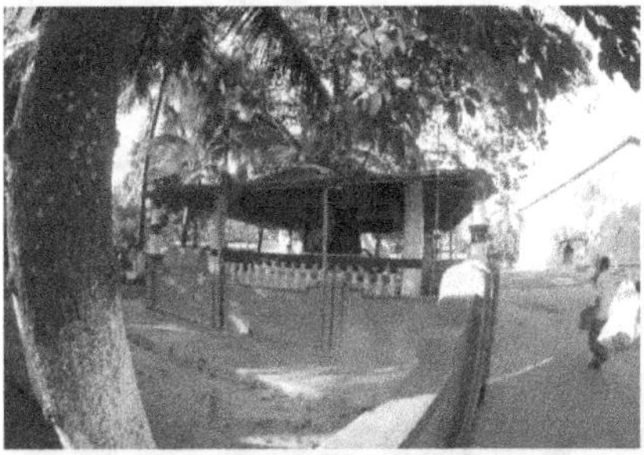

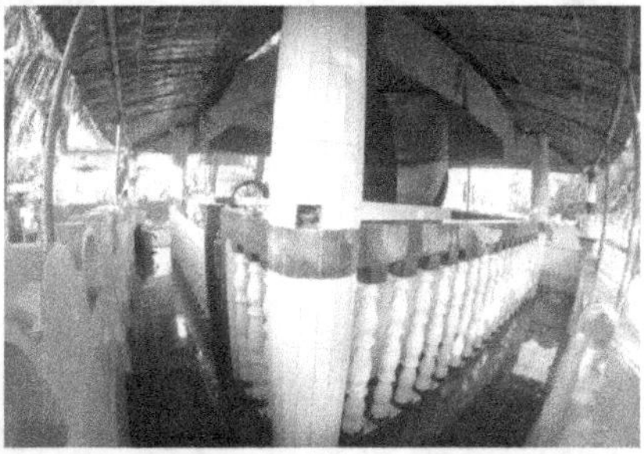

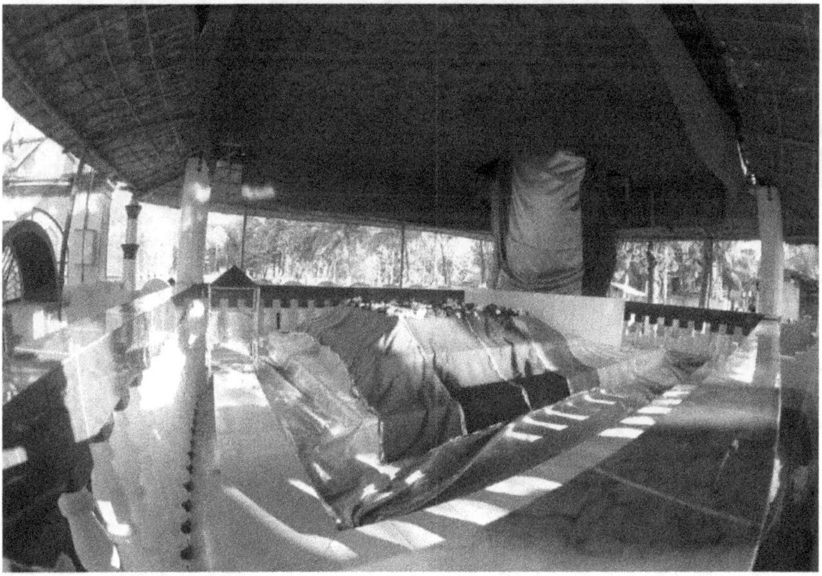

28.1.2011, 16:15

Shah Khuwaz*

Born in Ankara, Turkey

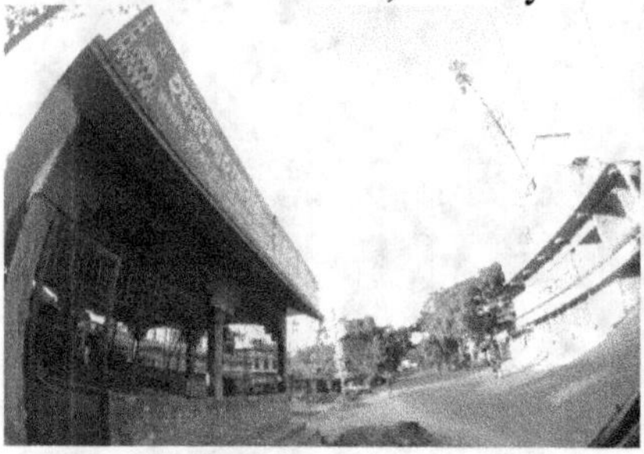

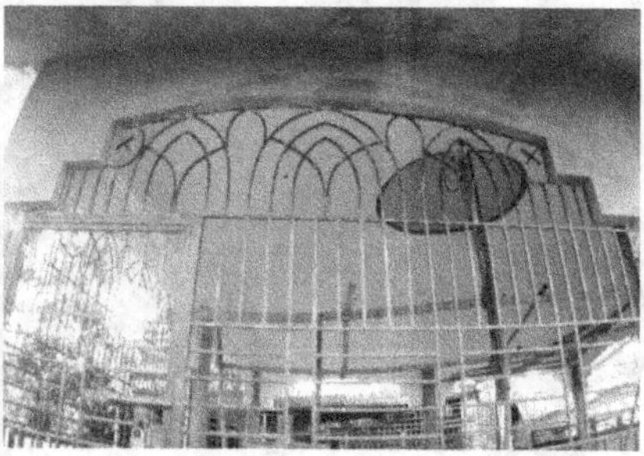

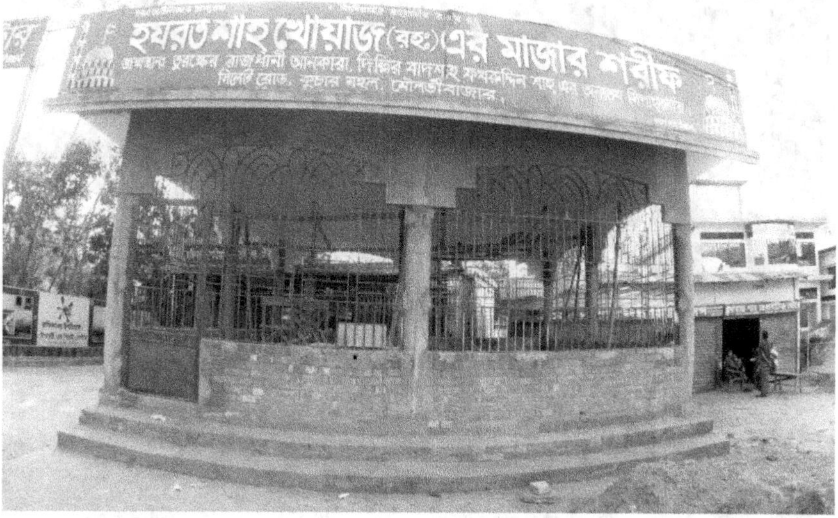
হযরত শাহ খোয়াজ (রহঃ) এর মাজার শরীফ

28.1.2011, 16:27

Shah Kamal*

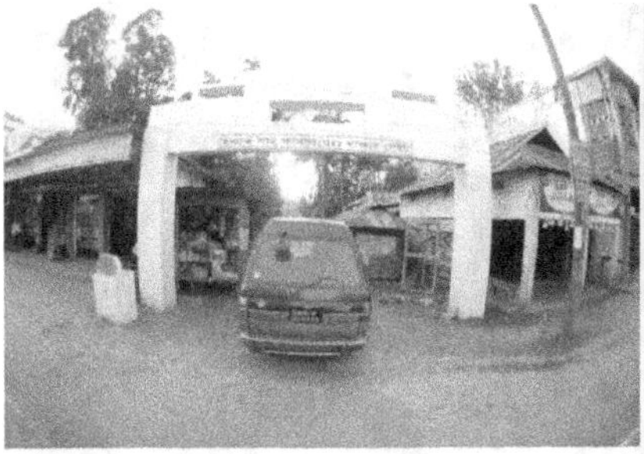

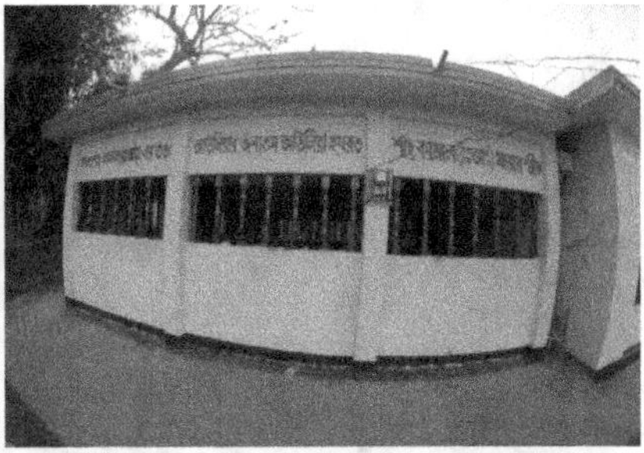

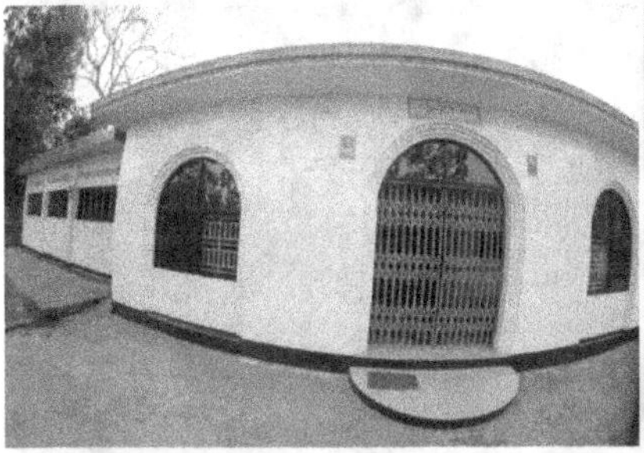

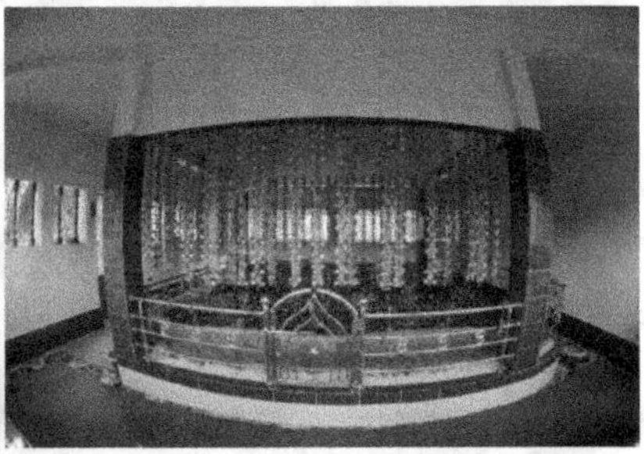

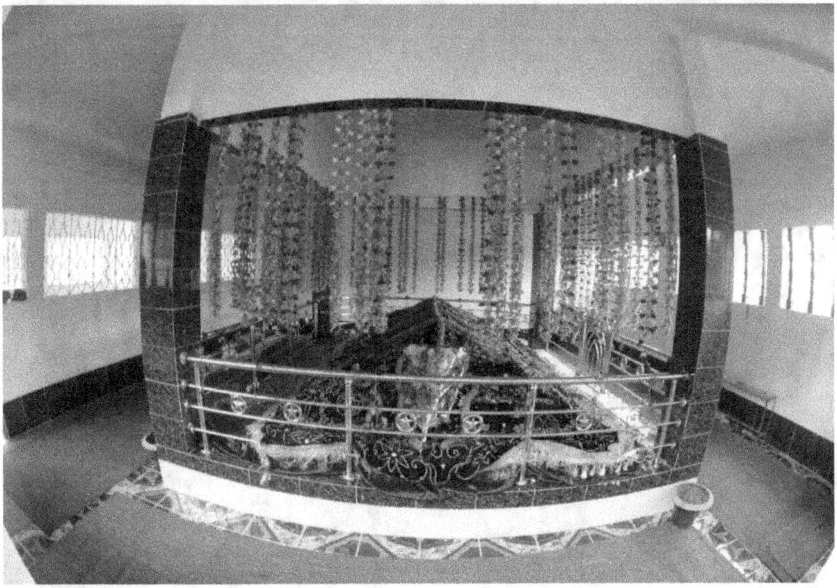

28.1.2011, 16:48

Shah Phatta

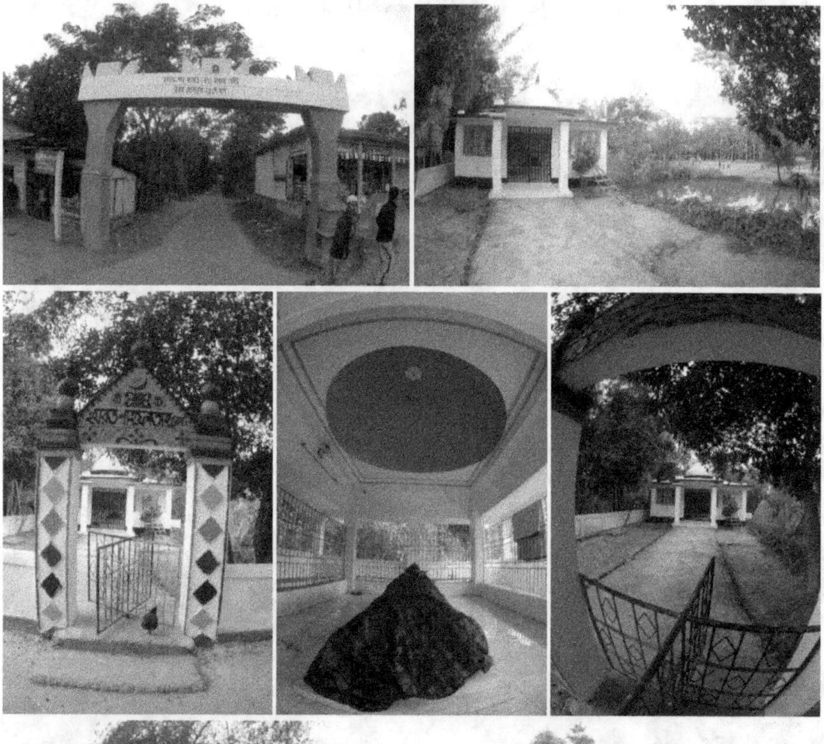

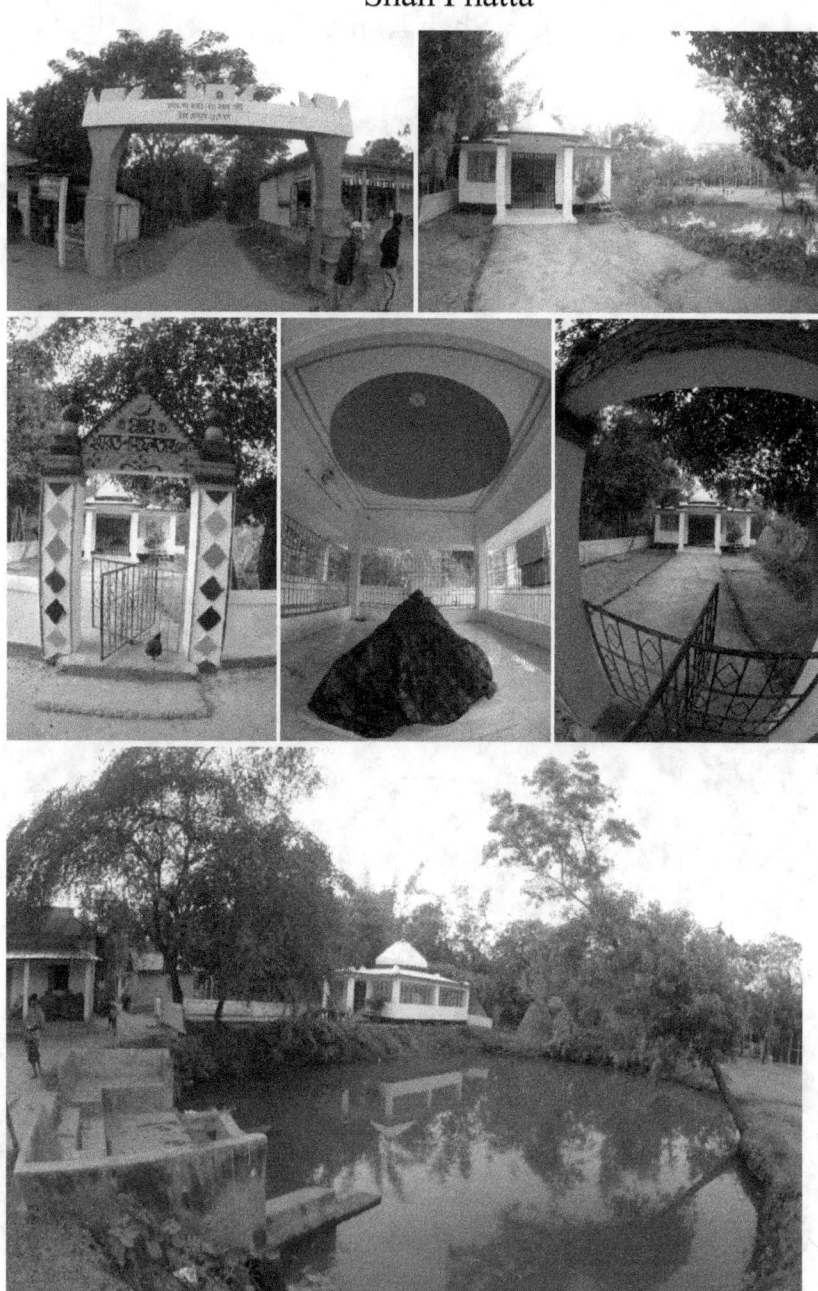

28.1.2011, 17:07

Soyod Shah Darang**

Bekhamura Soyod Bari

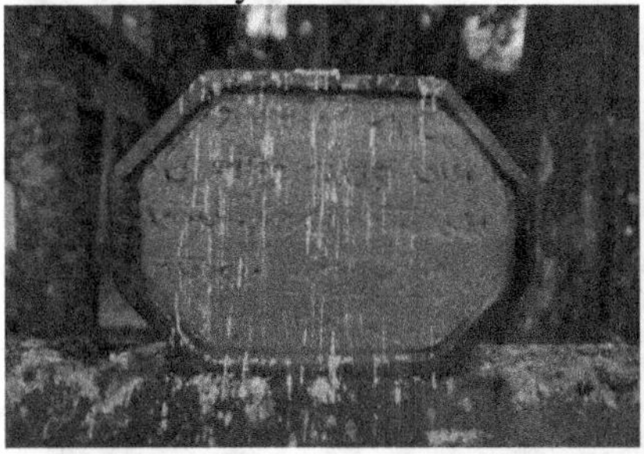
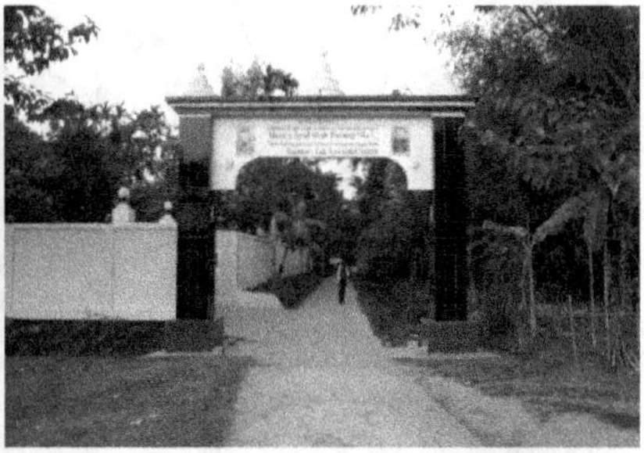
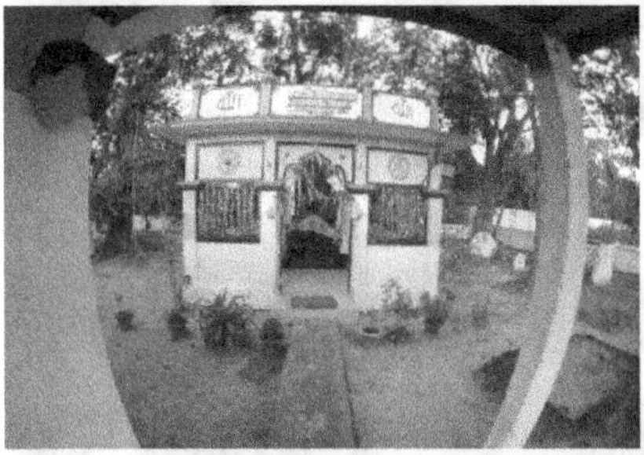
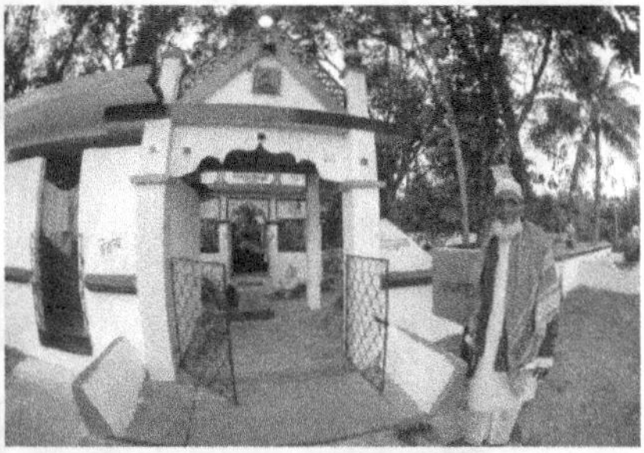
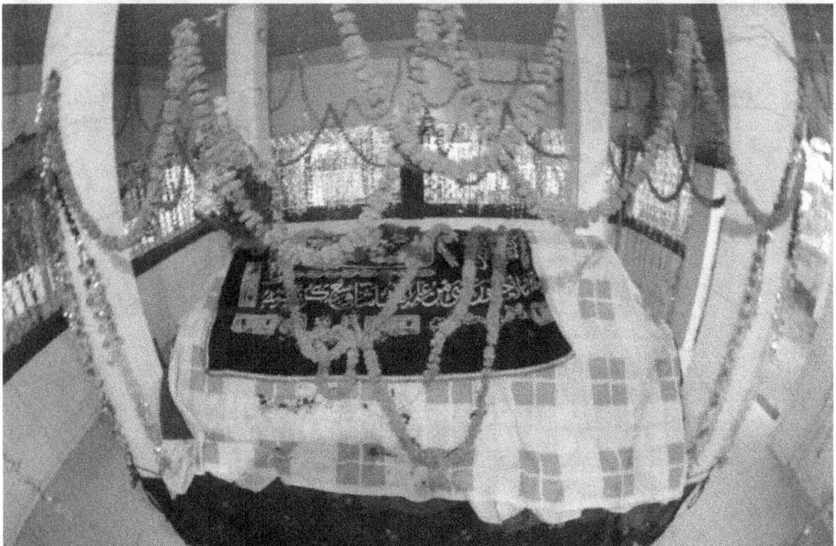

28.1.2011, 18:04

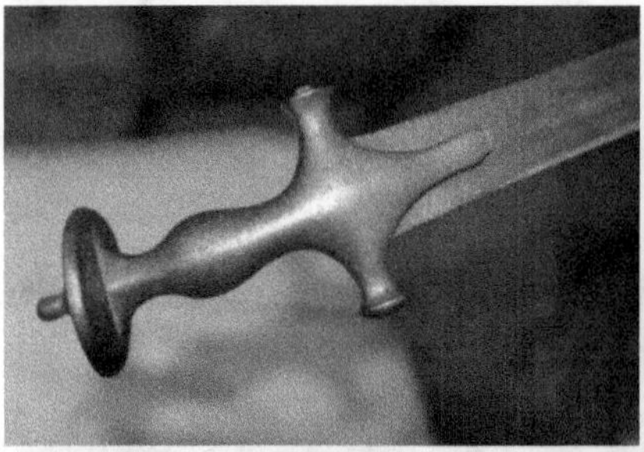
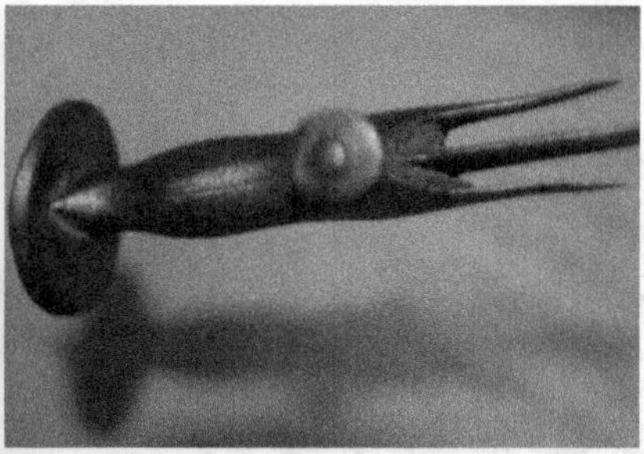

Hazrat Soyod Shah Dorang's swords and his cast iron bangle

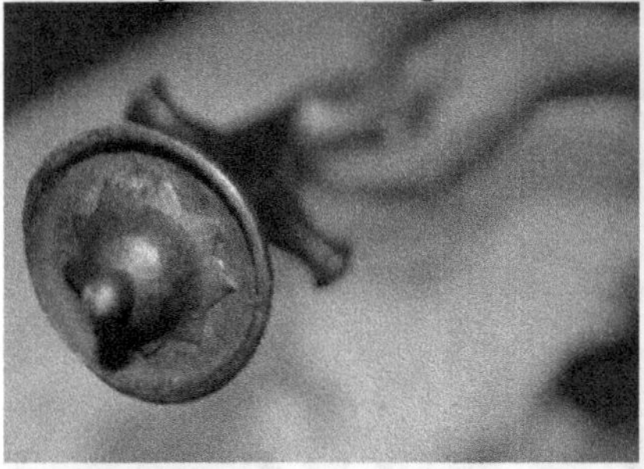
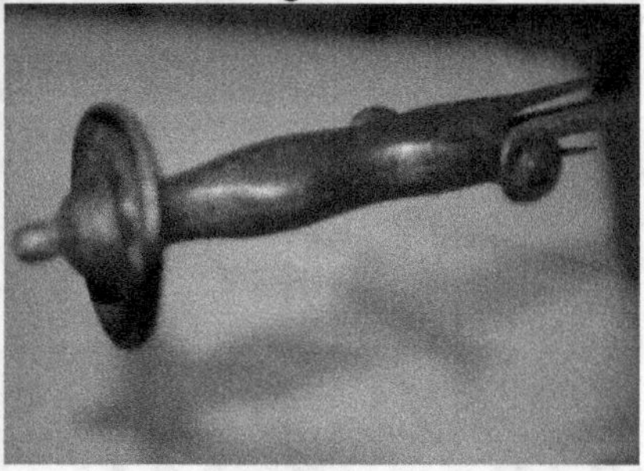
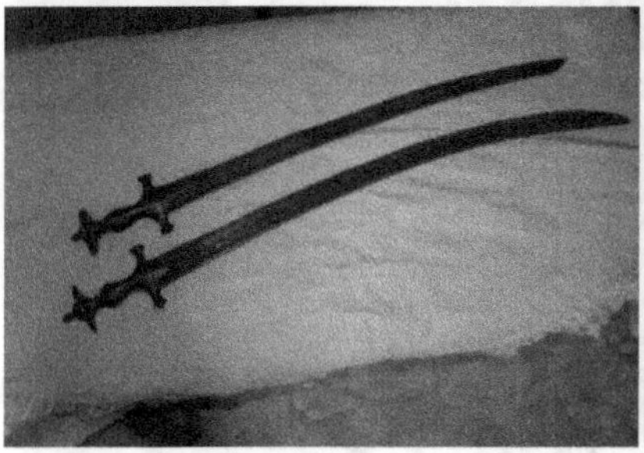
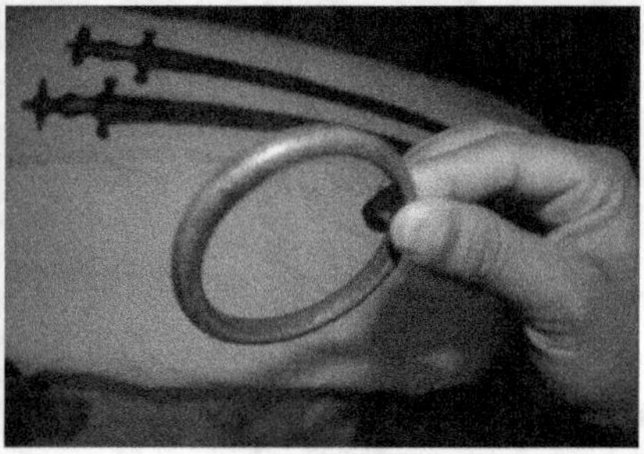
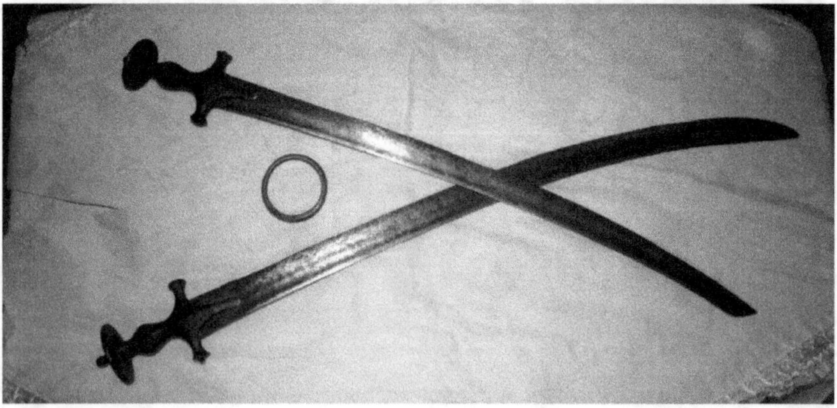

February 2011

Murarbond, Torof

Hazrat Nasir Uddin Sipah Salar**

Murarbond, Loshkorpur Habeli, Torof, Shayestagoinj, Hobigonj

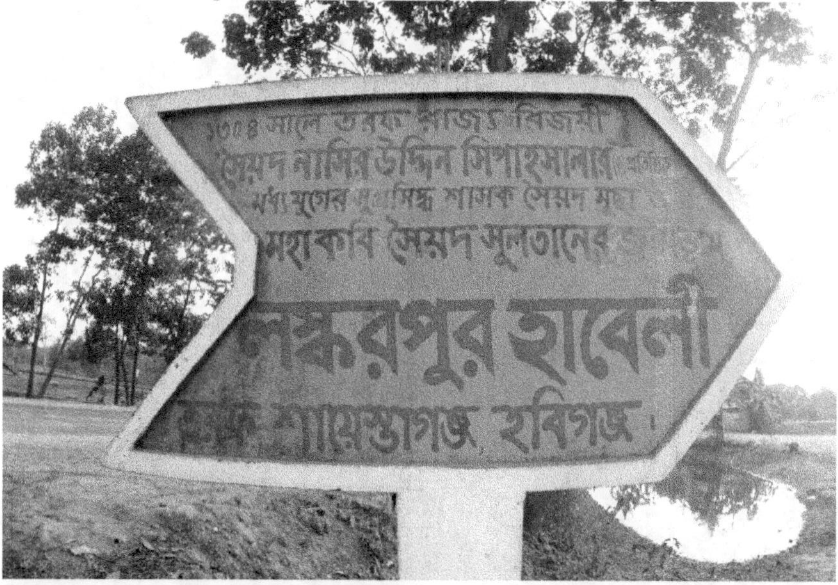
১৩০৪ সালে তরফ রাজ্য বিজয়ী
সৈয়দ নাসির উদ্দিন সিপাহসালার
মহা কবি সৈয়দ সুলতানের
লষ্করপুর হাবেলী
শায়েস্তাগঞ্জ, হবিগঞ্জ।

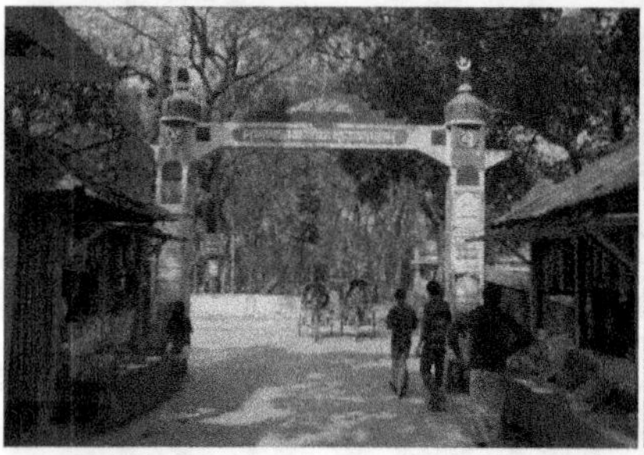

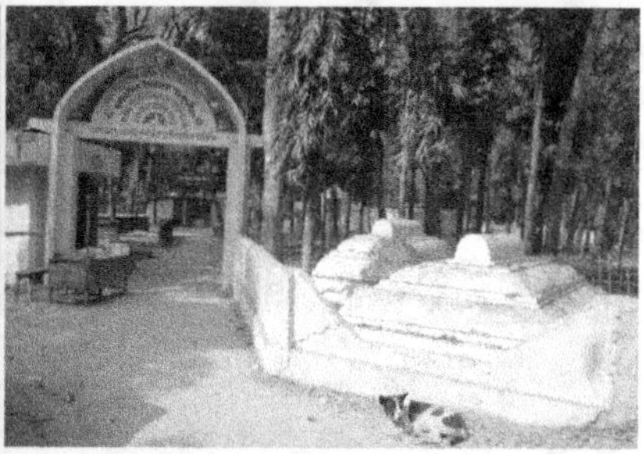

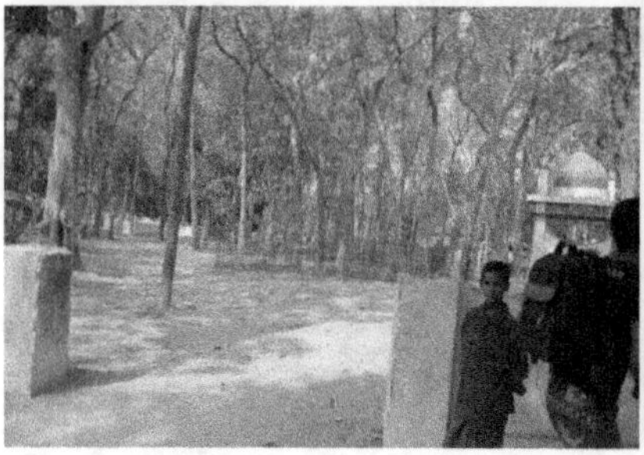

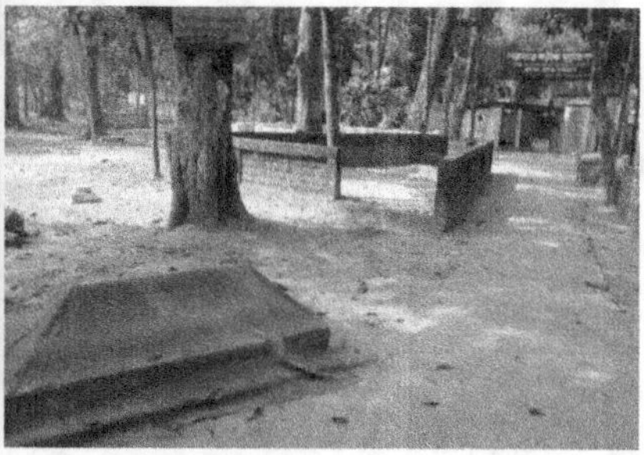

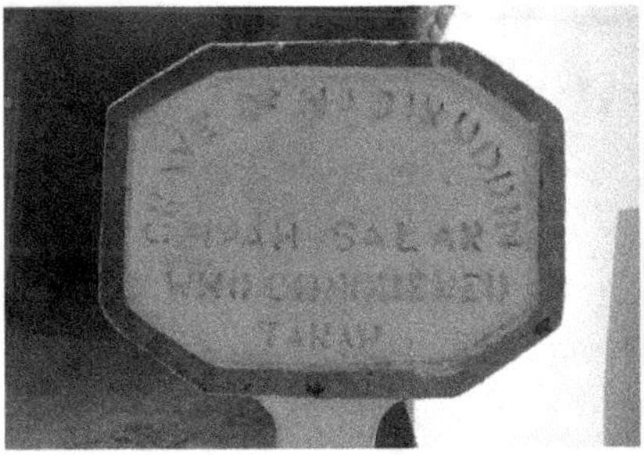
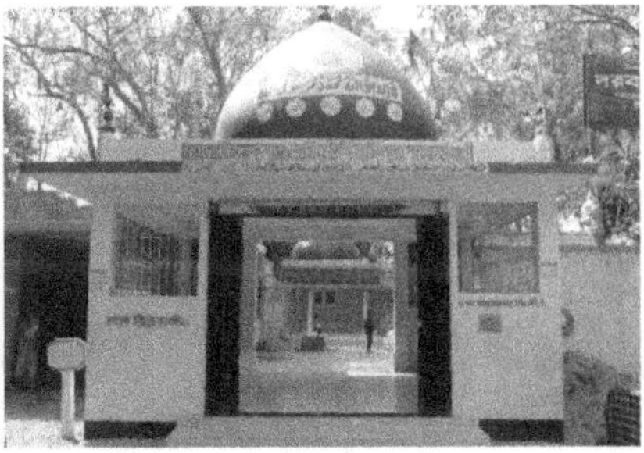
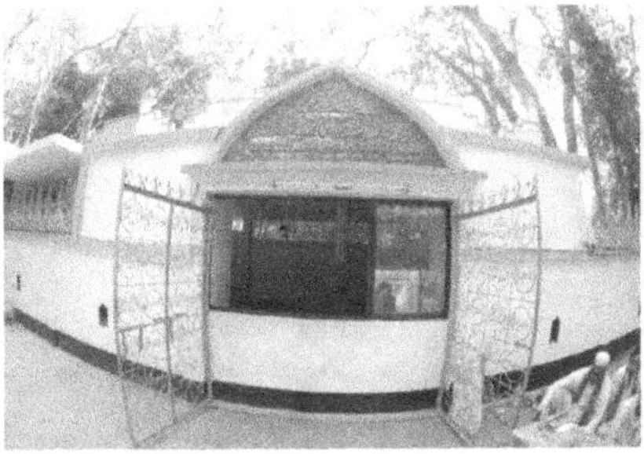
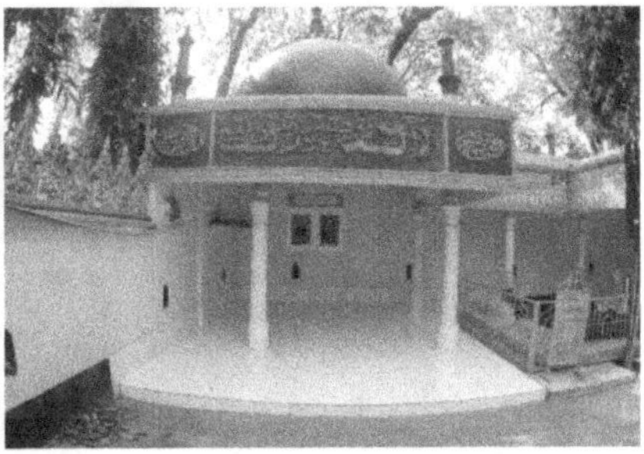
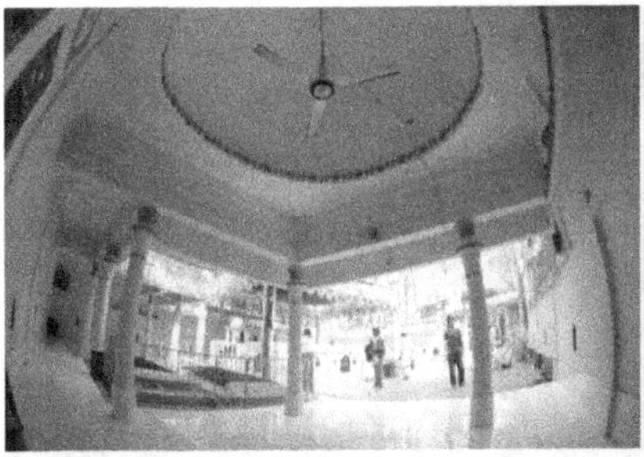
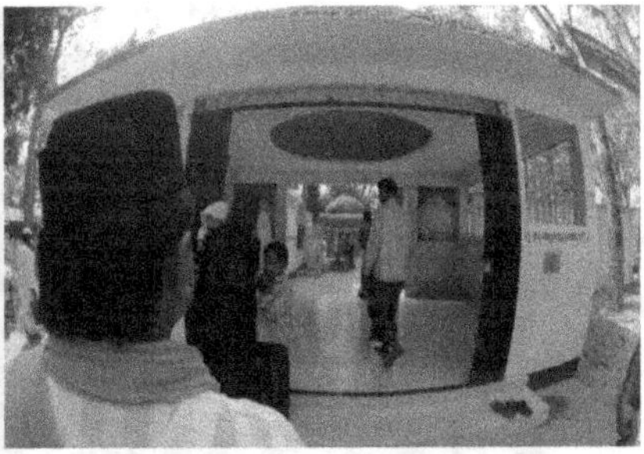
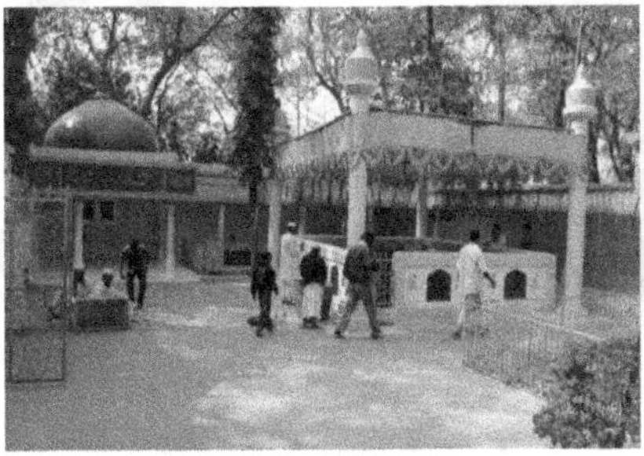
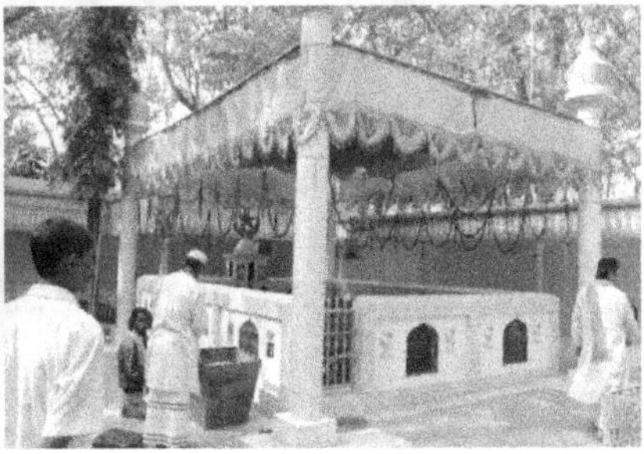

This is was an epic site - it has huge significance in the Sylheti Sufi history. Where the second of main battles took place with the Hindu Kings of the time.

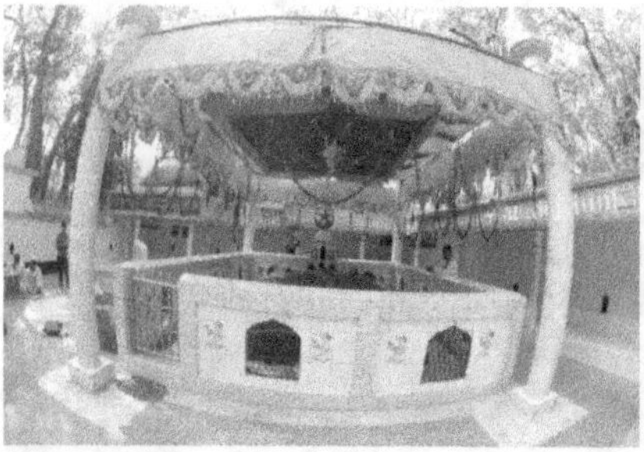

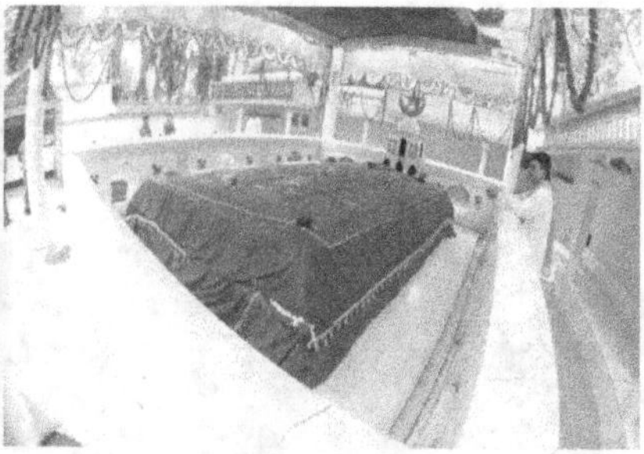

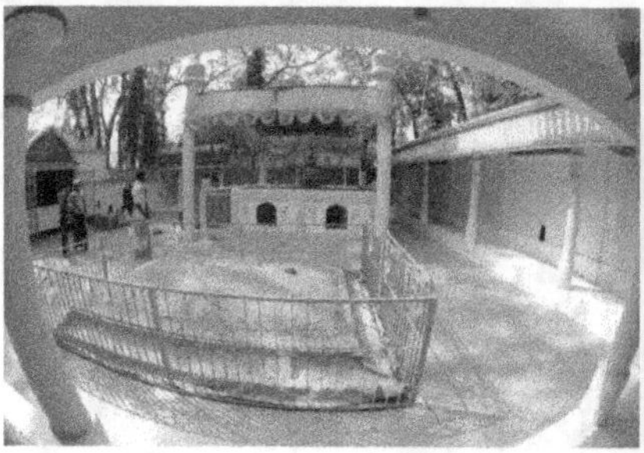

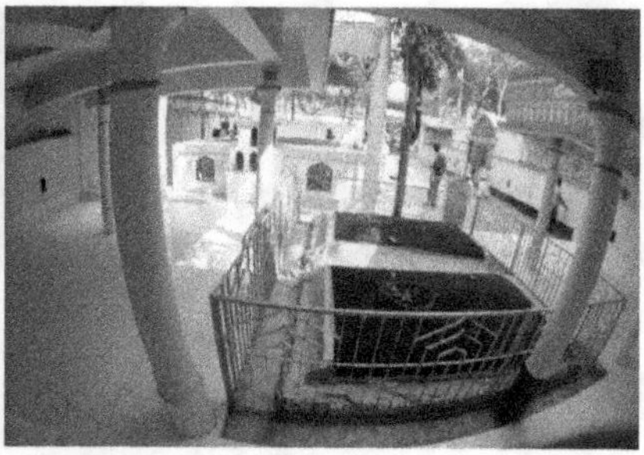

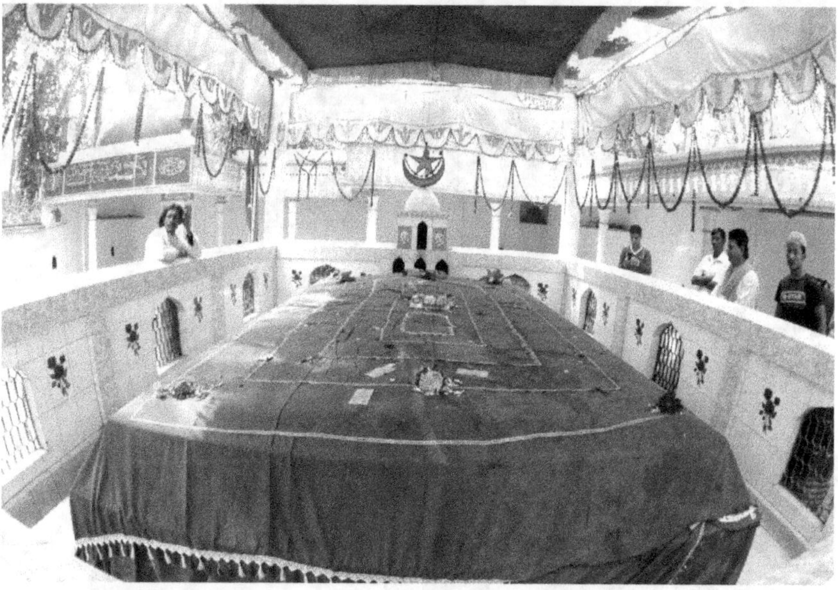

9.2.2011, 13:23

Plot of 120 lost missionaries**

Murarbond

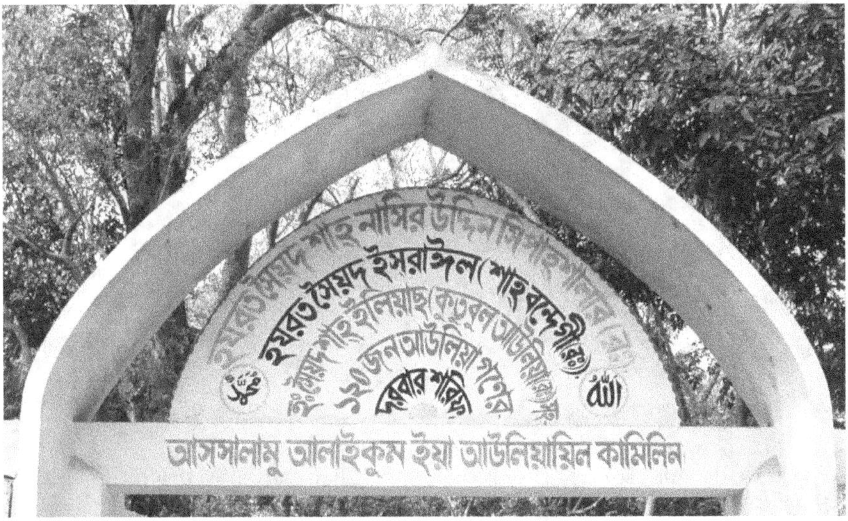
দরবার শরীফ
আসসালামু আলাইকুম ইয়া আউলিয়ায়িল কামিলিন

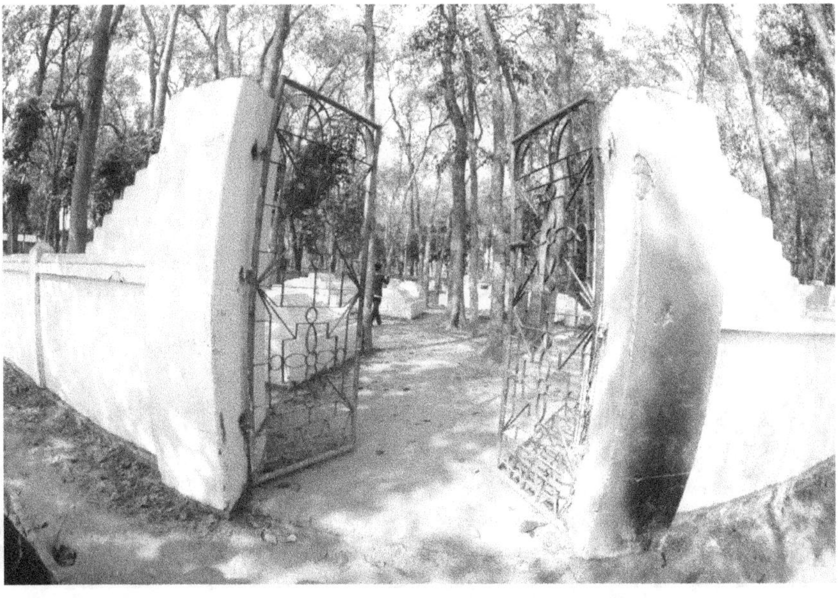

This is the entrance to the graves of the 120 of Hazrat Shah Jalal's companions, who had fallen – these graves have no names.

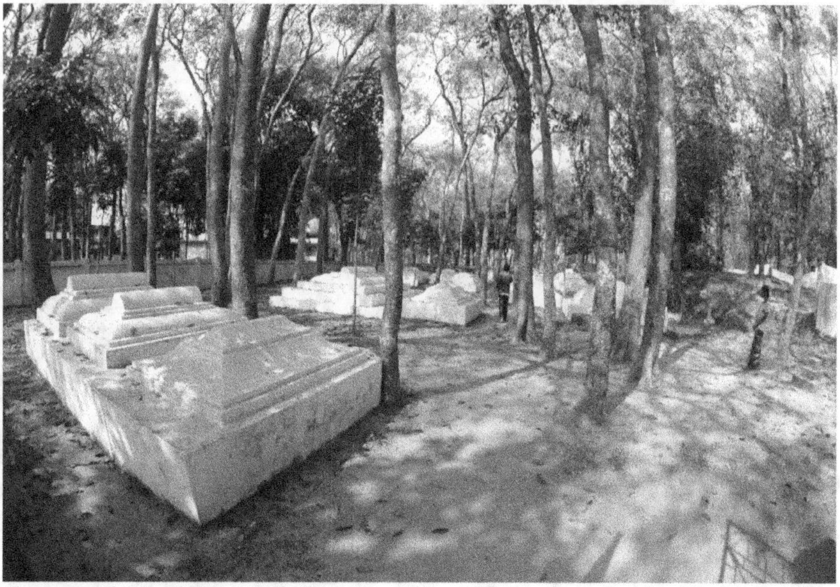

These are the burial grounds for some of the 120 missionaries that died in battle.

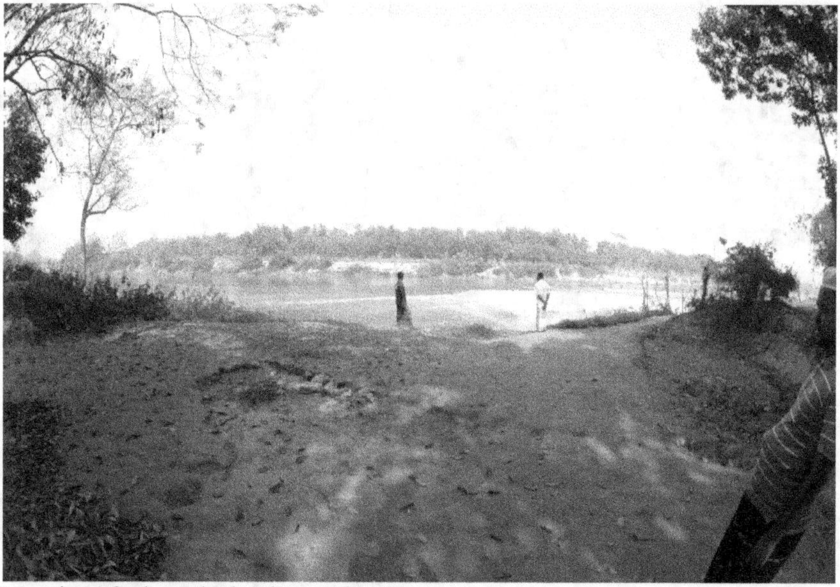

Location of where the battle was fought.

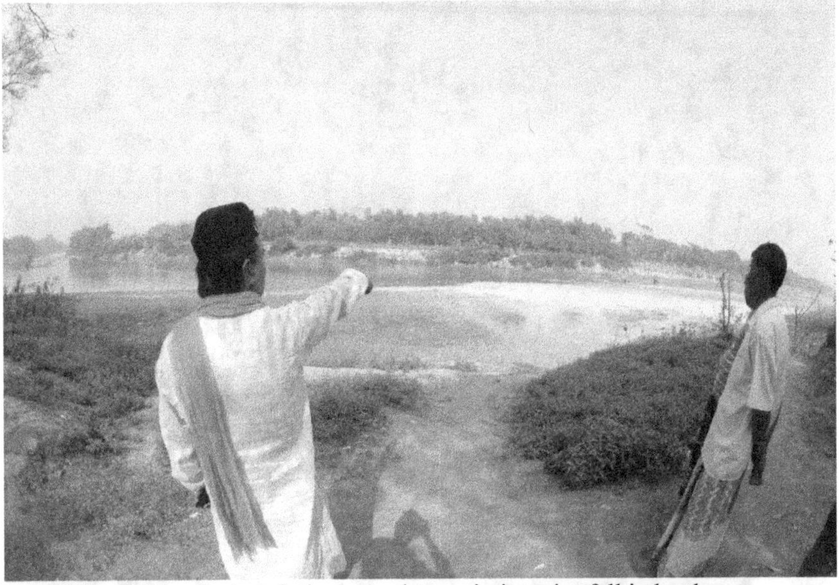

The Kadim of the site is pointing out where missionaries fell in battle.

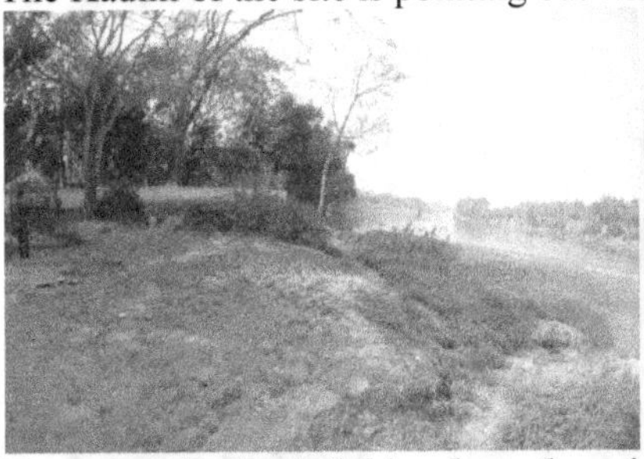

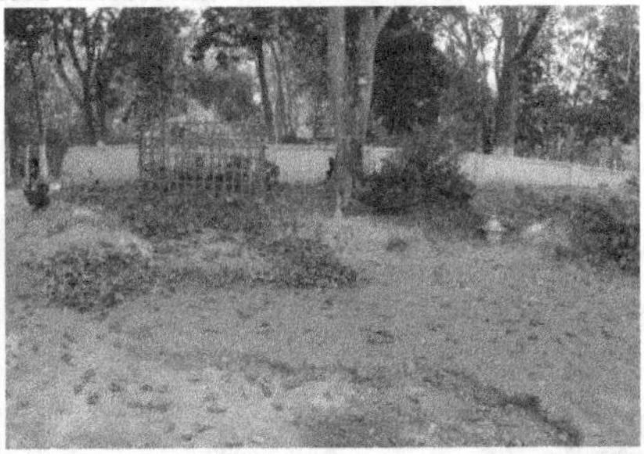

These are the battlefields where the missionaries died in battle. These are other tombs in Murarbond.

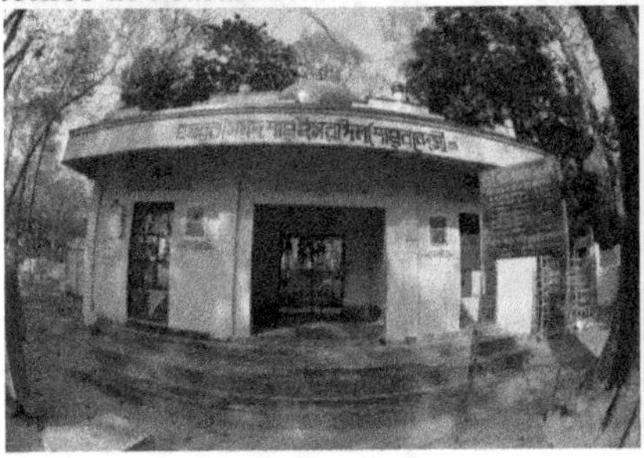

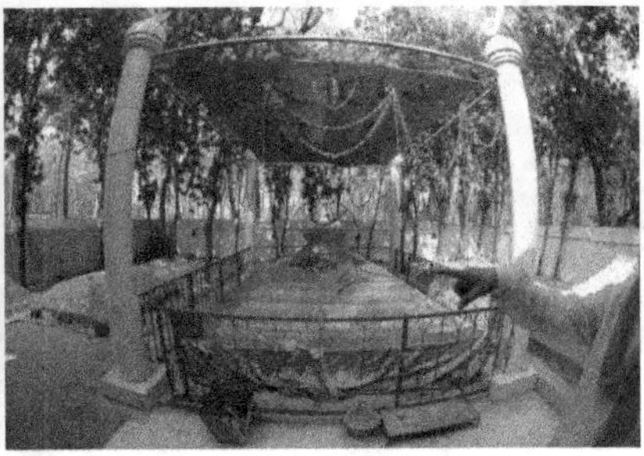

9.2.2011, 14:03.

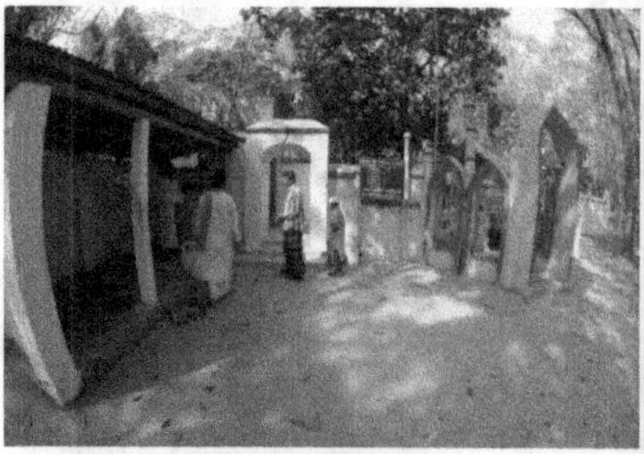
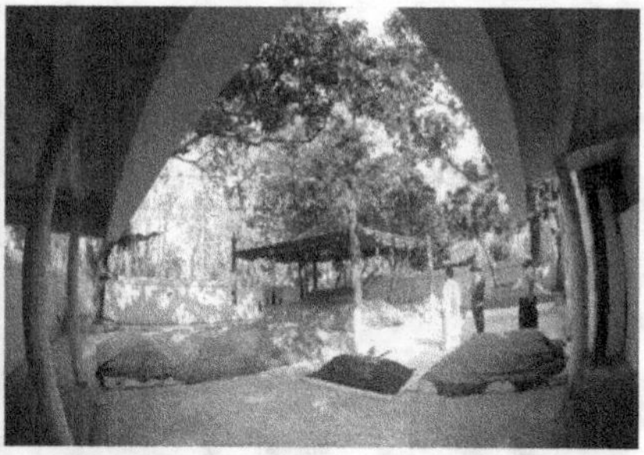
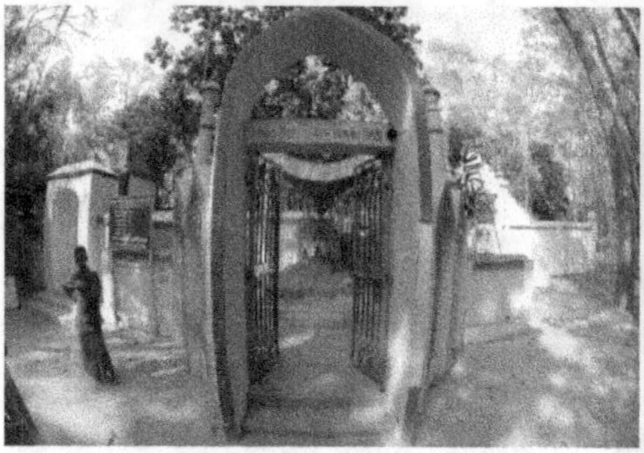
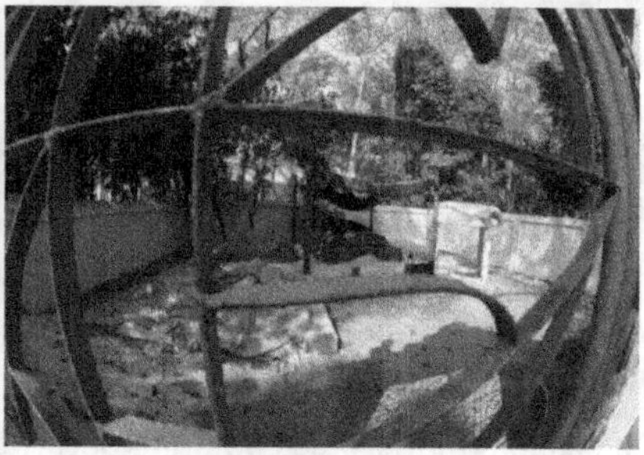
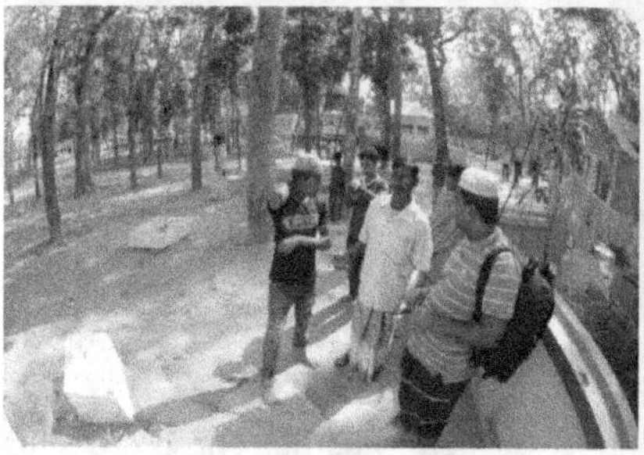
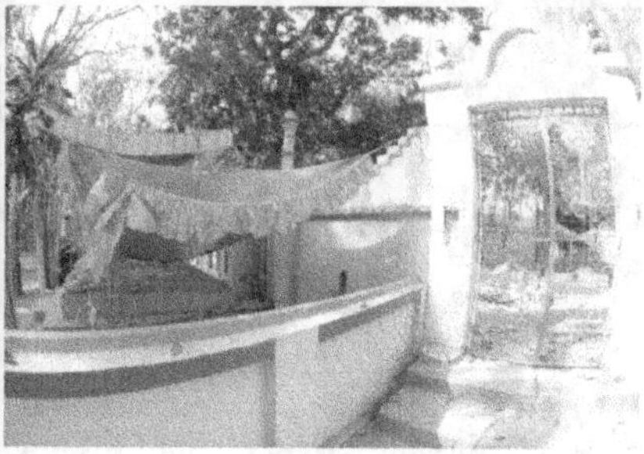
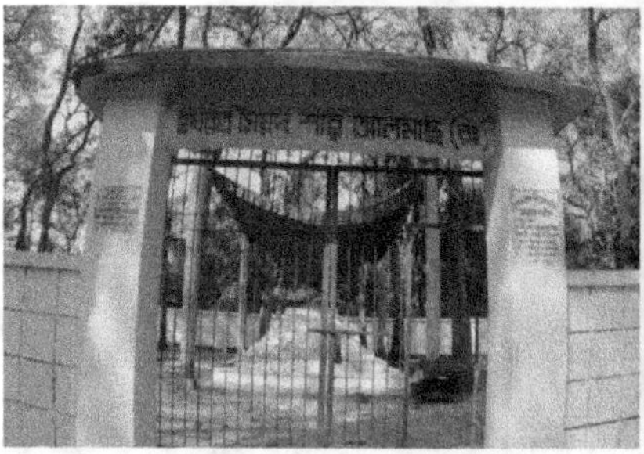
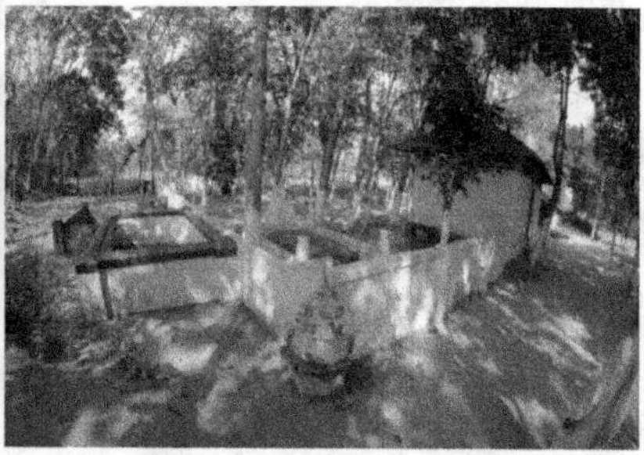

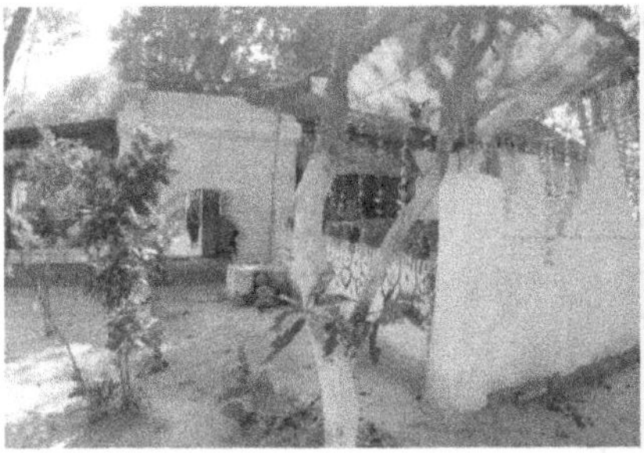

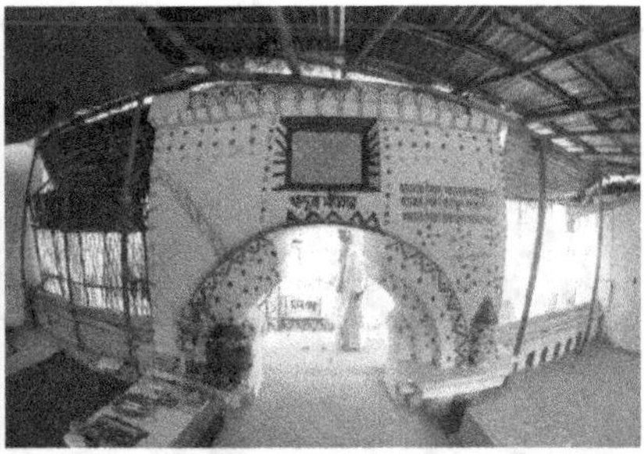

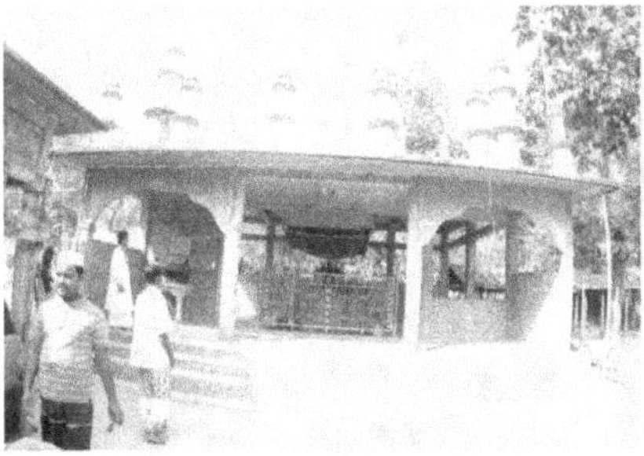

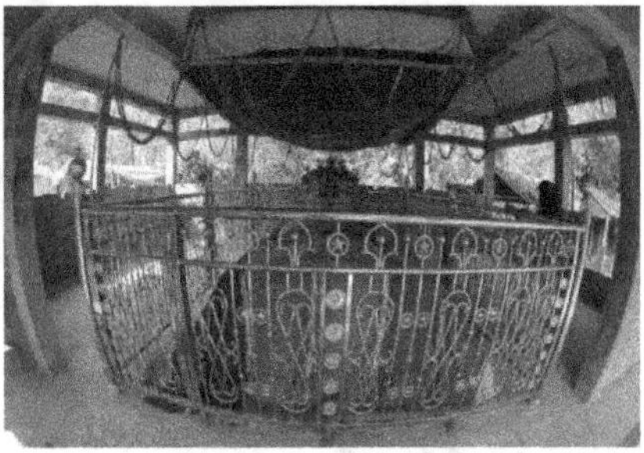

Soyod Shah Goda Hasan

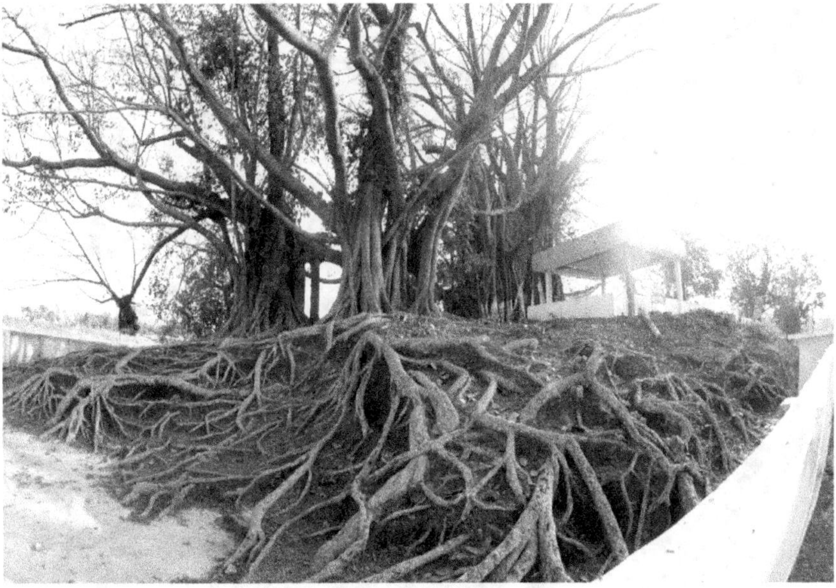

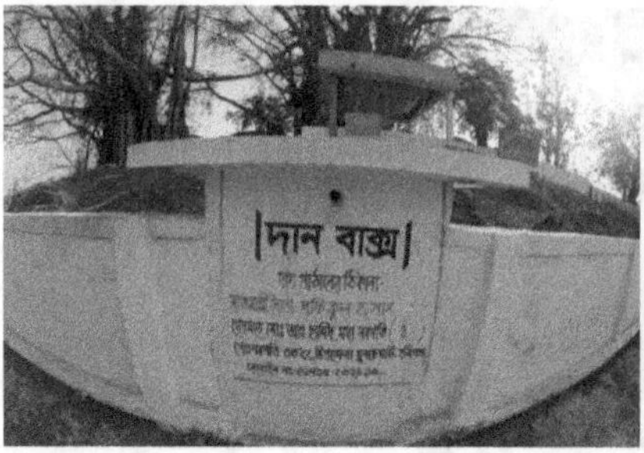
দান বাক্স

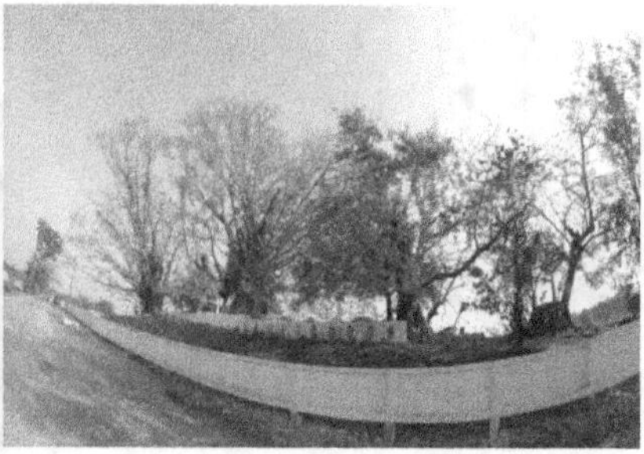

This not credited with the 8 sided plaque.

Dewan Soyod Mahbubur Reja

a.k.a., Madari Shah

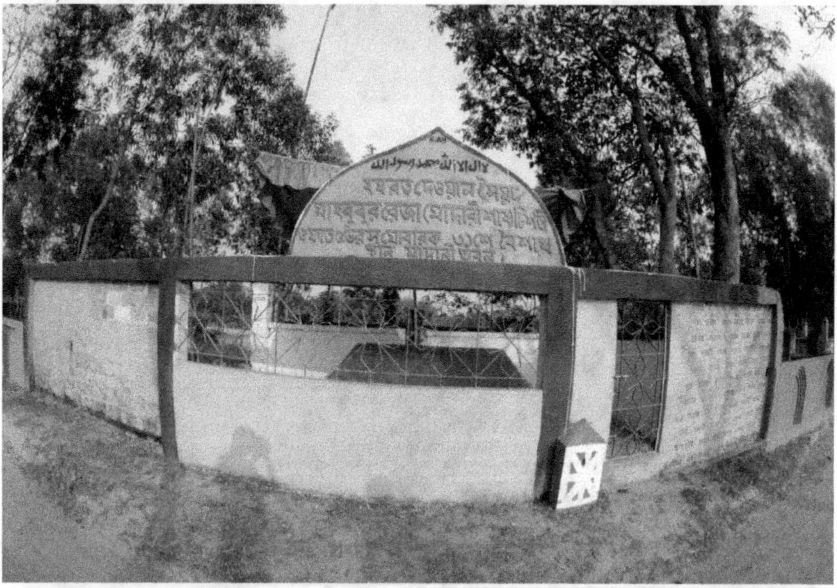
لا اله الا الله محمد رسول الله
হযরত দেওয়ান সৈয়দ
মাহবুবুর রেজা (মোদারী শাহ)

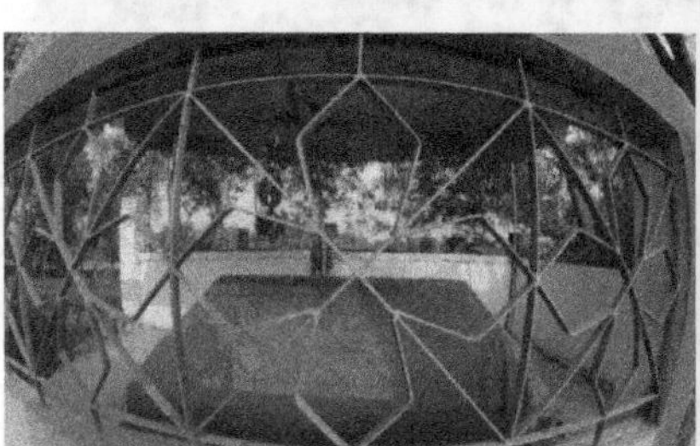

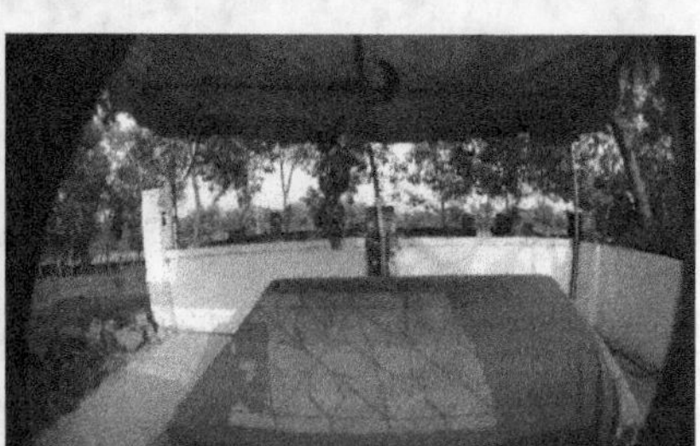

Soyod Shah Musa

a.k.a., Moina

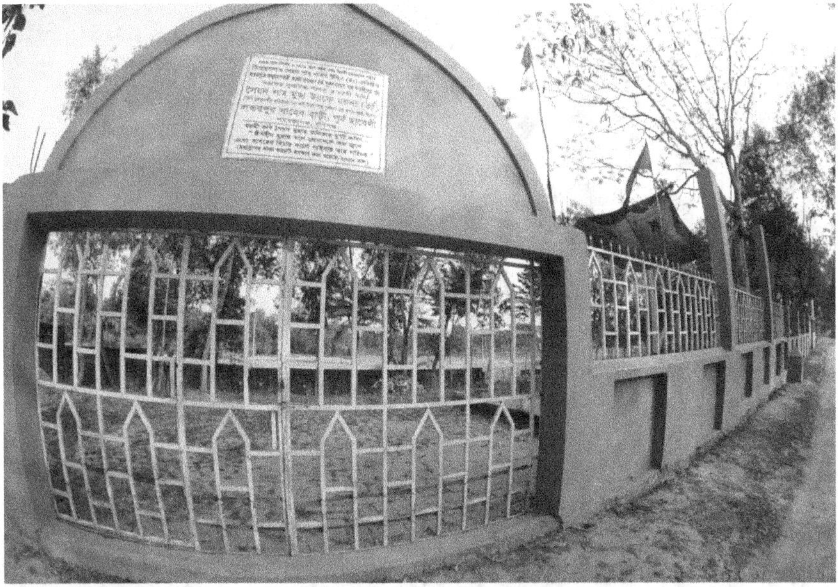

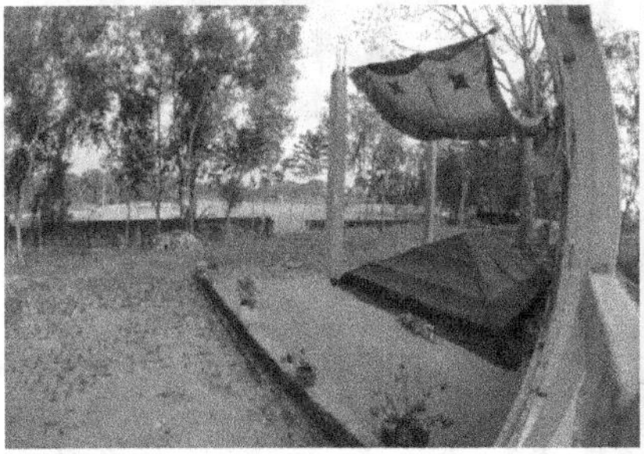

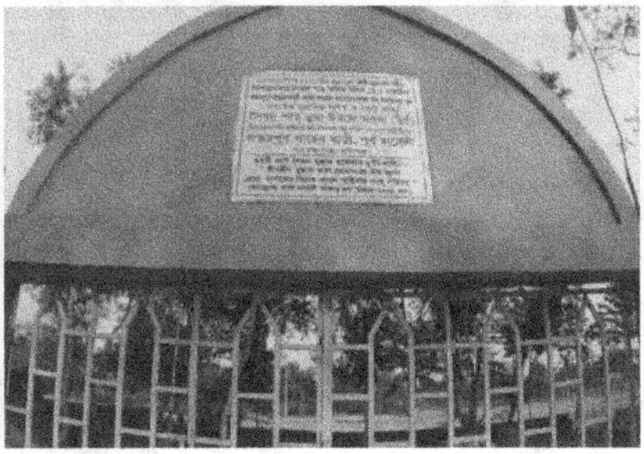

This place is not credited with the 8 sided plaque.

Recent discovery at Torof.

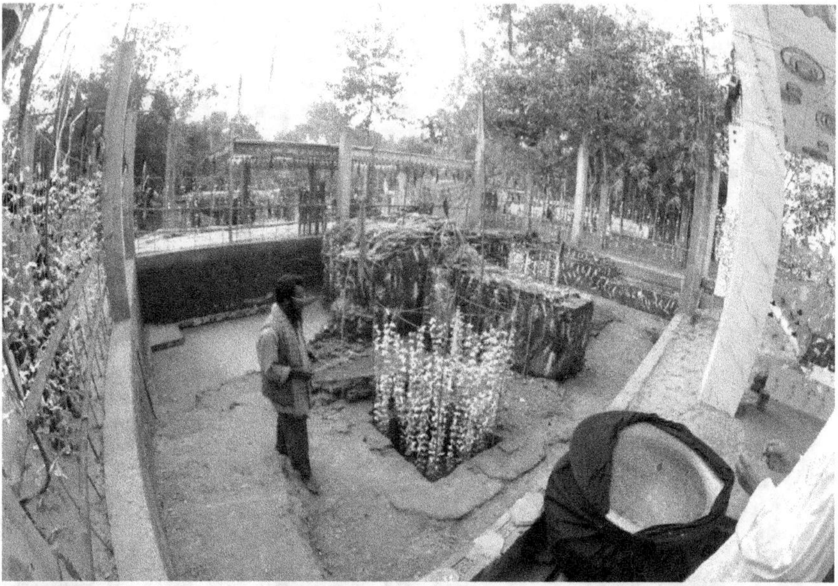

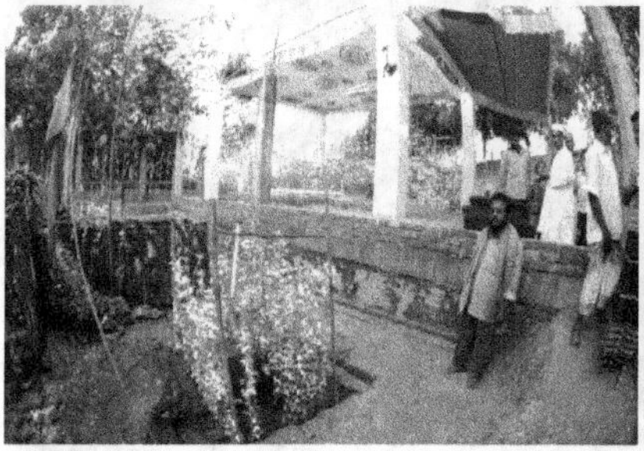

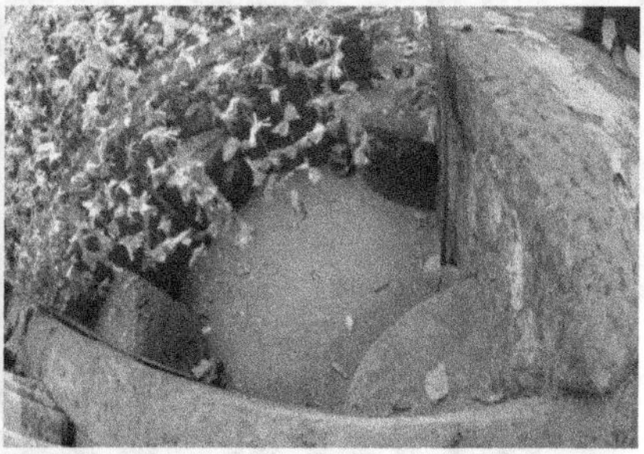

Bathing pool with corner stones to sit

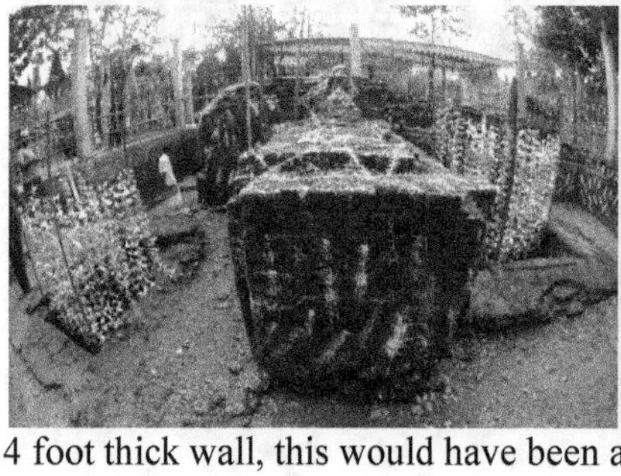

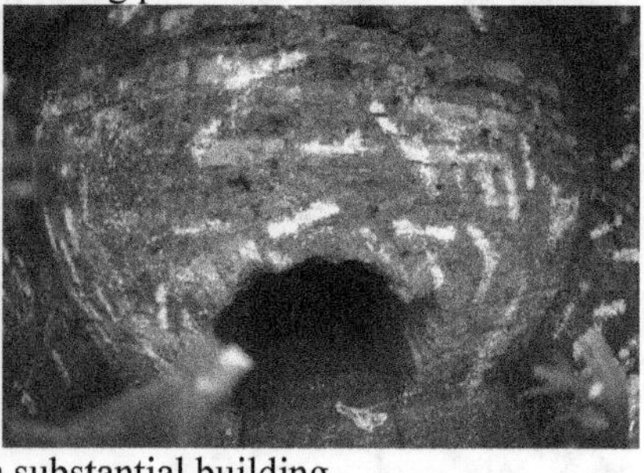

4 foot thick wall, this would have been a substantial building.

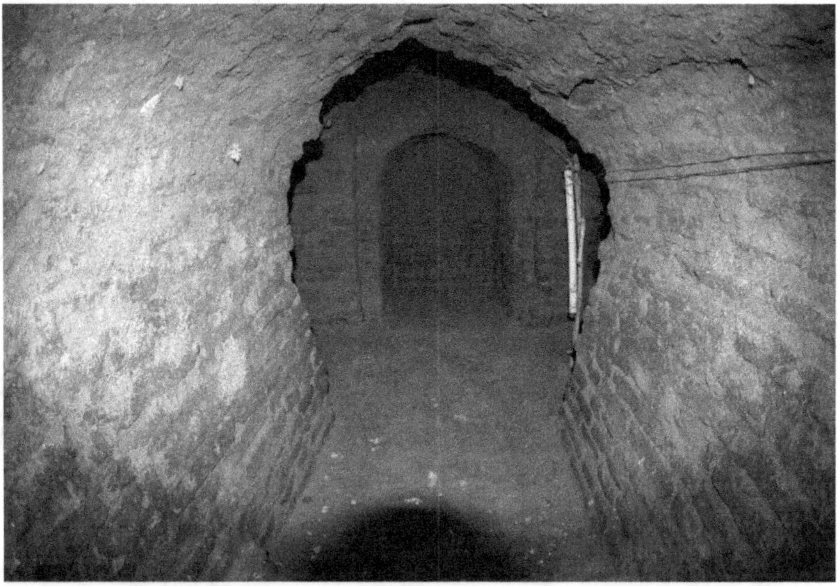

This is the tunnel leading into the contemplation room.

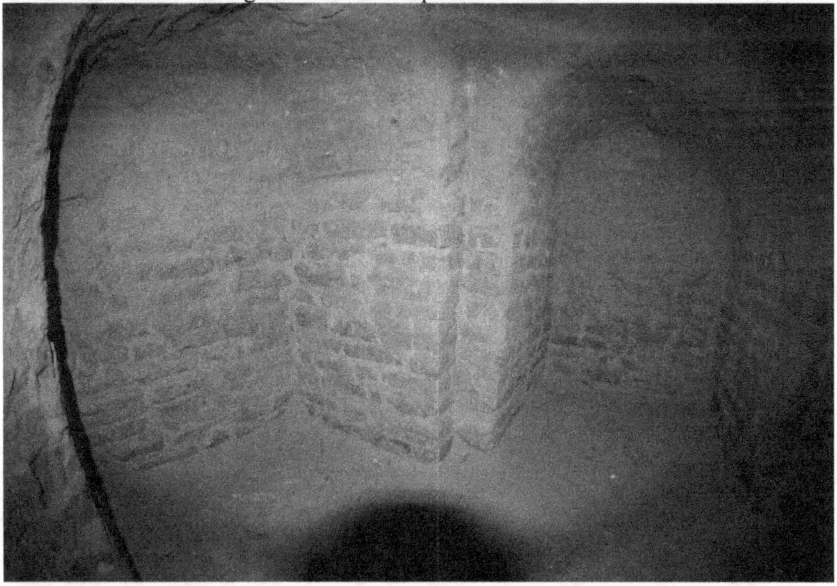

Inside there were 4 alcoves, 4 people can contemplate in silence and most importantly in the dark.

This place does give you a sense of "back in the old days."

This is a short entrance tunnel, in and out of the contemplation coves.

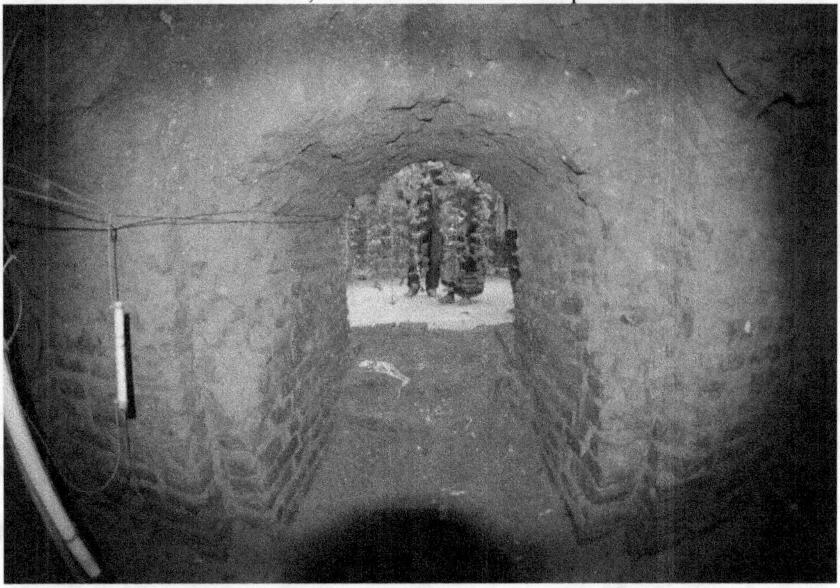

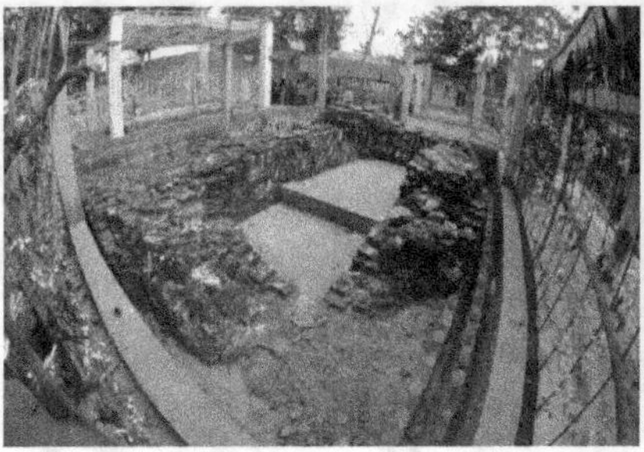

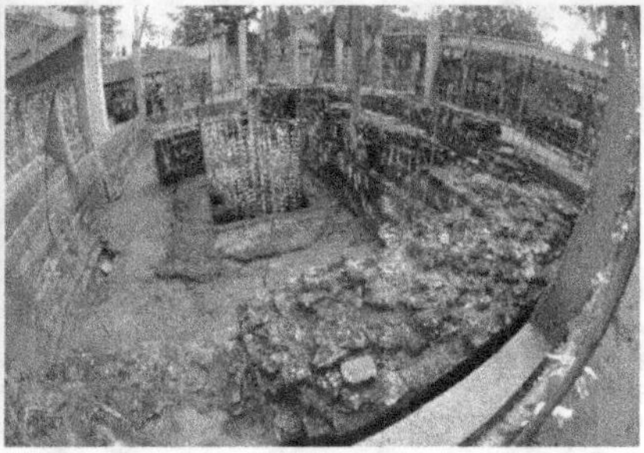

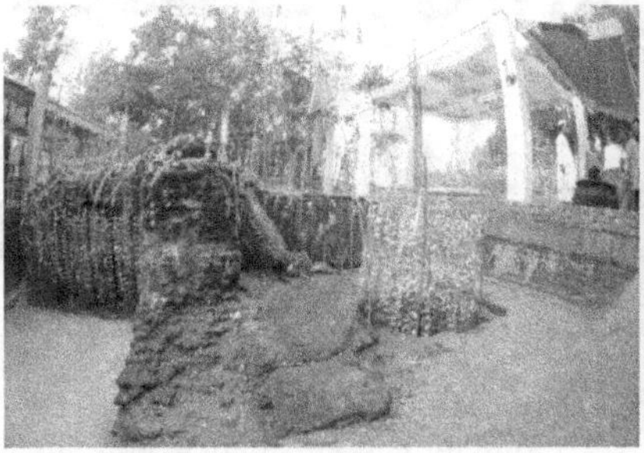

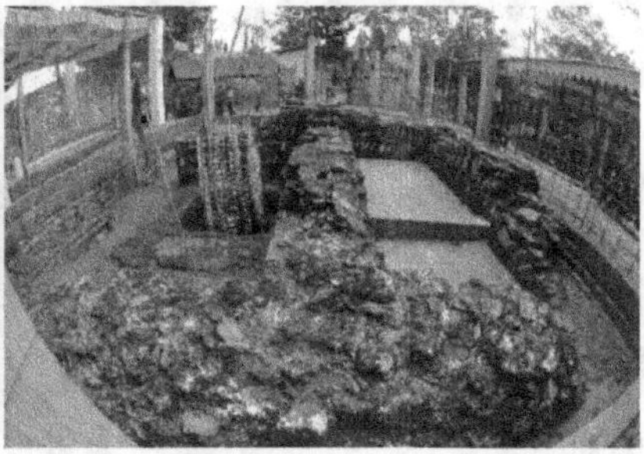

This discovery unearthed a bathing pool, and contemplation room. These were serious Sufi practitioners of that time.

9.2.2011, 16:47

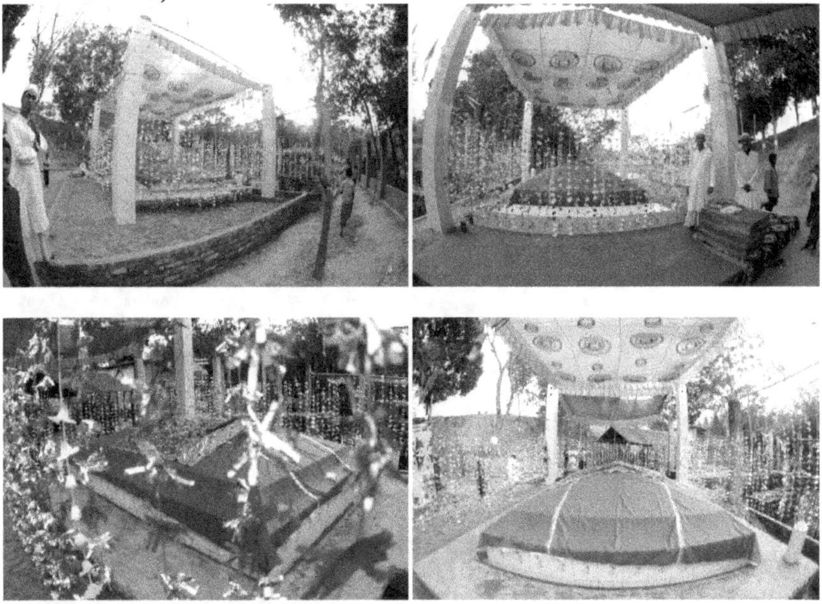

Mazar discovered in the vicinity.

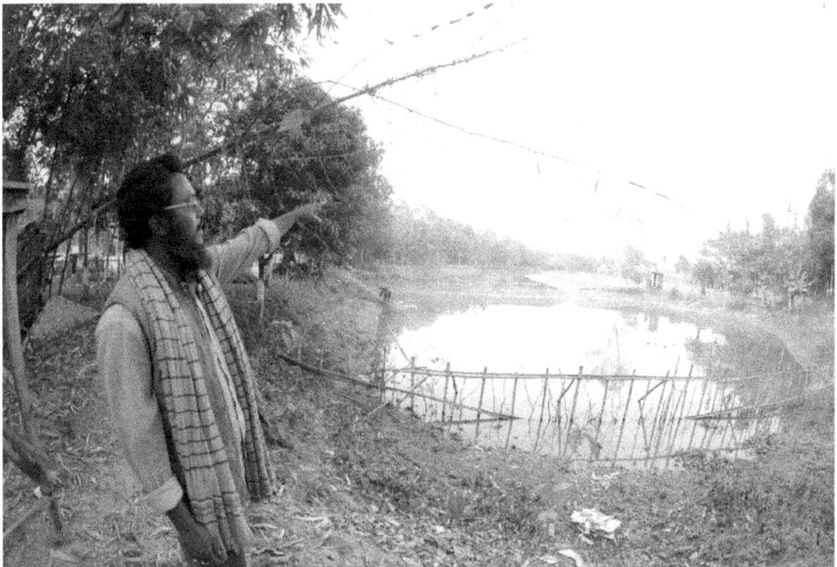

Torof battle ground, finger directing as to Hindu Kings of Torof who the missionaries faught.

Dhaka

Ibrahim Danishmand

Dhaka

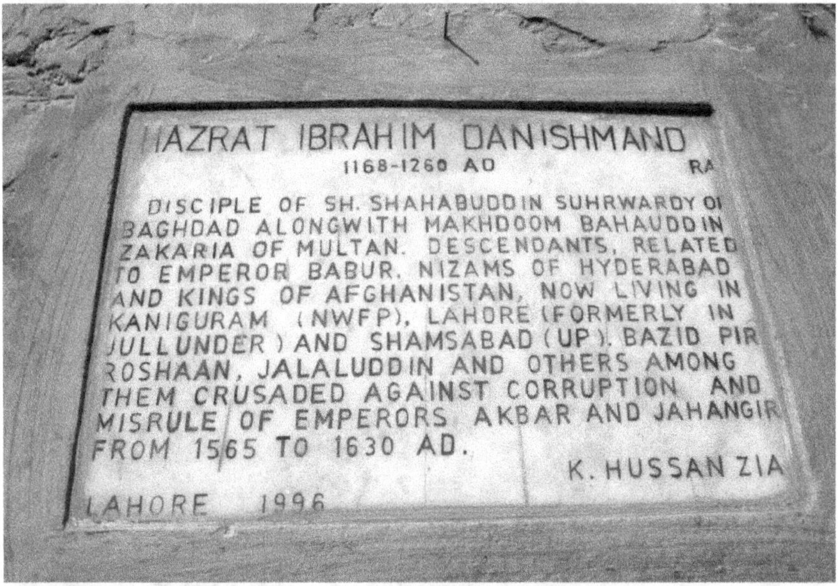
HAZRAT IBRAHIM DANISHMAND
1168-1260 AD
RA
DISCIPLE OF SH. SHAHABUDDIN SUHRWARDY OF BAGHDAD ALONGWITH MAKHDOOM BAHAUDDIN ZAKARIA OF MULTAN. DESCENDANTS, RELATED TO EMPEROR BABUR, NIZAMS OF HYDERABAD AND KINGS OF AFGHANISTAN, NOW LIVING IN KANIGURAM (NWFP), LAHORE (FORMERLY IN JULLUNDER) AND SHAMSABAD (UP). BAZID PIR ROSHAAN, JALALUDDIN AND OTHERS AMONG THEM CRUSADED AGAINST CORRUPTION AND MISRULE OF EMPERORS AKBAR AND JAHANGIR FROM 1565 TO 1630 AD.
K. HUSSAN ZIA
LAHORE 1996

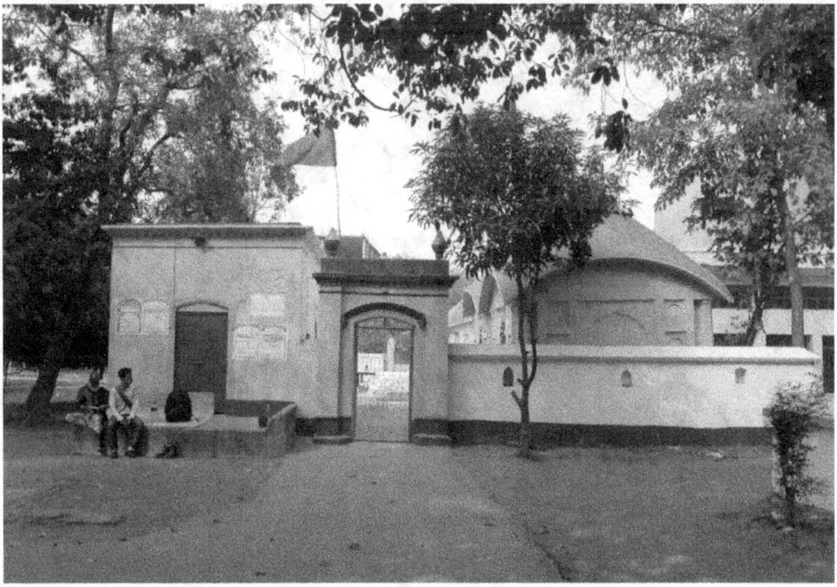

Dhaka was a different experience. Here you had history from the mogul times and history before Hazrat Shah Jalal. I only touched on few locations over a period of couple days.

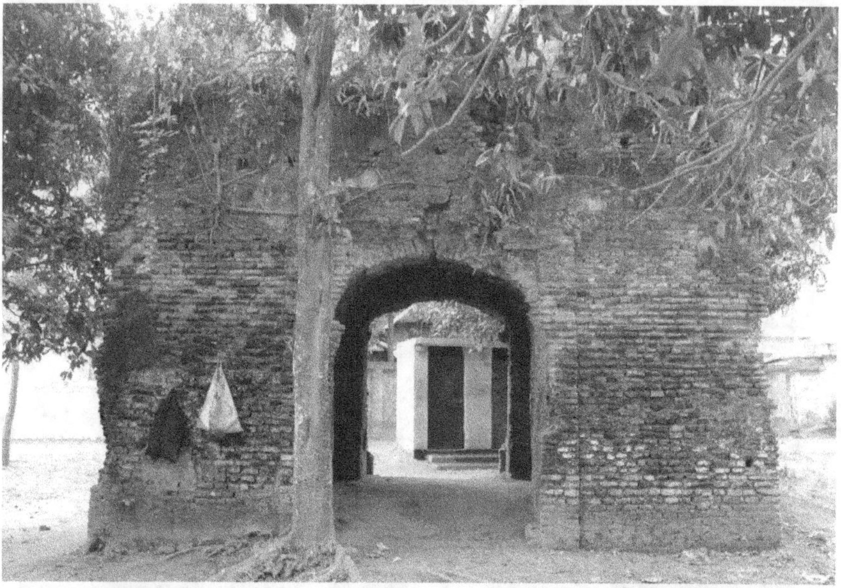

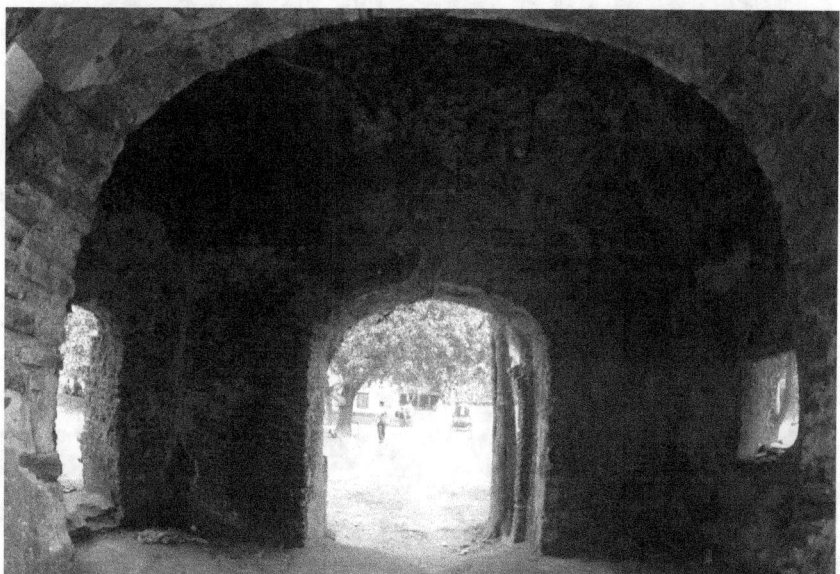

Old building with 2 feet deep walls, made to last, and parts of it lasted.

There are more Mazars and shrines there that I didn't get round to.

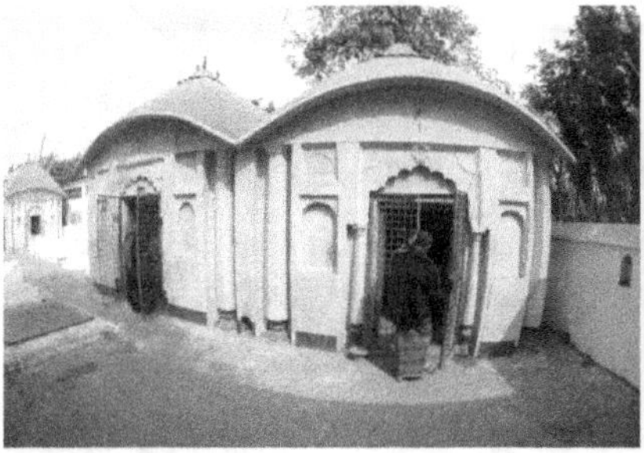
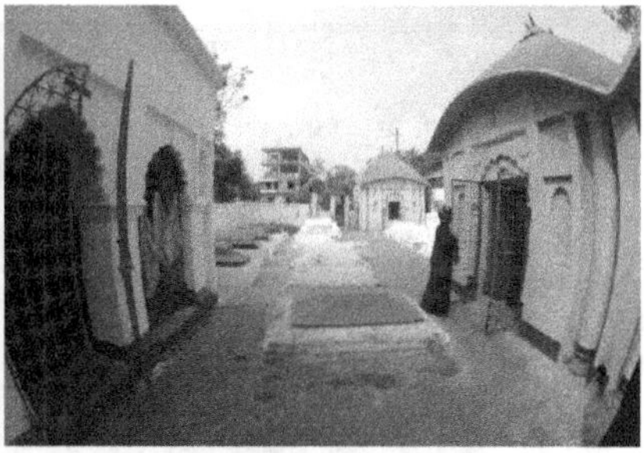
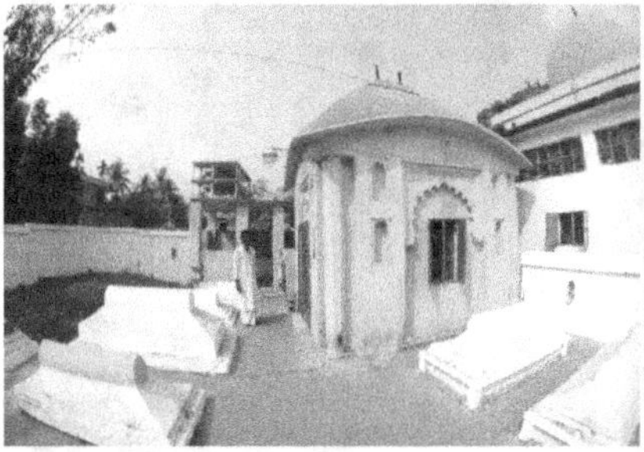
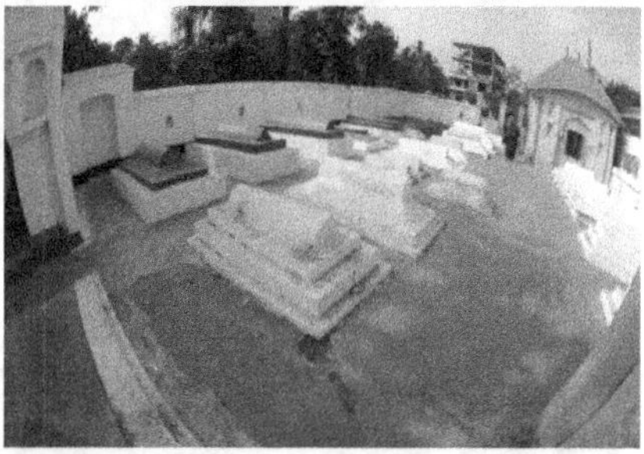
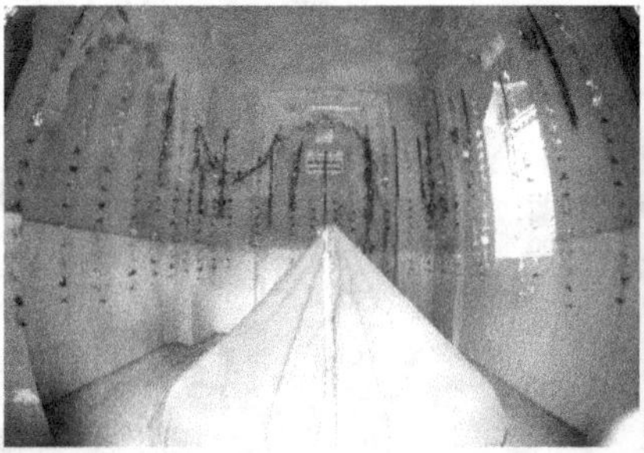
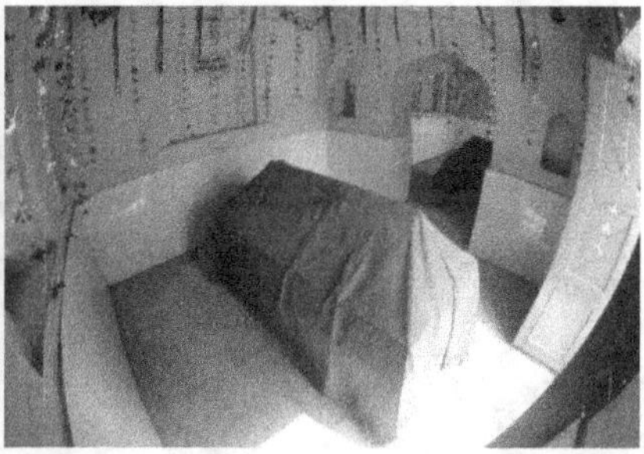
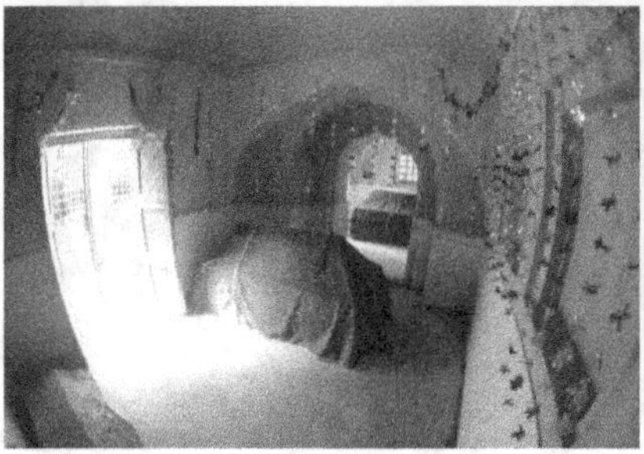
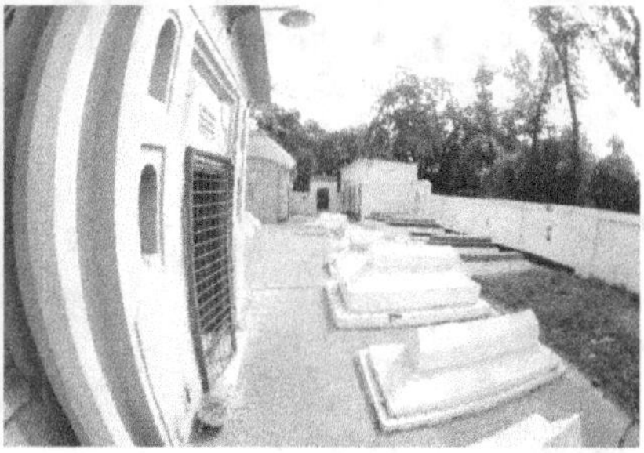

15.02.2011, 09:26:30

Sultan Giyash Uddin Azam Shah

Mograpara, Sonargoan, Dhaka

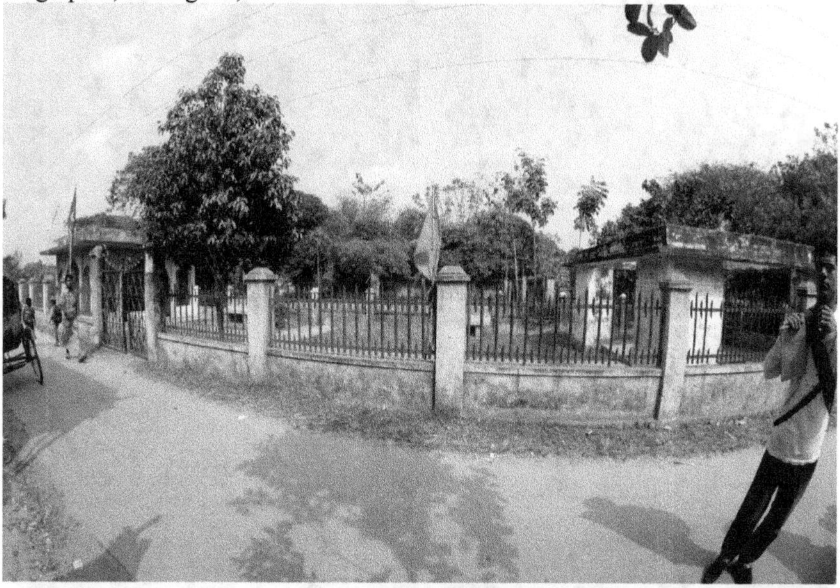

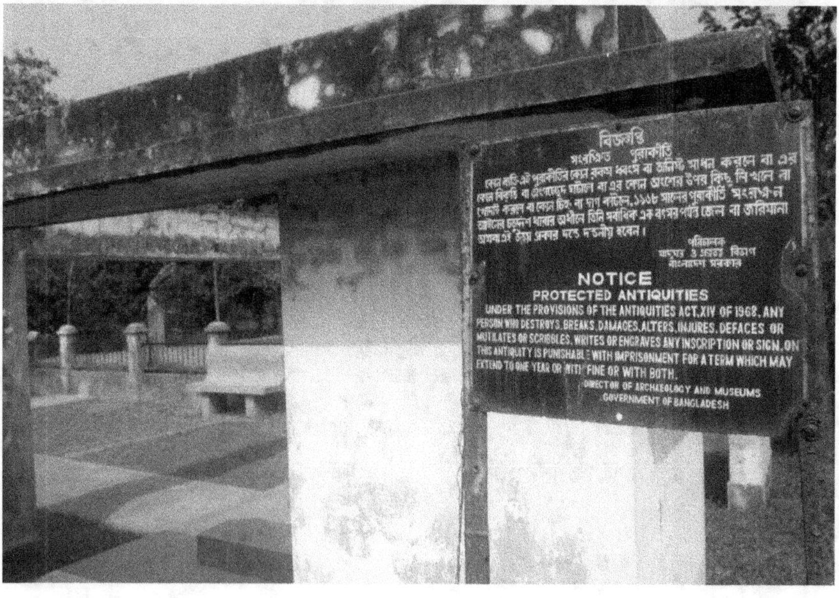
বিজ্ঞপ্তি
সংরক্ষিত পুরাকীর্তি
NOTICE
PROTECTED ANTIQUITIES
UNDER THE PROVISIONS OF THE ANTIQUITIES ACT, XIV OF 1968, ANY
PERSON WHO DESTROYS, BREAKS, DAMAGES, ALTERS, INJURES, DEFACES OR
MUTILATES OR SCRIBBLES, WRITES OR ENGRAVES ANY INSCRIPTION OR SIGN, ON
THIS ANTIQUITY IS PUNISHABL WITH IMPRISONMENT FOR A TERM WHICH MAY
EXTEND TO ONE YEAR OR WIT FINE OR WITH BOTH.
DIRECTOR OF ARCHAEOLOGY AND MUSEUMS
GOVERNMENT OF BANGLADESH

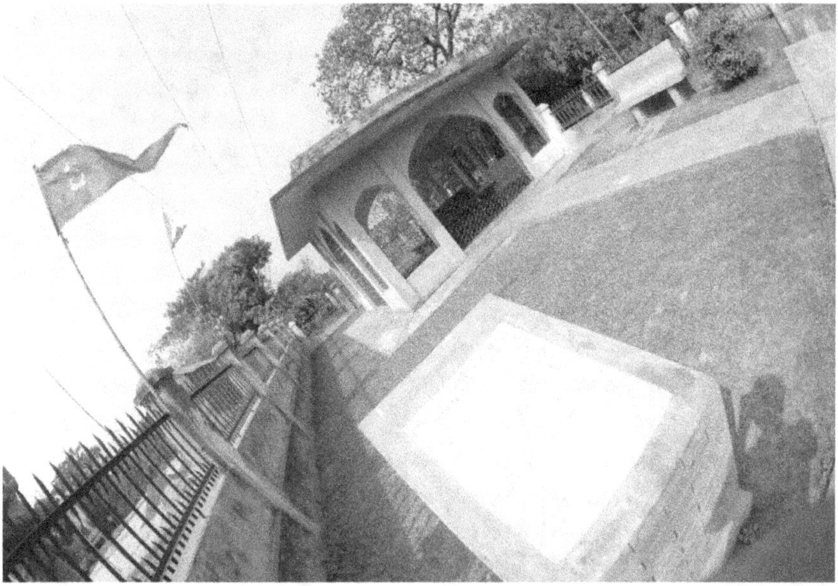

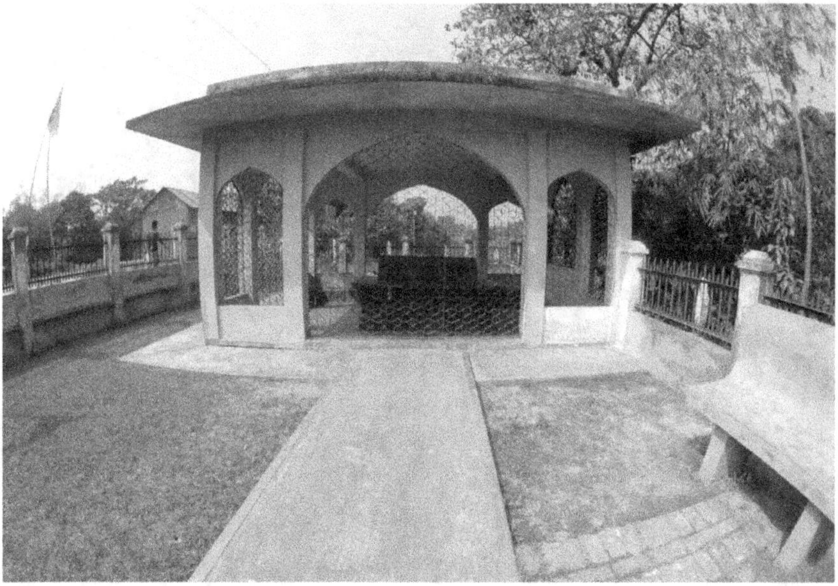

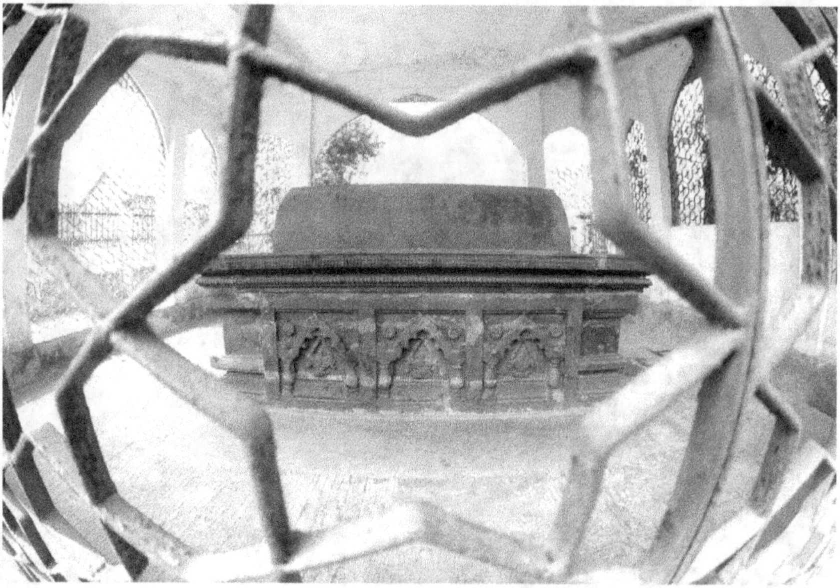

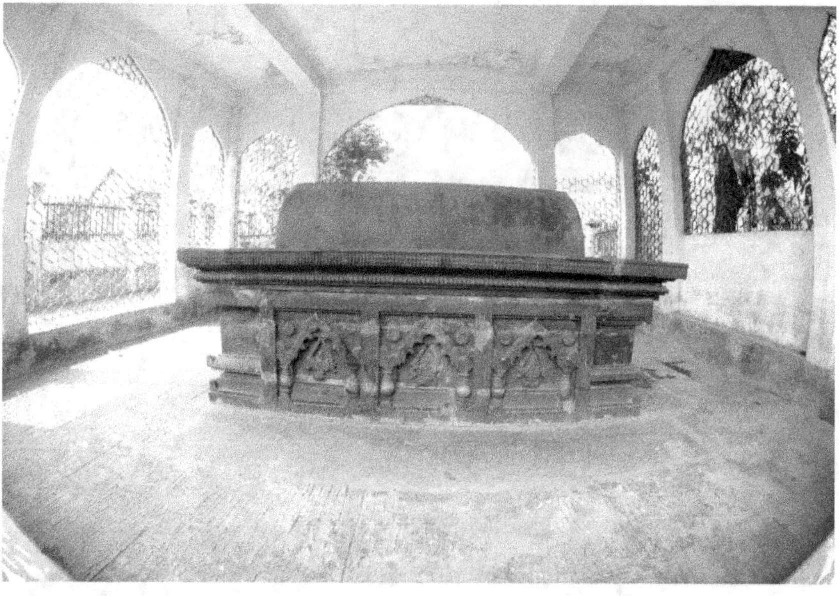

15.2.2011, 10:10:18

Fass Phirer Mazar

Sultan Shah Iliash Uddin
Sultan Shah Shams Uddin
Sultan Shah Giyash Uddin
Sultan Shah Gazi
Sultan Shah Kalu

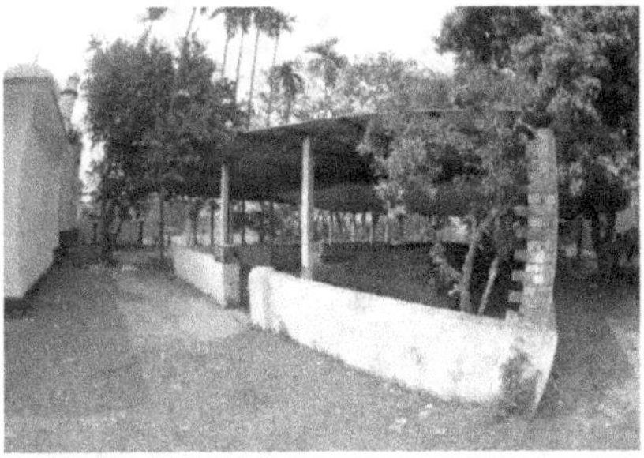

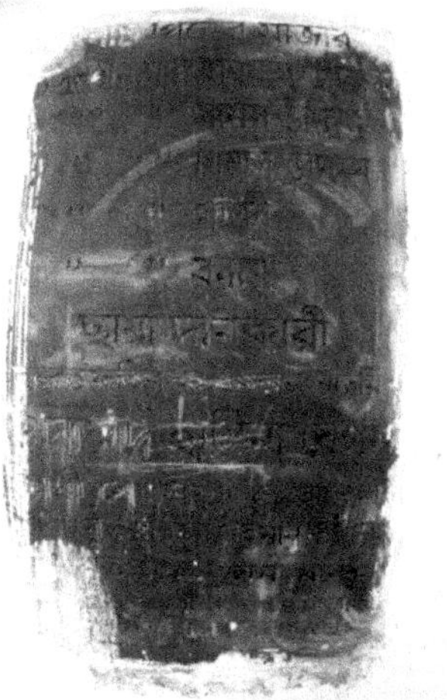

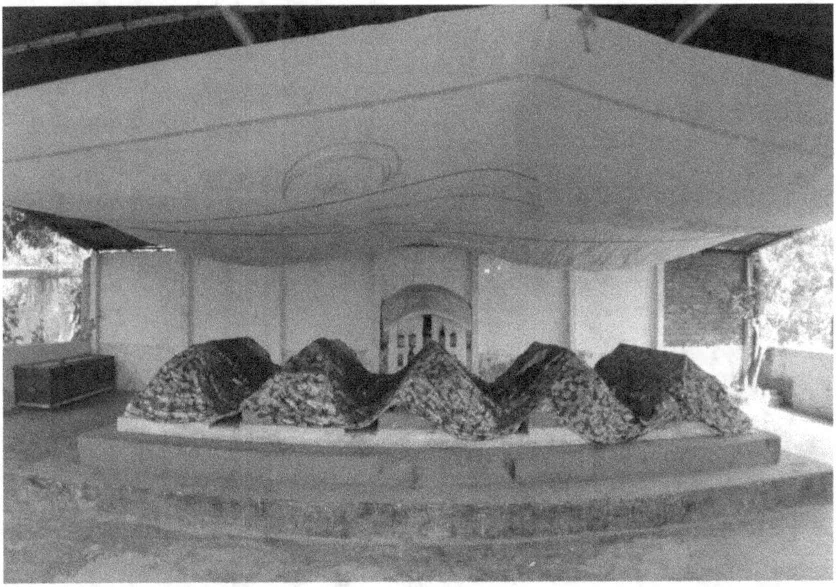

15.2.2011, 10:19:32

Mohojompur Shah

Lonkorshah

Dhaka, Outskirts

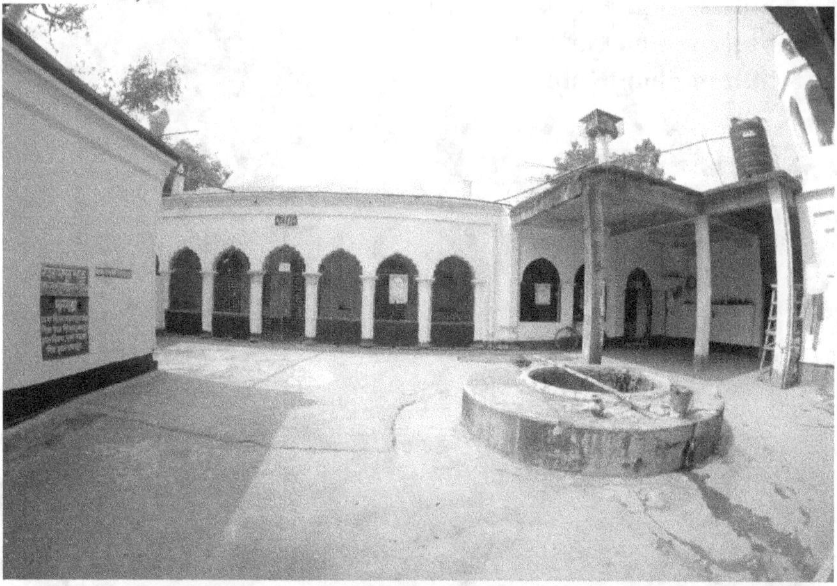

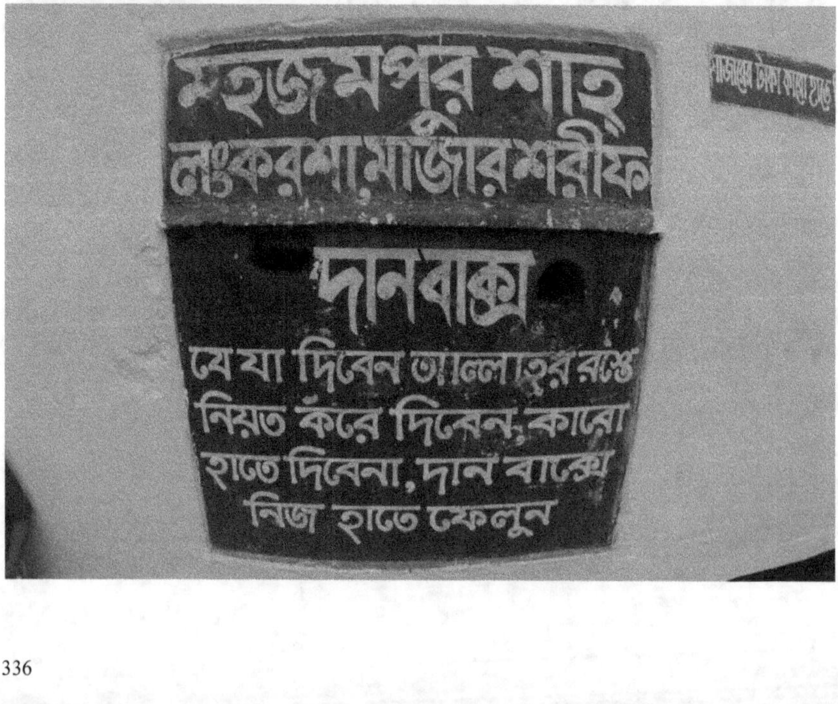
মহজমপুর শাহ্
লংকরশা মাজার শরীফ
দানবাক্স
যে যা দিবেন আল্লাহর রস্তে
নিয়ত করে দিবেন, কারো
হাতে দিবেনা, দান বাক্সে
নিজ হাতে ফেলুন

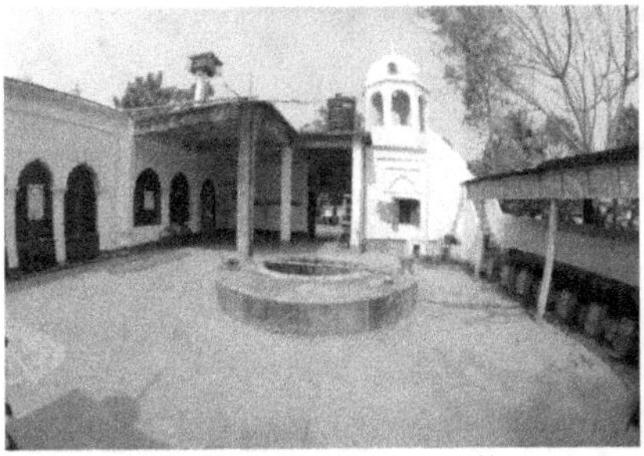

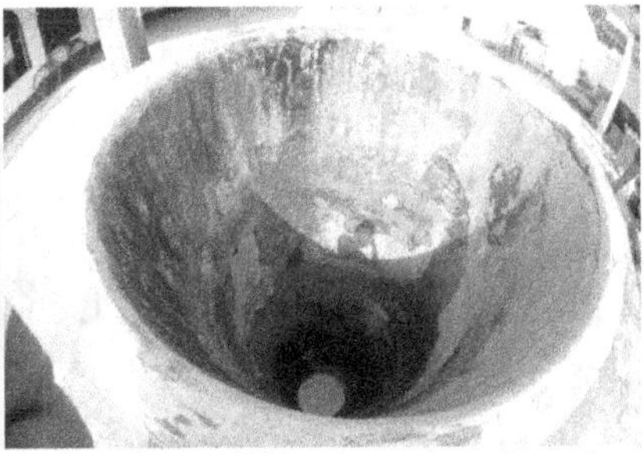

This mazar complex has a well, not seen many about. This place must have been well established and self sufficient set up.

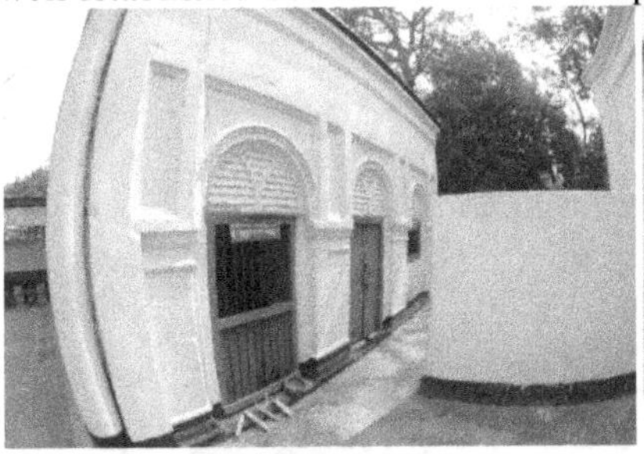

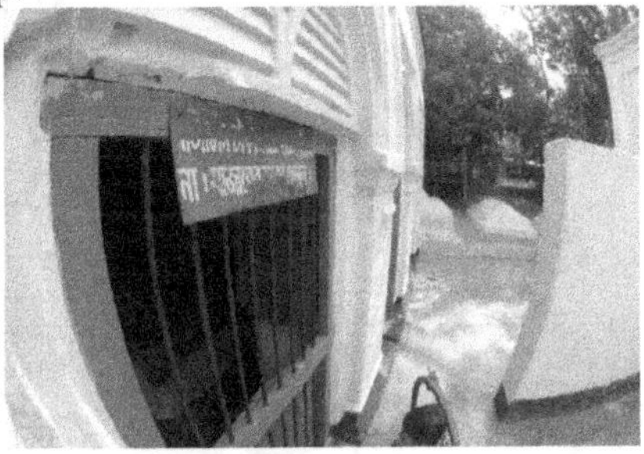

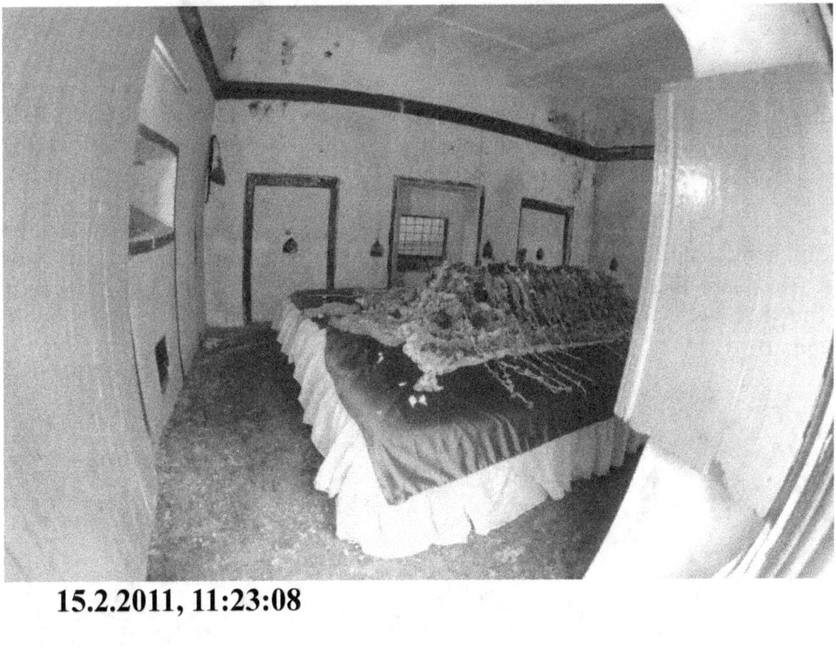

15.2.2011, 11:23:08

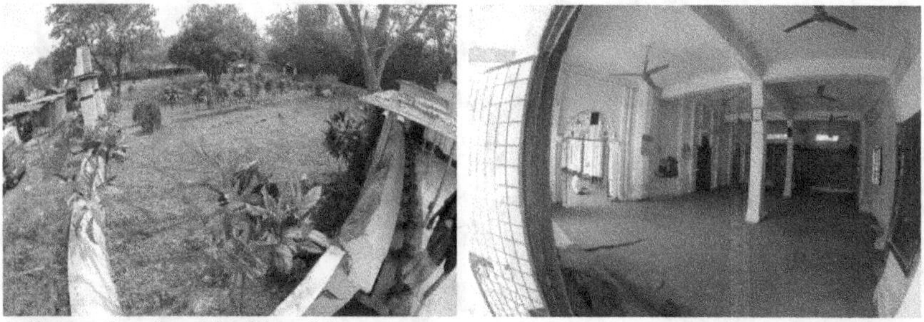

Adjacent land and inside of the mosque.

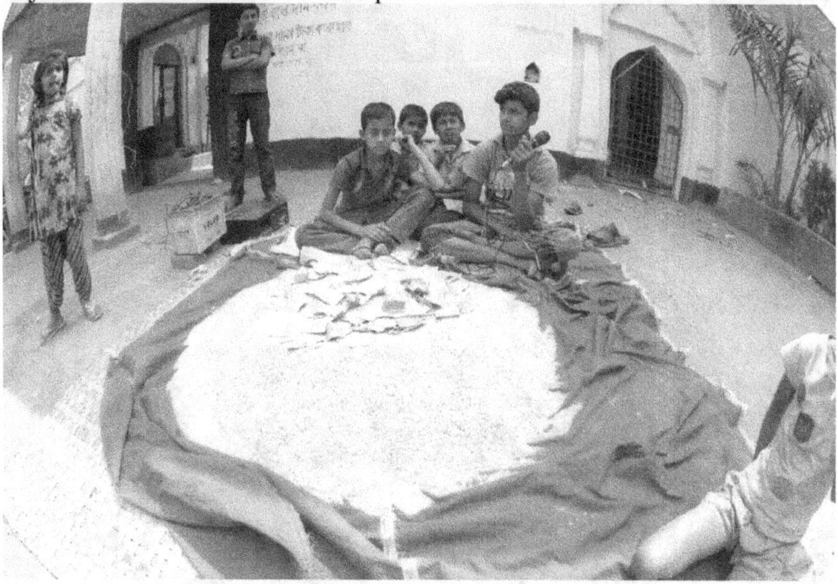

Children outside the Mosque by the road, sit on a cloth with rice and money on it. They are collected charity from passerby and tourist to that neck of the woods. The look very organised, with a mic. system, reciting various verses of the Quran.

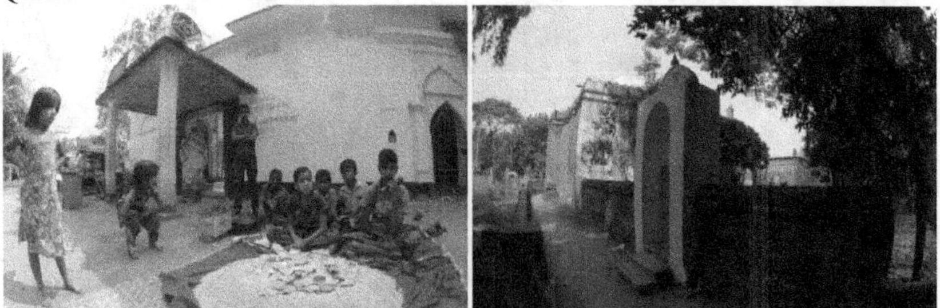

15.2.2011, 11:26:54

This place was more than meets the eye, on the side street, part of the complex held a very pleasant architectural surprise.

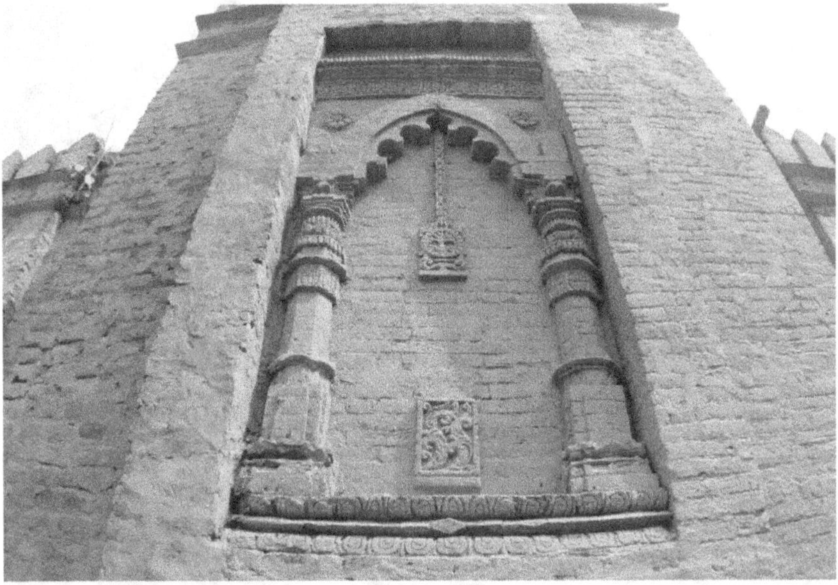

A pink wall, what seems to be a surviving wall.

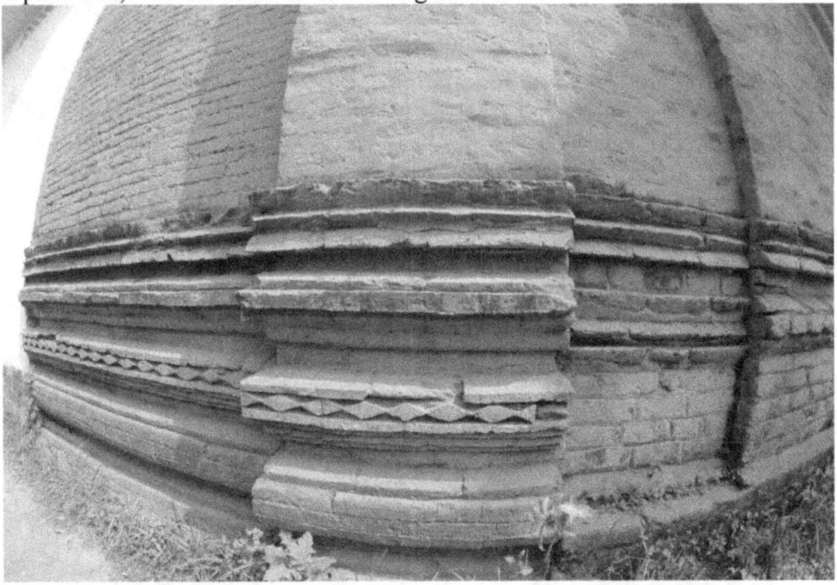

The brick work and the features were from the old time, Mugal time, the ornate brick work and pattern, as well as the carving. This was such a joy, bit of an eye candy, seeing something that would have been created hundreds of years ago.

Gulaf Shah

Dhaka City

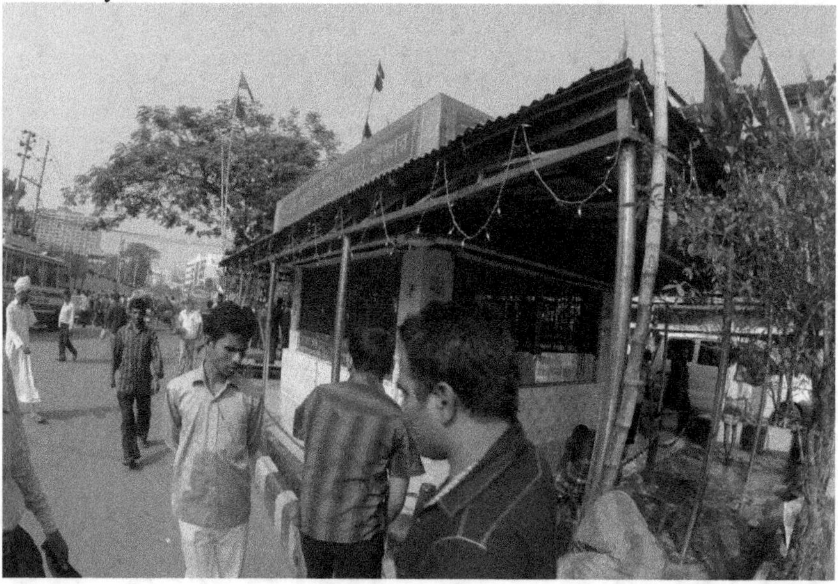

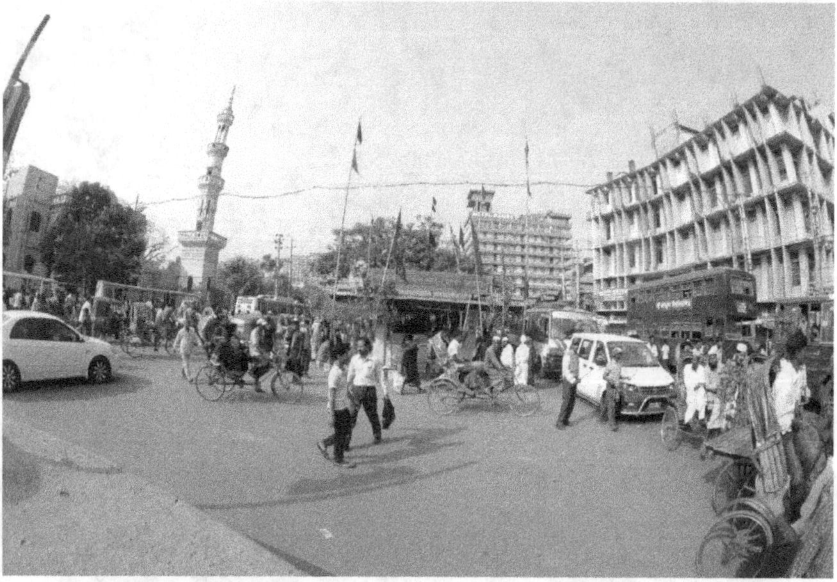

15.2.2011, 13:48:40

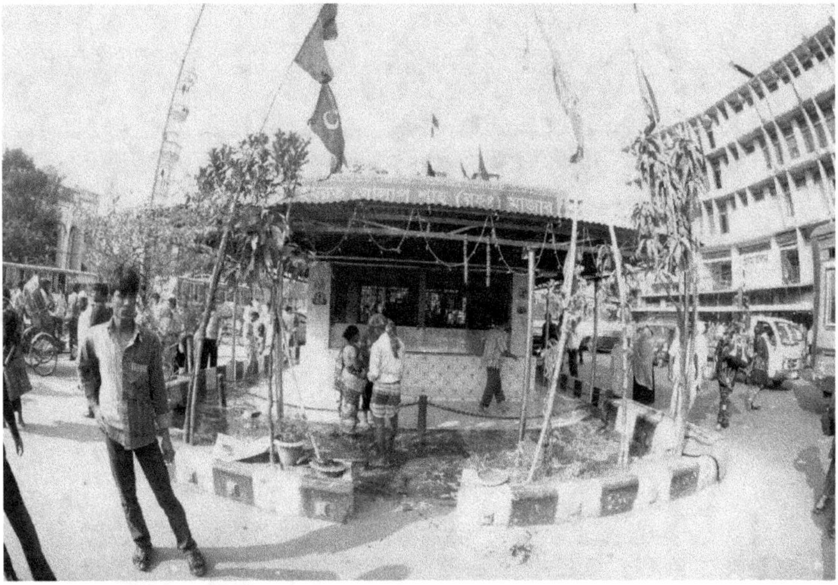

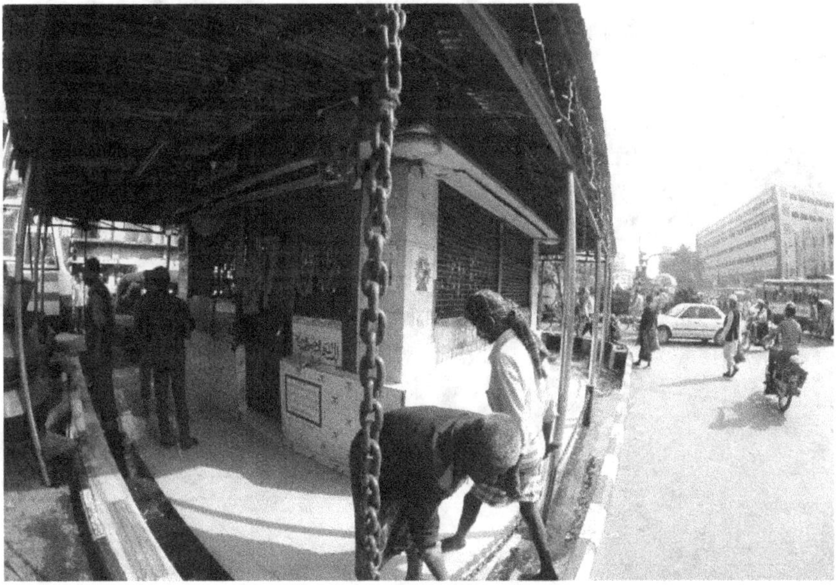

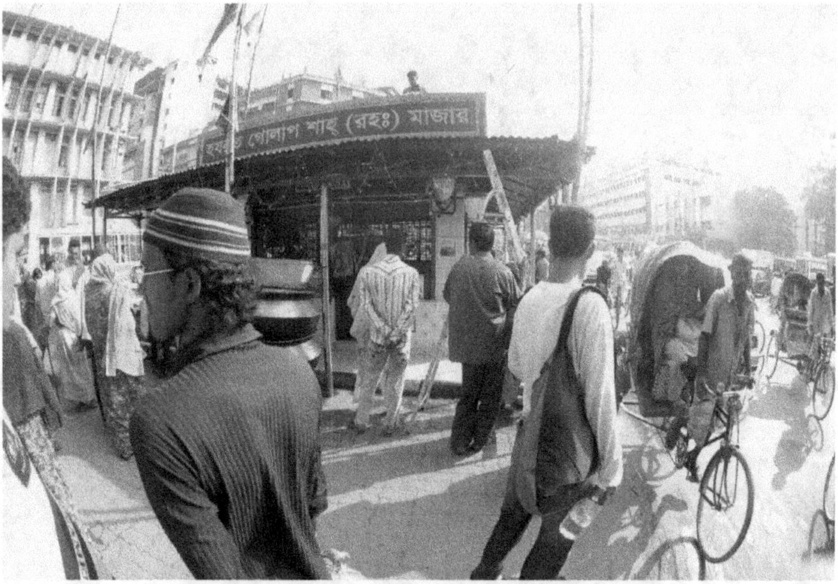
গোলাপ শাহ্ (রহঃ) মাজার

This mazar is in a triangle island, and has streets on all its 3 sides.

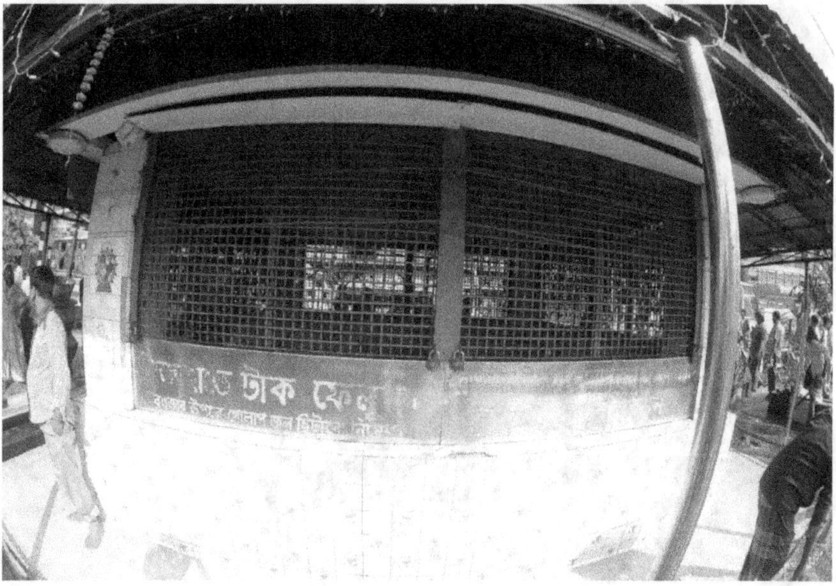

People offer the money, through the grill, a very busy hustling and bustling place.

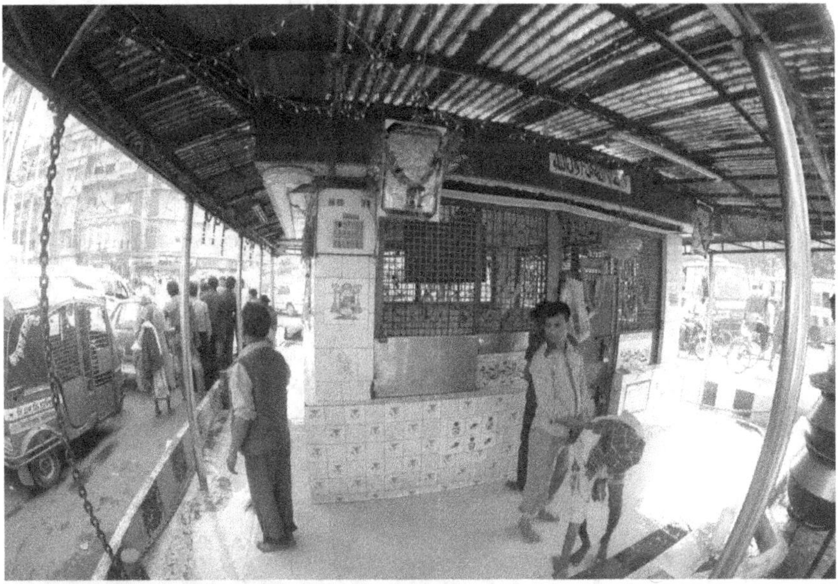

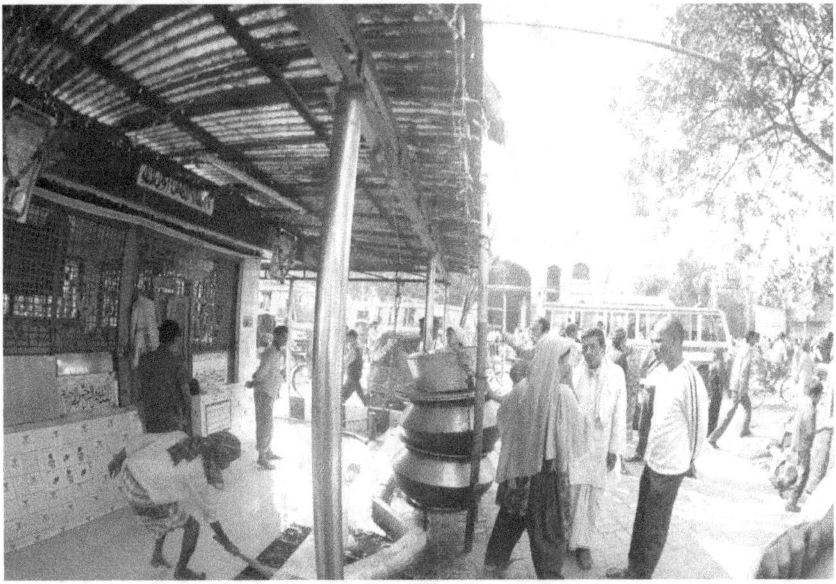

Hustle and bustle of the traffic and the people who commute daily.

Shah Khaza Sorfuddin Chisthti

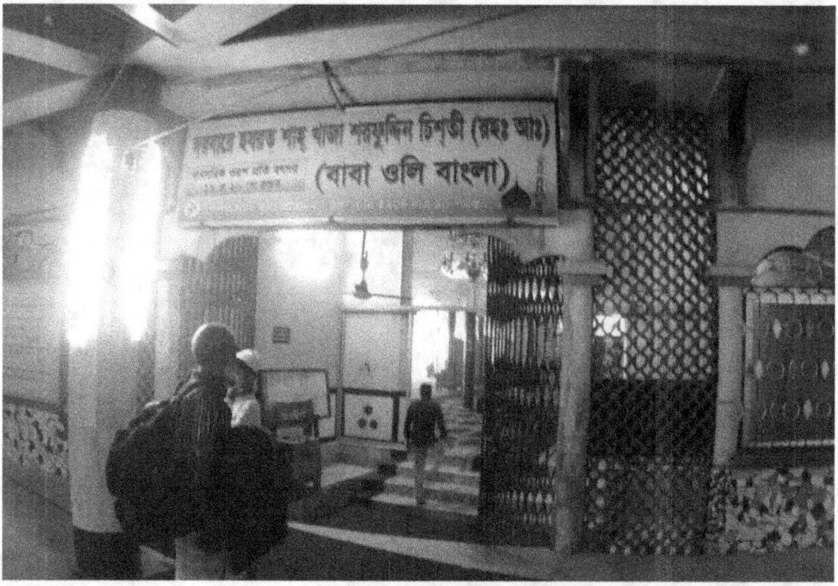
(বাবা ওলি বাংলা)

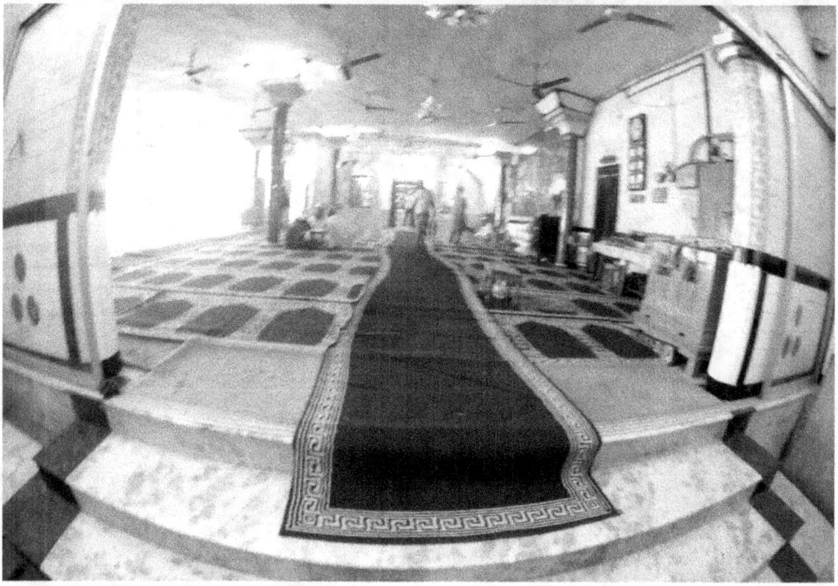

15.2.2011, 14:02:00

Gawshul Ajom Hazrat Shiraj Shah

Doniya, Shampur, Dhaka

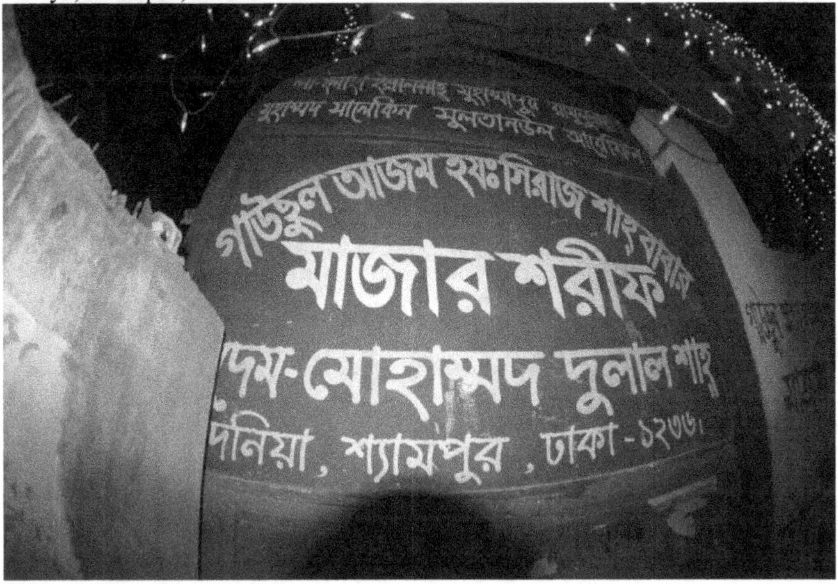
গাউছুল আজম হযঃ সিরাজ শাহ্
মাজার শরীফ
মোহাম্মদ দুলাল শাহ্
দনিয়া, শ্যামপুর, ঢাকা-১২৩৬।

15.2.2011, 20:43

Katwa (Tortoise) Mazar

Chittagong

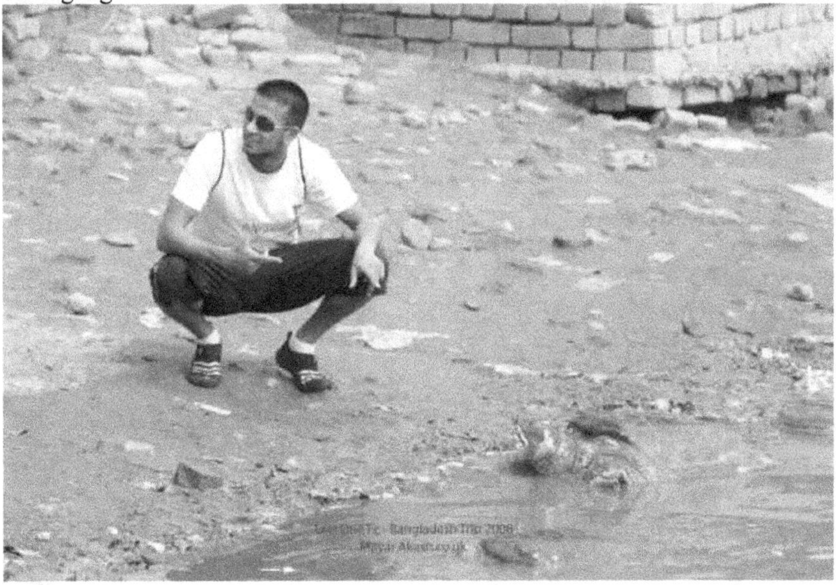

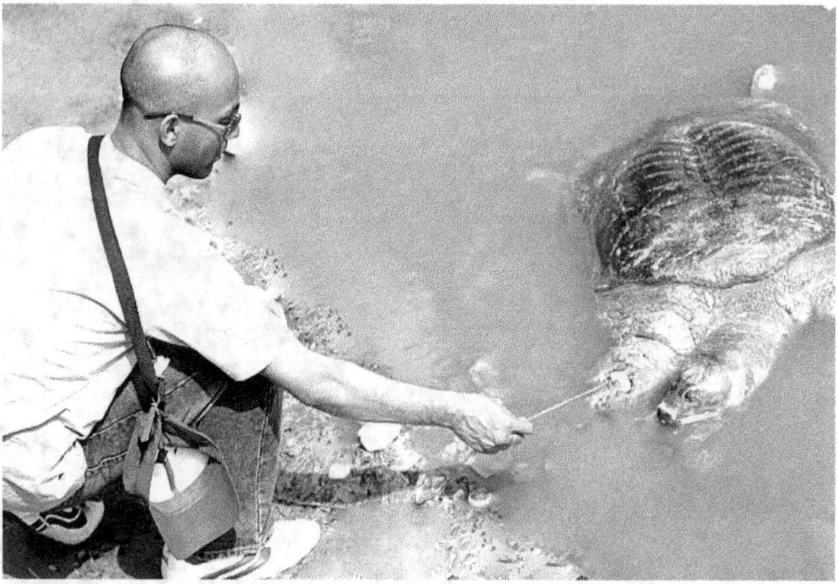

Feb 2008

When I went to this place in Chittagong with the group I went to Bangladesh with, I didn't take in the essence of what this place was, nor was it a personal contemplation moment for me either.

I didn't really appreciate it at that moment but on reflection many years later, it was awesome, and today I include it in this book as my list of gone to this place.

This place is revered by the people who visit it, I was dismayed with what I saw, witnessed; local visitor, a woman with child, went down to the murky water and cupped water with her hands and made her child drink it, so did she, and then rubbed the wet hand over his head.

There is no way that I would have drunk it or made any of my children drink it, cannot fathom the bacterias in it. But the locals have the stomach for it, I guess.

Nor did I get to learn the details about this place.

Index

Reference/Source

1. http://web.archive.org/web/20190209195823/http://www.mazaar.org.uk/Prayer%20Page.htm[12.12.2020]
2. Mazar Sharif, Mayar Akash, MAPublisher, London. 2017
3. Shah Jalal, Mayar Akash, MAPublisher, London, 2017
4. pininterest.com (Rabbir Ham Huma) [23.1.2021]
5. Hadrat-Wikipeadia (Hadrat) [23.1.2021]
6. Religions-Islam: Hajj: Pilgrimage to Mecca – BBC [23.1.2021]

www.ingramcontent.com/pod-product-compliance
Lightning Source LLC
Chambersburg PA
CBHW071248220526
45468CB00001B/46